PHILOSOPHY
and SEX

THIRD EDITION

PHILOSOPHY
and SEX

EDITED BY
ROBERT B. BAKER,
KATHLEEN J. WININGER,
and FREDERICK A. ELLISTON

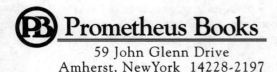 Prometheus Books

59 John Glenn Drive
Amherst, New York 14228-2197

Published 1998 by Prometheus Books

Inquiries should be addressed to
Prometheus Books
59 John Glenn Drive
Amherst, New York 14228–2197
VOICE: 716–691–0133, ext. 207
FAX: 716–564–2711
WWW.PROMETHEUSBOOKS.COM

06 05 04 03 02   6 5 4 3 2

Library of Congress Cataloging-in-Publication Data

Philosophy and sex / edited by Robert B. Baker, Kathleen J. Wininger, and Frederick
A. Elliston. — 3rd ed.
      p.   cm.
Includes bibliographical references.
ISBN 1-57392-184-X (alk. paper)
1. Sexual ethics. 2. Sex customs. 3. Marriage. 4. Moral conditions. I. Baker,
Robert, 1937–   . II. Wininger, Kathleen J. III. Elliston, Frederick.
HQ32.P5   1998
306.7′01—dc21   97-46446
                                                                                 CIP

Printed in the United States of America on acid-free paper

This volume is dedicated to the memory
of Frederick Elliston,
who lived his life believing that:

"Freedom is one of those things that our society values, and rightly so.
The ability to live one's life as one chooses is not only sought by most people,
but used as a standard against which particular practices and . . .
entire societies can be judged."

"Like health and wealth . . . love is a good thing,
something we would choose for ourselves and those close to us."

Contents

Part Two: Gender, Sexuality, and Perversion

Part Three: Desire, Pornography, and Rape

Introduction to the Third Edition

If political correctness arises from the identification of the personal with the political, the first edition of this book was undoubtedly an artifact of political correctness. The "correctness" in question, however, was not that of the editors but of others who sought to define and protect a certain established order of belief and, therefore, to limit what was publishable and discussible as philosophy. The first edition was conceived on the day in 1972 that Fred Elliston walked into the office of his colleague, Bob Baker, in search of teaching material for a new course he was offering, Sex and Society. Baker, ever a piler and seldom a filer, pointed to a motley stack of manuscripts decked out in the various hues characteristic of copies in the pre-photocopy era: carbon-copy gray, ditto-blue, mimeograph black. These were "samizdat" manuscripts circulated by philosophers who wrote about sexual issues in spite of the knowledge that the subject was considered unsuitable for philosophical reflection. Although unpublishable and undiscussible in formal philosophical fora, the manuscripts were nonetheless circulated and recirculated, and were discussed and commented upon at professional conventions—albeit always in the corridors and coffee shops, never from the podium at official sessions. Some of the manuscripts were unorthodox, others addressed their unorthodox subjects from behind an impeccable professional facade. Many expressed the dissenting voice of a generation of women philosophers who sought to challenge common practices and to reparse questions in a feminine and often a feminist voice. The common thread running through this motley group of unpublished and then unpublishable manuscripts was that they converted the personal into the philosophical. It was philosophy written from the heart, analyzed from the head, circulated, read and reread because of philosophers' personal investment in the issues.

After Elliston perused the stack of manuscripts from Baker's office, he returned them to Baker and said, "I know a publisher who will put these into print." Three years later, in 1975, with the backing of Paul Kurtz and Prometheus Books, the first edition of contemporary English-language essays on philosophy and sex was published. Resonating with defiance, the cover of the first edition paraded its previously unspeakable, unprintable, unpublishable, "unprofessional" subject matter in bright, neon-colored words displayed against a black background—"abortion," "adultery," "feminism," "homosexuality," "monogamy," "perversion," "promiscuity." The philosophy of sex had come out of the closet. At the time, no one knew how it would be received by the profession. Yet in the three years between the conception and the publication of *Philosophy and Sex,* professional philosophy had become receptive to what was later to be called "applied ethics." Richard Wasserstrom's trail-blazing *Today's Moral Problems* helped to make the idea of professional philosophical reflection about contemporary moral issues more palatable, a new subfield of applied ethics; "bioethics" was being formed, and at the same time feminist philosophers were demanding and increasingly gaining a voice in the public discourse of philosophy. What had once been unspeakable was now permissible, and was soon to become an acceptable and accepted part of the professional philosophy and of professional philosophical discourse.

Perhaps more importantly from the perspective of professionalization, it was being published in reputable philosophy journals. Alan Soble founded the Society for the Philosophy of Sex and Love, which was officially recognized as a special interest group by the American Philosophical Association (APA) and held meetings in conjunction with the APA. Philosophizing about sex had become philosophically respectable and *Philosophy and Sex* followed suit. The new acceptability of professional philosophical discourse about sexuality was reflected both on and within the covers of the second edition of *Philosophy and Sex,* which appeared in 1984. Although the cover design still consisted entirely of the words delineating once professionally undiscussible subjects, they were no longer displayed in neon on black, but in sedate baby blue or, in alternative printings, in feminine pink against white—color-coded gender equality, so to speak. Despite these hints at an earlier, more radical incarnation, the book now had the look and feel of an eminently respectable text. Inside its covers the subject's newly earned respectability was celebrated with a fifty-page bibliography (compiled by William Vitek, a former student of both Baker and Elliston; now a Professor of Philosophy at Clarkson University, who publishes extensively on environmental ethics) documenting the explosion of literature on the subject. The comprehensive bibliography of English-language literature on philosophy and sex in the first edition contained entries from 1697 to 1975, but filled fewer than seventeen full pages; by contrast, at fifty pages, the bibliography in the second edition was more than twice as long. More English-language literature had been written on philosophy and sex in the decade between 1975 and 1984 than in the previous three centuries.

Not unexpectedly, therefore, most of the articles in the second edition had been published previously in journals. For these articles *Philosophy and Sex* was no longer the sole route of entry into professional philosophical discourse; it was instead a form of canonization that converted them from contributions to an ongoing discussion into exemplars of a certain position to be taught and cited by professionals and their students. Yet all forms of professional discourse about sexuality were not treated equally between 1975 and 1984. Gay and lesbian perspectives found expression primarily in special fora created by, and for the most part addressed to, the gay and lesbian community. Following the precedent set in the first edition, therefore, Baker and Elliston allotted a significant amount of space to these articles in the second edition. They proudly introduced to a philosophical audience Jeremy Bentham's late eighteenth- and early nineteenth-century writings on "Paederasty." The manuscript had been ignored by professional philosophers entirely, and first appeared in print in the *Journal of Homosexuality* in 1978. The second edition also contained some of the earliest discussions of gay marriage, lesbianism as a choice, and the medicalization of homosexuality. It is interesting to note, in retrospect, that while these issues now seem integral to professional discourse on philosophy and sex, they were not well received by reviewers at the time.

Over a decade has passed since the publication of the second edition. A new edition was delayed for several reasons. Foremost among these was the tragic death of Frederick Elliston in a traffic accident. Baker and Elliston had been like salt and pepper, a partnership of opposites—Baker the piler, the conceptual-linguistic analyst, the old-fashioned liberal; Elliston the filer, the Husserlian phenomenologist who sought something beyond liberalism (and who might well have been a communitarian had he lived). What united the two was their shared belief in the liberating nature of the examined life, and hence the value of philosophy for the analysis and illumination of everyday life. No subject was so mundane or so profane that it was "off-limits" to professional philosophical inquiry. Everything should be open to the liberating force of the philosophical gaze, including human sexuality; and no area of philosophical scrutiny should be consigned to the limbo of unprofessionalism by virtue of its subject matter.

In the 1990s, however, nothing seemed closed to philosophical scrutiny. The impetus driving the first two editions was largely spent. Yet publishers abhor a vacuum. Steven Mitchell, who had edited the second edition, suggested that there was need for a new book that would take a fresh look at the subject. Ultimately Baker formed a new partnership with a Nietzsche scholar, a feminist, a philosopher of multiculturalism and former colleague, Kathleen J. Wininger, who chairs the Philosophy Department at the University of Southern Maine.

In the compiling this third edition Baker and Wininger reaped the bountiful harvest of more than two decades of fruitful philosophical work on sexuality. In striking contrast to the conditions under which the first two editions were published, the editors found no suppressed areas of philosophical discourse when preparing this edition. There was an abundance of material in print. As much to celebrate this achievement as to provide some criteria for selecting from the wealth of excellent material on philosophy and sex currently available, the editors attempted to limit the articles published in the third edition to those that had been published previously. Perhaps more controversially, in order to publish as many essays as possible the editors sacrificed the bibliography—which would have run to more than four times the fifty-page bibliography published in the second edition. They also decided to exclude essays about legal issues, and about feminist, gay and lesbian theory. Even with these exclusions, there are so many insightful analyses in the literature that one could easily have produced an alternative collection as good as, or better than, this one without including any of the essays that were chosen. There are many possible ways of presenting the rich philosophical literature on philosophy and sex; ours is but one way of presenting the material, it is certainly not the only way.

One major focus of the third edition is the philosophical discourse that has developed in recent years as Anglo-American philosophy joined European postmodern theorists, like Michel Foucault, in posing new questions about the history of sexual practice and its control. At the same time the sociobiological turn gave biology (and later anthropology) a philosophical voice that challenged many of the preconceptions of philosophers of the 1960s and 1970s. In those days, the philosophical analysis of sex and gender typically presupposed a binary biological distinction between female and male, paralleled by a socially constructed binary gender distinction between feminine and masculine. In the 1980s and 1990s, however, anthropologists, biologists, sociologists and some philosophers began to question both of these binaries; they began to reexamine the construction of the biological as well as of the social. In many ways these are the most exciting aspects of the recent literature and our attempt to represent this discussion constitutes one of the most important differences between the present and earlier editions. These discussions occur in the second section—Gender, Sexuality, and Perversion—which contains only four articles from earlier editions: Baker's " 'Pricks' and 'Chicks': A Plea for 'Persons' " (updated with a postscript), Bentham's "An Essay on Paederasty," Thomas Nagel's "Sexual Perversion," and Joyce Treblicot's "Taking Responsibility for Sexuality." Over a dozen new articles have been reprinted to introduce contemporary debates about the categorization and history of sexuality. The editors have blended European voices—Cixous, Foucault and Irigaray—with Anglo-Saxon analyses in a way that they believe will make the material accessible, lively, and illuminating.

There are, however, some important strands of continuity with the earlier editions. Like its predecessor, this edition opens by reproducing the Introduction to the first edition, and then turns to a dialogue between Firestone and Solomon about love and feminism. The rest of the first section addresses questions of love, marriage, and reproduction, and treats same-sex marriages as simply another form of marriage. Much of this material appeared in earlier editions, although the Vatican's position has been updated and a few articles have been replaced with more recent ones. The third and last section of the book speaks directly to everyday concerns about—Desire, Pornography, and Rape. These essays are all new to this edition and are designed to explore such basic questions as why men read pornography, who is to blame for rape, and whether rape is an expression of sexuality or an act of violence in sexual guise. The section closes with a discussion of the Antioch College Sexual Offense Policy.

One of the most famous Socratic dictums is that "the unexamined life is not worth living." It may not be a corollary that the unexamined sex life is not worth having, but it is a corollary that unexamined conceptions of sex and gender may trap us in sex lives and gender roles that may not be worth living. We have tried to compile a set of articles that will assist readers to examine questions of sex and gender, illuminating them with some of the best insights that philosophers have to offer after two decades of free and open reflection on the subject.

Books such as these are collaborative efforts. We would be remiss if we did not close with a word acknowledging the generosity of our contributors, the invaluable assistance of Deborah Elliston, Amy Geren, Ed Stein, David Gerhan, Jeannette Haas, Marianne Snowden, the editorial staff at Prometheus Books, particularly Steven Mitchell and Eugene O'Connor, and say a word of thanks to our families for their tolerance and generosity.

January 1998

Robert Baker
Union College
Schenectady, New York

Kathleen J. Wininger
University of Southern Maine
Portland, Maine

Introduction to the First Edition

In the "war" between philosophers and poets, the philosophers have all too willingly relinquished the field of sex to the poets. Their retreat is puzzling when one considers that all of us are born into this world as biological males or females, and that the attendant gender roles boy/girl, man/woman, husband/wife, father/ mother, adulterer/adulteress mediate and perhaps even determine our lives. If anatomy is not all of destiny, sex and sexuality—especially in the institutionalized forms of courtship, marriage, and the family—are crucial in molding individuals and cultures. Surely then, intellectuals who are committed to living the examined life should not fail to devote a goodly part of their work to the analysis of sex, sexuality, and gender.

Why then have philosophers surrendered sex to the poets? In part, their refusal to deal with sex can be traced to the tradition of rejecting the body and all things corporeal. For example, in the dialogue in which Plato introduces the "war" between the philosophers and the poets, he has the Prophetess advise Socrates that the contemplation of pure beauty "is the life for men to live." She goes on to say that he "will esteem [this pure beauty] far beyond . . . those lovely persons whom you and many others now gaze on with astonishment. . . ." Love between persons is contaminated with "the intermixture of human flesh and colors, and all other idle and unreal shapes attendant upon morality"; whereas pure beauty is "simple, pure and uncontaminated."[1]

Writing in a similar vein, Epictetus argued that rationality and sexuality are incompatible, and hence that there is no room for sex in the truly philosophical life.

> Every habit is confirmed and strengthened by corresponding acts. . . . So, if you lie in bed for ten days and then get up and try to take a fairly long walk, you will see how your legs lose their power. . . . When you yield to carnal passion you must take account not only of this one defeat, but of the fact that you fed your incontinence and strengthened it. . . .

Today when I saw a handsome woman I did not say "Would that she were mine!" and "Blessed is her husband!" . . . Nor do I picture the next scene: the woman present and disrobing and reclining by my side. . . . And if the woman, poor thing, is willing and beckons, and sends to me, and even touches me and comes close to me, I still hold aloof and conquer; the refutation of this argument is something greater than the argument of "the Liar" or the "Resting" argument This is a thing really to be proud of. . . .

The man who truly trains is he who disciplines himself to face such impressions. . . . Great is the struggle, divine the task; the stake is a Kingdom, freedom, peace, an unruffled spirit. . . . Can any storm be greater than that which springs from violent impressions to drive out reason?[2]

Except when planning utopias, the ancient philosophers tended to abandon sex to the poets because of the felt conflict between their commitment to reason and the inherent unreasonableness of sexual passion, because of a tendency to regard the sensual world as unworthy of philosophical contemplation, and—on a more personal level—because they tended to regard abnegation and the suppression of libido as intrinsically praiseworthy. For the most part the history of the philosophy of sex has been little more than a footnote to the ancients. Yet, a brief glance at this history is not altogether unrewarding.

In living their lives the great medieval philosophers Augustine and Aquinas followed the antisexual precedent of Plato and Epictetus. And while their writings form a somewhat different tradition, these medievals would undoubtedly have dismissed sex as quickly and disdainfully as their pagan predecessors if their inclinations had not been checked by the Biblical commandment to "increase and multiply and fill the earth."[3] This "blessing of fecundity," even more than St. Paul's grudging concession that marriage is better than hell, led them to consider, analyze, and defend the institution of monogamous marriage—thereby providing us not only with one of the very few bodies of philosophical literature dealing with sex, but also with a series of expositions and arguments that still shape contemporary views.

As is so frequently the case, the typical expression of medieval thought is found in the works of Thomas Aquinas, who developed what might be called the traditional eightfold truth on the subject: (1) seminal discharge defines the essence of sexual intercourse; (2) the only moral function of sexual intercourse is procreation (hence the emission of semen in any way that in itself prevents procreation is unnatural and immoral); (3) procreation naturally completes itself in the generation of an adult; (4) those who engage in sexual intercourse should provide whatever is necessary to rear any creature they procreate; (5) an unadulterous monogamous marriage is the best environment for rearing offspring to become adults; (6) females are inferior to males; (7) the male acts as the female's governor in marriage;[4] (8) divorce is improper (note that the seventh proposition renders it unjust for a male to divorce a female, while the sixth proposition makes female-generated divorces inappropriate).

It would be difficult to overestimate the significance of these eight theses for the subject of this book—indeed for the very nature of our society. To accept or reject any one of them, even the most innocuous, is to accept or reject a significant feature of one's culture. Consider proposition 1. If ever a proposition appeared to be a metaphysical irrelevancy, it does. Yet this seemingly superfluous bit of abstraction can—and possibly does—have the mundane and tragically real effect of ruining the sex life of half of the population.[5] If the implications of proposition 1 are somewhat subtle, those of the remaining seven are not. Between them they describe a monogamous, sexually inequitable, paternalistic patriarchy that proscribes divorce and alternative marital and sexual relationships, including recreational and nonprocreative sexual intercourse—for example, masturbation, contraception, oral intercourse, homosexual intercourse, and sodomy.

Contemporary society is not as rigidly traditional as the one described above, but it partakes of the tradition to a greater extent than might be apparent. This point can be underlined by considering what a society that rejects Thomas' eightfold truth might be like.

At the heart of the tradition lies the belief that sex is essentially procreative; a contratraditional view belies this "truth." So let us imagine a society that takes the essence of sex to be erotic fulfillment and that considers sex moral only to the extent that it is fulfilling. (We need not stop to consider whether this "fulfillment" is essentially self-centered, other-directed, or interactive, since this is a rough sketch rather than a blueprint.) Perhaps the most significant difference between the erotic and the procreative conceptions of sex is that if procreation is linked with parental responsibility it provides grounds for believing in a relatively stable relationship with a fair degree of permanence (and generates arguments for sexual exclusivity, and so forth); by contrast, erotic fulfillment has little need of permanence. Hence, in contratraditional society there would be no reason for linking parenthood (or, rather, what might be called "parenting"—that is, the activity of rearing a child) with sexual partnership. Such a society would be free to deny proposition 4 and to allow children to be parented by the state, by private charities, by individual volunteers, or by tribes of volunteers. The erotic act itself could be unburdened of the onus of possible parenthood by socially encouraged policies of sterilization, contraception, and abortion.

While the family has many functions in our society, its two primary functions are to provide for and protect an exclusive sexual relationship between a man and a woman and to provide for the parenting of children. Neither of these functions would be required of sex partners in contratraditional society. In such a society sex partners might be permanent "bachelors," impermanent trios, or tribes; "marriage" might exist in some vestigial form, but since there would be no sexual exclusivity and no sexually determined parenting, there would be no daughters, no sons, no husbands, no wives, no mothers, no fathers, no sisters, no brothers—at least not in the accepted sense. Sexual relations might occur in specially provided places in public buildings (say, in rooms located between the telephone booth and the toilet), or out in the open where everyone could enjoy them as either participant or spectator; or perhaps they might be restricted to more-ritual occasions or more-private locations. But sex-dictated residences, such as the family-oriented dwellings that have been a feature of Western culture since prehistoric times, would be superfluous. A contratraditional society might be the communalistic world of Plato's *Republic,* the libertine world of the Marquis de Sade, or the Harmonian world of Charles Fourier's passional phalansteries. But it would be a postmarital culture, a society without families; as such it would be different from any culture that has played a significant role in any civilization known to history.

Having sketched the possible outlines of postmarital society, we should like to suggest that however radical this society may appear, the contratraditional transfiguration of Western culture is possible—perhaps even probable—within the next few decades. And that change is the subject of this book. While no one essay deals with all aspects of this transfiguration, together they consider the advisability of rejecting the tradition. Yet, if a tradition is to be transformed rationally, it must first be understood.

The following is a selection of passages from Thomas Aquinas in which he develops the eightfold tradition:

> Now, it is good for each person to attain his end, whereas it is bad for him to serve away from his proper end. Now, this should be considered applicable to the parts, just as it is to the whole being; for instance, each and every part of man, and every one of his acts, should attain the proper end. Now, though the male semen is superfluous in regard to the preservation of the individual, it is nevertheless necessary in regard to the propagation of the species. Other superfluous things, such as excrement, urine, sweat, and such things, are not at all necessary; hence, their emission contributes to man's good. Now, this is not what is sought in the case of semen, but, rather, to emit it for the purpose of generation, to which purpose the sexual act is directed. But man's generative process would be frustrated unless it were followed by proper nutrition, because the offspring would not survive if proper nutrition were withheld. Therefore, the emission of semen ought to be so ordered that it will result in both the production of the proper offspring and in the upbringing of this offspring.
>
> It is evident from this that every emission of semen, in such a way that generation cannot follow, is contrary to the good for man. And if this be done deliberately, it must be a sin. Now, I am speaking of a way from which, *in itself,* generation could not result; such would be any emission of semen apart from the natural union of male and female. For which reason, sins of this type are called *contrary to nature.* But, if by accident generation cannot result from the emission of semen, then this is not a reason for it being against nature, or a sin; as for instance, if the woman happens to be sterile.
>
> Likewise, it must also be contrary to the good for man if the semen be emitted under conditions such that generation could result but the proper upbringing would be prevented. We should take into consideration the fact that, among some animals where the female is able to take care of the

upbringing of offspring, male and female do not remain together for any time after the act of generation. This is obviously the case with dogs. But in the case of animals of which the female is not able to provide for the upbringing of off-spring, the male and female do stay together after the act of generation as long as is necessary for the upbringing and instruction of the offspring. . . .

Now, it is abundantly evident that the female in the human species is not at all able to take care of the upbringing of offspring by herself, since the needs of human life demand many things which cannot be provided by one person alone. Therefore, it is appropriate to human nature that a man remain together with a woman after the generative act, and not leave her immediately to have such relations with another woman, as is the practice with fornicators. . . .

Now, we call this society *matrimony*. Therefore, matrimony is natural for man, and promiscuous performance of the sexual act, outside matrimony, is contrary to man's good. For this reason, it must be a sin.

Nor, in fact, should it be deemed a slight sin for a man to arrange for the emission of semen apart from the proper purpose of generating and bringing up children, on the argument that it is either a slight sin, or none at all, for a person to use a part of the body for a different use than that to which it is directed by nature (say, for instance, one chose to walk on his hands, or to use his feet for something usually done with the hands) because man's good is not much opposed by such inordinate use. However, the inordinate emission of semen is incompatible with the natural good; namely, the preservation of the species. Hence, after the sin of homicide whereby a human nature already in existence is destroyed, this type of sin appears to take next place, for by it the generation of human nature is precluded.

Moreover, these views which have just been given have a solid basis in divine authority. That the emission of semen under conditions in which off-spring cannot follow is illicit is quite clear. There is the text of Leviticus (18:22–23): "thou shalt not lie with mankind as with womankind . . . and thou shalt not copulate with any beast." And in I Corinthians (6:10): "Nor the effem-inate, nor liers with mankind . . . shall possess the Kingdom of God."

Also, that fornication and every performance of the act of reproduction with a person other than one's wife are illicit is evident. For it is said: "There shall be no whore among the daughters of Israel, nor whoremonger among the sons of Israel" (Deut[eronomy] 23:17); and in Tobias (4:13): "Take heed to keep thyself from all fornication, and beside thy wife never endure to know a crime"; and in I Corinthians (6:18): "Fly fornication."

By this conclusion we refute the error of those who say that there is no more sin in the emission of semen than in the emission of any other super-fluous matter, and also of those who state that fornication is not a sin.

If one will make a proper consideration, the preceding reasoning will be seen to lead to the conclusion not only that the society of man and woman of the human species, which we call matrimony, should be long lasting, but even that it should endure throughout an entire life.

Indeed, possessions are ordered to the preservation of natural life, and since natural life, which cannot be preserved perpetually in the father, is by a sort of succession preserved in the son in its specific likeness, it is naturally fitting for the son to succeed also to the things which belong to the father. So, it is natural that the father's solicitude for his son should endure until the end of the father's life. Therefore, if even in the case of birds the solicitude of the father gives rise to the cohabitation of male and female, the natural order demands that father and mother in the human species remain together until the end of life.

It also seems to be against equity if the aforesaid society be dissolved. For the female needs the male, not merely for the sake of generation, as in the case of other animals, but also for the sake of government, since the male is both more perfect in reasoning and stronger in his powers. In fact, a woman is taken into man's society for the needs of generation; then, with the disappearance of a woman's fecundity and beauty, she is prevented from association with another man. So, if any man took a woman in the time of her youth, when beauty and fecundity were hers, and then sent her away after she had reached an advanced age, he would damage that woman contrary to natural equity.

Again, it seems obviously inappropriate for a woman to be able to put away her husband, because a wife is naturally subject to her husband as governor, and it is not within the power of a person subject to another to depart from his rule. So, it would be against the natural order if a wife were able to abandon her husband. Therefore, if a husband were permitted to abandon his wife, the society of husband and wife would not be an association of equals, but, instead, a sort of slavery on the part of the wife.

Besides, there is in men a certain natural solicitude to know their offspring. This is necessary for this reason: the child requires the father's direction for a long time. So, whenever there are obstacles to the ascertaining of offspring they are opposed to the natural instinct of the human species. But, if a husband could put away his wife, or a wife her husband, and have sexual relations with another person, certitude as to offspring would be precluded, for the wife would be united first with one man and later with another.[6]

In the seventeenth and eighteenth centuries most of the philosophers were bachelor males dedicated to the life of reason who viewed sex as an antirational distraction unworthy of serious comment. Insofar as they addressed themselves to sexual issues at all, it was only to reinforce the traditional view of marriage. In "Of Polygamy and Divorces," for example, David Hume defends the classic Western marriage ("an engagement entered into by mutual consent and has for its end the propagation of the species"), argues that polygamy and divorce are inimical to these ends, and concludes that "the exclusion of polygamy and divorce sufficiently recommend our present European practices with regard to marriage."[7]

Kant, too, concludes his brief remarks on sex and marriage by defending the tradition. In his precritical work *Observations on the Feeling of the Beautiful and the Sublime* (1763),[8] he takes the stance of an aesthete and extols the virtues of femininity while decrying the education of women ("her philosophy is not to reason but to sense") as a perversion by which males, who are weakened by the power of women ("a single sly glance sets them more in confusion than the most difficult problem of science"), seek to alter the situation to their own advantage. Kant argues that since women are naturally irrational, while morality is essentially rational, they will avoid the wicked "not because it is unright, but because it is ugly." Reaffirming the traditional procreative view of the nature of sexual intercourse, Kant contends that whatever feelings or fascinations may appear to motivate us in sexual matters, "Nature pursues its great purpose, and all refinements that join together, though they may appear to stand as far from that as they will, are only trimmings and borrow their charm ultimately from that very source." Finally, he concludes that this great procreative purpose is best served by nonadulterous monogamous marriage, because promiscuity "degenerates into excess and dissoluteness." In matrimonial life the united pair should constitute a single moral person animated and governed by the understanding of the man and the taste of the wife.

In Kant's later (critical) work *Lectures on Ethics* the aesthete turns rationalist. Many of his earlier conclusions are retained, but the analyses that buttress them are radically different. He eschews the traditional conception of sexual intercourse as procreation marred by lust and reconceptualizes sex as mutual masturbation salvageable by human love. In a few key passages he originates the concept of a *sex object*. He argues that from the participants' point of view the purpose of coition is not procreation but orgasm, and develops the view that coition is essentially mutual masturbation—that is, that each participant uses the other as a *means* for attaining his own sexual satisfaction and hence does not treat the other as a full human being, as an *end* in himself. Since, for Kant, treating someone as a means rather than as an end is the essence of immorality, he has developed a rational proof of St. Paul's belief that coition is intrinsically evil. Like St. Paul, Kant allows one condition under which coition is morally permissible—nonadulterous monogamous marriage. For in marriage two persons become united as one in all things, and neither uses the other for his own purposes, but each gives himself over to the other. In other words, marriage transubstantiates immoral sexual intercourse into morally permissible human copulation by transforming a manipulative masturbatory relationship into one of altruistic unity.

Human love is good-will, affection, promoting the happiness of others and finding joy in their happiness. But it is clear that, when a person loves another purely from sexual desire, none of these factors enter into the love. Far from there being any concern for the happiness of the loved one, the lover, in order to satisfy his desire and still his appetite, may even plunge the loved one into the depths of misery. Sexual love makes of the loved person an Object of appetite; as soon as that appetite has been stilled, the person is cast aside as one casts away a lemon which has been sucked dry. Sexual love can, of course, be combined with human love and so carry with it the characteristics of the latter, but taken by itself and for itself, it is nothing more than appetite. Taken by itself it is a degradation of human nature; for as soon as a person becomes an Object of appetite for another, all motives of moral relationship cease to function, because as an Object of appetite for another a person becomes a thing and can be treated and used as such by every one. This is the only case in which a human being is designed by nature as the Object of another's enjoyment. Sexual desire is at the root of it; and that is why we are ashamed of it, and why all strict moralists, and those who had pretensions to be regarded as saints, sought to suppress and extirpate it. . . .

Because sexuality is not an inclination which one human being has for another as such, but is an inclination for the sex of another, it is a principle of the degradation of human nature, in that it gives rise to the preference of one sex to the other, and to the dishonoring of that sex through the satisfaction of desire. The desire which a man has for a woman is not directed towards her because she is a human being, but because she is a woman; that she is a human being is of no concern to the man; only her sex is the object of his desires. Human nature is thus subordinated. Hence it comes that all men and women do their best to make not their human nature but their sex more alluring and direct their activities and lusts entirely towards sex. Human nature is thereby sacrificed to sex. If then a man wishes to satisfy his desire, and a woman hers, they stimulate each other's desire; their inclinations meet, but their object is not human nature but sex, and each of them dishonors the human nature of the other. They make of humanity an instrument for the satisfaction of their lusts and inclinations, and dishonor it by placing it on a level with animal nature. Sexuality, therefore, exposes mankind to the danger of equality with the beasts. But as man has this desire from nature, the question arises how far he can properly make use of it without injury to his manhood. . . .

The sole condition on which we are free to make use of our sexual desire depends upon the right to dispose over the person as a whole—over the welfare and happiness and generally over all the circumstances of that person. If I have the right over the whole person, I have also the right over the part and so I have the right to use that person's *organa sexualia* for the satisfaction of sexual desire. But how am I to obtain these rights over the whole person? Only by giving that person the same rights over the whole of myself. This happens only in marriage. Matrimony is an agreement between two persons by which they grant each other equal reciprocal rights, each of them undertaking to surrender the whole of their person to the other with a complete right of disposal over it. We can now apprehend by reason how a *commercium sexuale* is possible without degrading humanity and breaking the moral laws. Matrimony is the only condition in which use can be made of one's sexuality. If one devotes one's person to another, one devotes not only sex but the whole person; the two cannot be separated. If, then, one yields one's person, body and soul, for good and ill and in every respect, so that the other has complete rights over it, and if the other does not similarly yield himself in return and does not extend in return the same rights and privileges, the arrangement is one-sided. But if I yield myself completely to another and obtain the person of the other in return, I win myself back; I have given myself up as the property of another, but in turn I take that other as my property, and so win myself back again in winning the person whose property I have become. In this way the two persons become a unity of will. Whatever good or ill, joy or sorrow befall either of them, the other will share in it. Thus sexuality leads to a union of human beings, and in that union alone its exercise is possible.[9]

Whether Kant's conception of marriage and sexual intercourse is defensible, or indeed whether it even makes sense, is a question for Kant scholars. What interests us is Kant's reconceptualization of the nature of sexual intercourse, which alters the tradition in at least three significant ways: first, coition has become an essentially hedonic and self-interested act, rather than a procreative one; second, the sexual act is analyzed in terms of the manipulation of an object by a subject; and, third, sexual intercourse (even sexual intercourse entered into with procreative intent) is considered to be moral only if it is done as part of an altruistic union of two human beings. As will shortly become apparent, each of those three alterations had significant influence on later philosophical writings on sex.

If Thomas Aquinas and Kant are the most influential sexual philosophers, Arthur Schopenhauer is unique in being the first Western philosopher to recognize the significance of the subject as such and to contrast the loquaciousness of the poets to the silence of the philosophers.

> We are accustomed to see poets principally occupied with describing the love of the sexes. . . .
>   . . . no one can doubt either the reality or the importance of the matter; and therefore, instead of wondering that a philosophy should also for once make its own this constant theme of all poets, one ought rather to be surprised that a thing which plays throughout so important a part in human life has hitherto practically been disregarded by philosophers altogether, and lies before us a raw material. The one who has most concerned himself with it is Plato, especially in the "Symposium" and the "Phaedrus." Yet what he says on the subject is confined to the sphere of myths, fables and jokes, and also for the most part concerns only the Greek love of youths. The little that Rousseau says upon our theme in the *Discours sur l'inégalité* is false and insufficient. Kant's explanation of the subject in the third part of the essay, *Über das Gefühl des Schönen und Erhabenen* is very superficial and without practical knowledge, therefore it is also partly incorrect. . . . On the other hand, Spinoza's definition, on account of its excessive näiveté, deserves to be quoted for the sake of amusement: *"Amor est titillatio, concomitante idea causae externae"* ["Love is joy with the accompanying idea of an external cause"]. *(Eth.* iv., prop. 44, dem.) Accordingly I have no predecessors either to make use of or to refute.[10]

Schopenhauer's scholarship is not all that one might have hoped it to be. He may be forgiven for having overlooked a page or so of Bishop Berkeley's *The Querist;* but his omission of Kant's critical reconceptualization of coition in the *Lectures on Ethics* and *The Philosophy of Law* and Johann Gottlieb Fichte's defense of the inequality of women in *The Science of Rights* (1795) is more serious. No less significant (but perhaps more understandable) was Schopenhauer's failure to mention William Godwin's call for the abolition of marriage in *Political Justice* (1793) and Mary Wollstonecraft's defense of the rights of women in *A Vindication of the Rights of Women* (1793).

Nonetheless, Schopenhauer's point was well taken: "one ought to be surprised," given the importance of sex and its attendant institutions, that it has been "disregarded by philosophers altogether." In reviewing the works of the major philosophers of the seventeenth and eighteenth centuries—Hobbes, Descartes, Spinoza, Leibniz, Malebranche, Locke, Berkeley, Rousseau, Fichte, Godwin, Hume, and Kant—one discovers that their writings on sex and its attendant institutions occupy less than twenty octavo-size pages, and almost all of that is by the last five philosophers named. A look at Lewis Selby-Bigge's classical anthology *British Moralists: Being Selections from Writers Principally of the Eighteenth Century*[11] makes clear that in their major essays on ethics the British moralists from Ralph Cudworth to Jeremy Bentham did not consider sexual intercourse, gender roles, marriage, or parental roles to be topics worthy of discussion. So while Schopenhauer was wrong to claim that he had no predecessors, he was essentially correct in holding that both modern and ancient philosophers had hitherto largely abandoned sex to the poets.

What then does Schopenhauer have to say in his "pioneering" work on the subject? First, that "all love, however ethereally it may bear itself, is rooted in the sexual impulse alone . . ."; second, that when we consider the power of love and love affairs, not only in our art and fiction but also in life, where it "constantly lays claim to half the powers and thoughts of the younger portion of mankind . . . embarrasses for a while even the greatest minds, [and] demands the sacrifice even of life and health," we are forced to conclude that what is involved in love and sex is more than a "trifle." Why is sexual love so significant? Because it is essentially procreative: it involves the will to life—not of individuals, but of generations. Love, Schopenhauer maintains, is a mechanism whereby the species manipulates the individual for its own ends and whereby individuals deceive themselves—not only as to their role as perpetuators of the species, but also in their relations with each other.

> . . . the sexual impulse, although in itself a subjective need, knows how to assume very skilfully the mask of an objective admiration, and thus to deceive our consciousness; for nature requires this stratagem to attain its ends. But yet that in every case of falling in love, however objective and sublime this admiration may appear, what alone is looked to is the production of an individual of a definite nature. [This] is primarily confirmed by the fact that the essential matter is not the reciprocation of love, but possession, i.e., the physical enjoyment. The certainty of the former can therefore by no means console us for the want of the latter; on the contrary, in such a situation many a man has shot himself. On the other hand, persons who are deeply in love, and can obtain no return of it, are contented with possession, i.e., with the physical enjoyment. This is proved by all forced marriages, and also by the frequent purchase of the favor of a woman, in spite of her dislike, by large presents or other sacrifices, nay, even by cases of rape. That this particular child shall be begotten is, although unknown to the parties concerned, the true end of the whole love story; the manner in which it is attained is a secondary consideration.[12]

In terms of the philosophical tradition, Schopenhauer is arguing Kant's point that although sexual intercourse is objectively procreative in nature, subjectively it is essentially hedonic and manipulative, and that, moreover, the objective aspect of sex ennobles and controls the subjective, giving it both its direction and its meaning.

> . . . every lover will experience a marvellous disillusion after the pleasure he has at last attained, and will wonder that what was so longingly desired accomplishes nothing more than every other sexual satisfaction; so that he does not see himself much benefited by it. That wish was related to all other wishes as the species is related to the individual, thus as the infinite to the finite. The satisfaction, on the other hand, is really only for the benefit of the species, and thus does not come within the consciousness of the individual, who, inspired by the will of the species, here served an end with every kind of sacrifice, which was not his own end at all. Hence, then, every lover, after the ultimate consummation of the great work, finds himself cheated; for the illusion has vanished by means of which the individual was here the dupe of the species.[13]

He concludes his analysis of love by indicating its relationship to marriage.

> Happy marriages are well known to be rare; just because it lies in the nature of marriage that its chief end is not the present but the coming generation. However, let me add, for the consolation of tender, loving natures, that sometimes passionate sexual love associates itself with a feeling of an entirely different origin—real friendship based upon agreement of disposition, which yet for the most part only appears when sexual love proper is extinguished in its satisfaction. This friendship will then generally spring from the fact that the supplementing and corresponding physical, moral, and intellectual qualities of the two individuals, from which sexual love arose, with reference to the child to be produced, are, with reference also to the individuals themselves, related to each other in a supplementary manner as opposite qualities of temperament and mental gifts, and thereby form the basis of a harmony of disposition.[14]

For all Schopenhauer's self-proclaimed iconoclasm, he does not really challenge any of the eight theses associated with the traditional view of sex and marriage: he agrees with all those he specifically mentions, and differs from Thomas only by emphasizing a point previously noted by Kant—the hedonic nature of sex when viewed subjectively. On this point Thomas is silent, but since he readily allows the importance of the concupiscible appetite, it seems doubtful that he would be prone to quarrel—or even to cavil. Indeed, with the exception of Plato (who argues that males and females are morally and intellectually equal and who embraces the ideal of communal marriage), all the philosophers considered thus far have been content to justify the indigenous practice current when they penned their analyses. Since Schopenhauer does much the same thing in his essay, there seems to be little call for noting disagreements. But the situation changes in the nineteenth century.

Centuries are shaggy creatures. The social and intellectual movements of one century tend to originate in the eighties or nineties of the previous one and to spill over into half the next. Thus, with a typical disdain for the aesthetics of chronology, the basic sexual issues of the nineteenth century start in the 1790s. And to further complicate matters, Hegel's writings of 1821 and Schopenhauer's essay of 1844 sit more easily with the "eighteenth-century" essays of Kant and Hume than with the "nineteenth century" works of Condorcet, Wollstonecraft, Godwin, Fichte, Mill, and Nietzsche. Why do we claim this? It seems significant that despite the existence of libertine lifestyles the philosophers of the seventeenth and eighteenth centuries did not seriously question the traditional view of sex and marriage, whereas, with the exceptions of the early Schopenhauer and of Hegel, the nineteenth-century writers either had serious reservations about the traditional conception of sex, gender roles, and marriage, or defended the tradition in the face of critics' objections. The polemical nature of these "later" works sets them apart in such a way that they form a "school" if not a "century."

Much of the polemic of the nineteenth-century writers had its roots in feminism, which surfaced as a political movement in France with the publication of *The Petition of the Women of the Third Estate to the King* (1789) and was quickly defended by Condorcet, who pointed out the absurdity of males crying out for equality, yet ignoring these same cries when they issued from the mouths of females. The first feminist manifesto, *Declaration of the Rights of Women,* published by Olympe des Gouges (Marie Gouze) in 1791, called for total equality between the genders ("Woman is born free and her rights are the same as those of men"), education for women, and the abolition of "the trade in women." Traditional marriage ("the tomb of trust and love") was to be replaced with a liberated marriage in which property was owned in common for the duration of the marriage, and in which bastards had full rights if acknowledged by either parent. (In nineteenth-century French law both legitimacy and property were entirely in the province of the male.)

By 1793 the political climate of France changed, causing, among other things, a strong political reaction against feminism. Olympe des Gouges was guillotined and the nascent feminist organizations withered. The ideals of feminism migrated across the channel, to be articulated and developed by Mary Wollstonecraft (and later disseminated by her daughter, Mary Shelley). By the mid-nineteenth century feminism returned to France to be espoused by Charles Fourier, Saint-Simon, and other socialists. It was embraced by Karl Marx and Friedrich Engels and accepted by all communist parties after the Second International.[15] The first self-conscious purely feminist political movement was organized in 1848 when 250 women met at Seneca Falls, New York, to found the American Women's Rights Movement. (Interestingly, most of the women were abolitionists—the impetus for the meeting was the exclusion of Lucretia Mott and Elizabeth Cady Stanton from the proceedings of the 1840 World Anti-Slavery Convention, in London.)

Although feminist arguments changed somewhat in the years between des Gouges and John Stuart Mill, the basic position remained the same—equality of gender roles through equal education; equal property rights; equal rights in marriage; and above all, absolute legal equality. Legal equality was stressed not because it was more significant but because it seemed to be the prerequisite of everything else. As Mill put this, his central point, in *On the Subjection of Women,* "the principle which regulates the existing relations between the two sexes—the legal subordination of one sex to the other—is wrong in itself, and now one of the chief hindrances to human improvement; and . . . it ought to be replaced by a principle of perfect equality, admitting to no power or privilege on the one side, nor disability on the other."[16]

Revolutions and counterrevolutions go hand in glove, and, not surprisingly, a counterrevolutionary antifeminism quickly developed. For the most part the ideology of the counterrevolution can be described as either traditional or libertine. Perhaps the most powerful antifeminist essay ever published in the traditionalist vein was penned by Johann Gottlieb Fichte as an appendix to his *The Science of Rights,* under the title "Fundamental Principles of the Rights of the Family" (1795). In the "Principles" he attempts to deal with the questions posed by the various feminist manifestos of the 1770s: "Has woman the same rights in the state which man has?" Noting that the answer to this question was "never a more urgent problem than in our days," he argues that since both males and females are equally endowed with freedom and reason, the genders do indeed have equal rights. Their apparent inequality arises because it is questionable "how far the female sex *can desire* to exercise these rights."

Fichte's doubts derive from a theory of the nature of males and females that has its roots in Aristotelian biology. In the *Generation of Animals*[17] Aristotle argued that the female is a passive receptacle in procreation, while the male is the active generative principle. Fichte not only accepted this view of procreation but endowed it with a special significance, since he also held (on independent grounds) that (1) "the individual is permanent only as a tendency to form the species"[18] and that (2) an individual is essentially a rational, self-realizing, active agent.[19] If proposition 1 is true, then, Fichte thought, it is also true (1 a) that since individuals can give form to species only as a couple, complete individuals can exist only in a coupled relationship of the two sexes (for example, a married couple); and (1 b) that since the natural role of individuals (both complete and incomplete) is to form a species, the nature of each is determined by its sexual role. Since Fichte accepted the Aristotelian view that the female sexual role is essentially passive and since (by proposition 1 a) in order to complete themselves females (and males) will couple (or marry), it follows (by proposition 1 b) that females will be led through their coupling to an essentially passive role. But passivity is irrational and suicidal for rational agents, since (by proposition 2) rationality is essentially active. Thus, the female sexual role appears to be self-annihilating.

The character of reason is absolute self-activity; pure passivity for the sake of passivity contradicts reason, and utterly cancels it. Hence, it is not against reason that the one sex should propose to itself the satisfaction of its sexual impulse as an end in itself, since it can be satisfied through activity; but it is absolutely against reason that the other sex should propose to itself the satisfaction of its sexual impulse as an end, because in that case it would make a pure passivity its end. Hence, the female sex is either not rational even in its tendencies, which contradicts our presupposition that all men should be rational, or this tendency can not be developed in that sex in consequence of its peculiar nature, which is a self-contradiction, since it assumes a tendency in nature which nature does not accept; or, finally, that sex can never propose to itself the satisfaction of its sexual impulse as its end. Such an end and rationality utterly cancel each other in that sex.

Nevertheless, the sexual impulse of this female sex, as well as its manifestation and satisfaction, are part of the plan of nature. Hence it is necessary that the sexual impulse should manifest itself in woman under another form; and, in order to be conformable to reason, it must appear as an impulse to activity; and as a characteristic impulse of nature, it must appear as an activity exclusively appertaining to the female sex.[20]

How does the sexual impulse appear to women? Or, given proposition 1 b, what is Fichte's view of the nature of the female gender?

Woman can not confess to herself that she gives herself up—and since, in a rational being, everything is only in so far as it arises in consciousness—woman can not give herself up to the sexual impulse merely to satisfy her own impulse. But since she can give herself up only in obedience to an impulse, this impulse must assume in woman the character of an impulse to satisfy the man. Woman becomes, in this act, the means for the end of another, because she can not be her own end without renouncing her ultimate end—the dignity of reason! This dignity she maintains, although she becomes means, because she voluntarily makes herself means in virtue of a noble natural impulse—*love!*

Love, therefore, is the form in which the sexual impulse appears to woman. But love is to sacrifice one's self for the sake of another not in consequence of a reasoning, but in consequence of a feeling. Mere sexual impulse should never be called love; to do so is a vulgar abuse of language, calculated to cause all that is noble in human nature to be forgotten. In fact, my opinion is that nothing should be called love but what we have just now described. Man *originally* does not feel love, but sexual impulse; and love in man is not an original, but a *communicated, derived* impulse, namely, an impulse developed through connection with a loving woman; and has, moreover, quite a different form in man to what it has in woman. Love, the noblest of all natural impulses, is unborn only in woman; and only through woman does it, like many other social impulses, become the common property of mankind. The sexual impulse received this moral form of love in woman, because in its original form it would have canceled all morality in woman. Love is the closest point of union of nature and reason; it is the only link wherein nature connects with reason, and hence it is the most excellent of all that is natural. The Moral Law requires that man should forget himself in the other; but love even sacrifices itself to the other.

Let me state it concisely: In an uncorrupted woman the sexual impulse does not manifest itself at all, but only love; and this love is the natural impulse of a woman to satisfy a man. It is certainly an impulse which urgently requires to be satisfied, but its being thus satisfied is not the satisfaction of the woman. On the contrary, it is the satisfaction of the man, and for woman it is only the satisfaction of her heart. Her only requirement is to love and to be loved. Only thus does the impulse which the woman feels to sacrifice receive that character of freedom and activity which it must have in order to be rational. Perhaps there does not exist a man who does not feel the absurdity to turn this around and to assume in man a similar impulse to satisfy a need of woman; a need, in fact, which he can neither presuppose in woman nor consider himself as its tool without feeling himself disgraced to the innermost depths of his soul.

Hence, also, woman in the sexual union is not in every sense means for the object of the man. She is means for her own end, to satisfy her heart; and she is means for the end of the man only in so far as physical satisfaction is concerned.[21]

Although Fichte does not accept the Kantian view that sexual intercourse is mutual masturbation, his asymmetrical analysis reveals intercourse to be problematic, not only because the female is used by the male merely as a means, but also because to be so used she must reject rationality. On a superficial level Fichte's solution to the problem of the immoral nature of sexual intercourse is similar to Kant's: for both philosophers the moral salvation of copulation is achieved by the marital union of a dominant rational male and a sensitive loving female. Yet, though the rather conventional outward forms of their solutions are identical, the substance is radically different. For Kant, marital union makes moral the essentially manipulative (and hence inherently immoral) nature of intercourse because the very fact of union dissolves the possibility of manipulation. One person can use another only if there is both a one and an other, a user and a used. But if a fusion of the one and the other truly exists, if there is but one entity and hence neither user nor used, then the very possibility of using an *other* as a means no longer exists. Thus Kant's resolution of the dilemma turns on the cataclysmic power of love to transform a coupling into a unity called a couple.

For Fichte, on the other hand, a marital union is very much a *duo*. As such, it does not eliminate the possibility of manipulation but rather provides the opportunity for reciprocal manipulation—a quid pro quo whereby each partner uses the other. The female accepts her status as a sex object in return for the male's acquiescence in his role as a love object. The function of union is to allow each to use the other for his or her own ends. Presumably this reciprocity will ensure the morality of the exchange. (Of course, this exchange would be just only if the role of love object was as desirable—or as undesirable—as that of sex object; the point of much feminist literature is that while it is not altogether unattractive to be a love object, the status of sex object is quite repellent.)

The modern reader might be tempted to dismiss Fichte as obscure, antiquated, and, hence, uninteresting. But however dated the form of his analysis may be, the substance is both contemporary and radical. For Fichte argues that women are intrinsically the equal of men and that the female gender role (femininity) is essentially antihuman. So far, his analysis is consistent with radical feminism. Like the radical feminist, he sees the situation as one in which a woman must sacrifice her femininity to her humanity or her humanity to her femininity. He opted for the latter alternative because he held the not uncommon view that the interests of the species override those of its members; hence given the species' compelling interest in preserving itself, procreation demands the sacrifice of women's humanity to their femininity. Interestingly, as radical feminists have been quick to point out, revolutionary biological innovations such as cloning, parthenogenesis, and artificial placentas are on the verge of rendering obsolete the species' interest in womankind's acquiescence in femininity. Moreover, the most radical feminists concur with Fichte's view that "man does not originally feel love, but only sexual impulse," agree with him in rejecting the female sexual role as antihuman, and hence view the nascent biological revolution as heralding a post-sexual or, perhaps, lesbian or homosexual society. Thus, had the biology of one hundred years ago been more advanced, Fichte might have been remembered as the (perhaps inadvertent) grandfather of radical feminism rather than as the godfather of male chauvinism.

Yet another ironic aspect of Fichte's work is that while he was the first philosopher to establish a cogent justification for exclusive monogamous marriage without parenting, the structure of his argumentation is basically the same as that used by Fourier to justify sexual communes and by Robert Rimmer and Nena and George O'Neill to justify open marriage (a "marriage" between cohabiting sexual partners who may share parenting but who deny any commitment to sexual exclusivity on the part of either partner). That is, Fichte was the first to advance the argument that the value of marriage is inherent in the relationship itself, and not merely, as the tradition held, a function of procreative responsibility.[22] For Fichte, as for Fourier, Rimmer, and Nena and George O'Neill, the value of marriage lay in the fact that only through marriage could one become a whole person, a full human being capable of both love and reason.

> Philosophers have hitherto considered it necessary to assign some end to marriage, and have specified that end variously. But marriage has no other end than itself; it is its own end. The marriage relation is the true mode of existence of grown persons of both sexes, required even by nature. In this relation all man's faculties develop; but out of it many, and among them the most remarkable faculties of man, remain uncultivated. Precisely as the whole existence of man has no relation to any sensuous end, so neither has its necessary mode, marriage.
>
> Marriage is a union between *two* persons—*one* man and *one* woman. A woman who has given herself up to one, can not give herself up to a second, for her whole dignity requires that she should belong only to this one. Again, a man who has to observe the slightest wish of one woman can not conform to the contradictory wishes of many. Polygamy presupposes that women are not rational

beings like men, but merely willess and lawless means to gratify man. Such is, indeed, the doctrine of the religious legislation which tolerates polygamy. This religion has—probably without being clearly conscious of the grounds—drawn one-sided conclusions from the destination of woman to remain passive.[23]

As we pointed out earlier, Fichte's writings on sexual philosophy were basically addressed to the question of the political rights of women. And here again he develops the classic male-chauvinist position.

As a rule, woman is either a maid or married. If a maid, she is still under the care of her father, precisely as the unmarried young man. Herein both sexes are perfectly equal. Both become free by marriage, and in regard to their marriage both are equally free; . . .

If she is *married,* her whole dignity depends upon her being completely subjected, and seeming to be so subjected, to her husband. Let it be well observed, what my whole theory expresses, but what it is perhaps necessary to repeat once more emphatically—woman is not subjected to her husband in such a manner as to give him a *right of compulsion* over her; she is subjected through her own continuous necessary wish—a wish which is the condition of her morality—to be so subjected. She has the *power* to withdraw her freedom, if she could have the *will* to do so; but that is the very point: she can not rationally will to be free. Her relation to her husband being publicly known, she must, moreover, will to appear to all whom she knows as utterly subjected to, and utterly lost in, the man of her choice.

Her husband is, therefore, the administrator of all her rights in consequence of her own necessary will; and she wishes those rights asserted and exercised only in so far as *he* wishes it. He is her natural representative in the state and in the whole society. This is her *public* relation to society. She can not even allow herself to think for a moment that she should exercise herself her rights in the state.

So far as her *private* and *internal* relation in the house is concerned, *the tenderness of the husband necessarily restores to her all and more than she has lost.* The husband will not relinquish her rights, because they are his own; and because, if he did so, he would dishonor himself and his wife before society. The wife has also rights in public affairs, for she is a citizen. I consider it the duty of the husband—in states which give to the citizen a vote on public matters—not to vote without having discussed the subject with his wife, and allowed her to modify his opinion through her own. His vote will then be the result of their common will. The father of a family, who represents not only his own but also the interests of his wife and children, ought indeed to have a greater influence and a more decisive vote in a commonwealth, than the citizen who represents only his own interests. The manner of arranging this is a problem for the science of politics.

Women, therefore, do really exercise the right of suffrage—not immediately, however, in their own person, because they can not wish to do so without lowering their dignity, but—through the influence which results from the nature of the marriage relation.[24]

Nineteenth-century antifeminism exhibited itself in the works of philosophical libertines as well as in the writings of traditionalists. The Magna Carta of libertinism is *Justine,* by the Marquis de Sade, a work that contains the defining theme of the libertine tradition—the view that in sexual matters the natural determines the moral, with a correlative rejection of social restraints on coition and sexuality. In the words of its greatest exponent, libertinism calls upon one to "break those bonds" of social constraint: "nature wills it; for a bridle have nothing but your inclinations, for laws your desires, for morality Nature's alone. . . ." Libertinism per se need not be antifeminist. Godwin's variety is certainly profeminist (see *Social Justice,* 1793), and even de Sade's version has notable profeminist elements, for example, the call for houses intended for women's libertinage and the advocacy of state institutions to relieve women of the labors of parenting. Nonetheless, it is reasonably clear that for de Sade nature dictates a somewhat lesser role for females than for males.

> It is certain, in a state of Nature, that women are born *vulguivaguous,* that is to say, are born enjoying the advantages of other female animals and belonging, like them and without exception, to all males; such were, without any doubt, both the primary laws of Nature and the only institutions of those earliest societies into which men gathered. *Self-interest, egoism,* and *love* degraded these primitive attitudes. . . .
>
> Never may an act of possession be exercised upon a free being; the exclusive possession of a woman is no less unjust than the possession of slaves; all men are born free, all have equal rights: never should we lose sight of those principles; according to which never may there be granted to one sex the legitimate right to lay monopolizing hands upon the other, and never may one of these sexes, or classes, arbitrarily possess the other. Similarly, a woman existing in the purity of Nature's laws cannot allege, as justification for refusing herself to someone who desires her, the love she bears another, because such a response is based upon exclusion, and no man may be excluded from the having of a woman as of the moment it is clear she definitely belongs to all men. The act of possession can only be exercised upon a chattel or an animal, never upon an individual who resembles us, and all the ties which can bind a woman to a man are quite as unjust as illusory.
>
> If then it becomes incontestable that we have received from Nature the right indiscriminately to express our wishes to all women, it likewise becomes incontestable that we have the right to compel their submission, not exclusively, for I should then be contradicting myself, but temporarily. It cannot be denied that we have the right to decree laws that compel woman to yield to the flames of him who would have her; violence itself being one of that right's effects, we can employ it lawfully. Indeed! has Nature not proven that we have that right, by bestowing upon us the strength needed to bend women to our will?[25]

The later nineteenth-century philosophical libertines tended to accept de Sade's view that nature dictates the bending of the female to the will of the male, without conceding that justice mandated some profeminist revisions of the status quo. Perhaps the purest example of libertine antifeminism is Schopenhauer's essay *On Women*, which was written after, and in partial reaction to, the feminist aspects of the libertarian revolutionary movements of 1848. This essay differs markedly from his treatise of 1844. Whereas *The Metaphysics of Sexual Love* was a traditionalist defense of a monogamous union of a rational, dominant male with a sensitive, loving, submissive female, the later work bears all the earmarks of libertinism—the assimilation of the natural to the proper and the concomitant call for the revision of "unnatural" norms. In addition it is informed by a bitter misogyny and takes the radical libertine stance of rejecting monogamy as an unnatural perversion. For nature, he argues, has determined that the female is merely a mechanism by which *man*kind reproduces himself; since monogamy limits man's ability to reproduce himself, it must be replaced by polygamy.

It is only the man whose intellect is clouded by his sexual impulses that could give the name of *the fair sex* to that undersized, narrow-shouldered, broad-hipped, and short-legged race; for the whole beauty of the sex is bound up with this impulse. Instead of calling them beautiful, there would be more warrant for describing women as the unaesthetic sex. . . .

And since women exist in the main solely for the propagation of the species, and are not destined for anything else, they live, as a rule, more for the species than for the individual. . . .

They form the *sexus sequior*—the second sex, inferior in every respect to the first; their infirmities should be treated with consideration; but to show them great reverence is extremely ridiculous, and lowers us in their eyes. When Nature made two divisions of the human race, she did not draw the line exactly through the middle. These divisions are polar and opposed to each other, it is true; but the difference between them is not qualitative merely, it is also quantitative.

This is just the view which the ancients took of a woman, and the view which people in the East take now; and their judgment as to her proper position is much more correct than ours, with our old French notions of gallantry and our preposterous system of reverence—that highest product of Teutonico-Christian stupidity.

The laws of marriage prevailing in Europe consider the woman as the equivalent of the man—start, that is to say, from a wrong position. In our part of the world where monogamy is the rule, to marry means to halve one's rights and double one's duties. Now, when the laws gave woman equal rights with man, they ought also to have endowed her with a masculine intellect. But the fact is that just in proportion as the honors and privileges which the laws accord to women, exceed the amount which nature gives, is there a diminution in the number of women who really participate in these privileges; and all the remainder are deprived of their natural rights by just so much as is given to the others over and above their share. For the institution of monogamy, and the laws of marriage which it entails, bestow upon the woman an unnatural position of privilege, by considering her throughout as the full equivalent of the man, which is by no means the case; and seeing this, men who are shrewd and prudent very often scruple to make so great a sacrifice and to acquiesce in so unfair an arrangement.

Consequently, whilst among polygamous nations every woman is provided for, where monogamy prevails the number of married women is limited; and there remains over a large number of women without stay or support, who, in the upper classes, vegetate as useless old maids, and in the lower succumb to hard work for which they are not suited; or else become *filles de joie,* whose life is as destitute of joy as it is of honor. But under the circumstances they become a necessity; and their position is openly recognized as serving the special end of warding off temptation from those women favored by fate, who have found, or may hope to find, husbands. In London alone there are eighty thousand prostitutes. What are they but the women, who, under the institution of monogamy have come off worse? Theirs is a dreadful fate: they are human sacrifices offered up on the altar of monogamy. The women whose wretched position is here described are the inevitable set-off to the European lady with her arrogance and pretension. Polygamy is therefore a real benefit to the female sex if it is taken as a whole. And, from another point of view, there is no true reason why a man whose wife suffers from chronic illness, or remains barren, or has gradually become too old for him, should not take a second. The motives which induce so many people to become converts to Mormonism appear to be just those which militate against the unnatural institution of monogamy.[26]

In Schopenhauer's work there is a devolution of the status of woman from the deceived but sublime ladies of *The Metaphysics of Sexual Love* to the basically supine in *On Women,* while the evolution of his conception of the male role is ever upward. In the works of the third libertine we shall consider, Friedrich Nietzsche, the subsidiary procreative role of women is a constant. The themes of libertinism abound in Nietzsche's works. Nature, albeit a nature much tempered by the "evolutionary laws" of the survival of the fittest, determines morality, and traditions that are unnatural must be rejected. Thus, since nature determines that woman's sole role is the propagation of the species, any other activity by females is perverse: "When a woman has scholarly inclinations there is generally something wrong with her sexual nature; barrenness itself conduces to a certain virility of taste; man, if I may say so, is the barren animal."[27]

If women are naturally incapable of creative intellectual endeavor, and if as essentially herd creatures they threaten to mire males in herd mentality (and hence must be subdued), they are nonetheless capable of fulfilling their procreative function in the service of evolution.

"Much hath Zarathustra spoken also to us women, but never spake he unto us concerning woman."

And I answered her: "Concerning woman, one should only talk unto men."

"Talk also unto me of woman," said she; "I am old enough to forget it presently."

And I obliged the old woman and spake thus unto her:

Everything in woman is a riddle, and everything in woman hath one solution—it is called pregnancy.

Man is for woman a means: the purpose is always the child. But what is a woman for man?

Two different things wanteth the true man: danger and diversion. Therefore wanteth he woman, as the most dangerous plaything.

Man shall be trained for war, and woman for the recreation of the warrior; all else is folly.

Too sweet fruits—these the warrior liketh not. Therefore liketh he woman;—bitter is even the sweetest woman.

Better than man doth woman understand children, but man is more childish than woman.

In the true man there is a child hidden: it wanteth to play. Up then, ye women, and discover the child in man!

A plaything let woman be, pure and fine like the precious stone, illumined with the virtues of a world not yet come.

Let the beam of a star shine in your love! Let your hope say: "May I bear the Superman."[28] . . .

Not only onward shalt thou propagate thyself, but upward! For that purpose may the garden of marriage help thee!

A higher body shalt thou create, a first movement, a spontaneously rolling wheel—a creating one shalt thou create.

Marriage: so call I the will of the twain to create the one that is more than those who created it. The reverence for one another, as those exercising such a will, call I marriage.

Let this be the significance and the truth of thy marriage. But that which the many-too-many call marriage, those superfluous ones—ah, what shall I call it?

Ah, the poverty of soul in the twain! Ah, the faith of soul in the twain! Ah, the pitiable self-complacency in the twain!

Marriage they call it all; and they say their marriages are made in heaven.

Well, I do not like it, that heaven of the superfluous! No, I do not like them, those animals tangled in the heavenly toils!

Far from me also be the God who limpeth thither to bless what he hath not matched!

Laugh not at such marriages! What child hath not had reason to weep over its parents? . . .

"Lo! now hath the world become perfect!"—thus thinketh every woman when she obeyeth with all her love.

Obey, must the woman, and find a depth for her surface. Surface is woman's soul, a mobile, stormy film on shallow water.

"Man's soul, however, is deep, its current gusheth in subterranean caverns: woman surmiseth its force, but comprehendeth it not.—

Then answered me the old woman: "Many fine things hath Zarathustra said, especially for those who are young enough for them.

Strange! Zarathustra knoweth little about woman, and yet he is right about them! Doth this happen, because with women nothing is impossible?

And now accept a little truth by way of thanks! I am old enough for it! Swaddle it up and hold its mouth: otherwise it will scream too loudly, the little truth."

"Give me, woman, thy little truth!" said I. And thus spake the old woman:
"Thou goest to women? Do not forget thy whip!"—
Thus spake Zarathustra.[29]

Nietzsche finished speaking in 1888 but actually died in 1900. Twentieth-century sexual philosophy opens with, and is almost immediately dominated by, Bertrand Russell—whose syncretic blend of feminism, libertinism, and traditionalism (best expounded in *Marriage and Morals*) constitutes virtually the entire philosophical literature on the subject until Jean-Paul Sartre's analysis in *Being and Nothingness* (1943; chapter three, section two). Aside from the works of Russell and Sartre, the only other major contributions were Ortega y Gasset's *On Love* (1939), Simon de Beauvoir's *The Second Sex* (1949), and the chapter on "The Body in Its Sexual Being" in Merleau-Ponty's *The Phenomenology of Perception* (1945). The views of these philosophers are too contemporary, too significant—and, above all, too interrelated with the essays we have anthologized—to receive the sort of summary historical treatment accorded to the works we have hitherto discussed. Unfortunately, to present their work in an appropriate manner would expand this introduction to such an extent that it would crowd out some of the works we would like to include. We believe that the least unsatisfactory resolution of this dilemma is to refrain from commenting on pre-1968 modern work on sexual philosophy and to refer interested readers to D. P. Verene's *Sexual Love and Western Morality,*[30] which contains a fine selection of and introduction to this literature.

Why do we speak of *pre-1968* literature? To appreciate the significance of the date it is important to take cognizance of the fact that of the major twentieth-century philosophers not previously mentioned—Austin, Carnap, Heidegger, Husserl, James, Peirce, Whitehead, and Wittgenstein—not one wrote on sexual philosophy. *The Encyclopedia of Philosophy* (published in 1967) has no entries under "adultery," "contraception," "engagement," "marriage," "feminism," "libertinism," "monogamy," "perversion," "procreation," "sex," or "women." *The Philosopher's Index* indicates that no articles were published on these topics in 1967. Yet in the very next year articles began to appear in philosophical journals—hence the significance of the date. But why did this begin to happen in 1968?

One hypothesis is that if the time lag between inspiration and publication is taken into account, the two primary causes were the newly emergent feminist movement, which dates from the foundation of NOW (National Organization of Women) in 1965, and the almost simultaneous rebirth of libertinism in the counter-cultural revolution of the late sixties (for example, the "Hippie" movement). In this the genesis of the newly renascent literature on sexual philosophy seems to follow the precedent of its nineteenth-century forbears, although they are unlike most of their nineteenth-century predecessors in their inclination to be favorable toward the feminist movement. Also, two new factors that influence the literature are gay liberation and the ecology movement.

This new literature is not only a response to changing social conditions but to a new philosophical climate as well. By 1968 the "linguistic turn" had been executed and logical positivism had spent itself, leaving Anglo-American philosophers receptive to refocusing philosophical inquiry. By contrast, the existential-phenomenological tradition of Husserl, Heidegger, Sartre, Merleau-Ponty, Marcel, Ricoeur, and Ortega had retained its preoccupation with man's concrete existence. The translations of their works into English, which began to appear in the late fifties and early sixties, increasingly challenged the "analytic" tradition to address itself to mundane realities such as sex. This challenge was taken up explicitly by Thomas Nagel in his pioneering essay of 1969 "Sexual Perversion," and others have since joined the discussion.

In the present volume we have attempted to bring together essays that reflect the most significant aspects of the post-1968 literature. We have acted in the belief that sex, gender, and parenting are too significant to be the exclusive domain of the poets and too important to be left to the pragmatics of revolutionary politics. For the sexual revolution is in our midst, and philosophers have only belatedly begun to contemplate it.

Robert B. Baker
Frederick A. Elliston

Notes

1. Plato, *Symposium,* trans. Percy Shelley (New York: Peter Pauper Press, 1967), pp. 64–65, Steph. 211–12.

2. Epictetus, *The Discourse and Manual,* trans. P. E. Matheson, (Oxford: Clarendon Press, 1916), Book 2, chap. 18, pp. 208–209.

3. Genesis 8:17.

4. Cf. Genesis 3:16.

5. Cf. Janice Moulton, "Sex and Reference," in *Philosophy and Sex,* 1st ed. (Amherst, N.Y.: Prometheus Books, 1975), pp. 34–44.

6. Thomas Aquinas, *On the Truth of the Catholic Faith,* Book 3: Providence, pt. 1, trans. Vernon J. Bourke (New York: Doubleday, 1956).

7. David Hume, *Essays Moral, Political and Literary,* vol. 1, ed. T. H. Green and T. H. Grose (London: Longmans, Green, 1875), pp. 231–39.

8. Immanuel Kant, *Observations on the Feeling of the Beautiful and the Sublime,* trans. John T. Goldthwait (Berkeley and Los Angeles: University of California Press, 1960). All quotes are from section three.

9. Immanuel Kant, *Lectures on Ethics,* trans. Louis Infield (London: Methuen and Co., Ltd., 1930), pp. 162–71.

10. Arthur Schopenhauer, "Metaphysics of the Love and the Sexes," in Edman, *The Philosophy of Schopenhauer* (New York: Random House, Modern Library), p. 334.

11. Oxford, 1893.

12. In Edman, *The Philosophy of Schopenhauer,* pp. 342–43.

13. Ibid., pp. 349–50.

14. Ibid., pp. 373–74.

15. For an exposition of the views of Fourier and Marx see David Palmer, "The Consolation of the Wedded," in *Philosophy and Sex,* 1st ed., pp. 178–89.

16. John Stuart Mill, "The Subjection of Women" (1869), reprinted in *Three Essays by J. S. Mill* (London: Oxford University Press, World Classics Series, 1966), p. 427.

17. Book 1, chaps. 20–23.

18. *The Science of Rights* (Philadelphia: Lippincott, 1869), chap. 1, sec. 1.

19. This is the argument of Book 1 of *The Science of Rights* (Philadelphia: Lippincott, 1869).

20. Fichte, *The Science of Rights,* p. 394.

21. Ibid., sec. 4, pp. 398–401.

22. Cf. Thomas' propositions 3–5.

23. Fichte, *The Science of Rights,* pp. 406–407.

24. Ibid., pp. 440–42.

25. Marquis de Sade, *The Complete Justine* (New York: Grove Press, 1965), p. 318.

26. *Essays on Women* (New York: Simon & Schuster, Philosophers Library, 1928), pp. 450–55.

27. "Beyond Good and Evil," sec. 144 in *The Philosophy of Nietzsche* (New York: Random House, Modern Library, 1970), pp. 465–66.

28. "Child and Marriage," chap. 28 of "Thus Spake Zarathustra," trans. Thomas Common, in ibid., pp. 72–73.

29. "Old and Young Women," chap. 18 of "Thus Spake Zarathustra," in ibid., pp. 68–69.

30. New York: Harper & Row, 1972.

PART ONE

LOVE, MARRIAGE, and REPRODUCTION

1

Love:
A Feminist Critique

Shulamith Firestone

A book on radical feminism that did not deal with love would be a political failure. For love, perhaps even more than childbearing, is the pivot of women's oppression today. I realize this has frightening implications: Do we want to get rid of love?

The panic felt at any threat to love is a good clue to its political significance. Another sign that love is central to any analysis of women or sex psychology is its omission from culture itself, its relegation to "personal life." (And whoever heard of logic in the bedroom?) Yes, it is portrayed in novels, even metaphysics, but in them it is described, or better, recreated, not analyzed. Love has never been *understood,* though it may have been fully *experienced,* and that experience communicated.

There is reason for this absence of analysis: *Women and Love are underpinnings. Examine them and you threaten the very structure of culture.*

The tired question "What were women doing while men created masterpieces?" deserves more than the obvious reply: Women were barred from culture, exploited in their role of mother. Or its reverse: Women had no need for paintings since they created children. Love is tied to culture in much deeper ways than that. Men were thinking, writing, and creating, because women were pouring their energy into those men; women are not creating culture because they are preoccupied with love.

That women live for love and men for work is a truism. Freud was the first to attempt to ground this dichotomy in the individual psyche: the male child, sexually rejected by the first person in his attention, his mother, "sublimates" his "libido"—his reservoir of sexual (life) energies—into long-term projects, in the hope of gaining love in a more generalized form; thus he displaces his need for love into a need for recognition. This process does not occur as much in the female: most women never stop seeking direct warmth and approval.

There is also much truth in the clichés that "behind every man there is a woman," and that "women are the power behind [read: voltage in] the throne." (Male) culture was built on the love of women, and at their expense. Women provided the substance of those male masterpieces; and for millennia they have done the work, and suffered the costs, of one-way emotional relationships the benefits of which went to men and to the work of men. So if women are a parasitical class living off, and at the margins of, the male economy, the reverse too is true: *(Male) culture was (and is) parasitical, feeding on the emotional strength of women without reciprocity.*

Moreover, we tend to forget that this culture is not universal, but rather sectarian, presenting only half the spectrum. The very structure of culture itself, as we shall see, is saturated with the sexual polarity, as well as being in every degree run by, for, and in the interests of male society. But while the male half is termed all of culture, men have not forgotten there is a female "emotional" half: They live it on the sly. As the result of their battle to reject the female in themselves . . . they are unable to take love seriously as a cultural matter; but they can't do without it altogether. Love is the underbelly of (male) culture just as love is the weak spot of every man, bent on proving his virility in that large male world of "travel and adventure." Women have always known how men need love, and how they deny this need. Perhaps this explains the peculiar contempt women so universally feel for men ("men are so dumb"), for they can see their men are posturing in the outside world.

I

How does this phenomenon "love" operate? Contrary to popular opinion, love is not altruistic. The initial attraction is based on curious admiration (more often today, envy and resentment) for the self-possession, the integrated unity, of the other and a wish to become part of this Self in some way (today, read: intrude or take over), to become important to that psychic balance. The self-containment of the other creates desire (read: a challenge); admiration (envy) of the other becomes a wish to incorporate (possess) its qualities. A clash of selves follows in which the individual attempts to fight off the growing hold over him of the other. Love is the final opening up to (or, surrender to the dominion of) the other. The lover demonstrates to the beloved how he himself would like to be treated. ("I tried so hard to make him fall in love with me that I fell in love with him myself.") Thus love is the height of selfishness: the self attempts to enrich itself through the absorption of another being. Love is being psychically wide-open to another. It is a situation of total emotional vulnerability. Therefore it must be not only the incorporation of the other, but an *exchange* of selves. Anything short of a mutual exchange will hurt one or the other party.

There is nothing inherently destructive about this process. A little healthy selfishness would be a refreshing change. Love between two equals would be an enrichment, each enlarging himself through the other: instead of being one, locked in the cell of himself with only his own experience and view, he could participate in the existence of another—an extra window on the world. This accounts for the bliss that successful lovers experience: Lovers are temporarily freed from the burden of isolation that every individual bears.

But bliss in love is seldom the case: For every successful contemporary love experience, for every short period of enrichment, there are ten destructive love experiences, post-love "downs" of much longer duration—often resulting in the destruction of the individual, or at least an emotional cynicism that makes it difficult or impossible ever to love again. Why should this be so, if it is not actually inherent in the love process itself?

Let's talk about love in its destructive guise—and why it gets that way, referring . . . to the work of Theodore Reik. Reik's concrete observation brings him closer than many better minds to understanding the *process* of "falling in love," but he is off insofar as he confuses love as it exists in our present society with love itself. He notes that love is a reaction formation, a cycle of envy, hostility, and possessiveness: he sees that it is preceded by dissatisfaction with oneself, a yearning for something better, created by a discrepancy between the ego and the ego-ideal; that the bliss love produces is due to the resolution of this tension by the substitution, in place of one's own ego-ideal, of the other; and finally that love fades "because the other can't live up to your high ego-ideal any more than you could, and the judgment will be the harsher the higher are the claims on oneself." Thus in Reik's view love wears down just as it wound up: Dissatisfaction with oneself (whoever heard of falling in love the week one is leaving for Europe?) leads to astonishment at the other person's self-containment; to envy; to hostility; to possessive love; and back again through exactly the same process. This is the love process *today.* But why must it be this way?

Many, for example Denis de Rougemont in *Love in the Western World,* have tried to draw a distinction between romantic "falling in love" with its "false reciprocity which disguises a twin narcissism" (the Pagan Eros) and an unselfish love for the other person as that person really is (the Christian Agape). De Rougemont attributes the morbid passion of Tristan and Iseult (romantic love) to a vulgarization of specific mystical and religious currents in Western civilization.

I believe instead that *love is essentially a simple phenomenon—unless it has become complicated, corrupted, or obstructed by an unequal balance of power.* We have seen that love demands a mutual vulnerability or it turns destructive: the destructive effects of love occur only in a context of inequality. But if, as we have seen, (biological) inequality has always remained a constant, existing to varying degrees, then it is understandable that "romantic love" would develop. . . .

How does the sex class system based on the unequal power distribution of the biological family affect love between the sexes? In discussing Freudianism, we have gone into the psychic structuring of the individual within the family and how this organization of personality must be different for the male and the female because of their very different relationships to the mother. At present the insular interdependency of the mother/child relationship forces both male and female children into anxiety about losing the mother's love, on which they depend for physical survival. When later (Erich Fromm notwithstanding) the child learns that the mother's love is conditional, to be rewarded the child in return for approved behavior (that is, behavior in line with the mother's own values and personal ego gratification—for she is free to mold the child "creatively," however she happens to define that), the child's anxiety turns into desperation. This, coinciding with the sexual rejection of the male child by the mother, causes, as we have seen, a schizophrenia in the boy between the emotional and the physical, and in the girl, the mother's rejection, occurring for different reasons, produces an insecurity about her identity in general, creating a lifelong need for approval. (Later her lover replaces her father as a grantor of the necessary surrogate identity—she sees everything through his eyes.) Here originates the hunger for love that later sends both sexes searching in one person after the other for a state of ego security. But because of the early rejection, to the degree that it occurred, the male will be terrified of committing himself, of "opening up" and then being smashed. . . . To the degree that a woman is like his mother, the incest taboo operates to restrain his total sexual/emotional commitment; for him to feel safely the kind of total response he first felt for his mother, which was rejected, he must degrade this woman so as to distinguish her from the mother. This behavior reproduced on a larger scale explains many cultural phenomena, including perhaps the ideal love-worship of chivalric times, the forerunner of modern romanticism.

Romantic idealization is partially responsible, at least on the part of men, for a peculiar characteristic of "falling" in love: the change takes place in the lover almost independently of the character of the love object. Occasionally the lover, though beside himself, sees with another rational part of his faculties that, objectively speaking, the one he loves isn't worth all this blind devotion; but he is helpless to act on this, "a slave to love." More often he fools himself entirely. But others can see what is happening ("How on earth he could love her is beyond me!"). This idealization occurs much less frequently on the part of women, as is borne out by Reik's clinical studies. A man must idealize one woman over the rest in order to justify his descent to a lower caste. Women have no such reason to idealize men—in fact, when one's life depends on one's ability to "psych" men out, such idealization may actually be dangerous—though a fear of male power in general may carry over into relationships with individual men, appearing to be the same phenomenon. But though women know to be inauthentic this male "falling in love," all women, in one way or another, require proof of it from men before they can allow themselves to love (genuinely, in their case) in return. For this idealization process acts to artificially equalize the two parties, a minimum precondition for the development of an uncorrupted love—we have seen that love requires a mutual vulnerability that is impossible to achieve in an unequal power situation. *Thus "falling in love" is no more than the process of alteration of male vision—through idealization, mystification, glorification—that renders void the woman's class inferiority.*

However, the woman knows that this idealization, which she works so hard to produce, is a lie, and that it is only a matter of time before he "sees through her." Her life is a hell, vacillating between an all-consuming need for male love and approval to raise her from her class subjection, to persistent feelings of inauthenticity when she does achieve his love. Thus her whole identity hangs in the balance of her love life. She is allowed to love herself only if a man finds her worthy of love.

But if we could eliminate the political context of love between the sexes, would we not have some degree of idealization remaining in the love process itself? I think so. For the process occurs in the same manner whoever the love choice: the lover "opens up" to the other. Because of this fusion of egos, in which each sees and cares about the other as a new self, the beauty/character of the beloved, perhaps hidden to outsiders under layers of defenses, is revealed. "I wonder what she sees in him," then, means not only, "She is a fool, blinded with romanticism," but, "Her love has lent her x-ray vision. Perhaps we are missing something." (Note that this phrase is most commonly used about women. The equivalent phrase about *men's* slavery to love is more often something like, "She has him wrapped around her finger," she has him so "snowed" that he is the last one to see through her.) Increased sensitivity to the real, if hidden, values in the other, however, is not "blindness" or "idealization" but is, in fact, deeper vision. It is only the *false* idealization we have described above that is responsible for the destruction. Thus it is not the process of love itself that is at fault, but its *political,* i.e., unequal *power* context: the who, why, when and where of it is what makes it now such a holocaust.

II

But abstractions about love are only one more symptom of its diseased state. (As one female patient of Reik so astutely put it, "Men take love either too seriously or not seriously enough.") Let's look at it more concretely, as we now experience it in its corrupted form. Once again we shall quote from the Reikian Confessional. For if Reik's work has any value it is where he might least suspect, i.e., in his trivial feminine urge to "gossip." Here he is, justifying himself (one supposes his Superego is troubling him):

A has-been like myself must always be somewhere and working on something. Why should I not occupy myself with those small questions that are not often posed and yet perhaps can be answered? The "petites questions" have a legitimate place beside the great and fundamental problems of psychoanalysis.

It takes moral courage to write about certain things, as for example about a game that little girls play in the intervals between classes. Is such a theme really worthy of a *serious* psychoanalyst who has passed his 77th year? (Italics mine)

And he reminds himself:

But in psychoanalysis there are no unimportant thoughts; there are only thoughts that pretend to be unimportant in order not to be told.

Thus he rationalizes what in fact may be the only valuable contribution of his work. Here are his patients of both sexes speaking for themselves about their love lives:

WOMEN:

Later on he called me a sweet girl. . . . I didn't answer . . . what could I say? . . . but I knew I was not a sweet girl at all and that he sees me as someone I'm not.

No man can love a girl the way a girl loves a man.

I can go a long time without sex, but not without love.

It's like H_2O instead of water.

I sometimes think that all men are sex-crazy and sex-starved. All they can think about when they are with a girl is going to bed with her.

Have I nothing to offer this man but this body?

I took off my dress and my bra and stretched myself out on his bed and waited. For an instant I thought of myself as an animal of sacrifice on the altar.

I don't understand the feelings of men. My husband has me. Why does he need other women? What have they got that I haven't got?

Believe me, if all wives whose husbands had affairs left them, we would only have divorced women in this country.

After my husband had quite a few affairs, I flirted with the fantasy of taking a lover. Why not? What's sauce for the gander is sauce for the goose. . . . But I was stupid as a goose: I didn't have it in me to have an extramarital affair.

I asked several people whether men also sometimes cry themselves to sleep. I don't believe it.

MEN (for further illustration, see *Screw*):

It's not true that only the external appearance of a woman matters. The underwear is also important.

It's not difficult to make it with a girl. What's difficult is to make an end of it.

The girl asked me whether I cared for her mind. I was tempted to answer I cared more for her behind.

"Are you going already?" she said when she opened her eyes. It was a bedroom cliché whether I left after an hour or after two days.

Perhaps it's necessary to fool the woman and to pretend you love her. But why should I fool myself?

When she is sick, she turns me off. But when I'm sick she feels sorry for me and is more affectionate than usual.

It is not enough for my wife that I have to hear her talking all the time—blah, blah, blah. She also expects me to hear what she is saying.

Simone de Beauvoir said it: "The word love has by no means the same sense for both sexes, and this is one cause of the serious misunderstandings which divide them." Above I have illustrated some of the traditional differences between men and women in love that come up so frequently in parlor discussions of the "double standard," where it is generally agreed: That women are monogamous, better at loving, possessive, "clinging," more interested in (highly involved) "relationships" than in sex per se, and they confuse affection with sexual desire. That men are interested in nothing but a screw (Wham, bam, thank you Ma'am!), or else romanticize the woman ridiculously; that once sure of her, they become notorious philanderers, never satisfied; that they mistake sex for emotion. All this bears out what we have discussed—the difference in the psychosexual organizations of the two sexes, determined by the first relationship to the mother.

I draw three conclusions based on these differences:

1) That men can't love. (Male hormones? Women traditionally expect and accept an emotional invalidism in men that they would find intolerable in a woman.)

2) That women's "clinging" behavior is necessitated by their objective social situation.

3) That this situation has not changed significantly from what it ever was.

Men can't love. We have seen why it is that men have difficulty loving and that while men may love, they usually "fall in love"—with their own projected image. Most often they are pounding down a woman's door one day, and thoroughly disillusioned with her the next; but it is rare for women to leave men, and then it is usually for more than ample reason.

It is dangerous to feel sorry for one's oppressor—women are especially prone to this failing—but I am tempted to do it in this case. Being unable to love is hell. This is the way it proceeds: as soon as the man feels any pressure from the other partner to commit himself, he panics and may react in one of several ways:

1) He may rush out and screw ten other women to prove that the first woman has no hold over him. If she accepts this, he may continue to see her on this basis. The other women verify his (false) freedom; periodic arguments about them keep his panic at bay. But the women are a paper tiger, for nothing very deep could be happening with them anyway; he is balancing them against each other so that none of them can get much of him. Many smart women, recognizing this to be only a safety valve on their man's anxiety, give him "a long leash." For the real issue under all the fights about other women is that the man is unable to commit himself.

2) He may consistently exhibit unpredictable behavior, standing her up frequently, being indefinite about the next date, telling her that "my work comes first," or offering a variety of other excuses. That is, though he senses her anxiety, he refuses to reassure her in any way, or even to recognize her anxiety as legitimate. For he *needs* her anxiety as a steady reminder that he is still free, that the door is not entirely closed.

3) When he *is* forced into (an uneasy) commitment, he makes her pay for it: by ogling other women in her presence, by comparing her unfavorably to past girlfriends or movie stars, by snide reminders in front of his friends that she is his "ball and chain," by calling her a "nag," a "bitch," "a shrew," or by suggesting that if he were only a bachelor he would be a lot better off. His ambivalence about women's "inferiority" comes out: by being committed to one, he has somehow made the hated female identification, which he now must repeatedly deny if he is to maintain his self-respect in the (male) community. This steady derogation is not entirely put on: for in fact every other girl suddenly does look a lot better, he can't help feeling he has missed something—and, naturally, his woman is to blame. For he has never given up the search for the ideal; she has forced him to resign from it. Probably he will go to his grave feeling cheated, never realizing that there isn't much difference between one woman and the other, that it is the loving that *creates* the difference.

There are many variations of straining at the bit. Many men go from one casual thing to another, getting out every time it begins to get hot. And yet to live without love in the end proves intolerable to men just as it does to women. The question that remains for every normal male is, then, *how do I get someone to love me without her demanding an equal commitment in return?*

Women's "clinging" behavior is required by the objective social situation. The female *response* to such a situation of male hysteria at any prospect of mutual commitment was the development of subtle methods of manipulation, to force as much commitment as *could* be forced from men. Over the centuries strategies have been devised, tested, and passed on from mother to daughter in secret tête-à-têtes, passed around at "kaffee-klatsches" ("I never understand what it is women spend so much time talking about!"), or, in recent times, via the telephone. These are not trivial gossip sessions at all (as women prefer men to believe), but desperate strategies for survival. More real brilliance goes into one-hour coed telephone dialogue about men than into that same coed's four years of college study, or for that matter, than into most male political maneuvers. It is no wonder, then, that even the few women without "family obligations" always arrive exhausted at the starting line of any serious endeavor. It takes one's major energy for the best portion of one's creative years to "make a good catch," and a good part of the rest of one's life to "hold" that catch. ("To be in love can be a full-time job for a woman, like that of a profession for a man.") Women who choose to drop out of this race are choosing a life without love, something that, as we have seen, most *men* don't have the courage to do.

But unfortunately The Manhunt is characterized by an emotional urgency beyond this simple desire for return commitment. It is compounded by the very class reality that produced the male inability to love in the first place. In a male-run society that defines women as an inferior and parasitical class, a woman who does not achieve male approval in some form is doomed. To legitimate her existence, a woman must be *more* than woman, she must continually search for an out from her inferior definition;[1] and men are the only ones in a position to bestow on her this state of grace. But because the woman is rarely allowed to realize herself through activity in the larger (male) society—and when she is, she is seldom granted the recognition she deserves—it becomes easier to try for the recognition of one man than of many; and in fact this is exactly the choice most women make. Thus once more the phenomenon of love, good in itself, is corrupted by its class context: women must have love not only for healthy reasons but actually to validate their existence.

In addition, the continued *economic* dependence of women makes a situation of healthy love between equals impossible. Women today still live under a system of patronage: With few exceptions, they have the choice, not between either freedom or marriage, but between being either public or private property. Women who merge with a member of the ruling class can at least hope that some of his privilege will, so to speak, rub off. But women without men are in the same situation as orphans: they are a helpless sub-class lacking the protection of the powerful. This is the antithesis of freedom when they are still (negatively) defined by a class situation: for now they are in a situation of *magnified* vulnerability. To participate in one's subjection by choosing one's master often gives the illusion of free choice; but in reality a woman is never free to choose love without external motivations. For her at the present time, the two things, love and status, must remain inextricably intertwined.

Now assuming that a woman does not lose sight of these fundamental factors of her condition when she loves, she will never be able to love gratuitously, but only in exchange for security:

1) the emotional security which, we have seen, she is justified in demanding.

2) the emotional identity which she should be able to find through work and recognition, but which she is denied—thus forcing her to seek her definition through a man.

3) the economic class security that, in this society, is attached to her ability to "hook" a man.

Two of these three demands are invalid as conditions of "love," but are imposed on it, weighing it down.

Thus, in their precarious political situation, women can't afford the luxury of spontaneous love. It is much too dangerous. The love and approval of men is all-important. To love thoughtlessly, before one has ensured return commitment, would endanger that approval. Here is Reik:

> It finally became clear during psychoanalysis that the patient was afraid that if she should show a man she loved him, he would consider her inferior and leave her.

For once a woman plunges in emotionally, she will be helpless to play the necessary games: her love would come first, demanding expression. To pretend a coolness she does not feel, *then,* would be too painful, and further, it would be pointless: she would be cutting off her nose to spite her face, for freedom to love is what she was aiming for. But in order to guarantee such a commitment, she *must* restrain her emotions, she *must* play games. For, as we have seen, men do not commit themselves to mutual openness and vulnerability until they are forced to.

How does she then go about forcing this commitment from the male? One of her most potent weapons is sex—she can work him up to a state of physical torment with a variety of games: by denying his need, by teasing it, by giving and taking it back, by jealousy, and so forth. A woman under analysis wonders why:

> There are few women who never ask themselves on certain occasions, "How hard should I make it for a man?" I think no man is troubled with questions of this kind. He perhaps asks himself only, "When will she give in?"

Men are right when they complain that women lack discrimination, that they seldom love a man for his individual traits but rather for what he has to offer (his class), that they are calculating, that they use sex to gain other ends, etc. For in fact women are in no position to love freely. If a woman is lucky enough to find "a decent guy" to love her and support her, she is doing well—and usually will be grateful enough to return his love. About the only discrimination women *are* able to exercise is the choice between the men who have chosen them, or a playing off of one male, one power, against the other. But *provoking* a man's interest, and *snaring* his commitment once he has expressed that interest, is not exactly self-determination.

Now what happens after she has finally hooked her man, after he has fallen in love with her and will do anything? She has a new set of problems. Now she can release the vise, open her net, and examine what she has caught. Usually she is disappointed. It is nothing she would have bothered with were *she* a man. It is usually way below her level. (Check this out sometime: Talk to a few of those mousy wives.) "He may be a poor thing, but at least I've got a man of my own" is usually more the way she feels. But at least now she can drop her act. For the first time it is safe to love—now she must try like hell to catch up to him emotionally, to really mean what she has pretended all along. Often she is troubled by worries that he will find her out. She feels like an impostor. She is haunted by fears that he doesn't love the "real" her—and usually she is right. ("She wanted to marry a man with whom she could be as bitchy as she really is.")

This is just about when she discovers that love and marriage mean a different thing for a male than they do for her: Though men in general believe women in general to be inferior, every man has reserved a special place in his mind for the one woman he will elevate above the rest by virtue of association with himself. Until now the woman, out in the cold, begged for his approval, dying to clamber onto this clean well-lighted place. But once there, she realizes that she was elevated above other women not in recognition of her real value, but only because she matched nicely his store-bought pedestal. Probably he doesn't even know who she is (if indeed by this time she herself knows). He has let her in not because he genuinely loved her, but only because she played so well into his preconceived fantasies. Though she knew his love to be false, since she herself engineered it, she can't help feeling contempt for him. But she is afraid, at first, to reveal her true self, for then perhaps even that false love would go. And finally she understands that for him, too, marriage had all kinds of motivations that had nothing to do with love. She was merely the one closest to his fantasy image: she has been named Most Versatile Actress for the multi-role of Alter Ego, Mother of My Children, Housekeeper, Cook, Companion, in *his* play. She has been bought to fill an empty space in his life; but her life is nothing.

So she has not saved herself from being like other women. She is lifted out of that class only because she now is an appendage of a member of the master class; and he cannot associate with her unless he raises her status. But she has not been freed, she has been promoted to "house-nigger," she has been elevated only to be used in a different way. She feels cheated. She has gotten not love and recognition, but possessorship and control. This is when she is transformed from Blushing Bride to Bitch, a change that, no matter how universal and predictable, still leaves the individual husband perplexed. ("You're not the girl I married.")

The situation of women has not changed significantly from what it ever was. For the past fifty years women have been in a double bind about love: under the guise of a "sexual revolution," presumed to have occurred ("Oh, c'mon Baby, where have you *been?* Haven't you heard of the sexual revolution?"), women have been persuaded to shed their armor. The modern woman is in horror of being thought a bitch, where her grandmother expected that to happen as the natural course of things. Men, too, in her grandmother's time, expected that any self-respecting woman would keep *them* waiting, would play all the right games without shame: a woman who did not guard her own interests in this way was not respected. It was out in the open.

But the rhetoric of the sexual revolution, if it brought no improvements for women, proved to have great value for men. By convincing women that the usual female games and demands were despicable, unfair, prudish, old-fashioned, puritanical, and self-destructive, a new reservoir of available females was created to expand the tight supply of goods available for traditional sexual exploitation, disarming women of even the little protection they had so painfully acquired. Women today dare not make the old demands for fear of having a whole new vocabulary, designed just for this purpose, hurled at them: "fucked up," "ballbreaker," "cockteaser," "a real drag," "a bad trip"—to be a "groovy chick" is the ideal.

Even now many women know what's up and avoid the trap, preferring to be called names rather than be cheated out of the little they can hope for from men (for it is still true that even the hippest want an "old lady" who is relatively unused). But more and more women are sucked into the trap, only to find out too late, and bitterly, that the traditional female games had a point; they are shocked to catch themselves at thirty complaining in a vocabulary dangerously close to the old I've-been-used-men-are-wolves-they're-all-bastards variety. Eventually they are forced to acknowledge the old-wives' truth: a fair and generous woman is (at best) respected, but seldom loved. Here is a description, still valid today, of the "emancipated" woman—in this case a Greenwich Village artist of the thirties—from *Mosquitoes,* an early Faulkner novel:

> She had always had trouble with her men. . . . Sooner or later they always ran out on her. . . . Men she recognized as having potentialities all passed through a violent but temporary period of interest which ceased as abruptly as it began, without leaving even the lingering threads of mutually remembered incidence, like those brief thunderstorms of August that threaten and dissolve for no apparent reason without producing any rain.
>
> At times she speculated with almost masculine detachment on the reason for this. She always tried to keep their relationships on the plane which the men themselves seemed to prefer—certainly no woman would, and few women could, demand less of their men than she did. She never made arbitrary demands on their time, never caused them to wait for her nor to see her home at inconvenient hours, never made them fetch and carry for her; she fed them and flattered herself that she was a good listener. And yet—She thought of the women she knew; how all of them had at least one obviously entranced male; she thought of the women she had observed; how they seemed to acquire a man at will, and if he failed to stay acquired, how readily they replaced him.

Women of high ideals who believed emancipation possible, women who tried desperately to rid themselves of feminine "hangups," to cultivate what they believed to be the greater directness, honesty, and generosity of men, were badly fooled. They found that no one appreciated their intelligent conversation, their high aspirations, their great sacrifices to avoid developing the personalities of their mothers. For much as men were glad to enjoy their wit, their style, their sex, and their candlelight suppers, they always ended up marrying The Bitch, and then, to top it all off, came back to complain of what a horror she was. "Emancipated" women found out that the honesty, generosity, and camaraderie of men was a lie: men were all too glad to use them and then sell them out, in the name of *true* friendship. ("I respect and like you a great deal, but let's be reasonable. . . ." And then there are the men who take her out to discuss Simone de Beauvoir, leaving their wives at home with the diapers.) "Emancipated" women found out that men were far from "good guys" to be emulated; they found out that by imitating male sexual patterns (the roving eye, the search for the ideal, the emphasis on physical attraction, etc.), they were not only achieving liberation, they were falling into something much worse than what they had given up. They were *imitating*. And they had inoculated themselves with a sickness that had not even sprung from their own psyches. They found that their new "cool" was shallow and meaningless, that their emotions were drying up behind it, that they were aging and becoming decadent: they feared they were losing their ability to love. They had gained nothing by imitating men: shallowness and callowness, and they were not so good at it either, because somewhere inside it still went against the grain.

Thus women who had decided not to marry because they were wise enough to look around and see where it led found that it was marry or nothing. Men gave their commitment only for a price: share (shoulder) his life, stand on his pedestal, become his appendage, or else. Or else—be consigned forever to that limbo of "chicks" who mean nothing or at least not what mother meant. Be the "other woman" the rest of one's life, used to provoke his wife, prove his virility and/or his independence, discussed by his friends as his latest "interesting" conquest. (For even if she had given up those terms and what they stood for, no male had.) Yes, love means an entirely different thing to men than to women: it means ownership and control; it means jealousy, where he never exhibited it before—when she might have wanted him to (who cares if she is broke or raped until she officially belongs to him: then he is a raging dynamo, a veritable cyclone, because his property, his ego extension have been threatened); it means a growing lack of interest, coupled with a roving eye. Who needs it?

Sadly, women do. Here are Reik's patients once more:

She sometimes has delusions of not being persecuted by men anymore. At those times of her nonpersecution mania she is very depressed.

And:

All men are selfish, brutal and inconsiderate—and I wish I could find one.

We have seen that a woman needs love, first, for its natural enriching function, and second, for social and economic reasons which have nothing to do with love. To deny her need is to put herself in an extra-vulnerable spot socially and economically, as well as to destroy her emotional equilibrium, which, unlike most men's, is basically healthy. Are men worth that? Decidedly no. Most women feel that to do such tailspins for a man would be to add insult to injury. They go on as before, making the best of a bad situation. If it gets *too* bad, they head for a (male) shrink:

A young woman patient was once asked during a psychoanalytic consultation whether she preferred to see a man or woman psychoanalyst. Without the slightest hesitation she said, "A woman psychoanalyst because I am too eager for the approval of a man."

Note

1. Thus the peculiar situation that women never object to the insulting of women as a class, *as long as* they individually are excepted. The worst insult for a woman is that she is "just like a woman," i.e., no better; the highest compliment that she has the brains, talent, dignity, or strength of a man. In fact, like every member of an oppressed class, she herself participates in the insulting of others like herself, hoping thereby to make it obvious that *she* as an individual is above their behavior. Thus women as a class are set against each other ["Divide and Conquer"], the "other woman" believing that the wife is a "bitch" who "doesn't understand him," and the wife believing that the other woman is an "opportunist' who is "taking advantage" of him—while the culprit himself sneaks away free.

2

Love and Feminism

Robert C. Solomon

"Love. Being in love. Yuck!" Val poured more wine. . . . "I mean, it's one of those things they've erected, a bunch of nonsense *erected*—and that's the crucial word—into truth by a bunch of intelligent *men*—another crucial word. What the particular nonsense is, isn't particularly important. What's important is why they do it."

Marilyn French, *The Women's Room*

Is romantic love—the perennial obsession of the Western world—unfair to women, perhaps even a systematic form of rape? So it has been charged.

The charge itself is simple and persuasive. It begins with a fact, that some (many? most? almost all?) women are unhappy and unfulfilled; the fact suggests a hypothesis, that the cause of this unhappiness is the promise of romantic love, which will turn household chores into meaningful and significant acts of devotion, which will transform the biological pains and daily difficulties of having babies into cosmic events, which is said to last "forever" but normally lasts but a few months or years, followed by a lifetime in which to dwell on one's wasted opportunities. The hypothesis in turn implies a theory: that romantic love is neither "natural" nor "divine," as the (male) poets have always insisted, but rather a cultural invention, created by men for the subjugation of women.

It is, when spelled out, an extremely persuasive polemic, far more so than the murky and pious praise of love and lessons on our alleged "need for love" that have been the topic of so many predominantly male theoreticians and theologians from Plato and St. Paul to Rollo May. But it is a polemic with a tragic double bind, one that is also evident in *The Women's Room* and in the work of other authors from Virginia Woolf to Doris Lessing. In its simplest formulation, it is the feeling that love is a lie but nevertheless one cannot live without it.

Adapted from *Love: Emotion, Myth & Metaphor* (Doubleday-Anchor, 1981)

A double bind is not a question of mere addiction, a romantic habit that we would like to break but cannot; it is rather an impossible confusion in which we both accept and at the same time reject an utterly absurd ideal of love. What I would like to do here is attack this ideal, and to suggest that we can continue to honor a more reasonable notion of romantic love, not in spite of or even in addition to but as a presupposition of feminism. The latter, I would argue, depends largely upon the former.

The "dump love" argument begins with the realization that romantic love, which has so often been promised to women (by men), is an illusion, a fraud, a myth. It does not, as promised, change one's life once and for all or turn the drudgery of housework into joy, much less forever. But not only that. It is the myth itself that has this as its ulterior motive; it is an illusion whose deconstruction reveals a political purpose. Love was invented by men, as an instrument of a kind of culture—which might be summarized as "capitalist"—in order to "keep women in their place," or in any case isolated and dependent on men, and if not happy then at least hopeful of love and complacent about their socially inferior but infinitely useful occupations. By preaching that love is always good and desirable, it is charged, men have convinced at least most women that love is more important than politics and power, thus limiting the competition to themselves. By teaching that love is "everything," men have convinced many women that it is also worth any sacrifice, and like generals in their luxurious tents behind the battle lines, they have succeeded in getting others to make the sacrifices without having to make them themselves. Within the realm of love itself, men have created an image of the "feminine," such that the virtues a woman finds or creates in herself for the sake of love are directly at odds with the virtues required for success in the world: soft, yielding, quiet, accepting versus hard, aggressive, outspoken and critical. A man can be sexy in pursuit of his career; a woman is sexy despite or in contrast to hers (unless, of course, sex is her career). For a woman, to be in love is to be submissive, and therefore disadvantaged and powerless within the relationship, second-class and degraded. If the lover or husband also insists on praising her effusely, worshipping the ground she walks on or putting her "on a pedestal," that is just so much worse, for he is disguising the fact that she is becoming the willing victim in her own political oppression even while being worshiped.

This is not the smirking cynicism of neo-Freudian male reductionist "love is nothing but . . ." theorists like Philip Slater who argue that "romantic love is a scarcity mechanism . . . whose only function is to transmute that which is plentiful [i.e., sex] into that which is in short supply. Although romantic love always verges on the ridiculous, Western peoples and Americans in particular have shown an impressive tendency to take it seriously."[1] The argument that is so well-presented in *The Women's Room* represents the personal outrage and bitter disappointment of a million or more women, only some of whom would identify themselves as "feminists" and few of whom would be able to articulate the precise mechanism by which they have been systematically shut out of power or what all of this has to do with love. But that means it is an argument to be taken especially seriously, for it is not just an academic theory that is at stake.

Now to begin with, there is much here that is no longer controversial, no longer deniable:

1. Much of what we believe about love is demonstrably false or hopelessly obscure, mere mythology and pious illusion—men merely masturbating with the archaic concept of *eros.*

2. Love is not "everything" nor is it "the answer"; it is not always good or desirable. Sometimes, and for some people, it is simply stupid.

3. Love provides private compensation for public impotence or anonymity. Indeed, it is the very essence of love that it allows us to play roles and feel "special" in our personal relationships even when—especially when—we feel overburdened or underappreciated in our jobs or in our social roles.

4. Love is a cultural creation, the product of a male-dominated society, and so, we may reasonably suppose, "erected by men," presumably not to their own disadvantage. Indeed, our current conception of romantic love is largely a literary creation, from Plato and the Bible, from the medieval poets to Shakespeare and the Brownings. On the other hand, romantic love is unknown and would be considered ludicrous in many societies around the world.

5. Love consists of personal roles which, more often than not, cast the women into the more submissive and subservient position. There cannot be any argument against the claim that the promise of love, at least, has long been used against women, by way of compensation for political impotence, as an excuse to keep them in the home (and away from the public positions of power) and as a ready rationalization for social inequities in everything from politics ("women are too emotional") to changing diapers ("women are naturally better at that sort of thing").

Indeed there can be no objection to the charge that the "feminine" role in love makes it difficult for a woman to be both romantically desirable and successful in the male-dominated world of money and power.

So what is left of love to defend?

What does not follow is the conclusion that love itself is exploitative, a source of inequity or an obstacle to equality between the sexes. The fact that much of what we believe about love is illusion does not mean that love itself is illusion, nor does it follow from the fact that love is a cultural artifact that it is simply artificial, a "fiction" or a manipulative ploy. It does not follow from the fact that it was (probably) invented by men that love is disadvantageous to women (a man may have invented the wheel and the toothbrush too). It does not follow from the fact that romantic love is often used to reinforce submissive and subservient female roles that those roles are intrinsic to romantic love as such.

If, as the feminist argument charges, romantic love *required* in its structure a division into distinctively male and female roles, strictly corresponding to what has traditionally been called "masculinity" and "femininity," then I would agree that love and the love world constitute archaic emotional structures that we would

be better off leaving behind us. But if, as I will argue, romantic roles are fundamentally sex-neutral and presuppose a significant degree of equality, then the
much-abused neo-Victorian crypto-caveman scenario of macho "me-Tarzan" and
passive-submissive, lovingly house-cleaning Jane is not at all a paradigm of love
but at most one of its many historical curiosities—like Quasimodo and Esmerelda.

The History of Love

Looking back at the history of romantic love, it is no doubt true that it was
"erected," in part by men, in order to fill a need in a certain kind of society, but
this does not warrant the leap into the antagonistic and somewhat paranoid conclusion that the need could only have been the suppression of women. Indeed,
if we look back to Plato, we find that at least one classical author of love introduced *eros* not as a weapon against women but rather as a relationship between
males and between men and the gods; eros simply excluded women or at least
dismissed the love of women as "vulgar" and "inferior." Reading Aristophanes,
on the other hand, gives a very different impression: relations between men and
women, even 2,500 years before birth control, were not that different from
today. There were the same battles for power, the same charges and counter-
charges, with women getting the upper hand as often as men.[2]

   If we follow the scholars and locate the origins of romantic love more properly in the chivalric spirit of twelfth-century France, however, we get a very different picture again; what we find is that romantic (or "courtly") love was
indeed the invention of wandering free-agent knights and their poetic brethren
the troubadours, but it was not at all an instrument of female oppression. Quite
the contrary; courtly love quite literally placed women (often married, their husbands off to the Crusades) on pedestals, but thereby freed them from their strict
identities in terms of their families, marriages, and household duties. We may
now look at the "reduction" of women to their physical appearance and attractiveness as "dehumanizing," a denial of the *person,* but at its origins this celebration of individual attractiveness and personality was the first step in the individualization of women, the recognition that a woman was something more than
a household convenience, an object for inter-family barter—a mother, mistress,
and, literally, a possession.

   It is often argued, nowadays, that romantic love is essentially an invention
of capitalism, a creation of industrialized society. This is by any measure not
true. Shakespeare described a fully developed conception of romantic love well
over a century before the Industrial Revolution in England. It has been argued
(by Linda Nicholson, for example) that the breakdown of feudalism and the origins of a market-based society gave rise to the breakdown as well of the old religious view of women as "creatures before God" and began our current capitalist

insistence on evaluating people according to what they are "good for." But the truth seems to be rather that under feudalism women were evaluated and considered "worth something" only according to what they were "good for," and it is with the rise of a less regimented society that individual identity—as opposed to mere market value—came to mean anything at all. It is true, for example, as Shulamith Firestone argued in her *Dialectic of Sex,* that romantic love became more important with industrialization, but her Marxist urge to equate sexism with capitalism ignores the historical facts: that romantic love and our current conception of the feminine predates capitalism in any guise by several centuries, and that the parallel, in any case, is not with capitalism or industrialism but with the idea of individualism. Romantic love became possible with the severing of "natural" ties between a person and his or her family, the historical drama of a society of individuals—wandering knights and poets and abandoned wives and daughters—finding themselves for the first time required to make commitments rather than merely recognize predetermined allegiances, free to "devote" themselves to a master or mistress of their choice, and no longer locked into a rigid structure of arranged marriages and obligations. Because these "natural" ties were broken, love became not only desirable but a need.

Love is indeed a cultural invention, created by males perhaps but certainly to the advantage and also with the cooperation of women. Love is a cultural creation, but it is not, therefore, either arbitrary or easily dispensable. Romantic love is our primary mode of forming intimate relationships in a society in which we are all systematically uprooted and sent away from our families and communities. Though love is not the only way of achieving intimacy (friendship certainly deserves mention here), it is eminently successful in doing so. This is as true for men as for women. So it is not in the purpose or original design of romantic love that we are going to find the origins of its use against women.

Love and Power

A distinction of fundamental importance in recent literature about sexual identity has been marked out between *sex* (that is, male and female) and gender (that is, masculine and feminine). Sex is essentially a biological category, though what we *make* out of sexual differences is a matter of culture, no matter how they may be tied to history or biology by habit or some very suspiciously self-serving arguments. (Women are "naturally" this or that because of the mating habits of some species of fish.) Romantic love is from its very origins neutral to sex; homosexual and Lesbian love is just as much romantic love as unkinky, heterosexual love.

But what about gender roles? What would become of our romantic literature without *her* soft and dutiful gaze, waiting for *him* to return from the battle and give her a hard and possessive embrace? But who cares? In our non-warrior society, in which the day's battle is more than likely a screaming telephone battle with the local tax office, we can switch the above pronouns all that we want, delete as well the adjectives "soft" and "hard," dispense with the roles as well as the sexes. Yet it is part of the history of romantic love, and so part of the "dump love" argument as well, that masculine and feminine gender roles are, if not essential, at least central to love.

Years ago, in one of the more virulent classics of the genre, Shulamith Firestone argued in her *Dialectic of Sex* that it is precisely the "liberation of women from their biology," not now but several generations ago, that brought about the distinctively male invention of romantic love:

> Romantic love developed in opposition to the liberation of women from their biology. . . . Male supremacy must shore itself up with artificial institutions or exaggerations of previous institutions.[3]

Romantic role models, she argues, the gender distinctions of "masculine" and "feminine," are developed *in place of* the no longer essential distinction between male and female. Gender depends not on nature but on culture; thus the question, for what purpose, and for whose benefit, has gender been created? The answer is not long forthcoming.

> Romanticism is a cultural tool of male power to keep women from knowing their condition. It is especially needed—and therefore strongest—in Western countries with the highest rate of industrialization.[4]

Romantic love is thus to be understood in terms of *power,* and so viewed, the main difference between masculine and feminine gender roles becomes obvious. The argument, interestingly enough, is traced to Freud. Freud is usually considered the nemesis of feminism, but Firestone rightly credits him "as having grasped the crucial problem of modern life, sexuality."[5] But where Freud takes sexuality to be a psycho-biological problem, Firestone sees it as a political problem. Where Freud mysteriously talks about the powers of the libido, Firestone talks concretely about *power* itself. And where Freud talks murkily and unconvincingly about penis envy and castration fears, Firestone substitutes the tangible fact of family power relationships, the all-powerful father and the privileged sons.[6] Penis envy becomes privilege envy, and Firestone quite plausibly suggests that the young girl who is said to envy her brother's curious genitalia is more likely feeling deprived because she is not allowed to play her brother's rough-and-tumble games. With this switch on Freud, the theory can begin: romantic love is the extension of this power-game into adult life, a more subtle way of depriving women of "male" roles and at the same time flattering her as a "lady." Promise her anything, but offer her only love.

What Firestone is arguing, from Freud, is what Freud and many neo-Freudians prefer to ignore: the institutional nature of romantic love and its functional role, not only in the individual psyche and the family but in the power structure of society as a whole. According to Firestone's argument, now that female sexuality as such is of much less importance for survival, the institution of romantic love serves the function of introducing femininity as a matter of emotional significance, as a way of continuing archaic male-dominated institutions and power-structures. Femininity, in a word, is *impotency*. Masculinity is *potency*. To reinforce the roles, femininity is isolated in the home, while masculinity gathers further power in the marketplace. Women, in turn, find themselves seeking approval—the test of success in their feminine roles—entirely from men, while men gain their support and approval as well in a variety of friendships and business or professional relationships. The power relations thus become self-perpetuating.

The isolation of women and the exclusively male-dominated world of power are starting to break down extremely quickly on any reasonable historical scale, and this changes at least one of the key connections between romantic love, gender identity, and power. Much of the power that was once the exclusive domain of males had to do not only with the fact that they had power, but with their variable sources of recognition and approval as well. Men were not solely dependent on women for their sense of self-esteem as women were upon men. But now, as women aggressively find friendships and alliances for themselves— even to the extent that a current popular argument maintains that *only* women are even *capable* of friendship—and as women are beginning to find professional, political, and other sources of self-esteem, this source of power is becoming open to them as well. Thus, in this sense, it has become evident that it is not romantic love or gender roles as such that determine one major traditional source of asymmetrical female dependency, but an entirely distinct set of inequities which might be summarized as unequal access to approval and self-esteem. This isolation of women is now at an end, once and for all, I would argue. Even the reactionary countermovement, the "total woman" syndrome, has the ironic outcome of helping to bring about the public visibility of women speakers and "women's issues," thus destroying this sense of isolation. Romantic love, consequently, no longer remains a woman's sole source of self-esteem, a burden that, in any case, no single emotion could ever be expected to sustain.

Romantic Roles: Beyond Androgyny, Too

Are romantic roles themselves oppressive? If by "romantic roles" one means gender roles—masculine and feminine—the answer is yes. For a woman, if being in love meant accepting a position of subservience and passivity, if being romantically attractive meant being quiet, unaggressive, and apparently helpless, then I doubt that I could argue in favor of romantic love at all. But the truth of the matter seems to be that these roles are not so automatically involved in male-female love as our cheaper novels and more reactionary politicians would suggest. Indeed, love tends to destroy these stereotypes rather than reinforce them, and in theory as well as in practice the concepts of femininity and masculinity ought to be rejected, not only in the public sphere, where they put the woman to a serious disadvantage, but in the personal sphere as well, where they still tend to turn even the best relationships into one-role, one-plot, television-like situation comedies, or worse.

There are at least three ways of overcoming sexual stereotypes. Two of them have become popularly known under the camp word "androgyny." The word is often confused with "bi-sexual," which is only one of its variations, but in any case, I tend to agree with Mary Daly when she writes that " 'androgyny' makes me think of Farrah Fawcett and John Travolta Scotch-taped together." The first form of androgyny (or "androgynism") insists that masculine and feminine characteristics exist together in everyone, and so it is unnecessary, the argument goes, for each individual to feel that he or she should develop only one set of sex-bound characteristics. In the public sphere, the argument is appealing, since what it says, in effect, is that everyone has the same potential and so should have the same opportunities. Its effect, in other words, is to deny the difference between men and women and to provide a single ideal of rights and potential for all, which leads one author, Joyce Trebilcot, to call it "monoandrogynism."[7] In the personal sphere, however, the same view leads logically to the idea of bi-sexuality; if we each have essentially the same masculine and feminine characteristics, then it would follow that we each also have the same masculine and feminine desires. This sounds like Freud's well-known bi-sexuality argument, but it isn't. For Freud, this was a sexual matter, a fact about biology; for the monoandrogynist, it is a matter of cultural potential, not biology at all. But here, too, we see a problem with this simple view; as a theory about *potentials,* it slips too easily between the idea that the various roles that we call "masculine" and "feminine" *can* be developed in everyone (whether or not they should be) and the idea that these roles are *already* lurking somewhere inside of us, waiting to be developed. But, alas, in our society, only one of the roles ever is, thus frustrating the other. The recognition of the cultural origins of these roles ought to lead us not to the view that they are "there in everybody" but to the more radical conclusion that they are unnecessary, unreal—they do not exist except in so far as we *will* them.

The second form of androgyny is more radical in just this sense; it denies the simple duality between masculinity and femininity and emphasizes the wide variety of gender roles, including any number of combinations of the two "pure" extremes. In effect, this breaks down the extremes while refocusing our attention on particular traits and roles rather than on the monolithic extremes, and opens up the possibility of a large variety of roles that are, traditionally speaking, neither masculine nor feminine. (Because of its pluralism, Trebilcot calls this "polyandrogynism.")

But this second form of androgyny or androgynism suggests a third possibility, which escapes the man-woman etymological orientation of "androgyny" by dismissing masculinity and femininity as roles, particularly where romantic love is involved. What we have been allowing without comment for too long is the idea that these two roles define, if not all, at least a large part of our romantic tradition. In fact, they had no place in Plato; there the crucial distinction was one of age and experience, the lover as teacher, the beloved as pupil. The notion of masculine-feminine may have played a significant part in courtly love, but the notions of chivalry and attractiveness were a matter of historical context, and not necessarily essential to the concept of love as such. As one looks at the structure of romantic love—apart from the grade "B" novels—divisions according to sex and gender have had a very small part to play, even where sex itself is concerned. Indeed, romantic love consists of roles, private roles that are only occasionally or coincidentally played out in public. But the point now to be made once and for all is that few of these roles have anything to do with sex or gender, and insofar as they do, it is not *because* they are male or female or masculine or feminine roles but only because they contain roles that are usually associated with sex and gender, such as domination and submissiveness, aggressiveness and passivity. But what happens in love is that these roles are continuously redefined, and whatever might be expected on the masculine-feminine model, what we actually do in love is something quite different. Indeed, this leads to the unexpected conclusion that masculinity and femininity are, in fact, *public* roles, and not private, and that love requires the overcoming of these roles rather than the realization of them. Femininity is a show, not an expression, and trying to be "feminine" in bed or in love is more like trying to be a comedian or a prima donna rather than a lover. Indeed, as soon as one begins to list the huge gamut of roles through which we are intimate with one another—not only the thousand varieties of sex that need have nothing to do with gender, but cooking, talking, walking, dancing, looking, scratching, fighting, driving cross country, feeding the squirrels, confessing, celebrating, crying, laughing, knowingly nodding to each other in a room full of people, sharing the events of the day, consoling one another in defeat, studying Spanish, staying in bed on Sunday, reading the funnies, bitching about the weather, whispering and occasionally whimpering—the emphasis that is so stressed on a single set of asymmetrical roles, "masculine and feminine," becomes more than embarrassing. Indeed, people who are too caught up in their "masculine" and "feminine" roles are inevitably, after the initial attraction, disappointing lovers. This has nothing to do with sexism, but only with boredom. How can you build your life around a one-act actor? Or perhaps, in some cases, a movie poster?

Beyond sex and gender means beyond *androgyny* too, beyond that one-dimensional set of man-woman identities that too many bad movies and sado-masochistic Freudian fantasies have set out for us. Love is a multiplex of personal roles of all kinds, which are being continuously redefined and reenacted and which need have nothing to do with sex or with those simple stereotypes of gender. In fact, to think of love in terms of masculinity and femininity is like having a conversation in which each party is allowed to say just one sentence. At most, one can expect a predictable performance, instead of the "anything goes" exhilaration of love.

Love and Equality

Romantic love, unlike many other emotions and other forms of love, *requires* equality. It may be, as Stendhal argued a century ago, that love creates rather than discovers equals; and it may also be that within the bounds of equality love divides into unequal roles, into domination and submission, for example, with sado-masochism as its extreme. But it is absolutely crucial to this emotion that one sees the other as an equal, which is not to deny either that it is possible for one person to love more than the other (which is not a question of the nature of love) or that there are other emotions, distinct from romantic love, that some-times borrow its promiscuous name (adoration, feeling motherly or fatherly, fear, and simple possessiveness). Indeed, in a still class-ridden and unequal society, romantic love is our favorite if not most effective political equalizer. Cinderella moves from maid to princess not only in the eyes of her prince but in the eyes of the law, too, whether or not she lives thereby "happily ever after." King Edward VIII found it necessary to lower his social status to match that of the woman he loved, and with a perverse twist of this perception, Shulamith Firestone argues in *Dialectic of Sex* that men "fall in love (with women) to jus-tify their descent into a lower caste." But what is *equality,* in a relationship?

"Equality" is one of those political glow-words with very little determinate content, like "liberty." One gives it a content by giving it a context, for example—equal work time, or equal say in an issue, equal responsibility for some specific activity or equal power. What counts as equality in a particular relationship may indeed be quite different from what counts as equality in another. The equality that is the precondition for love only consists in the demand that social differences do not matter, that both lovers are mutually willing to take up the various personal and private roles that make up intimacy. But as the notion of equality starts to become more "objective" and more con-cerned with social rather than personal status, once the private is measured by public criteria, the tacitly accepted roles within the relationship tend to be shat-tered. The quasi-political self-consciousness that replaces them undermines the intimacy of love. What was once a relationship now becomes a "partnership," which may well be more efficient, even a model of fairness and success in "having worked it out," but it isn't love. It is too dominated by foreign and crit-ical observers, external measurements and publicly defined if nominally private roles. It was a problem that many of us had with women's liberation in the six-ties (though that is by no means the only ideology that has that consequence; sex books and our modern therapeutic attitudes towards sex can do the same thing). The demands may all be completely reasonable. They may indeed force a relationship to conform with some more general and "objective" form of equity. But what is too often sacrificed is love, for love is not objective, not negotiable, not a "partnership." None of which is to say, let me quickly add, that love itself is inherently, "objectively" unequal, or that what inequality there may be necessarily gives the woman the disadvantage, or that our idea of "women's roles" cannot be changed, or that romantic love and feminism are incompatible. To the contrary, they even presuppose one another. But the problem that defies ideology and one-sided "consciousness raising" by its very nature is to bring these demands—if they must be demands rather than shared ideals—into the relationship itself. As a set of demands or ideals imposed from the outside, "equality" becomes antithetical to, rather than the precondition for, love.

The division between the public and the personal, and the quite different concerns for equality of the sexes in the public sphere (equal pay for equal work, equal access to jobs and careers, equal rights and responsibilities under the law) on the one hand and the sense of equality that is the precondition for intimacy on the other, have been commonly confused by both feminist theorists and anti-feminists alike. Shulamith Firestone is just one of the many theorists who have argued that romantic love and "the relegation of love to the personal" is part and parcel of the manipulative ploy to "keep women in their place" and to rationalize, even idealize, their class inferiority. But love is by its very nature personal, and if it isolates women in romantic relationships, it isolates men in exactly the same way. That is what we mean by a "personal" relationship. The mistake is to think that the *overemphasis* on the personal, which is foisted upon women, to the exclusion of public roles and interests, is a feature of romantic love itself, and that the indefensible inequality in the public sphere necessarily has its counterpart in the personal sphere as well. But these are quite distinct, and to treat them together as a single problem may mean blurring the very different strategies that are required to encounter each of them.

A more vicious version of the same confusion has given birth to the outlandish conception of the "total woman," who is in fact a medieval woman, more at home in Khomeini's Persia than contemporary America. The strategy of these anti-feminists is to systematically confuse questions about intimacy and personal relationships with questions about equality and public life. *Whatever* one says about the private, romantic, and family roles to which women have become accustomed (which is misleadingly described as their "natural" roles), nothing follows about the public roles or abilities or ambitions of women in society, in which sex and gender considerations simply drop out of the picture— or ought to. It is simply false, where public criteria are concerned, that "men and women are different by nature," since nature has nothing to do with most public functions (given, that is, that we no longer inherit our leaders through their birthright) and sex, in any case, is irrelevant to our roles. But in the personal sphere, questions of sex do indeed arise, but not of necessity, much less "by nature." They arise because we choose to make sex—and heterosexuality specifically—the basis of our most intimate relationships. But it is not difficult to find cultures in which sexual relationships are perfunctory, and other encounters—with friends or fellow workers or soldiers—are far more intimate and "meaningful." One need only look again at Plato to appreciate the power of love in which the difference in the sexes plays no part whatever. It is what we *make* of the sexes and sex that determines the roles in our personal relationships, and it is here that the slippery argument from the historical *public* place of women in certain kinds of roles, to an inference about what is "natural," and to a conclusion about the properly submissive and subservient place of women in love is particularly vicious. There is nothing "natural" about public roles, and there is nothing "natural" about personal roles either. Our roles in romance are in every case personally determined, if on the basis of public instruction, and the kinds of roles one chooses to play with one's lover cannot be dictated *a priori*. To say that a woman *ought* to be submissive, and also to say that she ought not, is nothing less than a kind of emotional fascism, a way of dismissing and degrading huge numbers of women who find that their personal preferences do not match up to the latest official line. "The totalitarian woman" might be a better designation for the conservative tendency to confuse questions about public equality with questions about personal roles; but the tendency to confuse the demand for social equality with an authoritarian attack on love is to be found on the other side as well. Romantic love *requires* equality, and to deny this or to enforce it from the outside is the denial of love as well.

Yet, it would be absurd to deny that one's personal self-image and one's public, social image are related and affect each other. So what does this mean about equality in love? First of all, that it is aided immensely by social-political-economic equality. Whatever truth may be in the argument that women have always wielded "the *real* power" at home, there is no question that status in public and status at home are mutually supportive. But more crucial to the argument here is the fact that equality in personal relationships is essential to seeing oneself as equal in social relationships as well, in part because we (unlike most people of the world) tend to take our personal identities as more real ("more myself") than our public identities. If love is an emotion *requiring* that we see one another as equals, it is therefore an important tool for equality in the public sphere as well.

But what does "equality" mean in relations? It does not mean "being the same." It does not exclude all sorts of asymmetrical and uneven roles and relationships, including the absolute domination of one person by the other. It does not require, as such, the equal division of housework or "bread earning" tasks, though these have become rather routine expectations (whether or not routinely fulfilled). Equality in love essentially means a mutually-agreed upon indeterminacy, more or less free from social strictures and limitations (short of violence and illegality, sometimes), a sense of reformulation in which one's self-images and personal roles and identity are up for grabs, in negotiation with one other person, in which there are no preordained roles or predestined status relation-ships, including, particularly, those which are traditionally labeled "masculine" and "feminine." Indeed, it is the heart of love that it involves the breakdown of these television stereotypes and an openness to change and mutual reevaluation which is available in very few of our experiences. It is not yet political equality (or "liberation") and equality in love is no guarantee that the public demand will be successful. But it is a self-effacing error, and an unrealistic demand for most women besides, that the demand for political equality *preclude* romantic love (with men). The latter is and has often been a means to the former.

Love and Illusion

The central argument of *The Women's Room* is an anti-romantic version of an old argument in philosophy that is usually called "the argument from illusion." It is the fallacious but persuasive inference from the fact that one is sometimes fooled to the paranoid supposition that one might always be deceived. Quite a few years ago, Shulamith Firestone exploited this argument by attacking what she called "idealization": the fact that women tend to imagine their lovers with virtues they never had, and in return men mock-worship women, which Firestone says is an effective substitution for physical abuse—and the result is the same. (How this is so is never quite clear.) What is so obvious in Firestone is the double bind asymmetry itself: men idealize women and thereby exploit them, women ide-alize men and are therefore exploited. Idealization and the argument from illu-sion also enter into the work of a new spokesperson for the "dump love" move-ment, Jill Tweedie (*In The Name of Love*), who argues that love is a pair of "rose colored glasses" that when removed . . . reveal "that what was taken to be pre-cious is simply a bare dull pebble, like any other." But the most spectacular description of idealization as illusion is in *The Women's Room* itself, as Val describes with exquisite irony the bloated idealization of love, followed by its inevitable collapse:

> Okay. Love is one of those things you think is supposed to happen, is a fact of life, and if it doesn't happen to you, you feel cheated. You're walking around feeling rotten, you know, because it's never happened to you. So one day you meet this guy, right? And, ZING! He is gorgeous! It doesn't matter what he's doing. He may be making a point in a debate, he may be chopping up concrete on a city street, with his shirt off and his back tanned. It doesn't matter. Even if you've met him before and not thought much about him, at some moment you look at him and everything you've thought about him before goes straight out of your head. You never really saw him before! You realize that in a split second! You never saw how totally gorgeous he was![8]

Val, the narrator, then proceeds in almost obscene detail to describe his wonderful arms, his sensual month, his pithy intelligence, the desperation with
which one wants him, and so on, for several salivating pages.

> Then one day, the unthinkable happens. You are sitting together at the break-
> fast table and you're a little hung over, and you look across at beloved, beau-
> tiful golden beloved, and beloved opens his lovely rosebud mouth showing his
> glistening white teeth, and beloved says something stupid. Your whole body
> stops midstream: your temperature drops. Beloved has never said anything
> stupid before. You turn and look at him; you're sure you misheard. You ask him
> to repeat. And he does . . .

Thus, the doubt begins, but that's only the start, and soon you see that he is
always saying stupid things—and suddenly you see that he's skinny, or flabby
or fat. His teeth are crooked, his toenails are dirty and he farts in bed. So on now
in the other direction. The initial idealizations were all *falsehoods*. Now you see
you've been had:

> And you hate yourself for having deluded yourself about him (you tell your-
> self it was HIM you were deluded about—not love), and you hate him for
> having believed your delusions, and you feel guilty and responsible and you
> try, slowly, to disengage. But now, just try to get rid of him! He clutches, he
> clings, he doesn't understand. How could you want to separate from a deity?

Love always involves idealization, and, indeed, idealization, like hallucination
and flattery, can be abused to deceive either oneself or a lover. But the problem with
the argument is that it flatly fails to make the distinction between innocent fantasy
and celebration on the one hand and self-deception and illusion on the other. All
emotions, not only love, are blind (that is, myopic) in that they see what they want
to see, emphasize what they want to emphasize, celebrate what they want to celebrate. Without that element of enthusiasm, birthdays and anniversaries would be just
another day, life would be grey, and even family and friends would be reduced to
social security numbers and vital statistics. *All* values are idealizations in this sense;
all hopes and plans are fantasies, and even daydreams are, in one sense, false. Yes,
we do disappoint one another (women as well as men, though this would never be
known from *The Women's Room*), but to infer from this that our fantasies are fraudulent, much less that love is itself an illusion, is a piece of painful self-deception.

The Double Bind

> Except for her [Camille's] passion for Bernard, she is tough and fun. Don't ask
> what it is about Bernard that makes her so adore him. It is not Bernard, but love

itself. She believes in love, goes on believing in it against all odds. Therefore, Bernard is a little bored. It is boring to be adored. At thirty-eight, she should be tough and fun, not adoring. When he leaves her, a month or two from now, she will contemplate suicide. Whereas, if she had been able to bring herself to stop believing in love, she would have been tough and fun and he would have adored her forever. Which would have bored her. She then would have had to be the one to tell him to clear out. It is a choice to give one pause.[9]

The genius of *The Women's* Room—perhaps as opposed to *The Dialectic of Sex*—is in its descriptions, presented for the most part in a flat matter-of-fact familiarity that leaves many people who reject the tone of the book incapable of saying what is wrong with it. But the first thing to see about the above illustration, and a hundred others like it, is its unwarranted one-sidedness. French tells us that the dilemma is symmetrical, that it is the same for Bernard as for Camille, but Bernard remains a mere name for us; the problem is all Camille's. It has been said that French is unsympathetic to her male characters, but this isn't true. She *has* no male characters, no men with problems and paradoxes themselves, just cardboard figures who periodically fall down on, blow away from or on occasion confess to their disappointed female lovers. But French, unlike Firestone, for example, doesn't put the blame on men. She blames love itself, and idealization is the key to love.

The Women's Room is built on a brutal dichotomy, between an overidealized and impossible form of love—expecting love to be everything: instant happiness, creativity, undying devotion, adoring and being adored "forever"—and the disillusioning facts of our lives: that love doesn't last, that love isn't everything, that one can be in love and still be unhappy, suffer from writer's block, feel insecure and inadequate. But what remains intact is the ideal itself, unattainable, a bitter disappointment and a cruel promise. What we do not get, unfortunately, is a less pregnant but still desirable promise of love that is more in tune with experience, and thus not so prone to disillusionment.

The refrain of *The Women's Room*, "but of course, she would not think of blaming love," should have been about blaming certain ideas we have about love, not love itself. The danger of confusing love with illusion is more than the personal unhappiness it causes: its cost also includes creating a serious obstacle in the public fight for women's equality. Even if one assumes that the battle for equality will entail antagonism with men on a public level, it is sheer folly, and also unnecessary, to carry that antagonism into intimate relationships which, despite certain utopian hopes and radical experiments to the contrary, may well be indispensable in our society, at least for the present and the foreseeable future. But the argument goes beyond this, too: for if, as I have argued, romantic love actually *requires* a sense of equality, then love provides, rather than works against, the ideal of feminism. Historically, romantic love (and Christian love, too) were powerful forces in breaking down the old hierarchies and roles. Today, that conception is still at work, in spite of the continuing overemphasis on sex and gender roles and despite the fact that too many feminists see love as the problem, instead of as part of the solution. Indeed, here as elsewhere in politics, projecting one's personal disappointments into the world as cynical "realism" is not the way to win adherents. Romantic love between men and women, from its very inception, has always been the primary vehicle of personal and, consequently, social equality. It has always been "feminist" in its temperament, whatever the mythologies that have sometimes been imposed on top of it. Romantic love and feminism are neither incompatible nor antagonistic; in fact, I would argue that, for the present at least, they should not try to do without one another.

Notes

1. Philip Slater, *The Pursuit of Loneliness: American Culture at the Breaking Point* (Boston: Beacon Press, 1970), p. 8.
2. In *Euripides at Bay,* for example, as well as in Aristophanes' best-known play, *Lysistrata.*
3. Shulamith Firestone, *The Dialectic of Sex: The Case for Feminist Revolution* (New York: Morrow, 1970), p. 165.
4. Ibid., p. 166.
5. Ibid., p. 49.
6. Ibid., p. 53.
7. Joyce Trebilcot, "Two Forms of Androgynism," in *Feminism and Philosophy* by Vetterling-Braggin, Elliston, and English, eds. (Totowa, N.J.: Littlefield Adams, 1977), pp. 70–78.
8. Marilyn French, *The Women's Room* (New York: Summit Books, 1977), p. 362.
9. Ibid., pp. 210–11.

3

In Defense of Promiscuity

Frederick A. Elliston

The Western tradition has been remarkably conservative in its reflections on sexual morality.[1] Whether this conservatism is due to the fact that practically every major philosopher before Hegel was a bachelor male dedicated to the pursuit of some form of reason is a moot point on which I shall not speculate. Whatever the explanation, most philosophers have tended to formulate and resolve sexual issues in favor of the status quo. Perhaps because sexual promiscuity (the only type I shall consider) has usually been a practice widely at variance with prevalent norms, it has scarcely arisen as an issue at all—much less been criticized or defended. Today, however, sexual norms have changed—at least for an increasingly significant number of society's members. This change challenges the philosophers to question the assumptions on which the conventions that regulate our sex lives are based, much as recent political changes have provided the motive for a radical critique of social practices and institutions.[2] My purpose here is to take up this challenge by offering a defense of promiscuity: first, I shall criticize current notions of promiscuity as inadequate and provide my own definition; second, I shall rebut some traditional arguments against promiscuity; and third, I shall defend it in terms of three sexual paradigms. I shall conclude with some reflections on the limits of my defense.

Linguistic Forays

What is meant by "promiscuity"? It may be that the word has no descriptive content, but only emotive and/or hortatory force. On this view, to condemn a practice or person as promiscuous is simply to express feelings of disapproval, or to issue a prohibitive "Stop!" This position attempts to resolve the issue of meaning by limiting "promiscuity" to its emotional or prescriptive force.[3] Even this restriction, though, does not eliminate all of the problems. For not all people oppose promiscuity, and hence the intended overtones are not always negative. And this position leaves an important question unanswered: To what kinds of persons or actions does the term apply? Only when this question has been answered are we in a position to ask how we should feel about, act toward, or react to promiscuous people or behavior.

The *Oxford English Dictionary* defines "promiscuous" as: "without distinction, discrimination or order." *Webster's New Twentieth Century Dictionary* adds: "engaging in sexual intercourse indiscriminately or with many persons." The root notion operative in these definitions is *indiscriminate,* sometimes signified quantitatively, according to *Webster's.*

But this definition is too broad and begs the question at hand. For the promiscuous person clearly does draw *some* distinctions: typically he or she does not derive sexual satisfaction from a lover's shoe or copulate with a dead body or a sibling. In such cases more precise terminology is applied—fetishism, necrophilia, or incest. Even a promiscuous person usually discriminates between things and persons, between living people and dead people, between people who are members of the family and those who are not. Since some distinctions are operative, the suggestion that a promiscuous person is *completely indiscriminate* is too strong.

Similar difficulties arise with *Webster's* numerical criterion: How many liaisons must a person engage in before he or she is promiscuous? Clearly more than one is required; anyone who has made love to only one person cannot (logically) be labeled "promiscuous." But is two enough? Perhaps a person who carries on two affairs would be called "promiscuous." But imagine someone who married at twenty and who remarried at forty, two years after his wife died. Clearly, under these conditions he is not promiscuous. If two is not enough, then increase the number to three and repeat the scenario: married at twenty, forty, and sixty, two years after each wife died. This twice-widowed "Romeo" satisfies *Webster's* numerical criterion, for he has engaged in sex with many (that is, three) people; and yet he is clearly not promiscuous. As more marriages are added it still remains uncertain at what point a person becomes promiscuous. And even if a clear line could be drawn, the question would immediately arise: Why draw it there, for what is the criterion for assessing the number of liaisons that suffice to justify the judgment "promiscuous"? This is a further legitimate question raised by *Webster's* definition but left unanswered.

Of course these examples deal with sequential liaisons, which may be more problematic than their simultaneous counterparts. But I think the basic problem remains: Is a person who carries on two serious loving affairs that endure for a lifetime promiscuous? I think not. Then again, if two are not enough, how many are required and on what grounds?

By these two counterattacks I am suggesting that it is *false* that a promiscuous person is indiscriminate and *facile* to assess promiscuity numerically. But what is it, then, that invites this judgment? More likely the condemnation arises not because such people do not discriminate *at all*, but because they fail to discriminate *according to the prevalent sexual code*. Promiscuous behavior challenges our sexual conventions, thereby giving this label its emotive force and prescriptive overtones.[4]

More precisely, promiscuity violates a very special principle that regulates our erotic life: "Sexual relations shall be exclusively heterosexual and . . . no sexual activity shall take place outside monogamous unions which are, intentionally at least, life-long."[5] It is this "Western norm," as Ronald Atkinson terms it, that prescribes the *distinctions* to be drawn, the *discriminations* to be made, and the *order* to be upheld in our sex lives, to which the definition in the *Oxford English Dictionary* alludes.

But to say that promiscuity violates the Western norm is still too broad, for so does coprophilia. Though many people use the term in this vague sense, a more precise definition is needed.

Promiscuity is sometimes identified with "free love." This persuasive definition (or redefinition) may induce some to accept this sexual pattern because freedom, like motherhood, is a good everyone is supposed to espouse. But what exactly is the sexual freedom in question? If it means freedom from all sexual prohibitions (including, for example, those against perversions), then this rephrasing is again too broad. And if it means freedom from just the Western norm (which would allow perverted sex within marriage), then it is no improvement. Moreover "free love" is a misleading expression: like everything else, sex has its price—assessed in terms of time, effort, emotional tensions, and a tradeoff of other benefits and burdens.

Promiscuity may be identified with recreational sex—intercourse just for the fun of it. But this definition is disquieting because of what might be hidden under the adverb "just"; and the term "fun" would align the defenders of promiscuity with that "vulgar hedonism" that some may want to reject in favor of a broader conception of the good life. Though when it harms no one promiscuity may be defensible simply on the grounds that it provides pleasure, this justification should not be built into the definition. A more neutral definition is preferable in order to avoid this commitment at the outset and thereby leave open the question of its justification.

Neither the definitions of the *Oxford English Dictionary* nor *Webster's New Twentieth Century Dictionary*, nor any of the current philosophic or popular notions is satisfactory. In view of the failure of these linguistic forays to uncover a viable definition I shall offer my own. In so doing I cross a thin but significant boundary between linguistic analysis and linguistic revision. And conceding Wittgenstein's insight that language is a form of life, the dispute over the definition of promiscuity cannot be regarded as merely semantic.

With these caveats (or concessions), I shall offer the following definition, or redefinition: "promiscuity" means sex with a series of other adults, not directly related through marriage, with no commitments. Let me explain each component in turn.

First, promiscuity demands *copulation*—its *telos* is sexual intercourse. Someone who engages in the rituals of seduction without this goal is perhaps a flirt or a "tease"—but is not promiscuous. Of course not every seduction succeeds. But at least the intention to consummate the relation must be present on all occasions and realized on some. Whether the sex is "straight" or perverted is irrelevant, for these are two different phenomena. One can be perverted and not promiscuous, or promiscuous and not perverted: a lifelong incestuous relation renders a person perverted but not promiscuous; and many promiscuous liaisons accord with the paradigm of natural sex—"the two-minute emissionary missionary male-superior ejaculation service."[6]

Second, *repetition* is essential—the pursuit of a new partner must recur. Promiscuity on only one occasion is logically impossible. If someone is remarkably casual about his or her one affair, he or she may be labeled "superficial" or "unfeeling," but cannot be called promiscuous. Different partners on several occasions must be sought. The *number* of affairs per se does not suffice to delineate promiscuity (the mistake of *Webster's* definition); plurality is a necessary but not a sufficient condition of promiscuity.

Third, both partners must be *adults*. If one partner is a child, then their behavior is pedophilia. If the child is a son or daughter, it is incest. In neither case is it promiscuity. Adulthood cannot be fixed chronologically; it signifies a degree of maturity some teenagers have and some elderly people lack. The other adult need not be of the opposite sex. Homosexuals and lesbians per se are not necessarily promiscuous. Some make significant personal sacrifices to maintain their relationship; though their behavior violates the Western norm, it is not promiscuous, because of the commitment their sacrifices signify.

Fourth, the couple cannot be directly related through *marriage*. It is logically impossible for husband and wife to engage in promiscuity with one another, though of course their sex play may sometimes bear a "family resemblance" to it. Similarly, sex between a brother and sister, even when they are adults, is a different phenomenon. It is possible to be promiscuous with distant cousins to whom one is not *directly* related through marriage; different societies draw the lines for incest in different ways.[7]

Finally and most decisively, promiscuity is *noncommittal* sex. It defies the traditional connection between sex and marriage—not just as a social institution, but as a symbol of a serious, loving, and intentionally lifelong relation. Promiscuity asserts a freedom from the obligation within or without marriage to "love, honor, and obey" and a freedom to engage in sex with any peer who agrees. These refusals to issue promissory notes for affection and support throughout an indefinite future and to issue a guarantee of sexual exclusivity are promiscuity's most significant departures from the traditional sexual norm.

Is such behavior defensible? I shall now turn to some familiar arguments against it.

Rebuttals and Rejoinders

Several arguments can be offered in defense of the Western norm and hence in opposition to promiscuity. As I shall try to demonstrate in my rejoinders, none are sound.

1. *The Western Norm and Technology.* At one time a strong argument might have been made in defense of the Western norm by invoking the causal connection between sex and reproduction: unless the natural processes are interrupted, intercourse leads to procreation; for the sake of children, on whom society's future depends, promiscuity is rightly prohibited in order to confine sex to marriage, as that secure and loving context within which children can best be raised. As stated, this argument relies on two claims, the first factual and the second normative.

The first premise has been falsified by technology: the advances of medicine have made available reliable birth-control devices and reasonably safe techniques for sterilization and abortion, thereby making sex possible without the risk of conception or birth. Second, the absolute value of the nuclear family as the *only* context for child rearing is at least problematic: experiments in communal living and the increasing number of single parents provide some evidence that the needs of the child can be met either through a plurality of parent figures or through just one individual. Moreover, even granting the risk of pregnancy, despite precautions, and the value of the nuclear family, despite alternatives, the prohibitions against promiscuity would not follow. First, pregnancies can be terminated. With the exception of the Roman Catholic Church, many concede the legitimacy of abortion, at least during the first trimester. Second, even if this option is disregarded, it should be emphasized that promiscuity is *logically* compatible with *some* commitments to one's partner in the event of pregnancy and to the child in the event of its birth. Promiscuity does not preclude such contingent agreements; it rules out only emotional and sexual commitments as a precondition of sex—the promise to love the other exclusively and to share a life completely.

This rejoinder asserts that available technology should be used as a safeguard against undesirable consequences. But "can" does not always entail "ought": not everything science is capable of doing should be done. Some, notably Roman Catholics, have argued strongly against the use of such means.

2. *The Inseparability Premise and Promiscuity.* The Roman Catholic position is that the sex act[8] has two inseparable functions: to foster the physical, emotional, and spiritual union of man and woman, and to reproduce the species. If this claim were true, then the use of birth-control devices or sterilization and abortion techniques would be prohibited. Promiscuity would then become more hazardous since without contraceptives the risk of pregnancy would be much greater; and it would become less frequent since only *coitus interruptus* and the rhythm method could be practiced to avoid conception. Of course abstinence and masturbation would be alternatives; but to practice them is to cease to be promiscuous.

The most recent defense of this inseparability premise is found in Pope Paul VI's *Humanae Vitae*: to violate the inseparability of the unitive and procreative aspect of sex is "to contradict the nature of both man and woman and of their most intimate relationship, and therefore it is to contradict also the plan of God and His will." [9]

Carl Cohen contends that this inseparability premise is false. [10] First, it has no basis in scripture or natural law, but rests only on a fallacious *argumentum ad verecundiam*. Second, the entailed prohibition against birth control would cause overpopulation and hunger. Third, the fear of pregnancy and the ensuing inhibitions thwart the conjugal love that the Church promulgates. Fourth, the assumption that all sexual processes must be completed is erroneous, for we recognize acts with erotic overtones that rightly remain unconsummated (for example, a father's love for his daughter). Fifth, the integrity of the spiritual and natural is frequently denied without transgressing a divine (or moral) command—for example, eating for pleasure rather than nourishment. And finally, if the Church sanctions drugs to promote physical health, it should permit drugs (for example, oral contraceptives) to promote sexual health.

Though Cohen's six points may not persuade all Catholics, [11] they do provide an impressive list of reasons for legitimizing birth control. Though admittedly his purpose is to defend their use within marriage, this limitation is not demanded by his logic. They serve to justify the use of the technology that severs the causal tie on which the earlier rebuttal of promiscuity depended.

3. *Promiscuity as a Threat to Monogamy.* Like adultery, promiscuity may be judged immoral on the grounds that it endangers one of our society's central and sacred institutions—monogamous marriage: [12] allowing people to achieve sexual gratification while escaping long-term commitments undermines this basic institution in a way that threatens the stability of our society; in self-defense, society rightly imposes social sanctions against the threatening promiscuous behavior.

This argument rests on two assumptions: first, that promiscuity has adverse effects on monogamy; and second, that monogamy is socially superior to the alternatives.

The first assumption is a questionable causal claim. For despite the recent weakening of sexual taboos, marriage continues to be a popular practice. Even conceding the high divorce rate does not weaken this claim, for many who are divorced remarry—thereby testifying to the value they accord this institution. Consequently, the so-called new morality is not clearly harming marriage. Indeed, two alternative hypotheses about the causal relation between promiscuity and monogamy are equally plausible: by providing for a broader range of sex partners from which to select a spouse promiscuity increases the probability of sexual compatibility within marriage, and hence the probability of a more "successful" marriage (at least according to this one criterion of success—the satisfaction of one need); and by eliminating the need to marry *merely* for sexual gratification (and hence to disregard those other factors that contribute to successful marriages, such as respect, considerateness, shared values, love, and compassion), promiscuity again increases the likelihood of a successful marriage. Perhaps the trouble with premarital unions, trial marriage, and open marriage is that they have not been tried, for the strong presumption that monogamy is the only way to institutionalize our sex life works against such experiments. Freeing sex of the monopoly of marriage could provide for new institutions that might satisfy more effectively the emotional and physical needs of society's members and offer greater scope for the exercise of personal freedom and initiative in creating new lifestyles. Though society once had the right to insist that its members have a "license to procreate," to use Michael Bayles's expression, with the development of new contraceptives it no longer has the right to insist on a license to copulate. Abolishing the demand for such a license by permitting promiscuity may ease the unnecessary and spurious pressures on monogamy, so as to promote rather than prevent healthy changes within this institution.

4. *Lying, Deceiving, and Exploiting.* According to the popular prototype, promiscuous people are unfaithful and unreliable: they break promises, say things that are not true, and use others for their own sexual gratification. If this prototype were true, promiscuity would indeed be wrong, because it would violate familiar moral rules: people are supposed to keep their promises, tell the truth, and not deceive or exploit others. But does promiscuity *necessarily* involve these forms of immorality?

At one time these subterfuges may have been necessary in order to obtain sex and yet avoid commitments. To circumvent the Western norm, which was justified when copulation entailed procreation, those who wanted *only* the "joys of sex" were forced to tease, tempt, and manipulate. Under these circumstances promiscuity is wrong—*not* because it is promiscuity, but because it violates well-established ethical principles. The moral fault lies not in noncommittal sex but in the lies, deceptions, and exploitation to which some *happen* to have recourse in order to have intercourse. Such immoral behavior is only contingently associated with promiscuity; logically, rather than empirically, it is not necessary. In some groups or societies openly promiscuous behavior is tolerated, if not encouraged. When the threat of pregnancy is minimized, sex for its own sake becomes possible, enjoyable, and desirable—thereby making many of the earlier reasons for lying, deceiving, and exploiting invalid. That promiscuity must involve immoral behavior then becomes an anachronism, an empirical claim that is no longer true. Promiscuity per se or prima facie is not wrong. At most, it is the immoral things promiscuous people sometimes happen to do that are wrong.

This defense is complicated by the fact that a double standard is operative within large segments of society: men are allowed to "sow their wild oats," whereas women are denigrated as "loose" or "fallen" for the same behavior. Though this sexual inequality may once have served to protect women who had more to lose through such "sins" (for it is women who become pregnant, and not men), now it discriminates against them. Because of this double standard, promiscuity is to the advantage of males and to the disadvantage of females. Consequently it becomes exploitive in a more subtle fashion: men receive sexual gratification; women receive social condemnation.

This argument invites the initial rejoinder that it is not promiscuity that is wrong, but the double standard. In this case it is not promiscuity that we should abandon, but the double standard that places promiscuous women at a disadvantage in comparison to promiscuous men. However, this response may be too facile, too theoretical in its disregard for the reality of the social inequality of the sexes. Yet, even conceding the inadequacy of this initial rejoinder, this argument against promiscuity on the grounds that it exploits women would not apply to all cases: women immune or indifferent to social reprobation and members of groups without a double standard could still be promiscuous and yet not necessarily exploit others or be exploited by them. Since promiscuity cannot be shown to be wrong in all cases, the charge that it necessarily violates generally accepted moral principles is false.

5. *Personal Emotional Security and Growth.* Peter Bertocci argues against premarital sex, and by implication against promiscuity, on the grounds that it threatens "personal emotional security."[13] He contends that the demand for sex outside marriage exhibits a lack of self-discipline in people who cannot control their desires, and a failure to show respect and consideration for those on whom the demand is placed. Such undisciplined and inconsiderate behavior places needless strain on the relationship, threatening to destroy whatever values it embodies.

Is it true that a promiscuous person is completely lacking in self-discipline? The ritual of seduction frequently has its own carefully observed logic in the selection of a suitable consort, the finesse of the "first approach," and the rhythms of attracting and repulsing, until the ceremony reaches its *telos*.[14] What Bertocci perceives as incoherent or irrational behavior is really a self-conscious refusal to be directed by the Western norm. But promiscuous people should not be faulted for failing to regulate their actions according to a principle they reject.

Does promiscuity entail inconsiderateness? The rejoinder here parallels the earlier refutation of the charge that promiscuity is necessarily exploitive. The fact that some promiscuous people are rude, brusque, or selfish does not establish this logical tie, any more than the fact that some doctors collect stamps establishes a logical tie between medicine and philately. Only if respect is defined in terms of the Western norm is promiscuity necessarily disrespectful. Though such a definition is possible, it would beg the question at hand, which must remain empirical. Acknowledging the other's freedom to engage or not engage in noncommittal sex demonstrates some degree of respect. And at each subsequent stage of the battle of the sexes, its dialectical impetus arises through the joint effort to preserve the other's freedom.[15] The reciprocity of initiatives whereby each person asserts his or her selfhood, presided over by moral rules that embody recognition for "man as an end in himself" (to use Kant's somewhat chauvinistic phrase), provides further testimony for respect.

Does promiscuity threaten what is valuable in the relation? Of course the answer depends in part on what is considered valuable; pleasure, freedom, and respect certainly *need not* be endangered. Bertocci believes that the emotional tensions and guilt feelings that arise from violating the taboos against nonmarital sex will corrode the relation. But this harm can alternatively be eliminated by abolishing the taboos instead, so that promiscuity would no longer count as an infraction and hence no longer generate the strain that it now does. Since the traditional supports for these taboos have collapsed through an advancing technology, abolishing the Western norm is the more rational solution.

It is not promiscuity that is bad, but the arguments that purport to rebut it. These rejoinders to those arguments, though, do not prove that promiscuity itself is morally good, for I have not considered all possible arguments against it. And even if I had, the conclusion would not follow logically: promiscuity could still be bad although no one has formulated a good argument to prove it.

Perhaps promiscuity is neither good nor bad in any moral sense, but purely a matter of individual taste. To categorize it as an aesthetic rather than ethical issue concedes its normative status, but removes it from the sphere of other-regarding virtues. But even granting this move, some critical issues would remain: Is promiscuity in good taste or bad taste, and how does one decide?

Alternatively, promiscuity might be dismissed as neither a moral nor an aesthetic issue but a prudential one—a question of what is to the advantage of the agent within the sphere of actions that affect only him or her. This approach too leaves critical issues unresolved: Is promiscuity to my advantage or disadvantage, and how do I decide? Moreover this reduction of the normative to the prudential seems to disregard the fact that it takes two people (minimally) to be promiscuous—that is, others are involved.

Such attempts to categorize promiscuity presuppose a clarity and consensus on the nature of good taste and personal advantage that is altogether lacking in the literature. So I shall eschew these ways of demonstrating that promiscuity is positively a good thing in favor of a less traditional defense.

Paradigms and Archetypes

Development of a satisfactory sexual philosophy is hindered in part by lack of knowledge: Just what are the contingent ties between sexual intercourse, love, marriage, and the things or activities we find valuable? This difficulty is further compounded by linguistic confusions: the language at our disposal is notoriously vague and radically ambiguous. Moreover these two shortcomings are aggravated by a third: the absence of accepted paradigms for conceptualizing our sex life and of corresponding archetypes to give substance to our ideals. I shall now turn to three descriptive and normative models for understanding and directing sexual activities. In each case, I shall argue, promiscuity plays a legitimate role.

1. *A Classical Liberal Defense.* According to John Stuart Mill's principle of liberty, "the sole end for which mankind are warranted, individually or collectively, in interfering with the liberty of action of any of their number is self-protection. That the only purpose for which power can be rightfully exercised over any member of a civilized community, against his will, is to prevent harm to others. His own good, either physical or moral, is not a sufficient warrant."[16]

Promiscuity falls within this domain of individual liberty provided those who engage in it satisfy two conditions: they must observe some traditional moral rules, and they must exercise extreme care to avoid unwanted births. The conventional prohibitions against lying, deceit, and exploitation serve to prevent harm to others—most immediately to the person exploited or deceived and less immediately, but no less importantly, to others indirectly affected. The second proviso is designed to avoid illegitimacy, abortion, adoption, and forced marriage—not to mention the social stigma of an unwanted pregnancy, unmarried motherhood, or bastardy. Assuming then that promiscuity (as defined earlier) satisfies these two negative conditions, what can be said in its defense?

For at least some of the people some of the time sex is fun. Whatever else may be true of it, at the barest level sex remains an intensely pleasing physical activity. Like the satisfaction of an appetite (such as eating) or the release of tension (such as a good drive in golf), sex is physically enjoyable. Midst the mystification of sex it should not be forgotten that sex is and continues to be sensual; the erotic appeal of another engages all of our senses in a way equaled by few (if any) other physical activities. One paradigm that must be acknowledged by all is that sex is a type of bodily interaction that can be intensely pleasing. Granted the two earlier provisos, sex is good for this reason, if no other.

This defense does not entail that pleasure alone is good. The underlying hedonism is not "vulgar," to use Michael Bayles's term, for no attempt need be made to reduce sex merely to a sensation of pleasure.[17] A variety of things good in themselves can be acknowledged while still insisting that pleasure as "the joy of sex" is one of them. Insofar as promiscuity maximizes the pleasures that can be derived from sex, it is good; and insofar as the prohibition against promiscuity is a limitation on the pleasures to be derived from sex, it is unwarranted—in a word, "bad."

Despite his insistence that pleasure and pleasure alone is good in itself,[18] Mill himself gives evidence that he is not a vulgar hedonist. In defending his principle of liberty he suggests that happiness is not so much a sensation of pleasure as the full development of an individual's "higher faculties." Quoting Wilhelm von Humbolt with enthusiastic agreement, Mill asserts that the end of man is "the highest and most harmonious development of his powers to a complete and consistent whole."[19] This remark suggests a second defense of promiscuity within classical liberalism: the freedom to be promiscuous can contribute to the full growth of the human personality.

In many areas, such as clothing, vocation, and recreation, the need for experimentation and diversity is recognized and conceded. Mill defends his principle of liberty, not just in the intellectual arena by arguing for freedom of thought and discussion, but in the practical domain with his insistence on the individual's right to form and carry out his own "plan of life."[20] The lack of commitment that characterizes promiscuity is a freedom to explore patterns of sexual behavior at variance with the tradition. This exploration can engage one's "higher faculties" of reason, judgment, and good taste.[21] Promiscuity opens up to each person a broader range of sex partners and practices.

From the standpoint of classical liberalism, then, promiscuity may increase the pleasures of individuals, enhance the cultivation of their higher faculties (happiness in the eudaemonian sense) and enrich society with the ensuing institution.

2. *Sex as Body Language*. The sexual paradigm operative in the liberal defense of promiscuity has its limitations. For though sex is admittedly a form of bodily interaction that leads to pleasure, it is clearly more than that in some sense. In his papers "Sexual Paradigms" and "Sex and Perversion,"[22] Robert Solomon suggests what this "more" might be: As body language, sex has "meaning" that goes beyond its physical dimensions.

Just as words are more than marks and sounds, sex is more than thrusts and moans, caresses and sighs. Just as verbal language has a dimension of meaning beyond phonemes and morphemes,[23] so body language has a significance beyond the intertwining of two bodies. The sentences and words of verbal languages have their analogues in the gestures and particular movements of body language. As in all language, these latter are subject to rules that demarcate well-formed formulae. Body language has its own semantics and syntax.

This type of language can serve to express feelings, to state intentions, and to issue commands or invitations. An embrace can express genuine affection. A nod toward the bedroom door conjures up a familiar series of events. A sly glance may frequently initiate the rituals of seduction. Of course not all body language is sexual. Canadian Prime Minister Pierre Trudeau's infamous shrug communicates political indifference.[24] A policeman's hand signal issues a legal command. And holding open an elevator door is an invitation to enter something far more prosaic than what a coy smile offers. Meaning here as elsewhere depends on context. What imparts sexual significance to body language is the kind of possibility intimated—namely, intercourse, or some incomplete moment in the dialectical movement toward it.

Promiscuity has instrumental value in that it can facilitate the mastery of one kind of body language. To be in command of a language is to possess an extensive vocabulary, clear diction, and rhetorical devices for conveying meaning. These verbal skills are acquired through social interaction. Sexual body language is learned through sexual interaction.

Sexual experiences enable an individual to develop a repertoire of gestures for communicating desire and affection and of decisive movements that clearly state intentions of love or amusement. People can be moved not only by the things we *say* but by the things we *do*—with them, for them, or to them. Desire and satisfaction can be communicated not only through verbal exchanges such as "please" and "thank you," but through a lingering look and an appreciative caress. To a shattered ego a physical embrace may express far more reassurance than its verbal counterparts, and a kiss may convey desire more eloquently than pleas or poems. The subjectivity of another, their autonomy and individuality, is confirmed in the dialectics of sex: in the reversals of their roles as the initiator and the initiated, the aggressor and the pursued, the lover and the loved, each can experience his or her own incarnate freedom and acknowledge that of the other. Like verbal etiquette, the sexual rituals of flirtation and seduction are subject to rules that prohibit interruption while another is "speaking," that prescribe that each be allowed to participate fully in the conversation, and that exclude insults, attacks, and abuses. The observance of this etiquette is an acknowledgment of the selfhood of the other. The acquisition of it is one of the opportunities promiscuity provides.

Strict adherence to the Western norm places our sex lives in a straitjacket that curtails body language to "I love you," the *only* message to be delivered to just *one* person, with *fixed* diction and intonation—until the disillusioned pair have become bored by the repetition.

Sex and eating are frequently compared, since both are appetites whose satisfaction is socially regulated. Consider a society where the following etiquette is operative. Each man is allowed to dine with only one woman. Before their first meal begins, each receives a solemn injunction: "Thou shalt dine with none other, so long as you both shall live." Their partnership is exclusive; no one may be invited to the meal ("three is a crowd"). Only the utensils already provided and accepted by others may be used; bringing a new gadget to the meal is an innovation attempted by many, though (curiously) condemned by all. Throughout the remaining meals the menu is fixed on the grounds that meat and potatoes are the most nourishing foods. The ways in which these meals are prepared and consumed is subject to strict regulation: one is not supposed to touch the food with one's hands; everyone must keep an upright position (it is considered an insult for one to stand while the other lies). Interaction is drastically curtailed: one is not allowed to exchange dishes; one must feed only oneself (for a man to place his spoon in his partner's mouth is a mortal sin). These rules prescribe that each person gratify his own appetite, but in the company of a select other (to eat alone is forbidden, though many do).[25] During the meal a typical conversation consists of compliments—how good the meal is and how agreeable the company—regardless of their truthfulness.

If food and sex were only the satisfaction of appetites, these restrictions might be defensible—though the prohibitions against some changes would still be contentious. However, some innovations, at least for some people, not only could enhance the efficiency of such practices, but could add to their *meaning* as well. To "dine" with several different people can make eating not only more pleasant, but more enlightening too. To vary the "menu" is a safeguard against boredom that not only expands the topic of conversation, but also has nutritional value. To invite a guest similarly intensifies the conversation, which need not dissolve into monologues if considerateness is shown by all.[26] People should be allowed to get their fingers sticky (sex is wet) and to eat alone (masturbation makes neither your eyesight grow dim nor your hair fall out). Sometimes it may be more convenient to eat standing up or lying down: the exceptions of one society may elsewhere be the rule. More interaction can make the experience more significant; for example, switching dishes when the desires are different (to the dismay of many, they frequently only *look* different) provides variety that, after all, is still "the spice of life." If the food is not well-cooked and the company is no longer mutually attractive, admit these shortcomings; such honesty may lead to better meals. Only recently have the stereotypes that determined who issued the invitations, and who prepared the meal and did the serving, begun to dissolve. Exchanging traditional sex roles by allowing the woman to show greater initiative (if not aggression) can enhance mutual understanding and respect by dramatizing what it is to be in the other person's place.

Loosening the restrictions of the Western norm in these ways is tantamount to permitting, if not promulgating, promiscuity. The ensuing changes promise to make our sex lives not only physically more satisfying, but also more meaningful. This second defense of promiscuity has expanded the model of sexual behavior from mere bodily interaction for pleasure to a form of corporeal dialogue. With the third defense, to be offered next, these models are expanded further, to envelop man in the totality of his concrete existence.

3. *Authentic Sexuality: An Existential Defense of Promiscuity.* Heidegger's insistence that Being-with (*Mitsein*) is an essential structure of existence correctly stresses that the human personality is always situated within a social matrix.[27] My world includes others to whom I relate in various modes of solicitude. To this Heideggerian insight Merleau-Ponty adds that sexuality is an irreducible dimension of the being of the self as body subject: the erotic contours of the world reflect my incarnate being as sexual within that *gestalt* that is my existence taken as a whole.[28] Conjoining these two insights yields *eros* as a dimension of all modalities of social existence.

Among the three basic ways to be with others—against them, for them, or indifferently passing them by—Heidegger distinguishes two positive modes of "solicitude" (*Fürsorge*): to leap-in (*einspringen*) is to perform some task for another; to leap-ahead (*vorausspringen*) is to prepare another for their genuine or authentic (*eigentlich*) possibilities.[29] This authenticity stands in contrast to the inauthenticity of everyday life, which is lived under the domination of the "they-self" (*das Man*) and distinguished a lack of distinction in public, anonymous ways of thinking and acting.[30]

This everyday immersion in the commonplace, with its uncritical assimilation of the traditional, is disrupted by the call of conscience,[31] which summons the self (*Dasein*) to the recognition and acceptance of its finitude, or what Heidegger somewhat misleadingly calls "guilt."[32] My choices (*Existenz*) are finite: in pursuing one path I must forego its alternatives. My power over the world into which I am thrown (*geworfen*) is finite: some aspects of my situation remain forever beyond my control. And finally, my genuine existence, even when attained, is bounded by inauthenticity: the accommodating and tranquilizing ruses of the mediocre (*durchschnittlich*), leveled-down public life constantly tempt me to abandon personal initiative and responsibility.[33] This finitude is also temporal: my death is the ever-present possibility of my no longer having a world in which to reside, an eventuality certain to overcome me, though the moment always remains indefinite.[34] Authenticity (*Eigentlichkeit*) arises as a resolve (*Entschluss*) to remain open (*Erschliessen*) to this finitude— to be responsive to the summons to guilt and to anticipate (*vorlaufen*) death.[35] In their everyday lives, and indeed throughout a philosophical tradition, people have closed themselves off (a kind of ontological untruth for Heidegger[36]) from guilt and death, hence from that reality that they are and from that totality of entities (*Ganzheit des Seienden*) to which they are inextricably bound.

Authentic sexuality—admittedly a rather un-Heideggerian conjunction— requires a similar openness to others. Commitments are chains that bind us to some and exclude us from others, blinders that narrow down the field of social praxis to a privileged one (monogamy) or few (friendship). To elicit the many facets of the human personality requires a dynamic network of social interaction. Full sexual growth similarly requires a receptivity to the many erotic dimensions of social existence. Promiscuity provides this openness through its freedom from emotional and sexual commitments.

In the Western tradition love has been mistakenly treated as exclusive because it is erroneously thought of as possessive (compare, to "have" a woman), or that in which I have invested my will, in Hegelian terms.[37] But another person (*Mitdaseiende*) is neither a tool (*Zuhandene*) to be appropriated to my ends, nor a mere object of cognition (*Vorhandene*) to be explored. Rather, others are entities like me, with whom I share a world. Consequently love should be construed in Heideggerian terms as a leaping-ahead that affirms another's genuinely human possibilities, or in R. D. Laing's terms, as the confirmation of that which is true and good in another.[38]

The tradition has reversed the relation between sex and love—for reasons that once applied but, as previously pointed out, that are now anachronistic. The nakedness of sexual intercourse is not only physical, but psychological and emotional too: by laying bare not just our bodies, but our thoughts and feelings, two people can achieve a privileged moment from which they may *then* decide what kinds of commitments subsequently to make to one another. Promiscuity prepares for this moment through its "lack of commitment." To insist on an emotional involvement that closes off the future as a condition of this sexual self-revelation to others is, ironically, to frustrate the growth of the very love that such commitments are intended to cultivate. And to insist that this commitment as love can be made to only one other person is to succumb to the ontological fallacy of confusing people with things.

With its freedom from emotional and sexual restrictions promiscuity can play an important role in the achievement of authentic sexuality. This negative freedom-from is a positive freedom-for a genuinely human mode of social and sexual interaction.

Concluding Unscientific Postscript

My remarks might suggest that I believe promiscuity is *always* right. But this conclusion overstates my position. The claim I have sought to defend is more modest: for some of the people some of the time promiscuity is a good thing. Such behavior is curtailed by moral obligations to tell the truth, to be honest, and to respect others. It is also limited in time: for some, on occasion, promiscuity may not yet, or no longer, be good. To put my defense in perspective I shall conclude with a nod to Kierkegaard.

Kierkegaard's refutation of the Don Juan complex locates promiscuity as one stage on life's way.[39] Aping the Hegelian dialectic, of which he is both master and critic, he notes that the cause of its ultimate demise is boredom: despite the novelty achieved through the rotation method (varying the fields on which one's "seed" is sown), the full pursuit of the life of the senses ultimately succumbs to a cycle of sameness from which it can be rescued only by advancing to a higher mode of existence—the principled life of the ethical stage.[40]

Applied to the preceding sexual paradigms, Kierkegaard's insight suggests three corresponding resolutions of promiscuity. First, the good sex life cannot be achieved through physical gratification alone. The moral commitment represented by the Western norm is an attempt to achieve the advance Kierkegaard extols: wedded love regulated by reason seeks to overcome and yet to preserve (*aufheben*) the fleeting pleasures of the body. To deny this dialectical movement is to deny one's full humanity, to be arrested at a lower level of existence. Second, it may be noted that what the dialogue carried on through the body achieves in breadth it may lose in depth: having talked with many, we may discover that our most meaningful dialogue can be carried on with one. The commitment to this one person becomes, henceforth, a "natural" way to safeguard and foster this corporeal dialogue. The prohibitions against multiple dialogues were overthrown at the earlier stage so that this one person might be found and now they serve only as superfluous restrictions that need not be enforced to be observed. Finally, the openness of authentic sexuality may likewise achieve a moment at which a full commitment to a single other is its natural fruition; through its own catharsis the promiscuous life may discover a completion in Buber's I-Thou relation.[41] On such occasions promiscuity ceases to be of value in the sexual life of the individual. Indeed, from this point on not to abandon it would be as wrong as the prohibitions against it were at the earlier stage.

From this temporal perspective promiscuity has definite but limited value in the movement toward a sexual ideal. Michael Bayles is correct in his insistence that the intentionally lifelong relationship is intrinsically more valuable, but wrong in his (implicit) suggestion that intentionally temporary relations are of no value.[42] The principled life represented by the traditional commitment "to love, honor, and obey" signifies a higher mode of existence that partially transcends the vicissitudes of time. Whether this ideal is expressed in Platonic terms, as the longing for a love that is eternal,[43] or in Buber's terms, as a full awareness of the other in their unity, totality, and uniqueness, it must be wrung from man's historical existence. The value of promiscuity is located in the pursuit of just such ideals.

Notes

1. I am grateful to Professors Willard Enteman and Jan Ludwig for suggestions and criticisms that helped to rescue this paper from some of its more egregious errors and confusions.
2. See, for example, Robert Paul Wolff's *In Defense of Anarchism* (New York: Harper & Row, 1970). Though I shall not pursue the parallels between political and sexual life, I believe anarchy represents a moment in Wolff's account of political obligation analogous to the promiscuous moment in sexual morality: each is marked by a radical freedom that serves as the transcendental ground for subsequent commitments and obligations.
3. This thesis was advanced by A. J. Ayer in *Language, Truth and Logic* (New York: Dover, 1946), chap. 6, in order to account for the nonscientific (that is, nondescriptive) character of moral discourse. See C. L. Stevenson, *Ethics and Language* (New Haven: Yale University Press, 1944) and R. M. Hare, *The Language of Morals* (London: Oxford University Press, 1952) for subsequent refinements of this thesis.
4. What is true of promiscuity is also true of perversion: violations of the operative code tend to make our adrenalin flow. For one explanation of this emotional reaction to unnatural sexual acts see Michael Slote, "Inapplicable Concepts and Sexual Perversion," in *Philosophy and Sex,* 1st ed. (Amherst, N.Y.: Prometheus Books, 1975), pp. 261–67.
5. Ronald Atkinson, *Sexual Morality* (London: Hutchinson, 1965), p. 45.
6. See Robert Solomon, "Sex and Perversion," *Philosophy and Sex,* 1st ed., p. 271.
7. The boundaries of incest vary from society to society and, indeed, between groups within society. Freud sought to account for these differences in the incest taboo in terms of myth, Darwinism, and anthropology. See *Totem and Taboo* (New York: New Republic, 1931), pp. 249ff. Some have tried to show it is instinctive (see Robert H. Lowrie, *Primitive Society* [New York: Liveright, 1920]). Others explain the prohibition as a safeguard against biological degeneration due to inbreeding (see Lewis H. Morgan, *Ancient Society* [New York, 1877], pp. 69, 378, 424), or as a way of expanding and hence protecting the tribe (E. B. Tylor, "On a Method of Investigating the Development of Institutions; Applied to Laws of Marriage & Descent," *Journal of the Anthropological Institute* 18 [1888]: 245–69), or as a consequence of the prohibition against shedding the blood of one's own totemic group (Émile Durkheim, "La prohibition de l'incest et ses origines," *L'Année Sociologique* 1 [1898]: 1–70). For a more recent treatment see S. Kirson Weinberg, *Incest Behavior* (New York: Citadel, 1955).
8. To refer to this as the "conjugal act," as the Roman Catholic Church does, is to beg the question of sex outside marriage. This restriction has a long and venerable tradition within Roman Catholicism, beginning with St. Paul's warning that it is better to marry than to burn in hell. See the following: Augustine, *De Genesi ad Litteram,* Book IX, chap. 7, n. 12; Thomas Aquinas, *On*

the Truth of the Catholic Faith, Book 3, parts 1 and 2; Pope Leo XIII, *Rerum Novarum* (1891); and Pope Pius XI, *Casti Connubii* (1930).

9. Pope Paul VI, *Humanae Vitae,* "Faithfulness to God's Design," issued July 28, 1968, at Rome.

10. Carl Cohen, "Sex. Birth Control, and Human Life," *Ethics* 79 (1969): 251–62.

11. See, for example, E. D. Watt, "Professor Cohen's Encyclical," *Ethics* 80 (1970): 218–21.

12. Richard Wasserstrom considers this point in his article "Is Adultery Immoral?" in *Today's Moral Problems,* ed. Richard Wasserstrom (New York: Macmillan Co., 1975).

13. See Peter Bertocci, *The Human Venture in Sex, Love and Marriage* (New York: Associated Press, 1949), chap. 2, and his *Sex, Love and the Person* (New York: Sheed & Ward, 1967).

14. For an entertaining description of this ritual see Soren Kierkegaard. *Diary of a Seducer,* trans. K. Fick (Ithaca, N.Y.: The Dragon Press, 1935).

15. In *Being and Nothingness* (Part 3, chap. 3) Sartre transmutes the celebrated Hegelian dialectical battle for prestige between the master and slave of *The Phenomenology of Mind* (pp. 228–40) into the notorious battle of the sexes. The intervening link between Sartre and Hegel is Alexander Kojève; see his *Introduction to the Reading of Hegel,* trans. J. H. Nichols (New York: Basic Books, 1969), pp. 31–70.

16. *The Essential Works of John Stuart Mill*, ed. Max Lerner (New York: Bantam, 1961), p. 263.

17. See Michael Bayles, "Marriage, Love, and Procreation," chapter 7 in this volujme.

18. Mill, *The Essential Works,* pp. 193ff.

19. Ibid., p. 306.

20. Ibid., p. 307. Mill's insistence on the freedom to create one's own mode of life and his emphasis on individuality and the cultivation of human faculties align him with the existential tradition of Sartre ("condemned to be free"; "fundamental project") and Heidegger (*Seinkönnen*— "potentiality for Being") more than Mill's interpreters have yet recognized. I quoted Wilhelm von Humbolt earlier because he (and Aristotle) may provide the historical link.

21. Mill, *The Essential Works,* p. 323.

22. R. C. Solomon, "Sexual Paradigms," *Journal of Philosophy* 71(1974): 336–45; and "Sex and Perversion."

23. Max Black, *The Labyrinth of Language* (New York: Praeger, 1968). chap. 2, provides one explanation of this terminology.

24. Those less familiar with the gallic (and galling) tendencies of Canadian politics should consult Walter Stewart, *Shrug: Trudeau in Power* (New York: Outerbridge, 1971).

25. Lest the analogy seem farfetched by this point, it is worth recalling that Kant was one respected moral philosopher who regarded sex as mutual masturbation, salvaged only by the sanctity of matrimony. See Immanuel Kant, *Lectures on Ethics,* trans. Louis Infield (London: Methuen, 1930), pp. 162–71.

26. The conclusion that group sex is necessarily dissatisfying may be a faulty inference from the failures of its unskilled practitioners who have not yet mastered the complexities of multi-person corporeal conversations.

27. See Martin Heidegger, *Being and Time,* trans. J. Macquarrie and E. Robinson (New York: Harper & Row, 1962), sec. 27.

28. Maurice Merleau-Ponty, *The Phenomenology of Perception,* trans. Colin Smith (New York: Humanities Press, 1962), part 1, chap. 6.

29. *Being and Time,* sec. 26. R. Weber, in "A Critique of Heidegger's Concept of 'Solicitude,'" *New Scholasticism* 42 (1965): 537–60, misinterprets mineness (*Jemeinigkeit*) and the nonrelational character of death, thereby generating her spurious paradoxes. For a more faithful but less direct account see J. Macquarrie's excellent book *Existentialism* (Baltimore: Penguin, 1973), chap. 5, "Existence and Others."

30. *Being and Time,* sec. 27. For an explication of inauthenticity see Ernest H. Freund, "Man's Fall in Martin Heidegger's Philosophy," *The Journal of Religion* 24 (1944): 180–87.

31. *Being and Time,* secs. 54–57.

32. Ibid., sec. 58. On Heidegger's existential notion of guilt see Michael Gelven, *Winter Friendship and Guilt* (New York: Harper & Row, 1972); D. V. Morano, *Existential Guilt: A Phenomenological Study* (Assen, The Netherlands: Van Gorcum, 1973); C. 0. Schrag, *Existence and Freedom* (Evanston, Ill.: Northwestern University Press, 1961), chap. 6.

33. *Being and Time,* secs. 25–27, 35–38.

34. Ibid., division C, chap. 1.

35. On Heidegger's existential notion of death see J. G. Gray, "Martin Heidegger: On Anticipating my own Death," *Personalist* 46 (1965): 439–58; R. Hinners, "Death as Possibility," *Continuum* 5 (1967): 470–82; and B. E. O'Mahoney, "Martin Heidegger's Existential of Death," *Philosophical Studies* (Ireland) 18 (1969): 58–75.

36. Heidegger explicates his ontological notion of truth and relates this to the epistemological concepts in section 44 of *Being and Time* and in his essay "On the Essence of Truth," in *Being and Existence,* ed. W. Brock (Chicago: Gateway, 1949). This central concept has attracted much discussion. Ernst Tugendhat's *Der Wahrheitsbegriff bei Husserl und Heidegger* (Berlin: W. de Gruyter, 1970) is perhaps the most noteworthy.

37. G. W. F. Hegel, *The Philosophy of Right,* trans. T. M. Knox (London: Oxford University Press, 1942), pp. 40–56.

38. R. D. Laing, *Self and Others* (Baltimore: Penguin, 1971), chap. 7.

39. See Soren Kierkegaard, "The Rotation Method" (reprinted from *Either/Or*), in *A Kierkegaard Anthology,* ed. R. Bretall (New York: Modern Library, 1946), pp. 21–32.

40. In his recourse to the rational to overcome the sensual (or the "aesthetic," as Kierkegaard somewhat misleadingly terms it), Kierkegaard's solution to the morality of sex resembles Kant's (see note 25).

41. I have not tried to develop a notion of authentic sexuality on the model of Buber's I-Thou, though such an interpretation could be provided, because what I find lacking in Buber but present in Heidegger is a fuller recognition of the historicity of such ideals. For a Buberian interpretation of sexuality see M. Friedman, "Sex in Sartre and Buber," in *Sexuality and Identity,* ed. H. Ruitenbeek (New York: Bantam, 1970), pp. 84–99.

42. Though Bayles does not quite say they are of no value whatsoever, he believes that they are not sufficiently valuable to warrant legal protection.

43. See D. P. Verene, "Sexual Love and Moral Experience," in *Philosophy and Sex,* 1st ed., pp. 105–15; and his *Sexual Love and Western Morality* (New York: Harper & Row, 1972), pp. 10–47.

4

The Purpose of Sex

Thomas Aquinas

The Reason Why Simple Fornication Is a Sin According to Divine Law, and That Matrimony Is Natural

(1) We can see the futility of the argument of certain people who say that simple fornication is not a sin. For they say: Suppose there is a woman who is not married, or under the control of any man, either her father or another man. Now, if a man performs the sexual act with her, and she is willing, he does not injure her, because she favors the action and she has control over her own body. Nor does he injure any other person, because she is understood to be under no other person's control. So, this does not seem to be a sin.

(2) Now, to say that he injures God would not seem to be an adequate answer. For we do not offend God except by doing something contrary to our own good, as has been said. But this does not appear contrary to man's good. Hence, on this basis, no injury seems to be done to God.

(3) Likewise, it also would seem an inadequate answer to say that some injury is done to one's neighbor by this action, inasmuch as he may be scandalized. Indeed, it is possible for him to be scandalized by something which is not in itself a sin. In this event, the act would be accidentally sinful. But our problem is not whether simple fornication is accidentally a sin, but whether it is so essentially.

(4) Hence, we must look for a solution in our earlier considerations. We have said that God exercises care over every person on the basis of what is good

From *Summa contra Gentiles,* Book Three, by St. Thomas Aquinas, translated by Vernon J. Bourke. Translation copyright © 1956 by Doubleday, a division of Bantam Doubleday Dell Publishing Group, Inc. Used by permissed of Doubleday, a division of Bantam Doubleday Dell Publishing Group, Inc.

for him. Now, it is good for each person to attain his end, whereas it is bad for him to swerve away from his proper end. Now, this should be considered applicable to the parts, just as it is to the whole being; for instance, each and every part of man, and every one of his acts, should attain the proper end. Now, though the male semen is superfluous in regard to the preservation of the individual, it is nevertheless necessary in regard to the propagation of the species. Other superfluous things, such as excrement, urine, sweat, and such things, are not at all necessary; hence, their emission contributes to man's good. Now, this is not what is sought in the case of semen, but, rather, to emit it for the purpose of generation, to which purpose the sexual act is directed. But man's generative process would be frustrated unless it were followed by proper nutrition, because the offspring would not survive if proper nutrition were withheld. Therefore, the emission of semen ought to be so ordered that it will result in both the production of the proper offspring and in the upbringing of this offspring.

(5) It is evident from this that every emission of semen in such a way that generation cannot follow, is contrary to the good for man. And if this be done deliberately, it must be a sin. Now, I am speaking of a way from which, *in itself,* generation could not result: such would be any emission of semen apart from the natural union of male and female. For which reason, sins of this type are called *contrary to nature.* But, if by accident generation cannot result from the emission of semen, then this is not a reason for it being against nature, or a sin; as for instance, if the woman happens to be sterile.

(6) Likewise, it must also be contrary to the good for man if the semen be emitted under conditions such that generation could result but the proper upbringing would be prevented. We should take into consideration the fact that, among some animals where the female is able to take care of the upbringing of offspring, male and female do not remain together for any time after the act of generation. This is obviously the case with dogs. But in the case of animals of which the female is not able to provide for the upbringing of offspring, the male and female do stay together after the act of generation as long as is necessary for the upbringing and instruction of the offspring. Examples are found among certain species of birds whose young are not able to seek out food for themselves immediately after hatching. In fact, since a bird does not nourish its young with milk, made available by nature as it were, as occurs in the case of quadrupeds, but the bird must look elsewhere for food for its young, and since besides this it must protect them by sitting on them, the female is not able to do this by herself. So, as a result of divine providence, there is naturally implanted in the male of these animals a tendency to remain with the female in order to bring up the young. Now, it is abundantly evident that the female in the human species is not at all able to take care of the upbringing of offspring by herself, since the needs of human life demand many things which cannot be provided by one person alone. Therefore, it is appropriate to human nature that a man remain together with a woman after the generative act, and not leave her immediately to have such relations with another woman, as is the practice with fornicators.

(7) Nor, indeed, is the fact that a woman may be able by means of her own wealth to care for the child by herself an obstacle to this argument. For natural rectitude in human acts is not dependent on things accidentally possible in the case of one individual, but, rather, on those conditions which accompany the entire species.

(8) Again, we must consider that in the human species offspring require not only nourishment for the body, as in the case of other animals, but also education for the soul. . . . Children must be instructed by parents who are already experienced people. Nor are they able to receive such instruction as soon as they are born, but after a long time, and especially after they have reached the age of discretion. Moreover, a long time is needed for this instruction. Then, too, because of the impulsion of the passions, through which prudent judgment is vitiated, they require not merely instruction but correction. Now, a woman alone is not adequate to this task; rather, this demands the work of a husband, in whom reason is more developed for giving instruction and strength is more available for giving punishment. Therefore, in the human species, it is not enough, as in the case of birds, to devote a small amount of time to bringing up offspring, for a long period of life is required. Hence, since among all animals it is necessary for male and female to remain together as long as the work of the father is needed by the offspring, it is natural to the human being for the man to establish a lasting association with a designated woman, over no short period of time. Now, we call this society *matrimony*. Therefore, matrimony is natural for man, and promiscuous performance of the sexual act, outside matrimony, is contrary to man's good. For this reason, it must be a sin.

(9) Nor, in fact, should it be deemed a slight sin for man to arrange for the emission of semen apart from the proper purpose of generating and bringing up children, on the argument that it is either a slight sin, or none at all, for a person to use a part of the body for a different use than that to which it is directed by nature (say, for instance, one chose to walk on his hands, or to use his feet for something usually done with the hands) because man's good is not much opposed by such inordinate use. However, the inordinate emission of semen is incompatible with the natural good; namely, the preservation of the species. Hence, after the sin of homicide, whereby a human nature already in existence is destroyed, this type of sin appears to take next place, for by it the generation of human nature is precluded.

(10) Moreover, these views which have just been given have a solid basis in divine authority. That the emission of semen under conditions in which offspring cannot follow is illicit is quite clear. There is the text of Leviticus (18:22–23): "thou shalt not lie with mankind as with womankind . . . and thou shalt not copulate with any beast." And in I Corinthians (6:10): "Nor the effeminate, nor liers with mankind . . . shall possess the kingdom of God."

(11) Also, that fornication and every performance of the act of reproduction with a person other than one's wife are illicit is evident. For it is said: "There shall be no whore among the daughters of Israel, nor whoremonger

among the sons of Israel" (Deut. 23:17); and in Tobias (4:13): "Take heed to keep thyself from all fornication, and beside thy wife never endure to know a crime"; and in I Corinthians (6:18): "Fly fornication."

(12) By this conclusion we refute the error of those who say that there is no more sin in the emission of semen than in the emission of any other superfluous matter, and also of those who state that fornication is not a sin. . . .

That Matrimony Should Be Indivisible

(1) If one will make a proper consideration, the preceding reasoning will be seen to lead to the conclusion not only that the society of man and woman of the human species, which we call matrimony, should be long-lasting, but even that it should endure throughout an entire life.

(2) Indeed, possessions are ordered to the preservation of natural life, and since natural life, which cannot be preserved perpetually in the father, is by a sort of succession preserved in the son in its specific likeness, it is naturally fitting for the son to succeed also to the things which belong to the father. So, it is natural that the father's solicitude for his son should endure until the end of the father's life. Therefore, if even in the case of birds the solicitude of the father gives rise to the cohabitation of male and female, the natural order demands that father and mother in the human species remain together until the end of life.

(3) It also seems to be against equity if the aforesaid society be dissolved. For the female needs the male, not merely for the sake of generation, as in the case of other animals, but also for the sake of government, since the male is both more perfect in reasoning and is stronger in his powers. In fact, a woman is taken into man's society for the needs of generation; then, with the disappearance of a woman's fecundity and beauty, she is prevented from association with another man. So, if any man took a woman in the time of her youth, when beauty and fecundity were hers, and then sent her away after she had reached an advanced age, he would damage that woman contrary to natural equity.

(4) Again, it seems obviously inappropriate for a woman to be able to put away her husband, because a wife is naturally subject to her husband as governor, and it is not within the power of a person subject to another to depart from his rule. So, it would be against the natural order if a wife were able to abandon her husband. Therefore, if a husband were permitted to abandon his wife, the society of husband and wife would not be an association of equals, but, instead, a sort of slavery on the part of the wife.

(5) Besides, there is in men a certain natural solicitude to know their offspring. This is necessary for this reason: the child requires the father's direction for a long time. So, whenever there are obstacles to the ascertaining of offspring they are opposed to the natural instinct of the human species. But, if a husband

could put away his wife, or a wife her husband, and have sexual relations with another person, certitude as to offspring would be precluded, for the wife would be united first with one man and later with another. So, it is contrary to the natural instinct of the human species for a wife to be separated from her husband. And thus, the union of male and female in the human species must be not only lasting, but also unbroken.

(6) Furthermore, the greater that friendship is, the more solid and long-lasting will it be. Now, there seems to be the greatest friendship between husband and wife, for they are united not only in the act of fleshly union, which produces a certain gentle association even among beasts, but also in the partnership of the whole range of domestic activity. Consequently, as an indication of this, man must even "leave his father and mother" for the sake of his wife, as is said in Genesis (2:24). Therefore, it is fitting for matrimony to be completely indissoluble. . . .

5

Humanae Vitae

Pope Paul VI

To the venerable Patriarchs, Archbishops and other local ordinaries in peace and communion with the Apostolic See, to priests, the faithful and to all men of good will.

Venerable brothers and beloved sons:

The Transmission of Life

1. The most serious duty of transmitting human life, for which married persons are the free and responsible collaborators of God the Creator, has always been a source of great joys to them, even if sometimes accompanied by not a few difficulties and by distress.

At all times the fulfillment of this duty has posed grave problems to the conscience of married persons, but, with the recent evolution of society, changes have taken place that give rise to new questions which the Church could not ignore, having to do with a matter which so closely touches upon the life and happiness of men. . . . [Sections 2–6 have been deleted.]

The encyclical *Humanae Vitae* was issued July 29, 1968, at Rome. This official translation published by permission of the Pontifical Council for Social Communications.

Doctrinal Principles

A Total Vision of Man

7. The problem of birth, like every other problem regarding human life, is to be considered, beyond partial perspectives—whether of the biological or psychological, demographic or sociological orders—in the light of an integral vision of man and of his vocation, not only his natural and earthly, but also his supernatural and eternal vocation. And since, in the attempts to justify artificial methods of birth control, many have appealed to the demands both of conjugal love and of "responsible parenthood," it is good to state very precisely the true concept of these two great realities of married life, referring principally to what was recently set forth in this regard, and in a highly authoritative form, by the Second Vatican Council in its pastoral constitution *Gaudium et Spes.*

Conjugal Love

8. Conjugal love reveals its true nature and nobility when it is considered in its supreme origin, God, who is love,[1] "the Father, from whom every family in heaven and on earth is named."[2]

Marriage is not, then, the effect of chance or the product of evolution of unconscious natural forces; it is the wise institution of the Creator to realize in mankind His design of love. By means of the reciprocal personal gift of self, proper and exclusive to them, husband and wife tend towards the communion of their beings in view of mutual personal perfection, to collaborate with God in the generation and education of new lives.

For baptized persons, moreover, marriage invests the dignity of a sacramental sign of grace, inasmuch as it represents the union of Christ and of the Church.

Its Characteristics

9. Under this light, there clearly appear the characteristic marks and demands of conjugal love, and it is of supreme importance to have an exact idea of these.

This love is first of all fully human, that is to say, of the senses and of the spirit at the same time. It is not, then, a simple transport of instinct and sentiment, but also, and principally, an act of the free will, intended to endure and to grow by means of the joys and sorrows of daily life, in such a way that husband

and wife become only one heart and one only soul, and together attain their human perfection.

Then, this love is total, that is to say, it is a very special form of personal friendship, in which husband and wife generously share everything, without undue reservations or selfish calculations. Whoever truly loves his marriage partner loves not only for what he receives, but for the partner's self, rejoicing that he can enrich his partner with the gift of himself.

Again, this love is faithful and exclusive until death. Thus, in fact, do bride and groom conceive it to be on the day when they freely and in full awareness assume the duty of the marriage bond. A fidelity, this, which can sometimes be difficult, but is always possible, always noble and meritorious, as no one can deny. The example of so many married persons down through the centuries shows, not only that fidelity is according to the nature of marriage, but also that it is a source of profound and lasting happiness and, finally, this love is fecund for it is not exhausted by the communion between husband and wife, but is destined to continue, raising up new lives. "Marriage and conjugal love are by their nature ordained toward the begetting and educating of children. Children are really the supreme gift of marriage and contribute very substantially to the welfare of their parents."[3]

Responsible Parenthood

10. Hence conjugal love requires in husband and wife an awareness of their mission of "responsible parenthood," which today is rightly much insisted upon, and which also must be exactly understood. Consequently it is to be considered under different aspects which are legitimate and connected with one another.

In relation to the biological processes, responsible parenthood means the knowledge and respect of their functions; human intellect discovers in the power of giving life biological laws which are part of the human person.[4]

In relation to the tendencies of instinct or passion, responsible parenthood means that necessary dominion which reason and will must exercise over them.

In relation to physical, economic, psychological and social conditions, responsible parenthood is exercised, either by the deliberate and generous decision to raise a large family, or by the decision, made for grave motives and with due respect for the moral law, to avoid for the time being, or even for an indeterminate period, a new birth.

Responsible parenthood also and above all implies a more profound relationship to the objective moral order established by God, of which a right conscience is the faithful interpreter. The responsible exercise of parenthood implies, therefore, that husband and wife recognize fully their own duties towards God, towards themselves, towards the family and towards society, in a correct hierarchy of values.

In the task of transmitting life, therefore, they are not free to proceed completely at will, as if they could determine in a wholly autonomous way the honest path to follow; but they must conform their activity to the creative intention of God, expressed in the very nature of marriage and of its acts, and manifested by the constant teaching of the Church.[5]

Respect for the Nature and Purpose of the Marriage Act

11. These acts, by which husband and wife are united in chaste intimacy, and by means of which human life is transmitted, are, as the Council recalled, "noble and worthy,"[6] and they do not cease to be lawful if, for causes independent of the will of husband and wife, they are foreseen to be infecund, since they always remain ordained towards expressing and consolidating their union. In fact, as experience bears witness, not every conjugal act is followed by a new life. God has wisely disposed natural laws and rhythms of fecundity which, of themselves, cause a separation in the succession of births. Nonetheless the Church, calling men back to the observance of the norms of the natural law, as interpreted by their constant doctrine, teaches that each and every marriage act (*quilibet matrimonii usus*) must remain open to the transmission of life.[7]

Two Inseparable Aspects: Union and Procreation

12. That teaching, often set forth by the magisterium, is founded upon the inseparable connection, willed by God and unable to be broken by man on his own initiative, between the two meanings of the conjugal act: the unitive meaning and the procreative meaning. Indeed, by its intimate structure, the conjugal act, while most closely uniting husband and wife, empowers them to generate new lives, according to laws inscribed in the very being of man and of woman. By safeguarding both these essential aspects, unitive and procreative, the conjugal act preserves in its fullness the sense of true mutual love and its ordination towards man's most high calling to parenthood. We believe that the men of our day are particularly capable of seizing the deeply reasonable and human character of this fundamental principle.

Faithfulness to God's Design

13. It is in fact justly observed that a conjugal act imposed upon one's partner without regard for his or her condition and lawful desires is not a true act of love,

and therefore denies an exigency of right moral order in the relationships between husband and wife. Hence, one who reflects well must also recognize that a reciprocal act of love, which jeopardizes the responsibility to transmit life which God the Creator, according to particular laws, inserted therein is in contradiction with the design constitutive of marriage, and with the will of the Author of life. To use this divine gift destroying, even if only partially, its meaning and its purpose is to contradict the nature both of man and of woman and of their most intimate relationship, and therefore, it is to contradict also the plan of God and His will. On the other hand, to make use of the gift of conjugal love while respecting the laws of the generative process means to acknowledge oneself not to be the arbiter of the sources of human life, but rather the minister of the design established by the Creator. In fact, just as man does not have unlimited dominion over his body in general, so also, with particular reason, he has no such dominion over his generative faculties as such, because of their intrinsic ordination towards raising up life, of which God is the principle. "Human life is sacred," Pope John XXIII recalled; "from its very inception it reveals the creating hand of God."[8]

Illicit Ways of Regulating Birth

14. In conformity with these landmarks in the human and Christian vision of marriage, we must once again declare that the direct interruption of the generative process already begun, and, above all, directly willed and procured abortion, even if for therapeutic reasons, are to be absolutely excluded as licit means of regulating birth.[9]

Equally to be excluded, as the teaching authority of the Church has frequently declared, is direct sterilization, whether perpetual or temporary, whether of the man or of the woman.[10] Similarly excluded is every action which, either in anticipation of the conjugal act, or in its accomplishment, or in the development of its natural consequences, proposes, whether as an end or as a means, to render procreation impossible.[11]

To justify conjugal acts made intentionally infecund, one cannot invoke as valid reasons the lesser evil, or the fact that such acts would constitute a whole together with the fecund acts already performed or to follow later, and hence would share in one and the same moral goodness. In truth, if it is sometimes licit to tolerate a lesser evil in order to avoid a greater evil or to promote a greater good,[12] it is not licit, even for the gravest reasons, to do evil so that good may follow therefrom,[13] that is, to make into the object of a positive act of the will something which is intrinsically disordered, and hence unworthy of the human person, even when the intention is to safeguard or promote individual, family, or social well-being. Consequently it is an error to think that a conjugal act which is deliberately made infecund and so is intrinsically dishonest could be made honest and right by the ensemble of a fecund conjugal life.

Licitness of Therapeutic Means

15. The Church, on the contrary, does not at all consider illicit the use of those therapeutic means truly necessary to cure diseases of the organism, even if an impediment to procreation, which may be foreseen, should result therefrom, provided such impediment is not, for whatever motive, directly willed.[14]

Licitness of Resource to Infecund Periods

16. To this teaching of the Church on conjugal morals, the objection is made today . . . that it is the prerogative of the human intellect to dominate the energies offered by irrational nature and to orientate them towards an end conformable to the good of man. Now, some may ask: in the present case, is it not reasonable in many circumstances to have recourse to artificial birth control if, thereby, we secure the harmony and peace of the family, and better conditions for the education of the children already born? To this question it is necessary to reply with clarity: the Church is the first to praise and recommend the intervention of intelligence in a function which so closely associates the rational creature with his Creator; but she affirms that this must be done with respect for the order established by God.

If, then, there are serious motives to space out births, which derive from the physical or psychological condition of husband and wife, or from external conditions, the Church teaches that it is then licit to take into account the natural rhythms immanent in the generative functions, for the use of marriage in the infecund periods only, and in this way to regulate birth without offending the moral principles which have been recalled earlier.[15]

The Church is consistent with herself when she considers recourse to the infecund periods to be licit, while at the same time condemning, as being always illicit, the use of means directly contrary to fecundation, even if such use is inspired by reasons which may appear honest and serious. In reality, there are essential differences between the two cases; in the former, the married couple make legitimate use of a natural disposition; in the latter, they impede the development of natural processes. It is true that, in the one and the other case, the married couple are in agreement in the positive will of avoiding children for plausible reasons, seeking the certainty that offspring will not arrive; but it is also true that only in the former case are they able to renounce the use of marriage in the fecund periods when, for just motives, procreation is not desirable, while making use of it during infecund periods to manifest their affection and to safeguard their mutual fidelity. By so doing, they give proof of a truly and integrally honest love.

Grave Consequences of Methods
of Artificial Birth Control

17. Upright men can even better convince themselves of the solid grounds on which the teaching of the Church in this field is based, if they care to reflect upon the consequences of methods of artificial birth control. Let them consider, first of all, how wide and easy a road would thus be opened up towards conjugal infidelity and the general lowering of morality. Not much experience is needed in order to know human weakness, and to understand that men—especially the young, who are so vulnerable on this point—have need of encouragement to be faithful to the moral law, so that they must not be offered some easy means of eluding its observance. It is also to be feared that the man, growing used to the employment of anticonceptive practices, may finally lose respect for the woman and, no longer caring for her physical and psychological equilibrium, may come to the point of considering her as a mere instrument of selfish enjoyment, and no longer as his respected and beloved companion.

Let it be considered also that a dangerous weapon would thus be placed in the hands of those public authorities who take no heed of moral exigencies. Who could blame a government for applying to the solution of the problems of the community those means acknowledged to be licit for married couples in the solution of a family problem? Who will stop rulers from favoring, from even imposing upon their peoples, if they were to consider it necessary, the method of contraception which they judge to be most efficacious? In such a way men, wishing to avoid individual, family, or social difficulties encountered in the observance of the divine law, would reach the point of placing at the mercy of the intervention of public authorities the most personal and most reserved sector of conjugal intimacy.

Consequently, if the mission of generating life is not to be exposed to the arbitrary will of men, one must necessarily recognize insurmountable limits to the possibility of man's domination over his own body and its functions; limits which no man, whether a private individual or one invested with authority, may licitly surpass. And such limits cannot be determined otherwise than by the respect due to the integrity of the human organism and its functions, according to the principles recalled earlier, and also according to the correct understanding of the "principle of totality" illustrated by our predecessor Pope Pius XII.[16] . . .
[Sections 18–20 have been deleted.]

Pastoral Directives

Mastery of Self

21. The honest practice of regulation of birth demands first of all that husband and wife acquire and possess solid convictions concerning the true values of life and of the family, and that they tend towards securing perfect self-mastery. To dominate instinct by means of one's reason and free will undoubtedly requires ascetical practices, so that the affective manifestations of conjugal life may observe the correct order, in particular with regard to the observance of periodic continence. Yet this discipline which is proper to the purity of married couples, far from harming conjugal love, rather confers on it a higher human value. It demands continual effort yet, thanks to its beneficent influence, husband and wife fully develop their personalities, being enriched with spiritual values. Such discipline bestows upon family life fruits of serenity and peace, and facilitates the solution of other problems; it favors attention for one's partner, helps both parties to drive out selfishness, the enemy of true love; and deepens their sense of responsibility. By its means, parents acquire the capacity of having a deeper and more efficacious influence in the education of their offspring; little children and youths grow up with a just appraisal of human values, and in the serene and harmonious development of their spiritual and sensitive faculties.

Creating an Atmosphere Favorable to Chastity

22. On this occasion, we wish to draw the attention of educators, and of all who perform duties of responsibility in regard to the common good of human society, to the need of creating an atmosphere favorable to education in chastity, that is, to the triumph of healthy liberty over license by means of respect for the moral order.

Everything in the modern media of social communications which leads to sense excitation and unbridled habits, as well as every form of pornography and licentious performances, must arouse the frank and unanimous reaction of all those who are solicitous for the progress of civilization and the defense of the common good of the human spirit. Vainly would one seek to justify such depravation with the pretext of artistic or scientific exigencies,[17] or to deduce an argument from the freedom allowed in this sector by the public authorities.

Appeal to Public Authorities

23. To Rulers, who are those principally responsible for the common good, and who can do so much to safeguard moral customs, we say: Do not allow the morality of your peoples to be degraded; do not permit that by legal means practices contrary to the natural and divine law be introduced into that fundamental cell, the family. Quite other is the way in which public authorities can and must contribute to the solution of the demographic problem: namely, the way of a provident policy for the family, of a wise education of peoples in respect of moral law and the liberty of citizens.

We are well aware of the serious difficulties experienced by public authorities in this regard, especially in the developing countries. To their legitimate preoccupations we devoted our encyclical letter *Populorum Progressio*. But with our predecessor Pope John XXIII, we repeat: No solution to these difficulties is acceptable "which does violence to man's essential dignity" and is based only on an utterly materialistic conception of man himself and of his life. The only possible solution to this question is one which envisages the social and economic progress both of individuals and of the whole of human society, and which respects and promotes true human values.[18] Neither can one, without grave injustice, consider divine providence to be responsible for what depends, instead, on a lack of wisdom in government, on an insufficient sense of social justice, on selfish monopolization, or again on blameworthy indolence in confronting the efforts and the sacrifices necessary to ensure the raising of living standards of a people and of all its sons.[19]

May all responsible public authorities—as some are already doing so laudably—generously revive their efforts. And may mutual aid between all the members of the great human family never cease to grow. This is an almost limitless field which thus opens up to the activity of the great international organizations. . . .

Notes

1. Cf. I John 4:8.
2. Cf. Eph. 3:15.
3. Cf. II Vatican Council, Pastoral Const. *Gaudium et Spes*, no. 50.
4. Cf. St. Thomas, *Summa Theologica*, I–II, q. 94, art. 2.
5. Cf. Pastoral Const. *Gaudium et Spes*, nos. 50, 51.
6. Ibid, no. 49.
7. Cf. Pius XI, encyc. *Casti Connubii*, in *AAS* XXII (1930), p. 560; Pius XII, in *AAS* XLIII (1951), p. 843.
8. Cf. John XXIII, encyc. *Mater et Magistra*, in *AAS* LIII (1961), p. 447.

9. Cf. *Catechismus Romanus Concilii Tridentini*, part 2, chap. 8; Pius XI, encyc. *Casti Connubii*, in *AAS* XXII (1930), pp. 562–64; Pius XII, *Discorsi e Radiomessaggi*, VI (1944), pp. 191–92; *AAS* XLIII (1951), pp. 842–43; pp. 857–59; John XXIII, encyc. *Pacem in Terris*, Apr. 11, 1963, in *AAS* LV (1963), pp. 259–60; *Gaudium et Spes*, no. 51.

10. Cf. Pius XI encyc. *Casti Connubii*, in *AAS* XXII (1930), p. 565; decree of the Holy Office, Feb. 22, 1940, in *AAS* L (1958), pp. 734–35.

11. Cf. *Catechismus Romanus Concilii Tridentini*, part 2, chap. 8; Pius XI, encyc. *Casti Connubii*, in *AAS* XXII (1930), pp. 559–61; Pius XII, *AAS* XLIII (1951), p. 843; *AAS* L (1958), pp. 734–35; John XXIII, encyc. *Mater et Magistra*, in *AAS* LIII (1961), p. 447.

12. Cf. Pius XII, alloc. to the National Congress of the Union of Catholic Jurists, Dec. 6, 1953, in *AAS* XLV (1953), pp. 798–99.

13. Cf. Rom. 3:8.

14. Cf. Pius XII, alloc. to Congress of the Italian Association of Urology, Oct. 8, 1953, in *AAS* XLV (1953), pp. 674–75; *AAS* L (1958), pp. 734–35.

15. Cf. Pius XII, *AAS* XLIII (1951), p. 846.

16. Cf. *AAS* XLV (1953), pp. 674–75; *AAS* XLVIII (1956), pp. 461–62.

17. Cf. II Vatican Council, decree *Inter Mirifica, On the Instruments of Social Communication*, nos. 6–7.

18. Cf. encyc. *Mater et Magistra* in *AAS* LIII (1961), p. 447.

19. Cf. encyc. *Populorum Progressio*, nos. 48–55.

6

Declaration on Certain Questions concerning Sexual Ethics

The Vatican

I

According to contemporary scientific research, the human person is so profoundly affected by sexuality that it must be considered as one of the factors which give to each individual's life the principal traits that distinguish it. In fact it is from sex that the human person receives the characteristics which, on the biological, psychological and spiritual levels, make that person a man or a woman, and thereby largely condition his or her progress towards maturity and insertion into society. Hence sexual matters, as is obvious to everyone, today constitute a theme frequently and openly dealt with in books, reviews, magazines and other means of social communication.

In the present period, the corruption of morals has increased, and one of the most serious indications of this corruption is the unbridled exaltation of sex. Moreover, through the means of social communication and through public entertainment this corruption has reached the point of invading the field of education and of infecting the general mentality.

In this context certain educators, teachers and moralists have been able to contribute to a better understanding and integration into life of the values proper to each of the sexes; on the other hand there are those who have put forward concepts and modes of behavior which are contrary to the true moral exigencies of the human person. Some members of the latter group have even gone so far as to favor a licentious hedonism.

As a result, in the course of a few years, teachings, moral criteria and modes

This Declaration on Sexual Ethics was issued in Rome by the Sacred Congregation for the Doctrine of the Faith on December 29, 1975. Reprinted by permission of the Pontifical Council for Social Communications.

of living hitherto faithfully preserved have been very much unsettled, even among Christians. There are many people today who, being confronted with widespread opinions opposed to the teaching which they received from the Church, have come to wonder what must still hold as true.

II

The Church cannot remain indifferent to this confusion of minds and relaxation of morals. It is a question, in fact, of a matter which is of the utmost importance both for the personal lives of Christians and for the social life of our time.[1]

The Bishops are daily led to note the growing difficulties experienced by the faithful in obtaining knowledge of wholesome moral teaching, especially in sexual matters, and of the growing difficulties experienced by pastors in expounding this teaching effectively. The Bishops know that by their pastoral charge they are called upon to meet the needs of their faithful in this very serious matter, and important documents dealing with it have already been published by some of them or by episcopal conferences. Nevertheless, since the erroneous opinions and resulting deviations are continuing to spread everywhere, the Sacred Congregation for the Doctrine of the Faith, by virtue of its function in the universal Church[2] and by a mandate of the Supreme Pontiff, has judged it necessary to publish the present Declaration.

III

The people of our time are more and more convinced that the human person's dignity and vocation demand that they should discover, by the light of their own intelligence, the values innate in their nature, that they should ceaselessly develop these values and realize them in their lives, in order to achieve an ever greater development.

In moral matters man cannot make value judgments according to his personal whim: "In the depths of his conscience, man detects a law which he does not impose on himself, but which holds him to obedience. . . . For man has in his heart a law written by God. To obey it is the very dignity of man; according to it he will be judged."[3]

Moreover, through His revelation God has made known to us Christians His plan of salvation, and He has held up to us Christ, the Savior and Sanctifier, in His teaching and example, as the supreme and immutable Law of life: "I am the light of the world; anyone who follows Me will not be walking in the dark, he will have the light of life."[4]

Therefore there can be no true promotion of man's dignity unless the essential order of his nature is respected. Of course, in the history of civilization many of the concrete conditions and needs of human life have changed and will continue to change. But all evolution of morals and every type of life must be kept within the limits imposed by the immutable principles based upon every human person's constitutive elements and essential relations—elements and relations which transcend historical contingency.

These fundamental principles, which can be grasped by reason, are contained in "the Divine Law—eternal, objective and universal—whereby God orders, directs and governs the entire universe and all the ways of the human community, by a plan conceived in wisdom and love. Man has been made by God to participate in this law, with the result that, under the gentle disposition of Divine Providence, he can come to perceive ever increasingly the unchanging truth."[5] This Divine Law is accessible to our minds. . . .

V

Since sexual ethics concern fundamental values of human and Christian life, this general teaching equally applies to sexual ethics. In this domain there exist principles and norms which the Church has always unhesitatingly transmitted as part of her teaching, however much the opinions and morals of the world may have been opposed to them. These principles and norms in no way owe their origin to a certain type of culture, but rather to knowledge of the Divine Law and of human nature. They therefore cannot be considered as having become out of date or doubtful under the pretext that a new cultural situation has arisen.

It is these principles which inspired the exhortations and directives given by the Second Vatican Council for an education and an organization of social life taking account of the equal dignity of man and woman while respecting their difference.[6]

Speaking of "the sexual nature of man and the human faculty of procreation," the Council noted that they "wonderfully exceed the dispositions of lower forms of life."[7] It then took particular care to expound the principles and criteria which concern human sexuality in marriage, and which are based upon the finality of the specific function of sexuality.

In this regard the Council declares that the moral goodness of the acts proper to conjugal life, acts which are ordered according to true human dignity, "does not depend solely on sincere intentions or on an evaluation of motives. It must be determined by objective standards. These, based on the nature of the human person and his acts, preserve the full sense of mutual self-giving and human procreation in the context of true love."[8]

These final words briefly sum up the Council's teaching—more fully expounded in an earlier part of the same Constitution[9]—on the finality of the sexual act and on the principal criterion of its morality: it is respect for its finality that ensures the moral goodness of this act.

This same principle, which the Church holds from Divine Revelation and from her authentic interpretation of the natural law, is also the basis of her traditional doctrine, which states that the use of the sexual function has its true meaning and moral rectitude only in true marriage.[10]

VI

It is not the purpose of the present Declaration to deal with all the abuses of the sexual faculty, nor with all the elements involved in the practice of chastity. Its object is rather to repeat the Church's doctrine on certain particular points, in view of the urgent need to oppose serious errors and widespread aberrant modes of behavior.

VII

Today there are many who vindicate the right to sexual union before marriage, at least in those cases where a firm intention to marry and an affection which is already in some way conjugal in the psychology of the subjects require this completion, which they judge to be connatural. This is especially the case when the celebration of the marriage is impeded by circumstances or when this intimate relationship seems necessary in order for love to be preserved.

This opinion is contrary to Christian doctrine, which states that every genital act must be within the framework of marriage. However firm the intention of those who practice such premature sexual relations may be, the fact remains that these relations cannot ensure, in sincerity and fidelity, the interpersonal relationship between a man and a woman, nor especially can they protect this relationship from whims and caprices. Now it is a stable union that Jesus willed, and He restored its original requirement, beginning with the sexual difference. "Have you not read that the Creator from the beginning made them male and female and that He said: This is why a man must leave father and mother, and cling to his wife, and the two become one body? They are no longer two, therefore, but one body. So then, what God has united, man must not divide."[11] St. Paul will be even more explicit when he shows that if unmarried people or widows cannot live chastely they have no other alternative than the stable union of marriage: ". . . it is better to marry than to be aflame with passion."[12] Through marriage, in fact, the love of married people is taken up into that love which Christ irrevocably has for the Church,[13] while dissolute sexual union[14] defiles the temple of the Holy Spirit which the Christian has become. Sexual union therefore is only legitimate if a definitive community of life has been established between the man and the woman.

This is what the Church has always understood and taught,[15] and she finds a profound agreement with her doctrine in men's reflection and in the lessons of history.

Experience teaches us that love must find its safeguard in the stability of marriage, if sexual intercourse is truly to respond to the requirements of its own finality and to those of human dignity. These requirements call for a conjugal contract sanctioned and guaranteed by society—a contract which establishes a state of life of capital importance both for the exclusive union of the man and the woman and for the good of their family and of the human community. Most often, in fact, premarital relations exclude the possibility of children. What is represented to be conjugal love is not able, as it absolutely should be, to develop into paternal and maternal love. Or, if it does happen to do so, this will be to the detriment of the children, who will be deprived of the stable environment in which they ought to develop in order to find in it the way and the means of their insertion into society as a whole.

The consent given by people who wish to be united in marriage must therefore be manifested externally and in a manner which makes it valid in the eyes of society. As far as the faithful are concerned, their consent to the setting up of a community of conjugal life must be expressed according to the laws of the Church. It is a consent which makes their marriage a Sacrament of Christ.

VIII

At the present time there are those who, basing themselves on observations in the psychological order, have begun to judge indulgently, and even to excuse completely, homosexual relations between certain people. This they do in opposition to the constant teaching of the Magisterium and to the moral sense of the Christian people.

A distinction is drawn, and it seems with some reason, between homosexuals whose tendency comes from a false education, from a lack of normal sexual development, from habit, from bad example, or from other similar causes, and is transitory or at least not incurable; and homosexuals who are definitively such because of some kind of innate instinct or a pathological constitution judged to be incurable.

In regard to this second category of subjects, some people conclude that their tendency is so natural that it justifies in their case homosexual relations within a sincere communion of life and love analogous to marriage, in so far as such homosexuals feel incapable of enduring a solitary life.

In the pastoral field, these homosexuals must certainly be treated with understanding and sustained in the hope of overcoming their personal difficulties and their inability to fit into society. Their culpability will be judged with prudence. But no pastoral method can be employed which would give moral justification to these acts on the grounds that they would be consonant with the condition of such people. For according to the objective moral order, homosexual relations are acts which lack an essential and indispensable finality. In Sacred Scripture they are condemned as a serious depravity and even presented as the sad consequence of rejecting God.[16] This judgment of Scripture does not of course permit us to conclude that all those who suffer from this anomaly are personally responsible for it, but it does attest to the fact that homosexual acts are intrinsically disordered and can in no case be approved of.

IX

The traditional Catholic doctrine that masturbation constitutes a grave moral disorder is often called into doubt or expressly denied today. It is said that psychology and sociology show that it is a normal phenomenon of sexual development, especially among the young. It is stated that there is real and serious fault only in the measure that the subject deliberately indulges in solitary pleasure closed in on self ("ipsation"), because in this case the act would indeed be radically opposed to the loving communion between persons of different sex which some hold is what is principally sought in the use of the sexual faculty.

This opinion is contradictory to the teaching and pastoral practice of the Catholic Church. Whatever the force of certain arguments of a biological and philosophical nature, which have sometimes been used by theologians, in fact both the Magisterium of the Church—in the course of a constant tradition—and the moral sense of the faithful have declared without hesitation that masturbation is an intrinsically and seriously disordered act.[17] The main reason is that, whatever the motive for acting this way, the deliberate use of the sexual faculty outside normal conjugal relations essentially contradicts the finality of the faculty. For it lacks the sexual relationship called for by the moral order, namely the relationship which realizes "the full sense of mutual self-giving and human procreation in the context of true love."[18] All deliberate exercise of sexuality must be reserved to this regular relationship. Even if it cannot be proved that Scripture condemns this sin by name, the tradition of the Church has rightly understood it to be condemned in the New Testament when the latter speaks of "impurity," "unchasteness" and other vices contrary to chastity and continence.

Sociological surveys are able to show the frequency of this disorder according to the places, populations or circumstances studied. In this way facts are discovered, but facts do not constitute a criterion for judging the moral value of human acts.[19] The frequency of the phenomenon in question is certainly to be linked with man's innate weakness following original sin; but it is also to be linked with the loss of a sense of God, with the corruption of morals engendered by the commercialization of vice, with the unrestrained licentiousness of so many public entertainments and publications, as well as with the neglect of modesty, which is the guardian of chastity.

On the subject of masturbation modern psychology provides much valid and useful information for formulating a more equitable judgment on moral responsibility and for orienting pastoral action. Psychology helps one to see how the immaturity of adolescence (which can sometimes persist after that age), psychological imbalance or habit can influence behavior, diminishing the deliberate character of the act and bringing about a situation whereby subjectively there may not always be serious fault. But in general, the absence of serious responsibility must not be presumed; this would be to misunderstand people's moral capacity.

In the pastoral ministry, in order to form an adequate judgment in concrete cases, the habitual behavior of people will be considered in its totality, not only with regard to the individual's practice of charity and of justice but also with regard to the individual's care in observing the particular precepts of chastity. In particular, one will have to examine whether the individual is using the necessary means, both natural and supernatural, which Christian asceticism from its long experience recommends for overcoming the passions and progressing in virtue. . . .

XI

As has been said above, the purpose of this Declaration is to draw the attention of the faithful in present-day circumstances to certain errors and modes of behavior which they must guard against. The virtue of chastity, however, is in no way confined solely to avoiding the faults already listed. It is aimed at attaining higher and more positive goals. It is a virtue which concerns the whole personality, as regards both interior and outward behavior.

Individuals should be endowed with this virtue according to their state in life: for some it will mean virginity or celibacy consecrated to God, which is an eminent way of giving oneself more easily to God alone with an undivided heart.[20] For others it will take the form determined by the moral law, according to whether they are married or single. But whatever the state of life, chastity is not simply an external state; it must make a person's heart pure in accordance with Christ's words: "You have learned how it was said: You must not commit adultery. But I say this to you: if a man looks at a woman lustfully, he has already committed adultery with her in his heart."[21]

Chastity is included in that continence which St. Paul numbers among the gifts of the Holy Spirit, while he condemns sensuality as a vice particularly unworthy of the Christian and one which precludes entry into the Kingdom of Heaven.[22] "What God wants is for all to be holy. He wants you to keep away from fornication, and each one of you know how to use the body that belongs to him in a way that is holy and honorable, not giving way to selfish lust like the pagans who do not know God. He wants nobody at all ever to sin by taking advantage of a brother in these matters. . . . We have been called by God to be holy, not to be immoral. In other words, anyone who objects is not objecting to a human authority, but to God, Who gives you His Holy Spirit."[23] "Among you there must not be even a mention of fornication or impurity in any of its forms, or promiscuity: this would hardly become the saints! For you can be quite certain that nobody who actually indulges in fornication or impurity or promiscuity—which is worshipping a false god—can inherit anything of the Kingdom of God. Do not let anyone deceive you with empty arguments: it is for this loose living that God's anger comes down on those who rebel against Him. Make sure that you are not included with them. You were darkness once, but now you are light in the Lord; be like children of light, for the effects of the light are seen in complete goodness and right living and truth."[24]

In addition, the Apostle points out the specifically Christian motive for practicing chastity when he condemns the sin of fornication not only in the measure that this action is injurious to one's neighbor or to the social order but because the fornicator offends against Christ Who has redeemed him with His blood and of Whom he is a member, and against the Holy Spirit of Whom he is the temple. "You know, surely, that your bodies are members making up the body of Christ. . . . All the other sins are committed outside the body; but to fornicate is to sin against your own body. Your body, you know, is the temple of the Holy Spirit, Who is in you since you received Him from God. You are not your own property; you have been bought and paid for. That is why you should use your body for the glory of God."[25]

The more the faithful appreciate the value of chastity and its necessary role in their lives as men and women, the better they will understand, by a kind of spiritual instinct, its moral requirements and counsels. In the same way they will know better how to accept and carry out, in a spirit of docility to the Church's teaching, what an upright conscience dictates in concrete cases. . . .

Finally, it is necessary to remind everyone of the words of the Second Vatican Council: "This Holy Synod likewise affirms that children and young people have a right to be encouraged to weigh moral values with an upright conscience, and to embrace them by personal choice, to know and love more adequately. Hence, it earnestly entreats all who exercise government over people or preside over the work of education to see that youth is never deprived of this sacred right."[26]

At the audience granted on Nov. 7th, 1975, to the undersigned Prefect of the Sacred Congregation for the Doctrine of the Faith, the Sovereign Pontiff by Divine Providence Pope Paul VI approved this Declaration "On certain questions concerning sexual ethics," confirmed it and ordered its publication.

Given in Rome, at the Sacred Congregation for the Doctrine of the Faith, on December 29th, 1975.

Franjo Card. Seper,
Prefect

Most Rev. Jerome Hamer, O.P.
Titular Archbishop of Lorium
Secretary

Notes

1. Cf. Second Vatican Ecumenical Council, Constitution on the Church in the Modern World "Gaudium et Spes," 47 *AAS* 58 (1966), p. 1067.
2. Cf. Apostolic Constitution "Regimini Ecclesiae Universae," 29 (Aug. 15, 1967) *AAS* 89 (1967): 1067.
3. "Gaudium et Spes," 16 *AAS* 58 (1966), p. 1037.
4. John 8:12.
5. Second Vatican Ecumenical Council, Declaration "Dignitatis Humanae," 3 *AAS* 58 (1966), p. 931.
6. Cf. Second Vatican Ecumenical Council, Declaration "Gravissimum Educationis," 1, 8: *AAS* 58 (1966): 729–30; 734–36 "Gaudium et Spes," 29, 60, 67 *AAS* 58 (1966): 1048 1049, 1080–81, 1088–89.
7. "Gaudium et Spes," 51 *AAS* 58 (1966): 1072.
8. Ibid.; cf also 49 loc. cit., pp. 1069–70.
9. Ibid., 49, 50 loc. cit., pp. 1069–72.
10. The present Declaration does not go into further detail regarding the norms of sexual life within marriage; these norms have been clearly taught in the encyclical letter "Casti Connubii" and "Humanae Vitae."
11. Cf. Matt. 19:4–6.
12. I Cor. 7:9.
13. Cf. Eph. 5:25–32.
14. Sexual intercourse outside marriage is formally condemned in I Cor. 5:1; 6:9; 7:2; 10:8 Eph. 5:5; I Tim. 1:10; Heb. 13:4; and with explicit reasons I Cor. 6:12–20.
15. Cf. Innocent IV, letter "Sub catholica professione," March 6, 1254, *DS* 835; Pius II, "Propos damn in Ep Cum sicut accepimus." Nov 13th, 1459, *DS* 1367; decrees of the Holy Office, Sept 24th, 1665, *DS* 2045; March 2nd, 1679, *DS* 2148 Pius XI, encyclical letter "Casti Connubii," Dec 31st, 1930 *AAS* 22 (1930): 558–59.
16. Rom. 1:24–27 "That is why God left them to their filthy enjoyments and the practices with which they dishonor their own bodies since they have given up Divine truth for a lie and have worshipped and served creatures instead of the Creator, Who is blessed forever. Amen! That is why God has abandoned them to degrading passions; why their women have turned from natural inter-

course to unnatural practices and why their menfolk have given up natural intercourse to be consumed with passion for each other, men doing shameless things with men and getting an appropriate reward for their perversion." See also what St. Paul says of "masculorum concubitores" in I Cor. 6:10; I Tim. 1:10.

17. Cf. Leo IX, letter "Ad splendidum nitentis," in the year 1054 *DS* 687–88, decree of the Holy Office, March 2, 1679: *DS* 2149; Pius XII, "Allocutio," Oct. 8, 1953 *AAS* 45 (1953): 677–78; May 19th, 1956 *AAS* 48 (1956): 472–73.

18. "Gaudium et Spes," 51 *AAS* 58 (1966): 1072.

19. ". . . if sociological surveys are useful for better discovering the thought patterns of the people of a particular place, the anxieties and needs of those to whom we proclaim the word of God, and also the opposition made to it by modern reasoning through the widespread notion that outside science there exists no legitimate form of knowledge, still the conclusions drawn from such surveys could not of themselves constitute a determining criterion of truth," Paul VI, apostolic exhortation "Quinque iam anni." Dec 8th 1970, *AAS* 63 (1971): 102.

20. Cf. I Cor. 7:7, 34; Council of Trent, Session XXIV, can 10 DS 1810; Second Vatican Council, Constitution "Lumen Gentium," 42 43, 44 *AAS* 57 (1965): 47–51 Synod of Bishops, "De Sacerdotio Ministeriali," part II, 4, b: *AAS* 63 (1971): 915–16.

21. Matt. 5:28.

22. Cf. Gal. 5:19–23; I Cor. 6:9–11.

23. I Thess. 4:3–8; cf. Col. 3:5–7; I Tim. 1:10.

24. Eph. 5:3–8; cf. 4:18–19.

25. I Cor. 6:15, 18–20.

26. "Gravissimum Educationis," 1: *AAS* 58 (1966): 730.

7

Marriage, Love, and Procreation

Michael D. Bayles

The current era is one of that vulgar form of hedonism rejected by philosophical hedonists such as Epicurus and John Stuart Mill.[1] Apologists thinly disguise the tawdriness of a hedonism of biological pleasures by appeals to individual rights and autonomy. Far too frequently these appeals merely mask a refusal to accept responsibility. This failure to accept personal responsibility is periodically atoned for by ritualistic and ill-conceived attempts to help the poor and underprivileged people of the world.

One of the central focuses of the current vulgar hedonism has been sexual liberation. Premarital intercourse, gay liberation, no-fault divorce, open marriage (read, "open adultery"), polygamy, and orgies all have their advocates. About the only forms of sexual behavior yet to have strong advocates are pedophilia and bestiality. Any day now one may expect grade-school children to assert their right to happiness through pedophilia and animal lovers to argue that disapproval of bestiality is unfair to little lambs.

The result, especially in Western society, is an emphasis on sex that is out of all proportion to its significance for a eudaemonistic life—that is, a life worth living, including elements besides pleasure. The only ultimate test for the value of a life is whether at its end it is found to have been worth living. It is difficult to conceive of a person's thinking his life significant because it was a second-rate approximation to the sexual achievements of the notorious rabbit. However, many people seem to think such a life offers the highest ideal of a "truly human" existence, forgetting Aristotle's insight that reproduction is characteristic of all living things, not just humans.[2] Consequently, the institution of marriage has been attacked for hindering the achievement of this vulgar hedonistic ideal.

Attacks on Marriage

Not all attacks on the institution of marriage have been based solely on the vulgar hedonistic ideal. A more broad ranging, although no more plausible, attack has recently been made by John McMurtry. His attack is directed not against marriage per se but against that form of it found in Western society—monogamy. McMurtry does not merely find that monogamous marriage hinders the achievement of the vulgar hedonistic ideal. He also claims it is at least one of the causes of the following social ills: (1) Central official control of marriage *"necessarily* alienates the partners from full responsibility for and freedom in their relationship."[3] (2) Monogamy restricts the sources of adult affection and support available to children.[4] (3) It "systematically promotes conjugal insecurity, jealousy, and alienation. . . ."[5] (4) It "prevents the strengths of larger groupings."[6] (5) It stimulates aggression, apathy, frustration, lack of spontaneity, perversion, fetishism, prostitution, and pornography.[7] (6) It serves to maintain the status quo and capitalism.[8] (7) It supports the powerlessness of the individual family by keeping it small.[9] (8) By promoting many small families it creates a high demand for homes and consumer goods and services.[10] (9) It makes it necessary for many more males to sell their labor than would be necessary if monogamy were not practiced.[11] (10) By limiting opportunities for sexual satisfaction it channels unsatisfied desire into support for various institutions and interests.[12] (11) Finally, it promotes financial profit for lawyers, priests, and so forth, in marriage and divorce proceedings.[13] Such a catalog of evils omits only a few social problems such as political corruption and environmental deterioration, although even they are hinted at in numbers 8 and 11.

Many people have hoped that the simple-mindedness that attributes all or most or even many of society's ills to a single factor would disappear. At one time private ownership of the means of production was the *bête noir* of society.[14] Recently it has been replaced in that role by unlimited population growth.[15] Both of these beasts have been slain by the St. George of reasonableness.[16] McMurtry has called forth yet another single-factor beast. There is no reason to suppose this one to be any more powerful than its predecessors.

No attempt will be made in this essay to examine in detail McMurtry's criticisms of monogamous marriage. In general they are characterized by a lack of historical and sociological perspective. It is unclear whether he is attacking the ideal of monogamous marriage as it perhaps existed a hundred years ago or as it exists today. Yet this difference is crucial. A century ago divorce was not widely recognized or accepted; today that is not true. When divorce was not recognized, concubinage and prostitution were quite prevalent, as was simply abandoning one's family.

Such practices certainly mitigated the effect of the strict social rules that McMurtry discusses. Also, he criticizes monogamy for limiting the access of children to adult affection and support, since they must rely upon their parents alone for care. But in the extended family, which existed until the urbanization of society, that limitation was considerably less common than it may be at present.

McMurtry seems to be unaware of the social realities of modern society. He emphasizes the law as it is written rather than the law in action. It is generally recognized that despite the wording of statutes, marriages can in practice now be dissolved by mutual consent.[17] Nor is adultery usually prosecuted in those states in which it is still a crime. Nor does McMurtry present any sociological evidence for the various effects that he claims monogamous marriage has. Sometimes the evidence may well be against him. For example, he claims that monogamy supports the high demand for homes. Yet, for a century in Ireland monogamy coincided with a low demand for new homes. Couples simply postponed marriage until the male inherited the home of his parents, and those who did not inherit often did not marry.[18]

Underlying McMurtry's view of monogamous marriage is the Kantian conception of the marriage contract. According to Kant, marriage "is the Union of two Persons of different sex for life-long reciprocal possession of their sexual faculties."[19] McMurtry takes the following principle to be the essential ground of monogamous marriage: "the maintenance by one man or woman of the effective right to exclude indefinitely all others from erotic access to the conjugal partner."[20] Since by "possession" Kant meant legal ownership and the consequent right to exclude others, these two views come to the same thing. They both view marriage as chiefly concerned with private ownership of the means to sexual gratification, thus combining capitalism with vulgar hedonism (although Kant was not a hedonist).

Such a view of marriage is pure nonsense. However, it has more plausibility in today's era of vulgar hedonism than it did in Kant's time. Historically, the official aims of marriage, according to the Catholic Church—which was the only church during the period of the establishment of monogamous marriage in Western society—were procreation and companionship. There was also a tendency to view it as a legitimate outlet for man's sinful nature.[21] It is this latter element that Kant and McMurtry have taken as the chief one.

In addition to the avowed purposes of marriage there were the actual social functions that it performed. The family unit was the basic social unit, not only for the education of children (that is, socialization, not formal schooling—which has only become widespread during the past century), but also for the production of necessities, including food and clothing, and for recreation. These historical functions of the extended-family unit based on monogamous marriage have been undermined by the development of industrial, urban society.[22] Consequently, the moral and legal status and functions of marriage require reexamination in the light of current social conditions.

Before undertaking such a reexamination it is necessary to distinguish between rules of marriage and attendant social rules. They are mixed together in the traditional social institution of monogamous marriage, but there is no necessity for this mix and it is probably unjustified. In particular one must distinguish between penal laws prohibiting various forms of sexual union—homosexual, premarital, adulterous—and private arranging laws granting legal recognition to the marital relationship.[23] Private arranging laws do not prescribe punishment for offenses; instead, they enable people to carry out their desires. People are not punished for improperly made marriages; instead, the marriages are invalid and unenforceable. Laws against fornication, prostitution, cohabitation, and homosexuality are almost always penal. Objections to them cannot be transferred directly to the marriage relationship. All of these penal laws could be abolished and monogamous marriage could still be retained.

It may be claimed that despite their nonpenal form, marriage laws do in fact penalize those who prefer other forms of relationship. If homosexual and polygamous relationships are not legally recognized as "marriages," then persons desiring these forms of relationship are being deprived of some degree of freedom. When considering freedom one must be clear about what one is or is not free to do. Consider, for example, the case of gambling. One must distinguish between laws that forbid gambling and the absence of laws that recognize gambling debts. The latter does not deprive people of the freedom to contract gambling debts; it simply does not allow the use of legal enforcement to collect them. Similarly, the absence of laws recognizing polygamous and homosexual marriages does not deprive people of the freedom to enter polygamous and homosexual unions. Instead, it merely fails to provide legal recourse to enforce the agreements of the parties to such unions. The absence of laws recognizing such marriages does not deprive people of a freedom they previously had, for they were never able to have such agreements legally enforced. Nor have people been deprived of a freedom they would have if there were no legal system, for in the absence of a legal system no agreements can be legally enforced. If there is a ground for complaint, then, it must be one of inequality—that one type of relationship is legally recognized but others are not. However, a charge of inequality is warranted only if there are no relevant reasonable grounds for distinguishing between relationships. To settle that issue one must be clear about the state's or society's interests in marriage.

The rest of this essay is concerned with the purposes or functions of the marriage relationship in which society has a legitimate interest. It is not possible here to set out and to justify the purposes for which governments may legislate. It is assumed that the state may act to facilitate citizens' engaging in activities that they find desirable and to protect the welfare and equality of all citizens, including future ones. Government has an especially strong responsibility for the welfare of children. Of course, these legitimate governmental or social interests and responsibilities must be balanced against other interests and values of citizens, including those of privacy and freedom from interference.

There is no attempt or intention to justify penal laws prohibiting forms of relationship other than monogamous marriage. Indeed, it is generally assumed that they ought not be prohibited and that more people will enter into them than has been the case. In such a context, monogamous marriage would become a more specialized form of relationship, entered into by a smaller proportion of the population than previously. Underlying this assumption are the general beliefs that many people are unqualified or unfit for a marital relationship and ought never to enter one and that many people marry for the wrong reasons. If true, these beliefs may explain why both marriage and divorce rates have been steadily rising in most Western countries during this century.[24]

Promoting Interpersonal Relationships

Alienation from others and loss of community are perceived by many to be among the most serious ills of modern, mass society. In such a situation it seems unlikely that many would deny the need for intimate interpersonal relationships of affection. The importance of such relationships for a good or *eudaemonistic* life have been recognized by philosophers as diverse as Aristotle and G. E. Moore.[25] In considering such interpersonal relationships to be among the most valuable elements of a good life, one must distinguish between the value of a good and the strength of the desire for it. Many people have a stronger desire for life than for such interpersonal relationships, but they may still recognize such relationships as more valuable than mere life. Life itself is of little value, but it is a necessary condition for most other things of value.

Among the most valuable forms of interpersonal relationship are love, friendship, and trust. These relationships are limited with respect to the number of persons with whom one can have them. Classically, there has been a distinction between agapeic and erotic love. Agapeic love is the love of all mankind— general benevolence. The concept of erotic love is more limited. In today's world erotic love is apt to be confused with sexual desire and intercourse. But there can be and always has been sex without love and love without sex. Personal love is more restricted than either agapeic love or sexual desire. It implies a concern for another that is greater than that for most people. Hence, it cannot be had for an unlimited number of other people.[26] Similar distinctions must be drawn between friendship and acquaintance, trust of a political candidate and trust of a friend.

Such interpersonal relationships require intimacy. Intimacy involves a sharing of information about one another that is not shared with others. Moreover, it often involves seclusion from others—being in private where others cannot observe.[27] In some societies where physical privacy is not possible, psychological privacy—shutting out the awareness of the presence of others—substitutes. Consequently, these valuable interpersonal relationships require intimacy and usually physical privacy from others, and at the very least nonintrusion upon the relationship.

Moreover, these forms of interpersonal relationship require acts expressing the concern felt for the other person. In most societies acts of sexual intercourse have been such expressions of love and concern. It is not physically or psychologically necessary that sexual intercourse have this quasi-symbolic function, but it is a natural function of sexual intercourse. All that is here meant by "natural" is that in most societies sexual intercourse has this function, for which there is some psychological basis even though it is not contrary to scientific laws for it to be otherwise. Intercourse usually involves an element of giving of oneself, and one's sexual identity is frequently a central element of one's self-image. It is not, however, sexual intercourse that is intrinsically valuable but the feelings and attitudes, the underlying interpersonal relationship, that it expresses. Nonsexual acts also currently express such relationships, but sexual intercourse is still one of the most important ways of doing so. If sexual intercourse ceases to have this function in society, some other act will undoubtedly replace it in this function. Moreover, sexual intercourse will have lost much of its value.

If these interpersonal relationships of personal love and trust are of major value, it is reasonable for the state to seek to protect and foster them by according legal recognition to them in marriage. The specific forms of this recognition cannot be fully discussed. However, there is some basis for treating the partners to a marriage as one person. Historically, of course, the doctrine that the parties to a marriage are one person has supported the subjugation of women in all sorts of ways, for example, in their disability from owning property. But there is an underlying rationale for joint responsibility. Two people who, without a special reason such as taxes, keep separate accounts of income and expenditures do not have the love and trust of a couple who find such an accounting unnecessary. Moreover, in such a joint economic venture there is no point to allowing one party to sue the other. Only the advent of insurance, whereby neither spouse, but a third party, pays, makes such suits seem profitable. Another recognition of these relationships—albeit one not frequently invoked—is that one is not forced to testify against his or her spouse. More important is that neither party is encouraged to violate the trust and intimacy of the relationship, for example, by encouraging one to inform authorities about bedroom comments of his or her spouse.[28]

The character of these valuable forms of interpersonal relationship provides an argument against according marriages of definite duration legal recognition equal to that accorded those that are intentionally of indefinite duration. For it to be "intentionally of indefinite duration," neither partner may, when entering the marriage, intend it to be for a specific period of time, for example, five years, nor may the marriage contract specify such a period. The following argument is not to show that marriages for a definite duration should not be recognized, but merely to show that they should not have equal standing with those intentionally of indefinite duration. The basic reason for unequal recognition is that interpersonal relationships that are not intentionally of indefinite duration are less valuable than those that are.

Suppose one were to form a friendship with a colleague, but the two mutually agree to be friends for only three years, with an option to renew the friend-ship at that time. Such an agreement would indicate a misunderstanding of friendship. Such agreements make sense for what Aristotle called friendships of utility, but in the modern world these friendships are business partnerships.[29] While there is nothing wrong with business friendships, they do not have the intrinsic value of personal friendships. In becoming close personal friends with someone, one establishes a concern and trust that would be seriously weakened or destroyed by setting a time limit to the friendship. It is sometimes claimed that time limits may be set because people will only be together for a while. But one need not see a person every day or even every year to remain friends. However, extended separation usually brings about a withering away of the friendship.

Similarly, the personal relationship of love and trust in marriage is of lesser value if it is intentionally for only a definite period of time. Moreover, the entering into a relationship that is intentionally of indefinite duration and legally recognized symbolizes a strength of commitment not found in other types of relationships. While two unmarried people may claim that there is no definite limit to their mutual commitment, their commitment is always questionable. Entering into a marital relationship assures the commitment more than does a mere verbal avowal.

There are two common objections to this argument. First, it is sometimes said that there may be special reasons for making marriages of short, definite duration, for example, if one partner will only live in the area for a while. But a personal love that is not strong enough to overcome difficulties of moving to another area and possible sacrifices of employment is not as close and strong as a love that can. Many married couples make such compromises and sacrifices. Second, it is sometimes claimed that commitment is in fact stronger when not legally reinforced, when one does not need the law to support the relationship. However, this claim overlooks the fact that when a married couple's relation-ship rests substantially upon their legal obligations, their relationship has already begun to deteriorate. The strength of commitment is established by the willingness to enter into a legal relationship that cannot be broken simply, without any difficulties. A person who is not willing to undertake the risk of the legal involvement in divorce should he desire to terminate the relationship is probably unsure of his commitment. Moreover, the legal relationship provides security against a sudden and unexpected change in one's life—the breakup of the social aspects will take some time, giving one a chance to prepare for a new style of life. Even then the change is often very difficult.

Hence, if marriage is for the purpose of providing legal recognition of some of the most valuable interpersonal relationships, it should grant more protection and recognition to those intentionally of indefinite duration than to others. Such a conclusion does not imply that divorce should be impossible or exceedingly difficult. Friendships frequently do not last forever despite their not being intended for a limited period of time. The same may happen to a marital rela-tionship. So while this argument supports not according legal recognition to relationships intended to be of definite duration equal to that accorded those intended to be of indefinite duration, it does not support restrictions on divorce in the latter case. Moreover, the average length of time of marriages has increased considerably since the seventeenth century. When a couple married then, one of them was likely to die within twenty years. With today's increased life expectancy, both parties may live close to fifty years after they marry.[30] Obviously, with such an increased possible length of marriage, there is a greater chance for marital breakdown and divorce. One may expect more divorces in marriages that have lasted twenty to twenty-five years simply because there are more such marriages. Nevertheless, such marriages are intentionally of indefinite duration—for life.

Protecting the Welfare of Children

Another area of pervasive social interest that has historically centered in marriage concerns the procreation and raising of children. Society has an interest not only in the number of children born but their quality of life. This fact is in deep conflict with the current emphasis on the freedom of individuals to make reproductive decisions unfettered by social rules and restrictions. Moreover, it is an area in which social control has traditionally been weak. Child abuse is widespread, and efforts to prevent it are mediocre at best. There are few general legal qualifications or tests for becoming a parent. Yet parenthood is one of the most potentially dangerous relationships that one person can have with another. If one is a poor college teacher, then at worst a few students do not receive a bit of education they might have. But as a parent one potentially can ruin completely the lives of one's children. At the least, they may develop into psychological misfits incapable of leading responsible and rewarding lives.

Essentially, there are three areas of social interest and responsibility with respect to procreation and the raising of children. First, there is a social interest in the sheer number of children born. The current emphasis on population control makes this interest abundantly clear.[31] Second, there is a social interest in the potentialities of children. This area includes concern for genetic and congenital birth defects and abnormalities. Over 5 percent of all children born have a genetic defect. The possibility of genetic control of those who are born will soon take on major significance. Already, approximately sixty genetic diseases as well as almost all chromosomal abnormalities can be detected *in utero,* and adult carriers of about eighty genetic defects can be identified.[32] Given the possibility of genetic control, society can no longer risk having genetically disadvantaged children by leaving the decision of whether to have children to the unregulated judgment of individual couples. Some social regulations with respect to genetic screening and, perhaps, eugenic sterilization are needed.

While potential parents have interests of privacy and freedom in reproductive decisions, the social interests in preventing the suffering and inequality of possibly defective children may outweigh them in certain types of cases.

Third, the care and development of those who are born is a social interest and responsibility. This interest has been recognized for some time in the form of children's homes and compulsory education. However, increasing knowledge about childhood development extends the area in which social interests and responsibility may be reasonably involved. To give an example at the most elementary level, the nutritional diet of children during their first three years is crucial for their future development. So also is their psychological support. The welfare of future generations is not a private but a social matter. It is a proper task of society, acting through its government, to ensure that the members of the next generation are not physical or psychological cripples due to the ignorance, negligence, or even indifference of parents.

Historically, society has attempted to control procreation through the institution of marriage. Society's means were primarily to stigmatize children born out of wedlock and to encourage the having of many children. It is now recognized that no useful purpose is served by stigmatizing children born out of wedlock as illegitimate. (However, some useful purpose may be served by not according children born out of wedlock all the rights of those born in wedlock, for example, inheritance without parental recognition.) The emphasis on having as many children as one can has also disappeared. It is not this historical concern with procreation that is misplaced in modern society but the forms that the concern has taken.

If society has the responsibility to protect the welfare of children, then some social regulation and control of human reproduction and development is justified. Such regulation and control need not be effected by penal laws. For example, social concern has traditionally been expressed in adoptions through regulations to ensure that those who adopt children are fit to care for them. That some regulations have been inappropriate and not reasonably related to the welfare of children is not in question. Rather, the point is that there has been regulation without penal laws, or at least without resorting primarily to penal laws. Nor can social regulation and control be solely by legislation. Legislation alone is usually ineffective; it must be supported by informal social rules and expectations.

Not only has modern biomedicine made sex possible without procreation; it has also made procreation possible without sex. The techniques of artificial insemination and fertilization, embryo transfer, ova donation, ectogenesis. and cloning now, or soon will, make it possible for people to reproduce without sexual intercourse.[33] Hence, not only may one have sex for pleasure, but one may reproduce for pleasure without sexual intercourse. Not only may people reproduce outside marriage; they are not even biologically required to have intercourse. Thus, sex and marriage may become dissociated from reproduction.

However, there are strong reasons for restricting procreation primarily to marriages of indefinite duration, which does not imply that such marriages should be restricted to procreation. Marriage has traditionally been the central social institution concerned with procreation. Consequently, if society is to exercise some control over procreation in the future, it would involve the least change in conditions to do so through marriage. Moreover, there is considerable evidence that the disruption of family life contributes to juvenile delinquency. Whether divorce or marital breakdown (with or without divorce) is a prime cause of such delinquency does not matter. The point is that the disruption of home life does seriously affect the development of children.[34] The chance of such disruption outside of a marriage that is intentionally of indefinite duration is higher than for that within. Moreover, there is some reason to believe that the presence of both mother and father is instrumental in the psychological development of children. In any case, the presence of two people rather than one provides the security that there will be someone to care for the children should one of the parents die. Generally, children are better off being with one parent than in a state orphanage, but better off still with both parents. Hence, for the welfare of children it seems best that procreation and child rearing primarily occur within the context of marriages intentionally of indefinite duration.

While society has a responsibility for the care and development of children, this general responsibility is best carried out if specific adults have obligations to care for specific children. In the past, the biological parent-child relation has reinforced the allocation of responsibility for specific children and has been a major factor in monogamy.[35] The separation of reproduction and sexual intercourse threatens disruption of this assignment. For example, if gestation occurs in an artificial womb in a laboratory, there may be no "parents," only a scientific research group. More realistically, if a woman has an embryo from ova and sperm donors transferred to her uterus, it is unclear who are the child's parents. However, if there is to be optimal care for children, specific adults must have obligations for specific children. It cannot be left to somebody in general, for then nobody in particular is likely to do it. "Let George do it" is too prevalent and careless an attitude to allow with regard to children.

McMurtry's contention that monogamy restricts the care for children is not well founded.[36] First, if there are no specific adults responsible for children, they may become "lost" in large groups and victims of the "it's not my job" syndrome. Second, monogamy per se does not cut children off from the support and care of others. One must distinguish the marital relationship from living arrangements. It is the isolated situation of the family that deprives children of such support. In many married-student housing complexes children have access to other adults. Even in general-residential neighborhoods with separate family housing units, such support is available if there is a sense of community in the neighborhood.

Given the social interests in and responsibility for the procreation and development of children, some more effective controls of parenthood appear desirable. If the primary locus of reproduction is to be within marriages of intentionally indefinite duration, then the easiest way to institute controls is to add requirements for people to enter such marriages. A few requirements such as blood tests are already generally prevalent. Alternatively, one might have a separate licensing procedure for procreation. Nonmarried couples and single people might also qualify for such licenses. Moreover, couples who want to marry but not have children would not have to meet requirements. However, the only requirements suggested below that might bar marriages are almost as important for those couples who do not have children as for those who do. If the requirements were tied to marriage they would be easier to administer. The only drawback is that unmarried people would not have to meet them. However, such requirements can and should be part of the medical practice of the "artificial" techniques of reproduction—artificial insemination and embryo transfer. And there are few if any effective methods, except generally accepted social rules, to control procreation outside of marriage.

One obvious requirement would be genetic screening. With modern medical techniques genetic problems do not imply that couples cannot become married, but they might be expected not to have children who are their genetic offspring. Artificial insemination and embryo transfer make it possible for almost everyone to have children, even though the children might not be genetically theirs. A general distinction between biological and social parenthood should be made, with legal emphasis on the latter.

More important, perhaps, is some general expectation of psychological fitness for family life and the raising of children. The difficulty with such an expectation is the absence of any clear criteria for fitness and reliable methods for determining who meets them. Perhaps, however, some formal instruction in family relations and child rearing would be appropriate. The Commission on Population Growth and the American Future has already called for an expansion of education for parenthood.[37] It is only a bit further to require some sort of minimal family education for marriage. Probably the easiest method for ensuring such education would be to make it a required subject in secondary schools. If that were done, few people would have difficulty meeting this requirement for marriage.

There should not be any financial or property qualifications for marriage.[38] Society's interest in and responsibility for the welfare of the population in general is such that governments should ensure an adequate standard of living for all persons. Were that to be done there would be no reason to impose any financial restrictions on marriage. Nonetheless, prospective parents should have more concern for their financial situation than is now frequently the case. The adequate care of children is an expensive task, financially as well as psychologically and temporally.

Conclusion

It may be objected that neither the argument from interpersonal relations nor that from the welfare of children specifically supports monogamous marriage.

While loving relationships cannot extend to an indefinite number of people, they can extend to more than one other person. Also, a polygamous union may provide a reasonable environment for procreation. Hence, neither of the arguments supports monogamous marriage per se.

Logically, the objection is quite correct. But it is a misunderstanding of social philosophy to expect arguments showing that a certain arrangement is always best under all circumstances. The most that can be shown is that usually, or as a rule, one social arrangement is preferable to another. Practically, polygamous marriage patterns will probably never be prevalent.[39] For centuries they have been gradually disappearing throughout the world. If a disproportionate sex distribution of the population occurs in some areas or age groups (such as the elderly), then they may increase in significance. Unless that occurs, most people will probably continue to prefer marital monogamy.

More important, the burden of this paper has not been to defend the traditional ideal of marital union or even the current practice. Many of the traditional rules of marriage have been unjust, for example, the inequality between the sexes, both legally and in terms of social roles. Instead, it has been to defend social recognition of marriage of intentionally indefinite duration as a unique and socially valuable institution that society has interests in promoting and regulating. In particular, society has interests in and responsibility for promoting a certain form of valuable interpersonal relationship and protecting the welfare of children. Both of these purposes can be well served by monogamous marriage.

The image, then, is of a society with various forms of living together, but one in which marriage of intentionally indefinite duration would have a distinctive though lessened role as a special kind of socially and legally recognized relationship. There would not be laws prohibiting nonmarital forms of cohabitation. Divorce would be based on factual marital breakdown or mutual consent, with due regard for the welfare of children.

Monogamous marriage would recognize a special form of personal relationship in which reproduction and child rearing primarily occur. Given the social interest in decreasing procreation, many people might marry but not have children, and others might not marry at all. Details of the legal marital relationship have not been specified, nor could they be in this brief essay except with respect to the main social interests. Questions of inheritance, legal residence and name, social-security benefits, and so on, have not been specified. Changes in laws with respect to many of these matters can be made without affecting the arguments for the value of, social responsibility for, and interests in marriage. Above all, it is an image in which sexual intercourse plays a much smaller role in the conception of marriage and the good life in general, a society in which vulgar hedonism has at least been replaced by a broader-based *eudaemonism*.

Notes

1. Epicurus, "Letter to Menoeceus," in *The Stoic and Epicurean Philosophers,* ed. Whitney J. Oates (New York: Modern Library, 1957), p. 31. Epicurus even wrote, "Sexual intercourse has never done a man good, and he is lucky if it has not harmed him" (Fragment 8 in *The Stoic and Epicurean Philosophers*). John Stuart Mill, *Utilitarianism,* chap. 2, especially paragraphs 1–9.

2. *De Anima* 2.4.

3. "Monogamy: A Critique," *The Monist* 56 (1972); in *Philosophy and Sex,* 1st ed. (Amherst, N.Y.: Prometheus Books, 1975), pp. 107–18. This quote appears on page 111 of the 1975 volume (italics added). Subsequent references to McMurtry's essay are to pages in that edition.

4. Ibid., p. 111

5. Ibid.

6. Ibid.

7. Ibid., p. 112.

8. Ibid., p. 114.

9. Ibid., p. 115.

10. Ibid.

11. Ibid.

12. Ibid.

13. Ibid.

14. Karl Marx and Friedrich Engels, "Manifesto of the Communist Party," in *Basic Writings on Politics and Philosophy,* ed. Lewis S. Feuer (Garden City, N.Y.: Doubleday, Anchor Books, 1959), especially p. 24.

15. Paul R. Ehrlich, *The Population Bomb* (New York: Ballantine Books, 1968).

16. Even new Marxists perceive other sources of problems. See Milovan Djilas, *The New Class* (New York: Praeger, 1964); and, more generally, Richard T. De George, *The New Marxism* (New York: Pegasus, 1968), chap. 2. The importance of population for pollution, with which it is most frequently connected, has been contested by Barry Commoner, *The Closing Circle* (New York: Knopf, 1971), pp. 133–35. Ehrlich now clearly recognizes that various causal factors are important, although he still disagrees with Commoner on the importance of population growth; see Paul R. Ehrlich et al., *Human Ecology* (San Francisco: W. H. Freeman and Company, 1973), chap. 7, esp. pp. 206, 213–15, 221.

17. Max Rheinstein, *Marriage Stability, Divorce, and the Law* (Chicago: University of Chicago Press, 1972), p. 251.

18. Edwin D. Driver, "Population Policies of State Governments in the United States: Some Preliminary Observations." *Villanova Law Review* 15 (1970): 846–47.

19. Immanuel Kant, *The Philosophy of Law,* trans. W. Hastie (Edinburgh: T. & T. Clark, 1887), p. 110.

20. McMurtry, "Monogamy," p. 112; italics in original omitted.

21. See John T. Noonan Jr., *Contraception* (Cambridge, Mass.: Harvard University Press, 1966), pp. 312–14.

22. Keith G. McWalter, "Marriage as Contract: Towards a Functional Redefinition of the Marital Status," *Columbia Journal of Law and Social Problems* 9 (1973): 615.

23. Robert S. Summers, "The Technique Element of Law," *California Law Review* 59 (1971): 736–37, 741–45.

24. Burton M. Leiser, *Liberty, Justice and Morals* (New York: Macmillan Co., 1973), p. 126; R[oland] Pressat, *Population,* trans. Robert and Danielle Atkinson (Baltimore: Penguin Books, 1970), pp. 84, 86; U.S. Commission on Population Growth and the American Future, *Population and the American Future* (New York: Signet, New American Library, 1972), pp. 102–103.

25. Aristotle, *Nicomachean Ethics* 9.9–12; George Edward Moore, *Principia Ethica* (Cambridge: At the University Press, 1903), pp. 188, 203–205.

26. It is thus misleading for McMurtry to write of monogamous marriage excluding "almost *countless* other possibilities of *intimate* union" with any number of persons (p. 109; my italics). On the limited nature of personal love or friendship see also Aristotle, *Nicomachean Ethics* 9.10.

27. For a discussion of these relationships and the need for privacy, see Charles Fried, "Privacy," in *Law, Reason, and Justice,* ed. Graham Hughes (New York: New York University Press, 1969), pp. 45–69.

28. See the discussion (in another context) of such a case in Nazi Germany by H. L. A. Hart, "Positivism and the Separation of Law and Morals," *Harvard Law Review* 71 (1958): 618–20; and Lon L. Fuller, "Positivism and Fidelity to Law—A Reply to Professor Hart," *Harvard Law Review* 71 (1958): 652–55.

29. *Nicomachean Ethics* 8.3. The vulgar hedonists treat marriage as a form of friendship for pleasure, but that is not the highest form of friendship.

30. Pressat, *Population,* p. 52.

31. For a more complete discussion see my "Limits to a Right to Procreate," in *Ethics and Population,* ed. Michael D. Bayles (Cambridge, Mass.: Schenkman Publishing Company, 1975).

32. Daniel Callahan, *The Tyranny of Survival* (New York: Macmillan Co., 1973), p. 219.

33. For a good general survey of these techniques and some suggestions for social controls, see George A. Hudock, "Gene Therapy and Genetic Engineering: Frankenstein Is Still a Myth, But It Should Be Reread Periodically," *Indiana Law Journal* 48 (1973): 533–58. Various ethical issues are discussed in Joseph Fletcher, *The Ethics of Genetic Control* (Garden City, N.Y.: Doubleday, Anchor Books, 1974). Successful human embryo implantation and growth to term after *in vitro* fertilization has been reported in Britain (see *Time,* July 29, 1974, pp. 58–59; and *Newsweek,* July 29, 1974, p. 70).

34. President's Commission on Law Enforcement and Administration of Justice, *The Challenge of Crime in a Free Society* (New York: Avon Books, 1968), pp. 184–89.

35. Daniel Callahan, "New Beginnings in Life: A Philosopher's Response," in *The New Genetics and the Future of Man,* ed. Michael P. Hamilton (Grand Rapids, Mich.: William B. Eerdmans Publishing Company, 1972), pp. 102–103.

36. "Monogamy," p. 111.

37. *Population and the American Future,* pp. 126–33, esp. p. 133.

38. For some suggested financial requirements as well as others, see Jack Parsons, *Population versus Liberty* (Amherst, N.Y.: Prometheus Books, 1971), p. 349.

39. Even McMurtry appears to recognize this fact; see "Monogamy," p. 107.

8

Marital Faithfulness

Susan Mendus

And so the two swore that at every time of their lives, until death took them, they would assuredly believe, feel and desire exactly as they had believed, felt and desired during the preceding weeks. What was as remarkable as the undertaking itself was the fact that nobody seemed at all surprised at what they swore.[1]

Cynicism about the propriety of the marriage promise has been widespread amongst philosophers and laymen alike for many years. Traditionally, the ground for suspicion has been the belief that the marriage promise is a promise about feelings where these are not directly under the control of the will. G. E. Moore gives expression to this view when he remarks that "to love certain people, or to feel no anger against them, is a thing which it is quite impossible to attain directly by the will" and concludes therefore that the commandment to love your neighbor as yourself cannot possibly be a statement of your duty, "all that can possibly be true is that it would be your duty if you were able."[2] Thus, as Mary Midgley has pointed out, Moore invests the commandment with "about as much interest for us as a keep-fit manual would have for paraplegics."[3] Moore's sentiments would presumably be endorsed by Russell, who tells of how his love for his wife "evaporated" during the course of a bicycle ride. He simply "realized," he says, that he no longer loved her and was subsequently unable to show any affection for her.[4] This, anyway, is the most familiar objection to the marriage promise: that it is a promise about feelings, where these are not directly under the control of the will.

A second objection to the marriage promise is that it involves a commitment which extends over too long a period: promising to do something next Wednesday is one thing, promising to do something fifty years hence is quite another, and it is thought to be improper either to give or to extract promises extending over such a long period of time. This second objection has found

Originally published in *Philosophy* 59 (1984). Reprinted by permission of the author and publisher.

recent philosophical favor in the writings of Derek Parfit. In "Later Selves and Moral Principles" Parfit refers to those who believe that only short-term promises can carry moral weight and counts it virtue of his theory of personal identity that it "supports" or "helps to explain" that belief.[5]

Here I shall not discuss Parfit's theory of personal identity as such, but only the plausibility of the consequent claim that short-term promises alone carry moral weight: for it is the supposed intuitive plausibility of the latter which Parfit appeals to in defense of his theory of personal identity. If, therefore, the belief that only short-term promises carry moral weight can be undermined, that will serve, indirectly, to undermine any theory of personal identity which supports it.

Claiming that longterm promises do not carry any moral weight seems to be another way of claiming that unconditional promises do not carry any moral weight. Such an unconditional promise is the promise made in marriage, for when I promise to love and to honor I do not mutter under my breath, "So long as you never become a member of the Conservative party," or "Only if your principles do not change radically." Parfit's suggestion seems to be that all promises (all promises which carry any moral weight, that is) are, and can be, made only on condition that there is no substantial change in the character either of promisor or promisee: if my husband's character changes radically, then I may think of the man before me not as my husband, but as some other person, some "later self." Similarly, it would seem that I cannot now promise to love another "till death us do part," since that would be like promising that another person will do something (in circumstances in which my character changes fundamentally over a period of time) and I cannot promise that another person will do something, but only that *I* will do something. Thus all promises must be conditional; all promises must be short-term. For what it is worth, I am not the least tempted to think that only short-term promises carry any moral weight and it is therefore a positive *disadvantage* for me that Parfit's theory has this consequence. But even if it were intuitively plausible that short-term promises alone carry moral weight, there are better arguments than intuitive ones and I hope I can mention some here.

The force of Parfit's argument is brought out by his "Russian nobleman" example, described in "Later Selves and Moral Principles":

> Imagine a Russian nobleman who, in several years, will inherit vast estates. Because he has socialist ideals, he intends now to give the land to the peasants, but he knows that in time his ideals may fade. To guard against this possibility he does two things. He first signs a legal document, which will automatically give away the land and which can only be revoked with his wife's consent. He then says to his wife, "If I ever change my mind and ask you to revoke the document, promise me that you will not consent." He might add, "I regard my ideals as essential to me. If I lose these ideals I want you to think that I cease to exist. I want you to think of your husband then, not as me, but only as his later self. Promise me that you would not do as he asks."[6]

Parfit now comments:

> This plea seems understandable and if his wife made this promise and he later asked her to revoke the document she might well regard herself as in no way released from her commitment. It might seem to her as if she had obligations to two different people. She might think that to do what her husband now asks would be to betray the young man whom she loved and married. And she might regard what her husband now says as unable to acquit her of disloyalty to this young man—to her husband's earlier self. [Suppose] the man's ideals fade and he asks his wife to revoke the document. Though she promised him to refuse, he now says that he releases her from this commitment . . . we can suppose she shares our view of commitment. If so, she will only believe that her husband is unable to release her from the commitment if she thinks that it is in some sense not *he* to whom she is committed is. . . . She may regard the young man's loss of ideals as involving replacement by a later self.[7]

Now, strictly speaking, and on Parfit's own account, the wife should not make such a promise: to do so would be like promising that another person will do something, since she has no guarantee that *she* will not change in character and ideals between now and the time of the inheritance. Further, there is a real question as to why anyone outside of a philosophical example should first draw up a document which can only be revoked with his wife's consent and then insist that his wife not consent whatever may happen. But we can let these points pass. What is important here, and what I wish to concentrate on, is the suggestion that my love for my husband is conditional upon his not changing in any substantial way: for this is what the example amounts to when stripped of its special story about later selves. (In his less extravagant moods Parfit himself allows that talk of later selves is, in any case, a mere *"façon de parler."*)[8]

The claim then is that all promises must be conditional upon there being no change in the character of the promisee: that if my husband's character and ideals change it is proper for me to look upon him as someone other than the person I loved and married. This view gains plausibility from reflection on the fact that people can, and often do, give up their commitments. There is, it will be said, such an institution as divorce, and people do sometimes avail themselves of it. But although I might give up my commitment to my husband, and give as my reason a change in his character and principles, this goes no way towards showing that only short-term promises carry any moral weight, for there is a vital distinction here: the distinction between, on the one hand, the person who promises to love and to honor but who finds that, after a time, she has lost her commitment (perhaps on account of change in her husband's character), and, on the other hand, the person who promises to love and to honor only on condition that there be no such change in character. The former person may properly be said, under certain circumstances, to have given up a commitment; the latter person was never committed in the appropriate way at all. The wife of the Russian nobleman, by allowing in advance that she will love her husband only so long as he doesn't change in any of the aforementioned ways, fails properly to commit herself to him: for now her attitude to him seems to be one of respect or admiration, not commitment at all. Now she *does* mutter under her breath, "So long as you don't become a member of the Conservative party." But the marriage promise contains no such "escape clause." When Mrs. Micawber staunchly declares that she will never desert Mr. Micawber, she means just that. There are no conditions, nor could there be any, for otherwise we would fail to distinguish between respect or admiration *for the principles* of another and the sort of unconditional commitment *to him* which the marriage vow involves. There are many people whose ideals and principle I respect, and that respect would disappear were the ideals and principles to disappear, but my commitment to my husband is distinct from mere respect or admiration in just this sense, that it is not conditional on there being no change in his ideals and principles. I am now prepared to admit that my respect for another person would disappear were he revealed to be a cheat and a liar. I am not now prepared to admit that my love for my husband, my commitment to him, would disappear were he revealed to be a cheat and a liar. Perhaps an analogy will be illuminating here: in his article "Knowledge and Belief," Norman Malcolm distinguishes between a strong and a weak sense of "know" and says:

> In an actual case of my using "know" in a strong sense I cannot envisage a possibility that what I say should turn out to be not true. If I were speaking of another person's assertion about something I *could* think both that he is using "know" in a strong sense and that none the less what he claims he knows to be so might turn out to be not so. But in my own case I cannot have this conjunction of thoughts, and this is a logical, not a psychological fact. When I say that I know, using "know" in the strong sense, it is unintelligible to me (although perhaps not to others) to suppose that anything could prove that it is not so and therefore that I do not know it.[9]

Such is the case with commitment of the sort involved in the marriage vow. I promise to love and to honor and in so doing I cannot now envisage anything happening such as would make me give up that commitment. But, it might be asked, how can I be clairvoyant? How can I recognize that there is such a thing as divorce and at the same time declare that nothing will result in my giving up my commitment? The explanation lies in the denial that my claim to know (in the strong sense) or commitment (here) has the status of a prediction. My commitment to another should not be construed as a prediction that I will never desert that other. Malcolm again: "The assertion describes my present attitude towards the statement . . . it does not prophesy what my attitude would be if various things happened."[10] But if my statement is not a prediction, then what is it? It is perhaps more like a statement of intention, where my claims about a man's intentions do not relate to his future actions in as simple a way as do my predictions about his future actions.

   If I predict that A will do x and A does not do x, then my prediction is simply false. If, on the other hand, I claim that A intends to do x and he does not, it is not necessarily the case that my statement was false: for he may have had that intention and later withdrawn it. Similarly with commitment: if I claim that A is unconditionally committed to B, that is not a prediction that A will never desert B, it is a claim that there is in A a present intention to do something permanently, where that is distinct from A's having a permanent intention. Thus Mrs. Micawber's claim that she will never desert Mr. Micawber, if construed as a commitment to him, is to that extent different from a prediction that she will never desert him, for her commitment need not be thought never to have existed if she does desert him. Thus an unconditional commitment to another person today, a denial today that anything could happen such as would result in desertion of Mr. Micawber, is not incompatible with that commitment being given up at a later date.

In brief, then, what is wrong in Parfit's example is that the wife *now* allows that her commitment will endure only so long as there is no substantial change in character. She should not behave thus, because her doing so indicates that she has only respect for her husband, or admiration for his principles, not a commitment to him: she need not behave thus, as there can be such a thing as unconditional commitment, analogous to intention and distinct from prediction in the way described.

All this points to the inherent oddity of the "trial marriage." It is bizarre to respond to "wilt thou love her, comfort her, honor her and keep her?" with "Well, I'll try." Again, the response "I will" must be seen as the expression of an intention to do something permanently, not a prediction that the speaker will permanently have that intention.

A further problem with the Russian nobleman example and the claim that only short-term promises carry any moral weight is this: when the wife of the Russian nobleman allows in advance that her commitment to her husband will cease should his principles change in any substantial way, she implies that a list of his present principles and ideals will give an exhaustive explanation of her loving him. But this is not good enough. If I now claim to be committed to my husband I precisely cannot give an exhaustive account of the characteristics he possesses in virtue of which I have that commitment to him: if I could do so, there would be a real question as to why I am not prepared to show the same commitment to another person who shares those characteristics (his twin brother, for example). Does this then mean that nothing fully explains my love for another and that commitment of this sort is irrationally based? I think we need not go so far as to say that: certainly, when asked to justify or explain my love I may point to certain qualities which the other person has, or which I believe him to have, but in the first place such an enumeration of qualities will not provide a complete account of why I love him, rather it will serve to explain, as it were, his "lovableness." It will make more intelligible my loving him, but will not itself amount to a complete and exhaustive explanation of my loving him. Further, it may well be that in giving my list of characteristics I cite some which the other person does not, in fact, have. If this is so, then the explanation may proceed in reverse order: the characteristics I cite will not explain or make intelligible my love, rather my love will explain my ascribing these characteristics. A case in point here is

Dorothea's love for Casaubon, which is irrationally based in that Casaubon does not have the characteristics and qualities which Dorothea thinks him to have. Similarly, in the case of infatuation the lover's error lies in wrongly evaluating the qualities of the beloved. In this way Titania "madly dotes" on the unfortunate Bottom, who is trapped in an ass's head, and addresses him thus:

> Come sit thee down upon this flowery bed
> While I thy amiable cheeks do coy
> And stick musk roses in thy sleek, smooth head
> And kiss thy fair, large ears my gentle joy.

and again

> I pray thee, gentle mortal, sing again.
> Mine ear is much enamored of thy note;
> So is mine eye enthralled to thy shape,
> And thy fair virtue's force perforce doth move me
> On the first view, to say, to swear, I love thee.[11]

Both cases involve some error on the part of the lover: in one case the error is false belief about the qualities the beloved possesses; in the other it is an error about the evaluation of the qualities the beloved possesses. These two combine to show that there can be such a thing as a "proper object" of love. This will be the case where there is neither false belief nor faulty evaluation. They do not, however, show that in ascribing qualities and characteristics to the beloved the lover exhaustively explains and accounts for his love. The distinction between "proper" love and irrationally based love, or between "proper" love and infatuation, is to be drawn in terms of the correctness of beliefs and belief-based evaluations. By contrast, the distinction between love and respect or admiration is to be drawn in terms of the explanatory power of the beliefs involved. In the case of respect or admiration the explanatory power of belief will be much greater than it is in the case of love. For this reason my respect for John's command of modal logic will disappear, and I am now prepared to admit that it will disappear, should I discover that my belief that he has a command of modal logic is false. Whereas I am not now prepared to admit that my commitment to and love for my husband will disappear if I discover that my beliefs about his qualities and characteristics are, to some extent, false.

W. Newton-Smith makes something like this point in his article "A Conceptual Investigation of Love":

> Concern and commitment cannot be terminated by some change in or revelation about the object of that concern or commitment. We are inclined to accept "I felt affection for her so long as I thought she was pure and innocent" but not "I was really concerned for her welfare as long as I thought she was pure and innocent." Being genuinely concerned or committed seems to involve a will-

ingness on my part to extend that concern or commitment even if I have been mistaken about the person with regard to some feature of her that led to the concern, and even if that person ceases to have those features which led me to be concerned or committed in the first place.[12]

This, though initially plausible, cannot be quite right, for on Newton-Smith's analysis it is difficult to see how I could ever give up a commitment without it being the case that I never was committed in the first place. But we can and do distinguish between those who had a commitment and have now given it up and those who never had a commitment at all. We need not, I think, go so far as to say that "love is not love which alters when it alteration finds," but only that love is not love which allows in advance that it will so alter. The love which shows that it will alter when it alteration finds is at best sentimentality, at worst opportunism. (Of course, the reasons which one cites for giving up a commitment will cast light on whether one was committed at all. Thus "I was committed to her as long as I thought she was an heiress" is highly dubious. "I was committed to her as long as I though she was pure and innocent" is, I think, not so dubious.) What is at least necessary is that one should not be prepared to say *now* "I will love her as long as she is pure and innocent, but no longer."

I turn now to a somewhat bizarre element in Parfit's talk of ideals. Parfit portrays the Russian nobleman as one who "finds" that his ideals have faded, as one who "loses" his ideals when circumstances and fortune change. What is bizarre in this talk is emphasized by the following extract from Alison Lurie's novel *Love and Friendship*:

"But, Will, promise me something."
"Sure."
"Promise me you'll never be unfaithful to me."
Silence.
Emily raised her head. "You won't promise?" she said incredulously.
"I can't, Emily. How can I promise how I'll feel for the next ten years? You want me to lie to you? You could change. I could change. I could meet somebody."
Emily pulled away. "Don't you have any principles?" she asked.[13]

The trouble with the inappropriately named Will and the Russian nobleman in Parfit's example is that it is doubtful whether either man has any genuine principles at all. Each is portrayed as almost infinitely malleable, as one whose principles will alter in accordance with changing circumstances. The point about a moral principle however is that it must serve in some sense to rule out certain options as options at all. In his article "Actions and Consequences," John Casey refers us to the example of Addison's Cato who, when offered life, liberty and the friendship of Caesar if he will surrender, and is asked to name his terms, replies:

Bid him disband his legions,
Restore the Commonwealth to liberty,

Submit his actions to the public censure
And stand the judgment of a Roman Senate.
Bid him do this and Cato is his friend.[14]

The genuine principles which Cato has determine that certain options will not ultimately be options at all for him. To say this, of course, is not to deny that life and liberty are attractive and desirable to him. Obviously he is, in large part, admirable precisely because they are attractive to him and yet he manages to resist their allure. The point is rather that not *any* sort of life is desirable. The sort of life he would, of necessity, lead after surrender—a life without honor—is not ultimately attractive to him and that it is not attractive is something which springs from his having the principles he does have. What Cato values above all else is honor and his refusal to surrender to Caesar is a refusal to lead a life without honor. By contrast, when the Russian nobleman draws up a legal document giving away his inheritance, we may suspect that he is concerned not with an honorable life or with a life which he now conceives of as honorable, but rather with his present principle. Where Cato values a certain sort of life, the Russian nobleman values a certain principle. It is this which is problematic and which generates, I believe, the bizarre talk of ideals fading. For Cato's adherence to his principles is strengthened, if not guaranteed, by the fact that he treats a certain sort of life as an end in itself and adopts the principles he does adopt because they lead to that end. The Russian nobleman, however, is portrayed more as a man who finds the principle important than as a man who finds the life to which the principle leads important. Obviously, in either case there may be temptation and inner struggle, but the temptation is less likely to be resisted by the Russian nobleman than by Cato, for the nobleman will find his principle undermined and threatened by the prospect of affluence, which is attractive to him. His ideals will fade. For Cato, on the other hand, things are not so simple. He is not faced by a choice between two things, each of which he finds attractive. The fact that he treats a life of honor as an end in itself precludes his finding life attractive under *any* circumstances. For him, life will ultimately be attractive and desirable only where it can be conducted honorably. Nevertheless, he finds life attractive and desirable, but this means only that if he surrenders he will have *sacrificed* his ideals, not that his ideals will have faded. Thus, the nobleman is a victim, waiting for and guarding against attack upon his principles; Cato is an agent who may sacrifice his principles after a struggle, but not one who would find that they had altered.

In conclusion, then, the claim that the marriage vow is either impossible or improper is false. It is possible to commit oneself unconditionally because commitment is analogous to a statement of intention, not to a prediction or a piece of clairvoyance. It is proper, since if we refuse to allow such unconditional commitment, we run the risk of failing to distinguish between, on the one hand, sentimentality and commitment and, on the other hand, respect or admiration and commitment. Further, it is simply not true that I am helpless in circumstances in which I find my commitment wavering: this is because my principles will initially serve to modify my view of the opportunities which present themselves, so that I simply will not see certain things as constituting success because my principles are such as to exclude such things being constitutive of success. In this way, my principles determine what is to count as a benefit and what is to count as an opportunity. As Shakespeare has it:

> Some glory in their birth, some in their skill,
> Some in their wealth, some in their body's force,
> Some in their garments though new fangled ill:
> Some in their hawks and hounds, some in their horse.
> And every humour has his adjunct pleasure,
> Wherein it finds a joy above the rest,
> But these particulars are not my measure,
> All these I better in one general best.
> Thy love is better than high birth to me,
> Richer than wealth, prouder than garments cost,
> Of more delight than hawks and horses be:
> And having these of all men's pride I boast.
> Wretched in this alone, that thou may'st take
> All this away, and me most wretched make.[15, 16]

Notes

1. Thomas Hardy *Jude the Obscure.*

2. G. E. Moore, "The Nature of Moral Philosophy," in *Philosophical Studies* (London: Routledge and Kegan Paul, 1922), 316.

3. Mary Midgley, "The Objection to Systematic Humbug," *Philosophy* 53 (1978): 147.

4. Bertrand Russell, *Autobiography* (London: George Allen and: Unwin, 1967–69).

5. Derek Parfit, "Later Selves and Moral Principles," in *Philosophy and Personal Relations,* A. Montefiore, ed. (London: Routledge and Kegan Paul, 1973), p. 144.

6. Ibid., p. 145.

7. Ibid., pp. 145–46.

8. Ibid., pp. 14, 161–62.

9. Norman Malcolm, "Knowledge and Belief," in *Knowledge and Belief,* A. Phillips Griffiths, ed. (Oxford University Press 1967), 81.

10. Ibid., p. 78.

11. W. Shakespeare, *A Midsummer Night's Dream*, Acts III and I.

12. W. Newton-Smith, "A Conceptual Investigation of Love," in *Philosophy and Personal Relations*, pp. 132–33.

13. Alison Lurie, *Love and Friendship* (Harmondsworth: Penguin, 1962), pp. 329–30.

14. As quoted in J. Casey, "Actions and Consequences," from *Morality and Moral Reasoning,* J. Casey, ed. (London: Methuen, 1971), p. 201.

15. W. Shakespeare, Sonnet 91.

16. I wish to thank my colleague, Dr. Roger Woolhouse, for many helpful discussions on the topic of this paper.

9

Is Adultery Immoral?

Richard Wasserstrom

Many discussions of the enforcement of morality by the law take as illustrative of the problem under consideration the regulation of various types of sexual behavior by the criminal law. It was, for example, the Wolfenden Report's recommendations concerning homosexuality and prostitution that led Lord Devlin to compose his now famous lecture "The Enforcement of Morals." And that lecture in turn provoked important philosophical responses from H. L. A. Hart, Ronald Dworkin, and others.

Much, if not all, of the recent philosophical literature on the enforcement of morals appears to take for granted the immorality of the sexual behavior in question. The focus of discussion, at least, is on whether such things as homosexuality, prostitution, and adultery ought to be made illegal even if they are immoral, and not on whether they are immoral.

I propose in this paper to consider the latter, more neglected topic, that of sexual morality, and to do so in the following fashion. I shall consider just one kind of behavior that is often taken to be a case of sexual immorality—adultery. I am interested in pursuing at least two questions. First, I want to explore the question of in what respects adulterous behavior falls within the domain of morality at all, for this surely is one of the puzzles one encounters when considering the topic of sexual morality. It is often hard to see on what grounds much of the behavior is deemed to be either moral or immoral, for example, private homosexual behavior between consenting adults. I have purposely selected adultery because it seems a more plausible candidate for moral assessment than many other kinds of sexual behavior.

The second question I want to examine is that of what is to be said about adultery if we are not especially concerned to stay within the area of its

Reprinted from Richard Wasserstrom, ed., *Today's Moral Problems* (New York: Macmillan Co., 1975), with the permission of the author.

morality. I shall endeavor, in other words, to identify and to assess a number of the major arguments that might be advanced against adultery. I believe that they are the chief arguments that would be given in support of the view that adultery is immoral, but I think they are worth considering even if some of them turn out to be nonmoral arguments and considerations.

A number of the issues involved seem to me to be complicated and difficult. In a number of places I have at best indicated where further philosophical exploration is required, without having successfully conducted the exploration myself. This essay may very well be more useful as an illustration of how one might begin to think about the subject of sexual morality than as an elucidation of important truths about the topic.

Before I turn to the arguments themselves, there are two preliminary points that require some clarification. Throughout the paper I shall refer to the immorality of such things as breaking a promise, deceiving someone, and so on. In a very rough way I mean by this that there is something morally wrong in doing the action in question. I mean that the action is, in a strong sense of "prima facie," prima facie wrong or unjustified. I do not mean that it may never be right or justifiable to do the action—just that the fact that it is an action of this description always counts against the rightness of the action. I leave entirely open the question of what it is that makes actions of this kind immoral in this sense of "immoral."

The second preliminary point concerns what is meant or implied by the concept of adultery. I mean by "adultery" any case of extramarital sex, and I want to explore the arguments for and against extramarital sex, undertaken in a variety of morally relevant situations. Someone might claim that the concept of adultery is conceptually connected with the concept of immorality and that to characterize behavior as adulterous is already to characterize it as immoral or unjustified in the sense described above. There may be something to this. Hence the importance of making it clear that I want to discuss extramarital sexual relations. If they are always immoral, this is something that must be shown by argument. If the concept of adultery does in some sense entail or imply immorality, I want to ask whether that connection is a rationally based one. If not all cases of extramarital sex are immoral (again, in the sense described above), then the concept of adultery should either be weakened accordingly or restricted to those classes of extramarital sex for which the predication of immorality is warranted.

One argument for the immorality of adultery might go something like this: What makes adultery immoral is that it involves the breaking of a promise, and what makes adultery seriously wrong is that it involves the breaking of an important promise. For, so the argument might continue, one of the things the two parties promise each other when they get married is that they will abstain from sexual relationships with third parties. Because of this promise both spouses quite reasonably entertain the expectation that the other will behave in conformity with it. Hence, when one of them has sexual intercourse with a third party, he or she breaks that promise about sexual relationships that was made when the marriage was entered into and defeats the reasonable expectations of exclusivity entertained by the spouse.

In many cases the immorality involved in breaching the promise relating to extramarital sex may be a good deal more serious than that involved in the breach of other promises. This is so because adherence to this promise may be of much greater importance to them than is adherence to many of the other promises given or received by them in their lifetime. The breaking of this promise may be much more hurtful and painful than is typically the case.

Why is this so? To begin with, it may have been difficult for the nonadulterous spouse to have kept the promise. Hence that spouse may feel the unfairness of having restrained himself or herself in the absence of reciprocal restraint having been exercised by the adulterous spouse. In addition, the spouse may perceive the breaking of the promise as an indication of a kind of indifference on the part of the adulterous spouse. If you really cared about me and my feelings, the spouse might say, you would not have done this to me. And third, and related to the above, the spouse may see the act of sexual intercourse with another as a sign of affection for the other person and as an additional rejection of the nonadulterous spouse as the one who is loved by the adulterous spouse. It is not just that the adulterous spouse does not take the feelings of the nonadulterous spouse sufficiently into account; the adulterous spouse also indicates through the act of adultery affection for someone other than the nonadulterous spouse. I will return to these points later. For the present it is sufficient to note that a set of arguments can be developed in support of the proposition that certain kinds of adultery are wrong just because they involve the breach of a serious promise that, among other things, leads to the intentional infliction of substantial pain on one spouse by the other.

Another argument for the immorality of adultery focuses not on the existence of a promise of sexual exclusivity but on the connection between adultery and deception. According to this argument adultery involves deception. And because deception is wrong, so is adultery.

Although it is certainly not obviously so, I shall simply assume in this essay that deception is always immoral. Thus, the crucial issue for my purposes is the asserted connection between extramarital sex and deception. Is it plausible to maintain, as this argument does, that adultery always involves deception and is, on that basis, to be condemned?

The most obvious person upon whom deceptions might be practiced is the nonparticipating spouse; and the most obvious thing about which the nonparticipating spouse can be deceived is the existence of the adulterous act. One clear case of deception is that of lying. Instead of saying that the afternoon was spent in bed with A, the adulterous spouse asserts that it was spent in the library with B or on the golf course with C.

There can also be deception even when no lies are told. Suppose, for instance, that a person has sexual intercourse with someone other than his or her spouse and just does not tell the spouse about it. Is that deception? It may not be a case of lying if, for example, he or she is never asked by the spouse about the situation. Still, we might say, it is surely deceptive because of the promises that were exchanged at marriage. As we saw earlier, these promises provide a foundation for the reasonable belief that neither spouse will engage in sexual relationships with any other person. Hence the failure to bring the fact of extramarital sex to the attention of the other spouse deceives that spouse about the present state of the marital relationship.

Adultery, in other words, can involve both active and passive deception. An adulterous spouse may just keep silent or, as is often the case, the spouse may engage in an increasingly complex way of life devoted to the concealment of the facts from the nonparticipating spouse. Lies, half-truths, clandestine meetings, and the like may become a central feature of the adulterous spouse's existence. These are things that can and do happen, and when they do they make the case against adultery an easy one. Still, neither active nor passive deception is inevitably a feature of an extramarital relationship.

It is possible, though, that a more subtle but pervasive kind of deceptiveness is a feature of adultery. It comes about because of the connection in our culture between sexual intimacy and certain feelings of love and affection. The point can be made indirectly by seeing that one way in which we can in our culture mark off our close friends from our mere acquaintances is through the kinds of intimacies that we are prepared to share with them. I may, for instance, be willing to reveal my very private thoughts and emotions to my closest friends or to my wife but to no one else. My sharing of these intimate facts about myself is, from one perspective, a way of making a gift to those who mean the most to me. Revealing these things and sharing them with those who mean the most to me is one means by which I create, maintain, and confirm those interpersonal relationships that are of most importance to me.

In our culture, it might be claimed, sexual intimacy is one of the chief currencies through which gifts of this sort are exchanged. One way to tell someone—particularly someone of the opposite sex—that you have feelings of affection and love for them is by allowing them, or sharing with them, sexual behaviors that one does not share with others. This way of measuring affection was certainly very much a part of the culture in which I matured. It worked something like this: If you were a girl, you showed how much you liked a boy by the degree of sexual intimacy you would allow. If you liked him only a little you never did more than kiss—and even the kiss was not very passionate. If you liked him a lot and if your feeling was reciprocated, necking and, possibly, petting were permissible. If the attachment was still stronger and you thought it might even become a permanent relationship, the sexual activity was correspondingly more intense and intimate, although whether it led to sexual intercourse depended on whether the parties (particularly the girl) accepted fully the prohibition on nonmarital sex. The situation for the boys was related but not exactly the same. The assumption was that males did not naturally link sex with affection in the way in which females did. However, since women did link sex with affection, males had to take that fact into account. That is to say, because a woman would permit sexual intimacies only if she had feelings of affection for the male and only if those feelings were reciprocated, the male had to have and express those feelings too, before sexual intimacies of any sort would occur.

The result was that the importance of a correlation between sexual intimacy and feelings of love and affection was taught by the culture and assimilated by those growing up in the culture. The scale of possible positive feelings toward persons of the other sex ran from casual liking, at one end, to the love that was deemed essential to, and characteristic of, marriage, at the other. The scale of possible sexual behavior ran from brief, passionless kissing or hand-holding, at one end, to sexual intercourse, at the other. And the correlation between the two scales was quite precise. As a result, any act of sexual intimacy carried substantial meaning with it, and no act of sexual intimacy was simply a pleasurable set of bodily sensations. Many such acts were, of course, more pleasurable to the participants because they were a way of saying what their feelings were. And sometimes they were less pleasurable for the same reason. The point is, however, that sexual activity was much more than mere bodily enjoyment. It was not like eating a good meal, listening to good music, lying in the sun, or getting a pleasant back rub. It was behavior that meant a great deal concerning one's feelings for persons of the opposite sex in whom one was most interested and with whom one was most involved. It was among the most authoritative ways in which one could communicate to another the nature and degree of one's affection.

If this sketch is even roughly right, then several things become somewhat clearer. To begin with, a possible rationale for many of the rules of conventional sexual morality can be developed. If, for example, sexual intercourse is associated with the kind of affection and commitment to another that is regarded as characteristic of the marriage relationship, then it is natural that sexual intercourse should be thought properly to take place between persons who are married to each other. And if it is thought that this kind of affection and commitment is only to be found within the marriage relationship, then it is not surprising that sexual intercourse should only be thought to be proper within marriage.

Related to what has just been said is the idea that sexual intercourse ought to be restricted to those who are married to each other, as a means by which to confirm the very special feelings that the spouses have for each other. Because our culture teaches that sexual intercourse means that the strongest of all feelings for each other are shared by the lovers, it is natural that persons who are married to each other should be able to say this to each other in this way. Revealing and confirming verbally that these feelings are present is one thing that helps to sustain the relationship; engaging in sexual intercourse is another.

In addition, this account would help to provide a framework within which to make sense of the notion that some sex is better than other sex. As I indicated earlier, the fact that sexual intimacy can be meaningful in the sense described tends to make it also the case that sexual intercourse can sometimes be more enjoyable than at other times. On this view, sexual intercourse will typically be more enjoyable if strong feelings of affection are present than it will be if it is merely "mechanical." This is so in part because people enjoy being loved, especially by those whom they love. Just as we like to hear words of affection, so we like to receive affectionate behavior. And the meaning enhances the independently pleasurable behavior.

More to the point, an additional rationale for the prohibition on extramarital sex can now be developed. For given this way of viewing the sexual world, extramarital sex will almost always involve deception of a deeper sort. If the adulterous spouse does not in fact have the appropriate feelings of affection for the extramarital partner, then the adulterous spouse is deceiving that person about the presence of such feelings. If, on the other hand, the adulterous spouse does have the corresponding feelings for the extramarital partner but not toward the nonparticipating spouse, the adulterous spouse is very probably deceiving the nonparticipating spouse about the presence of such feelings toward that spouse. Indeed, it might be argued, whenever there is no longer love between the two persons who are married to each other, there is deception just because being married implies both to the participants and to the world that such a bond exists. Deception is inevitable, the argument might conclude, because the feelings of affection that ought to accompany any act of sexual intercourse can only be held toward one other person at any given time in one's life. And if this is so, then the adulterous spouse always deceives either the partner in adultery or the nonparticipating spouse about the existence of such feelings. Thus extramarital sex involves deception of this sort and is for that reason immoral even if no deception vis-à-vis the occurrence of the act of adultery takes place.

What might be said in response to the foregoing arguments? The first thing that might be said is that the account of the connection between sexual intimacy and feelings of affection is inaccurate—not in the sense that no one thinks of things that way but in the sense that there is substantially more divergence of opinion than the account suggests. For example, the view I have delineated may describe reasonably accurately the concepts of the sexual world in which I grew up, but it does not capture the sexual *Weltanschauung* of today's youth at all. Thus, whether or not adultery implies deception in respect to feelings depends very much on the persons who are involved and the way they look at the "meaning" of sexual intimacy.

Second, the argument leaves unanswered the question of whether it is desirable for sexual intimacy to carry the sorts of messages described above. For those persons for whom sex does have these implications there are special feelings and sensibilities that must be taken into account. But it is another question entirely whether any valuable end—moral or otherwise—is served by investing sexual behavior with such significance. That is something that must be shown and not just assumed. It might, for instance, be the case that substantially more good than harm would come from a kind of demystification of sexual behavior —one that would encourage the enjoyment of sex more for its own sake and one that would reject the centrality both of the association of sex with love and of love with only one other person.

I regard these as two of the more difficult unresolved issues that our culture faces today in respect of thinking sensibly about the attitudes toward sex and love that we should try to develop in ourselves and in our children.

Much of the contemporary literature that advocates sexual liberation of one sort or another embraces one or the other of two different views about the relationship between sex and love. One view holds that sex should be separated from love and affection. To be sure, sex is probably better when the partners genuinely like and enjoy being with each other. But sex is basically an intensive, exciting sensuous activity that can be enjoyed in a variety of suitable settings with a variety of suitable partners. The situation in respect to sexual pleasure is no different from that of the person who knows and appreciates fine food and who can have a satisfying meal in any number of good restaurants with any number of congenial companions. One question that must be settled here is whether sex can be thus demystified; another, more important, question is whether it would be desirable to do so. What might we gain and what might we lose if we all lived in a world in which an act of sexual intercourse was no more or less significant or enjoyable than having a delicious meal in a nice setting with a good friend? The answer to this question lies beyond the scope of this essay.

The second view of the relationship between sex and love seeks to drive the wedge in a different place. On this view it is not the link between sex and love that needs to be broken, but rather the connection between love and exclusivity. For a number of the reasons already given it is desirable, so this argument goes, that sexual intimacy continue to be reserved to and shared with only those for whom one has very great affection. The mistake lies in thinking that any "normal" adult will have those feelings toward only one other adult during his or her lifetime—or even at any time in his or her life. It is the concept of adult love, not ideas about sex, that needs demystification. What are thought to be both unrealistic and unfortunate are the notions of exclusivity and possessiveness that attach to the dominant conception of love between adults in our culture and others. Parents of four, five, six, or even ten children can certainly claim, and sometimes claim correctly, that they love all of their children, that they love them all equally, and that it is simply untrue to their feelings to insist that the numbers involved diminish either the quantity or the quality of their love. If this is readily understandable in the case of parents and children, there is no necessary reason why it is an impossible or undesirable ideal in the case of adults. To be sure, there is probably a limit to the number of intimate, "primary" relationships that any person can maintain at any given time without affecting the quality of the relationship. But one adult ought surely to be able to love two, three, or even six other adults at any one time without that love being different in kind or degree from that of the traditional, monogamous, lifetime marriage. And between the individuals in these relationships, whether within a marriage or without, sexual intimacy is fitting and good.

The issues raised by a position such as the one described above are also surely worth exploring in detail and with care. Is there something to be called "sexual love" that is different from parental love or the nonsexual love of close friends? Is there something about love in general that links it naturally and appropriately with feelings of exclusivity and possession? Or is there something about sexual love, whatever that may be, that makes these feelings especially fitting? Once again, the issues are conceptual, empirical, and normative all at once: What is love? How could it be different? Would it be a good thing or a bad thing if it were different?

Suppose, though, that having delineated these problems we were now to pass them by. Suppose, moreover, that we were to be persuaded of the possibility and the desirability of weakening substantially either the links between sex and love or the links between sexual love and exclusivity. Would it not then be the case that adultery could be free from all of the morally objectionable features described thus far? To be more specific, let us imagine that a husband and wife have what is today sometimes characterized as an "open marriage." Suppose, that is, that they have agreed in advance that extramarital sex is—under certain circumstances—acceptable behavior for each to engage in. Suppose that as a result there is no impulse to deceive each other about the occurrence or nature of any such relationships and that no deception in fact occurs. Suppose, too, that there is no deception in respect to the feelings involved between the adulterous spouse and the extramarital partner. And suppose, finally, that one or the other or both of the spouses then have sexual intercourse in circumstances consistent with these understandings. Under this description, so the argument might conclude, adultery is simply not immoral. At a minimum adultery cannot very plausibly be condemned either on grounds that it involves deception or on grounds that it requires the breaking of a promise.

At least two responses are worth considering. One calls attention to the connection between marriage and adultery; the other looks to more instrumental arguments for the immorality of adultery. Both deserve further exploration.

One way to deal with the case of the "open marriage" is to question whether the two persons involved are still properly to be described as being married to each other. Part of the meaning of what it is for two persons to be married to each other, so this argument would go, is to have committed oneself to have sexual relationships only with one's spouse. Of course, it would be added, we know that that commitment is not always honored. We know that persons who are married to each other often do commit adultery. But there is a difference between being willing to make a commitment to marital fidelity, even though one may fail to honor that commitment, and not making the commitment at all. Whatever the relationship may be between the two individuals in the case just described, the absence of any commitment to sexual exclusivity requires the conclusion that their relationship is not a marital one. For a commitment to sexual exclusivity is a necessary but not a sufficient condition for the existence of a marriage.

Although there may be something to this suggestion, it is too strong as stated to be acceptable. To begin with it is doubtful that there are many, if any, *necessary* conditions for marriage; but even if there are, a commitment to sexual exclusivity is not such a condition.

To see that this is so, consider what might be taken to be some of the essential characteristics of a marriage. We might be tempted to propose that the concept of marriage requires the following: a formal ceremony of some sort in which mutual obligations are undertaken between two persons of the opposite sex; the capacity on the part of the persons involved to have sexual intercourse with each other; the willingness to have sexual intercourse only with each other; and feelings of love and affection between the two persons. The problem is that we can imagine relationships that are clearly marital and yet lack one or more of these features. For example, in our own society it is possible for two persons to be married without going through a formal ceremony, as in the common-law marriages recognized in some jurisdictions. It is also possible for two persons to get married even though one or both lacks the capacity to engage in sexual intercourse. Thus, two very elderly persons who have neither the desire nor the ability to have intercourse can nonetheless get married, as can persons whose sexual organs have been injured so that intercourse is not possible. And we certainly know of marriages in which love was not present at the time of the marriage, as, for instance, in marriages of state and marriages of convenience.

Counterexamples not satisfying the condition relating to the abstention from extramarital sex are even more easily produced. We certainly know of societies and cultures in which polygamy and polyandry are practiced, and we have no difficulty in recognizing these relationships as cases of marriages. It might be objected, though, that these are not counterexamples because they are plural marriages rather than marriages in which sex is permitted with someone other than one of the persons to whom one is married. But we also know of societies in which it is permissible for married persons to have sexual relationships with persons to whom they are not married, for example, temple prostitutes, concubines, and homosexual lovers. And even if we knew of no such societies, the conceptual claim would still, I submit, not be well taken. For suppose all of the other indicia of marriage were present: suppose the two persons were of the opposite sex; suppose they had the capacity and desire to have intercourse with each other; suppose they participated in a formal ceremony in which they understood themselves voluntarily to be entering into a relationship with each other in which substantial mutual commitments were assumed. If all these conditions were satisfied we would not be in any doubt as to whether or not the two persons were married, even though they had not taken on a commitment of sexual exclusivity and even though they had expressly agreed that extramarital sexual intercourse was a permissible behavior for each to engage in.

A commitment to sexual exclusivity is neither a necessary nor a sufficient condition for the existence of a marriage. It does, nonetheless, have this much to do with the nature of marriage—like the other indicia enumerated above, its presence tends to establish the existence of a marriage. Thus, in the absence of a formal ceremony of any sort an explicit commitment to sexual exclusivity would count in favor of regarding the two persons as married. The conceptual role of the commitment to sexual exclusivity can, perhaps, be brought out through the following example. Suppose we found a tribe that had a practice in which all the other indicia of marriage were present but in which the two parties were *prohibited* even from having sexual intercourse with each other. Moreover, suppose that sexual intercourse with others was clearly permitted. In such a case we would, I think, reject the idea that the two persons were married to each other, and we would describe their relationship in other terms, for example, as some kind of formalized, special friendship relation—a kind of heterosexual "blood-brother" bond.

Compare that case with the following one. Again suppose that the tribe had a practice in which all of the other indicia of marriage were present, but instead of a prohibition on sexual intercourse between the persons in the relationship there was no rule at all. Sexual intercourse was permissible with the person with whom one had this ceremonial relationship, but it was no more or less permissible than with a number of other persons to whom one was not so related (for instance, all consenting adults of the opposite sex). While we might be in doubt as to whether we ought to describe the persons as married to each other, we would probably conclude that they were married and that they simply were members of a tribe whose views about sex were quite different from our own.

What all of this shows is that a *prohibition* on sexual intercourse between the two persons involved in a relationship is conceptually incompatible with the claim that the two of them are married. The *permissibility* of intramarital sex is a necessary part of the idea of marriage. But no such incompatibility follows simply from the added permissibility of extramarital sex.

These arguments do not, of course, exhaust the arguments for the prohibition on extramarital sexual relations. The remaining argument that I wish to consider is—as I indicated earlier—a more instrumental one. It seeks to justify the prohibition by virtue of the role that it plays in the development and maintenance of nuclear families. The argument, or set of arguments, might, I believe, go something like this:

Consider first a far-fetched nonsexual example. Suppose a society were organized so that after some suitable age—say 18, 19, or 20—persons were forbidden to eat anything but bread and water with anyone but their spouse. Persons might still choose in such a society not to get married. Good food just might not be very important to them because they have underdeveloped taste buds. Or good food might be bad for them because there is something wrong with their digestive system. Or good food might be important to them, but they might decide that the enjoyment of good food would get in the way of the attainment of other things that were more important. But most persons would, I think, be led to favor marriage in part because they preferred a richer, more varied diet to one of bread and water. And they might remain married because the family was the only legitimate setting within which good food was obtainable. If it is important to have society organized so that persons will both get married and stay married, such an arrangement would be well suited to the preservation of the family, and the prohibitions relating to food consumption could be understood as fulfilling that function.

It is obvious that one of the more powerful human desires is the desire for sexual gratification. The desire is a natural one, like hunger and thirst, in the sense that it need not be learned in order to be present within us and operative on us. But there is in addition much that we do learn about what the act of sexual intercourse is like. Once we experience sexual intercourse ourselves—and, in particular, once we experience orgasm—we discover that it is among the most intensive, short-term pleasures of the body.

Because this is so it is easy to see how the prohibition on extramarital sex helps to hold marriage together. At least during that period of life when the enjoyment of sexual intercourse is one of the desirable bodily pleasures, persons will wish to enjoy those pleasures. If one consequence of being married is that one is prohibited from having sexual intercourse with anyone but one's spouse, then the spouses in a marriage are in a position to provide an important source of pleasure for each other that is unavailable to them elsewhere in the society.

The point emerges still more clearly if this rule of sexual morality is seen as being of a piece with the other rules of sexual morality. When this prohibition is coupled, for example, with the prohibition on nonmarital sexual intercourse, we are presented with the inducement both to get married and to stay married. For if sexual intercourse is only legitimate within marriage, then persons seeking that gratification that is a feature of sexual intercourse are furnished explicit social directions for its attainment, namely, marriage.

Nor, to continue the argument, is it necessary to focus exclusively on the bodily enjoyment that is involved. Orgasm may be a significant part of what there is to sexual intercourse, but it is not the whole of it. We need only recall the earlier discussion of the meaning that sexual intimacy has in our own culture to begin to see some of the more intricate ways in which sexual exclusivity may be connected with the establishment and maintenance of marriage as the primary heterosexual love relationship. Adultery is wrong, in other words, because a prohibition on extramarital sex is a way to help maintain the institutions of marriage and the nuclear family.

I am frankly not sure what we are to say about an argument such as the preceding one. What I am convinced of is that, like the arguments discussed earlier, this one also reveals something of the difficulty and complexity of the issues that are involved. So what I want now to do in the final portion of this essay is to try to delineate with reasonable precision several of what I take to be the fundamental, unresolved issues.

The first is whether this last argument is an argument for the *immorality* of extramarital sexual intercourse. What does seem clear is that there are differences between this argument and the ones considered earlier. The earlier arguments condemned adulterous behavior because it was behavior that involved breaking a promise, taking unfair advantage of or deceiving another. To the degree to which the prohibition on extramarital sex can be supported by arguments that invoke considerations such as these, there is little question but that violations of the prohibition are properly regarded as immoral. And such a claim could be defended on one or both of two distinct grounds. The first is that action such as promise-breaking and deception are simply wrong. The second is that adultery involving promise-breaking or deception is wrong because it involves the straightforward infliction of harm on another human being—typically the nonadulterous spouse—who has a strong claim not to have that harm so inflicted.

The argument that connects the prohibition on extramarital sex with the maintenance and preservation of the institution of marriage is an argument for the instrumental value of the prohibition. To some degree this counts, I think, against regarding all violations of the prohibition as obvious cases of immorality. This is so partly because hypothetical imperatives are less clearly within the domain of morality than are categorical ones, and even more because instrumental prohibitions are within the domain of morality only if the end that they serve or the way that they serve it is itself within the domain of morality.

What this should help us see, I think, is the fact that the argument that connects the prohibition on adultery with the preservation of marriage is at best seriously incomplete. Before we ought to be convinced by it, we ought to have reasons for believing that marriage is a morally desirable and just social institution. And such reasons are not quite as easy to find or as obvious as it may seem. For the concept of marriage is, as we have seen, both a loosely structured and a complicated one. There may be all sorts of intimate, interpersonal relationships that will resemble but not be identical with the typical marriage relationship presupposed by the traditional sexual morality. There may be a number of distinguishable sexual and loving arrangements that can all legitimately claim to be called *marriages*. The prohibitions of the traditional sexual morality may be effective ways to maintain some marriages and ineffective ways to promote and preserve others. The prohibitions of the traditional sexual morality may make good psychological sense if certain psychological theories are true, and they may be purveyors of immense psychological mischief if other psychological theories are true. The prohibitions of traditional sexual morality may seem obviously correct if sexual intimacy carries the meaning that the dominant culture has often ascribed to it, and they may seem equally bizarre if sex is viewed through the perspective of the counterculture. Irrespective of whether instrumental arguments of this sort are properly deemed moral arguments, they ought not fully convince anyone until questions such as these are answered.

10

Adultery and Fidelity

Mike W. Martin

Adultery has recently entered prominently into evaluations of public figures. Bill Clinton's 1992 presidential campaign was nearly derailed by allegations about a twelve-year extramarital affair. Shortly thereafter England's royal family engaged in extensive damage control as public revelations surfaced about the love trysts of Prince Charles and Lady Diana. Earlier, in 1987, Gary Hart's "womanizing" forced his withdrawal as the leading democratic presidential candidate. About the same time, charges of adultery contributed to the downfall of the leading television evangelist Jim Bakker.[1]

It is not clear what most upsets (or intrigues) the public in such cases. Is it the adultery *per se,* the deception used to conceal it (from spouses or the public), the hypocrisy in professing contrary religious beliefs, or the poor judgment in failing to keep it discrete (including the bravado of Gary Hart in baiting the press to uncover his affairs)? Nor is it clear how the adultery itself is pertinent to public service, even if we think the adultery is immoral. Character is not a seamless web, and integrity can be present in one context (public service) and absent in another setting (sexual conduct).[2] Many notable leaders had extramarital affairs, including Franklin D. Roosevelt, Dwight Eisenhower, John F. Kennedy, and Martin Luther King Jr., and public scrutiny of marital intimacy might discourage worthy candidates from seeking public office.

It is clear, however, that adultery is morally complex. Philosophers have devoted little attention to it,[3] largely leaving it as a topic for theology, social science, and literature. Certainly novelists have had much to say: "To judge by literature, adultery would seem to be one of the most remarkable of occupations in both Europe and America. Few are the novels that fail to allude to it."[4] In any case, whether as moral judges assessing the character of adulterers or as moral

From the *Journal of Social Philosophy* 25, no. 3 (Winter 1994). Reprinted by permission of the *Journal of Social Philosophy.*

agents confronted with making our own decisions about adultery, we often find ourselves immersed in confusions and ambiguities that are both personally and philosophically troublesome.

I will seek a middle ground between conventional absolute prohibitions and trendy permissiveness. A humanistic perspective should embrace a pluralistic moral outlook that affirms a variety of forms of sexual relationships, including many traditional marriages. It can justify a strong presumption against adultery for individuals who embrace traditional marital ideals.

The ethics of adultery divides into two parts: making commitments and keeping them. The ethics of making commitments centers primarily on commitments to love, where love is a value-guided relationship, and secondarily on the promise of sexual exclusivity (the promise to have sex only with one's spouse) which some couples make in order to support the commitment to love. The ethics of keeping commitments has to do with balancing initial marital commitments against other moral considerations.

Making Commitments

What is adultery? Inspired by the New Testament, some people employ a wide definition that applies to any significant sexual interest in someone besides one's spouse: "You have heard that it was said, 'Do not commit adultery.' But I tell you that anyone who looks at a woman lustfully has already committed adultery with her in his heart."[5] Other people define adultery narrowly to match their particular scruples: for them extramarital genital intercourse may count as adultery, but not oral sex; or falling in love with someone besides one's spouse may count as adultery but not "merely" having sex.[6] Whatever definition we adopt there will always be borderline cases, if only those created by "brinkmanship"—going as far as possible without having intercourse (e.g., lying naked together in bed).[7]

In this paper, "adultery" refers to married persons having sexual intercourse (of any kind) with someone other than their spouses.[8] I am aware that the word "adultery" is not purely descriptive and evokes a range of emotive connotations. Nevertheless, I use the word without implying that adultery is immoral; that is a topic left open for investigation in specific cases. Like "deception," the word "adultery" raises moral questions about possible misconduct but it does not answer them. By contrast, I will use a wider sense of "marriage" that refers to all monogamous (two-spouse) relationships formally established by legal or religious ceremonies *and* closely analogous moral relationships such as committed relationships between homosexual or heterosexual couples who are not legally married.

A moral understanding of adultery turns on an understanding of morality. If we conceive morality as a set of rules, we will object to adultery insofar as it violates those rules. "Do not commit adultery" is not an irreducible moral principle, but many instances of adultery violate other familiar rules. As Richard Wasserstrom insightfully explained, much adultery violates one or more of these rules: Do not break promises (*viz.*, the wedding vows to abjure outside sex, vows which give one's partner "reasonable expectations" of sexual fidelity); do not deceive (whether by lying, withholding information, or pretending about the affair); do not be unfair (by enjoying outside sex forbidden to one's spouse); and do not cause undeserved harm (to one's spouse who suspects or hears of the affair).[9] Wasserstrom points out that all these rules are *prima facie*: In some situations they are overridden by other moral considerations, thereby justifying some instances of adultery.

Moreover, adultery is not even *prima facie* wrong when spouses have an "open marriage" in which they give each other permission to have extramarital affairs. In this connection Wasserstrom raises questions about the reasonableness of traditional marital promises of sexual exclusivity. Wouldn't it be wiser to break the conventional ties between sex and love, so that the pleasures of adultery can be enjoyed along with those of marriage? Alternatively, should we maintain the connection between sex and love but break the exclusive tie between sexual love and one's spouse, thus tolerating multiple simultaneous loves for one's spouse and for additional partners? No doubt the linking of love, sex, and exclusivity has an *instrumental* role in promoting marriages, but so would the patently unreasonable practice of allowing people to eat decent meals (beyond bread and water) only with their spouses.

In my view, a rule-oriented approach to morality lacks the resources needed to answer the important questions Wasserstrom raises. We need an expanded conception of morality as encompassing ideals and virtues, in particular the moral ideals of love which provide the point of marital commitments and the virtues manifested in pursuing those ideals. The ethics of adultery centers on the moral ideals of and commitments to love—which include ideals of constancy (or faithfulness), honesty, trust, and fairness—that make possible special ways of caring for persons. The ideals are morally optional in that no one is obligated to embrace them. Nevertheless, strong obligations to avoid adultery arise for those couples who embrace the ideals as a basis for making traditional marital commitments. The primary commitment is to love each other, while the commitment of sexual exclusivity is secondary and supportive. This can be seen by focusing on three ideas that Wasserstrom devotes little attention to: love, commitments to love, and trust.

1. What is *love*? Let us set aside the purely descriptive (value-neutral) senses in which "love" refers to (a) a strong positive attraction or emotion[10] or (b) a complex attitude involving many emotions—not only strong affection, but also excitement, joy, pride, hope, fear, jealousy, anger, and so on.[11] Let us focus instead on the normative (value-laden) sense in which we speak of "true love" or "the real thing." Cogent disputes arise concerning the values defining true

love, though ultimately individuals have a wide area of personal discretion in the ideals they pursue in relationships of erotic love.

In its value-laded senses, "love" refers to special ways of valuing persons.[12] As an attitude, love is valuing the beloved, cherishing her or him as unique. Erotic love includes sexual valuing, but the valuing is focused on the person as a unity, not just a body. As a relationship, love is defined by reciprocal attitudes of mutual valuing. The precise nature of this valuing turns on the ideals one accepts, and hence those ideals are part of the very meaning of "love."

2. According to the traditional ideal (or set of ideals) of interest here, marriage is based on a *commitment to love:* "to have and to hold from this day forward, for better for worse, for richer for poorer, in sickness and in health, to love and to cherish, till death us do part." This is not a commitment to have continuous feelings of strong affection—feelings which are beyond our immediate voluntary control. Instead, it is a commitment to create and sustain a relationship conducive to those feelings, as well as conducive to the happiness and fulfillment of both partners. Spouses assume responsibility for maintaining conditions for mutual caring which in turn foster recurring emotions of deep affection, delight, shared enthusiasm, and joy. The commitment to love is not a promise uttered once during a wedding ceremony; it is an ongoing willingness to assume responsibility for a value-guided relationship.

The commitment to love implies a web of values and virtues. It is a commitment to create a lifelong relationship of deep caring that promises happiness through shared activities (including sexual ones) and through joining interests in mutually supportive ways involving shared decision-making, honesty, trust, emotional intimacy, reciprocity, and (at least in modern versions) fair and equal opportunities for self-expression and personal growth. This traditional ideal shapes how spouses value each other, both symbolically and substantively. Commitments to love throughout a lifetime show that partners value each other as having paramount importance and also value them as a unity, as persons-living-throughout-a-lifetime. Time-limited commitments, such as to remain together only while in college, express at most a limited affirmation of the importance of the other person in one's life.

Valuing each other is manifested in a willingness to make accommodations and sacrifices to support the marriage. For most couples, some of those sacrifices are sexual. The promise of sexual exclusivity is a distinct wedding vow whose supportive status is symbolized by being mentioned in a subordinate clause, "and, forsaking all others, keep thee only unto her/him." Hopefully, couples who make the vow of sexual exclusivity are not under romantic illusions that their present sexual preoccupation with each other will magically abolish sexual interests in other people and temptations to have extramarital affairs. They commit themselves to sexual exclusivity as an expression of their love and with the aim of protecting that love.

How does sexual exclusivity express and protect love? In two ways. First, many spouses place adultery at the top of the list of actions which threaten their marriage. They are concerned, often with full justification, that adultery might lead to another love that would damage or destroy their relationship. They fear that the affection, time, attention, and energy (not to mention money) given to an extramarital partner would lessen the resources they devote to sustaining their marriage. They also fear the potential for jealousy to disrupt the relationship.[13] As long as it does not become excessive, jealousy is a healthy reaction of anger, fear, and hurt in response to a perceived loss of an important good.[14] Indeed, if a spouse feels no jealousy whatsoever, the question is raised (though not answered) about the depth of love.

Second, sexual exclusivity is one way to establish the symbolism that "making love" is a singular affirmation of the partner. The love expressed is not just strong affection, but a deep valuing of each other in the ways defined by the ideals embedded in the marriage. Sex is especially well-suited (far more than eating) to express that love because of its extraordinary physical and emotional intimacy, tenderness, and pleasure. The symbolic meaning involved is not sentimental fluff; it makes possible forms of expression that enter into the substance of love.

In our culture sex has no uniform meaning, but couples are free to give it personal meanings. Janet Z. Giele notes two extremes: "On the one hand, the body may be viewed as the most important thing the person has to give, and sexual intercourse therefore becomes the symbol of the deepest and most far-reaching commitment, which is to be strictly limited to one pair-bond. On the other hand, participants may define sexual activity as merely a physical expression that, since it does not importantly envelop the whole personality nor commit the pair beyond the pleasures of the moment, may be regulated more permissively."[15] Between the two extremes lie many variations in the personal symbolism that couples give to sex, and here we are exploring only those variations found in traditional marital vows.

3. *Trust* is present at the time when couples undertake commitments to love, and in turn those commitments provide a framework for sustaining trust. Trust implies but is not reducible to Wasserstrom's "reasonable expectations" about a partner's conduct. Expectations are epistemic attitudes, whereas trust is a moral attitude of relying on others to act responsibly, with goodwill, and (in marriage) with love and support.[16] We have a reasonable expectation that the earth will continue to orbit the sun throughout our lifetime, but no moral relationship of trust is involved. As a way of giving support to others, underwriting their endeavors, and showing the importance of their lives to us, trust and trustworthiness is a key ingredient in caring.

To be sure, trust is not always good. It is valuable when it contributes to valuable relationships, in particular to worthwhile marriages.[17] Marital trust is confidence in and dependence upon a spouse's morally responsible love. As such, it provides a basis for ongoing intimacy and mutual support. It helps spouses undergo the vulnerabilities and risks (emotional, financial, physical) inherent in intimate relationships.

The trust of marital partners is broad-scoped. Spouses trust each other to actively support the marriage and to avoid doing things that might pull them away from it. They trust each other to maintain the conditions for preserving intimacy and mutual happiness. Violating marital trust does more than upset expectations and cause pain. It violates trust, honesty, fairness, caring, and the other moral ideals defining the relationship. It betrays one's spouse. And it betrays one's integrity as someone committed to these ideals.

To sum up, I have avoided Wasserstrom's narrow preoccupation with the promise of sexual exclusivity. Commitments of sexual exclusivity find their rationale in wider commitments to love each other *if* a couple decides that exclusivity will support their commitments to love *and* where love is understood as a special way to value persons within lasting relationships based on mutual caring, honesty, and trust. Accordingly, marital faithfulness (or constancy) in loving is the primary virtue; sexual fidelity is a supporting virtue. And sexual fidelity must be understood in terms of the particular commitments and understandings that couples establish.

I have also avoided saying that sexual exclusivity is intrinsically valuable or a feature of all genuine love, unlike Bonnie Steinbock: "[sexual] exclusivity seems to be an intrinsic part of 'true love.' Imagine Romeo pouring out his heart to both Juliet *and* Rosaline! In our ideal of romantic love, one chooses to forgo pleasure with other partners in order to have a unique relationship with one's beloved."[18] In my view, the intrinsic good lies in fulfilling love relationships, rather than sexual exclusivity *per se*, thereby recognizing that some couples sustain genuine love without sexual exclusivity. For some couples sexual exclusivity does contribute to the goods found in traditional relationships, but other couples achieve comparable goods through nontraditional relationships, for example open marriages that tolerate outside sex without love.[19] We can recognize the value of traditional relationships while also recognizing the value of alternative relationships, as chosen autonomously by couples.[20]

Keeping Commitments

A complete ethics of keeping commitments of exclusivity would focus on the virtues of responsibility, faithfulness, and self-control. Here, however, I wish to defend Wasserstrom's view that even in traditional relationships the prohibition against adultery is *prima facie*. However strong the presumption against adultery in traditional relationships, it does not yield an exceptionless, all-things-considered judgment about wrongdoing and blameworthiness in specific cases. I will discuss four of many complicating factors.[21] What if partners wish to change their commitments? What happens when love comes to an end? What if one spouse falls in love with an additional partner? And what about the sometimes extraordinary self-affirmation extramarital affairs may bring?

(i) *Changing Commitments.* Some spouses who begin with traditional commitments later revise them. Buoyed by the exuberance of romance, most couples feel confident they will not engage in adultery (much less be among the fifty percent of couples who divorce). Later they may decide to renegotiate the guidelines for their marriage in light of changing attitudes and circumstances, though still within the framework of their commitments to love each other.[22] One study suggests that 90% of couples believe sexual exclusivity to be essential when they marry, but only 60% maintain this belief after several years of marriage (with the changes occurring primarily among those who had at least one affair).[23]

Vita Sackville-West and Harold Nicolson provide an illuminating if unusual example. They married with the usual sexual attraction to each other and for several years were sexually compatible. As that changed, they gave each other permission to pursue extramarital affairs, primarily homosexual ones. Yet their original commitment to love each other remained intact. Indeed, for forty-nine years, until Vita died in 1962, their happy marriage was a model of mutual caring, deep affection, and trust: "What mattered most was that each should trust the other absolutely. 'Trust,' in most marriages means [sexual] fidelity. In theirs it meant that they would always tell each other of their infidelities, give warning of approaching emotional crises, and, whatever happened, return to their common center in the end."[24] Throughout much of their marriage they lived apart on weekdays, thereby accommodating both their work and their outside sexual liaisons. On weekends they would reunite as devoted companions, "berthed like sister ships."[25]

Just as we respect the mutual autonomy of couples in forming their initial understanding about their relationship, we should also respect their autonomy in renegotiating that understanding. The account I have offered allows us to distinguish between the primary commitment to love and the secondary commitment of sexual exclusivity. The secondary commitment is made in order to support the primary one, and if a couple agrees that it no longer is needed they are free to revoke it. Renegotiations can also proceed in the reverse directions: Spouses who initially agree on an open marriage may find that allowing extramarital affairs creates unbearable strains on their relationship, leading them to make commitments of exclusivity.

Changing commitments raise two major difficulties. First, couples are sometimes less than explicit about the sexual rules for their relationship. One or both partners may sense that their understandings have changed over the years but fail to engage in discussions that establish explicit new understandings. As a result, one spouse may believe that something is acceptable to the other spouse when in fact it is not. For example, Philip Blumstein and Pepper Schwartz interviewed a couple who, "when it came to a shared understanding about extramarital sex, . . . seemed not to be in the same marriage."[26] The man reported to them, "Sure we have an understanding. It's: 'You do what you want. Never go back to the same one [extramarital partner],' " presumably since that would threaten the relationship. By contrast, the wife reports: "We've never spoken about cheating, but neither of us believe in it. I don't think I'd ever forgive him [if he cheated on me]." Lack of shared understanding generates moral vagueness and ambiguity concerning adultery, whereas periodic forthright communication helps establish clear moral boundaries.[27]

Second, what happens when only one partner wants to renegotiate an original understanding? The mere desire to renegotiate does not constitute a betrayal, nor does it by itself justify adultery if one's spouse refuses to rescind the initial vow of sexual exclusivity. In such cases the original presumption against adultery continues but with an increased risk that the partner wishing to change it may feel adultery is more excusable. Such conflicts may or may not be resolved in a spirit of caring and compromise that enables good relationships to continue. Lacking such resolution, the moral status of adultery may become less clear-cut.

(ii) *Lost Love.* Couples who make traditional commitments sometimes fall out of love, singly or together, or for other reasons find themselves unwilling to continue in a marriage. Sometimes the cause is adultery, and sometimes adultery is a symptom of irresponsibility and poor judgment that erodes the relationship in additional ways.[28] But other times there is little or no fault involved. Lasting love is a creation of responsible conduct *and* luck.[29] No amount of conscientiousness can replace the good fortune of emotional compatibility and conducive circumstances.

In saying that traditional commitments to love are intended to be lifelong, we need not view them as unconditional.[30] Typically they are based on tacit conditions. One condition is embedded in the wedding ceremony in which *mutual* vows are exchanged, namely, that one's spouse will take the marital vows seriously. Others are presupposed as background conditions, for example, that the spouse will not turn into a murderer, rapist, spouse-beater, child-abuser, or psychopathic monster. Usually there are more specific tacit assumptions that evolve before the marriage, for example, that the spouses will support each other's careers. Above all, there is the background hope that with sincere effort the relationship will contribute to the overall happiness of both partners. All these conditions remain largely tacit, as a matter of faith. When that faith proves ill-founded or just unlucky, the ethics of adultery becomes complicated.

As relationships deteriorate, adultery may serve as a transition to new and perhaps better relationships. In an ideal world, marriages would be ended cleanly before new relationships begin. But then, in an ideal world people would be sufficiently prescient not to make traditional commitments that are unlikely to succeed. Contemplating adultery is an occasion for much self-deception, but at least sometimes there may be good reasons for pursuing alternative relationships before officially ending a bad marriage.[31]

(iii) *New Loves.* Some persons claim to (erotically) love both their spouse and an additional lover. They may be mistaken, as they later confess to themselves, but is it impossible to love two (or more) people simultaneously? "Impossible" in what sense?

Perhaps for some people it is a psychological impossibility, but, again, other individuals report a capacity to love more than one person at a time. For many persons it is a practical impossibility, given the demands of time, attention, and affection required in genuine loving. But that would seem to allow that resourceful individuals can finesse (psychologically, logistically, financially, and so forth) multiple simultaneous relationships. I believe that the impossibility is moral and conceptual—*if* one embraces traditional ideals that define marital love as a singular affirmation of one's spouse and *if* a couple establishes sex as a symbolic and substantive way to convey that exclusive love.[32] Obviously people can experience additional romantic attractions after they make traditional vows, but it is morally impossible for them to actively engage in loving relationships with additional partners without violating the love defined by their initial commitments.

Richard Taylor disagrees in *Having Love Affairs,* a book-length defense of adultery. No doubt this book is helpful for couples planning open marriages, but Taylor concentrates on situations where traditional vows have been made and then searches for ways to minimize the harm to spouses that results from extramarital love affairs.[33] In that regard his book is morally subversive in that it systematically presents only one side of the story. Here are five examples of this one-sidedness.

First, with considerable panache Taylor develops a long list of rules for *non*adulterous partners who should be tolerant of their partner's affairs. (a) "Do not spy or pry," since that is self-degrading and shows a lack of trust in one's spouse. (But is a commitment-breaking spouse trustworthy?) (b) "Do not confront or entrap," because that would humiliate the spouse. (But what about being humiliated oneself?) (c) "Stay out of it," since good marriages survive adultery. (No empirical support is offered for that generalization!) (d) "Stop being jealous," since jealousy disrupts marriages. (But what about the case for not provoking jealousy in the first place?)

Taylor also offers rules for the spouse having the affair: Maintain fidelity with one's lover, be honest with one's lover, be discrete rather than boasting about the affair, and do not betray or abandon the lover. In discussing these rules Taylor is oblivious to the infidelity, betrayal of trust, and failure to value one's spouse in the way called for by traditional commitments and the shared understanding between spouses.

Second, Taylor defines infidelity as "a betrayal of the promise to love" and faithfulness as "a state of one's heart and mind," rather than "mere outward conformity to rules." Infidelity can be shown in ways unrelated to adultery, such as in neglecting the spouse's sexual needs, selfishly using shared financial resources, and failing to be caring and supportive.[34] It is true that infidelity takes other forms, but what about the infidelity in violating marital vows and under-standings? Moreover, the only place we are reminded that "inner states" of faithfulness are manifested in outward conduct is when Taylor condemns infi-delity toward an extramarital lover, not one's spouse.

Third, love affairs are natural and avoiding them is unhealthy. "A man, by nature, desires many sexual partners"; "The suppression of the polygamous impulse in a man is . . . bought at a great price" of frustrated and rueful longing for outside love affairs.[35] Granted, most people (male and female) have desires for multiple sexual partners. Yet many people also have monogamous impulses, as shown in their decisions to enter into traditional marriages. The resulting con-flicts make sexual exclusivity notoriously difficult, but they need not result in frustration; often they contribute greatly to overall sexual satisfaction within secure and trusting relationships.

Fourth, "No one can tell another person what is and is not permissible with respect to whom he or she will love. . . . However inadvisable it may be to seek love outside the conventional restraints, the *right* to do so is about as clear as any right can be."[36] Taylor is equivocating of "right," which can mean (1) that others are obligated to leave one alone or (2) that one's conduct is all right. Having a right not to be interfered with by society as one engages in adultery does not imply that one's conduct is "all right" or morally permissible. Indeed, couples who make traditional commitments waive some rights in relation to each other; in particular they waive the right to engage in adultery which vio-lates their marital agreements.

Fifth, and most important, Taylor praises love affairs as inherently good and even the highest good: "the joys of illicit and passionate love, which include but go far beyond the mere joys of sex, are incomparably good."[37] On the same page he says, "This does not mean that love affairs are better than marriage, for they seldom are. Love between married persons can, in the long run, be so vastly more fulfilling" than affairs. I find it difficult to reconcile these claims: Those marriages which are vastly more fulfilling would thereby seem to provide the incomparable goods, not extramarital affairs which violate the commitments defining the marriage. Of course many people find joy in extramarital sex, and for some the joy may be the greatest they find in life. But Taylor provides no basis for saying that happy traditional marriages never produce comparable joys. Nor does he ever explain how extramarital joys are morally permissible for individuals who make traditional marriage vows.

Bonnie Steinbock affirms an opposite view. She suggests that to fall in love with someone other than one's spouse is already a betrayal: "Sexual infidelity has significance as a sign of a deeper betrayal—falling in love with someone else. It may be objected that we cannot control the way we feel, only the way we behave; that we should not be blamed for falling in love, but only for acting on the feeling. While we may not have direct control over our feelings, however, we are responsible for getting ourselves into situations in which certain feelings natu-rally arise."[38] I agree that spouses who make traditional vows are responsible for avoiding situations that they know (or should know) foster extramarital love.[39] Nevertheless, deeply committed people occasionally do fall in love with third parties without being blameworthy for getting into situations that spark that love. Experiencing a strong romantic attraction is not by itself an infidelity, and questions of betrayal may arise only when a person moves in the direction of acting on the love in ways that violate commitments to one's spouse.

Having said all this, I know of no argument that absolutely condemns all love-inspired adultery as immoral, all things considered and in all respects, even within traditional relationships. Nonetheless, as I have been concerned to emphasize, there is a serious betrayal of one's spouse. But to say that ends the matter would make the commitment to love one's spouse a moral absolute, with no exceptions whatsoever. Tragic dilemmas overthrow such absolutes, and we need to set aside both sweeping condemnations and wholesale defenses of love-inspired adultery.

To mention just one type of case, when marriages are profoundly unfulfilling, and when constricting circumstances prevent other ways of meeting important needs, there is a serious question whether love-inspired adultery is sometimes justifiable or at least excusable—witness *The Scarlet Letter*, *Anna Karenina*, *Madame Bovary*, *Lady Chatterly's Lover*, and *The Awakening*. Moreover, our deep ambivalence about some cases of love-inspired adultery reflect how there is some good and some bad involved in conduct that we cannot fully justify nor fully condemn.

(iv) *Sex and Self-Esteem.* Extramarital affairs are often grounded in attractions less grand than love. Affection, friendship, or simple respect may be mixed with a desire for exciting sex and the enhanced self-esteem from being found sexually desirable. The sense of risk may add to the pleasure that one is so desirable that a lover will take added risks. Are sex and self-esteem enough to justify violating marital vows? It would seem not. The obligations created through marital commitments are moral requirements, whereas sex and self-esteem pertain to one's self-interest. Doesn't morality trump self-interest?

But things are not so simple. Morality includes rights and responsibilities to ourselves to pursue our happiness and self-fulfillment. Some marriages are sexually frustrating or damaging in other ways to self-respect. Even when marriages are basically fulfilling, more than a few individuals report their extramarital affairs were liberating and transforming, whether or not grounded in love. For example, many women make the following report about their extramarital affair: "It's given me a whole new way of looking at myself . . . I felt attractive again. I hadn't felt that way in years, really. It made me very, very confident."[40]

In addition, the sense of personal enhancement may have secondary benefits. Occasionally it strengthens marriages, especially after the extramarital affair ends, and some artists report an increase in creative activity. These considerations do not automatically outweigh the dishonesty and betrayal that may be involved in adultery, and full honesty may never be restored when spouses decide against confessing an affair to their partners.[41] But nor are considerations of enhanced self-esteem and its secondary benefits irrelevant.

I have mentioned some possible justifications or excuses for specific instances of adultery after traditional commitments are made. I conclude with a caveat. Specific instances are one thing; general attitudes about adultery are another. Individuals who make traditional commitments and who are fortunate enough to establish fulfilling relationships based on those commitments ought to maintain a general attitude that for them to engage in adultery would be immoral (as well as stupid). The "ought" is stringent, as stringent as the commitment to sexual exclusivity. Rationalizing envisioned adultery with anecdotes about the joys of extramarital sex or statistics about the sometimes beneficial effects of adultery is a form of moral duplicity. It is also inconsistent with the virtues of both sexual fidelity and faithfulness in sustaining commitments to love.

Notes

1. Charles E. Shepard, *Forgiven: The Rise and Fall of Jim Bakker and the PTL Ministry* (New York: Atlantic Monthly Press, 1989).

2. Cf. Owen Flanagan, *Varieties of Moral Personality* (Cambridge, Mass.: Harvard University Press, 1991).

3. R. J. Connelly, "Philosophy and Adultery," in Philip E. Lampe, ed., *Adultery in the United States* (Amherst, N.Y.: Prometheus Books, 1987), pp. 131–64.

4. Denis de Rougemont, *Love in the Western World*, rev. ed., trans. Montgomery Belgion (New York: Harper and Row, 1974), p. 16. Two illuminating literary critics are Tony Tanner, *Adultery in the Novel: Contract and Transgression* (Baltimore: The Johns Hopkins University Press, 1979) and Donald J. Greiner, *Adultery in the American Novel: Updike, James, and Hawthorne* (Columbia: University of South Carolina Press, 1985).

5. Matthew 5:27–28, *New International Version*. In targeting males, this scripture presupposes that husbands are the primary adulterers. That presupposition is not surprising given a long history of indulging profligate husbands while severely punishing wayward wives, based in part on the view that wives are their husbands' property, duty-bound to maintain male lines of progeny, and in part on the view that women are chaste creatures who can be held to a higher standard than males. Today, husbands continue to lead in adultery statistics—well over half of them have extramarital affairs—although women are catching up. Annette Lawson cautiously estimates that somewhere between 25 percent and 50 percent of women have at least one extramarital lover during any given marriage, and 50–65 percent of husbands engage in adultery by the age of forty. *Adultery: An Analysis of Love and Betrayal* (New York: Basic Books, 1988), p. 75. A humanistic approach regards male and female adultery as on a par and also proceeds without invoking religious beliefs that condemn all adultery as sinful.

6. Morton Hunt, *The Affair* (New York: The World Publishing Company, 1969), p. 9.

7. This is not an imaginary case. See ibid., p. 80.

8. Michael J. Wreen plausibly widens the term "adultery" to apply to nonmarried persons who have sex with married persons, but since my focus is spouses, I will not widen the definition. "What's Really Wrong with Adultery?" *Journal of Applied Philosophy* 3 (1986): 45–49.

9. Richard Wasserstrom, "Is Adultery Immoral?" *Philosophical Forum* 5 (1974): 513–28. Wasserstrom's preoccupation with rules explains why the most interesting part of his essay—the discussion of the connections between sex, love, and sexually exclusive loving relationships—is approached so indirectly, in terms of "deeper deceptions" that violate the rule against deception, rather than directly in terms of violating moral ideals embedded in love.

10. Wasserstrom sometimes uses "love" this way, as on p. 518. But on p. 522 he hints at the value-laden meaning of "love": "the issues are conceptual, empirical, and normative all at once: What is love? How could it be different? Would it be a good thing or a bad thing if it were different?" These questions, which are posed but not pursued, adumbrate my approach.

11. Cf. Annette Baier, "Unsafe Loves," in *The Philosophy of (Erotic) Love*, ed. Robert C. Solomon and Kathleen M. Higgins (Lawrence, KS: University Press of Kansas, 1991), pp. 444 and 449, n. 29.

12. Irving Singer, *The Nature of Love*, 2nd ed. (Chicago: University of Chicago Press, 1984), I, pp. 3ff. In the third volume of this work, Singer sets forth a subjectivist view of the worth of persons. (Chicago: University of Chicago Press, 1987), III, p. 403. I share the more objectivist view of the unique worth of persons defended by Jeffrey Blustein in *Care and Commitment* (New York: Oxford University Press, 1991), pp. 203–16.

13. Roger Scruton, *Sexual Desire* (New York: Free Press, 1986), p. 339.

14. For an illuminating historical study of changing attitudes see Peter N. Stearns, *Jealousy* (New York: New York University Press, 1989).

15. Janet Z. Giele, as quoted by Philip E. Lampe, "The Many Dimensions of Adultery," in *Adultery in the United States*, p. 56.

16. Cf. H. J. N. Horsburgh, "The Ethics of Trust," *The Philosophical Quarterly* 10 (1960): 343–54; Annette Baier, "Trust and Antitrust," *Ethics* 96 (1986): 231–60; Lawrence Thomas, "Trust, Affirmation, and Moral Character. A Critique of Kantian Morality," in *Identity, Character, and Morality: Essays in Moral Psychology* (Cambridge, Mass.: MIT Press, 1990), pp. 235–57; and Mike W. Martin, "Honesty in Love," *The Journal of Value Inquiry* (1993).

17. Michael Slote, *Goods and Virtues* (Oxford: Clarendon Press, 1983), pp. 49, 65.

18. Bonnie Steinbock, "Adultery," in Alan Soble (ed.), *The Philosophy of Sex* (Savage, MD: Rowman & Littlefield, 1991), p. 191.

19. See Russell Vannoy, *Sex Without Love* (Amherst, N.Y.: Prometheus Books, 1980).

20. I am assuming that the consent involved in agreements between couples is fully voluntary and that a dominant partner does not exert pressures that make consent "intellectual" rather than emotionally wholehearted. Cf. J. F. M. Hunter, *Sex and Love* (Toronto: Macmillan, 1980), p. 42. To be sure, autonomy is not the sole value governing the making of marital commitments. There are reasons which need to be weighed in deciding what kind of commitments to make. Are partners being realistic in choosing between an exclusive relationship (with its element of sexual restriction) or an open relationship (with its risks of jealousy and new loves) as the best way to promote their happiness and love each other? And would permitting extramarital affairs negatively affect third parties (perhaps children)?

21. These are not the only factors—a book would be needed to discuss all relevant factors. For example, what about the effects on third parties, not just children and other family, but the extramarital lover? Ellen Glasgow describes the joys of her affair with a married man as "miraculous" in *The Woman Within* (New York: Hill and Wang 1980), p. 156. Again, there are factors about how affairs are conducted, including the risk of contracting AIDS and giving it to one's spouse.

22. The mutual renegotiation of relationships is a central aspect of marital equality, as argued by Robert C. Solomon, *About Love* (New York: Simon and Schuster, 1980), pp. 283–300.

23. Lawson, *Adultery*, pp. 72–73.

24. Nigel Nicolson, *Portrait of a Marriage* (New York: Atheneum, 1973), p. 188.

25. Ibid., p. 231.

26. Philip Blumstein and Pepper Schwartz, *American Couples* (New York. William Morrow, 1983), pp. 286–87.

27. Cf. J. E. and Mary Ann Barnhart, "Marital Faithfulness and Unfaithfulness," *Journal of Social Philosophy* 4 (April 1973): 10–15.

28. E.g., Herbert S. Strean, *The Extramarital Affair* (New York: Free Press, 1980); and Frank Pittman, *Private Lies: Infidelity and the Betrayal of Intimacy* (New York: W. W. Norton, 1989).

29. Cf. Martha C. Nussbaum, *The Fragility of Goodness* (New York. Cambridge University Press, 1980), pp. 259–362.

30. Contrary to Susan Mendus, "Marital Faithfulness," *Philosophy* 59 (1984): 246. For criticisms of Mendus, see Alan Soble, *The Structure of Love* (New Haven, Conn.: Yale University Press, 1990), p. 166; and Mike W. Martin, "Love's Constancy," *Philosophy* 68 (1993): 63–77.

31. An interesting example of deciding against adultery is the subject of Lotte Hamburger and Joseph Hamburger, *Contemplating Adultery* (New York: Fawcett Columbine, 1991).

32. Robert Nozick develops a slightly different argument based on the intimate mutual identification involved in forming a couple or a "'we." See *The Examined Life* (New York: Simon and Schuster, 1989), pp. 82, 84.

33. Richard Taylor, *Having Love Affairs* (Amherst, N.Y.: Prometheus Books, 1982), pp. 67–68.

34. Ibid., pp. 59–60.

35. Ibid., pp. 70, 72–73. The possible frustrations of monogamy are discussed by Edmund Leites in his illuminating book, *The Puritan Conscience and Modern Sexuality* (New Haven, CT: Yale University Press, 1986).

36. Ibid, p. 48. For these and other ambiguities of "rights" see Ronald Dworkin, *Taking Rights Seriously* (Cambridge, Mass.: Harvard University Press, 1977), pp. 188–89.

37. Ibid., p. 12.

38. Bonnie Steinbock, "Adultery," in Alan Soble, ed., *The Philosophy of Sex*, p. 192.

39. For an interesting example, see Janice Rosenberg, "Fidelity," in Laurie Abraham et al., *Reinventing Love* (New York: Plume, 1993), pp. 101–106.

40. Lynn Atwater, *The Extramarital Connection* (New York: Irvington Publishers, 1982), p. 143. The same theme is developed in Dalma Heyn, *The Erotic Silence of the American Wife* (New York: Signet, 1993).

41. Dalma Heyn (ibid.) urges that not confessing adultery to one's spouse is especially justified for women whose adultery is likely to provoke physical abuse or a divorce that would leave them and their children impoverished. Others argue that even when the adultery is immoral that confession wreaks more harm than the benefits of restoring full honesty in the relationship. (E.g., Laura Green, "Never Confess," in *Reinventing Love*, pp. 192–97.) The case for promoting honesty by confessing to one's spouse an infidelity is made by Frank Pittman in *Private Lies*.

11

Sexual Ontology and Group Marriage

Stephen R. L. Clark

Philosophers of earlier ages have usually spent time in considering the nature of marital, and in general familial, duty. Paley devotes an entire book to those "relative duties which result from the constitution of the sexes,"[1] a book notable on the one hand for its humanity and on the other for Paley's strange refusal to acknowledge that the evils for which he condemns any breach of pure monogamy are in large part the result of the fact that such breaches are generally condemned. In a society where an unmarried mother is ruined no decent male should put a woman in such danger: but why precisely should social feeling be so severe? Marriage, the monogamist would say, must be defended at all costs, for it is a centrally important institution of our society. Political community was, in the past, understood as emerging from or imposed upon families, or similar associations. The struggle to establish the state was a struggle against families, clans, and clubs; the state, once established, rested upon the social institutions to which it gave legal backing.

The political philosophy of our day has tended to assume that the state is made up of individual persons, and even that individuals should not give their loyalty to anything except the state, whether because we should forswear all lesser loyalties or because we should aim to make our class, for example, into the state—the ultimate authority within a given region. I do not myself share the apparent belief that the state is the proper arena, organ, or authority in all matters, nor that individual persons are, as such, the basic elements of society. To suppose that they are leads to the absurdity of contract-theory, that children and other noncontracting members of the family are not properly parts of the community. The state is only one social form. It seems proper, therefore, that philosophers should spend more time considering the communities within which we chiefly live: families, clubs, colleges. These are more real to most of

From *Philosophy* 58 (1983). Reprinted with the permission of Cambridge University Press.

us than the distant maneuverings of the high court of Parliament, or even of the local council. As Paley remarks, one benefit of marriage is "the better government of society, by distributing the community into separate families, and appointing over each the authority of a master of a family, which has more actual influence than all civil authority put together."[2] This point is not invalidated simply because such patriarchy is no longer as obviously desirable as it was to Paley, nor because parental authority in general has been severely limited by the continued rise of state power, as well as of a more child-orientated educational theory. The state has some interest, at different times, either in securing and enforcing marital rights and duties or in weakening those ties, to the point where no mediator stands between the individual and state power. But we are not yet reduced to this latter condition. We do not yet have to choose between "loyalty to self" (if such a concept makes sense) and loyalty to the state. We inhabit a more organic universe than that. There are forms of social life that lie between the self-sufficient individual and the total state. There are, in particular, families.

My concern is with a particular form of family, or "family-like structure," the group marriage. It is not an institution which philosophers have much considered. Alan Donagan allows that such a marriage might be in accord with rational morality, so long as steps were taken to ensure that each child knew its own father,[3] but I know of no other extended discussion. Polygamy is discussed occasionally, or polygyny. Paley does notice, from Caesar's account of British life and in the decent obscurity of a learned language, a polyandrous form like that found also amongst Tibetan tribes: the sharing of a wife between brothers.[4]

My second concern is with the nature of the sexual relationship in general, with what it is to be a sexual object, and this too has not received very much attention. Sex, after all, is supremely nonrational: one of Augustine's complaints against it is that you can't think clearly in the act.[5] The sexual act also seems to be a clear case of using a person directly for one's own pleasure—and only a contract of mutual use could be held to justify such a deeply immoral act (if that could: should we agree to such a bargain?). Either sexuality is not to be discussed or rationalized at all, or else it must fall under the normal rules for fair contracts. Liberals tend to assume that any just contract in this area is proper (how about necrophilia?),[6] and traditionalists that sex is a more or less unfortunate by-product of the real business of living and working together—never wholly admirable, but excusable if the partners' other intentions are sound.[7] I do not find either of these positions very attractive.

Now, after this preamble, for group marriage.

The Constantines define "multi-lateral marriage" as "consisting of three or more partners, each of whom considers him/herself to be married or committed in a functionally analogous way to more than one of the other partners."[8] "Group marriage," in the sociological literature, is a term reserved for associations of four or more partners, such that there is more than one partner of each sex. I shall use the term "group marriage" in the same sense as the Constantines' "multi-lateral marriage." Their data and such other published data as I have seen, are American in origin, but it seems very likely that similar phenomena are also to be found in Britain.

But what does their definition amount to? What is it to be "'committed in a functionally analogous way'"? What is it that distinguishes a merely polygynous or polyandrous association from a group *marriage*? What, for that matter, distinguishes polygamy from *group* marriage? In a society where group marriages are not recognized in law, and may even be, at least in theory, against the law (as instances of open evil-living), there is no institutional difference between those who merely live together and those who are "group-married." Participants in some group marriages, by the way, do not literally live together, although their children may migrate easily from house to house. Group marriages exist in the minds of the partners. Many plural relationships exist where not all the participants conceive themselves to be married to more than one, or even any of the others. Can I be the husband of someone who does not conceive herself to be my wife? Can I be someone's husband if she is married to someone else as well? What relationship do I have to the husband of my wife? Riddles and confusions must abound as we try to apply the language of monogamous (even of polygamous) marriage to this new thing: better perhaps to call the participants merely "partners."

One further preliminary: it does not immediately follow from the definition that the partners will be having sex with more than one person, but it is hardly surprising that the Constantines found no cases of what the participants called a group marriage where they did not have sex together in ways not licensed by the morality of monogamy. And perhaps this does follow, distantly, from the definition. How could the partners regard themselves as mutually committed in a way "functionally analogous" to marital commitment if they did not have sex together? Marital commitment is sealed at consummation, and failure to consummate is a ground of nullity, the declaration that no marriage exists. When male and female take each other as wife and husband they enter into a relationship requiring, among other things, that they have sex together. "The wife cannot claim her body as her own; it is her husband's. Equally the husband cannot claim his body as his own; it is his wife's. Do not deny yourselves to one another."[9] Obviously, this raises the crucial question, how can my body belong to two or more wives simultaneously? What, indeed, is the relationship of belonging?

Group marriages, or what the participants agree to call "group marriages," need not involve ordinarily homosexual relationships. Triads presumably do: why otherwise do the two same-sex partners wish to reckon themselves "married" to each other as well as to their common wife/husband? But in larger groupings the relationship of the co-husbands or the co-wives may not be directly marital: rather is one man the husband of another's wife, one woman the wife of another's husband? On the other hand the same-sex partners in any group with much chance of stability will presumably at least be friends, and perhaps more physically demonstrative than are ordinary members of straight society. A piece of popular, moralizing psychology that found no confirmation in the Constantines' study, namely that two men who willingly share a woman's favor must be secret homosexuals (the suggestion does not seem to be made about two women in the converse situation), perhaps says more about the assumptions of our patriarchalist society than about the personal realities, but there may sometimes be an element of this half-acknowledged excitement.[10]

Something rather like a group marriage is probably to be encountered rather more often than we suppose. In the far west of America they may arise from spouse-swapping circuits, as the participants discover that they actually wish some more permanent association with the people, or some of the people, whom they take to bed. It turns out, for some, that they cannot maintain the ultra-liberal convention that having sex is just like playing tennis—that people may play at sex without wishing to talk, work, or live together. In less determinedly "progressive" places, the rise of a "group marriage" may follow the opposite track. Any network of baby-care, child-care, mutual assistance and shared endeavor may well generate special relationships of affection and commitment between the participants. In straight society the almost inevitable sexual interest which such friends may begin to feel for each other is deflated, sublimated, relegated to fantasy, but the commitments involved may still be real ones, not merely friendships of convenience. The moment when such a network, loose association, becomes explicitly adulterous or is transformed into a conscious "group marriage" is difficult to catch with the tools of conceptual analysis. It is similarly difficult to maintain such a group marriage against the forces, internal or external, working against it. It is difficult enough, for example, to find two jobs together: how do you find three or more, each suitable for the individual involved? How are finances to be managed, and taxation? Many of these problems will also be those of communes, exacerbated by the much higher level of commitment to each other that the "group-married" must display. Few such marriages last very long, easily dissolving into component couples, or splitting on the question of one partner's involvement with someone outside the group—group marriages can be as moralistic about extramarital infidelities as any monogamist. Maybe, indeed, they must be more so: they are based, after all, upon an assumption of shared sexual experience that the monogamously married may not require. Petty adulteries may matter less to the monogamous.

But it is worth remembering that the average length of an American marriage is only seven years. The most long-lived group marriage that the Constantines discovered was only about three or four years old, but given the external pressures against success (if success is to be measured by longevity) it is perhaps only surprising that some such groups last as long as they do. Their dissolution may be traumatic, but perhaps less so than a conventional divorce. Some indeed would say that group marriages are not meant to last: they are temporary associations only, and their advantage is just this, that when a former partner leaves he or she leaves spouse and children in good hands. Given that people are beginning to abandon the traditional view that marriage is a lifelong commitment, it may seem very wise to try to create an enduring structure to care for the young and old and lonely: the membership of such a structure may be unstable, but that is perhaps only a fact of life. Group marriage may make it easier for someone to walk out, but it is not obvious that people find it all that difficult to do so now. Paley's words may none the less have some point to them: "If a man choose to have it in his power to dismiss the woman at his pleasure . . . [such a liaison] is not the same thing [as marriage]."[11]

By traditional standards the "group-married" are not married, and neither are such members of straight society as prefer to practice serial polygamy. This is not to say that some of the group-married may not intend just the sort of life-long commitment enjoined by tradition; but they must do so with the knowledge that the odds are against them, and may well prefer to intend to live together "as long as it seems to work," and then move on.

According to one model of individual life and marriage this is as it should be. Individuals, conceived as free and independent agents, enter into various explicit and tacitly understood compacts for the mutual provision of food, comfort, children, and sexual pleasure. There is no expectation of any further involvement in each other's life, and where the compacts can be mutually agreed there is nothing to be said against a multilateral, and strictly temporary, agreement. This model has gained some emotional support from the wish, modeled upon social ideals of masculinity, that women, too, should have "their own" lives to live, and marriage be regarded as a temporary alliance of agents who continue to be separate individuals, with their own secret ways, even before their convenient separation. The traditional view in the West has been that a marriage makes a new creature, by the woman's submerging her own policies and preferences in the common good (as defined by the male). It is understandable that those who think that such patriarchy is oppressive should prefer another model. But though the rise of liberal individualism and hostility to patriarchy make it understandable that people should treat the marital or quasi-marital relationship like this, it is surely a very inadequate account. Can personal relationships be treated as purely external compacts? Can marriage be reduced to the level of a finite contract, complete with comic details about how often each partner should do the washing up? That is not how the traditional Christian marriage was regarded, wherein the partners took each other "for better, for worse; for richer, for poorer; in sickness and in health; to love and to cherish, till death us do part, according to God's holy law."[12] Perhaps the program is to be rejected, along with the older requirement that the woman promise also to obey, but it does seem to embody a genuine picture of open-ended commitment more realistic than the supposition that one can decree beforehand what one will put up with or undertake in the particular circumstances of life together. To imagine the moment when one's spouse is just another person, even just another friend, is to imagine the end of a marital relationship. Couples who have separated, even with the intention of continued friendship, do not find each other to be, do not even find themselves to be, the same persons as they were. And if what I am depends in part on what social relationships meet in me, we cannot plausibly regard such relationships as merely external compacts. We get under each other's skins too much for that.

It is clearly *possible* for people to live and sleep together on a largely external basis. Many "marriages" now, and perhaps most marriages in the past (in fact if not in theory), have hardly expected more than that. The Manus, allegedly, mostly hate their sexual partners, reserving affection for their siblings and cross-cousins.[13] But it must be very difficult to maintain this sort of compresence unless the partners are not in fact present to each other much of the time. In a harem society, or in one that assigns the most important aspects of a male life to the world beyond the household, people may live and sleep together, even give each other some pleasure, without admitting each other within the circles of their own selfhood. But where the partners really, not only notionally, live together, sharing in bed, board, and the rearing of their children, they cannot easily avoid (whatever their enjoyment of the situation) a mutual infection. Each comes to internalize the other. One's knowledge of what the other will likely do itself becomes a factor in what oneself decides to do: not merely that one takes account of the outward event one has reason to expect, but that the reasonings and sentiments which will lead the other to act are modeled in oneself, and have their own effect on us. Spouses think alike, fill in the gaps in each other's colloquies, reflect each other's expressions, are familiars (precisely).

This mutual infection may afflict any people who live together, but sexual enjoyment of each other changes or accelerates the process. Here, after all, we may quite literally "get inside of each other," and only strict Cartesians can think that what their bodies do has nothing to do with what they do. There are, of course, occasions when we do feel detached from our bodies, but sexual congress should not be one of them. Where it is, where one or more of the partners are merely "going through the motions," there is no meeting. To meet, to have sexual knowledge of, the other is to be deeply involved in one's own body and the other's. We each carry from that meeting an awareness of what that other bodily presence is.

My description is intended to convey that this event is at least sometimes a desirable one. The effect of sexual enjoyment is to embody oneself in the body that is appreciated by the other, to know oneself at the same time as one knows the other. Even Sartre, in one of his more optimistic moments, concedes that one may be reconciled to one's own bodily existence as just the body one is by the fact that the other wills and enjoys that bodily presence.[14] But the tension involved in being at once a subject and an object is usually too much for Sartre. His account of sexuality rests upon the notion that the lover is endeavoring to fascinate the beloved, to become pure subject and turn the other into a pure object (once accomplished, the deed proves futile, for the beloved is then no more than another object in the world).[15] For Merleau-Ponty the operation is at least known to be a mutual one; spoilt if the beloved shows too great a freedom or detachment or if the beloved is entirely overmastered: "precisely when my value is recognized through the other's desire, he is no longer the person by whom I wished to be recognized, but a being fascinated, deprived of his freedom, and who therefore no longer counts in my eyes."[16] He suggests that the presence of a nonparticipating observer is resented or feared by sexual partners, for just this reason, that they are made aware of their own existence as nakedly objects, without any compensating awareness of the other's partial subjection.

This account does not seem to me to be a piece of accurate phenomenology. There is a strain of romanticism that fantasizes a return to the "state of nature" where each individual was aware of his or her self-existence only as a subject, unaware that anyone else is also a subject of experience.[17] But it is very doubtful that any such condition could exist, nor is there much reason to think it desirable if it could. There are surely ways of being with people that do not involve a perpetual oscillation between sadism and masochism, "getting the better of," and furiously submitting. But there is a point of substance here. If one is making love, then to become aware of oneself as an object (and perhaps a somewhat comic one) because of another's objectifying gaze is to be diverted from an unselfconscious absorption in the act and the beloved. But this absorption is unlikely ever to be complete in any case. *Pace* Ruddick, to make love to a sleeping woman is radically incomplete (unless the intention is to wake her up).[18] The lover needs to be aware of the beloved's awareness of the lover, though this way of expressing the point is itself misleading, suggesting as it does that *one* person is active and the other passive. The reality is that two lovers are absorbed in lovemaking and in being loved. To be made aware that one is also another's laughingstock or admired performer is to experience a dislocation of meaning: what is one doing—making love or performing? To be aware of another's presence (nonparticipatory) is to have an image of oneself and one's lover that makes it difficult to sustain the act.

Or maybe not. Others may find that such an image actually sustains them through the act, part of their endeavor to realize themselves as two together. Sometimes this seems neurotic, as the man who claimed never to have made love to his wife, not really, since he must always *imagine* himself doing so if the deed was to be done at all.[19] Would he have been helped if there had been a third party present to show him what he was doing? Even those whose neuroses are more normally manageable may occasionally fantasize: "exhibitionism" may be no more than a normal human desire to show off, or to share, something of beauty. Indeed, the wish to be alone with the one single other may be the artificial or abnormal desire: it must, after all, have been fairly uncommon for our forebears to be wholly private in the act, and many of them would have believed that, even if no other living man was near, God and His angels were their constant companions.

Some onlookers, of course, are bound to be disconcerting or unwelcome: they impose some vision on the lovers which really does distract or repel them. But why should we think that all onlookers are bound to be "objectifying," in the sense that they turn the lovers' motions into the merely mechanical or comical or disgusting? Suppose the onlooker is another participant, either actually (by whatever athletic mode) or *in potentia*? What is it like to be the lover of two lovers simultaneously? The loved lover of two lovers is a different being from a monogamous spouse, or even from the lover of two persons in an ordinarily polygamous marriage where these two are, as it were, merely alongside each other. The lovers in such a nexus are simultaneously the loved lovers of one and the other, and since these latter are different people, the persons that their lover is *with them* are also different. Different behavior patterns are simultaneously elicited, but also different self-images are simultaneously recalled. If these images are unduly diverse schizophrenia might be a likely result, or else the wakening of another personality, reacting to the joint presence of the two. It may be that this is part of the explanation for the emotional intensity of such multi-lateral encounters.

Group marriages, of course, do not necessarily or even often involve group sex. They may rather be networks of couples, even though the couples some-times exchange members. Nor do they rest upon the extreme version of group sex, the orgy—a device described by those who know (?) as almost entirely obliterating one's sense of self in favor of absorption in a single homogeneous mass.[20] The orgy is the practical expression of the theory that any flesh will do to produce certain orgasmic sensations, and is hardly manageable as long as the participants retain a sense of own-selfhood and sexual discrimination. The group marriage ceases to be anything like a marriage if it is transformed into an orgy that anyone can join, for marriage is a personal commitment to other per-sons. It is, perhaps, worth asking if the personal mode is worth maintaining at all times. It may also be worth speculating if the true ancestor of the orgy is not the sexual act indefinitely multiplied but rather the system of mutual grooming and cuddling that helps to cement a primate horde, and which seems to involve a regression to infantile modes of behavior: "*storge,*" it may be, not "eros" at all—"all in a squeaking, nuzzling heap, together; purrings, lickings, baby-talk, milk, warmth, the smell of young life."[21]

But though group marriages are not orgiastic, and need not involve group sex, this latter does offer a useful metaphor and test case for the sort of relation-ships that are involved in a nondyadic marriage. How is one to *belong* to, be available to more than one person at the same time? Part of this problem is merely (!) practical, and can be left to the practitioners: such difficulties as arise may well be canceled out by the great practical benefits (as a sufficiency of baby-sitters, cooks, house-tenders, etc.). But there is perhaps a more intractable aspect of the problem. To be on marital or "quasi-marital" terms with several people clearly produces the possibility that one may talk about one to the other: Aleph's relations with Gimel may be a matter of (amused? horrified? speculative?) con-versation between Beth and Gimel. And to be talked about is to be turned into a nonparticipating object in a way analogous to the Sartrean nightmare. Aleph may feel herself diminished by it, and Gimel too may be uneasy, just in that *his* being-with-Aleph is turned into something not himself, to be talked or laughed about. This constant self-transcendence *may* be a joy, but it is one of the greatest difficulties even for an adulterous relationship: a man may begin the affair with good intentions, but progressively be detached from that person he is with his lawful wife. Rules of confidentiality and nonintrusion may save the adulterous situation (or exacerbate the problem), but such rules as those can hardly obtain within a marriage: how are the partners married to each other if there are such large areas of agreed concealment? Jealousies, confusions, mutual misunderstandings must multiply according to the usual rules of hearsay: Gimel says something to Aleph which Aleph guardedly reports to Daleth, who comments on it to Beth, who is gravely offended at Gimel. The situation is even more confused when not all participants suppose themselves part of a group marriage. Kelly's words may sometimes be applicable: "the bitternesses and loathings, the hypersensitivities about domestic protocols and possessiveness, the paranoiac suspicions, have to be lived into in lived contact with polygamists. I feel for them."[22] The advantage of a "group marriage" is that it is unlikely ever to reach that pitch of hatred: the members will have gone long since. Nor has monogamy so startling a success rate that we can afford to be complacent.

There seem to be roughly two responses to this set of problems. One is to abandon the claim to be anything like a *marriage*: group members never wholly trust themselves to any other person, always remember the essential loneliness of the human individual, and accept that the others whom they now enjoy will prove to have been quite unknown to them all along. Any separation calls in question the years the couple have spent together (were they ever really as close, as much in accord as they thought they were? How could they have been, if now they part?); the constant passing of members out of the group, the constant splitting of the group into new factions must make it clear that everyone is on his, is on her own. Whether such a group, no longer purporting to be a group marriage, could bring up children with sufficient confidence, or sufficient coldness, to engage on such a life themselves, seems uncertain. But perhaps the message will get through: that you are never to trust anyone to stay around, however affectionate they now appear. The closest analogy for such a group would seem to be a club much more than a family. Perhaps that is the appropriate institution for liberal individualists, where no secrets will be asked nor any loyalty demanded beyond a year or two's obedience to the house rules.[23]

But perhaps there is another way in which a would-be group marriage might develop that is a little more like a *marriage*. The members might take seriously their quasi-marital commitment and attempt to live with all their spouses without secrecies and reservations. To do this might be to discover or create new and more authentic selves, the persons they can be with all their family. Such a development, whether or not it leads to literally "group sex," raises a difficulty for our traditional understanding of sexuality. The mating of male and female has often been an image, even an invocation, of the union of God and the Soul, or God and the Community, or Energy and Form. Medieval rabbis were urged to copulate with their wives on Sabbath night, in memory of God's union with the Shekinah in the temple.[24] Paul, too, explicitly compares marital love with the union of Christ and His church,[25] and Indian Tantric yogis seek to embody the union of Shiva and Sakti in their carefully controlled unions.[26] These are the images of mystagogues, but it is ingrained at least in Western culture that "a man shall leave his father and mother and be made one with his wife; and the *two* shall become one flesh."[27] Bigamy is an offense, or so it seems plausible to believe, because it conflicts with the demand that this pattern of sexual relationship, one man to one woman, be maintained.[28] So natural do we find it, so easy is it to think that "the animals went in two by two," that we impute the pattern to our nonhuman kin. The sexual bond of (one) male to (one) female is held to be the foundation of society, or else their bond as joint parents: "there was a Daddy Bear, and a Mummy Bear, and a Baby Bear. . . ."

If group marriages prove successful as marriages, they cast some doubt on the naturalness of the monogamous relationship. And perhaps this is just as well. For though there are some animals who do seem to form couples, at any rate for the arduous task of parenting the young (gibbons, amongst the primates), much the most common pattern amongst the primates is the group, the clan, the horde. Popular descriptions of this form usually suggest that the males gather harems to themselves, or own the females in common. But a much more plausible reading of the primate structure (as well as of the prides of lions), is that the core of the society is the continuing lineage of mothers and daughters. Males are evicted from this central group and must make their way back in, sometimes forming alliances with the other males (their brothers?) in order to secure a place within the family. The most common social form, amongst primates at any rate, is a group marriage (or rather, since no vows are sworn, a group "marriage"). It is difficult not to be reminded of an anecdote of the Constantines: the triad whose male believed he had a harem, and whose females knew they had a pet.[29] It is also worth remembering, more seriously, that though it is the males who most often initiate group marriages, it is the females who most happily sustain them. It may be that, as it were, nature never "meant" us to live as couples (still less as patriarchal couples), that for us, as for other primates, it is the small group, of both sexes, many ages, that is our proper home.[30]

Those for whom the words of Jesus are definitive may continue to believe that the pattern of one man/one woman is what God demands of us (always excepting those who are called to a life without such particular attachments). But as marriages continue to break down under the strains imposed by a rapidly changing society, a rapidly changing view of what women in particular should be prepared to put up with, the group marriage, considered as an attempt to provide support for mothers, and a chance for males, too, to practice parenting, should be taken seriously. The group marriage, in short, may be considered not as a decadent attempt to provide sexual variety, but as a realistic proposal to help with the problems faced by parents and children in a changing world. It is a great deal more like the primate norm than is the nuclear marriage.

Indeed, if we choose to look at the latter from the point of view of the group marriage, it is possible to see it not as a sexually bonded couple and their several hangers-on (children, aunts, grandparents), but as a partial attempt to achieve just the nexus of many ages and both sexes that our ancestry seems to require. Such a family is united by affections and attractions that may be more or less sexual even if no one but the husband and wife actually have sex together. Data from primate studies suggest that pederasty, so far from being a hideous perversion or inappropriate response, is no more than a misunderstanding of the normal male (and female) response to the young. It is the infants who unite a baboon troop, by eliciting affectionate responses even from threatening males.[31] It is perhaps the failure of the nuclear family to provide that close physical affection which generates the search for satisfaction in *sexual* relationships.[32] But that suggestion takes me too far afield.

The group marriage, with its more open sexual relationships, may manage things better. Those of us who continue to maintain straight marriages may at least learn from the experience of the group-married. But one last question obtrudes itself. If the group marriage is a reflection of the primate clan, maintained in unity by mutual grooming, cuddling, and the like, and not especially by the mating activity of adults, is it actually necessary for the group of many ages and both sexes to have sex together at all? May not two couples, and their children, live together in amity without bothering about bed? If they do indulge in "cross-couple" mating, all sorts of comedies ensue (who is sleeping with whom tonight?): might it not be better to avoid the problem by cuddles, mutual grooming (physical or symbolic) and keep their generative organs private? May *"storge"* not be enough after all? Why raise up "eros"?

The answer may be simply that "eros" is a fact of life. There are those who can manage to reserve themselves for some one partner; others cannot. The question certainly cannot be settled here. The choice before us—not the *political* choice, for the officers of the state have not yet busied themselves about this matter—is whether our descendants shall be reared to live as liberal individualists (making and breaking temporary contracts), as members of a sexually open group, or as partners in a Christian (traditional Christian) marriage that is sustained by the care and affection of a wider group (some of whom will be celibate). How far the state should take a hand in this decision is another question again. We should at least make clear to ourselves and to our legislators that there are other options to traditional patriarchy (whose legal base is slowly, very slowly, being eroded) than liberal individualism.[33]

Notes

1. W. Paley, *Works* (Edinburgh: Nelson & Brown, 1828), pp. 59ff. (*Moral and Political Philosophy*, Book III).

2. Ibid., p. 59.

3. Alan Donagan, *The Theory of Morality* (Chicago and London: University of Chicago Press, 1977), p. 103.

4. Paley, *Works*, p. 65.

5. Augustine, *Confessions* 8.5; *pace* T. Nagel, *Mortal Questions* (Cambridge: Cambridge University Press, 1979), p. 47, this is not what Paul means in *Romans* 7.23.

6. See E. Fromm, *The Anatomy of Human Destructiveness* (London: Cape, 1974).

7. See P. Geach, *The Virtues* (Cambridge: Cambridge University Press, 1977).

8. L. and J. Constantine, *Group Marriage* (New York: Macmillan, 1973), p. 28.

9. Paul, *I Corinthians* 7.4ff.: any acquaintance with other late Hellenic and early Christian thinkers shows how liberal and level-headed Paul was.

10. Indeed, without at least a strong bond of friendship between the same-sex partners we have only an interlocking series of couples, not a real *group*.

11. Paley, *Works,* p. 61.

12. Solemnization of Matrimony: *Prayer Book* (1928).

13. M. Mead, *Growing up in New Guinea* (Harmondsworth: Penguin, 1942).

14. J. P. Sartre. *Being and Nothingness,* trans. H. P. Barnes (London: Methuen, 1957), p. 371.

15. Ibid., pp. 317f.

16. M. Merleau-Ponty, *The Phenomenology of Perception,* trans. C. Smith (London: Routledge & Kegan Paul, 1962), p. 167.

17. A doctrine not unrelated to the assumption that nonhuman animals are all asocial beasts: see "Men, Animals and 'Animal Behaviour,' " in *Ethics and Animals,* ed. H. B. Miller and W. H. Williams (Clifton, N.J.: Humana Press, 1983).

18. Ruddick, "On Sexual Morality," *Amoral Problems,* ed. J. Rachels, 2d ed. (New York: Harper & Row, 1975), p. 23.

19. R. D. Laing, *The Divided Self* (Harmondsworth: Pelican, 1965), p. 86 (originally published in 1960).

20. See E. Jong, *How to Save Your Own Life* (London: Secker & Warburg, 1977, Panther, 1978), p. 264. This is not quite the point made by Nagel in his original paper, "Sexual Perversion," *Journal of Philosophy* 66 (1969), reprinted in Rachels, *Moral Problems,* pp. 3–15, that in an orgy there must be a degeneration "into mutual epidermal stimulation by participants otherwise isolated from each other" (omitted in Nagel, "Sexual Perversion," pp. 39–52)—the participants in an orgy do not feel themselves isolated.

21. C. S. Lewis, *The Four Loves* (London: Bles, 1960), Ch. 3.

22. M. Kelly, "Polygamy," *New Universities Quarterly* 32 (1978): 454ff.

23. M. Douglas points out that something like this sort of life is enjoyed by pygmies: *Natural Symbols* (London: Barrie & Rockcliff, 1970), pp. 15ff.

24. R. Patai, *The Hebrew Goddess* (New York: Ktav, 1967).

25. Paul, Ephesians 5.32.

26. See H. Zimmer, *Philosophies of India,* ed. J. Campbell (London: Routledge & Kegan Paul, 1952), pp. 581ff.

27. Matthew 19.5.

28. B. Mitchell, *Law, Morality and Religion* (London: Oxford University Press, 1967), pp. 27ff.

29. Constantines, *Group Marriage,* p. 85.

30. See L. Williams, *Challenge to Survival* (New York: Harper & Row, 1977), also S. R. L. Clark, *The Nature of the Beast* (Oxford University Press, 1982).

31. A. Jolly, *The Evolution of Primate Behavior* (New York: Mason, 1972), p. 253.

32. See G. Devereux, "Greek Pseudo-homosexuality and the Greek Miracle," *Symbolae Osloenses* 42 (1967): 69, on the connection between the failure of Greek fathers and the institutionalization of pederasty.

33. Earlier versions of this paper have been read in Lancaster, Edinburgh, Glasgow, and an Open University Summer School in York. I am grateful to all my auditors.

12

Is It Wrong to Discriminate on the Basis of Homosexuality?

Jeff Jordan

Much like the issue of abortion in the early 1970s, the issue of homosexuality has exploded to the forefront of social discussion. Is homosexual sex on a moral par with heterosexual sex? Or is homosexuality in some way morally inferior? Is it wrong to discriminate against homosexuals—to treat homosexuals in less favorable ways than one does heterosexuals? Or is some discrimination against homosexuals morally justified? These questions are the focus of this essay.

In what follows, I argue that there are situations in which it is morally permissible to discriminate against homosexuals because of their homosexuality. That is, there are some morally relevant differences between heterosexuality and homosexuality which, in some instances, permit a difference in treatment. The issue of marriage provides a good example. While it is clear that heterosexual unions merit the state recognition known as marriage, along with the attendant advantage—spousal insurance coverage, inheritance rights, ready eligibility of adoption—it is far from clear that homosexual couples ought to be accorded that state recognition.

The argument of this essay makes no claim about the moral status of homosexuality per se. Briefly put, it is the argument of this essay that the moral impasse generated by conflicting views concerning homosexuality, and the public policy ramifications of those conflicting views justify the claim that it is morally permissible, in certain circumstances, to discriminate against homosexuals.[1]

From the *Journal of Social Philosophy* 25, no. 1 (Spring 1995). Reprinted by permission of the *Journal of Social Philosophy*.

1. The Issue

The relevant issue is this: does homosexuality have the same moral status as heterosexuality? Put differently, since there are no occasions in which it is morally permissible to treat heterosexuals unfavorably, whether because they are heterosexual or because of heterosexual acts, are there occasions in which it is morally permissible to treat homosexuals unfavorably, whether because they are homosexuals or because of homosexual acts?

A negative answer to the above can be termed the "parity thesis." The parity thesis contends that *homosexuality has the same moral status as heterosexuality.* If the parity thesis is correct, then it would be immoral to discriminate against homosexuals because of their homosexuality. An affirmative answer can be termed the "difference thesis" and contends that there are morally relevant differences between heterosexuality and homosexuality which justify a difference in moral status and treatment between homosexuals and heterosexuals. The difference thesis entails that *there are situations in which it is morally permissible to discriminate against homosexuals.*

It is perhaps needless to point out that the difference thesis follows as long as there is at least one occasion in which it is morally permissible to discriminate against homosexuals. If the parity thesis were true, then on no occasion would a difference in treatment between heterosexuals and homosexuals ever be justified. The difference thesis does not, even if true, justify discriminatory actions on every occasion. Nonetheless, even though the scope of the difference thesis is relatively modest, it is, if true, a significant principle which has not only theoretical import but important practical consequences as well.[2]

A word should be said about the notion of discrimination. To discriminate against X means treating X in an unfavorable way. The word "discrimination" is not a synonym for "morally unjustifiable treatment." Some discrimination is morally unjustifiable; some is not. For example, we discriminate against convicted felons in that they are disenfranchised. This legal discrimination is morally permissible even though it involves treating one person unfavorably different from how other persons are treated. The difference thesis entails that there are circumstances in which it is morally permissible to discriminate against homosexuals.

2. An Argument for the Parity Thesis

One might suppose that an appeal to a moral right, the right to privacy, perhaps, or the right to liberty, would provide the strongest grounds for the parity thesis. Rights talk, though sometimes helpful, is not very helpful here. If there is reason to think that the right to privacy or the right to liberty encompasses sexuality (which seems plausible enough), it would do so only with regard to private acts and not public acts. Sexual acts performed in public (whether heterosexual or homosexual) are properly suppressible. It does not take too much imagination to see that the right to be free from offense would soon be offered as a counter consideration by those who find homosexuality morally problematic. Furthermore, how one adjudicates between the competing rights claims is far from clear. Hence, the bald appeal to a right will not, in this case anyway, take one very far.

Perhaps the strongest reason to hold that the parity thesis is true is something like the following:

1. Homosexual acts between consenting adults harm no one. And,

2. respecting persons' privacy and choices in harmless sexual matters maximizes individual freedom. And,

3. individual freedom should be maximized. But,

4. discrimination against homosexuals, because of their homosexuality, diminishes individual freedom since it ignores personal choice and privacy. So,

5. the toleration of homosexuality rather than discriminating against homosexuals is the preferable option since it would maximize individual freedom. Therefore,

6. the parity thesis is more plausible than the difference thesis.

Premise (2) is unimpeachable: if an act is harmless and if there are persons who want to do it and who choose to do it, then it seems clear that respecting the choices of those people would tend to maximize their freedom.[3] Step (3) is also beyond reproach: since freedom is arguably a great good and since there does not appear to be any ceiling on the amount of individual freedom—no "too much of a good thing"—(3) appears to be true.

At first glance, premise (1) seems true enough as long as we recognize that if there is any harm involved in the homosexual acts of consenting adults, it would be harm absorbed by the freely consenting participants. This is true, however, only if the acts in question are done in private. Public acts may involve more than just the willing participants. Persons who have no desire to participate, even if only as spectators, may have no choice if the acts are done in public. A real probability of there being unwilling participants is indicative of the public realm and not the private. However, since where one draws the line between private acts and public acts is not always easy to discern, it is clear that different moral standards apply to public acts than to private acts.[4]

If premise (1) is understood to apply only to acts done in private, then it would appear to be true. The same goes for (4): discrimination against homosexuals for acts done in private would result in a diminishing of freedom: since

(1)–(4) would lend support to (5) only if we understand (1)–(4) to refer to acts done in private. Hence, (5) must be understood as referring to private acts; and, as a consequence, (6) also must be read as referring only to acts done in private.

With regard to acts which involve only willing adult participants, there may be no morally relevant difference between homosexuality and heterosexuality. In other words, acts done in private. However, acts done in public add a new ingredient to the mix; an ingredient which has moral consequence. Consequently, the argument (1)–(6) fails in supporting the parity thesis. The argument (1)–(6) may show that there are some circumstances in which the moral status of homosexuality and heterosexuality are the same, but it gives us no reason for thinking that this result holds for all circumstances.[5]

3. Moral Impasses and Public Dilemmas

Suppose one person believes that X is morally wrong, while another believes that X is morally permissible. The two people, let's stipulate, are not involved in a semantical quibble; they hold genuinely conflicting beliefs regarding the moral status of X. If the first person is correct, then the second person is wrong; and, of course, if the second person is right, then the first must be wrong. This situation of conflicting claims is what we will call an "impasse." Impasses arise out of moral disputes. Since the conflicting parties in an impasse take contrary views, the conflicting views cannot all be true, nor can they all be false.[6] Moral impasses may concern matters only of a personal nature, but moral impasses can involve public policy. An impasse is likely to have public policy ramifications if large numbers of people hold the conflicting views, and the conflict involves matters which are fundamental to a person's moral identity (and, hence, from a practical point of view, are probably irresolvable) and it involves acts done in public. Since not every impasse has public policy ramifications, one can mark off "public dilemma" as a special case of moral impasses: those moral impasses that have public policy consequences. Public dilemmas, then, are impasses located in the public square. Since they have public policy ramifications and since they arise from impasses, one side or another of the dispute will have its views implemented as pubic policy. Because of the public policy ramifications, and also because social order is sometimes threatened by the volatile parties involved in the impasse, the state has a role to play in resolving a public dilemma.

A public dilemma can be actively resolved in two ways.[7] The first is when the government allies itself with one side of the impasse and, by state coercion and sanction, declares that side of the impasse the correct side. The American Civil War was an example of this: the federal government forcibly ended slavery by aligning itself with the Abolitionist side of the impasse.[8] Prohibition is another example. The Eighteenth Amendment and the Volstead Act allied the state with the Temperance side of the impasse. State-mandated affirmative action programs provide a modern example of this. This kind of resolution of a public dilemma we can call a "resolution by declaration." The first of the examples cited above indicates that declarations can be morally proper, the right thing to do. The second example, however, indicates that declarations are not always morally proper. The state does not always take the side of the morally correct; nor is it always clear which side is the correct one.

The second way of actively resolving a public dilemma is that of accommodation. An accommodation in this context means resolving the public dilemma in a way that gives as much as possible to all sides of the impasse. A resolution by accommodation involves staking out some middle ground in a dispute and placing public policy in that location. The middle ground location of a resolution via accommodation is a virtue since it entails that there are no absolute victors and no absolute losers. The middle ground is reached in order to resolve the public dilemma in a way which respects the relevant views of the conflicting parties and which maintains social order. The Federal Fair Housing Act and, perhaps, the current status of abortion (legal but with restrictions) provide examples of actual resolutions via accommodation.[9]

In general, governments should be, at least as far as possible, neutral with regard to the disputing parties in a public dilemma. Unless there is some overriding reason why the state should take sides in a public dilemma—the protection of innocent life, or abolishing slavery, for instance—the state should be neutral, because no matter which side of the public dilemma the state takes, the other side will be the recipient of unequal treatment by the state. A state which is partial and takes sides in moral disputes via declaration, when there is no overriding reason why it should, is tyrannical. Overriding reasons involve, typically, the protection of generally recognized rights.[10] In the case of slavery, the right to liberty; in the case of protecting innocent life, the right involved is the negative right to life. If a public dilemma must be actively resolved, the state should do so (in the absence of an overriding reason) via accommodation and not declaration since the latter entails that a sizable number of people would be forced to live under a government which "legitimizes" and does not just tolerate activities which they find immoral. Resolution via declaration is appropriate only if there is an overriding reason for the state to throw its weight behind one side in a public dilemma.

Is moral rightness an overriding reason for a resolution via declaration? What better reason might there be for a resolution by declaration than that it is the right thing to do? Unless one is prepared to endorse a view that is called "legal moralism"—that immorality alone is a sufficient reason for the state to curtail individual liberty—then one had best hold that moral rightness alone is not an overriding reason. Since some immoral acts neither harm nor offend nor violate another's rights, it seems clear enough that too much liberty would be lost if legal moralism were adopted as public policy.[11]

Though we do not have a definite rule for determining a priori which moral impasses genuinely constitute public dilemmas, we can proceed via a case-by-case method. For example, many people hold that cigarette smoking is harmful and, on that basis, is properly suppressible. Others disagree. Is this a public dilemma? Probably not. Whether someone engages in an imprudent action is, as long as it involves no unwilling participants, a private matter and does not, on that account, constitute a public dilemma. What about abortion? Is abortion a public dilemma? Unlike cigarette smoking, abortion is a public dilemma. This is clear from the adamant and even violent contrary positions involved in the impasse. Abortion is an issue which forces itself into the public square. So, it is clear that, even though we lack a rule which filters through moral impasses designating some as public dilemmas, not every impasse constitutes a public dilemma.

4. Conflicting Claims on Homosexuality

The theistic tradition, Judaism and Christianity and Islam, has a clear and deeply entrenched position on homosexual acts: they are prohibited. Now it seems clear enough that if one is going to take seriously the authoritative texts of the respective religions, then one will have to adopt the views of those texts, unless one wishes to engage in a demythologizing of them with the result that one ends up being only a nominal adherent of that tradition.[12] As a consequence, many contemporary theistic adherents of the theistic tradition, in no small part because they can read, hold that homosexual behavior is sinful. Though God loves the homosexual, these folk say, God hates the sinful behavior. To say that act X is a sin entails that X is morally wrong, not necessarily because it is harmful or offensive, but because X violates God's will. So, the claim that homosexuality is sinful entails the claim that it is also morally wrong. And, it is clear, many people adopt the difference thesis just because of their religious views: because the Bible or the Koran holds that homosexuality is wrong, they too hold that view.

Well, what should we make of these observations? We do not, for one thing, have to base our moral conclusions on those views, if for no other reason than not every one is a theist. If one does not adopt the religion-based moral view, one must still respect those who do; they cannot just be dismissed out of hand.[13] And, significantly, this situation yields a reason for thinking that the difference thesis is probably true. Because many religious people sincerely believe homosexual acts to be morally wrong and many others believe that homosexual acts are not morally wrong, there results a public dilemma.[14]

The existence of this public dilemma gives us reason for thinking that the difference thesis is true. It is only via the difference thesis and not the parity thesis, that an accommodation can be reached. Here again, the private/public distinction will come into play.

To see this, take as an example the issue of homosexual marriages. A same-sex marriage would be a public matter. For the government to sanction same-sex marriage—to grant the recognition and reciprocal benefits which attach to marriage—would ally the government with one side of the public dilemma and against the adherents of religion-based moralities. This is especially true given that, historically, no government has sanctioned same-sex marriages. The status quo has been no same-sex marriages. If the state were to change its practice now, it would be clear that the state has taken sides in the impasse. Given the history, for a state to sanction a same-sex marriage now would not be a neutral act.

Of course, some would respond here that by not sanctioning same-sex marriages the state is, and historically has been, taking sides to the detriment of homosexuals. There is some truth in this claim. But one must be careful here. The respective resolutions of this issue—whether the state should recognize and sanction same-sex marriage—do not have symmetrical implications. The asymmetry of this issue is a function of the private/public distinction and the fact that marriage is a public matter. If the state sanctions same-sex marriages, then there is no accommodation available. In that event, the religion-based morality proponents are faced with a public, state-sanctioned matter which they find seriously immoral. This would be an example of a resolution via declaration. On the other hand, if the state does not sanction same-sex marriages, there is an accommodation available: in the public realm the state sides with the religion-based moral view, but the state can tolerate private homosexual acts. That is, since homosexual acts are not essentially public acts, they can be, and historically have been, performed in private. The state, by not sanctioning same-sex marriages, is acting in the public realm, but it can leave the private realm to personal choice.[15]

5. The Argument from Conflicting Claims

It was suggested in the previous section that the public dilemma concerning homosexuality, and in particular whether states should sanction same-sex marriages, generates an argument in support of the difference thesis. The argument, again using same-sex marriages as the particular case, is as follows:

7. There are conflicting claims regarding whether the state should sanction same-sex marriages. And,

8. this controversy constitutes a public dilemma. And,

9. there is an accommodation possible if the state does not recognize same-sex marriages. And,

10. there is no accommodation possible if the state does sanction same-sex marriages. And,

11. there is no overriding reason for a resolution via declaration. Hence,

12. the state ought not sanction same-sex marriages. And,

13. the state ought to sanction heterosexual marriages. So,

14. there is at least one morally relevant case in which discrimination against homosexuals, because of their homosexuality, is morally permissible. Therefore,

15. the difference thesis is true.

Since proposition (14) is logically equivalent to the difference thesis, then, if (7)–(14) are sound, proposition (15) certainly follows.

Premises (7) and (8) are uncontroversial. Premises (9) and (10) are based on the asymmetry that results from the public nature of marriage. Proposition (11) is based on our earlier analysis of the argument (1)–(6). Since the strongest argument in support of the parity thesis fails, we have reason to think that there is no overriding reason why the state ought to resolve the public dilemma via declaration in favor of same-sex marriages. We have reason, in other words, to think that (11) is true.

Proposition (12) is based on the conjunction of (7)–(11) and the principle that, in the absence of an overriding reason for state intervention via declaration, resolution by accommodation is the preferable route. Proposition (13) is just trivially true. So, given the moral difference mentioned in (12) and (13), proposition (14) logically follows.

6. Two Objections Considered

The first objection to the argument from conflicting claims would contend that it is unsound because a similar sort of argument would permit discrimination against some practice which, though perhaps controversial at some earlier time, is now widely thought to be morally permissible. Take mixed-race marriages, for example. The opponent of the argument from conflicting claims could argue that a similar argument would warrant prohibition against mixed-race marriages. If it does, we would have good reason to reject (7)–(14) as unsound.

There are three responses to this objection. The first response denies that the issue of mixed-race marriages is in fact a public dilemma. It may have been so at one time, but it does not seem to generate much, if any, controversy today. Hence, the objection is based upon a faulty analogy.

The second response grants for the sake of the argument that the issue of mixed-race marriages generates a public dilemma. But the second response points out that there is a relevant difference between mixed-race marriages and same-sex marriages that allows for a resolution by declaration in the one case but not in the other. As evident from the earlier analysis of the argument in support of (1)–(6), there is reason to think that there is no overriding reason for a resolution by declaration in support of the parity thesis. On the other hand, it is a settled matter that state protection from racial discrimination is a reason sufficient for a resolution via declaration. Hence, the two cases are only apparently similar, and, in reality, they are crucially different. They are quite different because, clearly enough, if mixed-race marriages do generate a public dilemma, the state should use resolution by declaration in support of such marriages. The same cannot be said for same-sex marriages.

One should note that the second response to the objection does not beg the question against the proponent of the parity thesis. Though the second response denies that race and sexuality are strict analogues, it does so for a defensible and independent reason: it is a settled matter that race is not a sufficient reason for disparate treatment; but, as we have seen from the analysis of (1)–(6), there is no overriding reason to think the same about sexuality.[16]

The third response to the first objection is that the grounds of objection differ in the respective cases: one concerns racial identity; the other concerns behavior thought to be morally problematic. A same-sex marriage would involve behavior which many people find morally objectionable; a mixed-race marriage is objectionable to some, not because of the participants' behavior, but because of the racial identity of the participants. It is the race of the marriage partners which some find of primary complaint concerning mixed-race marriages. With same-sex marriage, however, it is the behavior which is primarily objectionable. To see this latter point, one should note that, though promiscuously Puritan in tone, the kind of sexual acts that are likely involved in a same-sex marriage are objectionable to some, regardless of whether done by homosexuals or heterosexuals.[17] So again, there is reason to reject the analogy between same-sex marriages and mixed-race marriages. Racial identity is an immutable trait and a complaint about mixed-race marriages necessarily involves, then, a complaint about an immutable trait. Sexual behavior is not an immutable trait and it is possible to object to same-sex marriages based on the behavior which would be involved in such marriages. Put succinctly, the third response can be formulated as follows: objections to mixed-race marriages necessarily involve objections over status, while objections to same-sex marriages could involve objections over behavior. Therefore, the two cases are not analogous since there is a significant modal difference in the grounds of the objections.

The second objection to the argument from conflicting claims can be stated so: if homosexuality is biologically based—if it is inborn[18]—then how can discrimination ever be justified? If it is not a matter of choice, homosexuality is an immutable trait which is, as a consequence, morally permissible. Just as it would be absurd to hold someone morally culpable for being of a certain race, likewise it would be absurd to hold someone morally culpable for being a homosexual. Consequently, according to this objection, the argument from conflicting claims "legitimizes" unjustifiable discrimination.

But this second objection is not cogent, primarily because it ignores an important distinction. No one could plausibly hold that homosexuals act by some sort of biological compulsion. If there is a biological component involved in sexual identity, it would incline but it would not compel. Just because one naturally (without any choice) has certain dispositions, it is not in itself a morally cogent reason for acting upon that disposition. Most people are naturally selfish, but it clearly does not follow that selfishness is in any way permissible on that account. Even if it is true that one has a predisposition to do X as a matter of biology and not as a matter of choice, it does not follow that doing X is morally permissible. For example, suppose that pyromania is an inborn predisposition. Just because one has an inborn and, in that sense, natural desire to set fires, one still has to decide whether or not to act on that desire.[19] The reason that the appeal to biology is specious is that it ignores the important distinction between being a homosexual and homosexual acts. One is status; the other is behavior. Even if one has the status naturally, it does not follow that the behavior is morally permissible, nor that others have a duty to tolerate the behavior.

But, while moral permissibility does not necessarily follow if homosexuality should turn out to be biologically based, what does follow is this: in the absence of a good reason to discriminate between homosexuals and heterosexuals, then, assuming that homosexuality is inborn, one ought not discriminate between them. If a certain phenomenon X is natural in the sense of being involuntary and nonpathological, and if there is no good reason to hold that X is morally problematic, then that is reason enough to think that X is morally permissible. In the absence of a good reason to repress X, one should tolerate it since, as per supposition, it is largely nonvoluntary. The argument from conflicting claims, however, provides a good reason which overrides this presumption.

7. A Second Argument for the Difference Thesis

A second argument for the difference thesis, similar to the argument from conflicting claims, is what might be called the "no-exit argument." This argument is based on the principle that:

A. No just government can coerce a citizen into violating a deeply held moral belief or religious belief.

Is (A) plausible? It seems to be since the prospect of a citizen being coerced by the state into a practice which she finds profoundly immoral appears to be a clear example of an injustice. Principle (A), conjoined with there being a public dilemma arising over the issue of same-sex marriages, leads to the observation that if the state were to sanction same-sex marriages, then persons who have profound religious or moral objections to such unions would be legally mandated to violate their beliefs since there does not appear to be any feasible "exit right" possible with regard to state-sanctioned marriage. An exit right is an exemption from some legally mandated practice, granted to a person or group, the purpose of which is to protect the religious or moral integrity of that person or group. Prominent examples of exit rights include conscientious objection and military service, home-schooling of the young because of some religious concern, and property used for religious purposes being free from taxation.

It is important to note that marriage is a public matter in the sense that, for instance, if one is an employer who provides health care benefits to the spouses of employees, one must provide those benefits to any employee who is married. Since there is no exit right possible in this case, one would be coerced, by force of law, into subsidizing a practice one finds morally or religiously objectionable.[20]

In the absence of an exit right, and if (A) is plausible, then the state cannot morally force persons to violate deeply held beliefs that are moral or religious in nature. In particular, the state morally could not sanction same-sex marriages since this would result in coercing some into violating a deeply held religious conviction.

8. A Conclusion

It is important to note that neither the argument from conflicting claims nor the no-exit argument licenses wholesale discrimination against homosexuals. What they do show is that some discrimination against homosexuals, in this case refusal to sanction same-sex marriages, is not only legally permissible but also morally permissible. The discrimination is a way of resolving a public policy dilemma that accommodates, to an extent, each side of the impasse and further, protects the religious and moral integrity of a good number of people. In short, the arguments show us that there are occasions in which it is morally permissible to discriminate on the basis of homosexuality.[21]

Notes

1. The terms "homosexuality" and "heterosexuality" are defined as follows. The former is defined as sexual feelings or behavior directed toward individuals of the same sex. The latter, naturally enough, is defined as sexual feelings or behavior directed toward individuals of the opposite sex.

Sometimes the term "gay" is offered as an alternative to "homosexual." Ordinary use of "gay" has it as a synonym of a male homosexual (hence, the common expression, "gays and lesbians"). Given this ordinary usage, the substitution would lead to a confusing equivocation. Since there are female homosexuals, it is best to use "homosexual" to refer to both male and female homosexuals, and reserve "gay" to signify male homosexuals, and "lesbian" for female homosexuals in order to avoid the equivocation.

2. Perhaps we should distinguish the weak difference thesis (permissible discrimination on *some* occasions) from the strong difference thesis (given the relevant moral differences, discrimination on *any* occasion is permissible).

3. This would be true even if the act in question is immoral.

4. The standard answer is, of course, that the line between public and private is based on the notion of harm. Acts which carry a real probability of harming third parties are public acts.

5. For other arguments supporting the moral parity of homosexuality and heterosexuality, see Richard Mohr, *Gays/Justice: A Study of Ethics, Society and Law* (New York: Columbia University Press, 1988); and see Michael Ruse, "The Morality of Homosexuality" in *Philosophy and Sex,* eds. R. Baker and F. Elliston, 2d ed. (Amherst, N.Y.: Prometheus Books, 1984), pp. 370–90.

6. Perhaps it would be better to term the disputing positions "contradictory" views rather than "contrary" views.

7. Resolutions can also be passive in the sense of the state doing nothing. If the state does nothing to resolve the public dilemma, it stands pat with the status quo, and the public dilemma is resolved gradually by sociological changes (changes in mores and in beliefs).

8. Assuming, plausibly enough, that the disputes over the sovereignty of the Union and concerning states' rights were at bottom disputes about slavery.

9. The Federal Fair Housing Act prohibits discrimination in housing on the basis of race, religion, and sex. But it does not apply to the rental of rooms in single-family houses, or to a building of five units or less if the owner lives in one of the units. See 42 U.S.C. Section 3603.

10. Note that overriding reasons involve generally recognized rights. If a right is not widely recognized and the state nonetheless uses coercion to enforce it, there is a considerable risk that the state will be seen by many or even most people as tyrannical.

11. This claim is, perhaps, controversial. For a contrary view see Richard George, *Making Men Moral* (Oxford: Clarendon Press, 1993).

12. See, for example, Leviticus 18:22, 21:3; and Romans 1:22–32; and Koran IV:13.

13. For an argument that religiously based moral views should not be dismissed out of hand, see Stephen Carter, *The Culture of Disbelief: How American Law and Politics Trivialize Religious Devotion* (New York: Basic Books, 1993).

14. "Two assumptions are these: that the prohibitions against homosexual activity are part of the religious doctrine and not just an extraneous addition; second, that if X is part of one's religious belief or religious doctrine, then it is morally permissible to hold X. Though this latter principle is vague, it is, I think, clear enough for our purposes here (I ignore here any points concerning the rationality of religious belief in general, or in particular cases).

15. This point has implications for the moral legitimacy of sodomy laws. One implication would be this: the private acts of consenting adults should not be criminalized.

16. An *ad hominem* point: if this response begs the question against the proponent of the parity thesis, it does not beg the question any more than the original objection does by presupposing that sexuality is analogous with race.

17. Think of the sodomy laws found in some states which criminalize certain sexual acts, whether performed by heterosexuals or homosexuals.

18. There is some interesting recent research which, though still tentative, strongly suggests that homosexuality is, at least in part, biologically based. See Simon LeVay, *The Sexual Brain* (Cambridge, Mass.: MIT Press 1993), pp. 120–22; and J. M. Bailey and R. C. Pillard "A Genetic Study of Male Sexual Orientation," *Archives of General Psychiatry* 48 (1991): 1089–96; and C. Burr, "Homosexuality and Biology," *The Atlantic* 271/3 (March, 1993): 64; and D. Hamer, S. Hu, V. Magnuson, N. Hu, A. Pattatucci, "A Linkage between DNA Markers on the X Chromosome and Male Sexual Orientation," *Science* 261 (July 16, 1993): 321–27; and see the summary of this article by Robert Pool, "Evidence for Homosexuality Gene," *Science* 261 (July 16, 1993): 291–92.

19. I do not mean to suggest that homosexuality is morally equivalent or even comparable to pyromania.

20. Is the use of subsidy here inappropriate? It does not seem so since providing health care to spouses, in a society where this is not legally mandatory, seems to be more than part of a salary and is a case of providing supporting funds for a certain end.

21. I thank David Haslett, Kate Rogers, Louis Pojman, and Jim Fieser for helpful and critical comments.

13

The Case for Gay Marriage

Richard D. Mohr

I. Introduction: Marital Stories

The climax of Harvey Fierstein's 1979 play, *Torch Song Trilogy,* is a dialogue—well, shouting match—between mother and son about traditional marriage and its gay variant. As is frequently the case, the nature and function of an institution flashes forth only when the institution breaks down or is dissolved—here by the death of Arnold's lover.

Arnold: [I'm] widowing . . .

Ma: Wait, wait, wait, wait, wait. Are you trying to compare my marriage with you and Alan? Your father and I were married for thirty-five years, had two children and a wonderful life together. You have the nerve to compare yourself to that? . . .

What loss did you have? . . . Where do you come to compare that to a marriage of thirty-five years? . . .

It took me two months until I could sleep in our bed alone, a year to learn to say "I" instead of "we." Are you going to tell me you were "widowing"? How dare you!

Arnold: You're right, Ma. How dare I. I couldn't possibly know how it feels to pack someone's clothes in plastic bags and watch the garbage-pickers carry them away. Or what it feels like to forget and set his place at the table. How about the food that rots in the refrigerator because you forgot how to shop for one? How dare I? Right, Ma? How dare I?

This article originally appeared in the *Notre Dame Journal of Law, Ethics & Public Policy* 9, no. 1 (1995). Reprinted by permission of the author.

Ma: May God strike me dead! Whatever I did to my mother to deserve a child speaking to me this way. The disrespect!

Arnold: Listen, Ma, you had it easy. You have thirty-five years to remember, I have five. You had your children and friends to comfort you, I had me! My friends didn't want to hear about it. They said "What're you gripin' about? At least you had a lover." 'Cause everybody knows that queers don't feel nothin'. How dare I say I loved him? You had it easy, Ma. You lost your husband in a nice clean hospital, I lost mine out there. They killed him there on the street. Twenty-three years old, laying dead on the street. Killed by a bunch of kids with baseball bats. Children. Children taught by people like you. 'Cause everybody knows that queers don't matter! Queers don't love! And those that do deserve what they get![1]

In its representation both of the day-to-day nature of gay relationships and of the injustices which beset these relationships because they are not socially, let alone legally, acknowledged as marriages, Fierstein's moving fictional account has its roots deep in the real life experience of lesbian and gay couples. Consider three true-life stories of gay couples:

Years of domesticity have made Brian and Ed familiar figures in the archipelago of middle-aged, middle-class couples who make up my village's permanent gay male community. Ed drives a city bus. Brian is a lineman for the power company—or rather he was until a freak accident set aflame the cherry-picker atop which he worked. He tried to escape by leaping to a nearby tree, but lost his grip and landed on his head. Eventually, it became clear that Brian would be permanently brain-damaged. After a few awkward weeks in the hospital, Brian's parents refused to let Ed visit anymore. Eventually they moved Brian to their village and home, where Ed was not allowed.

A similar case garnered national attention. In Minnesota, Karen Thompson fought a seven-year legal battle to gain guardianship of her lover, Sharon Kowalski. Sharon was damaged of body and mind in a 1983 car accident, after which Sharon's parents barred Karen for years from seeing her.[2] Although the Minnesota tragedy made headlines, the causes of such occurrences are everyday stuff in gay and lesbian lives. In both Sharon and Karen's and Brian and Ed's cases, if the government had through marriage allowed the members of each couple to be next-of-kin for each other, the stories would have had different endings—ones in keeping with our cultural belief that in the first instance those to whom we as adults entrust our tendency in crisis are people we choose, our spouses, who love us because of who we are, not people who are thrust upon us by the luck of the draw and who may love us only in spite of who we are.[3]

On their walk back from their neighborhood bar to the Victorian which, over the years, they had lovingly restored, Warren and Mark stopped along San Francisco's Polk Street to pick up milk for breakfast and for Sebastian, their geriatric cat. Just for kicks, some wealthy teens from the Valley drove into town to "bust some fags." Warren dipped into a convenience store, while Mark had a smoke outside. As Mark turned to acknowledge Warren's return, he was hit across the back of the head with a baseball bat. Mark's blood and vomit splashed across Warren's face. In 1987, a California appellate court held that under no circumstance can a relationship between two homosexuals—however emotionally significant, stable, and exclusive—be legally considered a "close relationship," and so Warren was barred from bringing any suit against the bashers for negligently causing emotional distress.[4]

Gay and lesbian couples are living together as married people do, even though they are legally barred from getting married. The legally aggravated injustices contained in the stories above suggest both that this bar deserves a close examination and that the law, if it aims at promoting justice, will have to be attentive and responsive to the ways couples actually live their lives rather than, as at present, preemptively and ignorantly determining which relationships are to be acknowledged and even created by it. America stands at a point where legal tradition is largely a hindrance to understanding what the law should be.

In this article, I advocate the legalization of gay marriage.[5] My analysis does not in the main proceed by appeal to the concept of equality; in particular, nothing will turn on distinctive features of equal protection doctrine. Rather, the analysis is substantive and turns on understanding the nature and meaning of marriage itself.

To count as a marriage, a relation must fulfill certain normative conditions. Marriage is norm-dependent. In the first half of the article, I examine this aspect of marriage. First, in Part II-A, I examine the going social and legal definitions of marriage and find them all wanting. I then in Part II-B tender a substantive, nonstipulative definition of marriage that is centered and analytically based on the norms which inform the way people actually live as couples. I go on to show that gay couples in fact meet this definition.

But marriage is also norm-invoking: when a relation is determined to be a marital one, that property, in turn, has normative consequences. In particular, it invokes a certain understanding of the relation of marriage to government. And so, Part III of this article examines, along several dimensions, various normative consequences and legal reforms that are suggested by the values that inform marriage. Along the way, I suggest that the lived experience of gay couples not only shows them as fulfilling the norms of marriage but can even indicate ways of improving marital law for everyone. The article concludes in Part IV with an examination of the social, religious, and legal reforms that are under way toward the recognition and support of gay marital relationships. Part of the chore of plumping for radical legal reform is to show that the reform is in fact possible—and that it does not cause the skies to fall.

II. Definitions of Marriage: Its Normative Content

A. Definitional Failures

1. Social and Legal Attempts to Define Marriage

Usually in religious, ethical, and legal thinking, issues are settled with reference to a thing's goodness. Yet oddly, the debate over gay marriage has focused not on whether the thing is good but on whether the thing can even exist. Those opposing gay marriage say that the very definition of marriage rules out the possibility that gay couples can be viewed as married.[6]

If one asks the average Jo(e) on the street what marriage is, the person generally just gets tongue-tied. Try it. The meaning of marriage is somehow supposed to be so obvious, so entrenched and ramified in daily life, that it is never in need of articulation.

Standard dictionaries, which track and make coherent common usages of terms, are unhelpfully circular. Most commonly, dictionaries define marriage in terms of spouses, spouses in terms of husband and wife, and husband and wife in terms of marriage.[7] In consequence, the various definitions do no work in explaining what marriage is and so simply end up assuming or stipulating that marriage must be between people of different sexes.

Legal definitions of marriage fare no better. Many state laws only speak of spouses or partners and do not actually make explicit that people must be of different sexes to marry.[8] During the early 1970s and again in the early 1980s, gays directly challenged these laws in four states, claiming that in accordance with common law tradition, whatever is not prohibited must be allowed, and that if these laws were judicially construed to require different-sex partners, then the laws constituted unconstitutional sex or sexual-orientation discrimination.[9] Gays lost all these cases, which the courts treated in dismissive, but revealing, fashion.[10]

The courts would first claim that the silence of the law notwithstanding, marriage automatically entails gender difference. The best known of these rulings is the 1974 case *Singer* v. *Hara,* which upheld Washington's refusal to grant a marriage license to two males. The case defined marriage as "the legal union of one man and one woman" as husband and wife.[11] This definition has become *the* legal definition of marriage, since it has been taken up into the standard law dictionary, *Black's Sixth Edition,* where the case is the only citation given in the section on marriage.[12]

Yet, the *Singer* definition tells us nothing whatever of the content of marriage. First, the qualification "as husband and wife" is simply circular. Since "husband" and "wife" mean people who are in a marriage with each other, the definition, as far as these terms go, presupposes the very thing to be defined. So what is left is that marriage is "the legal union of one man and one woman." Now, if the term "legal" here simply means "not illegal," then notice that a kiss after the prom can fit its bill: "the legal union of one man and one woman." We are told nothing of what "the union" is that is supposed to be the heart of marriage. The formulation of the definition serves no function other than to exclude from marriage—whatever it is—the people whom America views as destroyers of the American family, same-sex couples and polygamists: "*one* man and *one* woman." Like the ordinary dictionary definitions, the legal definition does no explanatory work.[13]

Nevertheless, the courts take this definition, turn around, and say that since this is what marriage *means,* gender discrimination and sexual-orientation discrimination is built right into the institution of marriage; therefore, since marriage itself is permitted, so, too, must be barring same-sex couples from it. Discrimination against gays, they hold, is not an illegitimate discrimination in marriage, indeed it is necessary to the very institution: No one would be married if gays were, for then marriage wouldn't be marriage. It took a gay case to reveal what marriage is, but the case reveals it, at least as legally understood, to be nothing but an empty space, delimited only by what it excludes—gay couples. And so the case has all the marks of being profoundly prejudicial in its legal treatment of gays.

2. Gender in Marital Law

If we shift from considering the legal definition of marriage to the legal practices of marriage, are there differences of gender that insinuate themselves into marriage, so that botched definitions aside, marriage does after all require that its pairings be of the male-female variety? There used to be major gender-based legal differences in marriage, but these have all been found to be unjust and have gradually been eliminated through either legislative or judicial means. For example, a husband used to have an obligation to take care of his wife's material needs without his wife (no matter how wealthy) having any corresponding obligation to look after her husband (however poor). Now both spouses are mutually and equally obliged.[14] At one time a husband could sell his wife's property without her consent; the wife had no independent power to make contracts. But these laws have not generally been in force since the middle of the last century and are now unconstitutional.[15] It used to be that a husband *by definition* could not rape his wife—one could as well rape oneself, the reasoning went. Now, while laws governing sexual relations between husbands and wives are not identical to those governing relations between (heterosexual) strangers, they are nearly so, and such differences as remain are in any case cast in gender-neutral terms.[16] Wives are legally protected from ongoing sexual abuse from husbands—whatever the nonlegal reality.

Now that gender distinctions have all but vanished from the legal *content* of marriage, there is no basis for the requirement that the legal form of marriage unite members of different sexes. The legal definition of marriage—"union of one man and one woman"—though doggedly enforced in the courts, is a dead husk that has been cast off by marriage as a living legal institution.[17]

3. Babies in Marital Law

Perhaps sensing the shakiness of an argument that rests solely on a stipulative definition of little or no content, the courts have tried to supplement the supposedly obvious requirement for gender disparity in access to marriage with appeal to reproduction. By assuming that procreation and rearing of children is essential to married life, the courts have implicitly given marriage a functional definition designed to eliminate lesbians and gay men from the ranks of the marriageable.[18] "As we all know" (the courts self-congratulatorily declare), lesbians are "constitutionally incapable" of bearing children by other lesbians, and gay men are incapable of siring children by other gay men.

But the legally acknowledged institution of marriage in fact does not track this functional definition. All states allow people who are over sixty to marry each other, with all the rights and obligations marriage entails, even though biological reality dictates that such marriages will be sterile. In Hawaii, the statute that requires women to prove immunity against rubella as a condition for getting a marriage license exempts women "who, by reason of age or other medically determined condition are not and never will be physically able to conceive children."[19] In 1984, Hawaii also amended its marriage statute to delete a requirement that "neither of the parties is impotent or physically incapable of entering into the marriage state."[20] This statutory latitude belies any claim that the narrow purpose of marriage is to promote and protect propagation.[21]

The functional definition is too broad as well. If the function of marriage is only to bear and raise children in a family context, then the state should have no objection to the legal recognition of polygamous marriages. Male-focused polygamous families have been efficient bearers of children; and the economies of scale afforded by polygamous families also make them efficient in the rearing of children.[22] So given the actual scope of legal marriage, reproduction and child rearing cannot be its purpose or primary justification.

This finding is further confirmed if we look at the rights and obligations of marriage, which exist independently of whether a marriage generates children and which frequently are not even instrumental to childbearing and rearing. While mutual material support might be viewed as guarding (indirectly) the interests of children, other marital rights, such as the immunity against compelled testimony from a spouse, can hardly be grounded in child-related purposes. Indeed, this immunity is waived when relations with one's own children are what is at legal stake, as in cases of alleged child abuse.[23]

The assumption that childrearing is a function uniquely tethered to the institution of heterosexual marriage also collides with an important but little acknowledged social reality. Many lesbian and gay male couples already are raising families in which children are the blessings of adoption, artificial insemination, surrogacy, or prior marriages. The country is experiencing something approaching a gay and lesbian baby boom.[24] Many more gays would like to raise or foster children. A 1988 study by the American Bar Association found that eight to ten million children are currently being raised in three million gay and lesbian households.[25] This statistic, in turn, suggests that around 6 percent of the U.S. population is made up of gay and lesbian families with children.[26] We might well ask what conceivable purpose can be served for these children by barring to their gay and lesbian parents the mutual cohesion, emotional security, and economic benefits that are ideally promoted by legal marriage.[27]

4. Marriage as a Creature of the State

If the desperate judicial and social attempts to restrict marriage and its benefits to heterosexual parents are conceptually disingenuous, unjust, and socially inefficient, the question arises: what is left of marriage? Given the emptiness of its standard justifications, should marriage as a legal institution simply be abolished? Ought we simply to abandon the legal institution in favor of a family policy that simply and directly looks after the interests of children, leaving all other possible familial relations on the same legal footing as commercial transactions?

Not quite; but to see what is left and worth saving, we need to take a closer look at the social realities of marriage. Currently, state-sanctioned marriage operates as a legal institution that defines and creates social relations. The law creates the status of husband and wife; it is not a reflection of or response to spousal relations that exist independently of law. This notion that the law "defines and creates social relations" can be clarified by looking at another aspect of family law, one which ordinary people might well find surprising, even shocking. If Paul consensually sires a boy and raises the boy in the way a parent does, then we are strongly inclined to think that he is the boy's father in every morally relevant sense. And we expect the law to reflect this moral status of the father. But the law does not see things this way; it does not reflect and respond to moral reality. For if it turns out that at the time of the boy's birth, his mother was legally married not to Paul but to Fred, the boy is declared by law to be Fred's son, and Paul is, legally speaking, a stranger to the boy. If the mother subsequently leaves Paul and denies him access to the child, Paul has no right at all even to explore legally the possibility that he might have some legislated rights to visit the boy—or so the Supreme Court declared in 1989.[28] Here the law defines and creates the relation of father and son—which frequently, but only by legal accident, happens to accord with the moral reality and lived experience of father and son.

Similarly, in the eyes of the law, marriage is not a social form that exists independently of the law and which marriage law echoes and manages. Rather, marriage is entirely a creature of the law—or as Hawaii's Supreme Court recently put it: "Marriage is a state-conferred legal partnership status."[29]

If we want to see what's left in the box of marriage, we need to abandon this model of legal marriage as constitutive of a status, and rather look at marriage as a form of living and repository of norms independent of law, a moral reality that might well be helped or hindered, but not constituted by the law.[30] Further, current legal marriage, at least as conceptualized by judges, with its definitional entanglements with gender and procreation, is likely to distract us from perceiving lived moral reality.

B. Marriage Defined

What is marriage? Marriage is intimacy given substance in the medium of everyday life, the day-to-day. Marriage is the fused intersection of love's sanctity and necessity's demand.

Not all loves or intimate relations count or should count as marriages. Culturally, we are disinclined to think of "great loves" as marriages. Antony and Cleopatra, Tristan and Isolde, Catherine and Heathcliff—these are loves that burn gloriously but too intensely ever to be manifested in a medium of breakfasts and tire changes. Nor are Americans inclined to consider as real marriages arranged marriages between heads of state who never see each other, for again the relations do not grow in the earth of day-to-day living.

Friendships, too, are intimate relations that we do not consider marital relations. Intimate relations are ones that acquire the character they have—that are unique—because of what the individuals in the relation bring to and make of it; the relation is a distinctive product of their separate individualities. Thus, intimate relations differ markedly from public or commercial transactions. For instance, there is nothing distinctive about your sales clerk that bears on the meaning of your buying a pair of socks from him. The clerk is just carrying out a role, one that from the buyer's perspective nearly anyone could have carried out. But while friendships are star cases of intimate relationships, we do not count them as marriages; for while a person might count on a friend in a pinch to take her to the hospital, friendly relations do not usually manifest themselves through such necessities of life. Friendships are for the sake of fun, and tend to break down when put to other uses. Friendships do not count as marriages, for they do not develop in the medium of necessity's demand.

On the other hand, neither do we count roommates who regularly cook, clean, tend to household chores and share household finances as married, even though they "share the common necessities of life." This expression is the typical phrase used to define the threshold requirement for being considered "domestic partners" in towns that have registration programs for domestic partners.[31] Neither would we even consider as married two people who were roommates and even blended their finances if that is all their relationship comprised. Sharing the day-to-day is, at best, an ingredient of marriage.

Marriage requires the presence and blending of both necessity and intimacy. Life's necessities are a mixed fortune: on the one hand, they frequently are drag, dross, and cussedness, yet on the other hand, they can constitute opportunity, abidingness, and prospect for nurture. They are the field across which, the medium through which, and the ground from which the intimacies which we consider marital flourish, blossom, and come to fruition.

III. The Normative and Legal Consequence of Marriage

A. The Legal Rights and Benefits of Marriage

This required blend of intimacy and everyday living explains much of the legal content of marriage. For example, the required blend means that for the relationship to work, there must be a presumption of trust between partners; and, in turn, when the relationship *is* working, there will be a transparency in the flow of information between partners—they will know virtually everything about each other. This pairing of trust and transparency constitutes the moral ground for the common law right against compelled testimony between spouses, and explains why this same immunity is not extended to (mere) friends.[32]

The remaining vast array of legal rights and benefits of marriage fit equally well this matrix of love and necessity—chiefly by promoting the patient tendency that such life requires (by providing for privacy, nurture, support, persistence) and by protecting against the occasions when necessity is cussed rather than opportune, especially when life is marked by crisis, illness, and destruction.[33]

First and foremost, state-recognized marriage changes strangers-at-law into next-of-kin with all the rights which this status entails. These rights include: the right to enter hospitals, jails and other places restricted to "immediate family" the right to obtain "family" health insurance and bereavement leave; the right to live in neighborhoods zoned "single family only"; and the right to make medical decisions in the event a partner is injured or incapacitated.

Both from the partners themselves and from the state, marriage provides a variety of material supports which ameliorate, to a degree, necessity's unfriendly intervals. Marriage requires mutual support between spouses. It provides income tax advantages, including deductions, credits, improved rates, and exemptions. It provides for enhanced public assistance in times of need. It governs the equitable control, division, acquisition, and disposition of community property. At death it guarantees rights of inheritance in the absence of wills—a right of special benefit to the poor, who frequently die intestate. For the wealthy, marriage virtually eliminates inheritance taxes between spouses, since spouses as of 1981 can make unlimited untaxed gifts to each other even at death.[34] For all, it exempts property from attachments resulting from one partner's debts. It confers a right to bring a wrongful death suit. And it confers the right to receive survivor's benefits.

Several marital benefits promote a couple's staying together in the face of changed circumstances. Included in the benefits are the right to collect unemployment benefits if one partner quits her job to move with her partner to a new location because the partner has obtained a new job there, and the right to obtain residency status for a noncitizen partner. Currently lesbians and gay men are denied all of these rights in consequence of being barred access to legal marriage, even though these rights and benefits are as relevant to committed gay relationships as to heterosexual marriages.

B. The Structuring of Lesbian and Gay Relationships

The portraits of gay and lesbian committed relationships that emerge from ethnographic studies suggest that in the way they typically arrange their lives, gay and lesbian couples fulfill in an exemplary manner the definition of marriage developed here.[35]

In gay relationships, the ways in which the day-to-day demands of necessity are typically fulfilled are themselves vehicles for the development of intimacy. It is true that gay and lesbian relationships generally divide duties between the partners—this is the efficient thing to do, the very first among the economies of scale that coupledom affords. But the division of duties is in the first instance a matter of personal preference and joint planning, in which decisions are made in part with an eye to who is better at doing any given task and who has free time—say, for ironing or coping with car dealerships. But adjustments are made in cases where one person is better at most things, or even everything. In these cases, the relation is made less efficient for the sake of equality between partners, who willingly end up doing things they would rather not do. Such joint decisions are made not from a sense of traditionally assigned duty and role, but from each partner's impulse to help out, a willingness to sacrifice, and a commitment to equality.[36] In these ways, both the development of intimacy through choice and the proper valuing of love are interwoven in the day-to-day activities of gay couples. Choice improves intimacy. Choice makes sacrifices meaningful. Choice gives love its proper weight.

C. Weddings and Licensing Considered

If this analysis of the nature of marriage is correct, then misguided is the requirement, found in most states, that beyond securing from government a marriage license, the couple, in order to be certifiably married, must also undergo a ceremony of solemnization, either in a church or before a justice of the peace.[37] For people are mistaken to think that the sacred valuing of love is something that can be imported from the outside, in public ceremonies invoking praise from God or community.[38] Even wedding vows can smack of cheap moral credit, since they are words, not actions. The sacred valuing of love must come from within and realize itself over time through little sacrifices in day-to-day existence. In this way, intimacy takes on weight and shine, the ordinary becomes the vehicle of the extraordinary, and the development of the marital relation becomes a mirror reflecting eternity. It is more proper to think of weddings with their ceremonial trappings and invocations as bon voyages than as a social institution which, echoing the legal institution of marriage, defines and confers marital status. In a gay marriage, the sanctifications that descend instantly through custom and ritual in many heterosexual marriages descend gradually over and through time—and in a way they are better for it. For the sacred values and loyal intimacies contained in such a marriage are a product of the relation itself; they are truly the couple's own.

The model of marriage advanced here is highly compatible with, indeed it recommends, what has been, until recently, by far the most usual form of marriage in Western civilization, namely, common-law marriage—in which there is no marriage license or solemnization. Currently only about one-fourth of the states legally acknowledge common-law marriages, but over the largest stretches of Western civilization, legally certifiable marriage was an arrangement limited almost exclusively to the wealthy, the noble—in short, the few.[39]

In a common-law arrangement, the marriage is at some point, as the need arises, culturally and legally acknowledged in retrospect as having existed all along. It is important to remember that as matter of law, the standard requirement of living together seven years is entirely evidentiary and not at all constitutive of the relation as a marriage.[40] So, for example, a child born in the third year of a common-law marriage is legitimate from the moment of its birth and need not wait four years as Mom and Dad log seven years together. The marriage was there in substance all along. The social and legal custom of acknowledging common-law marriage gives an adequately robust recognition to marriage as a lived arrangement and as a repository of values.

The securing of a marriage license is something the state may well want to encourage as a useful device in the administration of the legal benefits of marriage. But the licensing should not be seen as what legally constitutes the marriage when questions arise over whether the marriage in fact exists (say, in paternity, custody, or inheritance disputes). In turn, it is completely legitimate for the state to terminate marital benefits if in fact the couple gets a license but is not fulfilling the definition of marriage as a living arrangement. The state already investigates such cases of fraud when marriage licenses are secured simply to acquire an enhanced immigration status for one of the licensees.[41] Indeed, that immigration fraud through marriage licenses is even conceptually possible is a tacit recognition that marriage *simpliciter* is marriage as a lived arrangement, while legally certified marriage is and should be viewed as epiphenomenal or derivative—and not vice versa.

D. The Relation between Love and Justice

If intimate or private relations of a certain quality provide the content of marriage, what can the law and public policy provide to marriage? Why do we need legal marriage at all? Folk wisdom has it that both love and justice are blind. But they are blind in different ways, ways which reveal possible conflicts and tensions between love and justice in practice.[42]

Justice is blind—blindfolded—so that it may be a system of neutral, impersonal, impartial rules, a governance by laws, not by idiosyncratic, biased, or self-interested persons. Principles of justice in the modern era have been confected chiefly with an eye to relations at arm's length and apply paradigmatically to competitions conducted between conflicting interests in the face of scarce resources. Equal respect is the central concern of justice.[43]

Love is blind—(as the song goes) blinded by the light—because the lover is stutteringly bedazzled by the beloved. In love, we overlook failings in those whom we cherish. And the beloved's happiness, not the beloved's respect, is love's central concern.

Within the family, we agree that the distribution of goods should be a matter of feeling, care, concern, and sacrifice rather than one conducted by appeal to impartial and impersonal principles of equity. Indeed, if the impersonal principles of justice are constantly in the foreground of familial relations, intimacy is destroyed. If every decision in a family requires a judicial-like determination that each member got an equal share, then the care, concern, and love that are a family's breath and spirit are dead. Justice should not be front and center in family life.

But love may lead to intolerable injustices, even as a spinoff effect of one of its main virtues. In the blindness of love, people will love even those who beat them and humiliate them. Conversely, aggressors in these cases will feel more free to aggress against a family member than a stranger exactly because the family is the realm of love rather than of civic respect. Some of these humiliations are even occasioned by the distinctive opportunities afforded by traditional family life—in particular, society's misguided notion that everything that occurs behind the family's four walls is private, and so beyond legitimate inquiry.

Conflicts between love and justice can be relieved if we view marriage as a legal institution that allows for appeals to justice when they are needed. Justice should not be the motivation for loving relations, but neither should love and family exist beyond the reach of justice. Justice needs to be a reliable background and foundation for family life. Therefore, legal marriage should be viewed as a nurturing ground for social marriage, and not (as now) as that which legally defines and creates marriage and so tends to preclude legal examination of it.

E. The Contribution of Minorities to Family Law Reform

Marriage law should be a conduit for justice in moments of crisis—in financial collapse, in illness, at death—to guard against exploitation both in general and in the distinctive forms that marriage allows.

And, indeed, family law reform has generally been moving in this direction. State-defined marriage is an evolving institution, not an eternal verity. As noted, inequitable distributions of power by gender have been all but eliminated as a legally enforced part of marriage.[44] People at the margins of society have frequently provided the beacon for reform in family law. Already by the 1930s, black American culture no longer stigmatized children born out of wedlock, though whites continued to do so.[45] In 1968, the Supreme Court belatedly came to realize that punitively burdening innocent children is profoundly unjust, and subsequently, through a series of some thirty Supreme Court cases, illegitimacy has all but vanished as a condition legally affecting children born out of wedlock.[46] Further, black Americans provided to the mainstream the model of the extended family with its major virtue of a certain amount of open texture and play in the joints. In 1977, this virtue, too, was given constitutional status when the Supreme Court struck down zoning laws that discriminated against extended, typically black, families.[47]

Currently society and its discriminatory impulse make gay coupling very difficult. It is hard for people to live together as couples without having their sexual orientation perceived in the public realm, which in turn targets them for discrimination. Sharing a life in hiding is even more constricting than life in a nuclear family. Members of nongay couples are here asked to imagine what it would take to erase every trace of their own sexual orientation for even one week. Still, despite oppressive odds, gays have shown an amazing tendency to nest.[48] And those lesbian and gay male couples who have persevered show that the structure of more usual couplings is not a matter of destiny, but of personal responsibility. The so-called basic unit of society turns out not to be a unique immutable atom; it can adopt different parts, and be adapted to different needs.

F. Gay Couples As Models of Family Life

Gay life, like black culture, might even provide models and materials for rethinking family life and improving family law. I will now chart some ways in which this might be so—in particular drawing on the distinctive experiences and ideals of gay male couples.[49]

Take sex. Traditionally, a commitment to monogamy—to the extent that it was not simply an adjunct of property law, a vehicle for guaranteeing property rights and succession—was the chief mode of sacrifice imposed upon or adopted by married couples as a means of showing their sacred valuing of their relation. But gay men have realized that while couples may choose to restrict sexual activity in order to show their love for each other, it is not necessary for this purpose; there are many other ways to manifest and ritualize commitment. And so monogamy (it appears) is not an essential component of love and marriage. The authors of *The Male Couple* found that:

> [T]he majority of [gay male] couples, and *all* of the couples together for longer than five years, were not continuously sexually exclusive with each other. Although many had long periods of sexual exclusivity, it was not the ongoing expectation for most. We found that gay men *expect* mutual emotional dependability with their partners [but also believe] that relationship fidelity transcends concerns about sexuality and exclusivity.[50]

Both because marital sacrifices must be voluntary to be meaningful and because sexual exclusivity is not essential to marital commitment, the law should not impose monogamy on married couples. And, indeed, half the states have decriminalized adultery.[51]

Other improvements that take their cue from gay male couplings might include a recognition that marriages evolve over time. *The Male Couple* distinguishes six stages that couples typically pass through: blending (year one), nesting (years two and three), maintaining (years four and five), building (years six though ten), releasing (years eleven through twenty), and renewing (beyond twenty years).[52] Relations initially submerge individuality, and emphasize equality between partners, though the equality usually at first takes the form of complementarity rather than similarity.[53] With the passage of years individuality reemerges. Infatuation gives way to collaboration. The development of a foundational trust between the partners and a blending of finances and possessions, interestingly enough, occurs much later in the relationship—typically after ten years.[54] While the most important factor in keeping men together over the first ten years is finding compatibility, the most important factor for the second decade is a casting off of possessiveness, even as the men's lives become more entwined materially and by the traditions and rituals they have established.

The fact that relations evolve makes the top-down model of legal marriage as creator of relations particularly inappropriate for human life. Currently at law, the only recognition that marriages change and gather moral weight with time, is the vesting of one spouse's (typically the wife's) interests in the other's Social Security benefits after ten years of marriage.[55] More needs to be explored along these lines. For example, one spouse's guaranteed share of the other's inheritance might rise with the logging of years, rather than being the same traditionally fixed, one-third share, both on day one of the marriage and at its fiftieth anniversary.[56] Men's relations also suggest, however, that the emphasis that has been put on purely material concerns, like blended finances, as the marks of a relation in domestic partnership legislation and in a number of gay family law cases is misguided and fails to understand the dynamics and content of gay relations.[57]

In gay male relations, the relation itself frequently is experienced as a third element or "partner" over and above the two men.[58] This third element frequently has a physical embodiment in a home, business, joint avocation, or companion animal, but also frequently consists of joint charitable, civil, political, or religious work. The third element of the relation both provides a focus for the partners and relieves some of the confining centrifugal pressures frequently found in small families. Whether this might have legal implications deserves exploration—it certainly provides a useful model for small heterosexual families.

All longterm gay male relationships, *The Male Couple* reports, devise their own special ways of making the relations satisfying: "Their styles of relationship were developed without the aid of visible role models available to heterosexual couples."[59] This strongly suggests that legal marriage ought not to enforce any tight matrix of obligations on couples if their longterm happiness is part of the laws' stake. Rather the law ought to provide a ground in which relations can grow and change and even recognize their own endings.

IV. Conclusion: Religious and Legal Reforms Afoot

Given the nature of marriage and the nature of gay relations, it is time for the law to let them merge. And, indeed, there have been some general legal, social, and cultural shifts in the direction of acknowledging and supporting gay marriages. On January 1, 1995, gay marriages [became] legal in Sweden; they [became] legal in Denmark in 1989 and Norway in 1993.[60]

In 1993, Hawaii's Supreme Court ruled that Hawaii's marriage laws, which the court interpreted as requiring spouses to be of different sex presumptively violate Hawaii's Equal Rights Amendment, which bars sex discrimination. The court ruled that the laws could only be upheld on remand if shown to be necessary to further a compelling state interest.[61] The court preemptively found illegitimate the two standard justifications that have been used in other jurisdictions to claim state interests in restricting marriage to different-sex couples—namely, appeals to the very definition of marriage and procreation.[62] It looks promising, then, that the court will strike down the ban on same-sex marriages. And if one is married in Hawaii, one is married everywhere—thanks both to common-law tradition and to the U.S. Constitution's full faith and credit clause.[63]

As a matter of general cultural perception, recognitions of same-sex domestic partnerships are baby steps toward the legalization of gay marriage. A number of prestigious universities (including Harvard, Columbia, Stanford, the University of Chicago, and the University of Iowa) and prestigious corporations (including AT&T, Bank of America, Levi Strauss and Company, Lotus Development Corp., Apple Computer, Inc., Warner Brothers, MCA/Universal Inc., the *New York Times* and *Time* magazine) have extended to their employees' same-sex partners domestic partnership benefits, which include many of the privileges extended to their employees' heterosexual spouses.[64] These benefits typically include health insurance. Approximately thirty municipalities, beginning with Berkeley in 1984 and including San Francisco, Seattle, and New York City, have done the same, establishing in some cases a system of civic registrations for same-sex couples.[65]

In June 1994, Vermont became the first state to extend health insurance coverage to the same-sex partners of its state workers.[66] In August 1994, the California legislature passed a bill to establish a registry of domestic partners for both mixed-sex and same-sex couples and gave the partners three legal rights: (1) access to each other when one of them is hospitalized; (2) the use of California's short form will to designate each other as primary beneficiaries, and, most importantly; (3) the establishment of one's partner as conservator if one is incapacitated.[67] On September 11, Governor Pete Wilson vetoed the legislation, issuing a veto message that failed even to acknowledge the bill's impact on the lives of California's gay couples.[68]

In 1984, the General Assembly of the Unitarian-Universalist Association voted to "affirm the growing practice of some of its ministers in conducting services of union of gay and lesbian couples and urges member societies to support their ministers in this important aspect of our movement's ministry to the gay and lesbian community."[69]

In October 1993, the General Assembly of the Union of American Hebrew Congregations—which is the federation of U.S. and Canadian Reform synagogues—adopted a resolution calling for the legal and social recognition and support of gay domestic partners.[70]

Mainline Protestant denominations have ceased full-scale attacks on gay and lesbian relationships and are struggling with the issue of blessing them.[71] In June 1994, the General Assembly of the Presbyterian Church (U.S.A.) came within a few votes of permitting ministers to bless same-sex unions.[72] Also in June 1994, a draft proposal by the Episcopal bishops, after describing homosexuality as an orientation of "a significant minority of persons" that "cannot usually be reversed," went on to say that sexual relationships work best within the context of a committed life-long union: "We believe this is as true for homosexual relationships as for heterosexual relationships and that such relationships need and should receive the pastoral care of the church."[73] In October 1993, a draft report by a national Lutheran study group on sexuality had called for the blessing and even legal acknowledgment of loving gay relationships.[74]

These actions addressing the material dimensions of gay relationships through domestic partnership legislation and the spiritual dimensions of gay relationships through holy union ceremonies constitute true moral progress if they are steps toward the full legal and religious recognition of gay marriages. They are morally suspect, though, if they simply end up establishing and then entrenching a system of gay relations as separate but equal to heterosexual ones. To move from a position of no gay blessings and privileges to a structure of separate blessings and privileges is to traverse only the moral ground from the Supreme Court's 1857 *Dred Scott* ruling upholding the form of white supremacy under which blacks could not marry at all—slavery—to its 1896 *Plessy* v. *Ferguson* ruling upholding the reign of white supremacy that allowed blacks to marry blacks but not to marry whites.[75]

Whether domestic partnership legislation is a stepping-stone or a distracting impediment to gay marriage cannot be known categorically. Whether it is one or the other depends on a number of factors: the specific content of the legislation, the social circumstances of its passage, and the likely social consequences of its passage. I conjecture that states will take the route of domestic partnership legislation until they find out that a "separate but equal" structuring of gay and nongay relationships is hopelessly unwieldy. Then states will resort to the benefits of simplicity and recognize gay marriages straight out.

If the analysis of marriage in this article is correct, then marriage, like knowledge, is a common good, one which any number of people can share without its diminution for any one of the sharers. So heterosexuals have nothing to lose from the institutionalization of gay marriage. And the legalization of gay marriage is a moral advance over mere civil rights legislation. For civil rights legislation tends to treat gayness as though it were a property, like having an eye color or wearing an earring, which one could have in isolation from all other people. But gay marriage is an acknowledgement that gayness, like loving and caring, is a relational property, a connection between persons, a human bonding, one in need of tendance and social concern.

Notes

1. Harvey Fierstein, *Torch Song Trilogy* (New York: Villard Books, 1983; c. 1979), pp. 144–46.

2. See Karen Thompson and Julie Andrzejewski, *Why Can't Sharon Kowalski Come Home?* (San Francisco: Spinsters/Aunt Lute, 1988).

3. Eventually, Thompson did get guardianship of Kowalski, but only after Kowalski's parents withdrew from the field of battle. A Minnesota appeals court held that "this choice [of guardianship] is further supported by the fact that Thompson and Sharon are a family of affinity, which ought to be accorded respect." In re Guardianship of Kowalski, 478 N.W.2d 790, 796 (Minn. 1991).

4. *Coon* v. *Joseph*, 237 Cal. Rptr. 873, 877–78 (Cal. Ct. App. 1987).

5. As a subsidiary matter, I also advocate domestic partnership legislation to the extent that such legislation is a determinate step toward the realization of gay legal marriage and not a distraction from or new hurdle to this goal. See below, Part IV.

6. See, e.g., *Adams* v. *Howerton*, 486 F. Supp. 1119, 1123 (C.D. Cal. 1980) (holding that under the immigration and Nationality Act a gay man could not be considered an "immediate relative" of another with whom he had lived for years and had had a marriage ceremony). "Thus there has been for centuries a combination of scriptural and canonical teaching under which a 'marriage' between persons of the same sex was unthinkable and, by definition, impossible." Id.

Similarly, in 1991, Hawaii's Director of the Department of Health argued before Hawaii's Supreme Court: "The right of persons of the same sex to marry one another does not exist because marriage, by definition and usage, means a special relationship between a man and a woman." *Baehr* v. *Lewin* 852 P.2d 44, 61 (Haw. 1993).

7. *The Concise Oxford Dictionary* (3d ed., 1964), pp. 594, 746, 1241, 1478, 1493, for example, offers the following definitions:

"Marriage: relation between married persons, wedlock."

"Married: united in wedlock."

"Wedlock: the married state."

"Spouse: husband or wife."

"Husband: man joined to woman by marriage."

"Wife: married woman esp. in relation to her husband."

8. For example, "Kentucky statutes do not specifically prohibit marriage between persons of the same sex, nor do they authorize the issuance of a marriage license to such persons." *Jones* v. *Hallahan*, 501 S.W.2d 588, 589 (Ky. 1973). One of the very first gay marriage cases—one from Minnesota—also dealt with a state statute that failed to expressly prohibit same-sex marriages. *Baker* v. *Nelson*, 191 N.W.2d 185 (Minn. 1971), appeal dismissed, 409 U.S. 810 (1972).

9. *De Santo* v. *Bamsicy*, 476 A.2d 952 (Pa. 1984) (two persons of the same sex cannot contract a common-law marriage notwithstanding the state's recognition of common-law marriages between persons of different sexes); *Singer* v. *Hara*, 522 P.2d 1187 (Wash. 1974); *Jones*, 501 S.W.2d at 588; *Baker*, 191 N.W.2d at 185.

10. Other cases that, in one way or another, have held that gays cannot marry are *Adams*, 486 F. Supp. at 1119; Succession of Bascot, 502 So. 2d 1118, 1127–30 (La. 1987) (holding that a man cannot be a "concubine" of another man); *Slayton* v. *Texas*, 633 S.W.2d 934, 937 (Tex. 1982) (stating that same-sex marriage is impossible in Texas); *Jennings* v. *Jennings*, 315 A.2d 816, 820 n.7 (Md. 1974) (explaining that "Maryland does not recognize a marriage between persons of the same sex"); *Dean* v. *District of Columbia*, No. CA 90-13892, slip op. at 18–21 (D.C. Super. Ct. Dec. 30, 1991) (invoking passages from Genesis, Deuteronomy, Matthew, and Ephesians to hold that "societal recognition that it takes a man and a woman to form a marital relationship is older than Christianity itself"), in re Estate of Cooper, 564 N.Y.S.2d 684, 687 (N.Y. Sup. Ct. 1990) (refusing to "elevat[e] homosexual unions to the same level achieved by the marriage of two people of the opposite sex"); *Anonymous* v. *Anonymous*, 325 N.Y.S.2d 499, 500 (N.Y., Sup. CL. 1971) (stating that "[m]arriage is and always has been a contract between a man and a woman").

11. *Singer*, 522 P.2d at 1193.

12. *Black's Law Dictionary* (6th ed. 1990), p. 972.

13. Even the highly analytical historian John Boswell, in his recent book on the history of gay

marriage, fares no better in coming up with a definition of marriage: "It is my understanding that most modern speakers of English understand the term 'marriage' to refer to what the partners expect to be a permanent and exclusive union between two people, which would produce legitimate children if they chose to have children, and which creates mutual rights and responsibilities, legal, economic, and moral." John Boswell, *Same-Sex Unions in Premodern Europe* (New York: Villard Books, 1994), p. 10; cf. Boswell, p. 190. But if one asks "what partners?" "what union?" "what rights?" and "what responsibilities?" I fear the answer in each instance must be "marital ones," in which case the definition goes around in the same small circle as the law. And legitimate children just are children of a marriage, so that component of the definition is circular as well.

14. Harry D. Krause, *Family Law in a Nutshell*, 2d ed. (St. Paul, Minn.: West Publishing Co., 1986), p. 92 (hereinafter *Family Law*).

15. Ibid., pp. 96–103. See, e.g., *Kirchberg* v. *Feenstra*, 450 U.S. 455 (1981) (invalidated Louisiana's community property statute that gave the husband, as the family's "head and master," the unilateral right to dispose of property jointly owned with his wife without her consent).

16. *Family Law*, pp. 127–29.

17. "However unpleasant, outmoded or unnecessary, whatever sex discrimination remains in family law is trivial in comparison with the inequality of spouses that result from family facts, from the traditional role division which places the husband into the money-earner role and the wife into the home where she acquires neither property nor marketable skills." *Family Law*, p. 146.

18. See *Singer* v. *Hara*, 522 P.2d 1187, 1195 (Wash. 1974).

19. *Baehr* v. *Lewin*, 852 P.2d 44, 50 n.7 (Haw. 1993) (quoting Haw. Rev. Stat. §572–7[a] [Supp. 1992]).

20. Id. at 48 n.1 (quoting Haw. Rev. Stat. 580–21 [1985]).

21. Id. at 48.

22. See Dirk Johnson, "Polygamists Emerge from Secrecy, Seeking Not Just Peace, But Respect," *New York Times,* April 9, 1991, p. A22.

23. *Family Law*, p. 131.

24. See, e.g., Susan Chira, "Gay and Lesbian Parents Grow More Visible," *New York Times*, September 30, 1993, p. Al; Daniel Coleman, "Gay Parents Called No Disadvantage," *New York Times*, December 2, 1992, p. B7; "Homosexuality Does Not Make Parent Unfit, Court Rules," *New York Times*, June 22, 1994, p. A8.

25. Editors of the *Harvard Law Review, Sexual Orientation and the Law* 119 (1990).

26. Craig R. Dean, "Legalize Gay Marriage," *New York Times*, September 28, 1991 §1, p. 19.

27. Andrew Sullivan, "Here Comes the Groom: A (Conservative) Case for Gay Marriage," *New Republic*, August 1989, p. 22.

28. *Michael H.* v. *Gerald D.*, 491 U.S. 110 (1989).

29. *Baehr* v. *Lewin*, 852 P.2d 44, 58 (Haw. 1993).

30. The Supreme Court's three "right to marry" cases implicitly acknowledge that marriage is a social reality and repository of norms, indeed of rights, independent of statutory law, since the right to marry is a substantive liberty right which overrides, trumps, and voids statutory marital law. *Loving* v. *Virginia*, 388 U.S. 1, 12 (1967) (voiding laws barring blacks and whites from marrying each other); *Zablocki* v. *Redhail*, 434 U.S. 374 (1978) (voiding law barring child support scofflaws from marrying); *Turner* v. *Safley*, 482 U.S. 78, 94–99 (1987) (voiding regulation barring prisoners from marrying).

31. See, e.g., City of Berkeley, California, Domestic Partnership Policy, Statement of General Policy, December 4, 1984, quoted in Harry D. Krause, *Family Law: Cases, Comments and Questions*, 3rd ed. (1990), p. 159.

32. See *Family Law*, pp. 131–32.

33. *Baehr* 852 P.2d at 59 (catalogues the most salient rights and benefits that are contingent upon marital status). The benefits discussed in this section are drawn from this case and from a catalogue of marital privileges given in a 1993 Georgia Supreme Court case, *Van Dyck* v. *Van Dyck*, 425 S.E.2d 853 (Ga. 1993) (Sears-Collins, J., concurring) (holding that a state law authorizing

cutoff of alimony payments to a former spouse who enters into a voluntary cohabitation does not apply when the cohabitation in question is a lesbian one). See also 1 Hayden Curry and Denis Clifford, *A Legal Guide for Lesbian and Gay Couples,* R. Leonard, ed., 6th ed. (Berkeley, Calif.: Nole Press, 1991), p. 2.

34. *Family Law*, p. 107.

35. See Alan P. Bell and Martin S. Weinberg, *Homosexualities: A Study of Diversity among Men and Women* (New York: Simon and Schuster, 1978); Philip Blumstein and Pepper Schwartz, *American Couples: Money, Work, Sex* (New York: Morrow, 1983); David McWhirter and Andrew M. Mattison, *The Male Couple: How Relationships Develop* (Englewood Cliffs, N.J.: Prentice-Hall, 1984); Suzanne Sherman, *Lesbian and Gay Marriages: Private Commitments, Public Ceremonies* (Philadelphia: Temple University Press, 1992); Kath Weston, *Families We Choose: Lesbians, Gays, Kinship* (New York: Columbia University Press, 1991).

36. See Weston, *Families We Choose*, pp. 149–50.

37. *Family Law*, pp. 47–48.

38. On sacred values, see generally Douglas MacLean, "Social Values and the Distribution of Risk," in *Values at Risk*, Douglas MacLean, ed. (Totowa, N.J.: Rowman & Allanheld, 1986), pp. 85–93.

39. *Family Law*, p. 50. For a review of the literature on the vagaries of marriage as an institution, see Lawrence Stone, "Sex in the West: The Strange History of Human Sexuality," *New Republic,* July 8, 1985, pp. 25–37. See also Boswell, *Same-Sex Unions in Premodern Europe,* pp. 32–33, 35.

40. *Family Law,* p. 49.

41. Ibid. p. 47.

42. This section draws on some ideas in Claudia Mills and Douglas MacLean, "Love and Justice," *QQ: Report from the Institute for Philosophy and Public Policy,* Fall 1989, pp. 12–15.

43. For a classic statement of this position, see Ronald Dworkin, *Taking Rights Seriously* (Cambridge, Mass.: Harvard University Press, 1978), pp. 180–83, 272–78.

44. Ibid., 1944; text accompanying notes 14–17.

45. Gunnar Myrdal, *An American Dilemma* (New York: Harper & Row, 1944; 1962), p. 935.

46. *Family Law,* pp. 154-55.

47. *Moore* v. *City of East Cleveland, Ohio,* 431 U.S. 494 (1977).

48. Ibid., note 35 (studies of gay couples).

49. Lesbian legal theorists have generally supposed marriage too sexist an institution to be salvaged, and lesbian moral theorists also have found traditional forms of coupling highly suspect. Some recommend communal arrangements as the ideal for lesbians. Others have proposed that lovers should not even live together. See Paula L. Ettelbrick, "Since When Is Marriage a Path to Liberation?" *OUT/LOOK,* Fall 1989, pp. 9, 14–17; Nancy D. Polikoff, "We Will Get What We Ask For: Why Legalizing Gay and Lesbian Marriage Will Not 'Dismantle Legal Structure of Gender in Every Marriage,'" *Virginia Law Review* 79 (1993): 1535; Sarah Lucia Hoagland, *Lesbian Ethics: Toward New Value* (1988); Claudia Card, *Lesbian Choices* (1994).

50. McWhirter and Mattison, *The Male Couple,* p. 285.

51. *Family Law,* p. 130.

52. McWhirter and Mattison, *The Male Couple,* pp. 15–17.

53. Ibid., pp. 31–33.

54. Ibid., pp. 104–105.

55. *Family Law,* pp. 369, 386.

56. Ibid., p. 104.

57. I am thinking in particular of the 1989 case *Braschi* v. *Stahl,* 543 N.E.2d 49 (N.Y. 1989), in which New York's highest court ruled that two men who had been living together for years with blended finances—whom the court called "unmarried lifetime partners"—qualified as "family members" for the purposes of New York's law governing succession rights on apartment leases. At the time, this was considered the most progressive gay family law case of record. And in one regard

the case was progressive. It proposed that the concept "family" should be given an operational definition: if it waddles, flaps, and quacks like a family, then it is a family. But then the case went on to dwell almost exclusively on the material and monetary side of life, so much so that in the end it appeared almost to be a case promoting property fights rather than familial relations. And, indeed, this case has had no progeny.

Two years later, the same court abandoned any effort to define family relationships operationally or functionally and held that a lesbian had no rights at all to visit a daughter whom she had jointly reared with the girl's biological mother. *Alison D.* v. *Virginia M.,* 572 N.E.2d 27 (N.Y. 1991). Here only biology mattered. The same court held later that year that grandparents do have a right to visit their grandchildren even over the objections of both parents. In re *Emanuel S.,* 577 N.E.2d 77 (N.Y 1991). Clearly much work remains to be done in bringing law into accord with what families and marriages functionally are and operationally do. Mere reference to the material circumstances of marriage will not do that work.

58. McWhirter and Mattison, *The Male Couple,* p. 285.

59. Ibid., p. 286.

60. "A Swede Deal for Couples," *Advocate,* July 12, 1994, p. 16.

61. *Baehr* v. *Lewin,* 852 P.2d 44, 60–68 (Haw. 1993). Subsequently, Hawaii's legislature voted that marriages in Hawaii must have mixed-sex partners; but since the court had already evaluated this condition in its constitutional analysis of Hawaii's laws, the legislature's vote seems to be a case of moral grandstanding and political posturing. "Hawaii Legislature Blocks Gay Marriage," *New York Times,* April 27, 1994, at A18.

62. *Baehr,* 852 P.2d at 48 n.1, 61 (Haw. 1993).

63. "Full Faith and Credit shall be given in each State to the public Acts, Records, and judicial Proceedings of every other State." U.S. Const. art. IV, §1.

Gay marriage is also gradually coming into law through the back door of same-sex second parent adoptions. At least six states have allowed the lesbian partner of a woman with a child to adopt—become the second mother of—the child. But if Heather has at law two moms, what is the relation between her two parents? Strangers at law? Surely not. "Court Grants Parental Rights to Mother of Lesbian Lover," *New York Times,* September 12, 1993, §1, p. 42.

64. "Two Universities Give Gay Partners Same Benefits as Married Couples," *New York Times,* December 24, 1992, p. A10; "Domestic Partnership Benefits Found Not to Increase Employer Costs," *Windy City Times,* June 4, 1992, p. 9; *Frontiers* (Los Angeles), October 7, 1994, p. 16.

65. "Workers' Partners Get Benefit of Health Plan," *New York Times,* October 31, 1993, §1, p. 40.

66. "Vermont Union Wins Benefits for Partners," *New York Times,* June 13, 1994, p. A12. In some jurisdictions, including Vermont, such benefits are also extended to unmarried but cohabiting heterosexual couples.

67. "Senate Passes Historic Domestic Partners Bill," *Frontiers* (Los Angeles), September 9, 1994, p. 17.

68. "Domestic Partner Bill Vetoed in California," *New York Times,* September 13, 1994, p. A6; see *Frontiers* (Los Angeles), October 7, 1994, p. 36.

69. Paul H. Landen, "Unitarian-Universalist Views on Issues in Human Sexuality" (unpublished Ph.D. thesis, Michigan State University, 1992), p. 134.

70. General Assembly, Union of American Hebrew Congregations, Recognition for Lesbian and Gay Partnerships (October 21–25, 1993).

71. See William N. Eskridge Jr., "A History of Same-Sex Marriage," *Virginia Law Review* 79 (1993): 1419, 1497-1502.

72. "Presbyterians Try to Resolve Long Dispute," *New York Times,* June 17, 1994, p. A9.

73. "Episcopal Draft on Sexuality Tries to Take a Middle Course," *New York Times,* June 26, 1994, §1, p. 9.

74. "Lutherans to Decide Whether to Sanction Homosexual Unions," *New York Times,*

October 21, 1993, p. Al; "Lutheran Church Stalled in Drafting Sex Statement," *New York Times,* November 26, 1993, p. A14.

In marked contrast, the Catholic Church has dug in its heels on the issue. In February 1994, Pope John Paul II issued a hundred-page "Letter to Families." Among other things, the letter sent a message to Catholics to refrain from supporting the notion of gay and lesbian marriages, calling such unions "a serious threat to the family and society" and viewing them as "inappropriately conferring an institutional value on deviant behavior." The pope's own definition of marriage, however, seems to be as circular in its exclusion of gays as those definitions explored above (See above Part II, A.1): "Marriage . . . is constituted by the covenant whereby a man and a woman establish between themselves a partnership for their whole life." "Pope Calls Gay Marriage Threat to Family," *New York Times,* February 23, 1994, p. A2. The complete English language text of the Letter is published in *Origins: CNS Documentary Service* 23:37 (March 3, 1994): 637–59.

75. *Dred Scott* v. *Sandford,* 60 U.S. (19 How.) 393 (1857); *Plessy* v. *Ferguson,* 163 U.S. 537 (1896). in 1883, the Supreme Court in a cursory opinion had upheld against constitutional challenge anti-miscegenation laws. *Pace* v. *Alabama,* 106 U.S. 583 (1883). These laws were finally struck down in 1967. *Loving* v. *Virginia,* 388 U.S. 1 (1967).

14

Same-Sex Marriage:
A Philosophical Defense[*]

Ralph Wedgwood

1. Introductory

In this paper, I give what I will call a "philosophical defense" of same-sex marriage. More precisely, I argue that the present system, which reserves the institution of marriage for opposite-sex couples, and excludes same-sex couples, is intolerably unjust.

I call my defense of same-sex marriage a "philosophical" defense for two reasons. My first reason is to emphasize that I am not arguing about any *constitutional* or *legal* questions—such as, for example, whether the constitution of Hawaii, or the United States Constitution, implies that same-sex couples have a legal right to civil marriage. These questions have been dealt with by other writers elsewhere.[1] I am arguing about a *political* question: about what sort of laws or social institutions we *ought to* have. My argument is designed to apply just as effectively to societies that lack constitutionally guaranteed civil rights, such as Britain, as to societies that have such constitutional rights, such as the United States or South Africa.

My second reason for calling my argument a "philosophical defense" is to signal its most serious limitation—namely, the lack of any serious consideration of the relevant empirical questions, such as what the consequences of introducing same-sex marriage would be. My main focus throughout is not on these empirical questions, but on the fundamental values that are at stake—especially the values of justice and the common good, democracy, freedom, and equality. Of course, my argument will have to rely on empirical assumptions at certain

*For helpful comments on earlier drafts, I thank Alex Byrne, Erin Kelly, David Lyons, Vann McGee, Richard Mohr, Charles Morcom, Michael Otsuka, Andrew Sabl, Seana Shiffrin, Judith Thomson, Ramon Vela, and Stuart White.

points. I will carefully flag each of these assumptions when it first appears; but although I am convinced that these assumptions are true, I shall not try to defend these assumptions here.

The political question that I am concerned with, about whether the law should allow same-sex marriage, is clearly different from all the *ethical* questions that concern individual conduct, including the question whether it is right or wrong (ethically speaking) for two people of the same sex to get married. Indeed, my argument for same-sex marriage is not just focused on a different issue from these ethical views about whether it is right or wrong to marry someone of one's own sex, it is *independent* of all such views.

My reason for making my argument independent of such ethical views is simply that all such views are intensely controversial. Some people believe that entering into a same-sex marriage would sometimes be the right thing to do, while others are firmly convinced that it would always be wrong. This disagreement about same-sex marriage is typically rooted in a disagreement about homosexuality, since it is generally assumed that marriage involves sexual relations.

The advantage of my neutral defense of same-sex marriage is that it allows us simply to *agree to disagree* about these disputed ethical questions, and to decide the political question on other grounds. "Agreeing to disagree" about a question involves finding a way to live and act together with the people with whom you disagree that is itself based on agreement. Agreeing to disagree on some question is easiest if the disputed question is simply *irrelevant* to the collective decisions that you have to make together. Even if the disputed question is not simply irrelevant, however, it may be possible to agree that other principles are more important in the context, and so to base your collective decisions on those shared principles. Finding ways to agree to disagree is extremely important in any pluralistic society that aspires to be democratic. Perhaps certain fervent atheists believe that society would be better off if religious belief were to die out. Still, they may be able to "agree to disagree" with religious believers if they accept that, in the context, respecting freedom is more important than achieving their ideal of a postreligious society.

My argument then will rely, not on any disputed ethical view about homosexuality, but on the more widely held values of *democracy, freedom,* and *equality.* First, I argue that the values of freedom and democracy support a certain view of the essential rationale of the institution of marriage—that is, of the fundamental way in which marriage serves the common good (or at least would serve the common good if it were a just social institution). Assuming this account of marriage's rationale, I then argue that the ban on same-sex marriage conflicts with the value of equality, and is for that reason seriously unjust. Finally, in arguing against some proposed justifications for the ban on same-sex marriage, I appeal again to the values of freedom and democracy.[2]

In principle then, even people who believe that homosexual relationships are deviant and inferior to traditional heterosexual marriages should find my defense of same-sex marriage convincing—so long as they also believe that it is more important for social institutions to respect the values of democracy, freedom, and equality, than for them to affirm this view of the moral superiority of heterosexuality. I have also tried to rely on the least controversial ideas about democracy, freedom, and equality, that I could. My goal is to construct a defense of same-sex marriage on the basis of the weakest assumptions possible. In this way, I hope that something like the argument presented here could be the basis for a widespread consensus in favor of same-sex marriage.

Besides its political utility, my argument may also have some philosophical interest. Many philosophers find the institution of marriage puzzling: why, after all, should the state become involved in people's intimate personal relationships? Many people assume that marriage necessarily involves the state's "legitimizing," or encouraging approval of, certain intimate relationships—implicitly by contrast with other, less favored relationships. But if this assumption is correct, marriage itself seems quite dubious, since it is doubtful that it is appropriate for the state to "legitimize" certain intimate relationships at all, let alone to do so at the expense of other relationships.[3] Although I do not offer a full defense of marriage (I argue only that the ban on same-sex marriage is unjust), I do propose an alternative view of marriage; and my alternative view may make marriage seem at least somewhat less dubious.

2. What Is Marriage?

In spite of the large role that religion has played in its history, marriage is clearly not an essentially religious institution, since secular civil marriage is evidently a kind of marriage.[4] So what are the essential features of marriage?

It seems that marriage has always involved something like *marriage law.* In modern pluralistic societies, marriage law is part of civil law. In the past, marriage law was often part of religious law rather than civil law—such as Christian canon law, which was administered by the church courts, or Jewish religious law, which was administered by rabbinical courts. In those nonpluralistic societies, however, the religious authorities were just as much a valid source of law as the civil authorities. So it might seem that marriage is simply a *legal* institution, in the sense that its nature is entirely determined by the marriage laws that are laid down by some socially recognized authority.

This legalistic assumption has been common in recent discussions of same-sex marriage; but it is, I think, a mistake. The legal character of marriage is not enough by itself to explain the institution's special centrality and importance in the lives of so many people. To explain why marriage plays this central role in people's lives, we must appeal, not only to marriage's legal character, but also to its *social meaning,* the web of shared assumptions about marriage that are common knowledge in society.

It is essential to marriage, it seems to me, that it has such a social meaning—that is, that it is an extraordinarily *familiar* social institution, which practically everyone has heard about and has some understanding of. For marriage to exist, it is not enough that there are certain laws on the books; these laws must also be surrounded by a familiar social practice of the appropriate kind. Imagine a society that had some laws on the books that defined a certain legal relationship, which in fact involved all the legal rights and obligations that marriage confers in our society, but which no one except a few legal theorists had ever heard of. Suppose that this society also recognized a relationship that had a different name, which was undergirded by generally recognized religious laws very similar to Roman Catholic marriage laws, and was universally familiar and understood, and generally favored by couples who wanted to share their lives together. In this society, it seems to me, it is the second relationship that is marriage, while the first, purely legal relationship is just some obscure sort of legal covenant.

So it is essential to marriage that it has a social meaning. This social meaning is a cultural phenomenon, consisting above all in the great familiarity of the institution, and the prevalence of certain shared understandings about what the institution involves. These shared understandings or assumptions vary over time and from place to place, but there is a basic core which seems essential to marriage.

First, marriage is understood to be a relationship between exactly two people.[5] It is, I think, always assumed that a married couple will normally be living together and have at least at some time had sex together; that they have shared finances, or at least will support each other economically if necessary; and that the two married people have a serious commitment to sustaining their relationship. It is generally assumed that both spouses will share in the activity of running their household (even if they play very different roles in that activity). In particular, it is assumed that if the married couple have children together, then they will share the responsibilities of parenthood.[6]

Marriage enables the married couple to make it public that they are in this sort of relationship, simply by exploiting these general assumptions about marriage: you can tell people "We are married," with the result that they will immediately come to expect that you are living together, have had sex, have shared finances, are committed to sustaining this relationship, and so on.

Saying "We are married" has this effect only because of the great familiarity of marriage. Suppose that I told you, "John and I went to the Odin-worshiping temple last week and had a ceremony to become each other's gloggle." You would have no idea what I meant. I would have to offer a lengthy explanation. Or suppose that I told you, "John and I became each other's domestic partner at City Hall last week." You would not have to be extraordinarily ignorant to wonder, "Do domestic partnerships expire every year unless they are renewed? Should I assume that you are lovers, or just that you are roommates who want to make sure that each of you can continue to rent the apartment in case the other roommate dies? Have you made a commitment to support your domestic partner even if he loses his job, or do you just share the chore of buying groceries?" Again, I could not convey the information that I want to convey without a lengthy explanation.

This social meaning is, it seems to me, one of the essential features of marriage. But at least some of the legal aspects of marriage are no less essential, and closely bound up with its social meaning. The legal aspects of marriage fall into the following three categories.

First, it is the law that confers the marital status itself. When one learns that two people are married, one takes this to mean that those people have met all the legal requirements for being married. If people known not to be legally married say "We are married," they are understood to be speaking metaphorically or in jest. The fact that the marital status is conferred by law explains why it is not a controversial question whether or not two people are married. If two people are married, then there is typically general agreement that they are married, even among people who take very different views of those people and of the kind of life that they lead.

Second, marriage in many ways resembles a contract: each spouse has certain legally binding rights and obligations with respect to the other.[7] Many of these mutual rights and obligations have the function of assuring the spouses that they can rely economically on each other. Nowadays, these rights include, most notably, the right to spousal support; the right (in the event of divorce or separation) to alimony and an equitable division of property; and the right to inherit even if there is no will. Another group of mutual rights reflects the idea that spouses are each other's "next of kin." Nowadays, these rights include the legal authority to act for an incapacitated spouse; hospital visitation rights; and a right to priority in claiming human remains. These rights express the general assumption that spouses have a more intimate relationship with each other than with anyone else, and are committed to maintaining this relationship: hence, it is assumed, one's spouse will understand one's interests best, and is likely to have one's interests at heart; so one's spouse is best placed to act on one's behalf when necessary. The fact that marriage involves such legally binding obligations is crucial for reinforcing the assumption that married people have a serious commitment to maintaining their relationship.

Third, the state often provides certain special benefits for married couples, over and above the marital status itself and the enforcement of spousal obligations. (In a similar way, many nongovernment organizations, especially employers, have a policy of giving certain special benefits to married couples, most notably health insurance.) Some of these special legal benefits reflect the expectation that the married couple have shared finances: under current law, married couples can file their taxes jointly, and property transfers between spouses are not taxed. Other such special legal benefits include the right to visit one's spouse in prison; the right not to be compelled to testify against one's spouse; and the right of a foreign spouse to receive preferential immigration treatment. These benefits reflect the expectation that marriage is a longterm intimate relationship: it would be thought unacceptably cruel to deny spousal visits to prisoners, to keep spouses apart through immigration barriers, or to compel anyone to testify against his or her spouse.

This third legal aspect of marriage—the benefits that the state (like certain other organizations such as employers) provides for married couples, in addition to the marital status itself and the enforcement of spousal obligations—is certainly an important aspect of marriage today. But these special legal benefits do not seem to be *essential* to the institution of marriage itself. Marriage would still exist if there were no tax breaks for married couples. What is really essential to marriage, I propose, is the legally conferred marital status, the legally binding mutual commitments, and the social meaning of the relationship.

The claim that these special legal benefits are not essential to marriage implies that a justification of marriage need not itself involve a justification of these special benefits. There ought to be a *separate* justification for attaching these special legal benefits to marriage. Such a justification would have to show that in attaching these benefits to marriage alone, the state is not unjustly discriminating against single people, or against unmarried couples. (The most plausible justification may be that these benefits are uniquely appropriate for couples who have a longterm intimate relationship involving economic and domestic cooperation; and rather than employing some intrusive test to determine whether a couple has a relationship of this kind, it is reasonable for the state simply to attach these benefits to marriage. But we need not consider this question here.)

The essential elements of marriage—the legally binding mutual commitments, the legally conferred marital status, and the social meaning of marriage—together form a coherent package. The legally binding mutual commitments of marriage are at least roughly standardized throughout society, and, when necessary, enforced, thus providing an assurance that these commitments will be fulfilled.[8] This reinforces and standardizes society's shared assumptions about marriage, since the mutual commitments of marriage clearly reflect these shared assumptions; thus, marriage has a clear social meaning that is understood, not just by a limited subculture, but by society as a whole. If the law attaches certain standardized rights and obligations to marriage, then the law must determine who counts as married and who does not; and the fact that the law determines who counts as married also ensures that there is general agreement about who is married and who is not, thus allowing a married couple to be regarded as married, not just by their circle of friends, but by society as a whole.

Consider what might happen if the law did not determine who was married and who was not. Suppose that individuals were free to form whatever legally binding contracts they wished, and nongovernment associations (such as religious organizations) were free to call any relationship a "marriage" if they wished; but no public authority made any attempt to determine which relationships counted as marriages and which did not. The risk is that this situation would lead to ever-increasing confusion about what the term "marriage" implies. Different associations might take very different views of what is required for a couple to be married: some associations might regard certain vows that are not legally binding as sufficient for marriage; some associations might allow polygamous marriages; some associations might allow marriages that expire every year unless renewed; and some of these "marriages" might become common between pairs of friends whose relationship is entirely non-sexual. This would confuse the social meaning of marriage so much that there would no longer be any clear shared understanding of marriage. Except within limited subcultures, saying "We are married" would convey little information. The point is not that such confusion is necessarily the most likely result of this situation. The point is that if we are to be assured that marriage will not cease to have any clear social meaning in this way, then marriage must be insulated from the risk of such confusion; and the only effective way to insulate marriage from this risk is for marital status to be determined by law.[9]

For these reasons then, it is essential to marriage that it is undergirded by marriage law; and marriage law requires some generally recognized authority (such as the state or the religious authorities) as its source. In a pluralistic society, however, there is only one authority that is generally recognized as a valid source of law, namely, the state. So, in a pluralistic society, marriage law has to be part of the civil laws of the state.

In sum, marriage is a legally conferred relationship between two people, involving legally binding mutual commitments; the character of these commitments reflects society's shared understandings and assumptions about this relationship, assumptions that make this relationship uniquely familiar and well understood; and the core of these assumptions is that marriage involves both sexual intimacy and sharing the necessities of life.[10]

3. Why Marriage Might Further the Common Good

Several writers have argued that the chief justification for the institution of marriage is that it encourages married life, which tends (according to these writers) to be a particularly virtuous or valuable way of life.[11]

If this were the official justification for the institution of marriage, the government, in giving this justification, would have to appeal explicitly to this view about the value of married life—a view that we might call "conjugalism," perhaps. But the trouble is that this view, "conjugalism," is unnecessarily controversial. It is a view about the good life that many people quite reasonably reject. It seems far better for government not to take sides on controversial questions of this kind, if it can avoid it (just as it should take no sides in the dispute between Catholics and Protestants). The political process ought to involve a serious attempt to find ways of "agreeing to disagree," and of basing public policy decisions on the most inclusive possible consensus, since only then can such decisions be seen as collectively authorized by the people as a whole—that is, as democratically legitimate. The following principle encapsulates this point:

Inclusive Democracy

In a well-functioning democracy, the exercise of public authority should typically be adequately justified in public discussion on the basis of values that are as uncontroversial as possible.[12]

For example, wherever possible, laws and public policies should be justified by appeal to uncontroversial values like security, prosperity, freedom, and equality—not by appeal to controversial values about which there is deep, widespread, and intense disagreement. The controversial justification of marriage just considered will clearly conflict with *Inclusive Democracy* if there is an alternative justification of marriage that is less controversial. As I argue below, there is another, less controversial justification.

This controversial justification of marriage may also conflict with the value of freedom. This justification commits the state to promoting married life. But the existence of marriage will have the effect of encouraging married life only if a large proportion of the population desire to become and stay married—that is, presumably, only if it is widely believed that married life is a particularly good life to lead. So, the government, in giving this controversial justification, would also be committing itself to *promoting* the view that married life is an especially good life to lead. If the government is really committed to promoting this view, it would have to encourage a social climate in which people are put under *pressure* to accept this view.[13] But in causing people to be pressured into accepting a controversial view of the best way to lead intimate and personal aspects of one's life, the government would be compromising people's power to lead their lives in the light of the beliefs, values, and choices that they develop through their own autonomous deliberation. In so doing, it would violate the following principle:

Freedom

Government should respect and protect people's power to lead their own lives in the light of their own beliefs, values, and choices (unless, perhaps, it is uncontroversial that compromising freedom in some way brings great benefits, while imposing only relatively trivial burdens).[14]

For these reasons then, the justification in question is misguided.

Not all proposed justifications of marriage are misguided for these reasons. Some writers have suggested that marriage is justified because it helps to cement stable relationships of a kind that tend to be highly beneficial both to those involved and, more indirectly, to a wider circle of people. Moreover, if unmarried people are discouraged from having children, then marriage will also help children to be brought up in stable families of this kind. These justifications of marriage do not obviously conflict with the principles of *Freedom* and *Inclusive Democracy*. They appeal to values that are relatively uncontroversial; practically everyone agrees that it is good for *some* couples to form stable unions, and that it is usually good for children to be brought up in a stable family of this sort.

It may well be that marriage does help to cement stable relationships. One reason for this may be that the community tends to support married couples' relationships more than unmarried couples'. Since the married couple have made a legally binding commitment, and have typically also made their commitment public, in a way that is especially readily understood, typically more people know about their relationship and regard the relationship as serious and likely to last; so if these people have goodwill toward the couple, they will tend to support their relationship. It has been claimed that empirical evidence about modern Western societies suggests that couples who marry are significantly more likely to stay together than couples who stay unmarried, and that stable relationships are on balance good for people: single people are apparently more likely to commit suicide, to fall sick, to become dependent on public assistance, and so on.[15]

Still, I shall argue that these justifications at best pinpoint beneficial *side effects* of marriage, not the essential rationale for the institution. The "essential rationale" for an institution, I assume, must be both necessary and sufficient to justify the institution, in any possible situation in which it is justified. But we can easily imagine that marriage might not have had these beneficial effects: perhaps married couples were no more likely to stay together than unmarried couples, people in stable relationships no happier and no healthier than single people, and children brought up by two parents no better off than children brought up by single parents. This would not by itself show that marriage was not a good social institution to have. So long as marriage had no positively harmful consequences, and so long as people still wanted to be married, for reasons that were clearly serious and deserved to be respected, marriage would still be a good institution to have. On the other hand, if no one ever desired to marry, except perhaps for plainly frivolous or malicious reasons, then marriage would not be a good institution to have. So the essential rationale for marriage is simply that many people *want* to be married, for reasons that are clearly serious and deserve to be respected.

What do I mean by saying that people want to marry "for reasons that are clearly serious and deserve to be respected"? What I have in mind is that this desire is of a certain kind, such that it is generally agreed that there are strong reasons for public policy not to interfere with people's attempts to fulfill desires of this kind, and good reasons for public policy to support or assist people's attempts to fulfill such desires.[16] It is strong evidence that a desire is of this kind if the desire is extremely widespread and strongly held, and few people strongly resent those who succeed in fulfilling this desire.

It is plausible that the desire to marry is usually a serious desire in exactly this way. People want to get married in order to make a legally binding commitment, of a certain particularly familiar and widely recognized kind. This desire is both widespread and strongly held; and few people strongly resent those who satisfy this desire. Moreover, the typical reasons for wanting to marry all seem to be reasons that command respect. Some may want to get married as a gesture of love for their spouse; others because they wish to celebrate and share their happiness with their friends and family; others because they wish to cement their own relationship, by impressing on themselves their commitment to each other, and by enlisting the support of the community; and others may have the special legal benefits in view. All these reasons are clearly serious; none is frivolous or malicious.

Here is a plausible claim about one way in which social institutions can further the common good:

One way to further the common good

If a social institution is indispensable for enabling people to fulfill certain serious desires that they have, and if, at the same time, this institution does not impose any serious burdens on anyone else, and violates no principle of justice, then the institution furthers the common good.

Offhand, it seems plausible that marriage does further the common good in this way. People are impelled to marry by a serious desire to make a legally binding mutual commitment, of a certain uniquely familiar and well-understood kind: that is, people want some assurance that this commitment will have a clear social meaning of the relevant kind. As I argued in the previous section, we can only be assured that marriage will have a clear social meaning of this kind if marital status is determined by law. So legal marriage really is indispensable for enabling people to fulfill this serious desire that they have. Through undergirding the institution of marriage, the state provides a benefit that, in a pluralistic society, only the state can provide.[17]

Moreover, it might seem that marriage need not impose any burdens on anyone—not even on the taxpayer, since presumably the cost of maintaining the institution could be covered by the license fee (which could be means-tested to allow everyone to get married). So, on these assumptions, if the institution of marriage violates no principle of justice, it furthers the common good.

In the following section, however, I shall argue that marriage, in its present form, does not further the common good. This is because its present form involves a ban on same-sex marriage; and that ban violates a principle of justice.

4. The Demands of Equality

One might be tempted to argue that the ban on same-sex marriage is an unjustified restriction of freedom. The ban closes off a certain option, the option of marrying someone of one's own sex; surely people would be more free if this option were open to them. But, on second thoughts, it is not clear that failing to provide this option in itself limits people's freedom. It does not seem that a society that had never had the institution of marriage would thereby be less free than one that had it. So the most plausible objection to the ban on same-sex marriage is not that it denies an option that is essential to freedom, but that it denies an option to some that is *actually made available to others*. That is, the ban conflicts with the value of *equality*.

I am appealing here to the most basic and uncontroversial idea of equality—the idea that society, as a collective body, must treat all its members with equal respect. It must acknowledge that they are all equally members of society, and that they should not be impeded or obstructed in their participation in the life of society. I shall try to capture this idea with the following principle:

Minimal Equality

Every adult should have an equal, unabridged right to participate in the basic institutions of society (unless, perhaps, it is uncontroversial that a somewhat unequal or abridged right brings great benefits and imposes only relatively trivial burdens).

The basic point of this principle is to rule out certain unjust forms of discrimination. Among the basic institutions of society are various political and economic institutions. So violations of *Minimal Equality* include the following familiar examples: denying women the right to vote; denying Roman Catholics the right to own land; a ban on Jews or atheists serving as members of Parliament; and the apartheid system in South Africa, which specifically excluded black South Africans from a large number of social institutions.

These examples, all familiar from history, involve discrimination on the basis of sex, race, or religion. But there could be many other examples. For example, in many societies only property-owners had the right to vote or to serve on juries. Or we could imagine a society in which people born into a certain caste were prohibited from filing civil lawsuits or pressing criminal charges in a court of law; or a society where widows, or redheads, or left-handed people were regarded as unlucky and so forbidden to work in a large number of occupations; or a mostly vegetarian society where people known to eat meat were forbidden to own or edit newspapers; and so on.

Marriage seems also to be one of the basic institutions of society. So, according to *Minimal Equality*, everyone should have an equal unabridged legal right to participate in the institution: everyone should have an equal right to marry. But it might seem strange to claim that anyone is denied this right. After all, everyone, including those who wish to share their life with someone of the same sex, has the right to marry someone of the opposite sex (that, after all, is how many dictionaries define "marriage"); and no one has the right to "marry" someone of the same sex. So everyone has the same rights: no one is denied a right that is available to others.

But obviously a precisely parallel claim could be made about the ban on interracial marriage. You could say: everyone has the right to marry a member of her own race; and no one has the right to marry someone of a race different from her own. So everyone has the same rights: no one is denied a right that is available to others. But almost everyone today agrees that the ban on interracial marriages was an unjust form of discrimination.

This points to something important. Unless we impose some restrictions on how "rights to participate in society's basic institutions" are specified, then the demand for equal rights can be totally trivialized. Unless we impose some such restrictions, then any system of rights, no matter how unjust and discriminatory, could be specified in such a way that everyone can be said to have the same rights. Consider the old apartheid system, in which white South Africans could vote, while black South Africans could not. Suppose you say that the "form of political participation traditional for white South Africans" involved voting, running for office, and so on, while the "form of political participation traditional for black South Africans" consisted in holding political demonstrations until they were dispersed, often brutally, by the police. Then you could say that, under the apartheid system, everyone had an equal right to the form of political participation that was traditional for her ethnic group.

Clearly, this is outrageous. The rights in question have to be specified in the right sort of way. It was to signal this point that my formulation of *Minimal Equality* required that everyone's right to participate in society's basic institutions should be not only equal but also *unabridged*. But what does it mean for rights to be "unabridged" in this sense? What is the right way to specify such rights?

The key idea, I propose, is that each of the rights that we ought to have must be a right to something that is *desirable* or *worthwhile* in a certain way. Consider the right to participate in a certain social institution. Typically, it is part of the essential rationale of a social institution that there is something about participating in that institution that makes it an advantageous or worthwhile thing to do. If so, then the right in question must be specified terms of the features of exercising the right that make it advantageous or worthwhile. Whatever exactly the rationale for a democratic political process may be, it is clear that the reason why participating in such a process is worthwhile has nothing to do with the fact that one is participating in the way that is traditional for one's ethnic group. That fact is incidental to what makes participation in the process desirable or worthwhile. So the right to political participation should not be restricted to political participation of the kind traditional for one's ethnic group. Such a restriction would be arbitrary at best.

Similarly, the essential rationale of civil marriage, I have argued, is that it enables couples to fulfill their serious desire to make a legally binding commitment to each other, of a certain uniquely familiar and widely understood kind. Getting married is worthwhile because it enables the married couple to fulfill this serious desire. But—I claim—many same-sex couples have exactly the same desire, to make such a commitment to each other, as opposite-sex couples. So the reason why getting married is worthwhile has nothing to do with the fact that one is marrying someone of the opposite sex; that fact is incidental to what makes getting married valuable or worthwhile for the married couple. So the right to get married should not be specified as the right to marry someone of the opposite sex. That is at best an arbitrary restriction of this right.

My claim, that many same-sex couples have exactly the same desire as opposite-sex couples, might be controverted. Someone might object that a traditional opposite-sex marriage and a so-called same-sex marriage are so different in their nature and their worth that the desires must also be quite different in kind. But whether two couples' desires count as "the same desire" should not be decided on the basis of such controversial ethical views. It should be decided on *empirical* grounds, by finding out whether our best empirical psychology needs to draw a sharp distinction between the desires of same-sex couples and those of opposite-sex couples, or whether more or less the same psychological theory is true of both. So my claim is in fact the first of the empirical assumptions on which my defense of same-sex marriage is based:

1. Many same-sex couples desire to get married for essentially the same kinds of reasons as opposite-sex couples; that is, they are motivated by desires that empirical psychology would hardly ever need to treat differently, for theoretical or explanatory purposes.

As I warned at the outset, I am not going to defend this empirical assumption, although I am convinced that it is true. There is in my view ample evidence for this assumption, in the motives that move many same-sex couples to have "commitment ceremonies," or to enter registered domestic partnerships. But a full defense of the assumption would require a more extensive survey than I can undertake.

If this assumption is true, then we can see why anything less than full same-sex marriage is "separate and unequal." Commitment ceremonies, private contractual arrangements, and registered domestic partnerships are just not as familiar and well understood as marriage. They lack the resonance of marriage. Saying, "We had a commitment ceremony two years ago," or "We are registered domestic partners," signally lacks the social consequences of saying, "We are married." As a result, commitment ceremonies and registered partnerships are unlikely to be as effective as marriage for a couple who want to impress their commitment on themselves by affirming it publicly in a way that the community will readily understand, or to enlist the support of the community for their relationship. To fulfill these desires effectively, same-sex couples actually need to be able to *say that they are married.* The word "marriage" (or some word that means the same thing in the language of the community) is essential. Suppose that same-sex marriage had a different name—as it might be, "quarriage." Inevitably, there would be fewer same-sex quarriages than opposite-sex marriages; so, even if the term became more familiar over the years, "quarriage" would always be less familiar and well understood than "marriage." Hence the arrangement would still be separate and unequal.

When the right to marry is properly specified, in its genuine, unabridged form, as the right to get married to the person who wishes to marry you, it is clear that not everyone has this right. Those who wish to marry members of the opposite sex have it, while those who wish to marry members of the same sex do not. Prima facie, this is a violation of *Minimal Equality,* and so an unjust form of discrimination.

In fact, the first and third of my three empirical assumptions are sufficient to show that the ban on same-sex marriage is unjust. But there is also an additional factor that makes this form of discrimination, not merely unjust, but intolerably unjust. This is the second empirical assumption of my defense of same-sex marriage:

2. Many people are gay or lesbian: that is, they have an involuntary and effectively immutable homosexual orientation; they are, and will always be, sexually attracted only toward members of their own sex.

This point is sometimes denied; but it has been adequately confirmed by contemporary psychology. Sexual intimacy is typically an integral part of marriage. So gay and lesbian people have no hope of forming a satisfactory marriage except with a member of their own sex. Hence a ban on same-sex marriage excludes lesbian and gay people from marriage altogether. This makes the ban on same-sex marriage not just unjust, but intolerably unjust.

Still, I have formulated the minimal equality principle so that it allows for exceptions: if an unequal or abridged right uncontroversially brings great benefits, while imposing only relatively trivial burdens, it may be justified. For instance, it would be outrageous if people of Asian descent were denied driver's licenses. But it is not outrageous that blind people are denied driver's licenses. Denying blind people the right to drive does not deprive them of any benefit that they could realistically have, and is essential to maintaining road safety; so it is clearly justified. So, my defense of same-sex marriage also rests on a third empirical assumption:

3. The ban on same-sex marriage brings no uncontroversial benefits that could outweigh its obvious and serious burdens.

Many writers have claimed that same-sex marriage would have harmful effects. Typically, these writers allege that their claims are supported by empirical evidence; and, as before, I shall not assess this alleged empirical evidence here. But some writers appear to believe that the ban on same-sex marriage can be justified directly on the basis of the view that homosexual acts and relationships are morally wrong, or at least greatly inferior to heterosexual acts and relationships. In the remainder of this section, I shall argue that the ban on same-sex marriage cannot be justified in this way.

Some people argue, on the basis of this moral view of the inferiority of homosexuality, that same-sex marriage must be banned in order to discourage homosexual acts and relationships, or at least to affirm this moral view of homosexuality. But this argument does not reveal any *uncontroversial* benefits of the ban on same-sex marriage, since this moral view of homosexuality is clearly intensely controversial. No appeal to such controversial "benefits" could justify an exception to the principle of *Minimal Equality*.

The requirement that only uncontroversial benefits can justify exceptions to the principle of *Minimal Equality* reflects the principle of *Inclusive Democracy*, together with the assumption that equality itself is a value that is basically uncontroversial. Practically everyone agrees that equality is an important value, while this moral view about homosexuality is intensely controversial. Since it is important, in a pluralistic society that aspires to be democratic, to find ways of "agreeing to disagree," it is preferable to base our decision about same-sex marriage on the relatively uncontroversial value of equality, rather than on such controversial moral views.

Moreover, there is a general objection to laws that aim to discourage homosexuality, or to affirm the superiority of heterosexuality; and this objection is also grounded in another relatively uncontroversial value—namely, *freedom*. Laws that discourage homosexuality aim to put pressure on people to adopt a view that not only is highly controversial, but also concerns the best way to lead the most intimate and important aspects of one's life. This is connected with the fact that the kind of conduct stigmatized by this view consists of intimate interaction between *consenting adults:* while it is uncontroversial that nonconsensual sexual interactions are wrong, the consenting adults who engage in homosexual acts typically do not believe that these acts are wrong; indeed, they typically believe that their engaging in such acts is vital for their chances of living the best life that they can (even if they are wrong to believe this, this belief is clearly a considered, coherent part of their whole outlook on life). Laws that put pressure on people to adopt a view of this kind compromise people's power to lead their own lives in the light of their own beliefs, values, and choices. Thus, the principle of *Freedom* condemns all laws that aim to discourage or denigrate homosexuality. The ban on same-sex marriage cannot possibly be justified by any moral view of homosexuality.

By contrast, lifting the ban on same-sex marriage would not in itself express any ethical view about homosexuality. It is not plausible that marriage involves the state's expressing its approval of any particular relationship. After all, convicted wife-murderers, convicted child-abusers, and convicted rapists are all allowed to get married (indeed, they can even get married while in prison).[18] The state is not expressing approval of these relationships. So why should we think that if the state allows same-sex marriage, it is expressing any view about whether same-sex marriage is inferior to opposite-sex marriage? The state could even allow same-sex marriage while making a special proclamation that it values marriages that raise children properly, and has no position on whether or not same-sex marriages are inferior to opposite-sex marriages, no more than it has any official position on whether Christianity is better than Judaism or atheism.

5. The Role of Empirical Evidence

My "philosophical defense" of same-sex marriage is now complete. Before concluding, however, I shall briefly comment on the role of empirical evidence in answering the commonest objections to same-sex marriage.

My defense of same-sex marriage rested on three empirical assumptions: (1) same-sex couples typically want to get married for essentially the same sorts of reasons as opposite-sex couples; (2) the ban on same-sex marriage imposes intolerable burdens on some people; and (3) the ban brings no uncontroversial benefits. Of these three assumptions, the most controversial is the third. Clearly, further empirical investigation is needed to evaluate this assumption.

Still, it is not necessary to prove this third assumption beyond all reasonable doubt. It is fair to demand that we should be reasonably confident that introducing same-sex marriage will not cause serious harm. But the main burden of proof should be on those who wish to justify exceptions to *Minimal Equality* (although it may be arguable that there should also be some burden of proof on those who wish to achieve such equality by means of radical departures from the status quo).

Moreover, in assessing the empirical evidence for this third assumption, we need only consider whether there are any uncontroversial benefits that are *effectively inseparable* from the ban on same-sex marriage. Suppose for example—what seems to me almost certainly false[19]—that the empirical evidence shows that same-sex couples are bad parents. This does not show that the ban on same-sex marriage in itself brings any uncontroversial benefits, since it would always be possible to sever the connection between marriage and the legal right to adopt children. A ban on same-sex marriage would not be necessary in order to protect children, even if it were necessary to ban adoption by same-sex couples.

It might be thought that my account of marriage clearly supports the often-repeated claim that allowing same-sex marriage would weaken and undermine the institution of marriage. According to my account, it is essential to marriage that it has a clear and widely understood social meaning. But it is plainly part of the current social meaning of marriage that it is the union of one man and one

woman. If you say, "I'm getting married," people will assume that you are getting married to someone of the opposite sex. So wouldn't allowing same-sex
marriage confuse and destabilize the social meaning of marriage?

Introducing same-sex marriage would indeed *change* the social meaning of
marriage. But the social meaning of marriage has already changed in many
ways: most notably, it is now widely assumed that marriage ought to be a relationship of equals, whereas formerly it was assumed that the wife ought to be
subordinated under the authority of her husband. Few people really want the
social meaning of marriage to stay forever unchanged; what they fundamentally
want is that marriage have a *clear* social meaning, involving a certain *basic core*
of shared understandings about how marriage involves both intimacy and
sharing the necessities of life. Introducing same-sex marriage would not change
this basic core of marriage's social meaning, and it need not lead to great confusion about what marriage involves. So there is no need to fear that same-sex
marriage would undermine or weaken marriage in this way.

My argument's reliance on these three assumptions also suggests a reply to
the ever-popular "polygamy objection"—the objection that the arguments for
same-sex marriage can be automatically adapted to support polygamy. To
answer this objection, we should consider the empirical evidence for the three
corresponding assumptions with respect to polygamy. (1) Do those who are
already married and want to acquire a second spouse typically want this for the
same sorts of reasons as impel people to enter their first marriage? Or is the
motivation for entering polygamous marriages typically quite different, from a
psychological point of view? (2) Is there such a thing as a polygamous sexual
orientation? Is there any significant group of people whose only hope of a satisfactory marriage is to have more than one marriage at the same time? (3) Does
the ban on polygamy bring any uncontroversial benefits? Would allowing
polygamy cause serious harm? It is far from obvious that the answers to these
questions will be the same as the answers to the corresponding questions about
same-sex marriage.[20]

6. Conclusion

I have argued that if marriage is to be justifiable at all, it must be made available to same-sex couples as well as opposite-sex couples. I have also given an
account of the essential rationale for the institution of marriage—that is, of the
basic way in which marriage would further the common good, if it were a justifiable institution. I have not argued that marriage definitely would be a justifiable institution as soon as the ban on same-sex marriage is lifted. Perhaps marriage also violates a principle of justice in some other way (perhaps it still discriminates against women, for example); or perhaps people's reasons for

wanting to get married are in fact typically frivolous or malicious, rather than serious reasons that deserve to be respected. By itself, however, my argument does nothing to suggest that marriage is marred by any such flaws. My argument poses no threat to the justification of marriage itself—only to the existing ban on same-sex marriage.

Notes

1. See William N. Eskridge, Jr., *The Case for Same-Sex Marriage* (New York: Free Press, 1996); Cass R. Sunstein, "Homosexuality and the Constitution," in David Estlund and Martha Nussbaum, eds., *Sex, Preference, and Family: Essays on Law and Nature* (New York: Oxford University Press, 1997); and Mark Strasser, *Legally Wed: Same-Sex Marriage and the Constitution* (Ithaca, N.Y.: Cornell University Press, 1997).

2. The overall structure of my argument is similar to that of A. A. Wellington, "Why Liberals Should Support Same-Sex Marriage," *Journal of Social Philosophy* 26:3 (Winter 1995): 5–32. There are many differences between our arguments, however: I give a quite different account of the nature of marriage and of its essential rationale, and my appeal to equality is related to my account of marriage's rationale in a different way.

3. This argument has often been used to attack marriage; see, for example, Paula Ettelbrick, "Since When Is Marriage a Path to Liberation?" in Robert Baird and Stuart Rosenbaum, eds., *Same-Sex Marriage: The Moral and Legal Debate* (Amherst, N.Y.: Prometheus Books, 1997).

4. Indeed, even in the past, as recent historians have pointed out, "although the church had been trying to control marriage since the twelfth century, it had only been partially successful in doing so" (John Gillis, *For Better, for Worse: British Marriages, 1600 to the Present* [New York: Oxford University Press, 1985], p.15).

5. The existence of polygamy is no exception: the patriarch Jacob had a separate marriage with each of his two wives, not one "group marriage" in which all three of them married each other. Polygamy involves being in *more than one* marriage *simultaneously*.

6. Thus, if society draws a distinction between legitimate and illegitimate children, the child of a married couple will count as legitimate (since both parents are expected to assume full parental responsibilities for the child). But it is not essential to marriage that society should draw any distinction between legitimate and illegitimate children.

7. Marriage need not strictly speaking *be* a contract, however. In the United States, for example, marriage is not covered by the constitutional rule that "no state shall pass any law impairing the obligation of contracts." The rights and obligations of marriage can be changed by new legislation even without the consent of the parties involved (just as these rights and obligations change if the married couple move to another state). Under American law then, marriage is a legal *status,* which is entered by means of a contract. For this point, and an account of the mutual rights and obligations of marriage, see Harry D. Krause, *Family Law in a Nutshell,* 3rd edition (St. Paul, Minn.: West Pub. Co., 1995), pp. 88–90, and chapters 8, 25 and 26.

8. I say "roughly standardized," not only because of variations between the marriage laws of different states, but also because of the variations introduced by prenuptial agreements. Still, not all spousal rights and obligations can be waived by means of such agreements. For example, parties are not permitted to contract away their obligation to support their spouse during the marriage. There are numerous other restrictions as well; see Kraus, *Family Law in a Nutshell,* pp. 91–99.

9. Consider two social relationships and practices that are not undergirded by law: promising and friendship. Promising has a clear social meaning, but promising is a relatively simple social

practice, defined by a clear social norm whose utility is generally understood. Marriage is a much more complex practice, serving many different functions; and the social norms surrounding marriage are often contested. In this respect, friendship resembles marriage: it too is complex, serves many different functions, and is often contested. Unlike marriage, friendship is not undergirded by law, and has little in the way of a clear social meaning. Saying, "We are friends" conveys remarkably little information (as Brecht's Mother Courage says, "I don't trust him—he's a friend of mine").

10. I owe this formulation to Richard Mohr, "The Case for Gay Marriage," in Baird and Rosenbaum, *Same-Sex Marriage: The Moral and Legal Debate,* pp. 91–92.

11. Andrew Sullivan, *Virtually Normal: An Argument about Homosexuality* (New York: Knopf, 1995), p. 182; see also his "Three's a Crowd," in Andrew Sullivan, ed., *Same-Sex Marriage: Pro and Con* (New York: Vintage Books, 1997), pp. 278–82.

12. Thus, every proposed public policy decision should be given the most uncontroversial justification possible; and if, out of two alternative public policy decisions, one can be adequately justified on the basis of much less controversial values than the other, then typically the first decision is preferable to the second. Whether one value is more or less controversial than another depends on at least three factors: how widespread the disagreement is (how many people disagree); how deep it is (whether it is a rational disagreement about basic values, or just a matter of detail); and how intense it is (how much reasonable resentment would be felt if the value were a basis for public policy). (For similar ideas, compare John Rawls, *Political Liberalism* [New York: Columbia University Press, 1993], Lectures IV and V; and Joshua Cohen's unpublished "Deliberative Democracy.")

13. This consequence is explicitly embraced by Jonathan Rauch, "For Better or Worse?" in Sullivan, *Same-Sex Marriage: Pro and Con,* pp. 169–81.

14. By this contrast between relatively "serious" and relatively "trivial" benefits and burdens, I have in mind something like T. M. Scanlon's idea of "urgency"; see his "Preference and Urgency," *Journal of Philosophy* 82 (1975): 655–69, and "The Moral Basis of Interpersonal Comparisons," in Jon Elster and John Roemer, eds., *Interpersonal Comparisons of Well-Being* (Cambridge: Cambridge University Press, 1991). One burden is more "serious" than another if, other things equal, there are stronger reasons against public policies imposing the first burden than the second.

15. The Editors of *The Economist,* "Let Them Wed," in Sullivan, *Same-Sex Marriage: Pro and Con,* pp. 181–85.

16. The general idea of desires that are serious and deserve to be respected is also related to Scanlon's idea of "urgency" (see n. 14 above).

17. Of course, some marriages turn out very badly for the people concerned. But the state can still be described as "helping" these people, since they were harmed as the direct result of their own free choice, and the state was only enabling them to achieve their own freely chosen goals.

18. See William Eskridge, *The Case for Same-Sex Marriage,* pp. 106–108.

19. Compare the finding of Judge Kevin S. C. Chang in *Baehr v. Miike,* First Circuit Court, State of Hawaii, Civil Case No. 91–1394 (December 1996).

20. See Richard Posner, *Sex and Reason* (Cambridge, Mass.: Harvard University Press, 1992), pp. 253–60.

15

A Defense of Abortion

Judith Jarvis Thomson

Most opposition to abortion relies on the premise that the fetus is a human being, a person, from the moment of conception.[1] The premise is argued for, but, as I think, not well. Take, for example, the most common argument. We are asked to notice that the development of a human being from conception through birth into childhood is continuous; then it is said that to draw a line, to choose a point in this development and say "before this point the thing is not a person, after this point it is a person" is to make an arbitrary choice, a choice for which in the nature of things no good reason can be given. It is concluded that the fetus is, or that we had better say it is, a person from the moment of conception. But this conclusion does not follow. Similar things might be said about the development of an acorn into an oak tree, and it does not follow that acorns are oak trees, or that we had better say they are. Arguments of this form are sometimes called "slippery-slope arguments"—the phrase is perhaps self-explanatory—and it is dismaying that opponents of abortion rely on them so heavily and uncritically.

I am inclined to agree, however, that the prospects for "drawing a line" in the development of the fetus look dim. I am inclined to think also that we shall probably have to agree that the fetus has already become a human person well before birth. Indeed, it comes as a surprise when one first learns how early in its life the fetus begins to acquire human characteristics. By the tenth week, for example, it already has a face, arms and legs, fingers and toes; it has internal organs, and brain activity is detectable.[2] On the other hand, I think that the premise is false, that the fetus is not a person from the moment of conception. A newly fertilized ovum, a newly implanted clump of cells, is no more a person than an acorn is an oak tree. But I shall not discuss any of this. For it seems to me to be of greater

Judith Jarvis Thomson, "A Defense of Abortion," first published in *Philosophy & Public Affairs* 1, no. 1. Copyright © 1971 by Princeton University Press. Reprinted by permission of Princeton University Press.

interest to ask what happens if, for the sake of argument, we allow the premise. How, precisely, are we supposed to get from there to the conclusion that abortion is morally impermissible? Opponents of abortion commonly spend most of their time establishing that the fetus is a person, and hardly any time explaining the step from there to the impermissibility of abortion. Perhaps they think the step too simple and obvious to require much comment. Or perhaps they are simply being economical in argument. Many of those who defend abortion rely on the premise that the fetus is not a person, but only a bit of tissue that will become a person at birth; and why pay out more arguments than you have to? Whatever the explanation, I suggest that the step they take is neither easy nor obvious, that it calls for closer examination than it is commonly given, and that when we do give it this closer examination we shall feel inclined to reject it.

I propose, then, that we grant that the fetus is a person from the moment of conception. How does the argument go from here? Something like this, I take it. Every person has a right to life. So the fetus has a right to life. No doubt the mother has a right to decide what shall happen in and to her body; everyone would grant that. But surely a person's right to life is stronger and more stringent than the mother's right to decide what happens in and to her body, and so outweighs it. So the fetus may not be killed; an abortion may not be performed.

It sounds plausible. But now let me ask you to imagine this. You wake up in the morning and find yourself back to back in bed with an unconscious famous violinist. He has been found to have a fatal kidney ailment, and the Society of Music Lovers has canvassed all the available medical records and found that you alone have the right blood type to help. They have therefore kidnapped you, and last night the violinist's circulatory system was plugged into yours so that your kidneys could be used to extract poisons from his blood as well as your own. The director of the hospital now tells you: "Look, we're sorry the Society of Music Lovers did this to you—we would never have permitted it if we had known. But still, they did it and the violinist now is plugged into you. To unplug you would be to kill him. But never mind, it's only for nine months. By then he will have recovered from his ailment and can safely be unplugged from you." Is it morally incumbent on you to accede to this situation? No doubt it would be very nice of you if you did, a great kindness. But do you *have* to accede to it? What if it were not nine months but nine years? Or longer still? What if the director of the hospital said: "Tough luck, I agree, but you've now got to stay in bed, with the violinist plugged into you, for the rest of your life. Because remember this: All persons have a right to life, and violinists are persons. Granted you have a right to decide what happens in and to your body, but a person's right to life outweighs your right to decide what happens in and to your body. So you cannot ever be unplugged from him." I imagine you would regard this as outrageous, which suggests that something really is wrong with that plausible-sounding argument that was mentioned previously.

In this case, of course, you were kidnapped; you did not volunteer for the operation that plugged the violinist into your kidneys. Can those who oppose abortion on the grounds I mentioned make an exception for a pregnancy due to rape? Certainly. They can say that persons have a right to life only if they did not come into existence because of rape; or they can say that all persons have a right to life, but that some have less of a right to life than others, in particular, that those who came into existence because of rape have less. But these statements have a rather unpleasant sound. Surely the question of whether one has a right to life at all, or how much of a right one has, should not turn on the question of whether or not one is the product of a rape. And in fact the people who oppose abortion on the ground I mentioned do not make this distinction, and hence do not make an exception in case of rape.

Nor do they make an exception for a case in which the mother has to spend the nine months of her pregnancy in bed. They would agree that that would be a great pity and hard on the mother, but would insist all the same that all persons have a right to life, and that the fetus is a person. I suspect, in fact, that they would not make an exception for a case in which, miraculously enough, the pregnancy went on for nine years, or even for the rest of the mother's life.

Some would not even make an exception for a case in which continuation of the pregnancy is likely to shorten the mother's life; they regard abortion as impermissible even to save the mother's life. Such cases are nowadays very rare, and many opponents of abortion do not accept this extreme view. All the same, it is a good place to begin: a number of points of interest come out in respect to it.

1. Let us call the view that abortion is impermissible even to save the mother's life "the extreme view." I want to suggest, first, that it does not issue from the argument I mentioned earlier without the addition of some fairly powerful premises. Suppose a woman has become pregnant, and now learns that she has a cardiac condition such that she will die if she carries the baby to term. What may be done for her? The fetus, being a person, has a right to life; but as the mother is a person too, so has she a right to life. Presumably they have an equal right to life. How is it supposed to come out that an abortion may not be performed? If mother and child have an equal right to life, should not we perhaps flip a coin? Or should we add to the mother's right to life her right to decide what happens in and to her body, which everybody seems to be ready to grant—the sum of her rights now outweighing the fetus' right to life?

The most familiar argument here is the following. We are told that performing the abortion would be directly killing[3] the child, whereas doing nothing would not be killing the mother, but only letting her die. Moreover, in killing the child, one would be killing an innocent person, for the child has committed no crime and is not aiming at his mother's death. And then there are a variety of ways in which this argument might be continued. (1) As directly killing an innocent person is always and absolutely impermissible, an abortion may not be performed. Or, (2) as directly killing an innocent person is murder, and murder is always and absolutely impermissible, an abortion may not be performed.[4] Or, (3) as one's duty to refrain from directly killing an innocent person is more strin-

gent than one's duty to keep a person from dying, an abortion may not be performed. Or, (4) if one's only options are directly killing an innocent person or
letting a person die, one must prefer letting the person die, and thus an abortion
may not be performed.[5]

Some people seem to have thought that these are not further premises that
must be added if the conclusion is to be reached, but that they follow from the
very fact that an innocent person has a right to life.[6] But this seems to me a mistake, and perhaps the simplest way to show this is to point out that while we must
certainly grant that innocent persons have a right to life, the theses in arguments
1 through 4 are all false. Take argument 2 for example. If directly killing an innocent person is murder, and thus is impermissible, then the mother's directly
killing the innocent person inside her is murder, and thus is impermissible. But it
cannot seriously be thought to be murder if the mother performs an abortion on
herself to save her life. It cannot seriously be said that she *must* refrain, that she
must sit passively by and wait for her death. Let us look again at the case of you
and the violinist. There you are, in bed with the violinist, and the director of the
hospital says to you: "It's all most distressing, and I deeply sympathize, but you
see this is putting an additional strain on your kidneys, and you'll be dead within
the month. But you *have* to stay where you are all the same, because unplugging
you would be directly killing an innocent violinist, and that's murder, and that's
impermissible." If anything in the world is true, it is that you do not commit
murder, you do not do what is impermissible, if you reach around to your back
and unplug yourself from that violinist to save your life.

The main focus of attention in writings on abortion has been on what a third
party may or may not do in answer to a request from a woman for an abortion.
This is in a way understandable. Things being as they are, there is not much a
woman can safely do to abort herself. So the question asked is, What may a third
party do? And what the mother may do, if it is mentioned at all, is deduced,
almost as an afterthought, from what it is concluded that a third party may do.
But it seems to me that to treat the matter in this way is to refuse to grant to the
mother that very status of person that is so firmly insisted on for the fetus. For
we cannot simply read off what a person may do from what a third party may
do. Suppose you find yourself trapped in a tiny house with a growing child—I
mean a very tiny house, and a rapidly growing child; you are already up against
the wall of the house and in a few minutes you'll be crushed to death. The child,
on the other hand, will not be crushed to death; if nothing is done to stop him
from growing he will be hurt, but in the end he will simply burst open the house
and walk out a free man. Now I could well understand it if a bystander were to
say: "There's nothing we can do for you. We cannot choose between your life
and his, we cannot be the ones to decide who is to live, we cannot intervene."
But it cannot be concluded that you too can do nothing, that you cannot attack
the child to save your life. However innocent the child may be, you do not have
to wait passively while it crushes you to death. Perhaps a pregnant woman is
vaguely felt to have the status of a house, which we do not allow the right of

self-defense. But if the woman houses the child, it should be remembered that she is a person who houses it.

I should perhaps pause to say explicitly that I am not claiming that people have a right to do anything whatever to save their lives. I think, rather, that there are drastic limits to the right of self-defense. If someone threatens you with death unless you torture someone else to death, I think you have not the right, even to save your life, to do so. But the case under consideration here is very different. In our case there are only two people involved, one whose life is threatened, and one who threatens it. Both are innocent: the one who is threatened is not threatened because of any fault; the one who threatens does not threaten because of any fault. For this reason we may feel that we bystanders cannot intervene. But the person threatened can.

In sum, a woman surely can defend her life against the threat to it posed by the unborn child, even if doing so involves its death. And this shows not merely that the theses in arguments 1 through 4 are false; it shows also that the extreme view of abortion is false, and so we need not canvass any other possible ways of arriving at it from the argument I mentioned at the outset.

2. The extreme view could of course be weakened to say that while abortion is permissible to save the mother's life, it may not be performed by a third party, but only by the mother herself. But this cannot be right either. For what we have to keep in mind is that the mother and the unborn child are not like two tenants in a small house that has, by an unfortunate mistake, been rented to both: the mother *owns* the house. The fact that she does adds to the offensiveness of deducing that the mother can do nothing from the supposition that third parties can do nothing. But it does more than this; it also casts a bright light on the supposition that third parties can do nothing. Certainly it lets us see that a third party who says "I cannot choose between you" is fooling himself if he thinks this is impartiality. If Jones has found and fastened on a certain coat that he needs to keep himself from freezing but that Smith also needs to keep from freezing, then it is not impartiality that says "I cannot choose between you" when Smith owns the coat. Women have said again and again, "This body is my body!" and they have reason to feel angry, reason to feel that it has been like shouting into the wind. Smith, after all, is hardly likely to bless us if we say to him: "Of course it's your coat; anybody would grant that it is. But no one may choose between you and Jones who is to have it."

We should really ask what it is that says "no one may choose" in the face of the fact that the body that houses the child is the mother's body. It may be simply a failure to appreciate this fact. But it may be something more interesting, namely the sense that one has a right to refuse to lay hands on people, even where it would be just and fair to do so, even where justice seems to require that somebody do so. Thus justice might call for somebody to get Smith's coat back from Jones, and yet you have a right to refuse to be the one to lay hands on Jones, a right to refuse to do physical violence to him. This, I think, must be granted. But then what should be said is not "no one may choose," but only "*I* cannot choose"—indeed not even this, but rather "*I* will not act," leaving it open that somebody else can or should, in particular that anyone in a position of authority, with the job of securing people's rights, both can and should. So this is no difficulty. I have not been arguing that any given third party must accede to the mother's request that he perform an abortion to save her life, but only that he may.

I suppose that in some views of human life the mother's body is only on loan to her, the loan not being one that gives her any prior claim to it. One who held this view might well think it impartiality to say, "I cannot choose." But I shall simply ignore this possibility. My own view is that if a human being has any just, prior claim to anything at all, he has a just, prior claim to his own body. And perhaps this need not be argued for here anyway, since, as I mentioned, the arguments against abortion we are looking at do grant that the woman has a right to decide what happens in and to her body.

But although they do grant it, I have tried to show that they do not take seriously what is done in granting it. I suggest the same thing will reappear even more clearly when we turn away from cases in which the mother's life is at stake and attend, as I propose we now do, to the vastly more common cases in which a woman wants an abortion for some less weighty reason than preserving her own life.

3. Where the mother's life is not at stake the argument I mentioned at the outset seems to have a much stronger pull. "Everyone has a right to life, so the unborn person has a right to life." And isn't the child's right to life weightier than anything other than the mother's own right to life, which she might put forward as ground for an abortion?

This argument treats the right to life as if it were unproblematic. It is not, and this seems to me to be precisely the source of the mistake.

For we should now, at long last, ask what it comes to, to have a right to life. In some views having a right to life includes having a right to be given at least the bare minimum one needs for continued life. But suppose that what in fact *is* the bare minimum a man needs for continued life is something he has no right at all to be given? If I am sick unto death, and the only thing that will save my life is the touch of Henry Fonda's cool hand on my fevered brow, then all the same, I have no right to be given the touch of Henry Fonda's cool hand on my fevered brow. It would be frightfully nice of him to fly in from the West Coast to provide it. It would be less nice, though no doubt well meant, if my friends flew to the West Coast and carried Henry Fonda back with them. But I have no right at all against anybody that he should do this for me. Or again, to return to the story I told earlier, the fact that for continued life the violinist needs the continued use of your kidneys does not establish that he has a right to be given the continued use of your kidneys. He certainly has no right against you that *you* should give him continued use of your kidneys. For nobody has any right to use your kidneys unless you give him such a right; and nobody has the right against you that you shall give him this right. If you do allow him to go on using your kidneys, this is a kindness on your part, and not something he can claim from you as his due. Nor has he any right against anybody else that they should give him continued use of your kidneys. Certainly he had no right against the Society of Music Lovers that they should plug him into you in the first place. And if you now start to unplug yourself, having learned that you will otherwise have to spend nine years in bed with him, there is nobody in the world who must try to prevent you, in order to see to it that he is given something he has a right to be given.

Some people are rather stricter about the right to life. In their view it does not include the right to be given anything, but amounts to, and only to, the right not to be killed by anybody. But here a related difficulty arises. If everybody is to refrain from killing the violinist, then everybody must refrain from doing a great many different sorts of things. Everybody must refrain from slitting his throat, everybody must refrain from shooting him—and everybody must refrain from unplugging you from him. But does he have a right against everybody that they shall refrain from unplugging you from him? To refrain from doing this is to allow him to continue to use your kidneys. It could be argued that he has a right against us that *we* should allow him to continue to use your kidneys. That is, while he had no right against us that we should give him the use of your kidneys, it might be argued that he anyway has a right against us that we shall not now intervene and deprive him of the use of your kidneys. I shall come back to third-party interventions later. But certainly the violinist has no right against you that *you* shall allow him to continue to use your kidneys. As I said, if you do allow him to use them, it is a kindness on your part, and not something you owe him.

The difficulty I point to here is not peculiar to the right to life. It reappears in connection with all the other natural rights; and it is something that an adequate account of rights must deal with. For present purposes it is enough just to draw attention to it. But I would stress that I am not arguing that people do not have a right to life—quite the contrary, it seems to me that the primary control we must place on the acceptability of an account of rights is that it should turn out in that account to be a truth that all persons have a right to life. I am arguing only that having a right to life does not guarantee having either a right to be given the use of or a right to be allowed continued use of another person's body—even if one needs it for life itself. So the right to life will not serve the opponents of abortion in the very simple and clear way in which they seem to have thought it would.

4. There is another way to bring out the difficulty. In the most ordinary sort of case, to deprive someone of what he has a right to is to treat him unjustly. Suppose a boy and his small brother are jointly given a box of chocolates for Christmas. If the older boy takes the box and refuses to give his brother any of the chocolates, he is unjust to him, for the brother has been given a right to half of them. But suppose that having learned that otherwise it means nine years in bed with that violinist, you unplug yourself from him. You surely are not being unjust to him, for you gave him no right to use your kidneys, and no one else can have given him any such right. But we have to notice that in unplugging

yourself you are killing him; and violinists, like everybody else, have a right to life, and thus in the view we are considering, the right not to be killed. So here you do what he supposedly has a right that you shall not do, but you do not act unjustly to him in doing it.

The emendation that may be made at this point is this: the right to life consists not in the right not to be killed but rather in the right not to be killed unjustly. This runs a risk of circularity, but never mind: it would enable us to square the fact that the violinist has a right to life with the fact that you do not act unjustly toward him in unplugging yourself, thereby killing him. For if you do not kill him unjustly, you do not violate his right to life, and so it is no wonder you do him no injustice.

But if this emendation is accepted, the gap in the argument against abortion stares us plainly in the face: it is by no means enough to show that the fetus is a person, and to remind us that all persons have a right to life; we need to be shown also that killing the fetus violates its right to life, that is, that abortion is unjust killing. And is it?

I suppose we may take it as a datum that in a case of pregnancy due to rape the mother has not given the unborn person a right to the use of her body for food and shelter. Indeed, in what pregnancy could it be supposed that the mother has given the unborn person such a right? It is not as if there were unborn persons drifting about the world, to whom a woman who wants a child says, "I invite you in."

But it might be argued that there are other ways one can have acquired a right to the use of another person's body than by having been invited to use it by that person. Suppose a woman voluntarily indulges in intercourse, knowing of the chance that it will issue in pregnancy, and then she does become pregnant. Is she not in part responsible for the presence, in fact the very existence, of the unborn person inside her? No doubt she did not invite it in. But doesn't her partial responsibility for its being there itself give it a right to the use of her body?[7] If so, then her aborting it would be more like the boy's taking away the chocolates and less like your unplugging yourself from the violinist—doing so would be depriving it of what it does have a right to, and thus would be doing it an injustice.

And then, too, it might be asked whether or not she can kill it even to save her own life: If she voluntarily called it into existence, how can she now kill it, even in self-defense?

The first thing to be said about this is that it is something new. Opponents of abortion have been so concerned to make out the independence of the fetus, in order to establish that it has a right to life, just as its mother does, that they have tended to overlook the possible support they might gain from making out that the fetus is dependent on the mother, in order to establish that she has a special kind of responsibility for it, a responsibility that gives it rights against her that are not possessed by any independent person—such as an ailing violinist who is a stranger to her.

On the other hand, this argument would give the unborn person a right to its mother's body only if her pregnancy resulted from a voluntary act, under-taken in full knowledge of the chance that a pregnancy might result from it. It would leave out entirely the unborn person whose existence is due to rape. Pending the availability of some further argument, then, we would be left with the conclusion that unborn persons whose existence is due to rape have no right to the use of their mothers' bodies, and thus that aborting them is not depriving them of anything they have a right to and hence is not unjust killing.

And we should also notice that it is not at all plain that this argument really does go even as far as it purports to. For there are different kinds of cases, and the details make a difference. If the room is stuffy and I therefore open a window to air it and a burglar climbs in, it would be absurd to say, "Ah, now he can stay; she's given him a right to the use of her house—for she is partially responsible for his presence there, having voluntarily done what enabled him to get in, in full knowledge that there are such things as burglars, and that burglars burgle." It would be still more absurd to say this if I had had bars installed out-side my windows precisely to prevent burglars from getting in, and a burglar got in only because of a defect in the bars. It remains equally absurd if we imagine it is not a burglar who climbs in but an innocent person who blunders or falls in. Again, suppose it were like this: people-seeds drift about in the air like pollen, and if you open your windows one may drift in and take root in your carpet or upholstery. You do not want children, so you fix up your windows with fine mesh screens, the very best you can buy. As can happen, however, and on very rare occasions does happen, one of the screens is defective; and a seed drifts in and takes root. Does the person-plant who now develops have a right to the use of your house? Surely not, despite the fact that you voluntarily opened your windows, that you knowingly kept carpets and upholstered furniture, and that you knew that screens were sometimes defective. Someone may argue that you are responsible for its rooting, that it does have a right to your house because, after all, you *could* have lived out your life with bare floors and furniture, or with sealed windows and doors. But this will not do, for by the same token anyone can avoid a pregnancy due to rape by having a hysterectomy, or by never leaving home without a (reliable!) army.

It seems to me that the argument we are looking at can establish at most that there are some cases in which the unborn person has a right to the use of its mother's body, and therefore some cases in which abortion is unjust killing. There is room for much discussion and argument as to precisely which cases, if any, are unjust. But I think we should sidestep this issue and leave it open, for the argument certainly does not establish that all abortion is unjust killing.

5. There is, however, room for yet another argument here. We all surely must grant that there may be cases in which it would be morally indecent to detach a person from your body at the cost of his life. Suppose you learn that what the vio-linist needs is not nine years of your life but only one hour: all you need do to save his life is to spend one hour in that bed with him. Suppose also that letting him use your kidneys for that one hour would not affect your health in the

slightest. Admittedly you were kidnapped. Admittedly you did not give anyone permission to plug him into you. Nevertheless it seems to me plain you *ought* to allow him to use your kidneys for that hour—it would be indecent to refuse.

Again, suppose pregnancy lasted only an hour and constituted no threat to life or health. And suppose that a woman becomes pregnant as a result of rape. Admittedly she did not voluntarily do anything to bring about the existence of a child. Admittedly she did nothing at all that would give the unborn person a right to the use of her body. All the same it might well be said, as in the newly emended violinist story, that she *ought* to allow it to remain for that hour—that it would be indecent in her to refuse.

Now some people are inclined to use the term "right" in such a way that it follows from the fact that you ought to allow a person to use your body for the hour he needs, that he has a right to use your body for the hour he needs, even though he has not been given that right by any person or act. They may say that it follows also that if you refuse you act unjustly toward him. This use of the term is perhaps so common that it cannot be called wrong; nevertheless it seems to me to be an unfortunate loosening of what we would do better to keep a tight rein on. Suppose that the box of chocolates I mentioned earlier had not been given to both boys jointly, but was given only to the older boy. There he sits, stolidly eating his way through the box, his small brother watching enviously. Here we are likely to say: "You ought not to be so mean. You ought to give your brother some of those chocolates." My own view is that it just does not follow from the truth of this that the brother has any right to any of the chocolates. If the boy refuses to give his brother any, he is greedy, stingy, callous—but not unjust. I suppose that the people I have in mind will say it does follow that the brother has a right to some of the chocolates, and thus that the boy does act unjustly if he refuses to give his brother any. But the effect of saying this is to obscure what we should keep distinct, namely the difference between the boy's refusal in this case and the boy's refusal in the earlier case, in which the box was given to both boys jointly, and in which the small brother thus had what was from any point of view clear title to half.

A further objection to so using the term "right," that from the fact that A ought to do a thing for B it follows that B has a right against A that A do it for him, is that it is going to make the question of whether or not a man has a right to a thing turn on how easy it is to provide him with it; and this seems not merely unfortunate but morally unacceptable. Take the case of Henry Fonda again. I said earlier that I had no right to the touch of his cool hand on my fevered brow, even though I needed it to save my life. I said it would be frightfully nice of him to fly in from the West Coast to provide me with it, but that I had no right against him that he should do so. But suppose he isn't on the West Coast. Suppose he has only to walk across the room and place a hand briefly on my brow—and lo, my life is saved. Then surely he ought to do it; it would be indecent to refuse. Is it to be said, "Ah, well, it follows that in this case she has a right to the touch of his hand on her brow, and so it would be an injustice for him to refuse"? So that I have a right to it when it is easy for him to provide it, though no right when it is hard? It's rather a shocking idea that anyone's rights should fade away and disappear as it gets harder and harder to accord them to him.

So my own view is that even though you ought to let the violinist use your kidneys for the one hour he needs, we should not conclude that he has a right to do so; we should say that if you refuse you are, like the boy who owns all the chocolates and will give none away, self-centered and callous—indecent, in fact—but not unjust. And similarly, that even supposing a case in which a woman pregnant due to rape ought to allow the unborn person to use her body for the hour he needs, we should not conclude that he has a right to do so; we should conclude that she is self-centered, callous, indecent, but not unjust, if she refuses. The complaints are no less grave; they are just different. However, there is no need to insist on this point. If anyone does wish to deduce "he has a right" from "you ought," then all the same he must surely grant that there are cases in which it is not morally required of you that you allow that violinist to use your kidneys, and in which he does not have a right to use them, and in which you do not do him an injustice if you refuse. And so also for mother and unborn child. Except in such cases as the unborn person has a right to demand it—and we were leaving open the possibility that there may be such cases—nobody is morally *required* to make large sacrifices, of health, of all other interests and concerns, of all other duties and commitments, for nine years, or even for nine months, in order to keep another person alive.

6. We have in fact to distinguish between two kinds of Samaritans: the Good Samaritan and what we might call the Minimally Decent Samaritan. The story of the Good Samaritan, you will remember, goes like this:

> A certain man went down from Jerusalem to Jericho, and fell among thieves, which stripped him of his raiment, and wounded him, and departed, leaving him half dead.
>
> And by chance there came down a certain priest that way; and when he saw him, he passed by on the other side.
>
> And likewise a Levite, when he was at the place, came and looked on him, and passed by the other side.
>
> But a certain Samaritan, as he journeyed, came where he was; and when he saw him he had compassion on him.
>
> And went to him, and bound up his wounds, pouring in oil and wine, and set him on his own beast, and brought him to an inn, and took care of him.
>
> And on the morrow, when he departed, he took out two pence, and gave them to the host, and said unto him, "Take care of him; and whatsoever thou spendest more, when I come again, I will repay thee." (Luke 10:30–35)

The Good Samaritan went out of his way, at some cost to himself, to help one in need of it. We are not told what the options were, that is, whether or not the priest and the Levite could have helped by doing less than the Good Samaritan did; but assuming they could have, then the fact they did nothing at all shows they were not even Minimally Decent Samaritans, not because they were not Samaritans, but because they were not even minimally decent.

These things are a matter of degree, of course, but there is a difference; it comes out perhaps most clearly in the story of Kitty Genovese, who was murdered while thirty-eight people watched or listened and did nothing at all to help her. A Good Samaritan would have rushed out to give direct assistance against the murderer. Or perhaps we had better allow that it would have been a Splendid Samaritan who did this, on the ground that it would have involved a risk of death for himself. But the thirty-eight people not only did not do this; they did not even trouble to pick up a phone to call the police. Minimally Decent Samaritanism would call for doing at least that, and their not having done so was monstrous.

After telling the story of the Good Samaritan Jesus said, "Go, and do thou likewise." Perhaps he meant that we are morally required to act as the Good Samaritan did. Perhaps he was urging people to do more than is morally required of them. At all events it seems plain that it was not morally required of any of the thirty-eight that he rush out to give direct assistance at the risk of his own life and that it is not morally required of anyone that he give long stretches of his life—nine years or nine months—to sustaining the life of a person who has no special right (we were leaving open the possibility of this) to demand it.

Indeed, with one rather striking class of exceptions, no one in any country in the world is *legally* required to do anywhere near as much as this for anyone else. The class of exceptions is obvious. My main concern here is not the state of the law in respect to abortion, but it is worth drawing attention to the fact that in no state in this country is any man compelled by law to be even a Minimally Decent Samaritan to any person; there is no law under which charges could be brought against the thirty-eight people who stood by while Kitty Genovese died. By contrast, in most states in this country women are compelled by law to be not merely Minimally Decent Samaritans, but Good Samaritans, to unborn persons inside them. This does not by itself settle anything, because it may well be argued that there should be laws in this country—as there are in many European countries—compelling at least Minimally Decent Samaritanism.[8] But it does show that there is a gross injustice in the existing state of the law. And it shows also that the groups currently working against liberalization of abortion laws, in fact working toward having it declared unconstitutional for a state to permit abortion, had better start working for the adoption of Good Samaritan laws generally, or earn the charge that they are acting in bad faith.

I myself think that Minimally Decent Samaritan laws would be one thing, Good Samaritan laws quite another—and in fact highly improper. But we are not here concerned with the law. What we should ask is not whether anybody should be compelled by law to be a Good Samaritan but whether we must accede to a situation in which somebody is being compelled—by nature, perhaps—to be a Good Samaritan. We have, in other words, to look now at third-party interventions. I have been arguing that no person is morally required to make large sacrifices to sustain the life of another who has no right to demand them, and this even where the sacrifices do not include life itself; we are not morally required to be Good Samaritans, or anyway, Very Good Samaritans, to one another. But what if a man cannot extricate himself from such a situation? What if he appeals to us to extricate him? It seems to me plain that there are cases in which we can, cases in which a Good Samaritan would extricate him. There you are: you were kidnapped, and nine years in bed with the violinist lie ahead of you. You have your own life to lead. You are sorry, but you simply cannot see giving up so much of your life to the sustaining of his. You cannot extricate yourself, and ask us to do so. I should have thought that—in light of his having no right to the use of your body—it was obvious that we do not have to accede to your being forced to give up so much. We can do what you ask. There is no injustice to the violinist in our doing so.

7. Following the lead of the opponents of abortion, I have throughout been speaking of the fetus merely as a person; and what I have been asking is whether or not the argument we began with, which proceeds only from the fetus' being a person, really does establish its conclusion. I have argued that it does not.

But of course there are arguments and arguments, and it may be said that I have simply fastened on the wrong one. It may be said that what is important is not merely the fact that the fetus is a person but that it is a person for whom the woman has a special kind of responsibility issuing from the fact that she is its mother. It might be argued that all my analogies are therefore irrelevant—for you do not have that special kind of responsibility for that violinist and Henry Fonda does not have that special kind of responsibility for me. And our attention might be drawn to the fact that men and women both are compelled by law to provide support for their children.

I have in effect dealt (briefly) with this argument in section 4 above; but a (still briefer) recapitulation now may be in order. Surely we do not have any such "special responsibility" for a person unless we have assumed it, explicitly or implicitly. If a set of parents do not try to prevent pregnancy, do not obtain an abortion, and then at the time of birth of the child do not put it up for adoption but rather take it home with them, then they have assumed responsibility for it, they have given it rights, and they cannot *now* withdraw support from it at the cost of its life because they now find it difficult to go on providing for it. But if they have taken all reasonable precautions against having a child, they do not simply by virtue of their biological relationship to the child who comes into existence have a special responsibility for it. They may wish to assume responsibility for it, or they may not wish to. And I am suggesting that if assuming responsibility for it would require large sacrifices, then they may refuse. A Good Samaritan would not refuse, or, anyway, a Splendid Samaritan would not, if the sacrifices that had to be made were enormous. But then so would a Good Samaritan assume responsibility for that violinist; so would Henry Fonda, if he is a Good Samaritan, fly in from the West Coast and assume responsibility for me.

8. My argument will be found unsatisfactory on two counts by many of those who want to regard abortion as morally permissible. First, while I do

argue that abortion is not impermissible, I do not argue that it is always permissible. There may well be cases in which carrying the child to term requires only Minimally Decent Samaritanism of the mother, and this is a standard we must not fall below. I am inclined to think it a merit of my account precisely that it does *not* give a general yes or a general no. It allows for and supports our sense that, for example, a sick and desperately frightened fourteen-year-old schoolgirl, pregnant due to rape, may *of course* choose abortion, and that any law that rules this out is an insane law. And it also allows for and supports our sense that in other cases resort to abortion is even positively indecent. It would be indecent in the woman to request an abortion, and indecent in a doctor to perform it, if she is in her seventh month and wants the abortion just to avoid the nuisance of postponing a trip abroad. The very fact that the arguments I have been drawing attention to treat all cases of abortion, or even all cases of abortion in which the mother's life is not at stake, as morally on a par ought to have made them suspect at the outset.

Second, while I am arguing for the permissibility of abortion in some cases, I am not arguing for the right to secure the death of the unborn child. It is easy to confuse these two things in that up to a certain point in the life of the fetus it is not able to survive outside the mother's body; hence removing it from her body guarantees its death. But they are different in important ways. I have argued that you are not morally required to spend nine months in bed, sustaining the life of the violinist; but to say this is by no means to say that if when you unplug yourself there is a miracle and he survives, you have a right to turn round and slit his throat. You may detach yourself even if this costs him his life; you have no right to be guaranteed his death by some other means if unplugging yourself does not kill him. There are some people who will feel dissatisfied by this feature of my argument. A woman may be utterly devastated by the thought of a child, a bit of herself, put up for adoption and never seen or heard of again. She may therefore want not merely that the child be detached from her but, more, that it die. Some opponents of abortion are inclined to regard this as beneath contempt, thereby showing insensitivity to what is surely a powerful source of despair. All the same, I agree that the desire for the child's death is not one that anybody may gratify, should it turn out to be possible to detach the child alive.

At this place, however, it should be remembered that we have only been pretending throughout that the fetus is a human being from the moment of conception. A very early abortion is surely not the killing of a person and so is not dealt with by anything I have said here.

Notes

1. I am very indebted to James Thomson for discussion, criticism, and many helpful suggestions.

2. Daniel Callahan, *Abortion: Law, Choice, and Morality* (New York: Macmillan, 1970), p. 373. This book gives a fascinating survey of the available information on abortion. The Jewish tradition is surveyed in David M. Feldman, *Birth Control in Jewish Law* (New York: New York University Press, 1968), part 5; the Catholic tradition, in John T. Noonan Jr., "An Almost Absolute Value in History," in *The Morality of Abortion,* ed. John T. Noonan Jr. (Cambridge, Mass.: Harvard University Press, 1970).

3. The term "direct" in the arguments I refer to is a technical one. Roughly, what is meant by "direct killing" is either killing as an end in itself or killing as a means to some end, for example, the end of saving someone else's life. See note 6 for an example of its use.

4. Cf. *Encyclical Letter of Pope Pius XI on Christian Marriage,* St. Paul Editions (Boston, n.d.), p. 32: "However much we may pity the mother whose health and even life is gravely imperiled in the performance of the duty allotted to her by nature, nevertheless what could ever be a sufficient reason for excusing in any way the direct murder of the innocent? This is precisely what we are dealing with here." Noonan *(The Morality of Abortion,* p. 43) reads this as follows: "What cause can ever avail to excuse in any way the direct killing of the innocent? For it is a question of that."

5. The thesis in argument 4 is in an interesting way weaker than those in 1, 2, and 3: they rule out abortion even in cases in which both mother and child will die if the abortion is not performed. By contrast, one who held the view expressed in 4 could consistently say that one need not prefer letting two persons die to killing one.

6. Cf. the following passage from Pius XII, *Address to the Italian Catholic Society of Midwives:* "The baby in the maternal breast has the right to life immediately from God.—Hence there is no man, no human authority, no science, no medical, eugenic, social, economic or moral 'indication' which can establish or grant a valid juridical ground for a direct deliberate disposition of an innocent human life, that is a disposition which looks to its destruction either as an end or as a means to another end perhaps in itself not illicit.—The baby, still not born, is a man in the same degree and for the same reason as the mother" (quoted in Noonan, *The Morality of Abortion,* p. 45).

7. The need for a discussion of this argument was brought home to me by members of the Society for Ethical and Legal Philosophy, to whom this paper was originally presented.

8. For a discussion of the difficulties involved, and a survey of the European experience with such laws, see *The Good Samaritan and the Law,* ed. James M. Ratcliffe (New York: Peter Smith, 1966).

16

On the Moral and Legal Status of Abortion

Mary Anne Warren

We will be concerned with both the moral status of abortion, which for our purposes we may define as the act which a woman performs in voluntarily terminating, or allowing another person to terminate, her pregnancy, and the legal status which is appropriate for this act. I will argue that, while it is not possible to produce a satisfactory defense of a woman's right to obtain an abortion without showing that a fetus is not a human being, in the morally relevant sense of that term, we ought not to conclude that the difficulties involved in determining whether or not a fetus is human make it impossible to produce any satisfactory solution to the problem of the moral status of abortion. For it is possible to show that, on the basis of intuitions which we may expect even the opponents of abortion to share, a fetus is not a person, and hence not the sort of entity to which it is proper to ascribe full moral rights.

Of course, while some philosophers would deny the possibility of any such proof,[1] others will deny that there is any need for it, since the moral permissibility of abortion appears to them to be too obvious to require proof. But the inadequacy of this attitude should be evident from the fact that both the friends and the foes of abortion consider their position to be morally self-evident. Because pro-abortionists have never adequately come to grips with the conceptual issues surrounding abortion, most, if not all, of the arguments which they advance in opposition to laws restricting access to abortion fail to refute or even weaken the traditional antiabortion argument, i.e., that a fetus is a human being, and therefore abortion is murder.

These arguments are typically of one of two sorts. Either they point to the terrible side effects of the restrictive laws, e.g., the deaths due to illegal abortions, and the fact that it is poor women who suffer the most as a result of these

First published in *The Monist,* vol. 57 (1973). Copyright © 1973, *The Monist,* La Salle, Illinois, 61301. Reprinted by permission.

laws. or else they state that to deny a woman access to abortion is to deprive her of her right to control her own body. Unfortunately, however, the fact that restricting access to abortion has tragic side effects does not, in itself, show that the restrictions are unjustified, since murder is wrong regardless of the consequences of prohibiting it; and the appeal to the right to control one's body, which is generally construed as a property right, is at best a rather feeble argument for the permissibility of abortion. Mere ownership does not give me the right to kill innocent people whom I find on my property, and indeed I am apt to be held responsible if such people injure themselves while on my property. It is equally unclear that I have any moral right to expel an innocent person from my property when I know that doing so will result in his death.

Furthermore, it is probably inappropriate to describe a woman's body as her property, since it seems natural to hold that a person is something distinct from her property, but not from her body. Even those who would object to the identification of a person with his body, or with the conjunction of his body and his mind, must admit that it would be very odd to describe, say, breaking a leg, as damaging one's property, and much more appropriate to describe it as injuring *oneself*. Thus it is probably a mistake to argue that the right to obtain an abortion is in any way derived from the right to own and regulate property.

But however we wish to construe the right to abortion, we cannot hope to convince those who consider abortion a form of murder of the existence of any such right unless we are able to produce a clear and convincing refutation of the traditional antiabortion argument, and this has not, to my knowledge, been done. With respect to the two most vital issues which that argument involves, i.e., the humanity of the fetus and its implication for the moral status of abortion, confusion has prevailed on both sides of the dispute.

Thus, both proabortionists and antiabortionists have tended to abstract the question of whether abortion is wrong to that of whether it is wrong to destroy a fetus, just as though the rights of another person were not necessarily involved. This mistaken abstraction has led to the almost universal assumption that if a fetus is a human being, with a right to life, then it follows immediately that abortion is wrong (except perhaps when necessary to save the woman's life), and that it ought to be prohibited. It has also been generally assumed that unless the question about the status of the fetus is answered, the moral status of abortion cannot possibly be determined.

Two recent papers, one by B. A. Brody,[2] and one by Judith Thomson,[3] have attempted to settle the question of whether abortion ought to be prohibited apart from the question of whether or not the fetus is human. Brody examines the possibility that the following two statements are compatible: (1) that abortion is the taking of innocent human life, and therefore wrong; and (2) that nevertheless it ought not to be prohibited by law, at least under the present circumstances.[4] Not surprisingly, Brody finds it impossible to reconcile these two statements, since, as he rightly argues, none of the unfortunate side effects of the prohibition of abortion is bad enough to justify legalizing the *wrongful* taking of human life.

He is mistaken, however, in concluding that the incompatibility of (1) and (2), in itself, shows that "the legal problem about abortion cannot be resolved independently of the status of the fetus problem" (p. 369).

What Brody fails to realize is that (1) embodies the questionable assumption that if a fetus is a human being, then of course abortion is morally wrong, and that an attack on *this* assumption is more promising, as a way of reconciling the humanity of the fetus with the claim that laws prohibiting abortion are unjustified, than is an attack on the assumption that if abortion is the wrongful killing of innocent human beings then it ought to be prohibited. He thus overlooks the possibility that a fetus may have a right to life and abortion still be morally permissible, in that the right of a woman to terminate an unwanted pregnancy might override the right of the fetus to be kept alive. The immorality of abortion is no more demonstrated by the humanity of the fetus, in itself, than the immorality of killing in self-defense is demonstrated by the fact that the assailant is a human being. Neither is it demonstrated by the *innocence* of the fetus, since there may be situations in which the killing of innocent human beings is justified.

It is perhaps not surprising that Brody fails to spot this assumption, since it has been accepted with little or no argument by nearly everyone who has written on the morality of abortion. John Noonan is correct in saying that "the fundamental question in the long history of abortion is, How do you determine the humanity of a being?"[5] He summarizes his own antiabortion argument, which is a version of the official position of the Catholic Church, as follows:

> . . . it is wrong to kill humans, however poor, weak, defenseless, and lacking
> in opportunity to develop their potential they may be. It is therefore morally
> wrong to kill Biafrans. Similarly, it is morally wrong to kill embryos.[6]

Noonan bases his claim that fetuses are human upon what he calls the theologians' criterion of humanity: that whoever is conceived of human beings is human. But although he argues at length for the appropriateness of this criterion, he never questions the assumption that if a fetus is human then abortion is wrong for exactly the same reason that murder is wrong.

Judith Thomson is, in fact, the only writer I am aware of who has seriously questioned this assumption: she has argued that, even if we grant the antiabortionist his claim that a fetus is a human being, with the same right to life as any other human being, we can still demonstrate that, in at least some and perhaps most cases, a woman is under no moral obligation to complete an unwanted pregnancy.[7] Her argument is worth examining, since if it holds up it may enable us to establish the moral permissibility of abortion without becoming involved in problems about what entitles an entity to be considered human, and accorded full moral rights. To be able to do this would be a great gain in the power and simplicity of the proabortion position, since, although I will argue that these problems can be solved at least as decisively as can any other moral problem, we should certainly be pleased to be able to avoid having to solve them as part of the justification of abortion.

On the other hand, even if Thomson's argument does not hold up, her insight, i.e., that it requires *argument* to show that if fetuses are human then abortion is properly classified as murder, is an extremely valuable one. The assumption she attacks is particularly invidious, for it amounts to the decision that it is appropriate, in deciding the moral status of abortion, to leave the rights of the pregnant woman out of consideration entirely, except possibly when her life is threatened. Obviously, this will not do; determining what moral rights, if any, a fetus possesses is only the first step in determining the moral status of abortion. Step two, which is at least equally essential, is finding a just solution to the conflict between whatever rights the fetus may have, and the rights of the woman who is unwillingly pregnant. While the historical error has been to pay far too little attention to the second step, Ms. Thomson's suggestion is that if we look at the second step first we may find that a woman has a right to obtain an abortion *regardless* of what rights the fetus has.

Our own inquiry will also have two stages. In Section I, we will consider whether or not it is possible to establish that abortion is morally permissible even on the assumption that a fetus is an entity with a full-fledged right to life. I will argue that in fact this cannot be established, at least not with the conclusiveness which is essential to our hopes of convincing those who are skeptical about the morality of abortion, and that we therefore cannot avoid dealing with the question of whether or not a fetus really does have the same right to life as a (more fully developed) human being.

In Section II, I will propose an answer to this question, namely, that a fetus cannot be considered a member of the moral community, the set of beings with full and equal moral rights, for the simple reason that it is not a person, and that it is personhood, and not genetic humanity, i.e., humanity as defined by Noonan, which is the basis for membership in this community. I will argue that a fetus, whatever its stage of development, satisfies none of the basic criteria of personhood, and is not even enough *like* a person to be accorded even some of the same rights on the basis of this resemblance. Nor, as we will see, is a fetus's *potential* personhood a threat to the morality of abortion, since, whatever the rights of potential people may be, they are invariably overridden in any conflict with the moral rights of actual people.

I

We turn now to Professor Thomson's case for the claim that even if a fetus has full moral rights, abortion is still morally permissible, at least sometimes, and for some reasons other than to save the woman's life. Her argument is based upon a clever, but I think faulty, analogy. She asks us to picture ourselves waking up one day, in bed with a famous violinist. Imagine that you have been kidnapped, and your bloodstream hooked up to that of the violinist, who happens to have an ailment which will certainly kill him unless he is permitted to share your kidneys for a period of nine months. No one else can save him, since you alone have the right type of blood. He will be unconscious all that time, and you will have to stay in bed with him, but after the nine months are over he may be unplugged, completely cured, that is, provided that you have cooperated.

Now then, she continues, what are your obligations in this situation? The antiabortionist, if he is consistent, will have to say that you are obligated to stay in bed with the violinist: for all people have a right to life, and violinists are people, and therefore it would be murder for you to disconnect yourself from him and let him die. But this is outrageous, and so there must be something wrong with the same argument when it is applied to abortion. It would certainly be commendable of you to agree to save the violinist, but it is absurd to suggest that your refusal to do so would be murder. His right to life does not obligate you to do whatever is required to keep him alive; nor does it justify anyone else in forcing you to do so. A law which required you to stay in bed with the violinist would clearly be an unjust law, since it is no proper function of the law to force unwilling people to make huge sacrifices for the sake of other people toward whom they have no such prior obligation.

Thomson concludes that, if this analogy is an apt one, then we can grant the antiabortionist his claim that a fetus is a human being, and still hold that it is at least sometimes the case that a pregnant woman has the right to refuse to be a Good Samaritan toward the fetus, i.e., to obtain an abortion. For there is a great gap between the claim that x has a right to life, and the claim that y is obligated to do whatever is necessary to keep x alive, let alone that he ought to be forced to do so. It is y's duty to keep x alive only if he has somehow contracted a *special* obligation to do so; and a woman who is unwillingly pregnant, e.g., who was raped, has done nothing which obligates her to make the enormous sacrifice which is necessary to preserve the conceptus.

This argument is initially quite plausible, and in the extreme case of pregnancy due to rape it is probably conclusive. Difficulties arise, however, when we try to specify more exactly the range of cases in which abortion is clearly justifiable even on the assumption that the fetus is human. Professor Thomson considers it a virtue of her argument that it does not enable us to conclude that abortion is *always* permissible. It would, she says, be "indecent" for a woman in her seventh month to obtain an abortion just to avoid having to postpone a trip to Europe. On the other hand, her argument enables us to see that "a sick and desperately frightened schoolgirl pregnant due to rape may *of course* choose abortion, and that any law which rules this out is an insane law." So far, so good; but what are we to say about the woman who becomes pregnant not through rape but as a result of her own carelessness, or because of contraceptive failure, or who gets pregnant intentionally and then changes her mind about wanting a child? With respect to such cases, the violinist analogy is of much less use to the defender of the woman's right to obtain an abortion.

Indeed, the choice of a pregnancy due to rape, as an example of a case in which abortion is permissible even if a fetus is considered a human being, is extremely significant; for it is only in the case of pregnancy due to rape that the woman's situation is adequately analogous to the violinist case for our intuitions about the latter to transfer convincingly. The crucial difference between a pregnancy due to rape and the *normal* case of an unwanted pregnancy is that in the normal case we cannot claim that the woman is in no way responsible for her predicament; she could have remained chaste, or taken her pills more faithfully, or abstained on dangerous days, and so on. If, on the other hand, you are kidnapped by strangers, and hooked up to a strange violinist, then you are free of any shred of responsibility for the situation, on the basis of which it could be argued that you are obligated to keep the violinist alive. Only when her pregnancy is due to rape is a woman clearly just as nonresponsible.[8]

Consequently, there is room for the antiabortionist to argue that in the normal case of unwanted pregnancy a woman has, by her own actions, assumed responsibility for the fetus. For if x behaves in a way which he could have avoided, and which he knows involves, let us say, a 1 percent chance of bringing into existence a human being, with a right to life, and does so knowing that if this should happen then that human being will perish unless x does certain things to keep him alive, then it is by no means clear that when it does happen x is free of any obligation to what he knew in advance would be required to keep that human being alive.

The plausibility of such an argument is enough to show that the Thomson analogy can provide a clear and persuasive defense of a woman's right to obtain an abortion only with respect to those cases in which the woman is in no way responsible for her pregnancy, e.g., where it is due to rape. In all other cases, we would almost certainly conclude that it was necessary to look carefully at the particular circumstances in order to determine the extent of the woman's responsibility, and hence the extent of her obligation. This is an extremely unsatisfactory outcome, from the viewpoint of the opponents of restrictive abortion laws, most of whom are convinced that a woman has a right to obtain an abortion regardless of how and why she got pregnant.

Of course a supporter of the violinist analogy might point out that it is absurd to suggest that forgetting her pill one day might be sufficient to obligate a woman to complete an unwanted pregnancy. And indeed it *is* absurd to suggest this. As we will see, the moral right to obtain an abortion is not in the least dependent upon the extent to which the woman is responsible for her pregnancy. But unfortunately, once we allow the assumption that a fetus has full moral rights, we cannot avoid taking this absurd suggestion seriously. Perhaps we can make this point more clear by altering the violinist story just enough to make it more analogous to a normal unwanted pregnancy and less to a pregnancy due to rape, and then seeing whether it is still obvious that you are not obligated to stay in bed with the fellow.

Suppose, then, that violinists are peculiarly prone to the sort of illness the only cure for which is the use of someone else's bloodstream for nine months, and that because of this there has been formed a society of music lovers who agree that whenever a violinist is stricken they will draw lots and the loser will, by some means, be made the one and only person capable of saving him. Now then, would you be obligated to cooperate in curing the violinist if you had voluntarily joined this society, knowing the possible consequences, and then your name had been drawn and you had been kidnapped? Admittedly, you did not promise ahead of time that you would, but you did deliberately place yourself in a position in which it might happen that a human life would be lost if you did not. Surely this is at least a prima facie reason for supposing that you have an obligation to stay in bed with the violinist. Suppose that you had gotten your name drawn deliberately; surely *that* would be quite a strong reason for thinking that you had such an obligation.

It might be suggested that there is one important disanalogy between the modified violinist case and the case of an unwanted pregnancy, which makes the woman's responsibility significantly less, namely, the fact that the fetus *comes into existence* as the result of the woman's actions. This fact might give her a right to refuse to keep it alive, whereas she would not have had this right had it existed previously, independently, and then as a result of her actions become dependent upon her for its survival.

My own intuition, however, is that x has no more right to bring into existence, either deliberately or as a foreseeable result of actions he could have avoided, a being with full moral rights (y), and then refuse to do what he knew beforehand would be required to keep that being alive, than he has to enter into an agreement with an existing person, whereby he may be called upon to save that person's life, and then refuse to do so when so called upon. Thus, x's responsibility for y's existence does not seem to lessen his obligation to keep y alive, if he is also responsible for y's being in a situation in which only he can save him.

Whether or not this intuition is entirely correct, it brings us back once again to the conclusion that once we allow the assumption that a fetus has full moral rights it becomes an extremely complex and difficult question whether and when abortion is justifiable. Thus the Thomson analogy cannot help us produce a clear and persuasive proof of the moral permissibility of abortion. Nor will the opponents of the restrictive laws thank us for anything less; for their conviction (for the most part) is that abortion is obviously *not* a morally serious and extremely unfortunate, even though sometimes justified act, comparable to killing in self-defense or to letting the violinist die, but rather is closer to being a morally neutral act, like cutting one's hair.

The basis of this conviction. I believe, is the realization that a fetus is not a person, and thus does not have a full-fledged right to life. Perhaps the reason why this claim has been so inadequately defended is that it seems self-evident to those who accept it. And so it is, insofar as it follows from what I take to be perfectly obvious claims about the nature of personhood, and about the proper grounds for ascribing moral rights, claims which ought, indeed, to be obvious to both the friends and foes of abortion. Nevertheless, it is worth examining these claims, and showing how they demonstrate the moral innocuousness of abortion, since this apparently has not been adequately done before.

II

The question which we must answer in order to produce a satisfactory solution to the problem of the moral status of abortion is this: How are we to define the moral community, the set of beings with full and equal moral rights, such that we can decide whether a human fetus is a member of this community or not? What sort of entity, exactly, has the inalienable rights to life, liberty, and the pursuit of happiness? Jefferson attributed these rights to all *men,* and it may or may not be fair to suggest that he intended to attribute them *only* to men. Perhaps he ought to have attributed them to all human beings. If so, then we arrive, first, at Noonan's problem of defining what makes a being human, and second, at the equally vital question which Noonan does not consider, namely, What reason is there for identifying the moral community with the set of all human beings, in whatever way we have chosen to define that term?

1. On the Definition of 'Human'

One reason why this vital second question is so frequently overlooked in the debate over the moral status of abortion is that the term 'human' has two distinct, but not often distinguished, senses. This fact results in a slide of meaning, which serves to conceal the fallaciousness of the traditional argument that since (1) it is wrong to kill innocent human beings, and (2) fetuses are innocent human beings, then (3) it is wrong to kill fetuses. For if 'human' is used in the same sense in both (1) and (2) then, whichever of the two senses is meant, one of these premises is question-begging. And if it is used in two different senses then of course the conclusion doesn't follow.

Thus, (1) is a self-evident moral truth,[9] and avoids begging the question about abortion, only if 'human being' is used to mean something like "a full-fledged member of the moral community." (It may or may not also be meant to refer exclusively to members of the species *Homo sapiens.*) We may call this the *moral* sense of 'human'. It is not to be confused with what we will call the *genetic* sense, i.e., the sense in which *any* member of the species is a human being, and no member of any other species could be. If (1) is acceptable only if the moral sense is intended, (2) is non-question-begging only if what is intended is the genetic sense.

In "Deciding Who Is Human," Noonan argues for the classification of fetuses with human beings by pointing to the presence of the full genetic code, and the potential capacity for rational thought (p. 135). It is clear that what he needs to show, for his version of the traditional argument to be valid, is that fetuses are human in the moral sense, the sense in which it is analytically true that all human beings have full moral rights. But, in the absence of any argument showing that whatever is genetically human is also morally human, and he gives none, nothing more than genetic humanity can be demonstrated by the presence of the human genetic code. And, as we will see, the *potential* capacity for rational thought can at most show that an entity has the potential for *becoming* human in the moral sense.

2. Defining the Moral Community

Can it be established that genetic humanity is sufficient for moral humanity? I think that there are very good reasons for not defining the moral community in this way. I would like to suggest an alternative way of defining the moral community, which I will argue for only to the extent of explaining why it is, or should be, self-evident. The suggestion is simply that the moral community consists of all and only *people,* rather than all and only human beings;[10] and probably the best way of demonstrating its self-evidence is by considering the concept of personhood, to see what sorts of entity are and are not persons, and what the decision that a being is or is not a person implies about its moral rights.

What characteristics entitle an entity to be considered a person? This is obviously not the place to attempt a complete analysis of the concept of personhood, but we do not need such a fully adequate analysis just to determine whether and why a fetus is or isn't a person. All we need is a rough and approximate list of the most basic criteria of personhood, and some idea of which, or how many, of these an entity must satisfy in order to properly be considered a person.

In searching for such criteria, it is useful to look beyond the set of people with whom we are acquainted, and ask how we would decide whether a totally alien being was a person or not. (For we have no right to assume that genetic humanity is necessary for personhood.) Imagine a space traveler who lands on an unknown planet and encounters a race of beings utterly unlike any he has ever seen or heard of. If he wants to be sure of behaving morally toward these beings, he has to somehow decide whether they are people, and hence have full moral rights, or whether they are the sort of thing which he need not feel guilty about treating as, for example, a source of food.

How should he go about making this decision? If he has some anthropological background, he might look for such things as religion, art, and the manufacturing of tools, weapons, or shelters, since these factors have been used to distinguish our human from our prehuman ancestors, in what seems to be closer to the moral than the genetic sense of 'human'. And no doubt he would be right to consider the presence of such factors as good evidence that the alien beings were people, and morally human. It would, however, be overly anthropocentric of him to take the absence of these things as adequate evidence that they were not, since we can imagine people who have progressed beyond, or evolved without ever developing, these cultural characteristics.

I suggest that the traits which are most central to the concept of personhood, or humanity in the moral sense, are, very roughly, the following:

1. consciousness (of objects and events external and/or internal to the being), and in particular the capacity to feel pain;

2. reasoning (the *developed* capacity to solve new and relatively complex problems);

3. self-motivated activity (activity which is relatively independent of either genetic or direct external control);

4. the capacity to communicate, by whatever means, messages of an indefinite variety of types, that is, not just with an indefinite number of possible contents, but on indefinitely many possible topics;

5. the presence of self-concepts, and self-awareness, either individual or racial, or both.

Admittedly, there are apt to be a great many problems involved in formulating precise definitions of these criteria, let alone in developing universally valid behavioral criteria for deciding when they apply. But I will assume that both we and our explorer know approximately what (1)–(5) mean, and that he is also able to determine whether or not they apply. How, then, should he use his findings to decide whether or not the alien beings are people? We needn't suppose that an entity must have *all* of these attributes to be properly considered a person; (1) and (2) alone may well be sufficient for personhood, and quite probably (1)–(3) are sufficient. Neither do we need to insist that any one of these criteria is *necessary* for personhood, although once again (1) and (2) look like fairly good candidates for necessary conditions, as does (3), if 'activity' is construed so as to include the activity of reasoning.

All we need to claim, to demonstrate that a fetus is not a person, is that any being which satisfies *none* of (1)–(5) is certainly not a person. I consider this claim to be so obvious that I think anyone who denied it, and claimed that a being which satisfied none of (1)–(5) was a person all the same, would thereby demonstrate that he had no notion at all of what a person is—perhaps because he had confused the concept of a person with that of genetic humanity. If the opponents of abortion were to deny the appropriateness of these five criteria, I do not know what further arguments would convince them. We would probably have to admit that our conceptual schemes were indeed irreconcilably different, and that our dispute could not be settled objectively.

I do not expect this to happen, however, since I think that the concept of a person is one which is very nearly universal (to people), and that it is common to both proabortionists and antiabortionists, even though neither group has fully realized the relevance of this concept to the resolution of their dispute. Furthermore, I think that on reflection even antiabortionists ought to agree not only that (1)–(5) are central to the concept of personhood, but also that it is a part of this concept that all and only people have full moral rights. The concept of a person is in part a moral concept; once we have admitted that *x* is a person we have recognized, even if we have not agreed to respect, *x*'s right to be treated as a member of the moral community. It is true that the claim that *x* is a *human being* is more commonly voiced as part of an appeal to treat *x* decently than is the claim that *x* is a person, but this is either because 'human being' is here used in the sense which implies personhood, or because the genetic and moral senses of 'human' have been confused.

Now if (1)–(5) are indeed the primary criteria of personhood, then it is clear that genetic humanity is neither necessary nor sufficient for establishing that an entity is a person. Some human beings are not people, and there may well be people who are not human beings. A man or woman whose consciousness has been permanently obliterated but who remains alive is a human being which is no longer a person; defective human beings, with no appreciable mental capacity, are not and presumably never will be people; and a fetus is a human being which is not yet a person, and which therefore cannot coherently be said to have full moral rights. Citizens of the next century should be prepared to recognize highly advanced, self-aware robots or computers, should such be developed, and intelligent inhabitants of other worlds, should such be found, as people in the fullest sense, and to respect their moral rights. But to ascribe full moral rights to an entity which is not a person is as absurd as to ascribe moral obligations and responsibilities to such an entity.

3. Fetal Development and the Right to Life

Two problems arise in the application of these suggestions for the definition of the moral community to the determination of the precise moral status of a human fetus. Given that the paradigm example of a person is a normal adult human being, then (1) How like this paradigm, in particular how far advanced since conception, does a human being need to be before it begins to have a right to life by virtue, not of being fully a person as of yet, but of being *like* a person? and (2) To what extent, if any, does the fact that a fetus has the *potential* for becoming a person endow it with some of the same rights? Each of these questions requires some comment.

In answering the first question, we need not attempt a detailed consideration of the moral rights of organisms which are not developed enough, aware enough, intelligent enough, etc., to be considered people, but which resemble people in some respects. It does seem reasonable to suggest that the more like a person, in the relevant respects, a being is, the stronger is the case for regarding it as having a right to life, and indeed the stronger its right to life is. Thus we ought to take seriously the suggestion that, insofar as "the human individual develops biologically in a continuous fashion . . . the rights of a human person might develop in the same way."[11] But we must keep in mind that the attributes which are relevant in determining whether or not an entity is enough like a person to be regarded as having some of the same moral rights are no different from those which are relevant to determining whether or not it is fully a person—i.e., are no different from (1)–(5)—and that being genetically human, or having recognizably human facial and other physical features, or detectable brain activity, or the capacity to survive outside the uterus, are simply not among these relevant attributes.

Thus it is clear that even though a seven- or eight-month fetus has features which make it apt to arouse in us almost the same powerful protective instinct as is commonly aroused by a small infant, nevertheless it is not significantly more personlike than is a very small embryo. It is *somewhat* more personlike; it can apparently feel and respond to pain, and it may even have a rudimentary form of consciousness, insofar as its brain is quite active. Nevertheless, it seems safe to say that it is not fully conscious, in the way that an infant of a few months is, and that it cannot reason, or communicate messages of indefinitely many sorts, does not engage in self-motivated activity, and has no self-awareness. Thus, in the *relevant* respects, a fetus, even a fully developed one, is considerably less personlike than is the average mature mammal, indeed the average fish. And I think that a rational person must conclude that if the right to life of a fetus is to be based upon its resemblance to a person, then it cannot be said to have any more right to life than, let us say, a newborn guppy (which also seems to be capable of feeling pain), and that a right of that magnitude could never override a woman's right to obtain an abortion, at any stage of her pregnancy.

There may, of course, be other arguments in favor of placing legal limits upon the stage of pregnancy in which an abortion may be performed. Given the relative safety of the new techniques of artificially inducing labor during the third trimester, the danger to the woman's life or health is no longer such an argument. Neither is the fact that people tend to respond to the thought of abortion in the later stages of pregnancy with emotional repulsion, since mere emotional responses cannot take the place of moral reasoning in determining what ought to be permitted. Nor, finally, is the frequently heard argument that legalizing abortion, especially late in the pregnancy, may erode the level of respect for human life, leading, perhaps, to an increase in unjustified euthanasia and other crimes. For this threat, if it is a threat, can be better met by educating people to the kinds of moral distinctions which we are making here than by limiting access to abortion (which limitation may, in its disregard for the rights of women, be just as damaging to the level of respect for human rights).

Thus, since the fact that even a fully developed fetus is not personlike enough to have any significant right to life on the basis of its personlikeness shows that no legal restrictions upon the stage of pregnancy in which an abortion may be performed can be justified on the grounds that we should protect the rights of the older fetus; and since there is no other apparent justification for such restrictions, we may conclude that they are entirely unjustified. Whether or not it would be *indecent* (whatever that means) for a woman in her seventh month to obtain an abortion just to avoid having to postpone a trip to Europe, it would not, in itself, be *immoral,* and therefore it ought to be permitted.

4. Potential Personhood and the Right to Life

We have seen that a fetus does not resemble a person in any way which can support the claim that it has even some of the same rights. But what about its *potential,* the fact that if nurtured and allowed to develop naturally it will very probably become a person? Doesn't that alone give it at least some right to life? It is hard to deny that the fact that an entity is a potential person is a strong prima facie reason for not destroying it; but we need not conclude from this that a potential person has a right to life, by virtue of that potential. It may be that our feeling that it is better, other things being equal, not to destroy a potential person is better explained by the fact that potential people are still (felt to be) an invaluable resource, not to be lightly squandered. Surely, if every speck of dust were a potential person, we would be much less apt to conclude that every potential person has a right to become actual.

Still, we do not need to insist that a potential person has no right to life whatever. There may well be something immoral, and not just imprudent, about wantonly destroying potential people, when doing so isn't necessary to protect anyone's rights. But even if a potential person does have some prima facie right to life, such a right could not possibly outweigh the right of a woman to obtain an abortion, since the rights of any actual person invariably outweigh those of any potential person, whenever the two conflict. Since this may not be immediately obvious in the case of a human fetus, let us look at another case.

Suppose that our space explorer falls into the hands of an alien culture, whose scientists decide to create a few hundred thousand or more human beings, by breaking his body into its component cells, and using these to create fully developed human beings, with, of course, his genetic code. We may imagine that each of these newly created men will have all of the original man's abilities, skills, knowledge, and so on, and also have an individual self-concept, in short that each of them will be a bona fide (though hardly unique) person. Imagine that the whole project will take only seconds, and that its chances of success are extremely high, and that our explorer knows all of this, and also knows that these people will be treated fairly. I maintain that in such a situation he would have every right to escape if he could, and thus to deprive all of these potential people of their potential lives; for his right to life outweighs all of theirs together, in spite of the fact that they are all genetically human, all innocent, and all have a very high probability of becoming people very soon, if only he refrains from acting.

Indeed, I think he would have a right to escape even if it were not his life which the alien scientists planned to take, but only a year of his freedom, or, indeed, only a day. Nor would he be obligated to stay if he had gotten captured (thus bringing all these people-potentials into existence) because of his own carelessness, or even if he had done so deliberately, knowing the consequences. Regardless of how he got captured, he is not morally obligated to remain in captivity for *any* period of time for the sake of permitting any number of potential people to come into actuality, so great is the margin by which one actual person's right to liberty outweighs whatever right to life even a hundred thousand potential people have. And it seems reasonable to conclude that the rights of a woman will outweigh by a similar margin whatever right to life a fetus may have by virtue of its potential personhood.

Thus, neither a fetus's resemblance to a person, nor its potential for becoming a person provides any basis whatever for the claim that it has any significant right to life. Consequently, a woman's right to protect her health, happiness, freedom, and even her life,[12] by terminating an unwanted pregnancy, will always override whatever right to life it may be appropriate to ascribe to a fetus, even a fully developed one. And thus, in the absence of any overwhelming social need for every possible child, the laws which restrict the right to obtain an abortion, or limit the period of pregnancy during which an abortion may be performed, are a wholly unjustified violation of a woman's most basic moral and constitutional rights.[13]

Notes

1. For example, Roger Wertheimer, who in "Understanding the Abortion Argument," *Philosophy and Public Affairs* 1, no. 1 (Fall 1971), argues that the problem of the moral status of abortion is insoluble in that the dispute over the status of the fetus is not a question of fact at all, but only a question of how one responds to the facts.

2. B. A. Brody, "Abortion and the Law," *The Journal of Philosophy* 68, no. 12 (June 17, 1971): 357–69.

3. Judith Thomson. "A Defense of Abortion." *Philosophy and Public Affairs* 1, no. 1 (Fall 1971 [chapter 15 in this volume].

4. I have abbreviated these statements somewhat, but not in a way which affects the argument.

5. John Noonan, "Abortion and the Catholic Church: A Summary History," *Natural Law Forum* 12 (1967): 125.

6. John Noonan, "Deciding Who Is Human," *Natural Law Forum* 13 (1968): 134.

7. "A Defense of Abortion."

8. We may safely ignore the fact that she might have avoided getting raped, e.g., by carrying a gun. since by similar means you might likewise have avoided getting kidnapped, and in neither case does the victim's failure to take all possible precautions against a highly unlikely event (as opposed to reasonable precautions against a rather likely event) mean that she is morally responsible for what happens.

9. Of course, the principle that it is (always) wrong to kill innocent human beings is in need of many other modifications, e.g., that it may be permissible to do so to save a greater number of other innocent human beings, but we may safely ignore these complications here.

10. From here on, we will use 'human' to mean genetically human, since the moral sense seems closely connected to, and perhaps derived from, the assumption that genetic humanity is sufficient for membership in the moral community.

11. Thomas L. Hayes, "A Biological View," *Commonweal* 85 (March 17, 1967): 677–78; quoted by Daniel Callahan, in *Abortion, Law, Choice, and Morality* (London: Macmillan & Co., 1970).

12. That is, insofar as the death rate, for the woman, is higher for childbirth than for early abortion.

13. My thanks to the following people, who were kind enough to read and criticize an earlier version of this paper: Herbert Gold, Gene Glass, Anne Lauterbach, Judith Thomson, Mary Mothersill, and Timothy Binkley.

17

Abortion, Infanticide, and the Asymmetric Value of Human Life

Jeffrey Reiman

Why . . . has it been imagined that to die is an evil—when it is clear that not to have been, before our birth, was no evil?

—Voltaire

1. Love, Respect, and the Asymmetric Value of Human Life

The pro-life position on abortion is that abortion is morally wrong because a fetus is an innocent human being, and killing it is, at least morally speaking, murder.[1] This claim doesn't challenge our normal way of evaluating something morally as murder. On the contrary, it appeals to that normal evaluation and insists that, according to it, killing fetuses counts as murder. Our normal evaluation of a killing as murder hinges on our normal valuation of the lives of those whom we think it uncontroversially wrong to kill, namely, children and adults. Rational assessment of the pro-life position, then, requires determining whether there is something about fetuses that provides a plausible basis for applying to them the value we normally apply to the lives of children and adults.[2] In conducting this assessment, we are aided by a clue that has been largely overlooked in the abortion debate, namely, that the way we normally value human life is quite unusual, quite unlike the normal way in which we value other things. This has the consequence that only a very specific kind of feature of humans at any stage can provide a plausible basis for the normal valuation. I shall follow out

First published in *Journal of Social Philosophy* 27, no. 3 (Winter 1996). Reprinted by permission of the *Journal of Social Philosophy*.

this clue and show that there is something about children and adults that provides a plausible basis for the way we value their lives, but there is nothing about fetuses that will do the job. The result is a refutation of the pro-life position, and a defense of the pro-choice position on abortion.

The question whether killing fetuses is wrong for the same reasons we think it wrong to kill children or adults is more general than whether a fetus has a right to life. To avoid the mistake of thinking that having a right to life is the only moral basis for the wrongness of destroying a human life,[3] we look for whatever might make it wrong to kill humans generally and see if this applies to fetuses. Of course, if it is not wrong to kill fetuses for the same reasons that it is wrong to kill humans generally, it might be wrong on other grounds.[4] I shall not pursue this, however, since it seems extremely unlikely that such grounds could be strong enough to justify requiring a woman to stay pregnant against her will (especially in these days of abundant reproduction). In any event, it is an implication of my argument here that there is nothing about fetuses which could provide a plausible basis for thinking that their lives should be protected in the way we protect the lives of children or adults.

There are some pro-choicers who think that the abortion dispute can be settled without addressing the moral status of the fetus. They think the fact (and I regard it as a fact) that a woman has a right to control her body is enough to justify her right to abortion. But, this is not enough because the right to control one's body ends if it comes up against a being with comparable moral status—"your right to swing your fist ends where my nose begins," and all that.[5] So we shall still have to figure out if the fetus has a moral status comparable to that of the woman carrying it.

On the other hand, there are even some arguments in favor of a woman's right to abortion that accept *per argumentum* that killing a fetus is as seriously wrong as killing a human adult. But such arguments can at best give a woman a right to expel an unwanted fetus from her body, and only to end its life if necessary for the expulsion.[6] As early as a living fetus can be safely and easily removed from a pregnant woman, her right to abortion might be transformed into a duty to provide extrauterine care for her expelled fetus. If (when!) medical technology pushes this point back toward the earliest moments of pregnancy, the right to abortion will disappear entirely. The surest way to secure a woman's right to abortion is to show that nothing about fetuses warrants including them under our normal way of valuing human life. And for this, we get some help from Voltaire.

Voltaire's question, quoted at the outset,[7] reminds us that we normally believe the moral wrongness of killing human beings to be something much worse than not creating them (if the latter is bad at all). This implies that the loss that results from ending a human life under way is much worse than the loss that would have been the result of not starting that life. In short, we normally think that murder is much worse than failure to procreate via contraception or voluntary abstinence. But, this means that the value of a human life is quite unusual: it is temporally *asymmetric*.

The standard kind of value is temporally symmetric. Normally, if something has x units of value, then destroying it (after it exists) and intentionally not producing it (before it exists) equally deprive the world of x units of value. Or, equivalently, that it has that value is equally a reason (before it exists) for a suitably situated moral agent to produce one and a reason (after it exists) for that agent to refrain from destroying it.

One way the value of something existing may seem not to be symmetric is that destroying the existent thing wastes the effort that already went into producing it, while not producing it does not. Likewise, trying to produce a new one courts a risk of failure, while an existing one is a sure thing. Thus, it would be more precise to say that the standard way in which something is thought to have value is symmetric except for considerations of wasted effort and uncertainty. However, these considerations are not large enough to account for the very large moral difference that people generally think exists between killing an existing human being and not bringing a new one into existence. Consequently, I shall say that a value is symmetric if the only difference between the value of producing it and the value of not destroying it stem from considerations of already invested effort and newly faced risk.[8] Thus, I will continue to say the value of normally valued things is symmetric, while the value we place on human life is asymmetric.

The upshot is that to determine whether killing a fetus is morally wrong for the same reasons that killing human beings generally is thought to be wrong, we need to figure out whether there is anything about the fetus that provides a plausible basis for thinking it is asymmetrically disvaluable—or, as I shall sometimes say, asymmetrically wrong—to end its life. Is there anything about the fetus that makes it seriously worse to kill it than not to have produced it, because of contraception or voluntary abstinence practiced by fertile couples? Though I don't argue for it here, I think that contraception and abstinence are not morally wrong at all. Nonetheless, my argument will work even if these are thought to be moderately wrong, since even people who think contraception is wrong think that abortion is much worse, and very few people who think that abortion is gravely evil think that abstinence is.

To help us think about the different ways in which things might have value, I want to distinguish roughly between the ways in which *love* and *respect* each value their objects. Love, though it may be triggered by the appeal of certain traits or properties of the beloved, conies to value the beloved as such—"unconditionally," we sometimes say—and thus values the sheer existence of the beloved. Respect, though it is aimed at individuals, is, in my view, a way of honoring some property possessed by the respected one, where "honoring" involves at least not interfering with the normal functioning of that property. Thus, for Kant, we are to respect human beings because they possess the trait of rational agency, and we do so by honoring that property, which is to say, not interfering with or undermining the normal functioning of their rational agency.[9] Further, love is *given* freely by the lover, while respect is *deserved* by the respected because of the property she possesses. Love expresses the will of the lover, while respect responds to the worth of the respected.

Now, I think that there are only two possible ways in which something can have asymmetric value: either its existence itself (somehow) gives it a value that is not temporally symmetric, or its value is the value it has to itself or someone else. Some important writers—for example, Ronald Dworkin[10]—adopt the first alternative, and I think that the assumption that existence does add asymmetric value is tacitly held by many people who think that abortion is morally questionable. Consequently, I shall take it up in section 2, "The Priority of Morality over Metaphysics in the Abortion Question," and try to show that, to paraphrase Kant, existence is not a morally relevant property.[11] Since love cherishes the sheer existence of its object, while respect honors some property possessed by its object, I speculate that the widespread error of thinking that existence as such lends value is the result of confusing love with respect. And then "the priority of morality over metaphysics in the abortion question" implies "the priority of respect over love in the abortion question."

The second way in which something might have asymmetric value is more promising. If the value of something lies in its value to itself or to someone else, then its value only exists for itself or someone else. With our focus on the normal valuation of human life, we can eliminate the "someone else" from this formulation, since a human life is thought to have its value even if no one else cares about the individual whose life it is. If, then, the value of life is its value to the one whose life it is and who cares about its continuation, then its value only exists for the one who cares about it, and only once it is cared about and not before. And that gives us asymmetric value. Note that, here, respect has priority over love. It is not so much that we care about the one whose life it is, or care about what she cares about, as it is that we respect her because she possesses the property of caring about her life and we do so by honoring that property, which is to say, not interfering with or undermining her having what she cares about. I shall defend this account of the asymmetric value of human life in section 3. As confirmation, in section 4, I shall show how the account supports the widely held (but vaguely formulated) view that it is only once humans are *persons* that it is seriously wrong to kill them.

One implication of my argument that may trouble some readers is that the life of newborn infants is not yet asymmetrically valuable. However, this doesn't imply that it is okay to kill infants, but rather that, if infanticide is morally wrong, it is wrong on other grounds and in a different way than the killing of children and adults. I take this up in section 5, "The Priority of Love over Respect in the Infanticide Question."

2. The Priority of Morality over Metaphysics in the Abortion Question

There are, broadly speaking, two ways to approach the question of abortion, which we can call the metaphysical way and the moral way. The metaphysical way is to start with a human being that it seems uncontroversially wrong to kill and work backwards to see if the fetus is, so to speak, a phase of this same individual entity. For example, up until the end of the first two weeks of pregnancy, a zygote or embryo may split into identical twins, who have the same genetic code and yet become two unique human beings. Noting this, Norman Ford maintains that starting at two weeks the fetus is the same individual entity which, in the normal course of events, will become a full-fledged person and thus ought to have its life protected from then on.[12] One reason that this approach is bound to fail is that the assumption that being a human individual is enough to earn one moral protection of one's life smacks of *speciesism*—arbitrary or dogmatic preference for our own species.[13] Once we recognize that what makes the killing of human beings seriously wrong cannot be the sheer fact of their membership in the human species, the wrongness must be based on a property (it could be one or more features) that human beings normally have, but which could in principle turn up in other species.

Accordingly, we are looking for a property, not a kind. Of course, the property might be just that by which we identify beings as of a certain kind; but even then—even if the property is strictly coterminous with the kind (for example, rationality in the case of humans)—it will be the property that does the moral work, not the kind.[14] On the other hand, once it is clear that it is a property we seek, it cannot be taken for granted that the property is coterminous with the kind. We look for a property (ever) possessed by human beings which explains the wrongness of killing them, all the while leaving open the question whether the property is possessed by all human beings or at all stages. We answer the abortion question by determining whether that property is possessed by fetuses. This is the moral approach to the question, which I shall follow.

There is yet a deeper way in which morality has priority over metaphysics in answering the abortion question. Imagine that we found the special property that is the basis of our objection to killing humans, and suppose that this property is something (for example, a functioning cerebral cortex)[15] that emerges in the seventh month of pregnancy.

Someone following the metaphysical approach outlined in the previous paragraphs might be tempted to say that the fetus from two weeks on is the same continuous self-identical individual as will have the special property at seven months, and thus it would be as wrong to kill it at two weeks as it is at seven months. If this were so, it would follow as well that the fetus is entitled to vote, since it is also the same continuous self-identical individual as will have that right at age eighteen. What's wrong in this argument is not the assumption that the being that traverses the span from conception to death is a self-identical individual. That is a more or less natural extension of the common belief that a human being from birth to death is a self-identical individual—the one named by its proper name.

The argument goes wrong by confusing metaphysical identity with moral identity, or assuming that the former entails the latter. Metaphysical identity from conception on means that the being is the same individual in all its temporal phases. Moral identity would mean that it has the same moral status in all its temporal phases, or at least, that earlier phases have a moral claim on the properties (and thus the moral status) possessed at later phases. If we are to grant the metaphysical identity of the human from conception on and avoid the inference that the fetus currently has the right to vote, we must grant that metaphysical identity is not equivalent to, and does not imply, moral identity. Here morality is prior to metaphysics in the sense that metaphysical identity will not supply us with the moral status needed to answer the abortion question: rather than looking for the (metaphysical) beginning of the human individual that somewhere down the line has a life it is wrong to take, we must look for the (morally relevant) property that makes it wrong to take a human life, and see when the human individual starts to have that property.

The priority of morality over metaphysics has important implications for the significance of *existence* in the abortion debate. It may turn out that the fetus possesses from the moment of conception the property that makes killing it seriously wrong, and then its metaphysical and moral identity in this regard will coincide. However, given the possibility that this property is acquired later (either during pregnancy or later still), then the fetus may exist for some time without the property. Since the fetus's metaphysical identity with the human being that will have the property does not entail their moral identity, it follows that the pre-property fetus has no moral claim to the property. Moreover, since what the property gives is precisely the moral wrongness of stopping the fetus from continuing on to later phases, there is nothing morally wrong with ending the fetus's life before the property is there. The fetus's existence prior to its possession of the property gives it no moral claim to continue existing. And, if the pre-property fetus has no moral claim to get the property, then there is no moral difference between a fetus that stops existing before it gets the property and a fetus that never starts to exist.

If this seems counterintuitive, I think it's because we tend to read a kind of personal identity backwards into fetuses, and personal identity carries connotations of moral identity beyond mere metaphysical identity. If we think of the pre-property fetus as a kind of quasi-person "who" loses the chance to have the special property, then we will think of the pre-property fetus as a person-like victim—which is a moral status that a not-yet-existing fetus lacks. Just because it is so natural to us to think this way, I believe that this ("retroactive empersonment") is the single greatest source of confusion in the abortion debate. If we resist it, then that the fetus has already been existing has no bearing on the moral status of its loss of future existence. Consequently, that loss is morally equivalent to the simple failure of that future stretch of fetal life to begin. And, then, it is no worse morally to end the life of a pre-property fetus than to refuse to produce a new one. Existence as such cannot provide asymmetrical value.

Mistakes about this are so common in the abortion dispute that I think that my argument will be strengthened by a plausible explanation of the appeal of the mistaken view. Recall the difference between the respect and (unconditional) love sketched earlier. Respect is something that we have toward some property that an individual has: reason, moral agency, what have you, and we respect that individual because of that property. Love, by contrast, is directed at individuals as such. Then, love naturally cherishes the sheer existence of its object. If this is so, then it is our natural love of our fellows (the sentiment that Hume called "humanity,"[16] which leads us to cherish their sheer existence— before there is a moral warrant for this. And cherishing their sheer existence, we are naturally led to cherish their existence for as long as they can be said to exist as the same individual, metaphysically speaking. But that love is given freely by us, not deserved by the beloved. Thus, it does not imply anything about the beloved deserving to continue to exist. It tells us rather about our own sentiments. Consequently, the argument for the priority of morality over metaphysics is equally an argument for the priority of respect over love in the abortion question. This isn't to say that love counts for nothing in morality, only that it cannot justify the belief that its object possesses a moral standing of its own. Only possession of the appropriate property can do that.

3. Voltaire's Question

Voltaire's question reminds us that we view the ending of a human life under way as much worse than the failure of a life to start. This gives us a surprisingly exclusive requirement because it rules out any attempt to explain the wrongness of killing human beings by invoking their "objectively" good properties—by which I mean properties whose appeal (roughly speaking) is that their existence makes the world a better place than it would be without them. Such objectively good properties are symmetrically valuable. That human beings possess such objectively good properties as rationality, or capacity for joy and attachment, cannot explain the serious wrongness of killing humans because contraception and abstinence also cause the nonexistence of these good properties. Then, these properties cannot be the basis of the asymmetric wrongness of killing human beings.

It might be thought that destroying an existing being that has objectively good properties is inherently worse than not creating a being with those properties. But this runs afoul of the priority of morality over metaphysics because it counts existence itself as giving an existing being a moral claim to continue existing. Nor can the force of Voltaire's question be escaped by recourse to the so-called acts-omissions principle, which holds that acting to produce a bad outcome is always much worse than simply failing to prevent that same outcome. This principle is far from universally accepted, so we cannot assume that it holds in the controversial cases we are here considering. And, anyway, contraception and abstinence are acts, so they get no special dispensation from the principle.

The problem is to find a property whose nature involves existence in a way that makes the destruction of a being with that property significantly wrong while the noncreation of such a being is only mildly wrong if wrong at all. That this is just what objectively good properties lack suggests that it is a *subjective* property we need. I will argue that this suggestion is correct, but that not just any subjective property will do. For example, L. W. Sumner contends that sentience brings any creature into the realm of moral consideration, and therefore we should protect the lives of fetuses from the point at which they become sentient.[17] Now, aside from the fact that consistency would require that we extend the same protection to most animals, the most important fact for our purposes is that there is nothing about sentience as such that accounts for the asymmetric values of beings that possess it. It may be good that a six-month-old sentient being continue on for another six months, but this is no better than ending its life painlessly and replacing it with another that will have six months of sentience. There is nothing about being sentient that makes it worse to end a sentient being's life than to fail to create another sentient being.

The failure of sentience points us to the kind of subjective property that can do the job: The subjective awareness that one is already alive and counting on staying alive fits the requirement suggested by Voltaire's question. The loss to an aware individual of the life whose continuation she is counting on is a loss that can only exist once an aware individual exists. Moreover, it is a loss that remains a loss, a frustration of an individual's expectations, even if that individual is replaced by another, equally aware one. And thus it is a loss that can explain why ending a human life is significantly worse than not creating one.

The point is precisely *not* to say that it is good that such awareness or such aware individuals exist. That would turn the property into one whose goodness is objective, and then we would lose the distinction needed to cope with Voltaire's question. It would then be just as good to create new aware individuals as to continue existing ones, and the harm of killing will be no worse than that of contraception or abstinence.

We need a way to say how it is valuable that individuals who care about their lives going on get to live on, without entailing that it is good that such aware individuals exist. We can do this by adverting to the moral attitude of respect: The asymmetric value of human life is a function of our respecting human beings because they possess the property of caring about the continuation of their lives; and we express that respect by honoring that property, which is to say by not interfering with or undermining people's ability to have or get what they care about. If it be thought that care about one's life is too thin a reed upon which to rest respect, remember that that care is the affective response to awareness of oneself as a being living out a life, so to speak, a minute or a day at a time—and that awareness is available only to rational beings. Consequently, respecting beings because they possess the property of caring about the continuation of their lives is respecting them for caring as only a rational being can care. Thus it can account for the asymmetric value we place on human life.

Note that I am not arguing that ending the life of a human being who is aware of and caring about his life is wrong because it thwarts an occurrent desire to stay alive or a felt expectation that one will.[18] Rather, our inquiry has led us to a unique human vulnerability, and to a distinctive moral response to that vulnerability. Once a human being has begun to be aware of her life, that life unfolds before a kind of inner audience that has an expectation of its continuation, an affective stake in living on. This expectation persists until the audience shuts down for good—even if, before that, the audience dozes off for a while. We defeat this expectation even if we kill a temporarily sleeping or comatose individual who has begun to be aware of her life. Because of this special awareness, humans are vulnerable to a special harm from the ending of a life already under way.[19] And we protect people from this harm because we respect them, not because we love them—though, of course, we may also do that.

My argument here should not be confused with the "logic-of-rights" approach used by Michael Tooley and S. I. Benn, to which it bears a certain surface resemblance.[20] Tooley has argued that a necessary logical condition for having a right is having some interest that the right protects, and—he contends—fetuses can't have an interest in staying alive. Consequently, fetuses are logically disqualified from possessing a right to life, and abortion is okay. As interesting as this strategy is, it relies too heavily on the logic of the concept of a right. Tooley's mistake is not just that his argument only works against a fetal right to life—but that he supposes us to be so much the prisoners of our existing moral concepts, that we need only determine what their logic allows to answer our moral questions. The simple fact is that if a moral concept logically excludes some case that there is good reason to include, we need only modify the concept or create a new one. Benn takes the logic of rights even further than Tooley. Benn thinks that the concept of a right is so exclusive that it only applies to agents. Then, since neither fetuses nor newborns are agents, they cannot have rights, and abortion and infanticide are okay. Benn's version seems to me extreme enough to qualify as a reductio ad absurdum of the "logic-of-rights" approach. Surely it cannot be that our concept of a right is so locked into its connection with agency that we cannot pry it loose and use it for other defensible purposes. Suppose we agreed that our concept of a right applied only to agents, and found that, say, people on respirators (or, in comas), though unable to act, ought to be protected against certain forms of molestation. What would happen if we simply modified the concept of a right so that it could cover such cases? Or, if we created a new concept with all the attributes of rights, except the restriction to agents? Would we slide into an abyss of incoherence? Would our lexicographers go on strike?

As I see it, the answer to the question of whether we should protect fetal life with a right to life or some other way hinges on whether there are good reasons for doing so, not on the logical preconditions of applying the concepts of rights or protection. My argument is that the interest that conscious human beings have in the continuation of the lives of which they are already aware is a good reason for protecting their lives morally in the asymmetric way that we do, and that no such good reason obtains in the case of fetuses. The loss suffered by the aborted fetus is precisely the same sort of loss caused by contraception or by abstinence, and thus provides no better reason for protecting fetuses than for prohibiting contraception abstinence. Then, abortion can be no worse morally than these.

This train of argument may seem counterintuitive. It looks like abortion is different because it has a victim, while contraception and abstinence do not. But, recall the priority of morality over metaphysics: Since it is a property that makes it seriously wrong to kill something, the existing fetus before the property is not a victim in the morally relevant sense. The fetus's existence as such does not make the harm of depriving it of its future life morally different from the harm of the failure to produce a new fetus with its own future life, in the way that existing consciousness and expectation do for the harm of ending an aware human being's life.[21] *The loss to the fetus of its future life is no worse a loss than the loss to the world of any future life.*

4. Personhood Revisited

In an important article, Mary Anne Warren argues that it is personhood that warrants the right to life, and—appealing to common usage—she lists the traits of personhood as consciousness, reasoning, self-motivated activity, capacity to communicate, and the presence of self-concepts and self-awareness. Contending that the fetus lacks these elements, she concludes that the fetus doesn't have a right to life.[22] What we are not told is why any or all of these elements make it appropriate to hold the killing of a being with the elements seriously wrong. Warren's position then amounts to a report of our common practice of awarding rights to the beings we call persons.[23] And this renders her conclusion problematic because the pro-lifer can simply assert that the common practice is mistaken, or that there are grounds other than being a person for protecting fetuses. The only way out of these interminable disputes is to show that there is something about the nature of persons that explains the serious wrongness of killing them, and that there is no such thing about a fetus.

My argument to this point provides a way of showing what it is about persons that makes it asymmetrically wrong to kill them. Guided by Voltaire, I urged that the only plausible basis for asymmetrically valuing human life is that (and once) humans are aware of and counting on continuing the particular lives they already have. This is only possible for a being that is aware of his or her self as the same self enduring over time. And a hallowed philosophical tradition defines personhood by this very awareness. Locke defined a "person" as "a thinking intelligent being, that . . . can consider itself as itself . . . in different times and places."[24] And Kant wrote: "That which is conscious of the numerical identity of itself at different times is in so far a *person*."[25]

Not only does this rescue the idea that it is persons who are morally entitled to protection against killing; it reinforces my claim that the asymmetric value of human life is based on our respect for our fellows as beings who care about their lives. Persons are commonly thought to be proper objects of respect.

5. The Priority of Love over Respect in the Infanticide Question

The newborn infant does not yet have awareness that it is alive, much less that it is the self-same person enduring over time.[26] Its relationship to the future person that it is on the way to becoming is more like a fetus's than like an adult's or a child's relationship to the life of which she is already aware. If already being aware of one's life is the necessary condition of the objection to killing human beings, what follows about the moral status of infanticide? This question is important because some philosophers (and many nonphilosophers) take their intuition that infanticide is as wrong as killing adults or children so seriously as to rule out any account of the wrongness of killing that doesn't apply equally to infants.[27] What I shall say in response to this is not an attempt to settle the issue about the moral status of infanticide. I wish only to say enough to suggest how the wrongness of infanticide can be accounted for on terms that are compatible with what I have said about abortion and the wrongness of killing children and adults.

The attitude that we have when we think it wrong to kill a child or adult because they care about their lives going on is a form of respect. We respect the property of being aware of and caring about their lives (and all this brings in its wake), and we respect them for having this attribute. We show this respect by not undermining what they care about. We are not (necessarily) either caring about them independently of what they care about or directly caring about what they care about, either of which would characterize love rather than respect.[28]

Now, I think that the normal reaction to infants is a loving one (though of course it is not the only reaction, nor the only normal one). And, I think that this has probably been built into us as a result of evolution. Human babies are born at a very early stage of their development and must therefore be tended to by their parents (primarily their mothers, at least until recently) for a long time before they can get along on their own, and surely a long time before they can begin to pay their own way.[29] There are numerous evolutionary advantages from the long extrauterine development of humans. Most important, it allows adult human beings to have larger brains than could pass through a human female's birth canal. On the other hand, it is inconceivable that parents would have provided the necessary care for their helpless offspring over the hundreds of thousands of years of human evolution, if they had not developed a strong tendency to love infants. And this is love, rather than respect precisely, because it must happen automatically, before the infant can do anything to deserve or be worthy of it.

But there is more. The love that we naturally direct toward infants is arguably a necessary condition of the development of the infant into a being worthy of respect. This is so for at least two reasons, and probably more. First of all, by loving infants, we are moved to devote the energy and attention necessary to bring infants into the community of language-users, which in turn brings infants to awareness of their lives, which is also a necessary condition of their caring about their lives and our respecting them for that.[30] (The *Oxford English Dictionary* gives the root of "infant" as *infans*, Latin for "unable to speak.") Second of all, by loving infants we convey to them a positive valuation of their sheer existence, which in turn underlies their valuation of their own particular lives once they are capable of it. Indeed, since it is precisely people's own valuation of their lives that is the condition of our respect for them, we can say that our loving infants is part of the process by which they become worthy objects of respect.

In short, we might say that we respect the lives of children and adults because they love their own lives, and loving infants prepares them for loving their own lives and thus for being worthy of respect. *Love is respect's pioneer.* It goes on ahead, clears the field and prepares the soil where respect will take root. Respect is what infants will get once they qualify for full membership in the human moral community, but love is what reaches out and brings them into that community and necessarily does so before they qualify.

This gives us enough to characterize the special status that infants have as natural objects of adults' love. As I suggested earlier, love cherishes the sheer existence of its object. Thus, love makes us want very much to protect infants and make sure that they survive. On the other hand, since that love is unconditional—given rather than deserved—it is not based on anything that makes the infants worthy of it. Thus, we find ourselves strongly inclined to believe that it is wrong to kill infants, and unable to point to some property of infants (not shared by human fetuses, or even animals that we think may be acceptably killed) that justifies this belief.

If this is correct, then we can say that the strong belief in the wrongness of killing infants is the product of our natural love for them coupled with (or strengthened by) our respect for our fellows' love of them. And this love is worth supporting because it is respect's pioneer. That is, by loving infants we treat them as asymmetrically valuable before they really deserve it, but as part of the process by which they come really to deserve it. And then it will be wrong to kill infants because it will be wrong generally to block or frustrate this love, both because we and our fellows naturally feel it and because it is good that we feel it inasmuch as it is essential to infants' development into children and adults worthy of respect.

Note that this won't apply to fetuses. They may be objects of love, but not of such love as can play a role in their psycho-moral development. That requires a real, interactive social relation such as can only occur after birth. That is not to say that the fact that many people love fetuses counts for nothing. Much as respect for our fellows' love for infants justifies protecting infants' lives, respect for those who love fetuses, may, for example, justify treating aborted fetuses with special care. But since this is a matter of other people's love rather than fetuses' own worthiness for respect, it surely won't be enough to justify requiring women to stay pregnant against their wills.

This account does not say that killing infants is wrong for the same reasons as killing children or adults. Quite the contrary, killing children or adults is wrong because it violates the respect they are due as creatures aware of and caring about their lives. Killing infants is wrong because it violates the love we give them as a means to making them into creatures aware of and caring about their lives. The killing of children and adults is wrong because of properties they possess that make it wrong, while the killing of infants is wrong because of an emotion which we naturally and rightly have toward infants. Then, it will be harder to justify exceptions to the rule against killing adults and children than to the rule against killing infants, because adults and children possess in their own right a property that makes it wrong to kill them. Infants, for the moment, do not. Killing them collides with our love for them, not their love for their lives. For this reason, there will be permissible exceptions to the rule against killing infants that will not apply to the rule against killing adults or children. In particular, I think (as do many philosophers, doctors, and parents) that ending the lives of severely handicapped newborns will be acceptable because it does not take from the newborns a life that the yet care about and because it is arguably compatible with, rather than violative of, our natural love for infants. But, of course, I have not proven this here.

Notes

1. A few words about terminology are in order. "Pro-life" and "pro-choice" are political labels, not technically accurate philosophical terms. I use them because of their familiarity, not because I think that only pro-lifers are pro-life or that only pro-choicers are pro-choice. Further, I use the term "murder" in its moral sense, meaning any killing that is bad for the same reasons it is bad to kill children and adults; and when I speak of it being bad or wrong to kill children or adults, I mean killing that takes place voluntarily and in the absence of such conditions as mental illness

or duress that would normally block the imputation of wrongdoing. For the purpose of simplicity, I normally omit these necessary qualifications, and assume that the reader will fill them in where needed. Finally, I join in the widespread though technically incorrect practice of using the term "fetus" to refer to the being that develops in a pregnant woman from the moment of conception to the moment of birth. Speaking strictly, the single cell resulting from the fertilization of the egg is a zygote; shortly thereafter, when it becomes somewhat more complex, it is a blastocyst; when it implants in the uterine wall about six days after fertilization it is a called an embryo. It is only technically a fetus at about sixty days after conception. See Harold J. Morowitz and James S. Trefil, *The Facts of Life* (New York: Oxford University Press, 1992), p. 46.

2. The claim is rightly understood and evaluated as a rational claim inasmuch as it is meant to persuade citizens of a modern secular state, since religious claims (such as that the fetus has an immortal soul from conception on) are neither testable nor provable, and thus not (or, anyway, no longer) a plausible basis for securing widespread conviction or requiring compliance of nonbelievers.

3. This mistake is all too prevalent in the literature on the abortion question, although, in a recent article, James Q. Wilson makes the mistake in reverse. He distinguishes the rights-based approach to abortion from the moral approach. Apparently, he's never heard of moral rights. I shall try to steer clear of both errors. See James Q. Wilson, "On Abortion," *Commentary* 27, no. 1 (Jan. 1994): 21–29.

4. Arguments which focus on the fact that the fetus is a *potential* human being or person make such a claim, but they are widely thought to fail because having the potential to realize a status does not entail having time rights that come with the actual status. (That newborn babies are potentially eighteen-year-olds doesn't give them the right to vote now.) Perhaps those pro-lifers who exhibit pictures of fetuses to show that they look like babies are making an argument of this sort, since being a baby is a property that adult humans don't have. But, being a baby is something that fetuses share with animals widely thought acceptable to kill. It's that fetuses look like baby humans that is thought to make them special, and their membership in the human species is something that fetuses share with adult humans. In any event, the positive emotional response that most people will have to pictures of babylike fetuses cannot decide their moral status, contrary to a claim recently made by James Q. Wilson. He proposes that we show people films of fetuses at different stages of gestation, and that we outlaw abortion at the point at which the fetus looks like a baby to most people, and, so to speak, engages their moral sentiments in its favor. If this really were a moral test, one wonders why Wilson doesn't also recommend that we show people films of women at different stages of legally enforced involuntary pregnancy, and that we permit abortion from the point at which the woman looks like a human being to most people and engages their moral sentiments in her favor. But, of course, it is not a moral test. Our emotional responses to what things look like is, at best, a hint about what they really are and really are entitled to. To determine that, we must use our reason. Mere feelings will not do. See Wilson, "On Abortion"; and my "The Impotency of the Potentiality Argument for Fetal Rights: Reply to Wilkins," *Journal of Social Philosophy* 24, no. 3 (Winter 1993): 170–76.

5. But more technically: a pregnant woman has a right to control her body because she is a human being with the full complement of rights that humans are normally thought to have. If the fetus turns out to be a human being with the full complement of rights also, the woman's right will generally be thought to end at the point that it interferes with the fetus's control over its body. I am indebted to Karen Dolan for this clear statement of the principle.

6. For example, Judith Thomson argues that, even if the fetus is already a person with a right to life (like a normal human adult), at least in most pregnancies, and at least prior to viability, a woman has a right to abortion because a (fetus's) right to life doesn't entail the right to use another's resources (such as her uterus). Consequently, a woman has the right to expel the unwanted fetus, but only to kill it if that is the only way to expel it. Thomson's view might be thought to vindicate the idea, which I rejected above, that a woman's right to control her body suffices to establish her right to an abortion. However, Thomson's argument only works against the idea that the fetus has a right to life. It won't work if the fetus has some other special moral status

which requires us to save it rather than merely not to kill it unjustly. (Suppose you found an abandoned baby on your doorstep and had no means of bringing it to other shelter. Would you have no duty to take it in, even if it had no right to use your resources?) It will still be necessary to determine the moral status of the fetus. See Judith Jarvis Thomson, "A Defense of Abortion," *Philosophy and Public Affairs* 1, no. 1 (1971): 47–66. Cf., Nancy Davis, "Abortion and Self-Defense," *Philosophy and Public Affairs* 13, no. 3 (1984): 175–207. The question about the baby at the doorstep is raised by John Arthur, *The Unfinished Constitution: Philosophy and Constitutional Practice* (Belmont, Calif.: Wadsworth, 1989), pp. 198–200.

7. The question is from Voltaire's article, "The Whys," *A Philosophical Dictionary*, vol. 10, in *The Works of Voltaire*, trans. W. F. Fleming (Paris: E. R. DuMont, 1901), vol. XIV, p. 214. I make no claim about what Voltaire actually meant by this question.

8. Note that this formulation favors the pro-life camp. If the moral difference between killing and not procreating were due to the loss of investment that results from killing, then this will surely not be a large enough difference to make abortions as bad as killing children or adults, since abortions come when there is much less investment than goes into raising babies to become children and children to become adults. Similar things can be said about risk. The risk of not producing a fetus that reaches the stage at which most abortions occur is much less than the risk of not producing a being that survives until childhood or adulthood. In any event, until birth, both the investment and the risk are the pregnant woman's, and thus hers to waste or venture.

9. "When I observe the duty of respect," writes Kant, "I . . . keep myself within my own bounds in order not to deprive another of any of the value which he as a human being is entitled to put upon himself." Immanuel Kant, "The Metaphysical Principles of Virtue," Part 2 of the *Metaphysics of Morals*, in *Ethical Philosophy* (Indianapolis, Ind.: Hackett, 1983), p. 114; see also Kant's *Grounding for the Metaphysics of Morals* (Indianapolis, Ind.: Hackett, 1981), pp. 35–37. While I think my account of respect is in line with Kant's, I do not put it forth as a gloss on Kant's.

10. In *Life's Dominion,* Ronald Dworkin maintains that we regard human life as sacred: "The hallmark of the sacred as distinct from the incrementally valuable is that the sacred is intrinsically *valuable because*—and therefore only once—*it exists*" (my emphasis). Dworkin gives two examples of things we value as sacred, works of great art and distinct animal species. What our valuation of these shares, and which Dworkin calls "the nerve of the sacred," is that we value the process that has brought them into existence. Individual human life is, for Dworkin, all the more eligible for sacredness than works of art or nature because it is, so to speak, the product of both natural and human creative efforts. But our valuing of the natural processes and the human creative efforts that bring something into existence does not explain (much less justify) our asymmetric valuing of that thing. If it did, then we would value asymmetrically—find sacred—*every product* of human effort or natural process, which we obviously do not, and surely should not. See Ronald Dworkin, *Life's Dominion: An Argument about Abortion, Euthanasia, and Individual Freedom* (New York: Vintage Books, 1994), pp. 73–83.

11. " '*Being'* is obviously not a real predicate; that is, it is not a concept of something which could be added to the concept of a thing." Immanuel Kant, *Critique of Pure Reason,* trans. Norman Kemp Smith (London: Macmillan, 1963), p. 504.

12. Norman M. Ford, *When Did I Begin?* (Cambridge: Cambridge University Press, 1991), pp. xvi–xviii, inter alia. I suspect that Ford is a decent fellow trying to find a little space for a woman's autonomy within an otherwise strict rendition of the Roman Catholic condemnation of abortion. Nonetheless, it is difficult to understand why it would be okay to kill something while it still might become two things that it would be wrong to kill separately. Others who take some form of the metaphysical approach are Richard Werner, "Abortion: The Moral Status of the Unborn," *Social Theory and Practice* 3, no. 2 (Fall 1974): 201–22; Jean Beer Blumenfeld, "Abortion and the Human Brain," *Philosophical Studies* 32, no. 3 (Oct. 1977): 251–68; Warrren Quinn, "Abortion: Identity and Loss," *Philosophy and Public Affairs* 13, no. 1 (Winter 1981): 24–54; Michael Lockwood, "Warnock versus Powell (and Harradine): When Does Potentiality Count?" *Bioethics* 2, no. 3 (1988), pp. 187–213; John T. Noonan, "An Almost Absolute Value in History," Philip E. Devine, "The Scope

of the Prohibition against Killing," Norman C. Gillespie, "Abortion and Human Rights," and Joel Feinberg, "Potentiality, Development, and Rights," in Joel Feinberg, ed., *The Problem of Abortion,* 2d ed. (Belmont, Calif.: Wadsworth, 1984), pp. 9–14. 21–42, 94–101, and 145–50.

13. "That term, [speciesism], coined by the Oxford psychologist Richard Ryder in 1970, has now entered the *Oxford English Dictionary,* where it is defined as "discrimination against or exploitation of certain animal species by human beings, based on an assumption of mankind's superiority." As the term suggests, there is a parallel between our attitudes to nonhuman animals, and the attitudes of racists to those they regard as belonging to an inferior race." Peter Singer, *Rethinking Life and Death* (New York: St. Martin's Press, 1995), p. 173.

14. I think this will hold even if, say, one thought of morality as an agreement among human beings to protect their shared interests. Such an agreement will have to identify the stage of development at which humans have an interest in being protected that is strong enough to override women's interest in being protected against forced pregnancy. This stage will have to coincide with the possession of some property that accounts for how humans become vulnerable to the sort of injury it would be reasonable for all to protect against.

15. This is the defining property of our humanity according to Morowitz and Trefil, who then recommend that abortion be restricted from seven months on. Since this view cannot explain why it is worse to kill fetuses with functioning cerebral cortexes than to refuse to produce new ones who will have functioning cerebral cortexes, it is refuted by considerations raised in the present article. Morowitz and Trefil, *The Facts of Life,* pp. 17, 119, inter alia.

16. David Hume, *An Enquiry Concerning the Principles of Morals* (Indianapolis, Ind.: Hackett Publishing, 1983), p. 75.

17. Writes Summer, "If the creatures we meet have interests and are capable of enjoyment and suffering, we must grant them some moral standing. We thereby constrain ourselves not to exploit them ruthlessly for our own advantage." On these grounds, he proposes that we treat the advent of fetal sentience (sometime in the second trimester of pregnancy) as bringing with it an entitlement to protection. L. W. Sumner. "'A Third Way,'" in Feinberg, ed., *The Problem of Abortion,* pp. 71–93, esp. p. 84 Some scientists hold fetal sentience to be impossible before the beginning of the seventh month that "'before the wiring up of the cortex [around the twenty-fifth week], the fetus is simply incapable of feeling anything, including pain." See Morowitz and Trefil, *The Facts of Life,* p. 158.

18. The wrong involved in being killed is the loss of life of which we have begun to be aware, it is not the pain of being aware of losing one's life. Causing this pain is a wrong to be sure, one that may make it worse to kill someone who is aware of what's happening than, say, to kill him in his sleep. But killing someone in his sleep is bad enough to count as murder, and that's what counts here.

19. It isn't easy to capture the way in which staying alive becomes specially important to us once we are aware of it, though I think everyone can recognize it in his or her own experience. One writer who has given expression to part of what is at stake here is Richard Wollheim. Arguing that death is a misfortune even when life is bad, Wollheim writes, "It is not that death deprives us of some particular pleasure, or even of pleasure. What it deprives us of is something more fundamental than pleasure: it deprives us of that thing which we gain access to when, as persisting creatures, we enter into our present mental states. . . . It deprives us of phenomenology, and, having once tasted phenomenology, we develop a longing for it which we cannot give up: not even when the desire for cessation of pain, for extinction, grows stronger." Richard Wollheim, *The Thread of Life* (Cambridge, Mass.: Harvard University Press, 1984), p. 269. I say that this captures part of what is at stake because I think that we long for more than phenomenology understood simply as perceptual experience. We would not, I think, care so much about it continuing if we were and knew we were just experiencing fictional appearances, if our experience were, say, a continuing series of movies. It's because we seem to experience a real world in which people act and produce or fail to produce outcomes that matter, that we long for experience to go on. If philosophers' epistemological nightmare came true and we really were brains in vats, I think that our attachment to life would diminish.

20. See Michael Tooley, *Abortion and Infanticide* (Oxford: Clarendon Press, 1983); and S. I. Benn, "Abortion, Infanticide, and Respect for Persons," in Feinberg, ed., *The Problem of Abortion*, pp. 135–44.

21. This is what Don Marquis overlooks in holding that "loss of a future life" is what makes killing both human adults and human fetuses equally wrong: "Since the loss of the future to a standard fetus, if killed, is, however, at least as great a loss as the loss of the future to a standard adult human being who is killed, abortion . . . is presumptively very seriously wrong, where that presumption is very strong—as strong as the presumption that killing another adult human being is wrong." Don Marquis, "Why Abortion Is Immoral," *Journal of Philosophy* 86, no. 4 (April 1989): 183–202, the quote is from p.194. Responding to Marquis, Peter McInerney lists some of the many differences in the ways fetuses and adult humans are related to their futures. He concludes: "Although there is some biological continuity between them so that there is a sense in which the later person stages 'are the future' of the fetus, the fetus is so little connected to the later personal life that it cannot be deprived of that personal life. At its time, the fetus does not already 'possess' that future personal life in the way that a normal adult human already 'possesses' his future personal life," Peter K. McInerney, "Does a Fetus Already Have a Future-Like-Ours?" *Journal of Philosophy* 87, no. 5 (May 1990): 266–67. While McInerney raises enough concerns about the difference between a fetus's relation to its future and an adult's to its to show that Marquis cannot simply assert that abortion does the same thing to a fetus that murder does to a normal adult, McInerney does not do enough to support his conclusion that a fetus cannot be deprived of its future personal life. Indeed, since he admits that there is at least biological continuity between the fetus and the future personal life it will have if not aborted, there remains at least some sense in which abortion does deprive the fetus of its future. The question whether the fetus's loss is enough to make killing it morally like killing an adult requires a moral comparison of the various losses which McInerney doesn't undertake. Another case of failure to respect the priority of morality over metaphysics.

23. Warren, "On the Moral and Legal Status of Abortion," in Feinberg, ed., *The Problem of Abortion*, pp. 110–14.

24. This fact enables Jamie English to stymie Warren's attempt by claiming that, as it functions in our actual practice of recognizing some creatures as persons, the concept of a person is too indefinite to be captured in a straitjacket of necessary and/or sufficient conditions. Jane English, "Abortion and the Concept of a Person," in Feinberg, ed., *The Problem of Abortion*, p. 152.

24. John Locke, *An Essay Concerning Human Understanding*, (London: Routledge & Sons, 1984), bk. II, chap. 27, sec. 9, p. 246.

25. Kant, *Critique of Pure Reason*, p. 341.

26. One expert on infant cognitive development writes, "it is a most un-Proustian life, not thought, only lived. Sensorimotor schemata . . . enable a child to walk a straight line, but not to think about a line in its absence, to recognize his or her mother, but not to think about her when she is gone. It is a world difficult for us to conceive, accustomed as we are to spend much of our time ruminating about the past and anticipating the future. Nevertheless, this is the state that Piaget posits for the child before one-and-a-half, that is, an ability to recognize objects and events, but an inability to recall them in their absence. Because of this inability . . . the child cannot even remember what he or she did a few minutes ago. . . . The observations have been made by others as well, but more recently there have been occasional suggestions that recall may occur considerably earlier than Piaget believed, perhaps in the second 6 months of life." Jean M. Mandler, "Representation and Recall in Infancy," in Morris Moscovitch, ed., *Infant Memory: It Relation to Normal and Pathological Memory in Humans and Other Animals* (New York: Plenum Press, 1984), pp. 75–76.

27. See, for example, Lockwood, "Warnock versus Powell (and Harradine): When Does Potentiality Count?"; Werner, "Abortion: The Moral Status of the Unborn"; Noonan, "An Almost Absolute Value in History"; Devine, "The Scope of the Prohibition against Killing"; Feinberg, "Potentiality, Development, and Rights"—references in note 12 above. See also Loren E. Lomasky, "Being a Person—Does It Matter?" in Feinberg, ed., *The Problem of Abortion*, pp.

161–72.

28. Of course, we will normally also be caring in these ways too. The point is that our doing so is not necessary to the way we value the lives of children or adults. For that, all that's necessary is that we respect their caring about their lives.

29. "Human babies are the most helpless in the animal kingdom; they require many years of care before they can survive on their own." Mary Batten, *Sexual Strategies: How Females Choose Their Mates* (New York: G. P. Putnam's Sons, 1992), p. 142.

30. "When infants become attached to their mothers many language-critical processes are encouraged: the desire to engage in playful vocalization, including vocal exploration, the emergence of turn taking and dialogue structure, and the desire to imitate vocal patterns. In turn, mothers who are attached to and feeling nurturant toward their infants provide them with a number of opportunities to learn. Among the other processes encouraged by attachment are the use of eye gaze and manual gestures to signal attentional focus and convey labels, and the use of voice to designate and convey." John L. Locke, *The Child's Path to Spoken Language* (Cambridge, Mass.: Harvard University Press, 1993), p. 107. Elsewhere Locke points out that infants who do not find this emotional responsiveness in their mothers seek it elsewhere (ibid., pp. 109–10).

PART TWO

GENDER, SEXUALITY, and PERVERSION

18

"Pricks" and "Chicks": A Plea for "Persons"

Robert B. Baker

There is a school of philosophers who believe that one starts philosophizing not by examining whatever it is one is philosophizing about but by examining the words we use to designate the subject to be examined. I must confess my allegiance to this school. The import of my confession is that this is an essay on women's liberation.

There seems to be a curious malady that affects those philosophers who in order to analyze anything must examine the way we talk about it; they seem incapable of talking about anything without talking about their talk about it—and, once again, I must confess to being typical. Thus I shall argue, first, that the way in which we identify something reflects our conception of it; second, that the conception of women embedded in our language is male chauvinistic; third, that the conceptual revisions proposed by the feminist movement are confused; and finally, that at the root of the problem are both our conception of sex and the very structure of sexual identification.

Identification and Conception

I am not going to defend the position that the terms we utilize to identify something reflect our conception of it; I shall simply explain and illustrate a simplified version of this thesis. Let us assume that any term that can be (meaningfully) substituted for x in the following statements is a term used to identify something: "Where is the x?" "Who is the x?" Some of the terms that can be substituted for x in the above expressions are metaphors; I shall refer to such metaphors as metaphorical identifications. For example, southerners frequently say such things as "Where did that girl get to?" and "Who is the new boy that Lou hired to help out at the filling station?" If the persons the terms apply to are adult Afro-Americans, then "girl" and "boy" are metaphorical identifications. The fact that the metaphorical identifications in question are standard in the language reflects the fact that certain characteristics of the objects properly classified as boys and girls (for example, immaturity, inability to take care of themselves, need for guidance) are generally held by those who use identifications to be properly attributable to Afro-Americans. One might say that the whole theory of southern white paternalism is implicit in the metaphorical identification "boy" (just as the rejection of paternalism is implicit in the standardized Afro-American forms of address, "man" and "woman," as in, for example, "Hey, man, how are you?").

Most of what I am going to say in this essay is significant only if the way we metaphorically identify something is not a superficial bit of conceptually irrelevant happenstance but rather a reflection of our conceptual structure. Thus if one is to accept my analysis he must understand the significance of metaphorical identifications. He must see that, even though the southerner who identifies adult Afro-American males as "boys" feels that this identification is "just the way people talk"; but for a group to talk that way it must think that way. In the next few paragraphs I shall adduce what I hope is a persuasive example of how, in one clear case, the change in the way we identified something reflected a change in the way we thought about it.

Until the 1960s, Afro-Americans were identified by such terms as "Negro" and "colored" (the respectable terms) and by the more disreputable "nigger," "spook," "kink," and so on. Recently there has been an unsuccessful attempt to replace the respectable identifications with such terms as "African," and "Afro-American," and a more successful attempt to replace them with "black." The most outspoken champions of this linguistic reform were those who argued that nonviolence must be abandoned for Black Power (Stokely Carmichael, H. Rap Brown), that integration must be abandoned in favor of separation (the Black Muslims: Malcolm X, Muhammad Ali), and that Afro-Americans were an internal colony in the alien world of Babylon who must arm themselves against the possibility of extermination (the Black Panthers: Eldridge Cleaver, Huey Newton). All of these movements and their partisans wished to stress that Afro-Americans were different from other Americans and could not be merged with them because the difference between the two was as great as that between black and white. Linguistically, of course, "black" and "white" are antonyms; and it is precisely this sense of oppositeness that those who see the Afro-American as alienated, separated, and nonintegratable wish to capture with the term "black." Moreover, as any good dictionary makes clear, in some contexts "black" is synonymous with "deadly," "sinister," "wicked," "evil," and so forth. The new militants were trying to create just this picture of the black man—civil rights and Uncle Tomism are dead, the ghost of Nat Turner is to be resurrected, Freedom Now or pay the price, the ballot or the bullet, "Violence is as American as cherry pie." The new strategy was that the white man would either give the black man his due or pay the price in violence. Since conceptually a "black man" was an object to be feared ("black" can be synonymous with "deadly," and so on), while a "colored man" or a "Negro" was not, the new strategy required that the "Negro" be supplanted by the "black man." White America resisted the proposed linguistic reform quite vehemently, until hundreds of riots forced the admission that the Afro-American was indeed black.

Now to the point: I have suggested that the word "black" replaced the word "Negro" because there was a change in our conceptual structure. One is likely to reply that while all that I have said above is well and good, one had, after all, no choice about the matter. White people are identified in terms of their skin color as whites; clearly, if we are to recognize what is in reality nothing but the truth, that in this society people are conscious of skin color, to treat blacks as equals is merely to identify them by their skin color, which is black. That is, one might argue that while there was a change in words, we have no reason to think that there was a parallel conceptual change. If the term "black" has all the associations mentioned above, that is unfortunate; but in the context the use of the term "black" to identify the people formerly identified as "Negroes" is natural, inevitable, and, in and of itself, neutral; black is, after all, the skin color of the people in question. (Notice that this defense of the natural-inevitable-and-neutral conception of identification quite nicely circumvents the possible use of such seemingly innocuous terms as "Afro-American" and "African" by suggesting that in this society it is *skin color* that is the relevant variable.)

The great flaw in this analysis is that the actual skin color of virtually all of the people whom we call "black" is not black at all. The color tones range from light yellow to a deep umber that occasionally is literally black. The skin color of most Afro-Americans is best designated by the word "brown." Yet "brown" is not a term that is standard for identifying Afro-Americans. For example, if someone asked, "Who was the brown who was the architect for Washington, D.C.?" we would not know how to construe the question. We might attempt to read "brown" as a proper name ("Do you mean Arthur Brown, the designer?"). We would have no trouble understanding the sentence "Who was the black (Negro, colored guy, and so forth) who designed Washington, D.C.?" ("Oh, you mean Benjamin Banneker"). Clearly, "brown" is not a standard form of identification for Afro-Americans. I hope that it is equally clear that "black" has become the standard way of identifying Afro-Americans not because the term was natural, inevitable, and, in the context, neutral, but because of its occasional synonymy with "sinister" and because as an antonym to "white" it best fitted the conceptual needs of those who saw race relations in terms of intensifying and insurmountable antonymies. If one accepts this point, then one must admit that there is a close connection between the way in which we identify things and the way in which we conceive them—and thus it should be also clear why I wish to talk about the way in which women are identified in English.[1] (Thus, for example, one would expect Black Muslims, who continually use the term "black *man"*—as in "the black *man's* rights"—to be more male chauvinistic than Afro-Americans who use the term "black *people*" or "black *folk*.")

Ways of Identifying Women

It may at first seem trivial to note that women (and men) are identified sexually; but conceptually this is extremely significant. To appreciate the significance of this fact it is helpful to imagine a language in which proper names and personal pronouns do not reflect the sex of the person designated by them (as they do in our language). I have been told that in some oriental languages pronouns and proper names reflect social status rather than sex, but whether or not there actually exists such a language is irrelevant, for it is easy enough to imagine what one would be like. Let us then imagine a language where the proper names are sexually neutral (for example, "Xanthe"), so that one cannot tell from hearing a name whether the person so named is male or female, and where the personal pronouns in the language are "under" and "over." "Under" is the personal pronoun appropriate for all those who are younger than thirty, while "over" is appropriate to persons older than thirty. In such a language, instead of saying such things as "Where do you think *he* is living now?" one would say such things as "Where do you think *under* is living now?"

What would one say about a cultural community that employed such a language? Clearly, one would say that they thought that for purposes of intelligible communication it was more important to know a person's age grouping than the person's height, sex, race, hair color, or parentage. (There are many actual cultures, of course, in which people are identified by names that reflect their parentage; for example, Abu ben Adam means Abu son of Adam.) I think that one would also claim that this people would not have reflected these differences in the pronominal structure of their language if they did not believe that the differences between unders and overs were such that a statement would frequently have one meaning if it were about an under and a different meaning if it were about an over. For example, in feudal times if a serf said, "My lord said to do this," that assertion was radically different from "Freeman John said to do this," since (presumably) the former had the status of a command while the latter did not. Hence the conventions of Middle English required that one refer to people in such a way as to indicate their social status. Analogously, one would not distinguish between pronominal references according to the age differences in the persons referred to were there no shift in meaning involved.

If we apply the lesson illustrated by this imaginary language to our own, I think that it should be clear that since in our language proper nouns and pronouns reflect sex rather than age, race, parentage, social status, or religion, we believe one of the most important things one can know about a person is that person's sex. (And, indeed, this is the first thing one seeks to determine about a newborn babe—our first question is almost invariably "Is it a boy or a girl?") Moreover, we would not reflect this important difference pronominally did we not also believe that statements frequently mean one thing when applied to males and something else when applied to females. Perhaps the most striking aspect of the conceptual discrimination reflected in our language is that man is, as it were, essentially human, while woman is only accidentally so.

This charge may seem rather extreme, but consider the following synonyms (which are readily confirmed by any dictionary). "Humanity" is synonymous with "mankind" but not with "womankind." "Man" can be substituted for "humanity" or "mankind" in any sentence in which the terms "mankind" or "humanity" occur without changing the meaning of the sentence, but significantly, "woman" cannot. Thus, the following expressions are all synonymous with each other: "humanity's great achievements," "mankind's great achievements," and "man's great achievements." "Woman's great achievements" is not synonymous with any of these. To highlight the degree to which women are excluded from humanity, let me point out that it is something of a truism to say that "man is a rational animal," while "woman is a rational animal" is quite debatable. Clearly, if "man" in the first assertion embraced both men and women, the second assertion would be just as much a truism as the first.[2] Humanity, it would seem, is a male prerogative. (And hence, one of the goals of women's liberation is to alter our conceptual structure so that someday "mankind" will be regarded as an improper and vestigial ellipsis for "humankind," and "man" will have no special privileges in relation to "human being" that "woman" does not have.[3])

The major question before us is, How are women conceived of in our culture? I have been trying to answer this question by talking about how they are identified. I first considered pronominal identification; now I wish to turn to identification through other types of noun phrases. Methods of nonpronominal identification can be discovered by determining which terms can be substituted for "woman" in such sentences as "Who is that woman over there?" without changing the meaning of the sentence. Virtually no term is interchangeable with "woman" in that sentence for all speakers on all occasions. Even "lady," which most speakers would accept as synonymous with "woman" in that sentence, will not do for a speaker who applies the term "lady" only to those women who display manners, poise, and sensitivity. In most contexts, a large number of students in one or more of my classes will accept the following types of terms as more or less interchangeable with "woman." (An asterisk indicates interchanges acceptable to both males and females; a plus sign indicates terms restricted to black students only. Terms with neither an asterisk nor a plus sign are accepted by all males but are not normally used by females.)

A. NEUTRAL TERMS: *lady, *gal, *girl (especially with regard to a co-worker in an office or factory), *sister, *broad (originally in the animal category, but most people do not think of the term as now meaning pregnant cow)

B. ANIMAL: chick, bird, fox, vixen, filly, bitch (Many do not know the literal meaning of the term. Some men and most women construe this use as pejorative; they think of "bitch" in the context of "bitchy," that is, snappy, nasty, and so forth. But a large group of men claim that it is a standard nonpejorative term of identification—which may perhaps indicate that women have come to be thought of as shrews by a large subclass of men.)

C. PLAYTHING: babe, doll, cuddly

D. GENDER (association with articles of clothing typically worn by those in the female gender role): skirt, hem

E. SEXUAL: snatch, cunt, ass, twat, piece (of ass, and so forth), lay, pussy (could be put in the animal category, but most users associated it with slang expression indicating the female pubic region), hammer (related to anatomical analogy between a hammer and breasts). There are many other usages, for example, "bunny," "sweat hog," but these were not recognized as standard by as many as 10 percent of any given class.

The students in my classes reported that the most frequently used terms of identification are in the neutral and animal classifications (although men in their forties claim to use the gender classifications quite a bit) and that the least frequently used terms of identification are sexual. Fortunately, however, I am not interested in the frequency of usage but only in whether the use is standard enough to be recognized as an identification among some group or other. (Recall that "brown" was not a standardized term of identification and hence we could not make sense out of "Who was the brown who planned Washington, D.C.?" Similarly, one has trouble with "Who was the breasts who planned Washington, D.C.?" but not with "Who was the babe (doll, chick, skirt, and so forth) who planned Washington, D.C.?")

Except for two of the animal terms, "chick" and "broad"—but note that "broad" is probably neutral today—women do not typically identify themselves in sexual terms, in gender terms, as playthings, or as animals; *only males use nonneutral terms to identify women.* Hence, it would seem that there is a male conception of women and a female conception. Only males identify women as "foxes," "babes," "skirts," or "cunts" (and since all the other nonneutral identifications are male, it is reasonable to assume that the identification of a woman as a "chick" is primarily a male conception that some women have adopted).

What kind of conception do men have of women? Clearly they think that women share certain properties with certain types of animals, toys, and playthings; they conceive of them in terms of the clothes associated with the female gender role; and, last (and, if my classes are any indication, least frequently), they conceive of women in terms of those parts of their anatomy associated with sexual intercourse, that is, as the identification "lay" indicates quite clearly, as sexual partners.

The first two nonneutral male classifications, animal and plaything, are prima facie denigrating (and I mean this in the literal sense of making one like a "nigger"). Consider the animal classification. All of the terms listed, with the possible exception of "bird," refer to animals that are either domesticated for servitude (to *man*) or hunted for sport. First, let us consider the term "bird." When I asked my students what sort of birds might be indicated, they suggested chick, canary (one member, in his forties, had suggested "canary" as a term of identification), chicken, pigeon, dove, parakeet, and hummingbird (one member). With the exception of the hummingbird, which like all the birds suggested is generally thought to be diminutive and pretty, all of the birds are domesticated, usually as pets (which reminds one that "my pet" is an expression of endearment). None of the birds were predators or symbols of intelligence or nobility (as are the owl, eagle, hawk, and falcon); nor did large but beautiful birds seem appropriate (for example, pheasants, peacocks, and swans). If one construes the bird terms (and for that matter, "filly") as applicable to women because they are thought of as beautiful, or at least pretty, *then there is nothing denigrating about them.* If, on the other hand, the common properties that underlie the metaphorical identification are domesticity and servitude, then they are indeed denigrating (as for myself, I think that both domesticity and prettiness underlie the identification). "Broad," of course, is, or at least was, clearly denigrating, since nothing renders more service to a farmer than does a pregnant cow, and cows are not commonly thought of as paradigms of beauty.

With one exception all of the animal terms reflect a male conception of women either as domesticated servants or as pets, or as both. Indeed, some of the terms reflect a conception of women first as pets and then as servants. Thus, when a pretty, cuddly little chick grows older, she becomes a very useful servant—the egg-laying hen.

"Vixen" and "fox," variants of the same term, are the one clear exception. None of the other animals with whom women are metaphorically identified are generally thought to be intelligent, aggressive, or independent—but the fox is. A chick is a soft, cuddly, entertaining, pretty, diminutive, domesticated, and dumb animal. A fox too is soft, cuddly, entertaining, pretty, and diminutive, but it is neither dependent nor dumb. It is aggressive, intelligent, and a minor predator—indeed, it preys on chicks—and frequently outsmarts ("outfoxes") men.

Thus the term "fox" or "vixen" is generally taken to be a compliment by both men and women, and compared to any of the animal or plaything terms it is indeed a compliment. Yet, considered in and of itself, the conception of a woman as a fox is not really complimentary at all, for the major connection between *man* and fox is that of predator and prey. The fox is an animal that men chase, and hunt, and kill for sport. If women are conceived of as foxes, then they are conceived of as prey that it is fun to hunt.

In considering plaything identifications, only one sentence is necessary. *All the plaything identifications are clearly denigrating since they assimilate women to the status of mindless or dependent objects.* "Doll" is to male paternalism what "boy" is to white paternalism.

Up to this point in our survey of male conceptions of women, every male identification, without exception, has been clearly antithetical to the conception of women as human beings (recall that "man" was synonymous with "human," while "woman" was not). Since the way we talk of things, and especially the way we identify them, is the way in which we conceive of them, any movement dedicated to breaking the bonds of female servitude must destroy these ways of identifying and hence of conceiving of women. Only when both sexes find the terms "babe," "doll," "chick," "broad," and so forth, as objectionable as "boy" and "nigger" will women come to be conceived of as independent *human beings.*

The two remaining unexamined male identifications are gender and sex. There seems to be nothing objectionable about gender identifications per se. That is, women are metaphorically identified as skirts because in this culture, skirts, like women, are peculiarly female. Indeed, if one accepts the view that the slogan "female and proud" should play the same role for the women's liberation movement that the slogan "Black is beautiful" plays for the black-liberation movement, then female clothes should be worn with the same pride as Afro clothes. (Of course, one can argue that the skirt, like the cropped-down Afro, is a sign of bondage, and hence both the item of clothing and the identification with it are to be rejected—that is, cropped-down Afros are to Uncle Tom what skirts are to Uncle Mom.)

The terms in the last category are obviously sexual, and frequently vulgar. For a variety of reasons I shall consider the import and nature of these identifications in the next section.

Men Ought Not to Think of Women As Sex Objects

Feminists have proposed many reforms, and most of them are clearly desirable, for example, equal opportunity for self-development, equal pay for equal work, and free day-care centers. One feminist proposal, however, is peculiarly conceptual and deeply perplexing. I call this proposal peculiarly conceptual because unlike the other reforms it is directed at getting people to think differently. The proposal is that *men should not think of women (and women should not think of themselves) as sex objects.* In the rest of this essay I shall explore this nostrum. I do so for two reasons: first, because the process of exploration should reveal the depth of the problem confronting the feminists; and second, because the feminists themselves seem to be entangled in the very concepts that obstruct their liberation.

To see why I find this proposal puzzling, one has to ask what it is to think of something as a sex object.

If a known object is an object that we know, an unidentified object is an object that we have not identified, and a desired object is an object that we desire, what then is a sex object? Clearly, a sex object is an object we have sex with. Hence, to think of a woman as a sex object is to think of her as someone to have sexual relations with, and when the feminist proposes that men refrain from thinking of women in this way, *she is proposing that men not think of women as persons with whom one has sexual relations.*

What are we to make of this proposal? Is the feminist suggesting that women should not be conceived of in this way because such a conception is "dirty"? To conceive of sex and sex organs as dirty is simply to be a prude. "Shit" is the paradigm case of a dirty word. It is a dirty word because the item it designates is taboo; it is literally unclean and untouchable (as opposed to something designated by what I call a curse word, which is not untouchable but rather something to be feared—"damn" and "hell" are curse words; "piss" is a dirty word). If one claims that "cunt" (or "fuck") is a dirty word, then one holds that what this term designates is unclean and taboo; thus one holds that the terms for sexual intercourse or sexual organs are dirty, one has accepted puritanism. If one is a puritan and a feminist, then indeed one ought to subscribe to the slogan *men should not conceive of women as sexual objects.* What is hard to understand is why anyone but a puritan (or, perhaps, a homosexual) would promulgate this slogan; yet most feminists, who are neither lesbians nor puritans, accept this slogan. Why?

A word about slogans: Philosophical slogans have been the subject of considerable analysis. They have the peculiar property (given a certain seemingly sound background story) of being obviously true, yet obviously false. "Men should not conceive of women as sex objects" is, I suggest, like a philosophical slogan in this respect. The immediate reaction of any humanistically oriented person upon first hearing the slogan is to agree with it—yet the more one probes the meaning of the slogan, the less likely one is to give one's assent. Philosophical analysts attempt to separate out the various elements involved in such slogans—to render the true-false slogan into a series of statements, some of which are true, some of which are false, and others of which are, perhaps, only probable. This is what I am trying to do with the slogan in question. I have argued so far that one of the elements that seems to be implicit in the slogan is a rejection of women as sexual partners for men and that although this position might be proper for a homosexual or puritanical movement, it seems inappropriate to feminism. I shall proceed to show that at least two other interpretations of the slogan lead to inappropriate results; but I shall argue that there are at least two respects in which the slogan is profoundly correct—even if misleadingly stated.

One plausible, but inappropriate, interpretation of "men ought not to conceive of women as sex objects" is that men ought not to conceive of women *exclusively* as sexual partners. The problem with this interpretation is that everyone can agree with it. Women are conceived of as companions, toys, servants, and even sisters, wives, and mothers—and hence not exclusively as sexual partners. Thus this slogan loses its revisionary impact, since even a male chauvinist could accept the slogan without changing his conceptual structure in any way—which is only to say that men do not usually identify or conceive of woman as sexual partners (recall that the sexual method of identification is the least frequently used).

Yet another interpretation is suggested by the term "object" in "sex object," and this interpretation too has a certain amount of plausibility. Men should not treat women as animate machines designed to masturbate men or as conquests that allow men to "score" for purposes of building their egos. Both of these variations rest on the view that to be treated as an object is to be treated as less than human (that is, to be treated as a machine or a score). Such relations between men and women are indeed immoral, and there are, no doubt, men who believe in "scoring." Unfortunately, however, this interpretation—although it would render the slogan quite apt—also fails because of its restricted scope. When feminists argue that men should not treat women as sex objects they are not *only* talking about fraternity boys and members of the Playboy Club; they are talking about all males in our society. The charge is that in our society men treat women as sex objects rather than as persons; it is this universality of scope that is lacking from the present interpretation. *Nonetheless, one of the reasons that we are prone to assent to the unrestricted charge that men treat women as sex objects is that the restricted charge is entirely correct.*

One might be tempted to argue that the charge that men treat women as sex objects is correct since such a conception underlies the most frequently used identifications, as animal and plaything; that is, these identifications indicate a sexual context in which the female is used as an object. Thus, it might be argued that the female fox is chased and slayed if she is four-legged, but chased and layed if she is two. Even if one admits the sexual context *implicit* in *some* animal and plaything identifications, one will not have the generality required; because, for the most part, the plaything and animal identifications themselves are nonsexual—most of them do not involve a sexual context. A pregnant cow, a toy doll, or a filly are hardly what one would call erotic objects. Babies do not normally excite sexual passion; and anyone whose erotic interests are directed toward chicks, canaries, parakeets, or other birds is clearly perverse. The animals and playthings to whom women are assimilated in the standard metaphorical identifications are not symbols of desire, eroticism, or passion (as, for example, a bull might be).

What is objectionable in the animal and plaything identifications is not the fact that some of these identifications reflect a sexual context but rather that—regardless of the context—these identifications reflect a conception of women as mindless servants (whether animate or inanimate is irrelevant). The point is not that men ought not to think of women in sexual terms but that they ought to think of them as human beings; and the slogan *men should not think of women as sex objects* is only appropriate when a man thinking of a woman as a sexual partner automatically conceives of her as something less than human. It is precisely this antihumanism implicit in the male concept of sex that we have as yet failed to uncover—but then, of course, we have not yet examined the language we use to identify sexual acts.

Our Conception of Sexual Intercourse

There are two profound insights that underlie the slogan "men ought not conceive of women as sexual objects"; both have the generality of scope that justifies the universality with which the feminists apply the slogan; neither can be put as simply as the slogan. The first is that the conception of sexual intercourse that we have in this culture is antithetical to the conception of women as human beings— as persons rather than objects. (Recall that this is congruent with the fact we noted earlier that "man" can be substituted for "humanity," while "woman" cannot.)

Many feminists have attempted to argue just this point. Perhaps the most famous defender of this view is Kate Millett,[4] who unfortunately faces the problem of trying to make a point about our conceptual structure without having adequate tools for analyzing conceptual structures.

The question Millett was dealing with was conceptual—Millett, in effect, asking about the nature of our conception of sexual roles. She tried to answer this question by analyzing novels; I shall attempt to answer this question by analyzing the terms we use to identify coitus, or more technically, in terms that function synonymously with "had sexual intercourse with" in a sentence of the form "A had sexual intercourse with B." The following is a list of some commonly used synonyms (numerous others that are not as widely used have been omitted, for example, "diddled," "laid pipe with"):

    screwed
    laid
    fucked
    had
    did it with (to)
    banged
    balled
    humped
    slept with
    made love to

Now, for a select group of these verbs, names for males are the subjects of sentences with active constructions (that is, where the subjects are said to be doing the activity); and names for females require passive constructions (that is, they are the recipients of the activity—whatever is done is done to them). Thus, we would not say "Jane did it to Dick," although we would say "Dick did it to Jane." Again, Dick bangs Jane, Jane does not bang Dick; Dick humps Jane, Jane does not hump Dick. In contrast, verbs like "did it with" do not require an active role for the male; thus, "Dick did it with Jane, and Jane with Dick." Again, Jane may make love to Dick, just as Dick makes love to Jane; and Jane sleeps with Dick as easily as Dick sleeps with Jane. (My students were undecided about "laid." Most thought that it would be unusual indeed for Jane to lay Dick, unless she played the masculine role of seducer-aggressor.)

The sentences thus form the following pairs. (Those conconjoined singular noun phrases where a female subject requires a passive construction are marked with a cross. An asterisk indicates that the sentence in question is not a sentence of English if it is taken as synonymous with the italicized sentence heading the column.[5])

Dick had sexual intercourse with Jane
Dick screwed Jane†
Dick laid Jane†
Dick fucked Jane†
Dick had Jane†
Dick did it to Jane†
Dick banged Jane†
Dick humped Jane†
Dick balled Jane(?)
Dick did it with Jane
Dick slept with Jane
Dick made love to Jane

Jane had sexual intercourse with Dick
Jane was banged by Dick
Jane was humped by Dick
*Jane was done by Dick
Jane was screwed by Dick
Jane was laid by Dick
Jane was fucked by Dick
Jane was had by Dick
Jane balled Dick (?)
Jane did it with Dick
Jane slept with Dick
Jane made love to Dick
*Jane screwed Dick
*Jane laid Dick
*Jane fucked Dick
*Jane had Dick
*Jane did it to Dick
*Jane banged Dick
*Jane humped Dick

These lists make clear that within the standard view of sexual intercourse, males, or at least names for males, seem to play a different role than females, since male subjects play an active role in the language of screwing, fucking, having, doing it, and perhaps, laying, while female subjects play a passive role.

The asymmetrical nature of the relationship indicated by the sentences marked with a cross is confirmed by the fact that the form "–ed with each other" is acceptable for the sentences not marked with a cross, but not for those that require a male subject. Thus:

Dick and Jane had sexual intercourse with each other
Dick and Jane made love to each other
Dick and Jane slept with each other
Dick and Jane did it with each other
Dick and Jane balled with each other (*?)
*Dick and Jane banged with each other
*Dick and Jane did it to each other
*Dick and Jane had each other
*Dick and Jane fucked each other
*Dick and Jane humped each other
*(?) Dick and Jane laid each other
*Dick and Jane screwed each other

It should be clear, therefore, that our language reflects a difference between the male and female sexual roles, and hence that we conceive of the male and female roles in different ways. The question that now arises is, What difference in our conception of the male and female sexual roles requires active constructions for males and passive for females?

One explanation for the use of the active construction for males and the passive construction for females is that this grammatical asymmetry merely reflects the natural physiological asymmetry between men and women: the asymmetry of "to screw" and "to be screwed," "to insert into" and "to be inserted into." That is, it might be argued that the difference between masculine and feminine grammatical roles merely reflects a difference naturally required by the anatomy of males and females. This explanation is inadequate. Anatomical differences do not determine how we are to conceptualize the relation between penis and vagina during intercourse. Thus one can easily imagine a society in which the female normally played the active role during intercourse, where female subjects required active constructions with verbs indicating copulation, and where the standard metaphors were terms like "engulfing"—that is, instead of saying "he screwed her," one would say "she engulfed him." It follows that the use of passive constructions for female subjects of verbs indicating copulation does not reflect differences determined by human anatomy but rather reflects those generated by human customs.

What I am going to argue next is that the passive construction of verbs indicating coitus (that is, indicating the female position) can *also* be used to indicate that a person is being harmed. I am then going to argue that the metaphor involved would only make sense if we conceive of the female role in intercourse as that of a person being harmed (or being taken advantage of).

Passive constructions of "fucked," "screwed," and "had" indicate the female role. They also can be used to indicate being harmed. Thus, in all of the following sentences, Marion plays the female role: "Bobbie fucked Marion"; "Bobbie screwed Marion"; "Bobbie had Marion"; "Marion was fucked"; "Marion was screwed"; and "Marion was had." All of the statements are equivocal. They might literally mean that someone had sexual intercourse with Marion (who played the female role); or they might mean, metaphorically, that Marion was deceived, hurt, or taken advantage of. Thus, we say such things as "I've been screwed" ("fucked," "had," "taken," and so on) when we have been treated unfairly, been sold shoddy merchandise, or conned out of valuables. Throughout this essay I have been arguing that metaphors are applied to things only if what the term *actually* applies to shares one or more properties with what the term *metaphorically* applies to. Thus, the female sexual role must have something in common with being conned or being sold shoddy merchandise. The only common property is that of being harmed, deceived, or taken advantage of. *Hence we conceive of a person who plays the female sexual role as someone who is being harmed* (that is, "screwed," "fucked," and so on).

It might be objected that this is clearly wrong, since the unsignated terms do not indicate someone's being harmed, and hence we do not conceive of having intercourse as being harmed. The point about the unsignated terms, however, is that they can take both females and males as subjects (in active constructions) and thus *do not pick out the female role*. This demonstrates that we conceive of sexual roles in such a way that only females are thought to be taken advantage of in intercourse.

The best part of solving a puzzle is when all the pieces fall into place. If the subjects of the passive construction are being harmed, presumably the subjects of the active constructions are doing harm, and, indeed, we do conceive of these subjects in precisely this way. Suppose one is angry at someone and wishes to express malevolence as forcefully as possible without actually committing an act of physical violence. If one is inclined to be vulgar one can make the sign of the erect male cock by clenching one's fist while raising one's middle finger, or by clenching one's fist and raising one's arm and shouting such things as "screw you," "up yours," or "fuck you." In other words, one of the strongest possible ways of telling someone that you wish to harm him is to tell him to assume the female sexual role relative to you. Again, to say to someone "go fuck yourself" is to order him to harm himself, while to call someone a "mother fucker" is not so much a play on his Oedipal fears as to accuse him of being so low that he would inflict the greatest imaginable harm (fucking) upon that person who is most dear to him (his mother).

Clearly, we conceive of the male sexual role as that of hurting the person in the female role—but lest the reader have any doubts, let me provide two further bits of confirming evidence: one linguistic, one nonlinguistic. One of the English terms for a person who hurts (and takes advantage of) others is the term "prick." This metaphorical identification would not make sense unless the bastard in question (that is, the person outside the bonds of legitimacy) was thought to share some characteristics attributed to things that are literally pricks. As a verb, "prick" literally means "to hurt," as in "I pricked myself with a needle"; but the usage in question is as a noun. As a noun, "prick" is a colloquial term for "penis." Thus, the question before us is what characteristic is shared by a penis and a person who harms others (or, alternatively, by a penis and by being stuck by a needle). Clearly, no physical characteristic is relevant (physical characteristics might underlie the Yiddish metaphorical attribution "schmuck," but one would have to analyze Yiddish usage to determine this); hence the shared characteristic is nonphysical; the only relevant shared nonphysical characteristic is that both a literal prick and a figurative prick are agents that harm people.

Now for the nonlinguistic evidence. Imagine two doors: in front of each door is a line of people; behind each door is a room; in each room is a bed; on each bed is a person. The line in front of one room consists of beautiful women, and on the bed in that room is a man having intercourse with each of these women in turn. One may think any number of things about this scene. One may say that the man is in heaven, or enjoying himself at a bordello; or perhaps one might only wonder at the oddness of it all. One does not think that the man is being hurt or violated or degraded—or at least the possibility does not immediately suggest itself, although one could conceive of situations where this was what was happening (especially, for example, if the man was impotent). Now, consider the other line. Imagine that the figure on the bed is a woman and that the line consists of handsome, smiling men. The woman is having intercourse with each of these men in turn. It immediately strikes one that the woman is being degraded, violated, and so forth—"that poor woman."

When one man fucks many women he is a playboy and gains status; when a woman is fucked by many men she degrades herself and loses stature.

Our conceptual inventory is now complete enough for us to return to the task of analyzing the slogan that men ought not to think of women as sex objects.

I think that it is now plausible to argue that the appeal of the slogan "men ought not to think of women as sex objects," and the thrust of much of the literature produced by contemporary feminists, turns on something much deeper than a rejection of "scoring" (that is, the utilization of sexual "conquests" to gain esteem) and yet is a call neither for homosexuality nor for puritanism.

The slogan is best understood as a call for a new conception of the male and female sexual roles. If the analysis developed above is correct, our present conception of sexuality is such that to be a man is to be a person capable of brutalizing women (witness the slogans "The marines will make a man out of you!" and "The army builds *men!*" which are widely accepted and which simply state that learning how to kill people will make a person more manly). Such a conception of manhood not only bodes ill for a society led by such men, but also is clearly inimical to the best interests of women. It is only natural for women to reject such a sexual role, and it would seem to be the duty of any moral person to support their efforts—to redefine our conceptions not only of fucking, but of the fucker (man) and the fucked (woman).

This brings me to my final point. We are a society preoccupied with sex. As I noted previously, the nature of proper nouns and pronouns in our language makes it difficult to talk about someone without indicating that person's sex. This convention would not be part of the grammar of our language if we did not believe that knowledge of a person's sex was crucial to understanding what is said about that person. Another way of putting this point is that sexual discrimination permeates our conceptual structure. Such discrimination is clearly inimical to any movement toward sexual egalitarianism and virtually defeats its purpose at the outset. (Imagine, for example, that black people were always referred to as "them" and whites as "us" and that proper names for blacks always had an "x" suffix at the end. Clearly any movement for integration as equals would require the removal of these discriminatory indicators. Thus at the height of the melting-pot era, immigrants Americanized their names: "Bellinsky" became "Bell," "Burnstein" became "Burns," and "Lubitch" became "Baker.")

I should therefore like to close this essay by proposing that contemporary feminists should advocate the utilization of neutral proper names and the elimination of gender from our language (as I have done in this essay); and they should vigorously protest any utilization of the third-person pronouns "he" and "she" as examples of sexist discrimination (perhaps "person" would be a good third-person pronoun)—for, as a parent of linguistic analysis once said, "The limits of our language are the limits of our world."

Notes

1. The underlying techniques used in this essay were all developed (primarily by Austin and Strawson) to deal with the problems of metaphysics and epistemology. All I have done is to attempt to apply them to other areas; I should note, however, that I rely rather heavily on metaphorical identifications, and that first philosophy tends not to require the analysis of such superficial aspects of language. Note also that it is an empirical matter whether or not people do use words in a certain way. In this essay I am just going to assume that the reader uses words more or less as my students do; for I gathered the data on which words we use to identify women, and so on, simply by asking students. If the reader does not use terms as my students do, then what I say may be totally inapplicable to him.

2. It is also interesting to talk about the technical terms that philosophers use. One fairly standard bit of technical terminology is "trouser word." J. L Austin invented this bit of jargon to indicate which term in a pair of antonyms is important. Austin called the important term a "trouser word" because "it is the use which wears the trousers." Even in the language of philosophy, to be important is to play the male role. Of course, the antifeminism implicit in the language of technical philosophy is hardly comparable to the male chauvinism embedded in commonplaces of ordinary discourse.

3. Although I thought it inappropriate to dwell on these matters in the text, it is quite clear that *we* do *not* associate many positions with females—as the following story brings out. I related this conundrum both to students in my regular courses and to students I teach in some experimental courses at a nearby community college. Among those students who had not previously heard the story, only native Swedes invariably resolved the problem; less than half of the students from an upper-class background would get it (eventually), while lower-class and black students virtually

never figured it out. Radical students, women, even members of women's liberation groups fared no better than anyone else with their same class background. The story goes as follows: A little boy is wheeled into the emergency room of a hospital. The surgeon on emergency call looks at the boy and says, "I'm sorry I cannot operate on this child; he is my son." The surgeon was not the boy's father. In what relation did the surgeon stand to the child? Most students did not give any answer. The most frequent answer given was that the surgeon had fathered the boy illegitimately. (Others suggested that the surgeon had divorced the boy's mother and remarried and hence was not legally the boy's father.) Even though the story was related as a part of a lecture on women's liberation, at best only 20 percent of the written answers gave the correct and obvious answer—the surgeon was the boy's mother.

    4. *Sexual Politics* (New York: Doubleday, 1971); but see also *Sisterhood Is Powerful,* ed. Robin Morgan (New York: Vintage Books, 1970).

    5. For further analysis of verbs indicating copulation see "A Note on Conjoined Noun Phrases," *Journal of Philosophical Linguistics* 1, no. 2, Great Expectations, Evanston, Ill. Reprinted with "English Sentences without Overt Grammatical Subject," in Zwicky, Salus, Binnick, and Vanek, eds., *Studies Out in Left Field: Defamatory Essays Presented to James D. McCawley* (Edmonton: Linguistic Research, Inc., 1971). The puritanism in our society is such that both of these articles are pseudoanonymously published under the name of Quang Phuc Dong; Mr. Dong, however, has a fondness for citing and criticizing the articles and theories of Professor James McCawley, Department of Linguistics, University of Chicago. Professor McCawley himself was kind enough to criticize an earlier draft of this essay. I should also like to thank G. E. M. Anscombe for some suggestions concerning this essay.

"Pricks" and "Chicks":
A Postscript after Twenty-five Years

" 'Pricks' and 'Chicks': A Plea for 'Persons' " is a product of a period, of personal guilt, of a strategy of reform, and of an attempt to teach philosophy. The period has passed, the guilt is gone, the reformist strategy has, for the most part, succeeded, but the essay still contains an effective tool for the analysis of conceptions of sex and gender—even though the specific terms originally analyzed are dated. In this postscript I recall the spirit of the era in which the essay was written, I try to evoke the sense of guilt that originally gave it impetus, I defend "political correctness" as strategy of moral reform, and I show how the essay can be used to teach a new generation to articulate and analyze the conceptions of sexuality and gender that inform their lives and the lives of their peers.

    The period in which the essay was written was the late 1960s and early 1970s. The place was the Midwest, where I worked as a somewhat out-of-place New Yorker teaching at various state universities. Like most academics of the period, I lived a schizophrenic life split between "serious" scholarly research published in professional journals like *Nous* and the *Review of Metaphysics,* and active participation in the "underground press" and in the reform movements reshaping American culture—civil rights, educational reform, and resistance to the war in Vietnam.

At the end of the sixties, feminism came into my life and changed it forever. Chicago feminist Marlene Dixon came to the university at which I was teaching. Her lecture, uniquely for the time, provided free baby-sitting. My wife and I both attended and left a changed couple. I realized—we both realized—that as a male I had assumed a position of privileged status that she, as a female, had been denied by virtue of her sex and by the social construction of gender roles. I discovered that I myself was by social right, however unwittingly, the very creature whom I abhorred as a matter of moral principle. We began, that night, the process of rethinking and restructuring our lives.

As it happened, the restructuring process took place in another midwestern city. I had alienated the university administration and they declined to renew my contract. In retrospect, my offenses seem innocuous: teaching a class in the city jail (student anti-war demonstrators had been arrested for picketing a military recruitment center; and the University administration had threatened to expel any student not attending class the next day, making male anti-war student protesters draft-eligible. Since my entire political philosophy class had been jailed, I taught the next day's class in jail, thereby protecting my students from expulsion); and acting as faculty advisor for innumerable student organizations, including the Black Athlete's Union (which went on strike to protest the inequitable treatment of African-American athletes by white coaches). Fortunately, I was well published in professional journals and I soon received a job offer from another state university. The new job was to be in Detroit, which was a move east, and hence, or so I thought at the time, a move to a more urbane and tolerant environment.

When the three of us—my wife, my young son, and I—arrived in Detroit in the fall of 1968, we were utterly unprepared for the scene that awaited us. Since I had never had an on-campus interview for my new position, we were shocked when we exited the thruway onto block after block of burned-out buildings. The inner city of Detroit was in ashes. Yet arising from the ruin of the urban riots was an oasis of white-on-white glass-and-steel buildings that housed the university at which my wife and I would soon be teaching. The rioters had burned and looted every sort of building, but the university and the nearby museums had been left unscathed. Access to education had been one of the rioters' principal demands; the unbroken windows of the gleaming university standing among the ashes symbolized this demand dramatically.

The university, however, declined to lower standards to admit those it considered unqualified, and so a number of faculty members banded together to respond to the rioters' demand for education by forming an alternative institution. I soon joined their ranks. Collectively we agreed to teach courses, initially without pay, in an open-admission proto-community college that would hold classes in abandoned store fronts, in high schools, and in factories. Working with a logician (Robert Titiev) and an African-American philosophy graduate student (Nadine Philips), I set up a modular philosophy course with three tracks: an African-American philosophy track, an ethics track, and a logic track. Students could take any two-week module in any of the tracks, and—once the institution had been accredited—would earn one "course credit" for every five modules completed (for a maximum of three course credits).

We taught the course once a week, at night, in an inner city high school with a dreadful reputation, located in a part of the city in which middle-class people, black or white, were hesitant to venture. But our students were warm and welcoming. Many were self-educated school dropouts, most had a thirst for learning. Those in my section insisted that they *not* be given a "second-rate" or "watered-down" education; they insisted on being taught "from the same books" that we used at the state university. To satisfy their insistence on parity I invited students from my regular university ethics course to attend my evening ethics track, and I had some of my evening students attend my regular university ethics course. The parity requirement also meant that I had to find a way to teach techniques of conceptual analysis to a class of forty African-American students with little formal education. So I designed an exercise that would use linguistic-conceptual analytic techniques to articulate conceptions of race: we discussed the difference between "African-American," "Black," "Colored," and "Negro" and the question of why it was insulting to call a black *man* a "boy" and a black *woman* a "girl," and so forth. Toward the end of class the techniques of analysis were challenged. Students asked me to validate the techniques by demonstrating their applicability to issues other than race. Since I had adopted the techniques from metaphysics—an area of philosophy unlikely to be illuminating to the class—I promised a demonstration of their validity at the next class meeting.

When I returned the next week I used two questions to demonstrate that techniques of linguistic-conceptual analysis could be used to articulate conceptions of sexuality and gender implicit in our ordinary language. I was soon asked to repeat this exercise, first in my regular classes and later in various feminist fora. The poet Judith McCombs Benjamin suggested that I write out the exercise as an essay that could be published in the local feminist magazine *Moving Out*. Once published, I refined the analysis as a philosophical essay "'Pricks' and 'Chicks': A Plea for 'Persons' " that I circulated in the "samizdat" circuit. This version was actually awarded a prize. Thus emboldened, I submitted the essay to several professional journals, only to have it returned immediately as unsuitable for publication.

The essay was destined to play an even larger role in my life. The state university in Detroit was as intolerant of my involvement in anti-war, civil rights, egalitarian, and feminist causes as my earlier employer had been. When I was reviewed for tenure I submitted only articles published in professional journals for assessment by the review committee, but some unnamed party called the committee's attention to the version of "'Pricks' and 'Chicks'" published in *Moving Out*. The committee decided that the essay established my untenurability. In response, I sent it to a number of leading women philosophers; many, including G. E. M. Anscombe and Ruth Barcan Marcus, wrote letters on my behalf, but to no avail.

Once again I found myself seeking a job. Determined to find a tolerant academic environment I sent copies of the essay to every hiring committee that wished to interview me. Somewhat to my surprise, a number of institutions made me offers. I accepted a position at Union College, a small private liberal arts college in upstate New York. There I began the partnership with a colleague, Fred Elliston, that culminated in the publication of the first two editions of *Philosophy and Sex*.

I outlined this history of the essay—which went on to be widely anthologized, but which also provoked a conflict with obscenity laws—to give students today some sense of the revolutionary reshaping of American culture that took place in the 1960s and 1970s. It was a time when people began the process of rethinking their received values and roles; when men and women, more often thinking and working together than not, began to reconceptualize gender and sexuality. It was an extraordinarily difficult process, made even more difficult by forces in the culture resisting the critical analysis and reassessment of the status quo.

Today it is common to deride the conceptual aspects of social reform, dismissing it with the canard "political correctness." The canard reflects a failure to appreciate the historical relationship between conceptual and sociopolitical change. Exclusionary conceptual frameworks circumscribe lives. There is thus little conceptual room for women in a world of business*men,* chair*men,* congress*men,* fire*men,* mail*men,* police*men*—or in an academy of gentle*men* and fellows. The linguistic preference toward males explicit in this terminology accurately mirrors the social facts of life in pre-feminist American culture. One way in which feminists successfully changed these social arrangements was through a linguistic-conceptual challenge that served as the cutting edge of a political-social-economic struggle. The conceptual challenge and political change operated in tandem, as they had in the civil rights movement, in the earlier suffragette and abolitionist movements, and in the American Revolution itself. For just as "British colonial subjects" had to reconceptualize themselves as "American citizens" to rebel successfully against the British monarchy, just as the National Association for the Advancement of Colored *People* had to assert their claims as "people," rather than as a race apart, to desegregate America, feminists had to force a gender-neutral reconceptualization of the worlds of business, administration, politics, civil service—and the academy—to successfully open these worlds to women. Reconceptualization *alone* would have been insufficient to guarantee the success of any social reform or revolution, but no social or political revolution has ever succeeded without inventing a reconceptualization that delegitimates the status quo while simultaneously legitimating the reforms to which it aspires. Revolutions are conceived in the mind well before they shape the body politic.

Canards about "political correctness" are often supported by tales that parody conceptual reform. These tales presume a movement to replace words like 'fat' and 'short' with 'horizontally challenged' and 'vertically challenged'. Such tales conflate euphemisms with conceptual revisions. Euphemisms (the term originates from Greek and means "good sounds") merely substitute inoffensive terms for offensive ones. They seldom involve the reconceptualization of exploitive conceptions. Thus, while the first terms in the antonym pairs 'fat'/ 'thin' and 'short'/'tall' may be taken as offensive in some contexts, these terms are not integral to a conceptual framework of exclusion. There is no equivalent to the exclusionary 'business*men*'—an expression that expressly excludes women from the workplace—in our current use of the terms 'thin' and 'tall'. One might euphemistically describe a fat person as "hefty" or a short person as "diminutive," but such a substitution involves neither a reconceptualization of a classificatory framework nor an attempt to rectify an inequality. Euphemisms generally do not change meanings, they merely say the same thing in a less offensive manner. (Note, by this standard, that "vertically challenged" does not qualify as a euphemism, since, whatever offense short people might take in being characterized as "short," that offense is unlikely to be mitigated by the substitution of the term "vertically challenged"—terminology that, by virtue of its novelty, is more likely to call attention to physical stature than the seemingly blunter 'short'.)

In striking contrast, conceptual revisions always *change* meanings. 'Business*person*' and 'chair*person*' do not have the same meaning as 'business*men*' and 'chair*men*' precisely because the latter terms expressly exclude women, whereas the former do not. Conceptual revisions differ radically from euphemisms because they aspire not to make something "sound good" to a hearer, but to replace an exploitive or exclusionary conception with a morally acceptable alternative.

Another charge characteristically directed against proponents of linguistic-conceptual reform is that it is inefficacious and thus changes linguistic traditions unnecessarily. "Sticks and stones may break my bones," the old saying goes, "but names can never hurt me." Whoever invented this silly slogan could never have been subjected to racist or sexist epithets; for the power of words to hurt exceeds those of sticks and stones. Exclusion, exploitation, even extermination all presuppose conceptual frameworks that render permissible what is normally immoral. Racism, sexism, and eliminative extermination movements (like Nazism) characteristically presuppose a linguistic-conceptual framework permitting moral people to act in ways that would otherwise be considered morally impermissible. The Nazis, for example, reconceptualized those whom they exterminated as *Gemeinschaftfremde,* or "enemies of the community," *lebensunwertes Leben,* or "life unworthy of living," and *Untermenschen,* or "subhumans." Conversely, egalitarian social reform movements succeed only if they successfully challenge such systems of conceptual exclusion, thereby extending normal moral concepts and protection to the previously excluded and exploited groups.

Names can hurt and thus changing names can alter hurtful behavior. I shall offer one particularly striking example of a conceptual revision that paved the way for social reform; a revision that has nothing whatsoever to do with race or sex, but one involving age. In his 1975 book, *Why Survive? Growing Old in*

America, Dr. Robert Butler assembled a massive amount of data documenting discrimination against a group of Americans known as "old folks," "old codgers," "old hags," or, to use the epithets that epitomized the popular disdain for the elderly as useless and undesirable—"old bags," and "old farts." Butler referred to this group as "elderly" (as in "the wisdom of one's elders") and "senior citizens" (emphasizing the deference owed to "seniority" and to fellow "citizens"). Neither of these terms, however, was new to Butler's work. The term he added to the American-English lexicon was "ageism," which he defined as the "process of systematic stereotyping of and discrimination against people because they are old." The new concept "ageism" served two ends: first, it organized the disparate data about the mistreatment of the elderly into a coherent pattern of stereotyping and discrimination; second, because of the linguistic analogy to other "isms"—racism and sexism—"ageism" implicitly evoked a civil rights model.

Butler's research came to the attention of Dr. Arthur S. Flemming, Commissioner on Aging for the Department of Health, Education and Welfare and Chairman of the United States Commission on Civil Rights. Flemming quickly introduced Butler's new term into American political rhetoric. "Ageism," Flemming informed the House Education and Labor Committee in a 1975 speech, was equivalent to "racism" and "sexism" and he "hope[d] that the day will come when the Civil Rights Act will be amended to include age . . . as one of the factors that must be taken into consideration under the Civil Rights Act." Like skin color, race, sex, and handicap, age is a biophysiological fact. As testimony before the House Education and Labor Committee quickly established, this biological fact was used by businesses, private organizations, and governmental agencies to deny senior citizens access to credit, education, employment, housing, mortgage financing, and scarce medical resources, irrespective of their abilities or physical condition. Thus the biophysiological fact of old age, like that of race and sex, had become associated with negative stereotypes that effectively denied individuals the opportunity to fully function as persons.

When Martin Luther King Jr. took a stand against racism he dreamed of an America in which all persons would be judged by the content of their character, not the color of their skin. When Butler and Flemming took a stand against "ageism," they dreamed of an America in which all are judged by their ability, not the wrinkles on their face, or the date on their birth certificate. They dreamed about imposing an egalitarian moral vision upon a recalcitrant reality; for to envision all persons as equal is to accept a conceptual framework blind to a world in which everyone is different: differently abled, differently colored, differently raced, differently sexed—and differently aged. The egalitarian vision requires a conceptual framework that looks to the person underlying these biophysiological facts of race, gender, handicap—or chronological age. By the end of the year Congress accepted this vision and passed the Age Discrimination Act of 1975. The act categorically prohibited discrimination on the basis of age: "no person in the United States shall, on the basis of age, be excluded from participation in, be denied the benefits of, or be subjected to discrimination under, any program receiving Federal financial assistance."

The speed with which this particular reform moved from conception to social legislation is remarkable; it serves as apt illustration of the power of reconceptualization as an agent of reform—the power of "political correctness," so to speak.

One of the major functions of social and political philosophy is to develop tools for conceptual analysis that enable one to articulate and reconceptualize conceptual frameworks. One of the tools on the social philosopher's workbench is the set of questions that I developed in the late 1960s and early 1970s to enable my students to explore their own conceptions of race, gender, and sexual intercourse. The version of the instrument that I am currently using is divided into three parts: the first asks demographic information about the student, the second explores the language students use to identify members of the opposite sex, and the third explores the language used to characterize sexual intercourse. I typically administer the instrument twice: once to students individually, on the first day of class, and once later in the term, when I have students fill it out in small same-sex groups, subdivided further so that fraternity members are in one group, sorority members in another, and so forth. After the students have reported their collective results, I then distribute a sheet tabulating the results of the survey taken on the first day of class. A lively discussion invariably follows in which we analyze the answers and unpack the metaphors implicit in the language that students use to identify members of the opposite sex, comparing the language females use for males with that used by males for females, and so forth.

A few caveats: I always warn students in advance that we will be discussing descriptions of sexual intercourse in an open and frank manner, allowing anyone who wishes to opt out of the discussion to do so. The discussion, more-over, should always be conducted in terms of what "one's friends would say," a strategy that encourages open discussion and minimizes defensiveness. On a more technical level, it is important that students place an asterisk by the most frequently used expressions, and that the test administrator compare this with the frequency of use reported collectively, exploring differences as they emerge.

When analyzing the various ways in which students describe the situation in which "Jane and Richard had sexual intercourse after the social last night," it is important to assess whether Jane and Richard are seen as playing equally active roles, as in the expression "Jane and Richard *hooked up* last night," or whether one is playing a more active role than the other, as in the expression "Richard nailed Jane last night," or "Richard scored last night," which suggests an active male and a passive female. The "scoring" metaphor actually suggests that the female is irrelevant, except as a means to male status. Unpacking metaphors is important; thus the metaphor "nailing" not only suggests activity but activity painful to the passive partner who has been "nailed."

The expressions that students use change over time and it is interesting to supplement the exercise by comparing the current class report with reports from earlier years. At the height of the AIDS epidemic, for example, "doing the nasty" became one of the most frequently used terms for sexual intercourse. In recent years that expression has faded. "Hooked up" is now the most commonly used description by my male students; "made love" is now the most commonly used female description.

In some classes gay and lesbian students offer to discuss their language and conceptions of sexuality with the class. I always accept such offers, but, because we still live in a world that is too often inhospitable to nonheterosexuals, I never solicit them.

I always end the exercise by asking the students to envision an ideal gender-sexual world and to suggest the language and metaphors that would reflect that world. My essay ends on the same note, arguing for the elimination of the generic use of 'he' as a pronoun representing someone whose sex is unspecified, as in, "one should do the best *he* can." Such male preferences violate ideals of gender egalitarianism. It is currently fashionable, in some circles, to attempt to rectify centuries of linguistic-conceptual preference toward males by using pronouns preferencing females, as in "one should do the best *she* can." Preferencing females, however, affronts ideals of gender equality as deeply as preferencing males. Ideally, one's conceptual framework should be neutral between females and males, as in "everyone should do the best they can." It is interesting to note, for example, that once gender-neutral conceptions of certain female professions were introduced (the reconceptualization of "stewardesses" as "flight attendants," for example) men gravitated to occupations that were once thought too "feminine" for them. If we would strive for a world of gender equality, we should fashion our language so that our occupations are limited only by our ambitions, efforts, and talents. For, to repeat the quotation from Wittgenstein that closed my "Plea for 'Persons' " twenty-five years ago, "the limits of our language are the limits of our world."

QUESTIONNAIRE CONCEPTIONS OF GENDER AND SEX
(copyright © Robert Baker, 1997)

Are you male or female? (Circle one)	M	F		
Your class is (Circle one):	FR	SOPH	JR	SR
Do you live in coed housing?	Yes	No		
Single-Sex housing?	Yes	No		
Are you living in a (circle one)	Dormitory	Fraternity	Sorority	
	Student Apartment	Parents' Home		
	Other (explain)			

Imagine that you are having breakfast with some of your friends (all of whom are the same sex as you) on a Saturday morning. You remark that Friday night, M, a mutual acquaintance, was with someone of the opposite sex. You ask your friends "Who was that (boy/girl) M was with last night?"

1) Please list the various expressions *your friends* (all of whom are the same sex as you) might use in such a conversation with you to refer to the boy/girl; as in the sentence "The _____ M was with last night was from a local college." (For example, "The *gal/guy* M was with last night was from a local college.) "Please place an asterisk, '*', after the most commonly used expressions, but do not use more than three asterisks.

2) Suppose that your friends (all of whom are the same sex as you) suspect that Jane and Richard had sexual intercourse after the social last night. Please list the words and expressions that *your friends* might use to describe this situation to you. Please place an asterisk, '*', after the most commonly used expressions, but do not use more than three asterisks.

19

Linguistic Sexes and Genders

Luce Irigaray

Women's entry into the public world, the social relations they have among themselves and with men, have made cultural transformations, and especially linguistic ones, a necessity. If the male President of the Republic meets the Queen, to say *Ils se sont rencontrés* (they met) borders on a grammatical anomaly.[1] Instead of dealing with this difficult question, most people wonder whether it wouldn't be better if we were governed by just men or just women, that is, by one gender alone. The rules of language have so strong a bearing on things that they can lead to such impasses. Unfortunately, there's still little appreciation of what's at stake here. Faced with the need to transform the rules of grammar, some women, even feminists—though fortunately not all—readily object that provided they have the right to use it, the masculine gender will do for them. But neutralizing grammatical gender amounts to an abolition of the difference between sexed subjectivities and to an increasing exclusion of a culture's sexuality. We would be taking a huge step backward if we abolished grammatical gender, a step our civilization can ill afford; what we do need, on the other hand, and it's essential, is for men and women to have equal subjective rights—equal obviously meaning different but of equal value, subjective implying equivalent rights in exchange systems. From a linguistic perspective, therefore, the cultural injustices of language and its generalized sexism have to be analyzed. These are to be found in grammar, in vocabulary, in the connotations of a word's gender.

From *Je, Tu, Nous: Toward a Culture of Difference,* translated by Alison Martin (New York: Routledge, 1993). Reprinted by permission of the publisher.

More or Less Masculine

For centuries, whatever has been valorized has been masculine in gender, whatever devalorized, feminine. So the sun is masculine, and the moon feminine. Yet in our cultures, *le soleil* (the sun) is thought of as the source of life, *la lune* (the moon) as ambiguous, almost harmful, except perhaps by some peasants. The attribution of masculine gender to the sun can be traced in history, and so can the attribution of the sun to the men-gods. These aren't all immutable truths but rather facts that evolve over long periods of time and at different rates of speed depending upon the culture, country, and language. The positive connotation of the masculine as word gender derives from the time of the establishment of patriarchal and phallocratic power, notably by men's appropriation of the divine. This is not a secondary matter. It is very important. Without divine power, men could not have supplanted mother-daughter relations and their attributions concerning nature and society. But man becomes God by giving himself an invisible father, a father language. Man becomes God as the Word, then as the Word made flesh. Because the power of semen isn't immediately obvious in procreation, it's relayed by the linguistic code, the *logos*. Which wants to become the all-embracing truth.

Men's appropriation of the linguistic code attempts to do at least three things:

1. prove they are fathers;

2. prove they are more powerful than mother-women;

3. prove they are capable of engendering the cultural domain as they have been engendered in the natural domain of the ovum, the womb, the body of a woman.

To guarantee loyalty to its authority, the male people consciously or unconsciously represents whatever has value as corresponding to its image and its grammatical gender. Most linguists state that grammatical gender is arbitrary, independent of sexual denotations and connotations. In fact, this is untrue. They haven't really thought about the issue. It doesn't strike them as being important. Their personal subjectivity, their theory is content to be valorized like the masculine, passing for an arbitrary universal. A patient study of the gender of words almost always reveals their hidden sex. Rarely is this immediately apparent. And a linguist will be quick to retort that *un fauteuil* (a sofa) or *un chateau* (a castle) are not more "masculine" than *une chaise* (a chair) or *une maison* (a house). Apparently not. A degree of thought will show that the former connote greater value than the latter. While the latter are simply useful in our cultures, the others are more luxurious, ornamental, noted for their distinction as higher-class goods. A thorough analysis of all the terms of the lexicon would in this way make their secret sex apparent, signifying their adherence to an as yet uninterpreted syntax. Another example: *un ordinateur* (a computer) is of course a masculine noun and *la machine à écrire* (the typewriter) a feminine one. Value is what matters. . . . Whatever has it must be masculine. Again, *un avion* (an airplane) is superior to *une voiture* (a car), *le Boeing* to *la Caravelle,* not to mention *le Concorde.* . . . With each counterexample we find a more complex explanation: the gender could be due to the prefix or the suffix and not to the root of the word; it could depend upon the time when the term entered the lexicon and the relative value of the masculine and feminine genders then (in this respect, Italian is a less coherently sexist language than French); sometimes its determination is consequent upon the language it's borrowed from (English, for example, gives us a number of terms that become masculine in French).

Gender As Identity or As Possession

How is gender attributed to words? It's done on different levels and in different ways. At the most archaic level, I think there is an identification of the denominated reality with the sex of the speaking subject. *La terre* (the earth) *is* woman, *le ciel* (the sky) *is* her brother. *Le soleil* (the sun) *is* man, the god-man. *La lune* (the moon) is woman, sister of the man-god. And so on. Something of this first identification always remains in the gender of words. The degree to which it is explicit or hidden varies. But there is another mechanism at work apart from the identification of designated reality and gender. Living beings, the animate and cultured, become masculine; objects that are lifeless, the inanimate and uncultured, become feminine. Which means that men have attributed subjectivity to themselves and have reduced women to the status of objects, or to nothing. This is as true for actual women as it is for the gender of words. *Le moissonneur* (a harvester) is a man. But if, in line with current debate on the names of occupations, a linguist or legislator wishes to name a woman who harvests *la moissonneuse,*[2] the word is not available for a female subject: *la moissonneuse* (harvesting machine) is the tool the male harvester makes use of, or else it doesn't exist in the feminine. This state of affairs is even more ridiculous at a higher professional level where sometimes one is presented with hierarchies in the attribution of grammatical gender: *le secrétaire d'Etat/parti* (the secretary of state or a party) is masculine and *la secrétaire steno-dactylo* (the shorthand secretary) is feminine.

There is no sexed couple to create and structure the world. Men are surrounded by tools of feminine gender and by women-objects. Men don't manage the world with women as sexed subjects having equivalent rights. Only through a transformation of language will that become possible. But this transformation can only take place if we valorize the feminine gender once more. Indeed, the feminine, which was originally just different, is now practically assimilated to the nonmasculine. Being a woman is equated with not being a man. Which is what psychoanalysis calmly informs us in its theory and its practice of penis or phallus envy. Its reality only corresponds to one cultural period and one state of language. In that case, the way for women to be liberated is not by "becoming a man" or by envying what men have and their objects, but by female subjects once again valorizing the expression of their own sex and gender. That's completely different.

This confusion between liberation as equal ownership of goods and liberation as access to a subjectivity of the same value is currently upheld by several social theories and practices: psychoanalysis is one of them, but another is Marxism, to a certain extent. These discourses have been elaborated by men. They used Germanic languages. At the present time they have a relative degree of success among women in countries that speak these languages, because gender is expressed in subject-object relations. In these languages a woman can therefore have *her* (*sa*) phallus if not *her* (*sa*) penis.[3] Thus some German, English, or American women are able, for example, to demand equality in relation to the possession of goods and mark them with their gender. Having achieved this, they may abandon their right to denote gender in relation to the subject and criticize the conscious relationship made between the sexuate body and language as "materialistic," "ontological," "idealist," etc. This shows a lack of comprehension of the relations between individual bodies, social bodies, and the linguistic economy. A great deal of misunderstanding in the so-called world of women's liberation is perpetuated by this lack of comprehension. For many an Anglo-Saxon—and in general Germanic language—feminist, all she needs is her university post or to have written her book to be liberated. For them it's a question of *her* (*sa*) post and *her* (*sa*) book[4] and this appropriation of ownership seems to satisfy them. In my view, we have to be free female *subjects*. Language represents an essential tool of production for this liberation. I have to make it progress in order to have subjective rights equivalent to men, to be able to exchange language and objects with them. For one women's liberation movement, the emphasis is on equal rights in relation to the possession of goods: difference between men and women is located in the nature, the quantity, and sometimes the quality of goods acquired and possessed. For the other movement, sexual liberation means to demand access to a status of individual and collective *subjectivity* that is valid for them as women. The emphasis is on the difference of rights between male and female subjects.

The Sex of Occupations

Owning a few goods equivalent to those men have doesn't solve the problem of gender for women who speak Romance languages because these goods don't bear the mark of their owner's subject. We say *mon enfant* (my child) or *mon phallus* (?) (my phallus) whether we are men or women. For valuable "objects," then, the mark of ownership is the same. As for other "objects," they are generally devalorized when they are likely to be used or appropriated by women alone. The problem of the object and its conquest cannot therefore solve the problem of inequality of sexed rights in all languages. Furthermore, I don't think it can solve it in any language. But it can just about satisfy demands, more or less immediately.

If the issue of names for occupations has been taken up so extensively, it's because such names represent an intermediary space between subject and object, object and subject. Of course, it is a matter of possessing professional status, having a job, but this cannot be possessed just like any object can. It represents a necessary, though not sufficient, part of subjective identity. In addition, this demand fits in well with the social demands already being made in the male world. Therefore, the issue is relatively easy to raise. People generally go along with it. Often its only opposition is reality as it has already been coded linguistically (so *moissonneuse* and *médecine* have become the names of objects or designate a professional discipline and are no longer names for people, and sometimes the female name for an occupation doesn't exist or designates a different job) and social resistance depending upon the level of access available for women. But in this debate about the names of occupations the issue of language's sexism has hardly been broached, and proposed solutions often tend to try to skirt around the problems it raises.

Notes

1. Irigaray is referring to the rule of using the masculine plural in French whenever masculine and feminine are combined . . . , according primacy to the masculine, which in this case might be seen to contradict the social custom of according primacy to the one having majesty over the "ordinary" subject or citizen (even elected presidents). (Tr.)

2. The suffix *euse* designates a feminine term. (Tr.)

3. In French the possessive adjective agrees in gender (and number) with the object possessed rather than with the possessor, as in English. To illustrate the point of her companion Irigaray uses the possessive adjective for feminine singular nouns, *sa,* instead of the masculine *son,* for the masculine nouns *phallus* and *penis.*

4. University post (*poste universitaire*) and book (*livre*) are masculine, hence Irigaray here again replaces the masculine possessive adjective with the feminine one. (Tr.)

20

Where Is She in Language?

Hélène Cixous

Where is she?

Activity/passivity,
Sun/Moon,
Culture/Nature,
Day/Night,
Father/Mother,
Mind/feeling,
Intelligible/perceptible,
Logos/Pathos.
Form, convex, movement, advance, seed, progress.
Matter, concave, ground—upon which the movement treads, receptacle.

Man
Woman

Always the same metaphor: we follow it, it transports us, in all its various forms, wherever there is organization of discourse. The same thread, or double strand, leads us—whether we are reading or speaking—through literature, philosophy, criticism, through centuries of representation, of reflection.

Thought has always worked by opposition.
Speech/Writing
High/Low

By dual, hierarchical oppositions. Superior/Inferior. Myths, legends, books. Philosophical systems, in every place (where) an ordering occurs, a law organizes the thinkable by oppositions (dual, irreconcilable; or sublatable, dialec-

Originally published as Hélène Cixous, "La Jeune Née: An Excerpt," *Diacritics,* June 1977, pp. 65–68. Copyright © 1977 Johns Hopkins University Press. Reprinted by permission.

tical). And all the couples of oppositions are *couples*. Does that mean something? That logocentrism submits thought—all concepts, codes, values—to a system with two terms: is this in relation to "the" couple, man/woman?

Nature/History,
Nature/Art,
Nature/Spirit,
Passion/Action.

Theory of culture, theory of society, the ensemble of symbolic systems— art, religion, family, language—they all show the same patterns as they work themselves out. And the movement by which each opposition establishes itself in order to make sense is the movement by which the couple is destroyed. General battleground. Each time, a war is waged. Death is always at work.

Father/son   Relations of authority, of privilege, of force.
Logos/writing   Relations: opposition, conflict, sublation [*relève*], return.
Master/slave   Violence. Repression.

And it can be seen that the "victory" always amounts to the same thing: It's a matter of hierarchy. Hierarchization subjects the entirety of conceptual organization to man. Male privilege, which is evident in the opposition which sustains it, *activity* versus *passivity*. Traditionally, the question of sexual difference is dealt with by coupling it with the opposition: activity/passivity.

That already says a lot. If we examine the history of philosophy—insofar as philosophic discourse orders and reproduces all thought—we notice[1] that: it is marked by an absolute constant, an organizer of values, which is precisely the opposition activity/passivity.

That in philosophy woman is always on the side of passivity. Each time the question arises; when we examine kinship structures; whenever a model of the family comes into play; in fact as soon as the ontological question begins stirring; as soon as one wonders what is meant by the question "what is it"; as soon as there is any will-to-express [*vouloir-dire*]. Any will: desire, authority, you look into it, and you're led right back . . . to the father. You can even not notice that there is no place at all for woman in the process! Ultimately the world of "being" can function having foreclosed the mother. No need for a mother—so long as the maternal persists: and it is the father who then makes—is—the mother. Either woman is passive; or she does not exist. Anything else is unthinkable, unthought. Which means of course that she is not thought, that she does not enter into the oppositions, she does not form a couple with the father (who forms a couple with the son).

There is Mallarmé's tragic dream[2], this lamentation of the father on the mystery of paternity, which is wrenched from the poet by *the* grief, the sorrow of sorrows, the death of the cherished son: that dream of a marriage between the father and the son—and thus no mother. Dream of man facing death. Which always threatens him differently than it threatens woman.

"a marriage alliance,
a hymen, superb   And dreams of masculine

—and the life filiation, dreams of God the father
remaining in me going forther from himself
I will use it into his son—and
for . . . then no mother.
thus no mother?"

She does not exist, she *can* not be; but there must be some. Of woman, upon whom he no longer depends, he thus keeps nothing but this space, always virgin, matter subjected to the desire he wishes to imprint.

And if we examine literary history, it's the same story. Everything refers back to man, to *his* anguish, his desire to be (at) the origin. To the father. There is an intrinsic bond between the philosophical—and the literary (to the extent that it has meaning, literature is governed by philosophy)—and phallocentrism. Philosophy is constructed on the basis of the degradation of woman. Subordination of the feminine to the masculine order which then appears to be the condition necessary for the functioning of the machine.

The contestation of this solidarity of logocentrism and phallocentrism has today become urgent enough—the revelation of the fate reserved for woman and the way it's been concealed—to threaten the stability of the masculine edifice which has been passing itself off as eternal-natural; by giving rise to considerations, to hypotheses on the part of femininity which can only be disastrous for the bastion which still holds on to authority. What would become of logocentrism, of the great philosophical systems, of the world order in general if the stone upon which they have founded their church crumbled?

If one day it became glaringly apparent that the unacknowledgeable plan of logocentrism had always been to *found* phallocentrism, to ensure for the masculine order a justification equal to history, to itself?

Then all the stories would have to be told differently, the future would be incalculable, the historical forces would change, will change hands, bodies, an other thought still unthinkable will transform the functioning of every society. Now, we are living through precisely that age when the conceptual foundation of a millenary culture is in the process of being undermined by millions of a kind of mole [*taupe*] which is as yet unrecognized.

When they awaken from among the dead, from among the words, from among the laws.

Once upon a time . . .

We cannot yet say of the story which follows: "It's only a story." This tale remains true today. Most of the women who have awakened remember having slept, *having been put to sleep.*

Once upon a time . . . and still another time . . .

The beauties are sleeping, waiting for princes to come to awaken them. In their beds, in their glass coffins, in their childhood forests, as if dead. Beautiful, but passive; therefore desirable: from them emanates all mystery. It is the men who like to play with dolls. As we've known ever since Pygmalion. Their old dream: to be God the mother. The best mother, the second one, the one who gives the second birth.

She is sleeping, she is intact, eternal, absolutely helpless. He doesn't doubt that she has been waiting for him forever.

The secret of her beauty, kept for him: she has the perfection of that which is finished. Of that which hasn't begun. Nonetheless she breathes. Just enough life; not too much. Then he will kiss her. In such a way that when she opens her eyes she will see only *him;* him, taking up all the space, him-as-all.[3]

"This dream is so satisfying!" Whose is it? What wish is fulfilled by it?

He leans over her . . . Cut. It's the end of the story. Curtain. Once s/he has awakened, this would be another story altogether. Then maybe there would be two people. You never know, with women. And the voluptuous simplicity of the preliminaries would no longer take place.

Harmony, desire, achievement, research, all of these movements occur before—the arrival of woman. More precisely, before she *rises.* She lying down he on his feet. She gets up—end of dream—what follows pertains to the sociocultural, he keeps getting her pregnant, she spends her youth in childbirth; from bed to bed, till the age when that is no longer a woman.

"Bridebed, childbed, bed of death": so it is with the woman who makes her mark as she travels thus from bed to bed in Joyce's *Ulysses.* Excursion of Ulysses Bloom on his feet, ceaselessly wandering through Dublin. Walking, exploration. Excursion of Penelope-Everywoman: sickbed in which the mother never gets done with dying, hospital bed in which Madame Purefoy never gets done with giving birth, bed of Molly the wife, the adulteress, setting of an infinite erotic reverie, excursion of reminiscences. She wanders, but in bed. In dream. Ponders. Talks to herself. Voyage of woman: as a *body.* As if, separated from the outside world where cultural exchanges take place, apart from the social scene where History is made, she were destined to be, in the division which men set up, the nonsocial, nonpolitical, nonhuman half in the living structure, on the side of nature of course, listening tirelessly to what is happening within, to her womb, to her "house." In close touch with her appetites, her emotions.

And while he takes (for better or for worse) the risk and the responsibility of being a particle, an agent, of a public stage where transformations get played out, she represents indifference or resistance to this active tempo, she is the principle of constancy, in a certain way always the same, daily and eternal.

Man's dream: I love her, absent therefore desirable, inexistent, dependent, therefore adorable. Because she is not where she is. So long as she is not where she is. Then, how he looks at her! When she has her eyes closed; when he takes in all of her, and she is then but that form made for him: body captured in his look.

Or woman's dream? This is only a dream. I am sleeping. If I were not sleeping, he would not look for me, he would not cross his good lands and my bad lands in order to come to me. Above all don't let anyone awaken me! What anxiety! What if I must be entombed in order to attract him! And what if he kissed me? That kiss, how to want it? Do I want?

What does she want? To sleep, perchance to dream, to be loved in dream, to be approached, touched, almost—almost *jouir.* But not *jouir:* or she would wake up. But she has experienced *jouissance*[4] in dream, once upon a time. . . .

Once upon a time there was the same story, repeating through the centuries the amorous destiny of woman, its cruel and mystifying pattern. And every story, every myth tells her: "there is no place for your desire in our affairs of State." Love is a threshold affair. For us, men, who are made in order to succeed, in order to climb the social ladder, that temptation is good which urges us on, pushes us, nourishes our ambitions. But achievement is dangerous. Desire must not disappear. You, women, represent for us the eternal threat, the anti-culture. We do not remain in your homes, we are not going to linger in your beds. We roam. Entice us, provoke us, that's all we ask of you. Do not make of us spineless, feeble, feminine beings, careless about time and money. Your kind of love is death for us. A threshold affair:[5] its all in the suspense, in the "coming soon," always deferred. What lies beyond is downfall: the both of them enslaved, domesticated, imprisoned in the family, in a social role.

By reading this story-which-ends-well, she gets to know the roads which lead to the "loss" which is her fate. And she comes tumbling after. A kiss; and off he goes. His desire, fragile, nourishing itself on lack, keeps itself alive through absence: man pursues. As if he could not manage to have what he has. Where is she, the woman in all the spaces he covers, all the scenes he stages within the literary enclosure?

There are many answers, we know them: she is in the shadows. In the shadows which he casts upon her; which she is.

Night for his day, thus it has always been fantasized. Black for his whiteness. Excluded from the space of his system, she is the repressed element which assures that the system will function.

Kept at a distance, so that he may take pleasure in the ambiguous advantages of distance, so that she may, by her very remoteness, keep alive the enigma, delight-danger, of seduction, suspended in the role of "the abductress" Helen, she is in a certain way "outside." But she cannot appropriate this "outside" (only rarely does she even desire to do so), it is his outside: the outside, so long as it is not absolutely exterior, not the unfamiliar unknown which would escape him. She dwells in a domesticated outside.

Abductress abducted from herself

—not is she the element of strangeness—within his universe which reanimates his uneasiness and his desire. She is, within his economy, the strangeness which he likes to appropriate for himself. But that's not all—there is still the "dark continent" business: she has been kept at a distance from herself, she has been allowed to see (= not-to-see) woman from the perspective of what man wants to see of her, i.e. almost nothing; she has been forbidden the possibility of the proud "inscription above my door" which stands at the threshold of *The Joyful Wisdom.* It is not she who could have exclaimed:

> I inhabit my own house,
> Have never imited anyone . . .

Her "own" house, her body itself, she has not been able to inhabit. It is possible in effect to imprison her, to slow down monstrously, to bring off for too long a time this triumph of Apartheid—but only for a time. It is possible to teach her, as soon as she begins to talk, and at the same time as she learns her name, that her region is dark: because you are Africa, you are black. Your continent is dark. Darkness is dangerous. In darkness you cannot see, you are afraid. Don't move because you might fall down. Above all don't go into the forest. And we have interiorized the dread of darkness. She has had no eyes for herself. She has never explored her house. Her genitals appal her still today. She has not dared to take pleasure in her body, which has been colonized. Woman is frightened and disgusted by woman.

Against women they have committed the greatest crime of all: they have led them, insidiously, violently, to hate women, to be their own enemies, to mobilize their immense power against themselves, to be the executors of man's virile task.

They have given her anti-narcissism! A narcissism in which love of self comes only from making oneself loved for what one does not have! They have fabricated the vile logic of anti-love.

The "Dark Continent" is neither dark nor unexplorable: It is still unexplored only because we have been made to believe that it was too dark to be explorable. And because they want to make us believe that what interests us is the white continent, with its monuments to the Lack. And we have believed. They have fixed us between two horrifying myths: between Medusa and the abyss. It would be enough to make half the world roar with laughter, if it were not still going on. For phallo-logocentric continuity is still there, and it is militant, reproducing the old patterns, anchored in the dogma of castration. They haven't changed anything: they have theorized their desire *as* reality! Let them tremble, the priests, we are going to *show* them our sexts!

Too bad for them if they fall apart upon discovering that women are not men, or that the mother doesn't have one. But doesn't that fear suit them? The worst, wouldn't it be, isn't it, in truth, that woman is not castrated, that he has only to stop listening to the Sirens (for the Sirens were men) in order for history to change direction? One has only to look the medusa in the face to see her: and she is not deadly. She is beautiful and she is laughing.

They say that there are two things which cannot be represented: death and female genitals. For they need to associate femininity with death: they get "stiff" with fear! for themselves! they need to be afraid of us. Look, the trembling Perseuses are coming towards us armed with apotropes, backwards! Pretty backs! Not a minute to lose. Let's go.

She is coming back from death's door: from forever: from "outside," from the wastelands where the witches are still alive; from beneath, beside "culture"; *from her childhood* which they have so much trouble making her forget, which they condemn to the *in pace*. Walled up, the little girls with the "ill-mannered" bodies. Preserved, untouched by themselves, in ice. Frigidified. But underneath something is stirring, wildly! What efforts they must make, the sex police, always having to begin again in order to obstruct her threatening return. On both sides, a display of force so great that the struggle, for centuries, has been immobilized in the trembling equilibrium of a deadlock.

We the precocious, we the repressed of culture, our lovely mouths clogged with gags, pollen, constricted breath; we the labyrinths, the ladders, the trampled spaces; the *volées**—we are "black" *and* we are beautiful.

—Translated by Meg Bortin

Notes

1. As all of Derrida's work crossing-detecting the history of philosophy endeavors to bring to light. In Plato, Hegel, Nietzsche a similar operation is performed, repression, foreclusion, distancing or woman. Murder which is indistinguishable from history as manifestation and representation of male power.

2. "Pour un tombeau d'Anatole" (ed. du Seuil, p. 138), tomb in which Mallarmé keeps his son, protects him, he being the mother, from death.

3. "She will awaken only at the touch of love, and before that moment she is but a dream. But in this dream existence, two stages can be distinguished: first love dreams of her, then she dreams of love." Thus muses Kierkegaard's *Seducer*.

4. *Jouissance* (verb form: *jouir*): the experience, often sexual, of intense pleasure.

5. That pleasure is preliminary, as Freud says, is a "truth," but only in part. A point of view which has in fact been upheld since the formation of the male *imaginaire*, to the extent that it is animated by the threat of castration. . . .

---

*Voler: To steal and to fly; thus *volées*: the robbed, those who have flown away [translator's note].

21

The Man without a Penis:
Libidinal Economies That (Re)cognize
the Hypernature of Gender

Margaret M. Nash

The Scene: Father and three-and-a-half-year-old son, Alex, taking a bath together:

Son: I'm going to bite your penis off.
Father: Then what will I do?
Son: You'll be a woman.
Father: But isn't there more to being a woman than that?
Son: Yeah, you'd be a man without a penis.

So Alex recognizes that there is more to gender than meets the eye at the same time as he both reflects and resignifies conceptions of men and women in our culture. The cultural construction of woman which Alex reflects is that of a castrated male (a man without a penis) and yet, in thinking for only a moment, Alex takes up the challenge to move outside of a monological conception of gender, a conception that privileges a certain sight, the penis, as the site (mark) definitory of meaning, value and difference. The problem of bodies, of identifying and naming them, evinces itself in this playing with language as a problem endemic to language. Naming splits and fragments and in so doing orders reality. But this play that Alex initiates also involves experimenting with loss, identity, and power. Does Alex want to eradicate, eat, or just bite off Dad's penis? How ought we to figure the loss (or is it a gain)? Is this desire the expression of an identification through ingestion or a separation that evokes excremental imagery? Is this a labile oral expression of love and hostility, a consumption that discursively constitutes and binds those engaged in it? Consumption ultimately ends in expulsion so, in any case, the penis could be excess, something that could be removed,

Reprinted by permission of Sage Publications from Margaret Nash, "The Man without a Penis: Libidinal Economies That (Re)cognize the Hypernature of Gender," *Philosophy and Social Criticism* 18, no. 2 (1992).

exchanged, wasted, tossed away or circulated in other ways. The penis, especially Dad's penis, is "not-me"; it is a fetish that we can all do without.

First, we must be clear about what it means to say that the penis is a fetish. Freud, in an essay titled "Fetishism," (1927), connects the development of a fetish to castration fears. As is usual, Freud's treatment of psychosexual development reflects and privileges male projections and experience. "The fetish is a substitute for the woman's (the mother's) penis that the little boy once believed in and . . . does not want to give up."[1] Loss is at stake here—the recognition that if the mother can be castrated (remember: in the Freudian system, every mother is initially a phallic mother), then so too can the little boy. Such uncertainty and anxiety surrounding his own integrity (wholeness) and value may result in the erection of a replacement. The fetish is a substitute based on a compulsive displacement that stands in for the "missing" female penis. Such a replacement, like neurotic symptoms in general, both conceals and reveals the castration or loss that it is meant to figure. Now we know that, given the value our culture accords this pleasure site, the fetish (substitute) is never fully adequate; at least it is not adequate for Freud. The fetish turns out to be an inferior sexual prop and/or means to sexual satisfaction. And just as the fetish does not exchange equitably, so women, within this economy, come out on the inferior side of the equation. Women and fetishes are peripheral and yet vital to the system that marginalizes them. For the penis that women lack and which the fetish replaces is a fiction that keeps the symbolic economy intact, the very same fiction that underwrites the pretense of penis power. We must dismember the fetishistic penis, for the fetish as substitute for lack is not a neutral posit; it is itself productive of the power it is meant to merely signify.

In what follows, I will use Alex's text as a way to consider how to displace and denaturalize notions of gender that are tied to phallocentric power configurations. As the title of this essay indicates, gender is excessive. I will make the multiplicity which constitutes gender explicit so that those gendered possibilities and configurations already at work but often overlooked in our seeing and theorizing are given attention. This is important in that it calls attention to the indeterminacy of gender; this indeterminacy may be the ground for the liberatory potential of feminism. That we can imagine and realize a world with different and many more gendered power configurations is figured by Alex's conclusion. A youngster can decouple anatomy and gender and can refuse to confuse difference with lack. Identity need not be founded on a reductionist, fetishistic exchange. We can attend to the way language divides and marks the sexes and we can push the constraints of phallocentric discursive practices and institutions. We need to think about how we control, perform, and signify the meaning of gender.

Judith Butler, in *Gender Trouble*, develops a performative theory of gender. She critiques the naturalness of sex and gender as identity categories and encourages us to view identity, of which gender is but one category, as a signifying practice constituted in and by acts of performance. In moving us to an understanding of gender as something that is performed, Butler forces us to see ourselves as actresses who can be aware of how we repeat, play, and otherwise act out gender identity. This does not mean that Butler views us as subjects or agents who are in full control of the meaning of the signifying act. Nor does it mean that we, as subjects, exist and have "true" interests outside of our cultural construction and locatedness. The context sets limits on the resignifying process even though the context is never entirely stable or fully determinable. In advocating that we engage in or enact subversive performances in order to disrupt and displace binary sexed and gendered constructions, Butler does not appeal to a fixed, prediscursive notion of agency. Indeed, she explicitly rejects any unconstructed, foundational "I" set over against and viewed as independent of a world or some other Other. Her antifoundationalist, performative politics relies on a notion of agency which recognizes that we, as subjects, are constructed in and through our acts. By refusing to posit a prediscursive "I" or intentional subject in control of, and thus accountable for, her actions, Butler does not eschew the issue of responsibility. Rather she resituates it within a Foucaultian framework that focuses on the constructed nature of our identity, whereby we are the effects of power relations but can nevertheless resist and rebel against those relations. This does not entail that we view ourselves as hopelessly determined by discursive, constructive practices and power relations, but neither does it appeal to any intentional, transparent agency. Quoting Butler:

> If identity is asserted through a process of signification, if identity is always already signified, and yet continues to signify as it circulates within various interlocking discourses, then the question of agency is not to be answered through recourse to an "I" that preexists signification.[2]

A constructed self does not rule out agency. Butler rightfully argues that to fail to understand this is to remain trapped in the binary opposition between free will and determinism. Identity is an effect which "means that it is neither fatally determined nor fully artificial and arbitrary."[3] By starting with the assumption of a constructed subject, we allow for the possibility of reconstructing it. Agency resides in how we repeat and resignify our identities; in this repetition and resignification lies the possibility of challenging the power matrix in which identities are embedded. On this view, parodic practices that mock the idea of an original and in other ways disrupt and displace gendered norms could be subversive in the service of liberatory ends. The philosophical and political advantage to be gained in following Butler is that we stay honest with respect to the exercise of power. We cannot escape it though we can become aware of how we support and resist particular workings of it.

For example, feminist jurisprudence seeks to posit and write law so as to include and do justice to women's experiences and daily realities. The activity of pursuing justice involves deploying language so as to expose the coercive strategies that have produced and legitimated exclusions. In resisting one construal of reality we, of course, generate others, and such generativity is not free of the workings of power. Indeed, it is alternative configurations that need to be propagated and enforced.

In Butler's framework, "signification is not a founding act, but rather a regulated process of repetition that both conceals itself and enforces its rules precisely through the production of substantializing effects. . . . 'Agency,' then is to be located within the possibility of a variation on that repetition."[4] By rejecting a foundationalist approach, we avoid the hegemonic consequences of a substance ontology, an ontology which assumes a universal male subject whose contingent properties are left unexamined. The principles, measures, and evaluations that this phallocracy puts into circulation are precisely what critiques of phallogocentrism are designed to uncover.

But, before proceeding further, assuming what I have failed to argue for, I need to address the value of displacing the binary sex/gender system and the question of our desire to do so. To what extent are we ready and willing to give up gender? Are we really committed to not acting out gender? Do we want to dispense with the markings and the actions that we use to engender us? What goal would that serve and is it a liberating one? To answer this last question first, perhaps the most obvious answer is that gendered norms are problematic because they support institutionalized sexist and heterosexist privilege and because they coerce and regulate behavior and desires in support of this privilege. This circumstance is something we, as feminists, desire to disrupt and dismantle. But I suspect that gender is not something that we can readily give up and thus the more troubling question is the first one. Sometimes I find participation in these regulative, normalizing practices enjoyable. This enjoyment may speak to my own privilege, but I wonder how to honestly analyze the pleasure that we sometimes derive from performing gender. In speaking of gender performances here I include both the unreflective enactments and the self-conscious dramas, skits, and scenarios that constitute daily life.

Perhaps playing at a gender identity (and here I mean a self-conscious playing) could serve as both a space and a strategy within which to experiment with the answer to the question of our readiness. Even though there is no fixed or correct gender identity to express, it is difficult to assess our commitment to expressing one, whether it is one that we invent or one of the dominant cultural constructions. Desires and pleasures are also shaped and constructed, rendering them problematic starting points for assessing how to proceed. So regardless of what we desire to express, interrogating desire may be the wrong way to go. That we often desire to mark ourselves seems evident. Perhaps, as Butler's strategy suggests, we can render gender unbelievable and hence inoperable by exposing its constructed nature, thus denormalizing the binary system while at the same time proliferating possibilities outside of the binary frame. In a fully realized economy of excess neither "man" nor "woman" would be representable in their exclusive distinction from each other. Precisely because our project is to subvert the binary system, we need to reject the temptation to erect exclusive "female" categories, categories which would then elaborate all else in terms of its negative or deficient status with respect to the female.

So how are we to proceed in multiplying genders?

Enter laughter—a much overlooked but important phenomenon for our purposes. What does it do? It jogs and jolts us; it scares us; it threatens to overpower us; it exhausts us; it renews us. Laughter cannot speak or be captured in discourse. Laughter reminds us of our embodiment; it sometimes holds us in thrall to our embodiment. This expenditure which laughter allows us is an excessive substitute for what cannot be figured discursively, yet laughter can communicate. As Bataille remarks: "Laughter may not show respect but it does show horror."[5] Horror, which may be a response to the contamination or violation of borders, is often handled or managed by laughter. Laughter often hides horror, revealing the tenuousness and fragility of the borders meant to establish order. Inside and outside are called into question in surrendering ourselves to convulsive spasms. But laughter does more than subject us to our carnality; it transgresses the inner/outer distinctions which constitute ordered systems and so can either mock and negate or affirmatively displace those boundaries. There is a refusal embodied in laughter which involves an affirmation of uncontrolled multiplicity and a fight against surrender to the dictates of a dogged reason. Laughter is an expenditure that attests to an economy of excess, an economy that circulates unstable and multiple meanings. Loving, scary, threatening, horrific, ecstatic, satirical, playful, or just plain silly—all of these characterize the richness and fullness that comprise the lability of laughter. I am interested in a destabilizing laughter that leads to open-ended inquiry and not laughter that solidifies a fixed self or wordview. To react with laughter is sometimes a subversive act, whether it involves humiliation, affirmation, or the expressive refusal to shut out the horror ('the castrated woman," perhaps) that underlies everyday life. We need to keep these potentialities in mind and use them to our advantage, remembering the connections to others that the surrender to our bodies can bring about. Laughter opens up sensuous possibilities and ways of restructuring phenomena that we might otherwise not consider.

Of course, laughter, parody, and other playful repetitions are not sufficient as political or philosophical strategies for displacing and replacing gendered norms. Changing the material conditions which backstop and coerce gender choices is also fundamental. But *how* we do this will of necessity vary, and I am suggesting that attention to the how is also important. How we enact authority, intimacy, friendship, collegiality—how we work together to resist and fight for particular political ends—these hows constitute what we enact. As we work to change one set of power norms, we must resituate the old norms so that they no longer seem normal. Laughter can help render the "naturalness" of gender incredible just as it can suggest strategies for rendering psychological, legal, and other institutionalized categorizations in support of such naturalness suspect. But there are (man)euvers besides laughter. We will turn to some of these. Exit hilarity.

As Luce Irigaray has explicated, women have been "seen" and theorized in the space of and in terms of a phallogocentric order. Either a woman is a cas-trated male (lacking the vital organ) or she is reduced to, and her sexuality con-ceptualized in terms of, the phallus; her clitoris is a stunted penis. She is really a little man, the very same little man from whom a man seeks valuation. What a pity that what a man really wants he never gets in this compulsively hetero-sexist, phallocratic scheme. Irigaray offers us other options, options which pro-liferate locations for pleasure sites and resignify heterosexual and homosexual desire, opening up a space for the possibility of sexual desires which do not specify in advance the sexed object of that desire. Nor need there be a materi-ally embodied other object of desire at all; autoeroticism and polymorphous sexuality, conceived outside of the phallocratic order, are imagined and metaphorically inscribed on multiple surfaces. Maybe women are getting, or could be experiencing, pleasure all of the time because of the way they are built. Irigaray is self-consciously writing about other ways we might interpret and experience our bodies and our sexuality. None of this should be read as essen-tialist theorizing. Creating new myths and offering multiple ways to interpret anatomical difference highlight the role that discursive practices and formula-tions can play in freeing us from past productions. Bodily experience is not fixed; it, like identity, is an ideological construction and Irigaray wants to have a say in naming and enacting the body differently.

If we return to the scene of Alex and his father in the tub, we can follow Alex in resignifying the notion of man. In Alex's formulation, the penis is not replaced by a fetish, which is to say that Alex does not fetishize it. The "without" is asserted without melancholy. The loss is not a loss. To be outside a libidinal economy of phallocentrism does not require actual removal of the organ. Clearly, we are no longer in a strictly referential system. We can exchange the fetishized penis, that fictive ground that serves the interests of those who profit from its symbolic and institutionalized power, without de-manding a return on the investment. In other words, we can waste the fetishized penis; we can treat it as excess. In doing so, we refuse to let it serve as the mea-sure of value and the signifier of desire. Not everyone wants it; maybe no one wants this fetish as fetish. Different forms of power, organized around other senses than this site (sight), are realizable. The dream of wholeness, and the power that derives from a feeling of integrity, need not be tied to possession of the penis, or a privileged relation to the phallus. One can be, have, or enact a man without a penis.

What is a man anyway? When Alex recognizes that anatomy does not make the man, in one way he implicitly holds onto a fixed gender, albeit one without a specific feature of anatomy. Dad or any man whose penis he might bite off would still be a man. How do we want to follow Alex? Do we want to make "man" more problematic than Alex's assertion suggests? The construction that Alex reflects is no doubt filled with the dominant cultural images, markings, and activities that most men in our culture tend to adopt. To be a man is to speak from a position of control and power relative to others who are not men, though class and ethnicity certainly figure in the extent of the power and control. But what is this position of power and control? What relation to the symbolic phallus does it effect? Certainly this position is more than any one designator can capture. When we look at the possibilities that fall under the category "man," we find enactments (crossdressers, drag queens, sportsmen, actors, fathers, husbands, to name a few) that defy any initial, binary exclusion to which a heterosexist, phallocracy has pretense. To really think through these possibilities opens up numerous others. Drag queens are men who dress as women but who tend to desire men. Male crossdressers are men who dress as women but who desire women. Husbands, by far the strangest lot, may be unsure of who they desire, though legitimately they desire a woman, or perhaps they *need* a woman to be the being whom they identify with, a woman who represents the being they fear they may be. Husbandly demeanor and dress, in all likelihood, reflect both the complex ambivalence and the legitimacy that the position of husband exudes. Fathers, in name if nothing else, effect a syzygy that attests to the hypernature of man.

Perhaps "man" is contextual. You can be a man, of sorts, ("Be a man") by positioning yourself in a privileged relation to the phallus, where the phallus does not reduce to the penis. But there is a problem with this. As Jane Gallop's critique of Lacan's distinction between penis and phallus points out:

> As long as the attribute of power is a phallus which can only have meaning by referring to and being confused with a penis, this confusion will support a structure in which it seems reasonable that men have power and women do not.[6]

How do we allow for change and encourage movements beyond this confusion? In spite of the contingent, historic *impossibility* of thinking a masculine that is not phallic, Gallop urges us and indeed says that it is *necessary* for us "to think a masculine that is not phallic, to think a sexuality that is not arrested in the phallic phase."[7] This includes, I would argue, thinking a feminine which does not position itself with respect to the phallus. Alex's text attests to this paradoxical project and the problematic with which it deals. In separating phallus/penis we deceive ourselves about the exits out of a phallocracy. For if no one in the end "has" the phallus, then where is the location and what is the nature of the forces (presumably phallic) which shape the order in which we live? On the other hand, perhaps the very activity of separating the two, of realizing in language this disjunction, as Alex does, serves as a guideline for how to replace the phallus. As the fetishized penis was replaced with nothing essential, nothing fixed, indeed, nothing at all, so the phallus, too, may be abandoned, circumvented, eaten (which does not or need not entail devouring men) without fearing anarchy, loss or epistemological confusion over identity. This project of re-writing, re-creating, and re-cognizing can be both serious and playful, subversive and affirmative. The repetitions, maneuvers, gestures, and twists whether in language or deed that transgress and help erode phallocratic supports will entail a moment which places us in a position to locate and re-think privilege and how it is sustained. In this way we might move toward making the impossible (thinking a nonphallic masculine) possible.

The move outside the feminine/masculine bifurcation may be effected in multiple ways. At this point I think we need to politicize and destabilize all sexual categories so that the lability of sex, gender, and sexuality is left open and the regulation of these categories is rendered problematic. To give voice in multiple ways to our experiences of sexes, genders, and sexualities, to perform these experiences, is in some sense to bring them into existence and to allow for their existence. This endeavor involves an examination which includes philosophical reflection. Foucault in an interview (1980) states:

> The movement by which, not without effort and uncertainty, dreams and illusions, one detaches oneself from what is accepted as true and seeks other rules—that is philosophy. The displacement and transformation of frameworks of thinking, the changing of received values and all the work that has been done to think otherwise, to do something else, to become other than what one is—that, too, is philosophy.[8]

Without this movement, philosophy tends to be sterile and, although I am not advocating procreation, I am in favor of experimentation, risk, and collapses which effect recombinant hypergendered possibilities. Doing something else, becoming other than what one is—this, too, can be enriching. An expansion that embraces and acts on the hypernature of gender need not be one we fear. To be avatars of this hypergendered reality involves addressing ourselves to a query which simultaneously functions as an existential demand that I place on the reader: How do we manage the excess that we are?

Notes

1. Sigmund Freud, "Fetishism," in *The Standard Edition of the Complete Works of Sigmund Freud*, trans. James Strachey (London: Hogarth Press, 1961), 21:152.

2. Judith Butler, *Gender Trouble: Feminism and the Subversion of Identity* (New York: Routledge, 1990), p. 143.

3. Ibid., p. 147.

4. Ibid., p. 145.

5. George Bataille, *Erotism: Death and Sensuality*, trans. Mary Dalwood (San Francisco: City Lights Bookstore, 1962), p. 265.

6. Jane Gallop, *Thinking Through the Body* (New York: Columbia University Press, 1988), p. 127.

7. Ibid.

8. Michel Foucault, "The Masked Philosopher," in *Michel Foucault: Politics, Philosophy, Culture*, trans. Alan Sheridan et al. (New York: Routledge, 1988), p. 330.

22

Sexual Perversion

Thomas Nagel

There is something to be learned about sex from the fact that we possess a concept of sexual perversion. I wish to examine the idea, defending it against the charge of unintelligibility and trying to say exactly what about human sexuality qualifies it to admit of perversions. Let me begin with some general conditions that the concept must meet if it is to be viable at all. These can be accepted without assuming any particular analysis.

First, if there are any sexual perversions, they will have to be sexual desires or practices that are in some sense unnatural, though the explanation of this natural/unnatural distinction is of course the main problem. Second, certain practices will be perversions if anything is, such as shoe fetishism, bestiality, and sadism; other practices, such as unadorned sexual intercourse, will not be; about still others there is controversy. Third, if there are perversions, they will be unnatural sexual *inclinations* rather than just unnatural practices adopted not from inclination but for other reasons. Thus contraception, even if it is thought to be a deliberate perversion of the sexual and reproductive functions, cannot be significantly described as a *sexual* perversion. A sexual perversion must reveal itself in conduct that expresses an unnatural *sexual* preference. And although there might be a form of fetishism focused on the employment of contraceptive devices, that is not the usual explanation for their use.

The connection between sex and reproduction has no bearing on sexual perversion. The latter is a concept of psychological, not physiological, interest, and it is a concept that we do not apply to the lower animals, let alone to plants, all of which have reproductive functions that can go astray in various ways. (Think of seedless oranges.) Insofar as we are prepared to regard higher animals as perverted, it is because of their psychological, not their anatomical, similarity to humans. Fur-

First published in Thomas Nagel, *Mortal Questions* (New York: Cambridge University Press, 1979). Reprinted with the permission of Cambridge University Press.

thermore, we do not regard as a perversion every deviation from the reproductive function of sex in humans: sterility, miscarriage, contraception, abortion.

Nor can the concept of sexual perversion be defined in terms of social disapprobation or custom. Consider all the societies that have frowned upon adultery and fornication. These have not been regarded as unnatural practices, but have been thought objectionable in other ways. What is regarded as unnatural admittedly varies from culture to culture, but the classification is not a pure expression of disapproval or distaste. In fact it is often regarded as a *ground* for disapproval, and that suggests that the classification has independent content.

I shall offer a psychological account of sexual perversion that depends on a theory of sexual desire and human sexual interactions. To approach this solution I shall first consider a contrary position that would justify skepticism about the existence of any sexual perversions at all, and perhaps even about the significance of the term. The skeptical argument runs as follows:

"Sexual desire is simply one of the appetites, like hunger and thirst. As such it may have various objects, some more common than others perhaps, but none in any sense 'natural.' An appetite is identified as sexual by means of the organs and erogenous zones in which its satisfaction can be to some extent localized, and the special sensory pleasures which form the core of that satisfaction. This enables us to recognize widely divergent goals, activities, and desires as sexual, since it is conceivable in principle that anything should produce sexual pleasure and that a nondeliberate, sexually charged desire for it should arise (as a result of conditioning, if nothing else). We may fail to empathize with some of these desires, and some of them, like sadism, may be objectionable on extraneous grounds, but once we have observed that they meet the criteria for being sexual, there is nothing more to be said on *that* score. Either they are sexual or they are not: sexuality does not admit of imperfection, or perversion, or any other such qualification—it is not that sort of affection."

This is probably the received radical position. It suggests that the cost of defending a psychological account may be to deny that sexual desire is an appetite. But insofar as that line of defense is plausible, it should make us suspicious of the simple picture of appetites on which the skepticism depends. Perhaps the standard appetites, like hunger, cannot be classed as pure appetites in that sense either, at least in their human versions.

Can we imagine anything that would qualify as a gastronomical perversion? Hunger and eating, like sex, serve a biological function and also play a significant role in our inner lives. Note that there is little temptation to describe as perverted an appetite for substances that are not nourishing: we should probably not consider someone's appetites *perverted* if he liked to eat paper, sand, wood, or cotton. Those are merely rather odd and very unhealthy tastes: they lack the psychological complexity that we expect of perversions. (Coprophilia, being already a sexual perversion, may be disregarded.) If on the other hand someone liked to eat cookbooks, or magazines with pictures of food in them, and preferred these to ordinary food—or if when hungry he sought satisfaction by fondling a napkin or ashtray from his favorite restaurant—then the concept of perversion might seem appropriate (it would be natural to call it gastronomical fetishism). It would be natural to describe as gastronomically perverted someone who could eat only by having food forced down his throat through a funnel, or only if the meal were a living animal. What helps is the peculiarity of the desire itself, rather than the inappropriateness of its object to the biological function that the desire serves. Even an appetite can have perversions if in addition to its biological function it has a significant psychological structure.

In the case of hunger, psychological complexity is provided by the activities that give it expression. Hunger is not merely a disturbing sensation that can be quelled by eating; it is an attitude toward edible portions of the external world, a desire to treat them in rather special ways. The method of ingestion: chewing, savoring, swallowing, appreciating the texture and smell, all are important components of the relation, as is the passivity and controllability of the food (the only animals we eat live are helpless mollusks). Our relation to food depends also on our size: we do not live upon it or burrow into it like aphids or worms. Some of these features are more central than others, but an adequate phenomenology of eating would have to treat it as a relation to the external world and a way of appropriating bits of that world, with characteristic affection. Displacements or serious restrictions of the desire to eat could then be described as perversions, if they undermined that direct relation between man and food which is the natural expression of hunger. This explains why it is easy to imagine gastronomical fetishism, voyeurism, exhibitionism, or even gastronomical sadism and masochism. Some of these perversions are fairly common.

If we can imagine perversions of an appetite like hunger, it should be possible to make sense of the concept of sexual perversion. I do not wish to imply that sexual desire is an appetite—only that being an appetite is no bar to admitting of perversions. Like hunger, sexual desire has as its characteristic object a certain relation with something in the external world; only in this case it is usually a person rather than an omelet, and the relation is considerably more complicated. This added complication allows scope for correspondingly complicated perversions.

The fact that sexual desire is a feeling about other persons may encourage a pious view of its psychological content—that it is properly the expression of some other attitude, like love, and that when it occurs by itself it is incomplete or subhuman. (The extreme Platonic version of such a view is that sexual practices are all vain attempts to express something they cannot in principle achieve: this makes them all perversions, in a sense.) But sexual desire is complicated enough without having to be linked to anything else as a condition for phenomenological analysis. Sex may serve various functions—economic, social, altruistic—but it also has its own content as a relation between persons.

The object of sexual attraction is a particular individual who transcends the properties that make him attractive. When different persons are attracted to a single person for different reasons—eyes, hair, figure, laugh, intelligence—we nevertheless feel that the object of their desire is the same. There is even an inclination to feel that this is so if the lovers have different sexual aims, if they include both men and women, for example. Different specific attractive characteristics seem to provide enabling conditions for the operation of a single basic feeling, and the different aims all provide expressions of it. We approach the sexual attitude toward the person through the features that we find attractive, but these features are not the objects of that attitude.

This is very different from the case of an omelet. Various people may desire it for different reasons, one for its fluffiness, another for its mushrooms, another for its unique combination of aroma and visual aspect; yet we do not enshrine the transcendental omelet as the true common object of their affections. Instead we might say that several desires have accidentally converged on the same object: any omelet with the crucial characteristics would do as well. It is not similarly true that any person with the same flesh distribution and way of smoking can be substituted as object for a particular sexual desire that has been elicited by those characteristics. It may be that they recur, but it will be a new sexual attraction with a new particular object, not merely a transfer of the old desire to someone else. (This is true even in cases where the new object is unconsciously identified with a former one.)

The importance of this point will emerge when we see how complex a psychological interchange constitutes the natural development of sexual attraction. This would be incomprehensible if its object were not a particular person, but rather a person of a certain *kind.* Attraction is only the beginning, and fulfillment does not consist merely of behavior and contact expressing this attraction, but involves much more.

The best discussion of these matters that I have seen appears in part III of Sartre's *Being and Nothingness.*[1] Sartre's treatment of sexual desire and of love, hate, sadism, masochism, and further attitudes toward others, depends on a general theory of consciousness and the body which we can neither expound nor assume here. He does not discuss perversion, and this is partly because he regards sexual desire as one form of the perpetual attempt of an embodied consciousness to come to terms with the existence of others, an attempt that is as doomed to fail in this form as it is in any of the others, which include sadism and masochism (if not certain of the more impersonal deviations) as well as several nonsexual attitudes. According to Sartre, all attempts to incorporate the other into my world as another subject, i.e., to apprehend him at once as an object for me and as a subject for whom I am an object, are unstable and doomed to collapse into one or other of the two aspects. Either I reduce him entirely to an object, in which case his subjectivity escapes the possession or appropriation I can extend to that object; or I become merely an object for him, in which case I am no longer in a position to appropriate his subjectivity. Moreover, neither of these aspects is stable; each is continually in danger of giving way to the other. This has the consequence that there can be no such thing as a *successful* sexual relation, since the deep aim of sexual desire cannot in principle be accomplished. It seems likely, therefore, that the view will not permit a basic distinction between successful or complete and unsuccessful or incomplete sex, and therefore cannot admit the concept of perversion.

I do not adopt this aspect of the theory, nor many of its metaphysical underpinnings. What interests me is Sartre's picture of the attempt. He says that the type of possession that is the object of sexual desire is carried out by "a double reciprocal incarnation" and that this is accomplished, typically in the form of a caress, in the following way: "I make myself flesh in order to impel the Other to realize *for herself* and *for me* her own flesh, and my caresses cause my flesh to be born for me in so far as it is for the Other *flesh causing her to be born as flesh*" (*Being and Nothingness*, p. 391; Sartre's italics). The incarnation in question is described variously as a clogging or troubling of consciousness, which is inundated by the flesh in which it is embodied.

The view I am going to suggest, I hope in less obscure language, is related to this one, but it differs from Sartre's in allowing sexuality to achieve its goal on occasion and thus in providing the concept of perversion with a foothold.

Sexual desire involves a kind of perception, but not merely a single perception of its object, for in the paradigm case of mutual desire there is a complex system of superimposed mutual perceptions—not only perceptions of the sexual object, but perceptions of oneself. Moreover, sexual awareness of another involves considerable self-awareness to begin with—more than is involved in ordinary sensory perception. The experience is felt as an assault on oneself by the view (or touch, or whatever) of the sexual object.

Let us consider a case in which the elements can be separated. For clarity we will restrict ourselves initially to the somewhat artificial case of desire at a distance. Suppose a man and a woman, whom we may call Romeo and Juliet, are at opposite ends of a cocktail lounge, with many mirrors on the walls which permit unobserved observation, and even mutual unobserved observation. Each of them is sipping a martini and studying other people in the mirrors. At some point Romeo notices Juliet. He is moved, somehow, by the softness of her hair and the diffidence with which she sips her martini, and this arouses him sexually. Let us say that X senses Y whenever X regards Y with sexual desire. (Y need not be a person, and X's apprehension of Y can be visual, tactile, olfactory, etc., or purely imaginary; in the present example we shall concentrate on vision.) So Romeo senses Juliet, rather than merely noticing her. At this stage he is aroused by an unaroused object, so he is more in the sexual grip of his body than she of hers.

Let us suppose, however, that Juliet now senses Romeo in another mirror on the opposite wall, though neither of them yet knows that he is seen by the other (the mirror angles provide three-quarter views). Romeo then begins to notice in Juliet the subtle signs of sexual arousal, heavy-lidded stare, dilating pupils, faint flush, etc. This of course intensifies her bodily presence, and he not only notices but senses this as well. His arousal is nevertheless still solitary. But now, cleverly calculating the line of her stare without actually looking her in the eyes, he realizes that it is directed at him through the mirror on the opposite wall. That is, he notices, and moreover senses, Juliet sensing him. This is definitely a new development, for it gives him a sense of embodiment not only through his own reactions but through the eyes and reactions of another. Moreover, it is separable from the initial sensing of Juliet; for sexual arousal might begin with a person's sensing that he is sensed and being assailed by the perception of the other person's desire rather than merely by the perception of the person.

But there is a further step. Let us suppose that Juliet, who is a little slower than Romeo, now senses that he senses her. This puts Romeo in a position to notice, and be aroused by, her arousal at being sensed by him. He senses that she senses that he senses her. This is still another level of arousal, for he becomes conscious of his sexuality through his awareness of its effect on her and of her awareness that this effect is due to him. Once she takes the same step and senses that he senses her sensing him, it becomes difficult to state, let alone imagine, further iterations, though they may be logically distinct. If both are alone, they will presumably turn to look at each other directly, and the proceedings will continue on another plane. Physical contact and intercourse are natural extensions of this complicated visual exchange, and mutual touch can involve all the complexities of awareness present in the visual case, but with a far greater range of subtlety and acuteness.

Ordinarily, of course, things happen in a less orderly fashion—sometimes in a great rush—but I believe that some version of this overlapping system of distinct sexual perceptions and interactions is the basic framework of any full-fledged sexual relation and that relations involving only part of the complex are significantly incomplete. The account is only schematic, as it must be to achieve generality. Every real sexual act will be psychologically far more specific and detailed, in ways that depend not only on the physical techniques employed and on anatomical details, but also on countless features of the participants' conceptions of themselves and of each other, which become embodied in the act. (It is familiar enough fact, for example, that people often take their social roles and the social roles of their partners to bed with them.)

The general schema is important, however, and the proliferation of levels of mutual awareness it involves is an example of a type of complexity that typifies human interactions. Consider aggression, for example. If I am angry with someone, I want to make him feel it, either to produce self-reproach by getting him to see himself through the eyes of my anger, and to dislike what he sees— or else to produce reciprocal anger or fear, by getting him to perceive my anger as a threat or attack. What I want will depend on the details of my anger, but in either case it will involve a desire that the object of that anger be aroused. This accomplishment constitutes the fulfillment of my emotion, through domination of the object's feelings.

Another example of such reflexive mutual recognition is to be found in the phenomenon of meaning, which appears to involve an intention to produce a belief or other effect in another by bringing about his recognition of one's intention to produce that effect. (That result is due to H. P. Grice,[2] whose position I shall not attempt to reproduce in detail.) Sex has a related structure: it involves a desire that one's partner be aroused by the recognition of one's desire that he or she be aroused.

It is not easy to define the basic types of awareness and arousal of which these complexes are composed, and that remains a lacuna in this discussion. In a sense, the object of awareness is the same in one's own case as it is in one's sexual awareness of another, although the two awarenesses will not be the same, the difference being as great as that between feeling angry and experiencing the anger of another. All stages of sexual perception are varieties of identification of a person with his body. What is perceived is one's own or another's *subjection* to or *immersion* in his body, a phenomenon which has been recognized with loathing by St. Paul and St. Augustine, both of whom regarded "the law of sin which is in my members" as a grave threat to the dominion of the holy will.[3] In sexual desire and its expression the blending of involuntary response with deliberate control is extremely important. For Augustine, the revolution launched against him by his body is symbolized by erection and the other involuntary physical components of arousal. Sartre too stresses the fact that the penis is not a prehensile organ. But mere involuntariness characterizes other bodily processes as well. In sexual desire the involuntary responses are combined with submission to spontaneous impulses: not only one's pulse and secretions but one's actions are taken over by the body; ideally, deliberate control is needed only to guide the expression of those impulses. This is to some extent also true of an appetite like hunger, but the takeover there is more localized, less pervasive, less extreme. One's whole body does not become saturated with hunger as it can with desire. But the most characteristic feature of a specifically sexual immersion in the body is its ability to fit into the complex of mutual perceptions that we have described. Hunger leads to spontaneous interactions with food; sexual desire leads to spontaneous interactions with other persons, whose bodies are asserting their sovereignty in the same way, producing involuntary reactions and spontaneous impulses in *them*. These reactions are perceived, and the perception of them is perceived, and that perception is in turn perceived; at each step the domination of the person by his body is reinforced, and the sexual partner becomes more possessible by physical contact, penetration, and envelopment.

Desire is therefore not merely the perception of a preexisting embodiment of the other, but ideally a contribution to his further embodiment, which in turn enhances the original subject's sense of himself. This explains why it is important that the partner be aroused, and not merely aroused, but aroused by the awareness of one's desire. It also explains the sense in which desire has unity and possession as its object: physical possession must eventuate in creation of the sexual object in the image of one's desire, and not merely in the object's recognition of that desire, or in his or her own private arousal.

*   *   *

Even if this is a correct model of the adult sexual capacity, it is not plausible to describe as perverted every deviation from it. For example, if the partners in heterosexual intercourse indulge in private heterosexual fantasies, thus avoiding recognition of the real partner, that would, on this model, constitute a defective sexual relation. It is not, however, generally regarded as a perversion. Such examples suggest that a simple dichotomy between perverted and unperverted sex is too crude to organize the phenomena adequately.

Still, various familiar deviations constitute truncated or incomplete versions of the complete configuration, and may be regarded as perversions of the central impulse. If sexual desire is prevented from taking its full interpersonal form, it is likely to find a different one. The concept of perversion implies that a normal sexual development has been turned aside by distorting influences. I have little to say about this causal condition. But if perversions are in some sense unnatural, they must result from interference with the development of a capacity that is there potentially.

It is difficult to apply this condition, because environmental factors play a role in determining the precise form of anyone's sexual impulse. Early experiences in particular seem to determine the choice of a sexual object. To describe some causal influences as distorting and others as merely formative is to imply that certain general aspects of human sexuality realize a definite potential, whereas many of the details in which people differ realize an indeterminate potential, so that they cannot be called more or less natural. What is included in the definite potential is therefore very important, although the distinction between definite and indeterminate potential is obscure. Obviously a creature incapable of developing the levels of interpersonal sexual awareness I have described could not be deviant in virtue of the failure to do so. (Though even a chicken might be called perverted in an extended sense if it had been conditioned to develop a fetishistic attachment to a telephone.) But if humans will tend to develop some version of reciprocal interpersonal sexual awareness unless prevented, then cases of blockage can be called unnatural or perverted.

Some familiar deviations can be described in this way. Narcissistic practices and intercourse with animals, infants, and inanimate objects seem to be stuck at some primitive version of the first stage of sexual feeling. If the object is not alive, the experience is reduced entirely to an awareness of one's own sexual embodment. Small children and animals permit awareness of the embodiment of the other, but present obstacles to reciprocity, to the recognition by the sexual object of the subject's desire as the source of his (the object's) sexual self-awareness. Voyeurism and exhibitionism are also incomplete relations. The exhibitionist wishes to display his desire without needing to be desired in return; he may even fear the sexual attentions of others. A voyeur, on the other hand, need not require any recognition by his object at all: certainly not a recognition of the voyeur's arousal.

On the other hand, if we apply our model to the various forms that may be taken by two-party heterosexual intercourse, none of them seem clearly to qualify as perversions. Hardly anyone can be found these days to inveigh against oral-genital contact, and the merits of buggery are urged by such respectable figures as D. H. Lawrence and Norman Mailer. In general, it would appear that any bodily contact between a man and a woman that gives them sexual pleasure is a possible vehicle for the system of multilevel interpersonal awareness that I have claimed is the basic psychological content of sexual interaction. Thus a liberal platitude about sex is upheld.

The really difficult cases are sadism, masochism, and homosexuality. The first two are widely regarded as perversions and the last is controversial. In all three cases the issue depends partly on causal factors: do these dispositions result only when normal development has been prevented? Even the form in which this question has been posed is circular, because of the word "normal." We appear to need an independent criterion for a distorting influence, and we do not have one.

It may be possible to class sadism and masochism as perversions because they fall short of interpersonal reciprocity. Sadism concentrates on the evocation of passive self-awareness in others, but the sadist's engagement is itself active and requires a retention of deliberate control which may impede awareness of himself as a bodily subject of passion in the required sense. De Sade claimed that the object of sexual desire was to evoke involuntary responses from one's partner, especially audible ones. The infliction of pain is no doubt the most efficient way to accomplish this, but it requires a certain abrogation of one's own exposed spontaneity. A masochist on the other hand imposes the same disability on his partner as the sadist imposes on himself. The masochist cannot find a satisfactory embodiment as the object of another's sexual desire, but only as the object of his control. He is passive not in relation to his partner's passion but in relation to his nonpassive agency. In addition, the subjection to one's body characteristic of pain and physical restraint is of a very different kind from that of sexual excitement: pain causes people to contract rather than dissolve. These descriptions may not be generally accurate. But to the extent that they are, sadism and masochism would be disorders of the second stage of awareness—the awareness of oneself as an object of desire.

Homosexuality cannot similarly be classed as a perversion on phenomenological grounds. Nothing rules out the full range of interpersonal perceptions between persons of the same sex. The issue then depends on whether homosexuality is produced by distorting influences that block or displace a natural tendency to heterosexual development. And the influences must be more distorting than those which lead to a taste for large breasts or fair hair or dark eyes. These also are contingencies of sexual preference in which people differ, without being perverted.

The question is whether heterosexuality is the natural expression of male and female sexual dispositions that have not been distorted. It is an unclear question, and I do not know how to approach it. There is much support for an aggressive-passive distinction between male and female sexuality. In our culture the male's arousal tends to initiate the perceptual exchange, he usually makes the sexual approach, largely controls the course of the act, and of course penetrates, whereas the woman receives. When two men or two women engage in intercourse they cannot both adhere to these sexual roles. But a good deal of deviation from them occurs in heterosexual intercourse. Women can be sexually aggressive and men passive, and temporary reversals of role are not uncommon in heterosexual exchanges of reasonable length. For these reasons it seems to be doubtful that homosexuality must be a perversion, though like heterosexuality it has perverted forms.

Let me close with some remarks about the relation of perversion to good, bad, and morality. The concept of perversion can hardly fail to be evaluative in some sense, for it appears to involve the notion of an ideal or at least adequate sexuality which the perversions in some way fail to achieve. So, if the concept is viable, the judgment that a person or practice or desire is perverted will constitute a sexual evaluation, implying that better sex, or a better specimen of sex, is possible. This in itself is a very weak claim, since the evaluation might be in a dimension that is of little interest to us. (Though, if my account is correct, that will not be true.)

Whether it is a moral evaluation, however, is another question entirely—one whose answer would require more understanding of both morality and perversion than can be deployed here. Moral evaluation of acts and of persons is a rather special and very complicated matter, and by no means all our evaluations of persons and their activities are moral evaluations. We make judgments about people's beauty or health or intelligence which are evaluative without being moral. Assessments of their sexuality may be similar in that respect.

Furthermore, moral issues aside, it is not clear that unperverted sex is necessarily *preferable* to the perversions. It may be that sex which receives the highest marks for perfection *as sex* is less enjoyable than certain perversions; and if enjoyment is considered very important, that might outweigh considerations of sexual perfection in determining rational preference.

That raises the question of the relation between the evaluative content of judgments of perversion and the rather common *general* distinction between good and bad sex. The latter distinction is usually confined to sexual acts, and it would seem, within limits, to cut across the other: even someone who believed, for example, that homosexuality was a perversion could admit a distinction between better and worse homosexual sex, and might even allow that good homosexual sex could be better sex than not very good unperverted sex. If this is correct, it supports the position that if judgments of perversion are viable at all, they represent only one aspect of the possible evaluation of sex, even *qua sex*. Moreover it is not the only important aspect: sexual deficiencies that evidently do not constitute perversions can be the object of great concern.

Finally, even if perverted sex is to that extent not so good as it might be, bad sex is generally better than none at all. This should not be controversial: it seems to hold for other important matters, like food, music, literature, and society. In the end, one must choose from among the available alternatives, whether their availability depends on the environment or on one's own constitution. And the alternatives have to be fairly grim before it becomes rational to opt for nothing.

Notes

1. *L'Être et le Néant* (Paris: Gallimard, 1943), translated by Hazel E. Barnes (New York: Philosophical Library, 1956).
2. "Meaning," *Philosophical Review* 66, no. 3 (July 1957): 377–88.
3. See Rom. 7:23; and the *Confessions,* bk. 8, part 5.

23

Why Homosexuality Is Abnormal*

Michael Levin

1. Introduction

This paper defends the view that homosexuality is abnormal and hence undesirable—not because it is immoral or sinful, or because it weakens society or hampers evolutionary development, but for a purely mechanical reason. It is a misuse of bodily parts. Clear empirical sense attaches to the idea of *the use* of such bodily parts as genitals, the idea that they are *for* something, and consequently to the idea of their misuse. I argue on grounds involving natural selection that misuse of bodily parts can with high probability be connected to unhappiness. I regard these matters as prolegomena to such policy issues as the rights of homosexuals, the rights of those desiring not to associate with homosexuals, and legislation concerning homosexuality, issues which I shall not discuss systematically here. However, I do in the last section draw a seemingly evident corollary from my view that homosexuality is abnormal and likely to lead to unhappiness.

I have confined myself to male homosexuality for brevity's sake, but I believe that much of what I say applies *mutatis mutandis* to lesbianism. There may well be significant differences between the two: the data of Bell and Weinberg, for example, support the popular idea that sex *per se* is less important to women and in particular lesbians than it is to men. On the other hand, lesbians

Reprinted from *The Monist* 67, no. 2 (April 1984). Copyright © 1984 *The Monist,* LaSalle, Illinois 61301. Reprinted by permission.

*Arthur Caplan, R. M. Hare, Michael Slote, Ed Erwin, Steven Goldberg, Ed Sagarin, Charles Winnick, Robert Gary, Thomas Nagel, David Benfield, Michael Green, and my wife, Margarita, all commented helpfully on earlier drafts of this paper, one of which was read to the New York chapter of the Society for Philosophy and Public Policy. My definition of naturalness agrees to some extent with Gary's (1978), and I have benefited from seeing an unpublished paper by Michael Ruse.

are generally denied motherhood, which seems more important to women than is fatherhood—normally denied homosexual males—to men. . . . Overall, it is reasonable to expect general innate gender differences to explain the major differences between male homosexuals and lesbians.

Despite the publicity currently enjoyed by the claim that one's "sexual preference" is nobody's business but one's own, the intuition that there is something unnatural about homosexuality remains vital. The erect penis fits the vagina, and fits it better than any other natural orifice; penis and vagina seem made for each other. This intuition ultimately derives from, or is another way of capturing, the idea that the penis is not *for* inserting into the anus of another man— that so using the penis is not the way it is *supposed*, even *intended*, to be used. Such intuitions may appear to rest on an outmoded teleological view of nature, but recent work in the logic of functional ascription shows how they may be explicated, and justified, in suitably naturalistic terms. . . . Furthermore, when we understand the sense in which homosexual acts involve a misuse of genitalia, we will see why such misuse is bad and not to be encouraged. . . . Clearly, the general idea that homosexuality is a pathological violation of nature's intent is not shunned by scientists. Here is Gadpille (1972):

> The view of cultural relativity seems to be without justification. Cultural judgment is collective human caprice, and whether it accepts or rejects homosexuality is irrelevant. Biological intent . . . is to differentiate male and female both physiologically and psychologically in such a manner as to insure species survival, which can be served only through heterosexual union.

Gadpille refers to homosexuality as "an abiological maladaptation." The novelty of the present paper is to link adaptiveness and normality via the notion of happiness.

But before turning to these issues, I want to make four preliminary remarks. The first concerns the explicitness of my language in the foregoing paragraph and the rest of this paper. Explicit mention of bodily parts and the frank description of sexual acts are necessary to keep the phenomenon under discussion in clear focus. Euphemistic vagary about "sexual orientation" or "the gay lifestyle" encourage one to slide over homosexuality without having to face or even acknowledge what it really is. Such talk encourages one to treat "sexual preference" as if it were akin to preference among flavors of ice cream. Since unusual taste in ice cream is neither right nor wrong, this usage suggests, why should unusual taste in sex be regarded as objectionable? Opposed to this usage is the unblinkable fact that the sexual preferences in question are such acts as mutual fellation. Is one man's taste for pistachio ice cream really just like another man's taste for fellation? Unwillingness to call this particular spade a spade allows delicacy to award the field by default to the view that homosexuality is normal. Anyway, such delicacy is misplaced in a day when "the love that dare not speak its name" is shouting its name from the rooftops.[1]

My second, related, point concerns the length of the present paper, which has a general and a specific cause. The general cause is that advocates of an unpopular position—as mine is, at least in intellectual circles—assume the burden of proof. My view is the one that needs defending, my presuppositions the ones not widely shared. I would not have entertained so many implausible and digressive objections had not so many competent philosophers urged them on me with great seriousness. Some of these objections even generate a dialectic among themselves. For example, I have to defend my view on two sociobiological fronts—against the view that what is innate is polymorphous sexuality shaped by culture, and against the incompatible view that not only are the details of sexual behavior innate, but homosexuality is one such behavior, and hence "normal."

The third point is this. The chain of intuitions I discussed earlier has other links, links connected to the conclusion that homosexuality is bad. They go something like this: Homosexual acts involve the use of the genitals for what they aren't for, and it is a *bad* or at least *unwise* thing to use a part of your body for what it isn't for. Calling homosexual acts "unnatural" is intended to sum up this entire line of reasoning. "Unnatural" carries disapprobative connotations, and any explication of it should capture this. One can, stipulatively or by observing the ordinary usage of biologists, coin an evaluatively neutral use for "normal," or "proper function," or any cognate thereof. One might for example take the normal use of an organ to be what the organ is used for 95 percent of the time. But there is a normative dimension to the concept of abnormality that all such explications miss. To have anything to do with our intuitions—even if designed to demonstrate them groundless—an explication of "abnormal" must capture the analytic truth that the abnormality of a practice is a reason for avoiding it. If our ordinary concept of normality turns out to be ill-formed, so that various acts are at worst "abnormal" in some nonevaluative sense, this will simply mean that, as we ordinarily use the expression, *nothing is abnormal*. (Not that anyone really believes this—people who deny that cacophagia or necrophilia is abnormal do so only to maintain the appearance of consistency.) . . .

2. On "Function" and Its Cognates

To bring into relief the point of the idea that homosexuality involves a misuse of bodily parts, I will begin with an uncontroversial case of misuse, a case in which the clarity of our intuitions is not obscured by the conviction that they are untrustworthy. Mr. Jones pulls all his teeth and strings them around his neck because he thinks his teeth look nice as a necklace. He takes pureéd liquids supplemented by intravenous solutions for nourishment. It is surely natural to say that Jones is misusing his teeth, that he is not using them for what they are for, that indeed the way he is using them is incompatible with what they are for. Pedants might argue that Jones's teeth are no longer part of him and hence that he is not misusing any bodily parts. To them I offer Mr. Smith, who likes to play "Old MacDonald" on his teeth. So devoted is he to this amusement, in fact, that he never uses his teeth for chewing—like Jones, he takes nourishment intravenously. Now, not only do we find it perfectly plain that Smith and Jones are misusing their teeth, we predict a dim future for them on purely physiological grounds; we expect the muscles of Jones's jaw that are used for—that *are* for— chewing to lose their tone, and we expect this to affect Jones's gums. Those parts of Jones's digestive tract that are for processing solids will also suffer from disuse. The net result will be deteriorating health and perhaps a shortened life. Nor is this all. Human beings enjoy chewing. Not only has natural selection selected in muscles for chewing and favored creatures with such muscles, it has selected in a tendency to find the use of those muscles reinforcing. Creatures who do not enjoy using such parts of their bodies as deteriorate with disuse, will tend to be selected out. Jones, product of natural selection that he is, descended from creatures who at least tended to enjoy the use of such parts. Competitors who didn't simply had fewer descendants. So we expect Jones sooner or later to experience vague yearnings to chew something, just as we find people who take no exercise to experience a general listlessness. Even waiving for now my apparent reification of the evolutionary process, let me emphasize how little anyone is tempted to say "each to his own" about Jones or to regard Jones's disposition of his teeth as simply a deviation from a statistical norm. This sort of case is my paradigm when discussing homosexuality. . . .

3. Applications to Homosexuality

The application of this general picture to homosexuality should be obvious. There can be no reasonable doubt that one of the functions of the penis is to introduce semen into the vagina. It does this, and it has been selected in because it does this. . . . Nature has consequently made this use of the penis rewarding. It is clear enough that any proto-human males who found unrewarding the insertion of penis into vagina have left no descendants. In particular, proto-human males who enjoyed inserting their penises into each other's anuses have left no descendants. This is why homosexuality is abnormal, and why its abnormality counts prudentially against it. Homosexuality is likely to cause unhappiness because it leaves unfulfilled an innate and innately rewarding desire. And should the reader's environmentalism threaten to get the upper hand, let me remind him again of an unproblematic case. Lack of exercise is bad and even abnormal not only because it is unhealthy but also because one feels poorly without regular exercise. Nature made exercise rewarding because, until recently, we had to exercise to survive. Creatures who found running after game unrewarding were eliminated. Laziness leaves unreaped the rewards nature has planted in exercise, even if the lazy man cannot tell this introspectively. If this I is a correct description of the place of exercise in human life, it is by the same token a correct description of the place of heterosexuality.

It hardly needs saying, but perhaps I should say it anyway, that this argument concerns tendencies and probabilities. Generalizations about human affairs being notoriously "true by and large and for the most part" only, saying that homosexuals are bound to be less happy than heterosexuals must be understood as short for "Not coincidentally, a larger proportion of homosexuals will be unhappy than a corresponding selection of the heterosexual population." There are, after all, genuinely jolly fat men. To say that laziness leads to adverse affective consequences means that, because of our evolutionary history, the odds are relatively good that a man who takes no exercise will suffer adverse affective consequences. Obviously, some people will get away with misusing their bodily parts. Thus, when evaluating the empirical evidence that bears on this account, it will be pointless to cite cases of well-adjusted homosexuals. I do not say they are nonexistent; my claim is that, of biological necessity, they are rare. . . .

Utilitarians must take the present evolutionary scenario seriously. The utilitarian attitude toward homosexuality usually runs something like this: even if homosexuality is in some sense unnatural, as a matter of brute fact homosexuals take pleasure in sexual contact with members of the same sex. As long as they don't hurt anyone else, homosexuality is as great a good as heterosexuality. But the matter cannot end here. Not even a utilitarian doctor would have words of praise for a degenerative disease that happened to foster a certain kind of pleasure (as sore muscles uniquely conduce to the pleasure of stretching them). A utilitarian doctor would presumably try just as zealously to cure diseases that feel good as less pleasant degenerative diseases. A pleasure causally connected with great distress cannot be treated as just another pleasure to be toted up on the felicific scoreboard. Utilitarians have to reckon with the inevitable consequences of pain-causing pleasure.

Similar remarks apply to the question of whether homosexuality is a "disease." A widely quoted pronouncement of the American Psychiatric Association runs:

> Surely the time has come for psychiatry to give up the archaic practice of classifying the millions of men and women who accept or prefer homosexual object choices as being, by virtue of that fact alone, mentally ill. The fact that their alternative life-style happens to be out of favor with current cultural conventions must not be a basis in itself for a diagnosis.

Apart from some question-begging turns of phrase, this is right. One's taste for mutual anal intercourse is nothing "in itself" for one's psychiatrist to worry about, any more than a life of indolence is anything "in itself" for one's doctor to worry about. In fact, in itself there is nothing wrong with a broken arm or an occluded artery. The fact that my right ulna is now in two pieces is just a fact of nature, not a "basis for diagnosis." But this condition is a matter for medical science anyway, because it will lead to pain. Permitted to persist, my fracture will provoke increasingly punishing states. So if homosexuality is a reliable sign of present or future misery, it is beside the point that homosexuality is not "by virtue of that fact alone" a mental illness. High rates of drug addiction, divorce, and illegitimacy are in themselves no basis for diagnosing social pathology. They support this diagnosis because of what else they signify about a society which exhibits them. Part of the problem here is the presence of germs in paradigm diseases, and the lack of a germ for homosexuality (or psychosis). I myself am fairly sure that a suitably general and germ-free definition of "disease" can be extruded from the general notion of "function" . . . , but however that may be, whether homosexuality is a disease is a largely verbal issue. If homosexuality is a self-punishing maladaptation, it hardly matters what it is called.

4. Evidence and Further Clarification

I have argued that homosexuality is "abnormal" in both a descriptive and a normative sense because—for evolutionary reasons—homosexuals are bound to be unhappy. In Kantian terms, . . . it is possible for homosexuality to be unnatural even if it violates no cosmic purpose or such purposes as we retrospectively impose on nature. What is the evidence for my view? For one thing, by emphasizing homosexual unhappiness, my view explains a ubiquitous fact in a simple way. The fact is the universally acknowledged unhappiness of homosexuals. Even the staunchest defenders of homosexuality admit that, as of now, homosexuals are not happy. (Writers even in the very recent past, like Lord Devlin, could not really believe that anyone could publicly advocate homosexuality as intrinsically good: see Devlin, p. 87.) . . .

The usual environmentalist explanation for homosexuals' unhappiness is the misunderstanding, contempt, and abuse that society heaps on them. But this not only leaves unexplained why society has this attitude, it sins against parsimony by explaining a nearly universal phenomenon in terms of variable circumstances that have, by coincidence, the same upshot. Parsimony urges that we seek the explanation of homosexual unhappiness in the nature of homosexuality itself, as my explanation does. Having to "stay in the closet" may be a great strain, but it does not account for all the miseries that writers on homosexuality say is the homosexual's lot.

Incorporating unhappiness into the present evolutionary picture also smooths a bothersome ad-hocness in some otherwise appealing analyses of abnormality. Many writers define abnormality as compulsiveness. On this conception, homosexuality is abnormal because it is an autonomy-obstructing compulsion. Such an analysis is obviously open to the question, What if an autonomous homosexual comes along? To that, writers like van den Haag point out that homosexuality is, in fact, highly correlated with compulsiveness. The trouble here is that the definition in question sheds no light on why abnormal, compulsive, traits are such. The present account not only provides a criterion for abnormality, it encapsulates an explanation of *why* behavior abnormal by its lights is indeed compulsive and bound to lead to unhappiness.

One crucial test of my account is its prediction that homosexuals will continue to be unhappy even if people altogether abandon their "prejudice" against homosexuality. This prediction, that homosexuality being unnatural homosexuals will still find their behavior self-punishing, coheres with available evidence. It is consistent with the failure of other oppressed groups, such as American Negroes and European Jews, to become warped in the direction of "cruising," sado-masochism, and other practices common in homosexual life (see McCracken, 1979). It is consistent as well with the admission by even so sympathetic an observer of homosexuality as Rechy (1977) that the immediate cause of homosexual unhappiness is a taste for promiscuity, anonymous encounters, and humiliation. It is hard to see how such tastes are related to the dim view society takes of them. Such a relation would be plausible only if homosexuals courted multiple anonymous encounters *faute de mieux*, longing all the while to settle down to some sort of domesticity. But, again, Europeans abhorred Jews for centuries, but this did not create in Jews a special weakness for anonymous, promiscuous sex. Whatever drives a man away from women, to be fellated by as many different men as possible, seems independent of what society thinks of such behavior. It is this behavior that occasions misery, and we may expect the misery of homosexuals to continue.

In a 1974 study, Weinberg and Williams found no difference in the distress experienced by homosexuals in Denmark and the Netherlands, and in the U.S., where they found public tolerance of homosexuality to be lower. This would confirm rather strikingly that homosexual unhappiness is endogenous, unless one says that Weinberg's and Williams's indices for public tolerance and distress—chiefly homosexuals' self-reports of "unhappiness" and "lack of faith in others"—are unreliable. Such complaints, however, push the social causation theory toward untestability. Weinberg and Williams themselves cleave to the hypothesis that homosexual unhappiness is entirely a reaction to society's attitudes, and suggest that a condition of homosexual happiness is positive endorsement by the surrounding society. It is hard to imagine a more flagrantly *ad hoc* hypothesis. Neither a Catholic living among Protestants nor a copywriter working on the great American novel in his off hours asks more of society than tolerance in order to be happy in his pursuits.

It is interesting to reflect on a natural experiment that has gotten under way in the decade since the Weinberg-Williams study. A remarkable change in public opinion, if not private sentiment, has occurred in America. For whatever reason —the prodding of homosexual activists, the desire not to seem like a fuddy-duddy—various organs of opinion are now hard at work providing a "positive image" for homosexuals. Judges allow homosexuals to adopt their lovers. The Unitarian Church now performs homosexual marriages. Hollywood produces highly sanitized movies like *Making Love* and *Personal Best* about homosexuality. Macmillan strongly urges its authors to show little boys using cosmetics. Homosexuals no longer fear revealing themselves, as is shown by the prevalence of the "clone look." Certain products run advertising obviously directed at the homosexual market. On the societal reaction theory, there ought to be an enormous rise in homosexual happiness. I know of no systematic study to determine if this is so, but anecdotal evidence suggests it may not be. The homosexual press has been just as strident in denouncing pro-homosexual movies as in denouncing Doris Day movies. Especially virulent venereal diseases have very recently appeared in homosexual communities, evidently spread in epidemic proportions by unabating homosexual promiscuity. One selling point for a presumably serious "gay rights" rally in Washington, D.C., was an "all-night disco train" from New York to Washington. What is perhaps most salient is that, even if the changed public mood results in decreased homosexual unhappiness, the question remains of why homosexuals in the recent past, who suffered greatly for being homosexuals, persisted in being homosexuals.

But does not my position also predict—contrary to fact—that any sexual activity not aimed at procreation or at least sexual intercourse leads to unhappiness? First, I am not sure this conclusion is contrary to the facts properly understood. It is universally recognized that, for humans and the higher animals, sex is more than the insertion of the penis into the vagina. Foreplay is necessary to prepare the female and, to a lesser extent, the male. Ethologists have studied the elaborate mating rituals of even relatively simple animals. Sexual intercourse must therefore be understood to include the kisses and caresses that necessarily precede copulation, behaviors that nature has made rewarding. What my view does predict is that exclusive preoccupation with behaviors normally preparatory for intercourse is highly correlated with unhappiness. And, so far as I know, psychologists do agree that such preoccupation or "fixation" with, e.g., cunnilingus, is associated with personality traits independently recognized as disorders. In this sense, sexual intercourse really is virtually necessary for well-being. Only if one is antecedently convinced that "nothing is more natural than anything else" will one confound foreplay as a prelude to intercourse with "foreplay" that leads nowhere at all. One might speculate on the evolutionary advantages of foreplay, at least for humans: by increasing the intensity and complexity of the pleasures of intercourse, it binds the partners more firmly and makes them more fit for child-rearing. In fact, such analyses of sexual perversion as Nagel's (1969), which correctly focus on the interruption of mutuality as central to perversion, go wrong by ignoring the evolutionary role and built-in rewards of mutuality. They fail to explain why the interruption of mutuality is disturbing.

It should also be clear that my argument permits gradations in abnormality. Behavior is the more abnormal, and the less likely to be rewarding, the more its emission tends to extinguish a genetic cohort that practices it. The less likely a behavior is to get selected out, the less abnormal it is. Those of our ancestors who found certain aspects of foreplay reinforcing might have managed to reproduce themselves sufficiently to implant this strain in us. There might be an equilibrium between intercourse and such not directly reproductive behavior. It is not required that any behavior not directly linked to heterosexual intercourse lead to maximum dissatisfaction. But the existence of these gradations provides no entering wedge for homosexuality. As no behavior is more likely to get selected out than rewarding homosexuality—except perhaps an innate tendency to suicide at the onset of puberty—it is extremely unlikely that homosexuality can now be unconditionally reinforcing in humans to any extent.

Nor does my position predict, again contrary to fact, that celibate priests will be unhappy. My view is compatible with the existence of happy celibates who deny themselves as part of a higher calling which yields compensating satisfactions. Indeed, the very fact that one needs to explain how the priesthood can compensate for the lack of family means that people do regard heterosexual mating as the natural or "inertial" state of human relations. The comparison between priests and homosexuals is in any case inapt. Priests do not simply give up sexual activity without ill-effect; they give it up for a reason. Homosexuals have hardly given up the use of their sexual organs, for a higher calling or anything else. Homosexuals continue to use them, but, unlike priests, they use them for what they are not for.

I have encountered the thought that by my lights female heterosexuality must be abnormal, since according to feminism women have been unhappy down the ages. The datum is questionable, to say the least. Feminists have offered no documentation whatever for this extravagant claim; their evidence is usually the unhappiness of the feminist in question and her circle of friends. Such attempts to prove female discontent in past centuries as Greer's (1979) are transparently anachronistic projections of contemporary feminist discontent onto inappropriate historical objects. An objection from a similar source runs that my argument, suitably extended, implies the naturalness and hence rewardingness of traditional monogamous marriage. Once again, instead of seeing this as a *reductio*, I am inclined to take the supposed absurdity as a truth that nicely fits my theory. It is not a theoretical contention but an observable fact that women enjoy motherhood, that failure to bear and care for children breeds unhappiness in women, and that the role of "primary caretaker" is much more important for women than men. However, there is no need to be dogmatic. This conception of the family is in extreme disrepute in contemporary America. Many women work and many marriages last less than a decade. Here we have another natural experiment about what people find reinforcing. My view predicts that women will on the whole become unhappier if current trends continue. Let us see.

Not directly bearing on the issue of happiness, but still empirically pertinent, is animal homosexuality. I mentioned earlier that the overwhelmingly heterosexual tendencies of animals in all but such artificial and genetically irrele-

vant environs as zoos cast doubt on sheer polymorphous sexuality as a sufficiently adaptive strategy. By the same token, it renders implausible the claim in
Masters and Johnson (1979) that human beings are born with only a general sex
drive, and that the objects of the sex drive are *entirely* learned. If this were so,
who teaches male tigers to mate with female tigers? Who teaches male primates
to mate with female primates? In any case, the only evidence Masters and
Johnson cite is the entirely unsurprising physiological similarity between heterosexual and homosexual response. Plainly, the inability of the penile nerve
endings to tell what is rubbing them has nothing to do with the innateness of the
sexual object. The inability of a robin to tell twigs from clever plastic look-
alikes is consistent with an innate nest-building instinct.

The work of Beach (1976) is occasionally cited (e.g., in Wilson, 1978) to
document the existence of animal homosexuality and to support the contention
that homosexuality has some adaptive purpose, but Beach in fact notes certain
important disanalogies between mammalian homosexual behavior in the wild
and human homosexuality. Citing a principle of "stimulus-response complementarity," he remarks that a male chimpanzee will mount another male if the
latter emits such characteristically female behavior as display of nether parts.
Male homosexual humans, on the other hand, are attracted to maleness. More
significantly, the male chimpanzee's mounting is unaccompanied by erection,
thrusting or, presumably, intromission. Beach suggests that this display-
mounting sequence may be multipurpose in nature, signalling submission and
dominance when it occurs between males. In the same vein, Barash (1979: 60)
cites male-male rape in *Xylocanis maculipennis*, but here the rapist's sperm is
deposited in the rape victim's storage organs. This is a smart evolutionary move
. . . but it is not comparable in its effects to homosexuality in humans. . . .

5. On Policy Issues

Homosexuality is intrinsically bad only in a prudential sense. It makes for unhappiness. However, this does not exempt homosexuality from the larger categories
of ethics—rights, duties, liabilities. Deontic categories apply to acts which
increase or decrease happiness or expose the helpless to the risk of unhappiness.

If homosexuality is unnatural, legislation which raises the odds that a given
child will become homosexual raises the odds that he will be unhappy. The only
gap in the syllogism is whether legislation which legitimates, endorses, or protects homosexuality does increase the chances that a child will become homosexual. If so, such legislation is *prima facie* objectionable. The question is not
whether homosexual elementary school teachers will molest their charges. Pro-
homosexual legislation might increase the incidence of homosexuality in subtler
ways. If it does, and if the protection of children is a fundamental obligation of

society, legislation which legitimates homosexuality is a dereliction of duty. I am reluctant to deploy the language of "children's rights," which usually serves as one more excuse to interfere with the prerogatives of parents. But we do have obligations to our children, and one of them is to protect them from harm. If, as some have suggested, children have a right to protection from a religious education, they surely have a right to protection from homosexuality. So protecting them limits somebody else's freedom, but we are often willing to protect quite obscure children's rights at the expense of the freedom of others. There is a movement to ban TV commercials for sugar-coated cereals, to protect children from the relatively trivial harm of tooth decay. Such a ban would restrict the freedom of advertisers, and restrict it even though the last clear chance of avoiding the harm, and thus the responsibility, lies with the parents who control the TV set. I cannot see how one can consistently support such legislation and also urge homosexual rights, which risk much graver damage to children in exchange for increased freedom for homosexuals. (If homosexual behavior is largely compulsive, it is falsifying the issue to present it as balancing risks to children against the freedom of homosexuals.) The right of a homosexual to work for the Fire Department is not a negligible good. Neither is fostering a legal atmosphere in which as many people as possible grow up heterosexual.

It is commonly asserted that legislation granting homosexuals the privilege or right to be firemen endorses not homosexuality, but an expanded conception of human liberation. It is conjectural how sincerely this can be said in a legal order that forbids employers to hire whom they please and demands hours of paperwork for an interstate shipment of hamburger. But in any case legislation "legalizing homosexuality" cannot be neutral because passing it would have an inexpungeable speech-act dimension. Society cannot grant unaccustomed rights and privileges to homosexuals while remaining neutral about the value of homosexuality. Working from the assumption that society rests on the family and its consequences, the Judaeo-Christian tradition has deemed homosexuality a sin and withheld many privileges from homosexuals. Whether or not such denial was right, for our society to grant these privileges to homosexuals *now* would amount to declaring that it has rethought the matter and decided that homosexuality is not as bad as it had previously supposed. And unless such rethinking is a direct response to new empirical findings about homosexuality, it can only be a revaluing. Someone who suddenly accepts a policy he has previously opposed is open to the same interpretation: he has come to think better of the policy. And if he embraces the policy while knowing that this interpretation will be put on his behavior, and if he knows that others know that he knows they will so interpret it, he is acquiescing in this interpretation. He can be held to have intended, meant, this interpretation. A society that grants privileges to homosexuals while recognizing that, in the light of generally known history, this act can be interpreted as a positive reevaluation of homosexuality, is signalling that it now thinks homosexuality is all right. Many commentators in the popular press have observed that homosexuals, unlike members of racial minorities, can always "stay in the closet" when applying for jobs. What homosexual rights activists really want, therefore, is not access to jobs but legitimation of their homosexuality. Since this is known, giving them what they want will be seen as conceding their claim to legitimacy. And since legislators know their actions will support this interpretation, and know that their constituencies know they know this, the Gricean effect or symbolic meaning of passing anti-discrimination ordinances is to declare homosexuality legitimate (see Will, 1977).

Legislation permitting frisbees in the park does not imply approval of frisbees for the simple reason that frisbees are new; there is no tradition of banning them from parks. The legislature's action in permitting frisbees is not interpretable, known to be interpretable, and so on, as the reversal of long-standing disapproval. It is because these Gricean conditions are met in the case of abortion that legislation—or rather judicial fiat—permitting abortions and mandating their public funding are widely interpreted as tacit approval. Up to now, society has deemed homosexuality so harmful that restricting it outweighs putative homosexual rights. If society reverses itself, it will in effect be deciding that homosexuality is not as bad as it once thought.

Notes

1. "Sexual preference" typifies the obfuscatory language in which the homosexuality debate is often couched. "Preference" suggests that sexual tastes are voluntarily chosen, whereas it is a commonplace that one cannot decide what to find sexually stimulating. True, we talk of "preferences" among flavors of ice cream even though one cannot choose what flavor of ice cream to like; such talk is probably a carryover from the voluntariness of *ordering* ice cream. "Sexual preference" does not even sustain this analogy, however, since sex is a forced choice for everyone except avowed celibates, and especially for the relatively large number of homosexuals who cruise regularly.

2. Nagel attempts to meet these counterexamples in effect by accepting such consequences of the classical analysis as that the beat of the heart is sometimes for diagnosis. The only reply to this sort of defense is that this is *not* what people mean. Met with such a reply, many philosophers feel impelled to say, "Well, it ought to be what you mean." This invitation to change the subject is attractive or relevant only if we haven't meant anything the first time around. If a coherent thought can be found behind our initial words which maximizes coherence with all hypothetical usages, it is *that thought* we were expressing and whose articulation was the aim of the analytic exercise.

Bibliography

Barash, D. *The Whispering Within.* New York: Harper & Row, 1979.
Beach, F. "Cross-Species Comparisons and the Human Heritage." *Archives of Sexual Behavior* 5 (1976): 469–85.

Bell, A., and M. Weinberg. *Homosexualities.* New York: Simon and Schuster, 1978.

Devlin, P. *The Enforcement of Morals.* Oxford: Oxford University Press, 1965.

Gadpille, W. "Research into the Physiology of Maleness and Femaleness: Its Contribution to the Etiology and Psychodynamics of Homosexuality." *Archives of General Psychiatry* (1972): 193–206.

Gary, R. "Sex and Sexual Perversion." *Journal of Philosophy* 74 (1978): 189–99.

Greer, G. *The Obstacle Race.* New York: Farrar, Strauss & Giroux, 1979.

Masters, W. and V. Johnson. *Homosexuality in Perspective.* Boston: Little, Brown and Company, 1979.

McCracken, S. "Replies to Correspondents." *Commentary,* April 1979.

Mossner, E. *The Life of David Hume,* 1st. ed. New York: Nelson & Sons, 1954.

Nagel, E. "Teleology Revisited." *Journal of Philosophy* 74 (1977): 261–301.

———. "Sexual Perversion." *Journal of Philosophy* 66 (1969): 5–17. This discussion can be found elsewhere in the present volume.

Rechy, J. *The Sexual Outlaw.* New York: Grove Press, 1977.

Weinberg, M., and C. Williams. *Male Homosexuals: Their Problems and Adaptations.* Oxford: Oxford University Press, 1974.

Will, G. "How Far Out of the Closet?" *Newsweek,* 30 May 1977, p. 92.

Wilson, E. *Sociobiology: The New Synthesis.* Cambridge, Mass.: Harvard University Press, 1975.

———. *On Human Nature.* Cambridge, Mass.: Harvard University Press, 1978.

24

An Essay on "Paederasty"

Jeremy Bentham

Introduction to Bentham's Essay

> *I have been tormenting myself for years to find, if possible, a sufficient ground for treating them* [homosexuals] *with the severity with which they are treated at this time of day by all European nations: but upon the principle of utility I can find none.*

Had these words been penned by a famous social philosopher of the 1980s, they would be noteworthy but not exceptional; written by a social philosopher of the 1880s, they would have been both noteworthy and exceptional; but since the passage was written by a famous English social philosopher of the 1780s, Jeremy Bentham, and since it prefaces what appears to be the first philosophical treatment of homosexuality in the English language, the passage is extraordinary indeed.

Bentham and his fellow utilitarians sought a rational standard against which they could measure the customs and laws of their society. The device they hit upon was the calculus of utility. To employ the calculus one had to conceptualize the social world in terms of acts that were morally neutral in and of themselves, but which acquired value in terms of their consequences. Acts were then held to be moral insofar as their consequences were conducive to human happiness, and immoral insofar as their effects militated against happiness and/or promoted pain, suffering, or any other form of human misery.

The utilitarian project was to measure all customs and laws in terms of the calculus of utility—including, as it turned out, those relating to "unnatural" sexual acts. Bentham appraised the moral nature of these acts and the laws that criminalize them in three different sets of writings dated ca. 1774, ca. 1785, and 1814–1816. In each case, when the sexual acts in themselves were regarded as morally neutral and appraised only in terms of their consequences he found that, except in cases of homosexual rape, the most certain consequence of a homosexual act was the pleasure experienced by the participants. There was, therefore, a strong prima facie *case both against the moral opprobrium with which homosexuality was customarily viewed and against imposing criminal sanctions on homosexual acts. (According to some scholars[1] more than sixty people were hanged for "sodomy" and other homosexual acts in England during the years 1806–1835.) Bentham carefully examined all of the purported negative consequences of homosexual intercourse suggested by his nonutilitarian contemporaries, Blackstone, Montesquieu, and Voltaire—for example, its supposed tendency to corrupt and debilitate practitioners, its effects on population, and so on. Weighing these conjectured effects against the historical data supplied by Greek homosexuality, Bentham concluded that since the net consequences of homosexual sex appear not to be harmful, utilitarians must reject the proscription and criminalization of homosexuality.*

Like most of Bentham's writings, his work on homosexuality was not published in his lifetime. The first publication of any of this material occurred in 1931 when C. K. Ogden published some of the 1814–1816 materials as an appendix to his 1931 edition of Bentham's Theory of Legislation. *The essay on "Paederasty" was not published until 1978, when it appeared in the Fall and Summer editions of the* Journal of Homosexuality. *Louis Compton, a professor of English at the University of Nebraska, had rediscovered these materials among Bentham's papers and transcribed the manuscript (whose page numbers are given in square brackets).[1] Although the style of Bentham's writings reflects the period in which they were written, the thought is remarkably contemporary; the essay is undoubtedly one of the most significant publications in the recent literature on philosophy and sex.—R.B.*

To what class of offences shall we refer these irregularities of the venereal appetite which are styled unnatural? . . . I have been tormenting myself for years to find if possible a sufficient ground for treating them with the severity with which they are treated at this time of day by all European nations: but upon the principle of utility I can find none.

. . . In settling the nature and tendency of this offence we shall for the most part have settled the nature and tendency of all the other offences that come under this disgusting catalogue.

Paederasty: Does It Produce Any Primary Mischief?

1. As to any primary mischief, it is evident that it produces no pain in anyone. On the contrary it produces pleasure, and that a pleasure which, by their perverted taste, is by this supposition preferred to that pleasure which is in general reputed the greatest. The partners are both willing. If either of them be unwilling, the act is not that which we have here in view: it is an offence totally different in its nature of effects: it is a personal injury; it is a kind of rape.

As a Secondary Mischief Whether They Produce Any Alarm in the Community

2. As to any secondary mischief, it produces not any pain of apprehension. For what is there in it for any body to be afraid of? By the supposition, those only are the objects of it who choose to be so, who find a pleasure, for so it seems they do, in being so.

Whether Any Danger

3. As to any danger exclusive of pain, the danger, if any, must consist in the tendency of the example. But what is the tendency of this example? To dispose others to engage in the same practises: but this practise for anything that has yet appeared produces not pain of any kind to anyone.

Reasons That Have Commonly Been Assigned

Hitherto we have found no reason for punishing it at all: much less for punishing it with the degree of severity with which it has been commonly punished. Let us see what force there is in the reasons that have been commonly assigned for punishing it.

Whether Against the Security of the Individual

Sir W. Blackstone [argues that paederasty] is not only an offence against the peace, but it is of that division of offences against the peace which are offences against security. According to the same writer, if a man is guilty of this kind of filthiness, for instance, with a cow, as some men have been known to be, it is an offence / against somebody's security. He does not say whose security, for the law makes no distinction in its ordinances, so neither does this lawyer or any other English lawyer in his comments make any distinction between this kind of filthiness when committed with the consent of the patient and the same kind of filthiness when committed against his consent and by violence. It is just as if a man were to make no distinction between concubinage and rape.

Whether It Debilitates—Montesquieu

The reason that Montesquieu gives for reprobating it is the weakness which he seems to suppose it to have a tendency to bring upon those who practise it. *(Esp. des Loix,* L. 12, ch. 6. 11) This, if it be true in fact, is a reason of a very different complexion from any of the preceding and it is on the ground of this reason as being the most plausible one that I have ranked the offence under its present head. As far as it is true in fact, the act ought to be regarded in the first place as coming within the list of offences against one's self, of offences of imprudence: in the next place, as an offence against the state, an offence the tendency of which is to diminish the public force. If, however, it tends to weaken a man it is not any single act that can in any sensible degree have that effect. It can only be the habit: the act thus will become obnoxious as evidencing the existence, in probability, of the habit. This enervating tendency, be it what it may, if it is to be taken as a ground for treating the / [192] practise in question with a degree of severity which is not bestowed upon the regular way of gratifying the veneral appetite, must be greater in the former case than in the latter. Is it so? If the affirmative can be shown it must be either by arguments *a priori* drawn from considerations of the nature of the human frame or from experience. Are there any such arguments from physiology? I have never heard of any: I can think of none.

What Says History?

What says historical experience? The result of this can be measured only upon a large scale or upon a very general survey. Among the modern nations it is comparatively but rare. In modern Rome it is perhaps not very uncommon; in Paris probably not quite so common; in London still less frequent; in Edinburgh or Amsterdam you scarce hear of it two or three times in a century. In Athens and in ancient Rome in the most flourishing periods of the history of those capitals, regular intercourse between the sexes was scarcely much more common. It was upon the same footing throughout Greece; everybody practised it; nobody was ashamed of it. They might be ashamed of what they looked upon as an excess in it, or they might be ashamed of it as a weakness, as a propensity that had a tendency to distract men from more worthy and important occupations, / just as a man with us might be ashamed of excess or weakness in his love for women. In itself one may be sure they were not ashamed of it. . . .

What is remarkable is that there is scarce a striking character in antiquity, not one that in other respects men are in use to cite as virtuous, of whom it does not appear by one circumstance or another, that / he was infected with this inconceivable propensity. . . .

Many moderns, and among others Mr. Voltaire, dispute the fact, but that intelligent philosopher sufficiently intimates the ground of his incredulity—if he does not believe it, it is because he likes not to believe it. What the ancients called love in such a case was what we call Platonic, that is, was not love but friendship. But the Greeks knew the difference between love and friendship as well as we—they had distinct terms to signify them by: it seems reasonable therefore to suppose that when they say love they mean love, and that when they say friendship only they mean friendship only. And with regard to Xenophon and his master, Socrates, and his fellow-scholar Plato, it seems more reasonable to believe them to have been addicted to this taste when they or any of them tell us so in express terms than to trust to the interpretations, however ingenious and however well-intended, of any men who write at this time of day, when they tell us it was no such thing. / Not to insist upon Agesilaus and Xenophon, it appears by one circumstance or another that Themistocles, Aristides, Epaminondas, Alcibiades, Alexander and perhaps the greatest number of the heroes of Greece were infected with this taste. Not that the historians are at the pains of informing us so expressly, for it was not extraordinary enough to make it worth their while, but it comes out collaterally in the course of the transactions they have occasion to relate.

It appears then that this propensity was universally predominant among the ancient Greeks and Romans, among the military as much as any. The ancient Greeks and Romans, however, are commonly reputed as / a much stouter as well as a much braver people than the stoutest and bravest of any of the modern nations of Europe. They appear to have been stouter at least in a very considerable degree than the French in whom this propensity is not very common and still more than the Scotch in whom it is still less common, and this although the climate even of Greece was a great deal warmer and in that respect more enervating than that of modern Scotland.

If then this practise was in those ancient warm countries attended with any enervating effects, they were much more than counteracted by the superiority of [illegible] in the exertions which were then required by the military education over and above those which are now called forth by ordinary labour. But if there be any ground derived from history for attributing to it any such enervating effects it is more than I can find.

Whether It Enervates the Patient More Than the Agent

Montesquieu however seems to make a distinction—he seems to suppose these enervating effects to be exerted principally upon the person who is the patient in such a business. This distinction does not seem very satisfactory in any point of view. Is there any reason for supposing it to be a fixed one? Between persons of the same age actuated by the same incomprehensible desires would not the parts they took in the business be convertible? Would not the patient / be the agent in his turn? If it were not so, the person on whom he supposes these effects to be the greatest is precisely the person with regard to whom it is most difficult to conceive whence those consequences should result. In the one case there is exhaustion which when carried to excess may be followed by debility: in the other case there is no such thing.

What Says History?

In regard to this point too in particular, what says history? As the two parts that a man may take in this business are so naturally convertible however frequently he may have taken a passive part, it will not ordinarily appear. According to the notions of the ancients, there was something degrading in the passive part which was not in the active. It was ministering to the pleasure, for so we are obliged to call it, of another without participation, it was making one's self the property of another man, it was playing the woman's part: it was therefore unmanly. (*Paedicabo vos et irrumabo, Antoni* [*sic*] *pathice et cinaede Furi.* [*Carm. 16*] Catullus. *J.B.*) On the other hand, to take the active part was to make use of another for one's pleasure, it was making another man one's property, it was preserving the manly, the commanding character. Accordingly, Solon in his laws prohibits slaves from bearing an active part where the passive is borne by a freeman. In the few instances in which we happen to hear of a person's taking the passive part there is nothing to favour / the above-mentioned hypothesis. The beautiful Alcibiades, who in his youth, says Cornelius Nepos, after the manner of the Greeks, was beloved by many, was not remarkable either for weakness or for cowardice: at least, [blank] did not find it so. The Clodius whom Cicero scoffs at for his servile obsequiousness to the appetite of Curio was one of the most daring and turbulent spirits in all Rome. Julius Caesar was looked upon as a man of tolerable courage in his day, notwithstanding the complaisance he showed in his youth to the King of Bithynia, Nicomedes, Aristotle, the inquisitive and observing Aristotle, whose physiological disquisitions are looked upon as some of the best of his works—Aristotle, who if there had been anything in this notion had every opportunity and inducement to notice and confirm it—gives no intimation of any such thing. On the contrary he sits down very soberly to distribute the male half of the species under two classes: one class having a natural propensity, he says, to bear a passive part in such a business, as the other have to take an active part. (*Probl.* Sect. 4 art. 27: The former of these propensities he attributes to a peculiarity of organization, analogous to that of women. The whole passage is abundantly obscure and shows in how imperfect a state of anatomical knowledge was his time. *J.B.*) This observation it must be confessed is not much more satisfactory than that other of the same philosopher when he speaks of two sorts of men—the one born to be masters, the other to be slaves. If however there had appeared any reason for supposing this practise, either with regard to the passive or the active part of it, to have had any remarkable effects in the way of debilitation upon those who were addicted to it, he would have hardly said so much / [194] upon the subject without taking notice of that circumstance.

Whether It Hurts Population?

A notion more obvious, but perhaps not much better founded than the former is that of its being prejudicial to population. Mr. Voltaire appears inclined in one part of his works to give some countenance to this opinion. He speaks of it as a vice which would be destructive to the human race if it were general. "How did it come about that a vice which would destroy mankind if it were general, that an infamous outrage against nature . . . ?" (*Questions sur l'Encyclop.* "Amour Socratique." *J.B.*)

A little further on, speaking of Sextus Empiricus who would have us believe that this practise was "recommended" in Persia by the laws, he insists that the effect of such a law would be to annihilate the human race if it were literally observed. "No", says he, "it is not in human nature to make a law that contradicts and outrages nature, a law that would annihilate mankind if it were observed to the letter." This consequence however is far enough from being a necessary one. For a law of the purport he represents to be observed, it is sufficient that this unprolific kind of venery be practised; it is not necessary that it should be practised to the exclusion of that which is prolific. Now that there should ever be wanting such a measure of the regular and ordinary inclination of desire for the proper object / as is necessary for keeping up the numbers of mankind upon their present footing is a notion that stands warranted by nothing that I can find in history. To consider the matter *a priori* [?], if we consult Mr. Hume and Dr. Smith, we shall find that it is not the strength of the inclination of the one sex for the other that is the measure of the numbers of mankind, but the quantity of subsistence which they can find or raise upon a given spot. With regard to the mere object of population, if we consider the time of gestation in the female sex we shall find that much less than a hundredth part of the activity a man is capable of exerting in this way is sufficient to produce all the effect that can be produced by ever so much more. Population therefore cannot suffer till the inclination of the male sex for the female be considerably less than a hundredth part as strong as for their own. Is there the least probability that [this] should ever be the case? I must confess I see not any thing that should lead us to suppose it. Before this can happen the nature of the human composition must receive a total change and that propensity which is commonly regarded as the only one of the two that is natural must have become altogether an unnatural one.

I have already observed that I can find nothing in history to countenance the notion I am examining. On the contrary the country in which the prevalence of this practise / is most conspicuous happens to have been remarkable for its populousness. The bent of popular prejudice has been to exaggerate this populousness: but after all deductions [are] made, still it will appear to have been remarkable. It was such as, notwithstanding the drain of continual wars in a country parcelled out into paltry states as to be all of it frontier, gave occasion to the continued necessity of emigration.

This reason however well grounded soever it were in itself could not with any degree of consistency be urged in a country where celibacy was permitted, much less where it was encouraged. The proposition which (as will be shown more fully by and by) is not at all true with respect to paederasty, I mean that were it to prevail universally it would put an end to the human race, is most evidently and strictly true with regard to celibacy. If then merely out of regard to population it were right that paederasts should be burnt alive, monks ought to be roasted alive by a slow fire. If a paederast, according to the monkish canonist Bermondus, destroys the whole human race Bermondus destroyed it I don't know how many thousand times over. The crime of Bermondus is I don't know how many times worse than paederasty. /

Whether It Robs Women

A more serious imputation for punishing this practise [is] that the effect of it is to produce in the male sex an indifference to the female, and thereby defraud the latter of their rights. This, as far as it holds good in point of fact, is in truth a serious imputation. The interest of the female part of the species claim just as much attention, and not a whit more, on the part of the legislator, as those of the male. A complaint of this sort, it is true, would not come with a very good grace from a modest woman; but should the woman be estopped from making complaint in such a case it is the business of the men to make it for them. This then as far as it holds good in point of fact is in truth a very serious imputation: how far it does it will be proper to enquire.

In all European countries and such others on which we bestow the title of civilized, this propensity, which in the male sex is under a considerable degree of restraint, is under an incomparably greater restraint in the female. While each is alike prohibited from partaking of these enjoyments but on the terms of marriage by the fluctuating and inefficacious influence of religion, the censure of the world denies it [to] the female part of the species under the severest penalties while the male sex is left free. No sooner is a woman known to have infringed this prohibition than either she is secluded from all means of repeating the offence, or upon her escaping from that vigilance she throws herself into that degraded class whom the want of company of their own sex render unhappy, and the abundance of it on the part of the male sex unprolific. This being the case, it appears the contribution which the male part of the species are willing as well as able to bestow is beyond all comparison greater than what the female part are permitted to receive. If a woman has a husband she is permitted to receive it only from her husband; if she has no husband she is not permitted to receive it from any man without being degraded into the class of prostitutes. When she is in that unhappy class she has not indeed less than she would wish, but what is often as bad to her—she has more.

It appears then that if the female sex are losers by the prevalence of this practise it can only be on this supposition—that the force with which it tends to divert men from entering into connection with the other sex is greater than the force with which the censure of the world tends to prevent those connections by its operation on the women. [196]

As long as things are upon that footing there are many cases in which the women can be no sufferers for the want of solicitation on the part of the men. If the institution of the marriage contract be a beneficial one, and if it be expedient that the observance of it should be maintained inviolate, we must in the first place deduct it from the number of the women who would be sufferers by the prevalence of this taste all married women whose husbands were not infected with it. In the next place, upon the supposition that a state of prostitution is not a happier state than a state of virginity, we must deduct all those women who by means of this prevalence would have escaped being debauched. The women who would be sufferers by it *ab initio* are those only who, were it not for the prevalence of it, would have got husbands.

The question then is reduced to this. What are the number of women who by the prevalence of this taste would, it is probable, be prevented from getting husbands? These and these only are they who would be sufferers by it. Upon the following considerations it does not seem likely that the prejudice sustained by the sex in this way could ever rise to any considerable amount. Were the prevalence of this taste to rise to ever so great a heighth the most considerable part of the motives to marriage would remain entire. In the first place, the desire of having children, in the next place the desire of forming alliances between families, thirdly the convenience of having a domestic companion whose company will continue to be agreeable throughout life, fourthly the convenience of gratifying the appetite in question at any time when the want occurs and without the expence and trouble of concealing it or the danger of a discovery.

Were a man's taste even so far corrupted as to make him prefer the embraces of a person of his own sex to those of a female, a connection of that preposterous kind would therefore be far enough from answering to him the purposes of a marriage. A connection with a woman may by accident be followed with disgust, but a connection of the other kind, a man must know, will for certain come in time to be followed by disgust. All the documents we have from the ancients relative to this matter, and we have a great abundance, agree in this, that it is only for a very few years of his life that a male continues an object of desire even to those in whom the infection of this taste is at the strongest. The very name it went by among the Greeks may stand instead of all other proofs, of which the works of Lucian and Martial alone will furnish any abundance that can be required. Among the Greeks it was called *Paederastia,* the love of boys, not *Andrerastia,* the love of men. Among the Romans the act was called *Paedicare* because the object of it was a boy. There was a particular name for those who had passed the short period beyond which no man hoped to be an object of desire to his own sex. They were called *exoleti.* No male therefore who was passed this short period of life could expect to find in this way any reciprocity of affection; he must be as odious to the boy from the beginning as in a short time the boy would be to him. The objects of this kind of sensuality would therefore come only in the place of common prostitutes; they could never even to a person of this depraved taste answer the purposes of a virtuous woman.

What says history?

Upon this footing stands the question when considered *a priori:* the evidence of facts seems to be still more conclusive on the same side. There seems no reason to doubt, as I have already observed but that population went on altogether as fast and that the men were altogether as well inclined to marriage among the Grecians in whom this vitious propensity was most prevalent as in any modern people in whom it is least prevalent. In Rome, indeed, about the time of the extinction of liberty we find great complaints of the decline of population: but the state of it does not appear to have been at all dependent on or at all influenced by the measures that were taken from time to time to restrain the love of boys: it was with the Romans, as with us, what kept a man from marriage was not the preferring boys to women but the preferring the convenience of a transient connection to the expense and hazard of a lasting one.

If it were more frequent than the regular connection in what sense could it be termed unnatural?

The nature of the question admits of great latitude of opinion: for my own part I must confess I cannot bring myself to entertain so high a notion of the alluringness of this preposterous propensity as some men appear to entertain. I cannot suppose it to [be] possible it should ever get to such a heighth as that the interests of the female part of the species should be materially affected by it: or that it could ever happen that were they to contend upon equal ground the eccentric and unnatural propensity should ever get the better of the regular and natural one. Could we for a moment suppose this to be the case, I would wish it to be considered what meaning a man would have to annex to the expression, when he bestows on the propensity under consideration the epithet of unnatural. If contrary to all appearance the case really were that if all men were left perfectly free to choose, as many men would make choice of their own sex as of the opposite one, I see not what reason there would be for applying the word natural to the one rather than to the other. All the difference would be that the one was both natural and necessary whereas the other was natural but not necessary. If the mere circumstance of its not being necessary were sufficient to warrant the terming it unnatural it might as well be said that the taste a man has for music is unnatural.

My wonder is how any man who is at all acquainted with the most amiable part of the species should ever entertain any serious apprehensions of their yielding the ascendent to such unworthy rivals.

Among the ancients—whether it excluded not the regular taste

A circumstance that contributes considerably to the alarms entertained by some people on this score is the common prejudice which supposes that the one propensity is exclusive of the other. This notion is for the most part founded on prejudice as may be seen in the works of a multitude of ancient authors in which we continually see the same person at one time stepping aside in pursuit of this eccentric kind of pleasure but at other times diverting his inclination to the proper object. Horace, in speaking of the means of satisfying the venereal appetite, proposes to himself as a matter of indifference a prostitute of either sex: and the same poet, who forgetting himself now and then says a little here and there about boys, says a great deal everywhere about women. The same observation will hold good with respect to every other personage of antiquity who either by his own account or that of another is represented to us as being infected with this taste. It is so in all the poets who in any of their works have occasion to say anything about themselves. Some few appear to have had no appetite for boys, as is the case for instance with Ovid, who takes express notice of it and gives a reason for it. But it is a never failing rule wherever you see any thing about boys, you see a great deal more about women. Virgil has one Alexis, but he has Galateas [blank] in abundance. Let us be unjust to no man: not even to a paederast. In all antiquity there is not a single instance of an author nor scarce an explicit account of any other man who was addicted exclusively to this taste. Even in modern times the real women-haters are to be found not so much among paederasts, as among monks and Catholic priests, such of them, be they more or fewer, who think and act in consistency with their profession.

Reason why it might be expected so to do

I say even in modern times; for there is one circumstance which should make this taste where it does prevail much more likely to be exclusive at present than it was formerly. I mean the severity with which it is now treated by the laws and the contempt and abhorrence with which it is regarded by the generality of the people. If we may so call it, the persecution they meet with from all quarters, whether deservedly or not, has the effect in this instance which persecution has and must have more or less in all instances, the effect of rendering those persons who are the objects of it more attached than they would otherwise be to the practise it proscribes. It renders them the more attached to one another, sympathy of itself having a powerful tendency, independent of all other motives, to attach a man to his own companions in misfortune. This sympathy has at the same time a powerful tendency to beget a proportionable antipathy even towards all such persons as appear to be involuntary, much more to such as appear to be the voluntary, authors of such misfortune. When a man is made to suffer it is enough on all other occasions to beget in him a prejudice against those by whose means or even for whose sake he is made to suffer. When the hand of every man is against a person, his hand, or his heart at least, will naturally be against every man. It would therefore be rather singular if under the present system of manners these outcasts of society should be altogether so well disposed towards women as in ancient times when they were left unmolested.

Whether, if it robbed women, it ought at all events to be punished?

The result of the whole is that there appears not any great reason to conclude that, by the utmost increase of which this vice is susceptible, the female part of the species could be sufferers to any very material amount. If however there was any danger of their being sufferers to any amount at all this would of itself be ample reason for wishing to restrain the practise. It would not however follow absolutely that it were right to make use of punishment for that purpose, much less that it were right to employ any of those very severe punishments which are commonly in use. It will not be right to employ any punishment, 1. if the mischief resulting from the punishment be equal or superior to the mischief of the offence, nor 2. if there be any means of compassing the same end without the expense of punishment. Punishment, says M. Beccaria, is never just so long as any means remain untried by which the end of punishment may be accomplished at a cheaper rate. [200c and 200d are blank]/ [201]

Inducements for punishing it not justified on the ground of mischievousness

When the punishment [is] so severe, while the mischief of the offence is so remote and even so problematical, one cannot but suspect that the inducements which govern are not the same with those which are avowed. When the idea of the mischievousness of an offence is the ground of punishing it, those of which the mischief is most immediate and obvious are punished first: afterwards little by little the legislator becomes sensible of the necessity of punishing those of which the mischief is less and less obvious. But in England this offence was punished with death before ever the malicious destruction or fraudulent obtainment or embezzlement of property was punished at all, unless the obligation of making pecuniary amends is to be called a punishment; before even the mutilation of or the perpetual disablement of a man was made punishable otherwise than by simple imprisonment and fine. (It was the custom to punish it with death so early as the reign of Ed. 1st.)

But on the ground of antipathy

In this case, in short, as in so many other cases the disposition to punish seems to have had no other ground than the antipathy with which persons who had punishment at their disposal regarded the offender. The circumstances from which this antipathy may have taken its rise may be worth enquiring to. 1. One is the physical antipathy to the offence. This circumstance indeed, were we to think and act consistently, would of itself be nothing to the purpose. The act is to the highest degree odious and disgusting, that is, not to the man who does it, for he does it only because it gives him pleasure, but to one who thinks [?] of it. Be it so, but what is that to him? He has the same reason for doing it that I have for avoiding it. A man loves carrion—this is very extraordinary—much good may it do him. But what is this to me so long as I can indulge myself with fresh meat? But such reasoning, however just, few persons have calmness to attend to. This propensity is much stronger than it is to be wished it were to confound physical impurity with moral. From a man's possessing a thorough aversion to a practise himself, the transition is but too natural to his wishing to see all others punished who give into it. Any pretense, however slight, which promises to warrant him in giving way to this intolerant propensity is eagerly embraced. Look the world over, we shall find that differences in point of taste and opinion are grounds of animosity as frequent and as violent as any opposition in point of interest. To disagree with our taste [and] to oppose our opinions is to wound our sympathetic feelings and to affront our pride. James the 1st of England, a man [more] remarkable for weakness than for cruelty, conceived a violent antipathy against certain persons who were called Anabaptists on account of their differing from him in regard to certain speculative points of religion. As the circumstances of the times were favorable to [the] gratification of antipathy arising from such causes, he found means to give himself the satisfaction of committing one of them to the flames. The same king happened to have an antipathy to the use of tobacco. But as the circumstances of the times did not afford the same pretenses nor the same facility for burning tobacco-smokers as for burning Anabaptists, he was forced to content himself with writing a flaming book against it. The same king, if he be the author of that first article of the works which bear his name, and which indeed were owned by him, reckons this practise among the few offences which no Sovereign ever ought to pardon. This must needs seems rather extraordinary to those who have a notion that a pardon in this case is what he himself, had he been a subject, might have stood in need of.

Philosophical pride

This transition from the idea of physical to that of moral antipathy is the more ready when the idea of pleasure, especially of intense pleasure, is connected with that of the act by which the antipathy is excited. Philosophical pride, to say nothing at present of superstition, has hitherto employed itself with effect in setting people a-quarreling with whatever is pleasurable even to themselves, and envy will always be disposing them to quarrel with what appears to be pleasurable to others. In the notions of a certain class of moralists we ought, not for any reason they are disposed to give for it, but merely because we ought, to set ourselves against every thing that recommends itself to us under the form of pleasure. Objects, it is true, the nature of which it is to afford us the highest pleasures we are susceptible of are apt in certain circumstances to occasion us still greater pains. But that is not the grievance: for if it were, the censure which is bestowed on the use of any such object would be proportioned to the probability that could be shewn in each case of its producing such greater pains. But that is not the case: it is not the pain that angers them but the pleasure.

How far the antipathy is a just ground

Meanwhile the antipathy, whatever it may arise from, produces in persons how many soever they be in whom it manifests itself, a particular kind of pain as often as the object by which the antipathy is excited presents itself to their thoughts. This pain, whenever it appears, is unquestionably to be placed to the account of the mischief of the offence, and this is one reason for the punishing of it. More than this—upon the view of any pain which these obnoxious persons are made to suffer, a pleasure results to those by whom the antipathy is entertained, and this pleasure affords an additional reason for the punishing of it. There remain however two reasons against punishing it. The antipathy in question (and the appetite of malevolence that results from it) as far as it is not warranted by the essential mischievousness of the offence is grounded only in prejudice. It may therefore be assuaged and reduced to such a measure as to be no longer painful only in bringing to view the considerations which shew it to be ill-grounded. The case is that of the accidental existence of an antipathy which [would have] no foundation [if] the principle of utility were to be admitted as a sufficient reason for gratifying it by the punishment of the object; in a word, if the propensity to punish were admitted in this or any case as a sufficient ground for punishing, one should never know where to stop. Upon monarchical principles, the Sovereign would be in the right to punish any man he did not like; upon popular principles, every man, or at least the majority of each community, would be in the right to punish every man upon no better reason.

If it were, so would heresy

If this were admitted we should be forced to admit the propriety of applying punishment, and that to any amount, to any offence for instance which the government should find a pleasure in comprising under the name of heresy. I see not, I must confess, how a Protestant, or any person who should be for looking upon this ground as a sufficient ground for burning paederasts, could with consistency condemn the Spaniards for burning Moors or the Portuguese for burning Jews: for no paederast can be more odious to a person of unpolluted taste than a Moor is to a Spaniard or a Jew to an orthodox Portuguese.

Note

1. Louis Compton, "Gay Genocide," in L. Crewe, *The Gay Academic* (Palm Springs, Calif.: ETC Publications, 1978).

25

Pathologizing Homosexuality

Robert B. Baker

What counts as madness? acting out? batty? bizarre? breaking down? cracked? crazy? daft? demented? depressed? deranged? erratic? frenzied? gaga? hysterical? idiotic? inane? insane? irrational? imbecile? jerky? kooky? lunatic? lulu? manic? melancholic? mentally ill? moronic? neurotic? nuts? off one's rocker? paranoid? possessed? psycho? psychotic? raving? schizoid? touched? unglued? wacky? weird? yo-yo? Shakespeare, through Polonius, suggests that the phenomenon is indefinable: "to define true madness, What is't but to be nothing else but mad?" (*Hamlet* 2.2.93–94). Yet Western law, medicine, philosophy, and sociology have attempted to define the elusive phenomenon of madness. This article introduces these various conceptions and comments on their implications for bioethics.

In traditional societies illness tends to be thought of in ethico-religious terms, as a punishment for a moral or a religious transgression: A "diagnosis" is a determination of the afflicted party's transgression; "treatment" involves atonement or prayer. Ethico-religious accounts of illnesses are common in the Hebrew Bible (e.g., 1 Kings 16). In the New Testament, however, Jesus replies to the question, "Rabbi, who hath sinned, this man or his parents, that he should be born blind?" by rejecting the ethico-religious association of illness with transgression: "Neither hath this man sinned, nor his parents" (John 9:1–3). In general, Christian societies have followed Jesus' precedent and accepted nonethico-religious conceptions of most disabilities and illnesses. Madness has tended to be an exception: Ethico-religious accounts of madness lingered into the sixteenth and seventeenth centuries. Thus the sixteenth-century physician Andrew Boorde (1490–1549), bishop of Chichester, discusses two kinds of

"Mental Illness: Conceptions of Mental Illness," by Robert B. Baker. Reprinted by permission of Macmillan Library Reference USA, a Simon & Schuster Co., from *Encyclopedia of Bioethics,* Rev. Edn., Warren T. Reich, Editor in Chief, Vol. 3, pp. 1731–43. Copyright © 1995 by Warren T. Reich.

madness, medical and ethico-religious: "When it is not illness, madness is named 'Demonici' . . . mad and possessed of the devyll or devylls. . . . This matter doth passe all manner of sickness and diseases" (Hunter and Macalpine, 1963, p. 12). Later in the same century another physician, Timothy Bright (ca. 1551–1615), published *A Treatise of Melancholie* (1586), the first English-language book on madness. Bright argued that melancholy and other forms of madness are afflictions of the brain, not of the soul. By the eighteenth century most educated people, and all physicians, treated madness as a form of illness.

Madness As Illness: The Hippocratic Model

The Western tradition of treating madness as illness is rooted in the Hippocratic Corpus, a collection of texts from the fifth, fourth, and third centuries B.C.E. written by physicians associated with the school of Hippocrates of Cos. According to the Hippocratics, diseases arise from an imbalance, or *dyscrasia*, of four basic humors: wetness, dryness, heat, and cold. In various passages, the writers expressly reject ethico-religious accounts of madness. The best known is the following: Men ought to know that from the brain, and from the brain only, arise our . . . pains, grief and tears. . . . It is the same thing which makes us mad or delirious. . . . These things that we suffer all come from the brain when it is not healthy, but becomes abnormally hot, cold, moist, or dry" ("On the Sacred Disease," in *Hippocrates,* vol. 2, p. 175; dates from the fifth century B.C.E.). Implicit in these few words is the following medical model of madness:
    1. Madness is a form of illness. Therefore, (a) it is a natural phenomenon, not a punishment for an ethico-religious transgression inflicted by "demonici," gods, or spirits; (b) no special stigma attaches to madness—it is not a fall from grace, but a physical state like "pain, grief and tears," and arises from "the brain alone"; (c) it is involuntary—people afflicted cannot control their actions; (d) those afflicted are sick and thus excused from normal obligations; (e) it is to be diagnosed and treated by physicians, not priests or shamans.
    2. The mad are patients. They enjoy the special protections provided for patients within the Hippocratic Corpus, and in all successive formulations of Western medical ethics. The best-known of these is the famous obligation stated in the Hippocratic oath to "use treatment to benefit the sick . . . but never with a view to injury or wrong-doing" (*Hippocrates,* vol. 1, p. 164).
    3. Madness is a symptom (an impairment of functionality) of a disease process (a dysfunction) internal to the organism. Thus the Hippocratics treat mad behavior as a symptom of an underlying dyscrasia of the humors within the brain.
    4. Madness, like other diseases, can be diagnosed in terms of its causes. In the Hippocratic Corpus there are several attempts to develop a comprehensive classi-

fication of illnesses (a nosology), based on their characteristic patterns of development (a course), their cause (etiology), or associated abnormalities (pathology).

Madness As Mental Illness

Initially, when the Hippocratics created the medical model of illness they extended it to madness, treating madness as just another symptom of dyscrasia, like a fever or a rash. They made no distinction whatsoever between physical and mental illness; all illness was biophysiological. For madness to be conceptualized as a different type of illness, as mental illness, medicine had to accept an entirely different worldview, one that accorded ontological status to minds as well as to bodies. Historically, the requisite dualistic metaphysic was supplied by René Descartes (1596–1650), through the agency of the philosopher-physician John Locke (1632–1704), who in turn influenced three other philosopher-physicians: William Battie (1703–1776), David Hartley (1705–1757) and, most important, Philippe Pinel (1745–1826). The second edition of Locke's *Essay Concerning Human Understanding* (1690, 1700) intrigued these three practicing physicians because it provided an elaborate account of mind and body as discrete but interacting substances, each operating under distinct principles.

Within Locke's framework "madness" could be explained as a symptom of physical pathology, or as an impairment to a conduit of body-mind interaction (caused, for example, by alcohol or some other neurotoxin), or, in a radical break with the Hippocratic tradition, as a disease of the mind itself, a mental illness—a misassociation of ideas or "passions." Locke's account of mental illness as confused ideas or passions derives from his empiricism (the hypothesis that the contents of the mind are ultimately derived from sensory experience). For if the entire contents of the mind derive from sensory experience, then it is reasonable to assume that disordered or deranged states of the mind are the product of disordering or traumatic experiences. Battie and Pinel, moreover, carried Locke's analysis one step further. They believed that it was possible to *reverse* the disordered ideas and passions of mad people. The reversal process, which they called "moral therapy," consisted of immersing the mad person in an orderly, pleasant, sedating environment in which "every unruly appetite [is] checked, every fixed imagination . . . diverted" (Battie, 1962, p. 69).

Eighteenth-century madhouses like Bedlam were the polar opposites of the ordered and pleasant environments required by moral therapy. Moral therapy called for peace, quiet, and order. But in eighteenth-century hospitals mad people lived in squalor and were often put on display to amuse "those who think it pastime to converse with madmen and to play upon their passions" (Battie, 1962, p. 69). Lockean moral therapists were thus forced to call for the radical reform of mental hospitals. Pinel became the symbolic leader of this reform in

October 1793 when he unchained a madman at Bicêtre Hospital in Paris. Sixty years later, on November 15, 1853, the first issue of *Asylum Journal* (still published as *Journal of Mental Science*) pronounced the Lockean reformers victorious: "From the time when Pinel obtained the permission . . . to try the humane experiment of releasing from fetters some of the insane citizens chained to the dungeon walls of Bicêtre, to the date when [Dr. John] Connolly announced, that in the vast asylum over which he presided, mechanical constraint in the treatment of the insane had been entirely abandoned, and superseded by moral influence, a new school of special medicine has been gradually forming" (Hunter and Macalpine, 1963, p. 1009). The "new school of special medicine" came to ascendancy a bit earlier in the United States, where, on October 16, 1844, thirteen asylum superintendents committed to moral therapy founded the American Association of Medical Superintendents, now known as the American Psychiatric Association.

The Evolution of Psychiatry

The struggle for moral therapy thus culminated in "a new school of medicine," one that treats madness as mental illness, and that ultimately called itself "psychiatry"—mind (*psyche*) healing (*iatria*). In retrospect it is amazing that psychiatry, or rather moral therapy, remained a branch of medicine. The eighteenth-century medical establishment was implacably hostile. The leading theorist of the period, Dr. William Cullen (1710–1790), professor of medicine at Edinburgh University, wrote two influential books, *First Lines in the Practice of Physic* (1784) and *Nosology* (1800), in which he classified madness as "neurosis," by which he meant a physical dysfunction of nerves, or "nervous breakdown" (both terms are Cullen's). Cullen held that there were four forms of neurosis: comata, adynamiae, spasmi, vesaniae. Vesaniae were subdivided into four categories, among them "insanity," derangement of the intellect: "Although this disease seems to be chiefly and sometimes solely an affection of the mind; yet the connection between mind and body in this life is such, that these affections of the mind must be considered as depending upon a certain state of our corporeal part" (Hunter and Macalpine, 1963, p. 476). By the "corporeal part," Cullen meant the nervous system, including the brain. Since he thought of neuroses as physiological conditions, he believed that any cure must also be physiological:

> Restraint, therefore, is useful and ought to be complete . . . the straight waist-coat answers every purpose better than any other that has thus been thought of. . . . Fear being a passion that diminishes excitement, may, therefore be opposed to the excess of it; and particularly to the angry and irascible excitement of maniacs . . . it appears to me to be commonly useful. In most cases it has

appeared to me to be necessary to employ a very common impression of fear; and therefore to inspire them with awe and dread . . . by one means or another . . . sometimes it may be necessary to acquire it even by stripes and blows. (Hunter and Macalpine, 1963, p. 475)

Cullen's enthusiasm for restraint inspired one of his American students, Benjamin Rush (1745–1813), to invent a totally immobilizing chair, "The Tranquilizer." In 1811 the Philadelphia Medical Museum proudly proclaimed "The Tranquilizer" a wonderful treatment for madness: "the most complete restraint of a patient's every movement ever devised" (Hunter and Macalpine, 1963, p. 671).

Restraint, immobilization, and other physical therapies were, as the Philadelphia Museum told the world, the practical corollaries of the advanced neurophysiological science of the day. Moral therapy, by contrast, seemed an atavistic reversion to ethico-religious conceptions of madness. Its leading proponents were religiously inspired humanitarian reformers: people like the Quaker merchant William Tuke (1732–1822), who had founded the York Retreat in 1796 to create "a quiet haven in which the shattered bark might find the means of reparation or safety" (Hunter and Macalpine, 1963, p. 685). Moral therapy was thus dismissed by physicians as misguided humanism. Pinel, however, set out to reclaim it as legitimate medicine. In 1785 he had translated the fourth edition of Cullen's *First Lines* into French, so he knew that Cullen was worried about the lack of empirical data supporting his neurophysiological account of madness. Cullen had written: "Although we cannot doubt that the operations of our intellect always depend on certain motions taking place in the brain . . . yet these motions have never been objects of our senses" (Hunter and Macalpine, 1963, pp. 476–77).

As a Lockean, Pinel did not believe that the operations of the intellect depend on motions in the brain, so he stood Cullen's observations on their head. In his *Traité médico-philosophique sur l'aliénation mentale* (1801), Pinel condemned as "error" the "supposition" that "derangement of the understanding is . . . an effect of an organic lesion of the brain." This supposition, he argued, is "contrary to anatomical fact" and should therefore be dismissed as nonempirical "prejudice" (Pinel, 1962, pp. 3–4). Cullen's physical restraints were also condemned as prejudice unsupported by empirical evidence. Hospitals practicing physical restraint considered their patients incurable and institutionalized them for life; however, hospitals practicing moral therapy were curing patients and returning them to their normal life. Thus, Pinel argued, a serendipitous, if inadvertent, natural experiment had been conducted, and "experience affords ample and daily proofs of the happier effect of a mild, conciliating treatment," that is, experience supports moral therapy, not physical restraint (Pinel, 1962, pp. 3–4).

Pinel's two examples of successful moral therapy, the York Retreat and Bicêtre, were both run by nonphysicians. So the evidence Pinel adduced to demonstrate the superior efficacy of moral therapy could also have been used to argue that nonphysicians, and nonmedical treatments, could effectively cure mad people. Pinel personally attested to the "expertise" of the superintendent at Bicêtre, Jean-Baptiste Pussin (1746–ca. 1809): "A man of great experience in the management of the insane . . . the advantages which I have derived from [his experience] will stamp a greater value on my observations in the present treatise. . . . For in diseases of the mind . . . it is an art of much greater and more difficult acquisition to know when to suspend [medicines] or altogether to omit them" (*Treatise*, 1962, p. 4). Yet it never seemed to occur to Pinel that if Pussin and Tuke were successfully treating mental derangement without medicine, the treatment of madness required no medical expertise and hence was not a medical matter. Pinel, in effect, accepted the traditional Hippocratic conception of madness as medical.

His theories are strikingly similar to Cullen's in *First Lines*, except that, instead of conceptualizing madness as a breakdown or derangement of nerves, Pinel conceived it as a derangement of ideas: Mental breakdown was substituted for nervous breakdown; psychopathology for neuropathology; and moral pacification for physical pacification. The parallelism left intact the assumptions about the medical model that Cullen inherited from the Hippocratics: Madness was still treated as an illness (albeit a mental illness) that bore no stigma and excused people from their normal responsibilities. As an illness, madness was properly diagnosed and treated only by physicians (not nonphysicians, like Pussin); mad people, moreover, were properly thought of as patients rather than citizens or clients. In other words, "moral therapy" as practiced by Pussin and Tuke could have been treated as a successful nonmedical model for dealing with madness. It is a precursor to such twentieth-century nonmedical models as "therapeutic communities" and "group therapy"—neither of which need involve physicians, or need use the concepts "illness," "disease," and "patient." Thus when Pinel invented psychiatry, he did not invent moral therapy: He reimposed a medical model on moral therapy, thereby inventing a psychiatric medical model of madness as "mental illness." . . .

The Antipsychiatric Critique of Mental Illness

"Antipsychiatry" is a term used to designate the views of historians (David Rothman), philosophers (Michel Foucault), psychiatrists (R. D. Laing, Thomas Szasz), and sociologists (Erving Goffman) who challenge one or more aspects of the psychiatric medical model of madness. Antipsychiatrists are united only by the object of their critique, not by any common ideology, methodology, or set of beliefs—except, perhaps, the critical spirit of the 1960s, the decade when most of their critiques were published. Foucault's methodology, for example, is "genealogy." Friedrich Nietzsche (1844–1900) pioneered the technique in *Towards a Genealogy of Morals* (1887) when he dug up the history of moral concepts to reveal their "real" nature. In *Folie et déraison* (1961, 1965) Foucault uses the genealogical method to "reveal" that psychiatry's outward humanism masks the Enlightenment's repressive intolerance of unreason, which it construed as "unchained animality [that] could be mastered only by discipline and brutalizing" (Foucault, 1965, pp. 74–75). Thus, in Foucault's analysis, Pinel sought to control unreason by imposing the "patient role" on mad people and by setting up physicians as warders: Pinel did not really unchain the mad, he merely exchanged their fetters, replacing physical manacles with "mind-forg'd manacles" (Porter, 1987, p. xi).

The British psychiatrist R. D. Laing developed an entirely different style of antipsychiatric critique. In the most accessible of his works, *The Politics of Experience* (1967), Laing argues that the phenomenon characterized as "schizophrenia" cannot be an illness because it is not dysfunctional. On the contrary, schizophrenia is really a coping strategy that helps people survive otherwise unlivable situations; it is a mechanism by which the psyche reconstitutes itself, and hence schizophrenia serves as a (frequently successful) form of self-therapy. Ironically, therefore, attempts at "therapeutic" intervention by traditional psychiatrists can actually disrupt the patient's self-curative process. (For a more detailed account see Laing, 1960.)

Thomas Szasz is the best-known American antipsychiatrist theorist. In a 1960 essay, "The Myth of Mental Illness," and in subsequent articles and books, he contrasts the patient-physician relationship in the Hippocratic and the Pinelian medical models. Drawing on Parsons's analysis of the sick role, Szasz points out that in the Hippocratic model, patients seek out physicians in the hope of finding relief from their illnesses. In a sense, therefore, when Hippocratic physicians treat their patients, they are applying their causal knowledge to satisfy the patient's values. On the Pinelian psychiatric model, however, it is often quite different. It is not the mad person who complains of being "sick" and seeks medical assistance; it is others in society who pronounce him or her "sick." Insofar as the pronounced party does not consider himself or herself to be "sick," however, the psychiatric label and any consequent "therapeutic" intervention really amount to others' imposing their values on the "mad" person. This is evident from the psychiatric diagnoses of previous eras. Looking back, it seems apparent that "masturbatory insanity" is really puritanism masquerading as medicine; similarly, Szasz contends, the diagnosis "sexual inversion" is really homophobia in medical guise. In each of these instances, what is nominally "therapy" is really a technique of repression (Baker, 1980; Szasz, 1970).

Szasz argues further that those imposing the sick role are not practicing scientific medicine. Medicine is scientific because its diagnoses rest on intersubjectively observable pathologies; thus a diagnosis of aneurysm or ulcer can be empirically confirmed by X-ray or postmortem examination. Physical illnesses, like diabetes, can be diagnosed even when they are asymptomatic. But there are no comparable diagnostic tests for mental illnesses. The psychopathology of other people's minds can never be intersubjectively observed; no one can examine anyone else's thought processes by X-ray or postmortem. Psychiatric diagnoses are thus incorrigible: There is no way of demonstrating that a psychiatric diagnosis is wrong. Scientific explanation, however, is always corrigible and subject to empirical disconfirmation. So, Szasz concludes, psychiatry is not a branch of scientific medicine.

Antipsychiatry was enormously influential in the 1960s and 1970s, decades concerned with civil rights and the empowerment of the oppressed. Reformers seeking to release the mentally ill from asylums and treat them in community programs appropriated the rhetoric of antipsychiatry. Antipsychiatric theory was also appropriated by psychologists, social workers, and others who sought to level a mental-health hierarchy dominated by psychiatrists. At the same time, mounting empirical evidence seemed to support the antipsychiatric analysis. Diaries from eastern Europe (e.g., Medvedev and Medvedev, 1971) revealed that Soviet psychiatrists were incarcerating dissidents in mental hospitals as "antisocial personalities"—corroborating the antipsychiatric charge that "mental illness" merely served as a myth to justify the incarceration of social undesirables. In America, David Rosenhan's "On Being Sane in Insane Places" (1973) cast further doubt on the scientific status of psychiatric diagnosis. Rosenhan's experiment tested "labeling theory," the theory that a psychiatric diagnostic label, once applied, tends to stick, even without supporting symptoms (Scheff, 1963; Goffman, 1961). Rosenhan had eight colleagues pose as "pseudo patients" who falsely reported hearing an unclear voice that seemed to say "empty," "hollow," and "thud." Upon admission to hospital, however, the pseudo patients ceased reporting these symptoms. Nonetheless, their hospitalization continued—on average for almost three weeks. Thus, just as the antipsychiatrists contended, psychiatric diagnoses seem to be unconfirmable stigmatizing labels, empty of empirical content.

Although a younger generation continues the critique (Cohen, 1990), antipsychiatry has lost much of its sting. Roy Porter and other historians have challenged Foucault's genealogies. Foucault contends that "sequestering the mad was basically an act of anathematization and quarantine. But [Porter argues] the ideology and expectations typically found in England, from Bedlam to the ritziest asylum, principally endorsed curability—incidentally explaining why *separate* institutions for incurables were set up" (Porter, 1987, p. 280). Even as historians were rethinking the antipsychiatric portrait of psychiatry's past, problems were becoming evident in the present. Antipsychiatrists rejected the insanity defense and had joined with civil libertarians to urge tightening the rules for involuntary commitment to mental institutions. They argued that a diagnosis of mental illness should not provide sufficient grounds for involuntary commitment. Persons deemed mentally ill should be committed to a hospital, against their wishes, only if there was also a legal determination that they posed a danger to themselves or to others.

These reforms were adopted and, throughout the Western world, the walls of the asylums came tumbling down. Thousands of involuntarily committed mentally ill people were found to have been illegally institutionalized and were discharged into their communities. The results were not as beneficial as antipsychiatrists had predicted. Once patients left the hospital, they were free: free of therapeutic supervision, free not to report to clinics for therapy, free not to take their medications. Deinstitutionalized patients availed themselves of these freedoms and consequently tended to become symptomatic, and hence problems for their communities. More tragically still, former mental patients were often unable to cope with the outside world. They swelled the ranks of the homeless and became easy targets for criminals. Ironically, one of the primary effects of deinstitutionalization was to reinvigorate Tuke's moral therapeutic ideal of the asylum as a "quiet haven," a refuge from the world for mad people (Scull, 1977, 1984).

In large measure, however, the antipsychiatric critique lost its sting because the American psychiatric profession appropriated it and used it as a basis for revising its diagnostic and statistical manuals. To appreciate how this came about, it is helpful to reflect on Szasz's critique and the general problem of developing a reliable system of valid psychiatric diagnoses, a nosology.

The Validity of Psychiatric Nosology

Szasz challenges the validity of psychiatric diagnoses on two primary grounds: that they are value-laden, and that they are immune to empirical disconfirmation. Although the first challenge may disturb those who subscribe to the ideal of objective, value-free medicine, contemporary philosophers, in a rare display of unanimity, concur with Szasz's analysis. They are just as unanimous, however, in rejecting Szasz's conclusion: that the mere presence of values invalidates diagnoses. The consensus of philosophical opinion is that all diagnoses are indelibly value-laden (Peset and Gracia, 1992). H. Tristram Engelhardt (1974) believes that medicine (not merely psychiatry) is the systematic deployment of science to eliminate physical or psychological conditions that someone dislikes and therefore dubs "illness." Christopher Boorse (1975) takes the opposite view: "Illness" is systematically incapacitating disease; "disease" is a deviation from the natural or normal functional organization of an individual, or of organic subsystems; these natural functions, in turn, are those designed to ensure the "apical goals" of survival and reproduction. Apical goals, according to Boorse, are the "empirically determined" values of evolutionary survival.

Robert Baker (1978, 1980) argues for a position midway between Engelhardt's entirely subjective conception of illness and Boorse's functionalist analysis. He agrees that all diagnoses contain values, but he denies that every value can be medicalized as a diagnosis. Medicine is a public art; its nosologies aspire to a common diagnostic language. Consequently a disvalued condition can be designated a "symptom" of an "illness" only if: (1) it is potentially incapacitating; (2) the condition is involuntary (an incapacity rather than a choice); and (3) there is a reliable way for practitioners to recognize this condition and its course (its standard pattern of development). Medical nosologies, moreover, classify diseases in terms of underlying causal pathologies. Therefore (4) any characterization of a condition as a "symptom" is effectively an empirically testable causal claim about pathology that, therefore, (5) presupposes a theory of pathology and consequently a theory of normal functionality.

All three of these philosophical positions undercut Szasz's claim that psychiatric diagnoses are invalid because they are value-laden. Consider again the contrast Szasz draws between the supposedly valid diagnosis of diabetes and two "mythical" mental illnesses, masturbatory insanity and homosexuality (or sexual inversion). Engelhardt would agree with Szasz that the diagnoses "masturbatory insanity" and "homosexuality" reflect puritanical social values. In his analysis, however, "diabetes" is also value-laden, since comas violate the Puritan work ethic just as surely as masturbation does. Boorse, in contrast, holds that determinations of illnesses depend on the empirical fact of incapacitation. Insofar as diabetes is typically incapacitating, while homosexuality and masturbation are not, the former is an illness and the latter two are not. Diabetes and homosexuality, however, are both diseases since both are abnormal deviations from the functional norms for organ systems and individuals. On Boorse's account, therefore, Szasz is wrong in arguing that homosexuality is not a disease. It is a disease, even though it is not an illness. However, because homosexuality is not an illness, neither homosexuals nor psychiatrists have a good reason to pursue treatment.

Baker holds that diabetes is a paradigm case of a disease (an incapacitating, diagnosable dysfunction with a clear pathology), and that masturbatory insanity is neither an illness nor a disease, since it is not involuntary, incapacitating, or associated with any pathology. Homosexuality's status is uncertain at present. Whether it is a disease will depend upon whether the condition can be shown to be avolitional, and whether it can be linked to a clear pathology (for example, an atypical gene, like Xq28). Even if these two conditions were to be satisfied, however, homosexuality, like any other illness, would be an illness only if homosexuals found their condition undesirable. Thus although Baker, unlike Boorse and Engelhardt, believes that the status of homosexuality remains open, he, too, states that the presence of values in the diagnosis does not undermine its validity. On this point these three representative philosophers agree: The presence of values in psychiatric diagnoses renders psychiatry neither more nor less problematic than other forms of medicine—all diagnoses are informed by values.

Szasz's second line of critique, however, focuses on an area of real vulnerability: the empirical validation of the psychiatric model. Pinel had established the idea of madness as mental illness in the context of an empiricist critique of Cullen's neurophysiological model. The argument over which model of madness, mental or neurophysiological, is validated by empirical evidence has been raging ever since. Pinel's student Jean-Étienne Dominique Esquirol (1772–1840) published a psychiatric nosology in 1838, and Emil Kraepelin (1856–1926) published his neurophysiologically inclined *Lehrbuch* in 1883; for a while both vied for the honor of being accepted as the psychiatric standard. Kraepelin's neurophysiological nosology appeared to win, but was then supplanted by the psychopathological nosology of Sigmund Freud (1856–1939). Like Pinel, Freud believed both that madness is a form of mental illness and that any psychopathological nosology must be empirically validated by therapeutic success.

Freud and Pinel part company only with respect to their theories of mind and, consequently, their conceptions of psychopathology and treatment. Pinel, like his mentor Locke, had envisioned an entirely conscious mind governed by laws of association. Freud posited an unconscious mind with different components whose interactions change as a person matures. The resulting psychodynamic model offers rich possibilities for psychopathology and psychotherapy, so Freudian nosology rapidly eclipsed those of Esquirol and Kraepelin. Unlike Pinel's moral therapy, however, no one empirically established the superior curative efficacy of Freudian therapy. Psychodynamic models and therapeutic techniques became standard in psychiatry by virtue of their theoretical richness, not on the basis of empirical validation. They are thus vulnerable to the charge, not only from antipsychiatrists but also from respected philosophers of science (for example, Grünbaum, 1984), that they lack empirical validity.

Reliability and the Creation of Standard Psychiatric Nosologies (DSM, ICD)

Diagnoses, nosologies, and the issues surrounding them are important to anyone attempting to count, to analyze, to indemnify, or to do research on illness. They are thus crucial not only to practitioners but also to census bureaus, to statisticians, to insurance companies, and to scientists. All of these parties would prefer to work with valid diagnoses, but they appreciate that validity is elusive. At a minimum, however, they need to work with reliable diagnoses. The difference between *validity* and *reliability* is as follows: A diagnosis is *valid* to the extent that it accurately differentiates one form of illness from another; a diagnosis is *reliable* to the extent that different practitioners will diagnose identical cases in the same way. If a diagnosis is unreliable, it cannot be valid; it is, moreover, useless for all administrative, therapeutic, or research purposes. In the 1890s various international committees recognized that reliability is a prelude to validity and tried to develop a single, universal standard list of causes of death.

In the 1920s the League of Nations began to publish a standard international nosology, and the task was continued by the World Health Organization (WHO). The first *International List of Causes of Death* (ICD-1) excluded mental illnesses because they are not significant causes of death. In 1948, however, the WHO expanded its list to include all diseases and disorders, and began to list mental disorders in the section "Diseases of the Nervous System and Sense Organs." As the title indicates, the 1948 ICD nosology was neurophysiological; so was the revised list issued in 1955. By the 1950s, however, almost all psychiatric practitioners were using psychodynamic diagnoses. To remedy the situation, in 1952 the American Psychiatric Association (APA) played Pinel to the WHO's Cullen, and produced its *Diagnostic and Statistical Manual* (DSM-I) based on commonly used psychodynamic diagnoses. The manual was updated in 1968 (DSM-II). The WHO introduced psychodynamic concepts into ICD-9 (1977). By the end of the 1970s there were thus two "official" psychiatric nosologies, DSM-II and ICD-9.

Both DSM-II and ICD-9 were criticized by gay activists for classifying homosexuality as a sexual abnormality. ICD-9, for example, classifies homosexuality as a sexual deviation because "[S]exual activity directed primarily towards people not of the opposite sex" cannot "serve approved social and biological purposes" (WHO, 1977, 302.0). This explanation presumes (as Engelhardt does) that society can stigmatize what it disapproves as a "disorder," and presupposes (as Boorse does) that the function of sexual intercourse is procreation, not recreation, not bonding, not even expressing love. Since homosexual intercourse is neither socially approved nor procreative, it follows that it is dysfunctional. DSM-II, while not as blatantly judgmental, also listed homosexuality as a disorder. Gay psychiatrists contested these classifications, protesting that since their homosexuality did not impair their functionality, that is, their ability to function in the world, they could not be sick. Their protests attracted the attention of psychiatrist Robert Spitzer, one of the authors of DSM-II and a member of the committee revising the DSM nosology, who subsequently proposed a new diagnosis to the Nomenclature Committee, "sexual orientation disturbance." If a homosexual was disturbed by his or her sexual orientation to the point that it impaired his or her ability to function, he or she suffered "sexual orientation disturbance," otherwise not (Bayer, 1981; note the similarity to Baker's analysis). In 1973 the APA's trustees approved the diagnosis, acting on a vote of the members: 58 percent in favor, 37 percent against.

DSM-III and DSM-III-R

Spitzer's successful resolution of the debate over homosexuality inspired the strategy that guided the creation of DSM-III and its revision, DSM-III-R. He had resolved the debate not by arguing over the value-laden question of the function of sexual intercourse but by focusing on the empirical questions of functionality: Can homosexuals function well in our society? Answering yes (provided they themselves are not disturbed by their sexual orientation), he concluded that homosexuality per se is not a disorder. In DSM-III and III-R this solution is generalized to all diagnoses in an attempt to resolve the perpetual nosological disputes between the neurophysiological, psychopathological, and behavioral theories of madness that had vexed psychiatry since its founding in the eighteenth century.

[1] In DSM-III-R each of the mental disorders is conceptualized as a clinically significant behavioral or psychological syndrome or pattern that occurs in a person and is associated with present distress (impairment in one or more important areas of functioning) or with a significantly increased risk of suffering death, pain, disability, or an important loss of freedom. [2] In addition, this syndrome or pattern must not be an expectable response to a particular event, e.g., the death of a loved one. [3] Whatever its original cause, it must currently be considered a manifestation of behavioral, psychological, or biological dysfunction in the person. [4] Neither deviant behavior, e.g., political, religious, or sexual, nor conflicts that are primarily between the individual and society are mental disorders, unless the deviance or conflict is a symptom of a dysfunction in the person, as described above. (American Psychiatric Association, 1987, p. xxii [numbers added])

In this passage the DSM declares its ideological neutrality by the condescending ecumenism of [3] that relegates the three classic accounts of madness, 'behavioral, psychological, or biological dysfunction," to mere "consider[ations]." Point [1] in contrast, declares the DSM's new approach: "Disorders" are to be defined exclusively in terms of observable behaviors—"distress (impairment in . . . functioning) or . . . increased risk of suffering death, pain, disability or . . . loss of freedom."

The DSM-III definition not only attempts to pacify disputes between different schools of psychiatry, it also responds directly to the antipsychiatric critique. Point [4] explicitly lists, and expressly excludes, the abuses that the antipsychiatric critics had documented. Strictly speaking, this list is redundant because the medicalization of political, religious, and sexual conflicts between individuals and society are ruled out by the criteria set forth in [1]; that is, unless a person is distressed, incapable of functioning, or at increased risk of death, he or she cannot be diagnosed as ill by DSM-III-R criteria, however distasteful a society finds her or his politics, religion, or sexual orientation. Yet Szasz and other critics of psychiatry had documented the abuses of psychiatry so effectively that redundancy must have appeared more prudent than elegant. Thus, although [1] effectively appropriates the antipsychiatric critique, [4] explicitly accommodates it.

DSM-III and its successor, DSM-III-R, thus defuse the major external criticisms of psychiatry while rendering quiescent, at the nosological level, the theoretical disputes that previously had divided the profession. It answered the need of its time, providing a theory-neutral, externally observable, nonrepressive, seemingly reliable nosology; it currently enjoys worldwide acceptance by psychologists and psychiatrists of all schools of thought.

Despite their undeniable successes, DSM-III and III-R are not without problems. One of the factors that motivated the revision of DSM-II was that empirical researchers, of all theoretical stripes, had found DSM-II's diagnostic categories unreliable (Kirk and Kutchins, 1992). Spitzer was one of the first to appreciate the gravity of these findings: "The validity, i.e., the usefulness, of a classification system is limited by its reliability. Therefore, to the extent that a classification system of psychiatric disorders is unreliable, a limit is placed on its validity for any clinical research or administrative use" (Spitzer et al., 1975, pp. 210–211). To resolve the problem of reliability, Spitzer devised a standardized "checklist" system of diagnosis, which was used extensively in DSM-III and then revised, after extensive field testing, for DSM-III-R. Nonetheless, psychiatrists and other professionals still found the diagnostic checklists difficult to use. Stuart Kirk and Herb Kutchins have analyzed all published empirical studies of the reliability of DSM-III and DSM-III-R diagnoses and concluded that they are no more reliable than their predecessor, DSM-II. Since Spitzer had claimed that DSM-II was so unreliable that it verged on uselessness, they argue that the same thing can be said of DSM-III.

Other critics urge a return to traditional nosological patterns of classification in DSM-II and ICD-9. This argument is usually parsed as the claim that DSM-III and DSM-III-R sacrifice validity to reliability (Eysenck, 1986; Kirk and Kutchins, 1992; Wakefield, 1992a, 1992b). These appeals to "validity" are odd because no one—not Cullen, not Pinel, not Esquirol, not Kraepelin, not Freud—has developed an empirically validated theory of physiopathology or psychopathology. What they did, however, was offer theoretically grounded diagnoses that made intuitive sense to those familiar with their theories. DSM-III and its successors take an atheoretical stance on diagnosis and thus deliberately sacrifice the intuitive clarity that these theories provide. Whether the sacrifice is worthwhile will depend upon whether DSM-IV generates reliable diagnoses.

Bioethical Implications

Ethics presupposes conflict. In the absence of any possibility of conflict, there is no need for ethics. As a rich source of potential conflicts between, on the one hand, patients' desires, goals, interests, and values, and, on the other hand, physicians' therapeutic goals, entrepreneurial interests, and traditional values, the patient-physician encounter has inspired an equally rich body of ethics. Most of the conflicts dealt with in medical ethics are unmistakable. We may not know the proper way to deal with a Jehovah's Witness who refuses a lifesaving blood transfusion, we may not know how to respond to the dying cancer patient who requests assisted suicide, or to the family of a patient in a persistent and irreversible vegetative state who, nonetheless, assert the patient's "right" to the last bed in the intensive-care unit (knowing that to do so will deprive other, potentially curable, patients of a bed); but in each of these cases, we know, unmistakably, that we are caught up in a conflict. Psychiatric ethics is no different. We may not know how to deal with a patient's declaration of an intent to kill some innocent third party, but the conflict between the duty to protect patient confidentiality and duty to warn an innocent third party is unmistakable.

Psychiatric diagnoses, however, have the insidious property of anesthetizing our sense of conflict; they tend to disguise moral issues in medical terminology. Masturbation, for example, is considered sinful by the three great Middle Eastern religions: Christianity, Islam, and Judaism. The practice is a battleground between the sacred spark religion finds in the human body and the profane uses to which real people put their bodies. The conflict between sacred and profane conceptions of the body, however, is unmistakably that: a conflict. When Freud and other psychiatrists medicalized the sin of onanism (named for Onan, whom God condemned for spilling his seed on the ground; Gen. 38:9), it dulled our sense of conflicting values. Masturbation was no longer condemned as sinful; it was a disease called onanism. Benjamin Rush used "The Tranquilizer" on masturbators; later physicians sometimes recommended surgery, including scarification of the penis and clitoridectomies—removal of the clitoris (see Barker-Benfield, 1976, for details). It is easy to look askance, and even in anger, at the extremity of these treatments. The more subtle point to appreciate, however, is that only the creation of a diagnosis, only medicalization, made these extreme measures permissible. No eighteenth-, nineteenth-, or twentieth-century Western religion claimed the right to immobilize a masturbator, or to scarify his penis, or to remove her clitoris, or to commit her or him to an institution, or even to require counseling. Only medicine could exercise this kind of power; individuals and society would tolerate these treatments only in the name of therapy.

This article has used the genealogical method, not to delegitimate psychiatry (as Foucault and Szasz have attempted to do) but to illuminate the extent to which psychiatric diagnoses encapsulate values, and to suggest how medicalization desensitizes ethical concerns. Most classical nosologists (Cullen, Esquirol, Freud, Kraepelin, Pinel) treated psychiatric diagnoses as objective and value-free; contemporary analysts and nosologists (APA, Baker, Boorse, Engelhardt, Foucault, Parsons, Porter, Spitzer, Szasz, WHO) appreciate that values play an inextricable role in diagnosis. Once the role of values is recognized, we must face the question of how best to handle the value conflicts inherent in psychiatric diagnoses. Do we avoid conflicts by abolishing psychiatric diagnoses altogether, as Szasz recommends? Do we presume that society's values ought properly to prevail over those of the individual, as the WHO appears to do in ICD-9? Or do we bring these conflicts to the surface and attempt to accommodate a compromise between individual and societal values, as the APA attempted to do in DSM-III and III-R? Or is some other form of resolution possible?

References and Bibliography

Adams, David. 1992. *Philosophical Problems in the Law.* Belmont, Calif.: Wadsworth. A particularly accessible, well-edited introduction to the philosophy of law.

American Law Institute. 1957. Model Penal Code: *Reprint. Tentative Drafts Nos. 5, 6, and 7.* Philadelphia: Author.

American Psychiatric Association. 1952, 1968, 1980, 1987. *Diagnostic and Statistical Manual of Mental Disorders.* Washington, D.C.: Author. 1st—rev. 3d eds., referred to as DSM-I, DSM-II, DSM-III, and DSM-III-R. Internationally recognized standard classifications of mental disorders. DSM-IV was published in 1994.

Baker, Robert. 1978. "Mental Illness: Conceptions of Mental Illness." In *Encyclopedia of Bioethics,* vol. 3, pp. 1090–97. Edited by Warren Reich. New York: Free Press, Macmillan.

———. 1980. "Thomas Szasz, Founder of the Philosophy of Psychiatry." In *Proceedings of Asclepius at Syracuse: Thomas Szasz, Libertarian Humanist,* vol. 1, pp. 292–313. Edited by M. F. Grenander. Albany: Institute for Humanistic Studies, State University of New York.

Barker-Benfield, G. J. 1976. *The Horrors of the Half-Known Life: Male Attitudes toward Women and Sexuality in Nineteenth-Century America.* New York: Harper & Row.

Battie, William. 1962. [1758]. *A Treatise on Madness.* Facsimile edited by Richard Hunter and Ida Macalpine. Psychiatric Monograph series, no. 3. London: Dawson's. 1st ed. London: Whiston and White.

Bayer, Ronald. 1987. [1981]. *Homosexuality and American Psychiatry: The Politics of Diagnosis.* Princeton, N.J.: Princeton University Press. The definitive account of the American Psychiatric Association's decision that homosexuality is not a disorder.

Benedict, Ruth. 1966. "Anthropology and the Abnormal." In *Issues and Problems in Social Psychiatry,* pp. 17–38. Edited by Bernard J. Bergen and Claudewell S. Thomas. Springfield, Ill.: Charles C. Thomas. The standard account of the cultural variability of "abnormality."

Boorse, Christopher. 1975. "On the Distinction between Disease and Illness." *Philosophy and Public Affairs* 5, no. 1:49–68.

Bynum, William F. 1985. "The Nervous Patient in Eighteenth- and Nineteenth-Century Britain: The Psychiatric Origins of British Neurology." In *The Anatomy of Madness,* vol. 1, *People and Ideas,* pp. 89–102. Edited by William F. Bynum, Roy Porter, and Michael Shepard. London: Tavistock. An overview of the development of neurological models of madness, in an excellent two-volume collection of recent work by historians of psychiatry.

Caplan, Arthur L., H. Tristam Engelhardt Jr., and James J. McCartney, eds. 1981. *Concepts of Health and Disease: Interdisciplinary Perspectives.* Reading, Mass.: Addison-Wesley. A collection of some of the best essays in the philosophy of medicine.

Cohen, D., ed. 1990. "Challenging the Therapeutic State: Critical Perspectives on Psychiatry and the Mental Health System." *Journal of Mind and Behavior* 11, nos. 3–4. Special Issue.

Durham v. *United States.* 1954. 214 F. 2d 862.

Engelhardt, H. Tristram Jr. 1974. "The Disease of Masturbation: Values and the Concept of Disease." *Bulletin of the History of Medicine* 48, no. 2: 234–48.

Eysenck, Hans Jurgen. 1986. "A Critique of Contemporary Classification and Diagnosis." In *Contemporary Directions in Psychopathology: Toward the DSM-IV,* pp. 73–98. Edited by Theodore Millon and Gerald L. Klerman. New York: Guilford.

Foucault, Michel. 1961. *Folie et déraison: Histoire de la folie à l'âge classique.* Paris: Librairie Plon. Translated by Richard Howard as *Madness and Civilization: A History of Insanity in the Age of Reason.* New York: Pantheon Books, 1965. A compelling antipsychiatric genealogical study of the birth of psychiatry.

Goffman, Erving. 1961. *Asylums: Essays on the Social Institution of Mental Patients and Other Inmates.* Garden City, N.Y.: Doubleday.

Grünbaum, Adolph. 1984. *The Foundations of Psychoanalysis: A Philosophical Critique.*

Berkeley: University of California Press. A comprehensive analysis of the logical and episte-mological foundations of psychoanalysis by a famous philosopher of science.

Hart, Herbert L. A. 1961. *The Concept of Law.* Oxford: At the Clarendon Press. A classic study.

Hippocrates. 1923–1931. *Hippocrates: Collected Works.* 4 vols. Translated by W. H. S. Jones. Loeb Classical Library. New York: G. P. Putnam's Sons.

Hunter, Richard, and Ida Macalpine. 1963. *Three Hundred Years of Psychiatry, 1535–1860.* London: Oxford University Press. A wonderful documentary history designed to introduce readers to psychiatry before Freud.

Kirk, Stuart A., and Herb Kutchins. 1992. *The Selling of DSM: The Rhetoric of Science in Psychiatry.* New York: Aldine de Gruyter. A sociological critique of DSM-III.

Laing, Ronald David. 1960. *The Divided Self: An Existential Study of Sanity and Madness.* London: Tavistock. New York: Pantheon, 1969.

———. 1967. *The Politics of Experience.* New York: Pantheon.

Langland, William. 1886. [1380]. *The Vision of William Concerning Piers the Plowman.* Edited by W. W. Skeat. Early English Text Society. London: Oxford University Press.

Medvedev, Zhores, and Roy Medvedev. 1971. *A Question of Madness.* London: Macmillan.

Offer, Daniel, and Melvin Sabshin. 1966. *Normality: Theoretical and Clinical Concepts of Mental Health.* New York: Basic Books. A classic study of "normality."

Parsons, Talcott. 1951. *The Social System.* Glencoe, Ill.: Free Press. Still the foundation for the sociological study of illness; see especially pp. 428–79.

———. 1958. "Definitions of Health and Illness in the Light of American Values and Social Structure." In *Patients, Physicians and Illness: A Sourcebook in Behavioral Science and Health,* pp. 165–87. Edited by E. Gartly Jaco. Glencoe, Ill.: Free Press.

Peset, José, and Diego Gracia, eds. 1992. *The Ethics of Diagnosis.* Dordrecht, Netherlands: Kluwer Academic. A comprehensive overview of the role of values in diagnosis.

Percival, Thomas. 1985. [1803]. *Medical Ethics; or, A Code of Institutes and Precepts, Adapted to the Professional Conduct of Physicians and Surgeons.* Manchester: S. Russell for J. Johnson and R. Bickerstaff. Facsimile reissue, with an introduction by Edmund D. Pellegrino. Birmingham, Ala.: Classics of Medicine Library.

Pinel, Philippe. 1801. *Traité médico-philosophique sur l'aliénation mentale, ou la manie.* Paris: Richard. Translated by David P. Davis as *A Treatise on Insanity, in Which Are Contained the Principles of a New and More Practical Nosology of Maniacal Disorders Than Has Yet Been Offered to the Public.* London: Cadell and Davis, 1806. Facsimile edition, New York Academy of Medicine, History of Medicine Series, no. 14. New York: Hafner, 1962.

Porter, Roy. 1987. *Mind-Forg'd Manacles: A History of Madness in England from the Restoration to the Regency.* Cambridge, Mass.: Harvard University Press. A well-written, historiographically sensitive history of Enlightenment psychiatry that challenges antipsychiatric genealogies.

Rosenhan, David. 1973. "On Being Sane in Insane Places." *Science* 179, no. 7: 250–58. A frequently cited, insightful, and frightening study of psychiatric diagnosis as labeling.

Rothman, David J. 1971. *The Discovery of the Asylum: Social Order and Disorder in the New Republic.* Boston: Little, Brown. A well-researched antipsychiatric history of asylums.

Scheff, Thomas J. 1963. "The Role of the Mentally Ill and the Dynamics of Mental Disorder: A Research Framework." *Sociometry* 26, no. 4: 436–53. A classic statement of labeling theory.

Scull, Andrew T. 1977. *Decarceration.* Englewood Cliffs, N.J.: Prentice-Hall. 2d ed. Cambridge: Oxford Polity Press, 1984. A definitive study of deinstitutionalization's failures.

Spitzer, Robert L., Jean Endicott, and Eli Robins. 1975. "Clinical Criteria of Psychiatric Diagnosis and DSM-III." *American Journal of Psychiatry* 132, no. 11: 1187–92.

Szasz, Thomas S. 1960. "The Myth of Mental Illness." *American Psychologist* 15: 113–18.

———. 1970. *The Manufacture of Madness: A Comparative Study of the Inquisition and the Mental Health Movement.* New York: Harper & Row.

Wakefield, Jerome C. 1992a. "The Concept of Mental Disorder: On the Boundary between Biological Facts and Social Values." *American Psychologist* 47, no. 3: 373–88.

Wakefield, Jerome C. 1992b. "Disorder as Harmful Dysfunction: A Conceptual Critique of DSM-III-R's Definition of Mental Disorder." *Psychological Review* 99, no. 2: 232–47. This and the preceding item are exceptionally insightful analyses of DSM-III and DSM-III-R.

Wasserstrom, Richard A. 1980. "The Therapeutic Model." In *Philosophical Problems in the Law,* pp. 493–98. Edited by David M. Adams. Belmont, Calif.: Wadsworth.

World Health Organization. 1939. Manual *of the International List of Causes of Death.* 5th rev. Geneva: Author.

————. 1948, 1955, 1969, 1977. *Manual of the International Statistical Classification of Diseases, Injuries and Causes of Death.* 6th, 7th, 8th, and 9th revs. Geneva: Author. Referred to as ICD, this classificatory scheme rivals DSM; ICD-9 classifies homosexuality as a mental disorder.

26

Essentialism and Constructionism in Sexual Orientation

Edward Stein

I. Introduction

In the past several years, scientific research on human sexual orientation—in particular, research that claims male homosexuality is innate—has garnered a great deal of attention among scientists and the general public. Although research of this sort has been ongoing for over one hundred years (Bullough, 1994), its current popularity stems from Simon LeVay's neuroanatomical research (LeVay, 1992) and two genetic studies (Bailey and Pillard, 1991; Hamer, et al., 1993). Although some have criticized this scientific approach (see, for example, Byne and Parsons, 1993, and Fausto-Sterling, 1992), most scientists doing work on sexual orientation claim that there is strong support for the view that sexual orientations are innate, very difficult to change, and come in two or three flavors (heterosexual, homosexual, and perhaps bisexual).

At the same time as this scientific paradigm for thinking about sexual orientation has been emerging, lesbian and gay studies, a new interdisciplinary field, has developed within the humanities and some of the social sciences (see Abelove et al., 1993). Within lesbian and gay studies, the reigning but not uncontested paradigm (see, for example, Boswell, 1982–83, and Mohr, 1992) for thinking about sexual orientation is constructionism, a view with roots in the work of Michel Foucault (1978) and in various approaches to sociology (for example, McIntosh, 1968). Constructionism about sexual orientation emphasizes the historical and cultural contingencies of sexual orientation and sexuality (Stein, ed., 1992). Constructionism is in conflict with the reigning scientific approach to sexual orientation because such scientific research assumes essentialism, the view that our contemporary categories of sexual orientation can be applied to people in any culture and at any point in history. What should be made of this conflict between the two models for thinking about human sexual orientation used by these two important approaches to human sexuality?

In this essay, I explicate the debate between essentialism and constructionism about sexual orientation. This debate has been conflated with questions concerning the causes of sexual orientation and questions about how the sexual desires of people in other cultures ought to be understood. These questions, while related to essentialism and constructionism, are distinct from them. In the next section, I develop precise characterizations of essentialism and constructionism. Following that, I explain the relationship between this debate and the question of whether our categories of sexual orientation can be applied to historical cultures (section III) and between this debate and the question of whether a person's sexual orientation is the result of genetic or environmental factors (section IV). Having differentiated these questions, I discuss in detail Simon LeVay's neuroanatomical research to show how scientific research does not provide evidence for essentialism, but rather assumes it and thereby ignores a whole range of plausible theories concerning human sexual desires (section V).

II. Natural Human Kinds

Underlying the conflict between essentialism and constructionism is a question concerning *natural kinds*. A natural kind is a grouping of entities that plays a central role in the correct scientific laws and explanations. A group is a natural kind in virtue of the properties its members share or the functions they play independent of how we conceive of them. For example, if current chemical, physical, and physiological theories are correct, then gold, electrons, hemoglobin, and hearts are natural kinds, while chairs, teddy bears, and diet soft drinks are not. Some groups that we think are natural kinds probably will turn out not to be. As a historical example, consider phlogiston. Until the late 1700s, scientists thought that phlogiston was an element found in high concentrations in substances that burned while exposed to air. Air that absorbed a lot of phlogiston would not support further combustion and was not suitable for living creatures to breathe because air was supposed to remove phlogiston from the body through respiration. We now know that there is no such substance as phlogiston. Although phlogiston was thought to be a natural kind, the scientific laws in which phlogiston played an explanatory role are false. There is no single substance that has the properties attributed to phlogiston. The category "phlogiston" fails to pick out any actual stuff. I call such groupings *empty kinds*.

Some natural kinds apply to people. I call these groupings of people that play a central role in scientific explanations and laws *natural human kinds* (for a related discussion, see Hacking, 1986). Examples of natural human kinds include groupings of people by blood types, for example, people with blood type AB, and groupings of people by genetic structures, for example, people with XY sex chromosomes. People with blood type AB constitute a natural human kind because having blood type AB plays a role in laws about what sorts of people a person can donate blood to and receive blood from; a person with blood type AB can, for example, receive transfusions of red blood cells from a person of any blood type. Just as there are many groups of things that are not natural kinds, there are many groups of people that are not natural human kinds; I call them *social human kinds*. Examples include registered members of the Democratic party, matriculated students at an Ivy League college, and convicted felons. These groupings may play a social role, but they do not play an explanatory role in scientific explanation. Similarly, just as there are empty natural kinds, there are empty human kinds, that is, groupings of people supposed to be natural human kinds, but which fail to match the way nature actually groups people. As an example, consider the concept of a hysterical woman. The idea that there are women who suffer from a particular disease called hysteria dates back to early Egyptian culture and continued to the middle of the twentieth century. The symptoms of this disease included uncontrollable outbursts as well as symptoms of any number of bodily diseases, though most typically spasms, paralysis, swelling, blindness, and deafness. Originally thought to be caused by a "wandering" womb, hysteria came to be seen as a specific neurotic illness primarily affecting women. Many people were diagnosed as having hysteria when, in fact, they had some other unidentified illness or were depressed, tired, or nervous. Today, no one believes that hysteria is an actual medical condition. The hysteric is, in a sense, a human kind, but, as there are no hysterics, the hysteric is an empty human kind. Other examples of empty human kinds include witches and warlocks, namely, women and men, respectively, with supernatural powers. These are empty human kinds, I would argue, because people with such supernatural powers simply do not exist.

It is relatively straightforward to use these notions to define constructionism about sexual orientation and its opposite, essentialism. Essentialism about sexual orientation is the view that the categories of sexual orientation refer to natural human kinds, while constructionism about sexual orientation is the view that the categories of sexual orientation do not refer to natural human kinds. Some people think that there are no natural kinds. From this it follows that there are no natural human kinds, and, thus, that our categories of sexual orientation do not refer to natural human kinds. While the position that there are no natural human kinds is an interesting general philosophical position (known as antirealism as well as by other names), it is not an interesting position about sexual orientation. Constructionism about sexual orientation at least implicitly involves the claim that the categories of sexual orientation do not refer to natural kinds but other categories, as being a proton or being a person with blood type B do. If there are no natural kinds, then there is nothing special about sexual orientation; sexual orientations would not be natural kinds but neither would having a Y chromosome or being a proton. The point here is that constructionism is an interesting position about sexual orientation only if there are some natural kinds. Given this, constructionism about sexual orientation is the view that, although there are some natural kinds, the categories of sexual orientation do not refer to natural human kinds but instead refer to empty human kinds or social human kinds. Having clarified what essentialism and constructionism claim, I turn to a discussion of how these views are frequently misunderstood.

III. A Historical Example

Consider Aristophanes' speech in the *Symposium*. In this speech, Aristophanes offers a myth about the origins of love according to which the human race was once made up of three sexes: "male and female, . . . [and] a third which partook of the nature of both, [called] . . . 'hermaphrodite,' . . . a being which was half male and half female" (Plato, 1935, 189d–e). The human race, besides having an additional sex, looked rather different. Each human was "globular in shape, with . . . four arms and legs, and two faces, both on the same cylindrical neck, and one head, with one face on one side and one on the other, and four ears, and two lots of privates . . ." (189e–190). Because these humans were too powerful, Zeus split each human in half down the middle, leaving "each half with a desperate yearning for the other . . ." (191). The three globular types of humans gave rise, once they had been divided, to different types of people defined by the type of person (other half) he or she was longing for:

> The man who is a slice of the hermaphrodite sex . . . will naturally be attracted by women . . . and the women who run after men are of similar descent. . . . But the woman who is a slice of the original female is attracted by women rather than by men . . . while men who are slices of the male are followers of the male. . . . (191d–e)

A natural interpretation of this myth is that Aristophanes is talking about male heterosexuals, female heterosexuals, lesbians and gay men, respectively, and that he is arguing that sexual orientation is an important, inborn, and defining feature of a person (Boswell, 1982–83). This reading of the myth depends on the appropriateness of applying our categories of sexual orientation to people living in Athens centuries ago. There is, however, an alternate interpretation of Aristophanes' myth. Some scholars have argued that Aristophanes' speech is not about sexual orientation at all (Halperin, 1990). This alternative reading draws support from historical evidence that the Greeks thought about people's sexual interests in a quite different way than we do. In ancient Greece, a person's social status, that is, whether the person was a citizen or noncitizen, a slave or a free person, an adult or a child, a woman or a man, was important to how the culture viewed his or her sexual interests. In terms of law and social custom, a citizen was allowed to penetrate but not be penetrated by noncitizens, those who lacked full civic rights (that is, slaves, children, women, and foreigners), and was not allowed to penetrate or to be penetrated by other citizens (Kaplan, 1997). This historical evidence is supposed to indicate that Aristophanes and his contemporaries could not have used anything like our categories of sexual orientation because these categories simply did not exist in their vocabulary. According to this view, it is anachronistic to interpret Aristophanes as talking about lesbians, heterosexuals, and gay men; it would be like claiming that someone in ancient Greece was talking about telephones or computers.

Supporters of the view that Aristophanes was talking about homosexuals in roughly the sense of the term as used by most people in contemporary North America (the first interpretation) might admit that due to the social institutions of ancient Greece, homosexual desire there took a very different form than it takes in our society (in particular, it took an "age-asymmetric" form whereby adult males are primarily attracted to teenaged boys). There are, on this view, homosexuals and heterosexuals in both contemporary times and in ancient Greece, but these types of people express their sexual desires in different ways in different eras. Aristophanes can, on this view, still be interpreted as talking about heterosexuals, lesbians, and gay men, even though he is talking about social structures surrounding sexual behaviors that seem foreign to us. The general point is that just because there are different social structures surrounding some human phenomena in the past and the present, that does not necessarily mean that the two phenomena are different. Consider pregnancy. In earlier times, people thought about pregnancy in ways very different from how we do today. For example, many people in ancient Greece believed that males were solely responsible for the form of human offspring; they thought that each sperm contained an exact blueprint for a human being. On the other hand, according to this view, females provided the material from which a human is constructed and acted as incubators in which this material develops according to the blueprint of the sperm. The fact that the Greeks believed this does not mean that females in ancient Greece failed to contribute genetic material to their offspring in the form of eggs. Even though the Greeks had a dramatically different understanding of pregnancy than we do today, and even though pregnancy had a quite distinct meaning in their culture than in ours, pregnancy then and now is the same biological phenomenon. I can say with confidence that a female in ancient Greece became pregnant when an egg fertilized by a sperm became attached to the wall of her uterus. Returning to sexual orientation, someone who favored the first interpretation would reply to the second interpretation of Aristophanes' speech in a way that parallels my points about pregnancy: just because homosexuality took a different form and was understood differently, it does not mean that our categories of sexual orientation fail to apply to people in ancient Greece. Our contemporary medical and biological categories apply to them; why should our sexual categories fail to do so?

A friend of the second interpretation might reply to this line of argument by admitting that some of our categories (for example, that of pregnant women) are appropriate to people in ancient Greece. She could argue, however, that sexual orientation is not like these concepts. The difference between us and the Greeks is not just that we have different concepts concerning sexual orientation; we also live our lives in different ways. We and the ancient Greeks have different forms of desire; gender is among the most important features of a person that determine whether we might be attracted to him or her; for the Greeks, age, social class, and citizenship status were of greater or equal importance.

The question of how Aristophanes' speech in the *Symposium* should be interpreted (as well as similar interpretive questions) is often connected to the debate between essentialists and constructionists. Essentialists think that our categories of sexual orientation are applicable to people in every culture because the categories refer to natural human kinds. The first interpretation of Aristophanes' speech, according to which he is talking about heterosexuals and homosexuals, thus fits well with essentialism about sexual orientation. In contrast, constructionists say that it does not make sense to apply the categories of sexual orientation to other cultures such as ancient Greece because our categories of sexual orientation do not refer to natural human kinds. Constructionists admit that there were people in ancient Greece who had sex with people of the same sex, and perhaps even that there were people who were sexually attracted primarily to people of the same sex, but they deny that this entails that there were homosexuals (in our sense of the term) in ancient Greece. To apply our sexual-orientation terms to another culture, we need to have evidence that people in that culture had sexual orientations in roughly our sense of the term. In fact, say constructionists, no one in any culture before the mid-1800s had sexual orientations.

What then is the relationship between the essentialist-constructionist debate and the interpretive question about Aristophanes' speech in the *Symposium*? If the first reading of Aristophanes' speech is right and Aristophanes is talking about lesbians, gay men, and heterosexuals, this shows that we share our categories for thinking about sexual orientation with the people of ancient Greece. This alone does not show that essentialism about sexual orientation is true. A person who believed that a witch was a natural human kind would not establish the truth of this belief by showing that people in another culture, say the colonists of Massachusetts in the 1600s, shared their categories. Contemporary believers in witches could use the same category that the colonists did, but this would not prove that a witch is a natural human kind. Although showing that the Greeks had the same categories that we do does not establish the truth of essentialism, it does count as inductive evidence for this thesis. If almost every culture divides people up into the same categories, then this suggests (but does not prove) that these categories capture some truth about human nature.

However, even if we were sure that Aristophanes is not talking about lesbians, gay men, and heterosexuals, this would not establish the truth of constructionism about sexual orientation. No one in ancient Greece talked about blood types, but, then and now, the categories of blood type still pick out natural human kinds. That most cultures lack a concept does not establish the truth of constructionism with respect to this concept. A culture might not have the concept, but the people in that culture might still fit it. If not, we could eliminate epilepsy, for example, just by eliminating the concept (Stein, 1992).

Just as the appropriateness of the first interpretation does not establish the truth of essentialism, and the appropriateness of the second interpretation does not establish the truth of constructionism, the truth of essentialism does not entail the truth of the first interpretation and the truth of constructionism does not entail the appropriateness of the second interpretation. First, suppose that essentialism is true and that sexual orientations are natural human kinds. It is perfectly consistent with this that the Greeks lacked these categories and, hence, that Aristophanes could not have been talking about homosexuals and heterosexuals in the *Symposium*. A parallel point can be made about pregnancy. It is perfectly consistent with the fact that females in ancient Greece contributed genetic material to their offspring through eggs that the Greeks lacked a concept of a human egg. Second, suppose that constructionism is true and that our categories of sexual orientation do not refer to natural human kinds. It is consistent with this that the Greeks might still have the same categories of sexual orientation that we do. Two cultures can have the same category even if the category does not refer to a natural kind.

The debate between essentialism and constructionism has often been equated with that over how various cultures categorized people in terms of their sexual desires. It is easy to see why this has happened. Our access to the sexual orientation of people in cultures that no longer exist (like ancient Greece) is dramatically limited. We cannot observe their sexual behavior and we cannot ask them about their sexual desires. Our access is limited to their expressions of their desires in the form of their writings, art, laws, and the like. This limitation on our access to other cultures should not, however, cause us to confuse what is at issue between essentialism and constructionism. Even if the Greeks lacked our categories, our categories still might refer to natural kinds; even if the Greeks had our categories, our categories still might not refer to natural kinds. There are, however, some links between the interpretive question and the ontological one. First, if we find that people in many other cultures have the same categories we do, this provides some suggestive evidence for essentialism. Second, keeping in mind the constructionist thesis helps us appreciate cultural differences. This is a useful antidote to simply seeing all cultures through the lens of our categories of sexual desire; in section IV, I will show that this is important for science as well as for history.

IV. Nature versus Nurture

The debate between essentialists and constructionists is also often understood as reducing to whether sexual orientation is the result of a person's genetic makeup or her environment. As typically discussed, this question of nature versus nurture is based on a false dichotomy. No human trait is strictly the result of either genes or environmental factors; all human traits are partly the result of both. There are genetic factors that affect even the most seemingly environmental traits, like, for example, what a person's major will be in college. On the other hand, environmental and developmental factors contribute to the development of even the most seemingly genetic traits, for example, eye color. Although every human trait is affected by both genetic and environmental factors, there does seem to be some variance in degree. That my eyes are hazel and that my blood type is B are more tightly constrained by genetic factors than that my major in college was philosophy and that I associate the word "tree" with tall, leafy plants found in forests. I have genes that make it almost certain that my eyes will be hazel, but I do not have genes that make it almost certain that I will major in philosophy; I do not even have genes that make it almost certain that if I live in a culture where there are colleges that offer philosophy degrees, I will major in philosophy. The nature-nurture debate about sexual orientation, properly understood, concerns where sexual orientation fits on the continuum between eye color, on the one hand, and college major, on the other.

Many people assume that essentialism entails that sexual orientation is strongly constrained by genes and constructionism entails that sexual orientation is primarily shaped by the environment. Neither is the case. In general, it is possible for a category to refer to a natural human kind without it being the case that a person fits into that category in virtue of her genes. For example, being a person with tuberculosis is a natural human kind, as is being a person who is immune to polio, but whether or not one is a member of either group is not genetically determined. Whether one is involves the presence of a particular rod-shaped bacterium or certain antibodies in the blood stream, respectively. Neither condition is determined genetically, but both are associated with natural human kinds. With respect to sexual orientation, if a simplified version of the Freudian theory of the origins of male sexual orientation were true and a man has the sexual orientation he does in virtue of his relationship with his parents, namely, if he has a resolved or unresolved Oedipal complex, then essentialism about sexual orientation would be true. Once a boy has settled into a particular Oedipal status, he has a naturalistically determinate sexual orientation: his brain instantiates a particular psychological state that makes him a heterosexual or homosexual. In virtue of this psychological state, certain scientific laws apply to him. If this theory were right, then sexual orientations would be natural human kinds, but they would not be primarily genetic. This shows that the truth of essentialism does not entail the truth of nativism; not all natural human kinds have a genetic basis. The same example will suffice to show that if sexual orientation is shaped primarily by environmental factors, the truth of constructionism does not necessarily follow. If this simple Freudian theory were true, then sexual orientation would not be innate, but constructionism would be false (because sexual orientation, in virtue of its psychological basis, would be a natural human kind). The simple connections commonly thought to hold between the nature of the categories of sexual orientation and the cause of sexual orientation do not in fact hold: essentialism does not entail nativism and environmentalism does not entail constructionism.

The commonly held view that there is a connection between the essentialism-constructionism debate and the nature-nurture debate about sexual orientation is not, however, completely wrong. If sexual orientation is innate, then constructionism about sexual orientation is false and essentialism is true. If a person's sexual orientation is primarily determined by genetic factors, then there are natural human kinds associated with sexual orientations in virtue of the genes responsible for sexual orientation. If this were the case, constructionism would be false. This does not, however, constitute an objection to constructionism; it just makes clear that constructionism and essentialism are empirical theses; in particular, they are empirical theses related to whether sexual orientation is innate. If nativism is true, then constructionism is false and essentialism is true. The contrapositive of this claim, that the truth of constructionism entails that nativism about sexual orientation is false, follows directly from the same line of argument: if sexual orientation is not a natural human kind, then it cannot be innate.

V. The Example of LeVay's Neuroanatomical Research

In the previous section, I concluded that the issue between essentialism and constructionism is empirical; if, for example, sexual orientation is innate, then essentialism is true. It might seem to follow from this that current scientific research on sexual orientation, which claims that sexual orientation is innate, supports essentialism. In fact, rather than proving it, current scientific research assumes essentialism. As an example of this, I consider LeVay's (1992) widely cited neuroanatomical study.

LeVay reported a neurological difference between heterosexual and gay men. He examined the interstitial nuclei of the anterior hypothalamus (INAH) of the brains of forty-one people. Nineteen were inferred to be homosexual or bisexual men (based on their medical records' accounts of their sexual activity) who died of complications due to AIDS; six were men of undetermined sexual orientation who also died of AIDS (LeVay presumed they were heterosexual);

ten were men also of undetermined sexual orientation who died of other causes (and also presumed to be homosexual); and six were women, all presumed to be heterosexual, one who died of AIDS and five who died from other causes. LeVay reported that one of the four sections of the INAH of the homosexual and bisexual men were significantly smaller than those of the men of undetermined sexual orientation. On this basis, he concluded that there is a correlation between hypothalami and sexual orientation and, further, that this correlation suggests there is something biological about sexual orientation. For various reasons concerning the details of its experimental design, this study should be viewed with great skepticism (see Byne and Parsons, 1993; Byne, 1996). However, for the purposes of this essay, I want to focus on two general features of LeVay's project, features that it shares with most research on sexual orientation in the reigning scientific paradigm; namely, it assumes that homosexuality is a form of sex inversion and it assumes a simplistic picture of what a sexual orientation is. Examining these features of LeVay's project underscores that essentialism is an assumption, not a conclusion, of his study. Doing so also points to the role constructionism can play in ferreting out the cultural biases implicit in scientific research on sexual orientation.

LeVay's study is premised on seeing sexual orientation as a trait with two forms, a male form that causes sexual attraction to women (shared by heterosexual men and lesbians) and a female form that causes sexual attraction to men (shared by heterosexual women and gay men). I call this assumption that homosexuality results from a sex-reversed brain or physiology the *inversion assumption*. This assumption is evident, for example, in the equation of same-sex sexual activity in men with effeminacy. Research premised on the inversion assumption typically proceeds by first trying to identify sex differences and then seeing if any alleged sex difference is reversed in homosexuals.

There are alternatives to the inversion assumption. Perhaps, from the physiological point of view, gay men and lesbians should be grouped together and heterosexual men and women should be grouped together. This would be the case if heterosexuals had a brain structure or physiology that disposed them to be sexually attracted to people of the opposite sex, while lesbians and gay men had a brain that disposed them to be sexually attracted to people of the same sex. Or, more plausibly, there might be no interesting generalizable differences in brains that correlate with these categories of sexual orientation. This would be the case if sexual orientation were not simply dimorphic but rather took many different forms. The conscious and unconscious motivations associated with sexual attraction could differ even among individuals of the same sex and sexual orientation. A myriad of experiences (and subjective interpretations of them) could interact to lead different individuals to the same relative degree of sexual attraction to men, women, or both. Because sexual attraction to women, for example, could be driven by various different psychological factors, there is no reason to expect that all individuals attracted to women should share any particular physiology that distinguishes them from individuals attracted to men.

This does not imply that a person's sexual orientation is not represented in her brain. Sexual orientation must of course be represented in the brain, but so must all of my other desires, proclivities, and preferences, including whether I prefer Brahms or Beethoven and whether I enjoy tennis (preferences that are probably not innate, that is, these preferences are closer to the origins of one's college major than one's eye color).

When reviewing evidence like LeVay's that is based on the inversion assumption, it is important to remember both that there are alternatives to this assumption and that it is as yet scientifically unsupported. This is not to deny that the inversion assumption is intuitively plausible to many people in our culture. This is not because the assumption is intrinsically more plausible than either of the two rivals I mentioned; rather, it is because of our cultural bias in favor of thinking that gay men are feminine and lesbians are masculine. This cultural view is hardly universal. For example, in some cultures, sexual activity between males was associated with warrior status (see, for example, Watanabe and Iwata, 1989), while in others receptive same-sex sexual activity was universally practiced by males and believed to be essential to their virility (Herdt, 1984). The fact that the inversion assumption would not have been plausible in some cultures does not show that it is false. Together, however, the lack of scientific evidence to support the inversion assumption and the fact that it is not culturally universal suggest that it may be based as much on our cultural biases as anything else. Turning to the second general feature of LeVay's study that I want to consider, note that one of the reasons LeVay looked to the hypothalamus is based on an analogy with rodents: hormonal exposure in the early development of rodents exerts organizational influences on their hypothalamus, which determines the balance between male-typical and female-typical patterns of mating behaviors displayed in adulthood. There are two problems with this analogy. First, it is unclear whether humans and rodents have relevantly similar hypothalami (Byne, 1996). Second, it is highly problematic to extrapolate from behaviors in rodents to psychological phenomena in humans. According to some researchers and many popular accounts, a male rat that is castrated at birth and subsequently shows a sexually receptive posture called lordosis when mounted by another male is homosexual. This receptive posture, however, is basically a reflex. A neonatally castrated male will assume the same posture if a handler strokes its back. Further, while the male who displays lordosis when mounted by another male and the female who mounts another female are counted as homosexual, the male that mounts another male is considered heterosexual, as is the female that displays lordosis when mounted by another female. In this laboratory paradigm, sexual orientation is defined in terms of specific behaviors and postures. In contrast, in the human case, both the male who penetrates and the male who is penetrated (as well as the male who engages in or desires to engage in various acts that do not involve penetration at all) are counted as gay. Sexual orientation in humans is defined not by what "position" one takes in sexual intercourse, but by one's pattern of erotic responsiveness and the sex of one's preferred sex partner. Some researchers acknowledge the problem of equating behaviors in rodents with their sexual desires, and employ a variety of strategies to reveal the sexual preferences of animals (for example, an animal is given the choice of pressing a bar that will allow access to a male conspecific or a bar that will allow access to a female conspecific; if the animal presses the bar to gain access to the animal of the same sex, this establishes that the animal is homosexual). Even these studies may, however, have little to do with human sexual orientation. In rodents, in order for a genetic male rodent to behave as a female rodent typically does with respect to partner preference (as well as sexual position), he must be exposed to extreme hormonal abnormalities that are unlikely to occur outside the neuroendocrine laboratory. First, he must either be castrated as a neonate, depriving him of androgens, or particular androgen-responsive regions of his brain must be destroyed. In addition, in order to activate the display of female-typical behaviors and preferences, he must also be injected with estrogens in adulthood (Byne, 1996). Because gay men and lesbians have hormonal profiles that are indistinguishable from those of their heterosexual counterparts (Meyer-Bahlburg, 1984), it is difficult to see how this situation has any bearing on human sexual orientation.

LeVay's study begins with a particular picture of sexual orientations. He assumes that homosexuality goes along with general sex inversion and, in virtue of the analogy to rodents, that human sexual orientation can be usefully analyzed in terms of the sexual positions one takes and the preferences for the company of males or females one exhibits. Neither of these assumptions are adequately justified, although both fit with a commonly accepted picture of sexual orientations (see LeVay, 1996; also see Stein, in press). Constructionism challenges us to look beyond our cultural assumptions about sexual orientation to the possibility that our categories of sexual orientation are not natural human kinds. This may be a difficult thing to do because we see ourselves and others through the categories of sexual orientation; these categories may thus seem natural when, in fact, they are not. Like the inversion assumption, essentialism is an assumption, not a conclusion, of current scientific research on sexual orientation.

VI. Conclusion

It is easy to picture what it would be like for essentialism to be true, but it is trickier to imagine how constructionism could be true. If the categories of sexual orientation are not natural kinds, how could we explain the fact that some people are attracted primarily to people of the same sex while others are not? Presumably, we would do so in the same way we would explain other differences among people that do not seem to be primarily explicable in terms of their genetic makeup, like, for example, differences in musical tastes, dietary preferences (Halperin, 1990), and sleep positions (Stein, 1992). We do not think, for example, that categories associated with whether a person typically sleeps on her back or her stomach will play a role in any significant scientific laws, yet we can imagine giving an explanation of how such an "orientation" develops. Constructionism about sexual orientation does not preclude an explanation of how people's sexual tastes develop; it just precludes that such explanations will involve natural kinds associated with the categories of sexual orientation. Scientists exploring sexual orientation need to take special care not to introduce unjustified cultural assumptions about the organization and nature of human sexual desires into their research. Constructionism (and the field of lesbian and gay studies from which it emerges) can make an important contribution to such research because they highlight these assumptions.

References

Abelove, Henry, Michle Barale, and David Halperin, eds. *The Lesbian and Gay Studies Reader*. New York, Routledge, 1993.

Bailey, J. Michael, and Richard Pillard. "A Genetic Study of Male Sexual Orientation." *Archives of General Psychiatry* 48 (1991): 1089–96.

Boswell, John. "Revolutions, Universals and Sexual Categories." *Salmagundi* 58–59 (1982–83): 89–113.

Boyd, Richard. "Realism, Anti-Foundationalism and the Enthusiasm for Natural Kinds." Philosophical Studies 61 (1991): 127–48.

Bullough, Vern. *Science in the Bedroom: The History of Sex Research*. New York: Basic Books, 1994.

Byne, William. "Biology and Sexual Orientation: Implications of Endocronological and Neuroanatomical Research." In R. Cabaj and T. Stein, eds. *Comprehensive Textbook of Homosexuality*. Washington, D.C.: American Psychiatric Press, 1996.

Byne, William, and Bruce Parsons. "Sexual Orientation: The Biological Theories Reappraised." *Archives of General Psychiatry* 50 (1993): 228–39.

Byne, William, and Edward Stein. "Ethical Implications of Scientific Research on the Causes of Sexual Orientation." *Health Care Analysis* 4 (1997).

Fausto-Sterling, Anne. *Myths of Gender: Biological Theories about Women and Men*. Rev. ed. New York: Basic Books, 1992.

Foucault, Michael. *The History of Sexuality*, vol. 1: *An Introduction*. Robert Hurley, trans. New York: Random House, 1978.

Hacking, Ian. "Making Up People." In Thomas Heller, Morton Sosna, and David Wellbery, eds. *Reconstructing Individualism: Autonomy, Individuality, and the Self in Western Thought*. Stanford: Stanford University Press, 1986, pp. 222–236; reprinted in Stein, ed., 1992, pp. 69–88.

———. "A Tradition of Natural Kinds." *Philosophical Studies* 61 (1991): 109–26.

Halperin, David. *One Hundred Years of Homosexuality and Other Essays in Greek Love*. New York: Routledge, 1990.

Hamer, Dean, et al. "A Linkage between DNA Markers on the X Chromosome and Male Sexual Orientation." *Science* 261 (1993): 321–27.

Herdt, Gil. "Semen Transactions in Sambia Culture." In *Ritualized Homosexuality in Melanesia*, Gil Herdt, ed. Berkeley and Los Angeles: University of California Press, 1984, pp. 167–210.

Kaplan, Morris. *Sexual Justice: Democratic Citizenship and the Politics of Desire*. New York: Routledge, 1997.

LeVay, Simon. "A Difference in the Hypothalamic Structure between Heterosexual and Homosexual Men." *Science* 253 (1992): 1034–37.

———. *Queer Science: The Use and Abuse of Research into Homosexuality*. Cambridge: MIT Press, 1996.

McIntosh, Mary. "The Homosexual Role." *Social Problems* 16 (1968): 182–92; reprinted in Stein, ed., 1992, pp. 25–42.

Meyer-Bahlburg, Heino. "Psychoendocrine Research on Sexual Orientation: Current Status and Future Options." *Progress in Brain Research* 71 (1984): 375–97.

Mohr, Richard. "The Thing of It Is: Some Problems with Models for the Social Construction of Homosexuality." In Richard Mohr, ed. *Gay Ideas*. Boston: Beacon, 1992.

Plato. *Symposium*. Michael Joyce, trans. New York: Everyman's Library, 1935.

Stein, Edward. "The Essentials of Constructionism and the Construction of Essentialism." In Stein, ed., 1992, pp. 325–54.

———. "Review of LeVay." *Journal of Homosexuality*. In press.

———. *Sexual Desires: Science, Theory and Ethics*. New York: Oxford University Press, forthcoming.

———. ed. *Forms of Desire: Sexual Orientation and the Social Constructionist Controversy*. New York: Routledge, 1992.

Watanabe, T., and J. Iwata. *The Love of the Samurai: A Thousand Years of Japanese Homosexuality*. London: GMP, 1989

27

Taking Responsibility for Sexuality*

Joyce Trebilcot

It is fundamental to feminism that women should take responsibility for ourselves, collectively and individually. In this essay I explore a central aspect of this project: taking responsibility for sexuality. I am particularly concerned here with women taking responsibility for our sexual identities as lesbian or heterosexual.

I write in part out of the struggle within feminism over whether feminism precludes women having affectional-sexual ties with men. As those familiar with feminist theory know, feminists advocate lesbianism on a variety of grounds. Some emphasize, for instance, that because virtually everyone's first erotic relationship is with a woman (mother), lesbianism is "natural" for women, as heterosexuality is for men. Another argument is based on the claim that, in patriarchy, equality in a heterosexual relationship is impossible; even if a man undertakes to renounce male privileges, he cannot do so entirely. A third argument holds that women who are committed to feminism should give *all* their energies to women. I am not concerned here to explore these arguments. Rather, I want to develop the idea of women taking responsibility for our own sexuality, whatever it may be. Feminism requires at least this of us.

Notice first that to take responsibility for a state of affairs is not to claim responsibility for having caused it. So, for example, if I take responsibility for cleaning up the kitchen I am not thereby admitting to any role in creating the mess; the state of the kitchen may be the consequence of actions quite independent of me. Similarly, in taking responsibility for her sexuality, a woman is not

*This paper was originally prepared as a talk for a conference on Women and Mental Health at the University of Oklahoma in the spring of 1982. That version appears in *Women and Mental Health: Conference Proceedings,* edited by Elaine Barton, Kristen Watts-Penny, and Barbara Hillyer Davis (Norman, Okla.: Women's Studies Program, University of Oklahoma, 1982). The paper was also presented at Union College, Schenectady, New York, in the spring of 1983.

I especially appreciate conversations about the topic of this essay with Sandra Lee Bartky.

thereby claiming responsibility for what her sexuality has been, but only for what it is now and what it will be in the future.

In taking responsibility, a woman chooses to make a commitment about a specific state of affairs. The role of choice here constitutes an important link between the idea of taking responsibility and feminist values, for in feminist value schemes choice often has a central place.[1] Indeed, a feminist theory of responsibility might well involve the thesis that one is not to be held responsible for anything one has not agreed ahead of time to be responsible for.[2]

To take responsibility for one's sexuality, broadly conceived, is to take responsibility for the whole range of erotic/sexual/gender phenomena that are aspects of one's actions, attitudes, thoughts, wishes, style, and so on. In particular, it includes taking responsibility for oneself as lesbian or heterosexual or bisexual, or the celibate version of any of these: celibate lesbian, celibate heterosexual, celibate bisexual. It is to be expected that many women find these male-created labels and perhaps even their feminist redefinitions unsatisfactory.[3] Nevertheless, taking responsibility for one's sexuality does include locating oneself in terms of some such categories—categories that are already available or that one may invent.[4]

A paradigm case of taking responsibility for one's sexuality is coming out as a lesbian.[5] It is characteristic of first coming out, of coming out to oneself, that a woman does not know whether to say that she has *discovered* that she is a lesbian, or that she has *decided* to be a lesbian. The experience is one of acknowledging, of realizing what is already there, and at the same time of creating something new, a new sense of oneself, a new identity. In coming out, one connects up an already existing reality—one's feelings, one's sensations, one's identification with women—with one's values, i.e., with one's understanding or concept of who one is. This is the sort of process I mean to refer to here when I speak of taking responsibility for sexuality.

The process, then, is one of *discovery/creation*. Notice that there is no simple term for this process in patriarchal language, at least not in English. It might be suggested, for example, that coming out is a matter of interpretation, of interpreting or reinterpreting one's experiences and feelings in a certain way, as evidence of or elements in one's lesbianism. But this way of understanding coming out is incomplete because it captures only part of the process, the discovery part. To discover that one has been a lesbian all along is certainly to interpret past experiences in a new way, as experiences of a closeted lesbian. But coming out involves also deciding to be a lesbian, for now and in the future, which is to say, deciding not to participate in the institution of heterosexuality and to go on loving women. Coming out then is not merely a matter of reinterpreting one's past; it involves taking responsibility for being a lesbian both in the past and in the future.

Another received term that might be thought to apply to coming out is "conversion experience." There is certainly ample patriarchal literature about people undergoing conversions, mostly religious ones. But the idea of conversion doesn't capture coming out either. The patriarchal convert becomes what he was not. The lesbian becomes what she is.

But, it might be suggested, what about the expression "coming out" itself? Doesn't that convey the experience? This expression has been adopted by lesbians from gay male culture and by gay males presumably from the custom of debutantes coming out into society. It emphasizes not the creation of the self, but the presentation of the self to others. It omits, I think, the inwardness of lesbian experience, the fact that coming out is not merely (or at all) a social exercise but a subjective one, a kind of growth.

It is no accident, of course, that there is no term in patriarchy for the experience I am concerned with here, that there is no brief and clear way of accurately referring to it. Taking responsibility for one's own sexuality is not in the interest of patriarchy, which insists, for its own protection, that sexuality is only a given, that we have no role in creating it. The power of men over women in patriarchy, and of some men over others, is maintained in large part through the institution of heterosexuality, which requires not that women take responsibility for our own sexuality but, rather, that women act on rules that are given to us.[6]

Now, before I go on to discuss the meaning of taking responsibility for one's sexuality for heterosexual women, I want to trace briefly how patriarchy insists that sexuality is wholly given, even through changing ways of thinking about sexuality, through changing sexual values.

Consider first the traditional view that establishes heterosexuality as the norm, and lesbianism as a deviation or disease. On this view, one's sexuality is clearly a given only; it is inherited, or acquired in childhood; it is something that happens *to* an individual. This way of thinking about sexuality tends to keep one docile: one is passive, submissive, with respect to it; it is something received entire, not something one contributes to or creates. On this model, the lesbian, who is described as deviant or as suffering some illness or pathology, is supposed to require treatment by an expert: her sexuality, her "deviance," is not something she can take care of herself. On this traditional model, the question of taking responsibility for one's sexuality does not arise for either lesbian or heterosexual. Sexual identity for everyone is something one "gets," something that happens to one; and if it is not okay, then an expert is called in, but the woman herself remains passive.

In some circles this traditional way of conceiving sexuality has been replaced by pluralism. Pluralism rejects the view that only heterosexuality is normal and holds instead, in the spirit of liberalism, that there are alternative "sexual preferences"—lesbianism, bisexuality, heterosexuality—which are all equally acceptable and which can all be equally "healthy." According to pluralism, sexual identity alone does not determine whether one is healthy or ill, normal or deviant. Such determinations are made in terms of how one "adjusts" to one's sexual identity, how well it satisfies one's needs, whatever they may be.

This way of thinking about sexual identity is equivalent to the more traditional view in terms of keeping women docile. Pluralism's message is: "Look, whatever you are, it's okay—don't worry about it. There are differences among us, but we can all live together happily." This message, of course, seeks to drown out the voice of the lesbian who understands lesbianism as part of the struggle against patriarchy. *Her* message is: "Pay attention to what each form of sexuality means for women. They are *not* all the same in terms of equality, in terms of power, in terms of domination." But this thinking is forbidden by an ethic that insists that all the alternatives are equally okay. So laissez-faire pluralism works against women thinking seriously about our sexuality as we must do if we are to take responsibility for it.

A third way of thinking about sexuality is to hold that everyone ought to be pansexual or at least bisexual, and so open to sexual encounters with persons of both sexes. This position is connected with the ideology, if not the practice (which was mainly heterosexual), of the "sexual revolution" of the sixties, and with leftist theories that advocate the release of sexuality from repression. On this view, the theoretical ideal is that everyone should be the same, bisexual. The theory itself tells us what to be. But if we don't have to decide for ourselves, we don't have to compare the different kinds of sexuality and consider reasons for and against them. We are simply to be obedient, to be bisexual, to be open to anything. This position, of course, has special potential for the exploitation of women. And, like the traditional and pluralistic models, it provides no support for individuals' taking responsibility for and defining their own sexuality.

None of these male-created value systems allows room for the idea that one might discover/create one's own sexuality on the basis of one's feelings and one's politics, on the basis of reasons, on the rational-emotional weighing of all one deems relevant. The same is true, of course, of patriarchal science. The scientific study of sexuality seeks to discover causes of lesbianism, and sometimes also of heterosexuality, and there is no space in these causal accounts for women to participate in the creating of our own sexual identities. A feminist theory of sexuality will not be a causal theory in any familiar sense, and will surely include an account of the role a woman herself may play in the development of her sexuality.[7]

It is, I believe, in the interest of all women to take responsibility for our sexuality. "Coming out," as I have suggested, provides a model for this process. But what could it possibly mean to "come out" as a heterosexual? Most heterosexual women accept the identities their conditioning provides for them, and so, it would seem, there is little or nothing for them to discover or create.

But to think in this way is again to fall into the trap of taking sexuality as merely given. Virtually all women can take responsibility for our sexuality. For a heterosexual woman to take responsibility for herself as heterosexual involves acknowledging the experiences and feelings she has that are parts of her heterosexuality, and also making the decision to participate or not in the institution of heterosexuality. Notice that the institution has many facets. It consists not just of sexual activity, but of a myriad of values and practices, including, for example, concepts of love, of couples, of faithfulness; meanings given to various fashions in clothes and personal appearance; ways of behaving with men and with women; and so on. A heterosexual woman taking responsibility decides which of the aspects of the institution she wishes to participate in (if any), and why. She may participate wholly, but if she is responsible, she does so not without thinking, but for reasons that she takes to be good ones.

Some women object to the idea that they should take responsibility for their own sexual identity on the ground that they have no choice, that they are what they are—lesbian, heterosexual—and cannot change. For example, it is not unusual for a feminist to claim that although the weight of *reason,* for her, is on the side of lesbianism, her *feelings* (perhaps as expressed in her fantasies), are irredeemably heterosexual, for she is sexually aroused by men but not by women. If such women sometimes identify as heterosexuals, they may claim that they cannot change the fact that they are sexually attracted to men, which they experience as a given, and so that they cannot take responsibility for their sexuality—that they are caught in a conflict between reason and feeling.

The peculiarity of this position is the assumption that one's feelings must determine one's sexual identity, that is, that one's genital twinges must determine whether one is lesbian, or heterosexual, or both. Granting that some women are sexually aroused only by men, they are not therefore locked into any of the familiar identities or excluded from any. Such women may, in the first place, choose for or against heterosexual *activity.* We know that there are many sexual impulses that ought to be suppressed rather than acted on, and women for whom the weight of reason is on the side of lesbianism have reason not to participate in heterosexual intercourse. It is also true that a woman may choose to make love to or with women, even though she is not sexually aroused. A woman's claim that she is not erotically responsive to women but only to men does not in itself limit her choices as between lesbianism, heterosexuality, or bisexuality, or celibacy of whatever variety. Sexuality is socially constructed; in reconstructing it we need not assume either that erotic feelings should lead to lovemaking or that love-making ought to occur only where there are erotic feelings.

Genital *sensations,* then, are not definitive of sexual identity; but clearly genital *activity* has a central role. Although there are, for example, lesbians who regularly engage in sexual intercourse with men (particularly, married lesbians and lesbian prostitutes), lesbian identity in these cases depends on there being special reasons (often economic) for continued heterosexual behavior. In the absence of such special reasons, regular heterosexual activity defeats the claim that one is a lesbian; such a woman would have instead to be identified as het-erosexual or bisexual. Similarly, women who believe themselves to be hetero-sexual or bisexual, but who regularly engage in sexual activity with women but not with men, cannot, in the absence of special circumstances, sustain the claim of heterosexuality.

But what about the heterosexual feminist whose purported reason for engaging in heterosexual activity is just that she takes physical pleasure in it, physical pleasure she can experience in no other way? It would be too great a sacrifice, she says, to give up this pleasure, even for the political and personal benefits she thinks would come from an identification other than heterosexual. In exploring this issue, it often turns out that the physical pleasure is not after all separable from the economic, emotional, social, and other advantages that she gains from heterosexual relationships. For such a woman identification as heterosexual is frequently based not primarily on some genital pleasure, but on a complex understanding of the role of heterosexual activity in her life.

A woman who has such an understanding can correctly be said to be taking responsibility for her own sexuality, even though the inconsistency between her reason (lesbian) and her genital feelings and behavior (heterosexual) remains. For she has come to understand her heterosexual identity not as a fate irrevo- cably determined by genital sensations, but as a choice she has made on the basis of a variety of factors, a choice pushed upon her, to be sure, by the power of the institution of heterosexuality, but also one that she might not have made and might yet revoke. Indeed, as she comes to understand her sexuality in the process of taking responsibility for it, her sexual identity may itself change, for the process of discovery/creation dialectically transforms preexisting reality.

It seems then that it does make sense to speak of all women—whatever our sexuality is and whatever it may become—as capable of taking responsibility for our sexuality, for discovering/creating our sexuality. I believe that we should take responsibility, for a variety of reasons I can only touch on here. First, if we define our own sexuality, if we are in control, we are more likely to be strong, self-creating, and independent, not merely about sexuality but generally, than if we simply do what is expected of us, that is, conform without question to the norms of heterosexuality. But also, to take responsibility for sexuality requires study and thought about the meanings of the different sexualities, and this con- sciousness-raising has important political implications. It means that there will be greater understanding among women of how patriarchy operates. It also means that there will be fewer heterosexuals, insofar as serious thought about heterosexuality leads women to withdraw from that institution. It not only con- tributes to a greater closeness in the women's community but also to a greater solidarity among all women through a lessening of heterosexism, lesbophobia, and lesbian-hating.

Let me focus briefly on this last idea, the connection between taking responsibility and overcoming these forms of lesbian oppression. Heterosexism is the conviction that heterosexuality is superior to other sexual identities; it includes heterosexist solipsism, that is, ignoring the existence of identities other than heterosexual. Heterosexism is commonly manifested in the assumption that everyone is heterosexual, or that lesbians are distant and rare, not one's friends and associates. Taking responsibility for sexual identity raises con- sciousness about lesbians and so makes women more aware of the presence of lesbians among their families, their friends, and in their workplaces. Hetero- sexism is expressed also, of course, by overt or subtle denigration of lesbians and lesbian culture. But a woman who takes seriously the project of defining her own sexuality has to consider the possibility that she herself could be a lesbian; having done this, I think, she is less likely to put down lesbians and things lesbian. If she rejects lesbianism, it is a reasoned rejection, not a prejudice (that is, not a judgment made prior to conscientious consideration of the issue). Heterosexism also takes the form of insensitivity, in heterosexual women, to the fact that the special privileges they enjoy as heterosexuals—privileges in jobs, housing, travel, and the like—are not privileges they *deserve* and lesbians do not, but rather, are privileges unfairly awarded to them by the heterosexual/patriarchal system and unfairly denied to their lesbian sisters. Again, women who take seriously their own sexual autonomy are likely to be more aware than others of the injustice of this system of privilege.

Lesbophobia, like heterosexism, may be lessened as one becomes conscious of one's sexual identity as something one has control over. Lesbophobia has a variety of forms. One is simply fear of the unknown: lesbians seem alien and threatening because one does not know what to expect from them. But part of taking responsibility for one's sexuality is finding out about lesbians and lesbianism.

Another form of lesbophobia is fear that I might be or become one too. But a woman who has a sense of responsibility about her sexuality, while she might find the idea of becoming a lesbian scary, knows that if she does identify as lesbian she does so because of her own discovery/decision; she knows that she herself is in control of her sexual identity, and whatever fear she has will be within her control as well.

Finally, lesbophobia may be a fear of being rejected by lesbians, of not being acceptable to them, or to some specific group of them, in terms of their values or standards or styles. This sort of lesbophobia is common among lesbians. But again, for lesbians and nonlesbians, the consciousness of creating one's own values and style mitigates the fear: the question is not after all whether one is acceptable to them, but, perhaps, whether one wants to expand one's own value system so as to include at least parts of theirs, so that one can be part of their group. This is something one can decide for oneself.

Hatred of lesbians, which frequently accompanies both heterosexism and lesbophobia, is, like misogyny, especially sad among women, for it is hatred of oneself, or of parts of oneself. Both lesbian and nonlesbian women can get into hating parts of ourselves and projecting those parts and that hatred onto lesbians. But taking responsibility involves getting in touch with dissonant, unacceptable, threatening, puzzling aspects of ourselves; if we acknowledge those aspects we are less likely both to project them and to hate them. Also, taking responsibility tends to increase self-esteem, and so to squeeze out self-hatred.

There are, then, excellent reasons why women, all women, should take responsibility for our own sexuality. We all *can* do so. For taking responsibility does not require a woman to be in a position to change the material conditions of her life; it requires only that she be able to understand her sexual identity as discovered and created by her in response to the pressures of patriarchy and the promise of the realization of feminism.

Notes

1. This is so even though choice is associated with hierarchy and dualism, which most feminist theorists understand to be inconsistent with feminist values.

2. In feminist discourse, the concept of responsibility tends to drop out and is partially replaced by the notion of accountability. Accepting accountability is like taking responsibility in that one chooses what one is accountable for (one is not accountable if one did not make the commitment). Accepting accountability differs from taking responsibility in emphasizing relationships, in emphasizing those to whom one is accountable—one's community, friends, and lover. To urge that women should accept accountability for their sexuality is to urge them to accept membership in a community or to make a commitment to some relationship. In this essay I use the more patriarchal concept of responsibility because my focus is not so much on a woman's relationship to other women as on her giving reasons, perhaps only to herself, for the forms in which she expresses her sexual feelings.

3. For a discussion of feminist definitions of lesbianism, see Ann Ferguson, "Patriarchy, Sexual Identity, and the Sexual Revolution," *Signs* 7 (Autumn 1981): 158–72.

4. Some rebellious women may resist avowing an identity in these terms on the ground that they do not want to be labeled. But compare rejecting all labels to adopting a deviant's label with respect to their potential for expressing rebelliousness.

5. For accounts of coming out see *The Coming Out Stories,* edited by Julia Penelope Stanley and Susan J. Wolfe (Watertown, Mass.: Persephone Press, 1980).

6. In patriarchy, women may be expected to take some responsibility for aspects of their sexuality, for example, for allowing sexual access only to certain males or for birth control. But the idea that a woman can take responsibility for herself as lesbian or as heterosexual is foreign to patriarchy.

7. Heterosexuality is compulsory (Adrienne Rich, "Compulsory Heterosexuality and Lesbian Existence," *Signs* 5 [Summer 1980]: 631–60) and chosen (Marilyn Frye, Assignment: NWSA—Bloomington—1980: Speak on "Lesbian Perspectives on Women's Studies," *Sinister Wisdom* 14 [1980]: 3–7).

Notice, too, that it may be politically advantageous for gay men to interpret homosexuality as caused, as something they did not choose, in order to protect themselves from being perceived by straight men as breaking the bonds of fraternity.

28

Domain

Michel Foucault

Sexuality must not be described as a stubborn drive, by nature alien and of necessity disobedient to a power which exhausts itself trying to subdue it and often fails to control it entirely. It appears rather as *an especially dense transfer point for relations of power*: between men and women, young people and old people, parents and offspring, teachers and students, priests and laity, an administration and a population. Sexuality is not the most intractable element in power relations, but rather one of those endowed with the greatest instrumentality: useful for the greatest number of maneuvers and capable of serving as a point of support, as a linchpin, for the most varied strategies.

There is no single, all-encompassing strategy, valid for all of society and uniformly bearing on all the manifestations of sex. For example, the idea that there have been repeated attempts, by various means, to reduce all of sex to its reproductive function, its heterosexual and adult form, and its matrimonial legitimacy fails to take into account the manifold objectives aimed for, the manifold means employed in the different sexual politics concerned with the two sexes, the different age groups and social classes.

In a first approach to the problem, it seems that we can distinguish four great strategic unities which, beginning in the eighteenth century, formed specific mechanisms of knowledge and power centering on sex. These did not come into being fully developed at that time; but it was then that they took on a consistency and gained an effectiveness in the order of power, as well as a productivity in the order of knowledge, so that it is possible to describe them in their relative autonomy.

1. *A hysterization of women's bodies:* a threefold process whereby the feminine body was analyzed—qualified and disqualified—as being thoroughly saturated with sexuality; whereby it was integrated into the sphere of medical practices, by reason of a pathology intrinsic to it; whereby, finally, it was placed in organic communication with the social body (whose regulated fecundity it was supposed to ensure), the family space (of which it had to be a substantial and functional element), and the life of children (which it produced and had to guarantee, by virtue of a biologico-moral responsibility lasting through the entire period of the children's education): the Mother, with her negative image of "nervous woman," constituted the most visible form of this hysterization.

2. *A pedagogization of children's sex:* a double assertion that practically all children indulge or are prone to indulge in sexual activity; and that, being unwarranted, at the same time "natural" and "contrary to nature," this sexual activity posed physical and moral, individual and collective dangers; children were defined as "preliminary" sexual beings, on this side of sex, yet within it, astride a dangerous dividing line. Parents, families, educators, doctors, and eventually psychologists would have to take charge, in a continuous way, of this precious and perilous, dangerous and endangered sexual potential: this pedagogization was especially evident in the war against onanism, which in the West lasted nearly two centuries.

3. *A socialization of procreative behavior:* an economic socialization via all the incitements and restrictions, the "social" and fiscal measures brought to bear on the fertility of couples; a political socialization achieved through the "responsibilization" of couples with regard to the social body as a whole (which had to be limited or on the contrary reinvigorated), and a medical socialization carried out by attributing a pathogenic value—for the individual and the species—to birth-control practices.

4. *A psychiatrization of perverse pleasure:* the sexual instinct was isolated as a separate biological and psychical instinct; a clinical analysis was made of all the forms of anomalies by which it could be afflicted: it was assigned a role of normalization or pathologization with respect to all behavior; and finally, a corrective technology was sought for these anomalies.

Four figures emerged from this preoccupation with sex, which mounted throughout the nineteenth century—four privileged objects of knowledge, which were also targets and anchorage points for the ventures of knowledge: the hysterical woman, the masturbating child, the Malthusian couple, and the perverse adult. Each of them corresponded to one of these strategies which, each in its own way, invested and made use of the sex of women, children, and men.

What was at issue in these strategies? A struggle against sexuality? Or were they part of an effort to gain control of it? An attempt to regulate it more effectively and mask its more indiscreet, conspicuous, and intractable aspects? A way of formulating only that measure of knowledge about it that was acceptable or useful? In actual fact, what was involved, rather, was the *very production of sexuality*. Sexuality must not be thought of as a kind of natural given which power tries to hold in check, or as an obscure domain which knowledge tries gradually to uncover. It is the name that can be given to a historical construct: not a furtive reality that is difficult to grasp, but a great surface network in which the stimulation of bodies, the intensification of pleasures, the incitement to discourse, the formation of special knowledges, the strengthening of controls and resistances, are linked to one another, in accordance with a few major strategies of knowledge and power.

It will be granted no doubt that relations of sex gave rise, in every society, to a *deployment of alliance*: a system of marriage, of fixation and development of kinship ties, of transmission of names and possessions. This deployment of alliance, with the mechanisms of constraint that ensured its existence and the complex knowledge it often required, lost some of its importance as economic processes and political structures could no longer rely on it as an adequate instrument or sufficient support. Particularly from the eighteenth century onward, Western societies created and deployed a new apparatus which was superimposed on the previous one, and which, without completely supplanting the latter, helped to reduce its importance. I am speaking of the *deployment of sexuality*: like the *deployment of alliance,* it connects up with the circuit of sexual partners, but in a completely different way. The two systems can be contrasted term by term. The deployment of alliance is built around a system of rules defining the permitted and the forbidden, the licit and the illicit, whereas the deployment of sexuality operates according to mobile, polymorphous, and contingent techniques of power. The deployment of alliance has as one of its chief objectives to reproduce the interplay of relations and maintain the law that governs them; the deployment of sexuality, on the other hand, engenders a continual extension of areas and forms of control. For the first, what is pertinent is the link between partners and definite statutes; the second is concerned with the sensations of the body, the quality of pleasures, and the nature of impressions, however tenuous or imperceptible these may be. Lastly, if the deployment of alliance is firmly tied to the economy due to the role it can play in the transmission or circulation of wealth, the deployment of sexuality is linked to the economy through numerous and subtle relays, the main one of which, however, is the body—the body that produces and consumes. In a word, the deployment of alliance is attuned to a homeostasis of the social body, which it has the function of maintaining; whence its privileged link with the law; whence too the fact that the important phase for it is "reproduction." The deployment of sexuality has its reason for being, not in reproducing itself, but in proliferating, innovating, annexing, creating, and penetrating bodies in an increasingly detailed way, and in controlling populations in an increasingly comprehensive way. We are compelled, then, to accept three or four hypotheses which run counter to the one on which the theme of a sexuality repressed by the modern forms of society is based: sexuality is tied to recent devices of power; it has been expanding at an increasing rate since the seventeenth century; the arrangement that has sustained it is not governed by reproduction; it has been linked from the outset with an intensification of the body—with its exploitation as an object of knowledge and an element in relations of power.

It is not exact to say that the deployment of sexuality supplanted the deployment of alliance. One can imagine that one day it will have replaced it. But as things stand at present, while it does tend to cover up the deployment of alliance, it has neither obliterated the latter nor rendered it useless. Moreover, historically it was around and on the basis of the deployment of alliance that the deployment of sexuality was constructed. First the practice of penance, then that of the examination of conscience and spiritual direction, was the formative nucleus: . . . what was at issue to begin with at the tribunal of penance was sex insofar as it was the basis of relations; the questions posed had to do with the commerce allowed or forbidden (adultery, extramarital relations, relations with a person prohibited by blood or statute, the legitimate or illegitimate character of the act of sexual congress); then, coinciding with the new pastoral and its application in seminaries, secondary schools, and convents, there was a gradual progression away from the problematic of relations toward a problematic of the "flesh," that is, of the body, sensation, the nature of pleasure, the more secret forms of enjoyment or acquiescence. "Sexuality" was taking shape, born of a technology of power that was originally focused on alliance. Since then, it has not ceased to operate in conjunction with a system of alliance on which it has depended for support. The family cell, in the form in which it came to be valued in the course of the eighteenth century, made it possible for the main elements of the deployment of sexuality (the feminine body, infantile precocity, the regulation of births, and to a lesser extent no doubt, the specification of the perverted) to develop along its two primary dimensions: the husband-wife axis and the parents-children axis. The family, in its contemporary form, must not be understood as a social, economic, and political structure of alliance that excludes or at least restrains sexuality, that diminishes it as much as possible, preserving only its useful functions. On the contrary, its role is to anchor sexuality and provide it with a permanent support. It ensures the production of a sexuality that is not homogeneous with the privileges of alliance, while making it possible for the systems of alliance to be imbued with a new tactic of power which they would otherwise be impervious to. The family is the interchange of sexuality and alliance: it conveys the law and the juridical dimension in the deployment of sexuality; and it conveys the economy of pleasure and the intensity of sensations in the regime of alliance.

This interpenetration of the deployment of alliance and that of sexuality in the form of the family allows us to understand a number of facts: that since the eighteenth century the family has become an obligatory locus of affects, feelings, love; that sexuality has its privileged point of development in the family; that for this reason sexuality is "incestuous" from the start. It may be that in societies where the mechanisms of alliance predominate, prohibition of incest is a functionally indispensable rule. But in a society such as ours, where the family is the most active site of sexuality, and where it is doubtless the exigencies of the latter which maintain and prolong its existence, incest—for different reasons altogether and in a completely different way—occupies a central place; it is constantly being solicited and refused; it is an object of obsession and attraction, a dreadful secret and an indispensable pivot. It is manifested as a thing that is strictly forbidden in the family insofar as the latter functions as a deployment of alliance; but it is also a thing that is continuously demanded in order for the family to be a hotbed of constant sexual incitement. If for more than a century the West has displayed such a strong interest in the prohibition of incest, if more or less by common accord it has been seen as a social universal and one of the points through which every society is obliged to pass on the way to becoming a culture, perhaps this is because it was found to be a means of self-defense, not against an incestuous desire, but against the expansion and the implications of this deployment of sexuality which had been set up, but which, among its many benefits, had the disadvantage of ignoring the laws and juridical forms of alliance. By asserting that all societies without exception, and consequently our own, were subject to this rule of rules, one guaranteed that this deployment of sexuality, whose strange effects were beginning to be felt—among them, the affective intensification of the family space—would not be able to escape from the grand and ancient system of alliance. Thus the law would be secure, even in the new mechanics of power. For this is the paradox of a society which, from the eighteenth century to the present, has created so many technologies of power that are foreign to the concept of law: it fears the effects and proliferations of those technologies and attempts to recode them in forms of law. If one considers the threshold of all culture to be prohibited incest, then sexuality has been, from the dawn of time, under the sway of law and right. By devoting so much effort to an endless reworking of the transcultural theory of the incest taboo, anthropology has proved worthy of the whole modern deployment of sexuality and the theoretical discourses it generates.

What has taken place since the seventeenth century can be interpreted in the following manner: the deployment of sexuality which first developed on the fringes of familial institutions (in the direction of conscience and pedagogy, for example) gradually became focused on the family: the alien, irreducible, and even perilous effects it held in store for the deployment of alliance (an awareness of this danger was evidenced in the criticism often directed at the indiscretion of the directors, and in the entire controversy, which occurred somewhat later, over the private or public, institutional or familial education of children[1]) were absorbed by the family, a family that was reorganized, restricted no doubt, and in any case intensified in comparison with the functions it formerly exercised in the deployment of alliance. In the family, parents and relatives became the chief agents of a deployment of sexuality which drew its outside support from doctors, educators, and later psychiatrists, and which began by competing with the relations of alliance but soon "psychologized" or "psychiatrized" the latter. Then these new personages made their appearance: the nervous woman, the frigid wife, the indifferent mother—or worse, the mother beset by murderous obsessions—the impotent, sadistic, perverse husband, the hysterical or neurasthenic girl, the precocious and already exhausted child, and the young homosexual who rejects marriage or neglects his wife. These were the combined figures of an alliance gone bad and an abnormal sexuality; they were the means by which the disturbing factors of the latter were brought into the former; and yet they also provided an opportunity for the alliance system to assert its prerogatives in the order of sexuality.

Then a pressing demand emanated from the family: a plea for help in reconciling these unfortunate conflicts between sexuality and alliance; and, caught in the grip of this deployment of sexuality which had invested it from without, contributing to its solidification into its modern form, the family broadcast the long complaint of its sexual suffering to doctors, educators, psychiatrists, priests, and pastors, to all the "experts" who would listen. It was as if it had suddenly discovered the dreadful secret of what had always been hinted at and inculcated in it: the family, the keystone of alliance, was the germ of all the misfortunes of sex. And lo and behold, from the mid-nineteenth century onward, the family engaged in searching out the slightest traces of sexuality in its midst, wrenching from itself the most difficult confessions, soliciting an audience with everyone who might know something about the matter, and opening itself unreservedly to endless examination. The family was the crystal in the deployment of sexuality: it seemed to be the source of a sexuality which it actually only reflected and diffracted. By virtue of its permeability, and through that process of reflections to the outside, it became one of the most valuable tactical components of the deployment.

But this development was not without its tensions and problems. Charcot doubtless constituted a central figure in this as well. For many years he was the most noteworthy of all those to whom families, burdened down as they were with this sexuality that saturated them, appealed for mediation and treatment. On receiving parents who brought him their children, husbands their wives, and wives their husbands, from the world over, his first concern was to separate the "patient" from his family, and the better to observe him, he would pay as little attention as possible to what the family had to say.[2] He sought to detach the sphere of sexuality from the system of alliance, in order to deal with it directly through a medical practice whose technicity and autonomy were guaranteed by the neurological model. Medicine thus assumed final responsibility, according to the rules of a specific knowledge, for a sexuality which it had in fact urged families to concern themselves with as an essential task and a major danger. Moreover, Charcot noted on several occasions how difficult it was for families to "yield" the patient whom they nonetheless had brought to the doctor, how they laid siege to the mental hospitals where the subject was being kept out of view, and the ways in which they were constantly interfering with the doctor's work. Their worry was unwarranted, however: the therapist only intervened in order to return to them individuals who were sexually compatible with the family system; and while this intervention manipulated the sexual body, it did not authorize the latter to define itself in explicit discourse. One must not speak of these "genital causes": so went the phrase—muttered in a muted voice— which the most famous ears of our time overheard one day in 1886, from the mouth of Charcot.

This was the context in which psychoanalysis set to work; but not without substantially modifying the pattern of anxieties and reassurances. In the beginning it must have given rise to distrust and hostility, for, pushing Charcot's lesson to the extreme, it undertook to examine the sexuality of individuals outside family control; it brought this sexuality to light without covering it over again with the neurological model; more serious still, it called family relations into question in the analysis it made of them. But despite everything, psychoanalysis, whose technical procedure seemed to place the confession of sexuality outside family jurisdiction, rediscovered the law of alliance, the involved workings of marriage and kinship, and incest at the heart of this sexuality, as the principle of its formation and the key to its intelligibility. The guarantee that one would find the parents-children relationship at the root of everyone's sexuality made it possible—even when everything seemed to point to the reverse process—to keep the deployment of sexuality coupled to the system of alliance. There was no risk that sexuality would appear to be, by nature, alien to the law: it was constituted only through the law. Parents, do not be afraid to bring your children to analysis: it will teach them that in any case it is you whom they love. Children, you really shouldn't complain that you are not orphans, that you always rediscover in your innermost selves your Object-Mother or the sovereign sign of your Father: it is through them that you gain access to desire. Whence, after so many reticences, the enormous consumption of analysis in societies where the deployment of alliance and the family system needed strengthening. For this is one of the most significant aspects of this entire history of the deployment of sexuality: it had its beginnings in the technology of the "flesh" in classical Christianity, basing itself on the alliance system and the rules that governed the latter; but today it fills a reverse function in that it tends to prop up the old deployment of alliance. From the direction of conscience to psychoanalysis, the deployments of alliance and sexuality were involved in a slow process that had them turning about one another until, more than three centuries later, their positions were reversed; in the Christian pastoral, the law of alliance codified the flesh which was just being discovered and fitted it into a framework that was still juridical in character: with psychoanalysis, sexuality gave body and life to the rules of alliance by saturating them with desire.

Hence the domain we must analyze . . . is that deployment of sexuality: its formation on the basis of the Christian notion of the flesh, and its development through the four great strategies that were deployed in the nineteenth century: the sexualization of children, the hysterization of women, the specification of the perverted, and the regulation of populations—all strategies that went by way of a family which must be viewed, not as a powerful agency of prohibition, but as a major factor of sexualization.

The first phase corresponded to the need to form a "labor force" (hence to avoid any useless "expenditure," any wasted energy, so that all forces were reduced to labor capacity alone) and to ensure its reproduction (conjugality, the regulated fabrication of children). The second phase corresponded to that epoch of *Spätkapitalismus* in which the exploitation of wage labor does not demand the same violent and physical constraints as in the nineteenth century, and where the politics of the body does not require the elision of sex or its restriction solely to the reproductive function; it relies instead on a multiple channeling into the controlled circuits of the economy—on what has been called a hyperrepressive desublimation.

If the politics of sex makes little use of the law of the taboo but brings into play an entire technical machinery, if what is involved is the production of sexuality rather than the repression of sex, then our emphasis has to be placed elsewhere; we must shift our analysis away from the problem of "labor capacity" and doubtless abandon the diffuse energetics that underlies the theme of a sexuality repressed for economic reasons.

Notes

1. Molière's *Tartuffe* and Jakob Michael Lenz's *Tutor,* separated by more than a century, both depict the interference of the deployment of sexuality in the family organization. apropos of spiritual direction in *Tartuffe* and education in *The Tutor.*

2. Jean Martin Charcot, *Leçons de Mardi*, January 7, 1888: "In order to properly treat a hysterical girl, one must not leave her with her father and mother; she needs to be placed in a mental hospital. . . . Do you know how long well-behaved little girls cry for their mothers after they part company? Let us take the average, if you will; it's not very long, a half-hour or thereabouts."

February 21, 1888: "In the case of hysteria of young boys, what one must do is to separate them from their mothers. So long as they are with their mothers, nothing is of any use. . . . The father is sometimes just as unbearable as the mother; it is best, then, to get rid of them both."

29

Is There a History of Sexuality?

David M. Halperin

Sex has no history.[1] It is a natural fact, grounded in the functioning of the body, and, as such, it lies outside of history and culture. Sexuality, by contrast, does not properly refer to some aspect or attribute of bodies. Unlike sex, sexuality is a cultural production: it represents the *appropriation* of the human body and of its physiological capacities by an ideological discourse.[2] Sexuality is not a somatic fact; it is a cultural effect. Sexuality, then, does have a history—though (as I shall argue) not a very long one.

To say that, of course, is not to state the obvious—despite the tone of assurance with which I just said it—but to advance a controversial, suspiciously fashionable, and, perhaps, a strongly counterintuitive claim. The plausibility of such a claim might seem to rest on nothing more substantial than the prestige of the brilliant, pioneering, but largely theoretical work of the late French philosopher Michel Foucault.[3] According to Foucault, sexuality is not a thing, a natural fact, a fixed and immovable element in the eternal grammar of human subjectivity, but that "set of effects produced in bodies, behaviors, and social relations by a certain deployment" of "a complex political technology."[4] "Sexuality," Foucault insists in another passage,

> must not be thought of as a kind of natural given which power tries to hold in check, or as an obscure domain which knowledge tries gradually to uncover. It is the name that can be given to a historical construct [*dispositif*]: not a furtive reality that is difficult to grasp, but a great surface network in which the stimulation of bodies, the intensification of pleasures, the incitement to discourse, the formation of special knowledges, the strengthening of controls and resistances, are linked to one another, in accordance with a few major strategies of knowledge and power.[5]

First published in *History and Theory* 28, no. 3 (1989). Reprinted by permission of the author.

Is Foucault right? I believe he is, but I also believe that more is required to establish the historicity of sexuality than the mere weight of Foucault's authority. To be sure, a great deal of work, both conceptual and empirical, has already been done to sustain Foucault's central insights and to carry forward the historicist project that he did so much to advance.[6] But much more needs to be accomplished if we are to fill in the outlines of the picture that Foucault had time only to sketch—hastily and inadequately, as he was the first to admit[7]—and if we are to demonstrate that sexuality is indeed, as he claimed, a uniquely modern production.

The study of classical antiquity has a special role to play in this historical enterprise. The sheer interval of time separating the ancient from the modern world spans cultural changes of such magnitude that the contrasts to which they give rise cannot fail to strike anyone who is on the lookout for them. The student of classical antiquity is inevitably confronted in the ancient record by a radically unfamiliar set of values, behaviors, and social practices, by ways of organizing and articulating experience that challenge modem notions about what life is like, and that call into question the supposed universality of "human nature" as we currently understand it. Not only does this historical distance permit us to view ancient social and sexual conventions with particular sharpness; it also enables us to bring more clearly into focus the ideological dimension—the purely conventional and arbitrary character—of our own social and sexual experiences.[8] One of the currently unquestioned assumptions about sexual experience which the study of antiquity calls into question is the assumption that sexual behavior reflects or expresses an individual's "sexuality."

Now that would seem to be a relatively harmless and unproblematic assumption to make, empty of all ideological content, but what exactly do we have in mind when we make it? What, in particular, do we understand by our concept of "sexuality"? I think we understand "sexuality" to refer to a positive, distinct, and constitutive feature of the human personality, to the characterological seat within the individual of sexual acts, desires, and pleasures—the determinate source from which all sexual expression proceeds. "Sexuality" in this sense is not a purely descriptive term, a neutral representation of some objective state of affairs or a simple recognition of some familiar facts about us; rather, it is a distinctive way of constructing, organizing, and interpreting those "facts," and it performs quite a lot of conceptual work.

First of all, sexuality defines itself as a separate, sexual domain within the larger field of human psychophysical nature. Second, sexuality effects the conceptual demarcation and isolation of that domain from other areas of personal and social life that have traditionally cut across it, such as carnality, venery, libertinism, virility, passion, amorousness, eroticism, intimacy, love, affection, appetite, and desire—to name but a few of the older claimants to territories more recently staked out by sexuality. Finally, sexuality generates sexual identity: it endows each of us with an individual sexual nature, with a personal essence defined (at least in part) in specifically sexual terms; it implies that human beings are individuated at the level of their sexuality, that they differ from one another in their sexuality and, indeed, belong to different types or kinds of being by virtue of their sexuality.

These, at least, appear to me to be some of the significant ramifications of "sexuality," as it is currently conceptualized. I shall argue that the outlook it represents is alien to the recorded experience of the ancients. Two themes, in particular, that seem intrinsic to the modern conceptualization of sexuality but that hardly find an echo in ancient sources will provide the focus of my investigation: the autonomy of sexuality as a separate sphere of existence (deeply implicated in other areas of life, to be sure, but distinct from them and capable of acting on them at least as much as it is acted on by them), and the function of sexuality as a principle of individuation in human natures. In what follows, I shall take up each theme in turn, attempting to document in this fashion the extent of the divergence between ancient and modern varieties of sexual experience.

First, the autonomy of sexuality as a separate sphere of existence. The basic point I should like to make has already been made for me by Robert Padgug in a now-classic essay on conceptualizing sexuality in history. Padgug argues that

> what we consider "sexuality" was, in the pre-bourgeois world, a group of acts and institutions not necessarily linked to one another, or, if they were linked, combined in ways very different from our own. Intercourse, kinship, and the family, and gender, did not form anything like a "field" of sexuality. Rather, each group of sexual acts was connected directly or indirectly—that is, formed part of—institutions and thought patterns which we tend to view as political, economic, or social in nature, and the connections cut across our idea of sexuality as a thing, detachable from other things, and as a separate sphere of private existence.[9]

The ancient evidence amply supports Padgug's claim. In classical Athens, for example, sex did not express inward dispositions or inclinations so much as it served to position social actors in the places assigned to them, by virtue of their political standing, in the hierarchical structure of the Athenian polity. Let me expand this formulation.

In classical Athens a relatively small group made up of the adult male citizens held a virtual monopoly of social power and constituted a clearly defined élite within the political and social life of the city-state. The predominant feature of the social landscape of classical Athens was the great divide in status between this superordinate group, composed of citizens, and a subordinate group, composed of women, children, foreigners, and slaves—all of whom lacked full civil rights (though they were not all equally subordinate). Sexual relations not only respected that divide but were strictly polarized in conformity with it.

Sex is portrayed in Athenian documents not as a mutual enterprise in which two or more persons jointly engage but as an action performed by a social superior upon a social inferior. Consisting as it was held to do in an asymmetrical gesture—the penetration of the body of one person by the body (and, specifically, by the phallus)[10] of another—sex effectively divided and distributed its participants into radically distinct and incommensurable categories ("penetrator" versus "penetrated"), categories which in turn were wholly congruent with superordinate and subordinate social categories. For sexual penetration was thematized as domination: the relation between the insertive and the receptive sexual partner was taken to be the same kind of relation as that obtaining between social superior and social inferior.[11] Insertive and receptive sexual roles were therefore necessarily isomorphic with superordinate and subordinate social status; an adult male citizen of Athens could have legitimate sexual relations *only* with statutory minors (his inferiors not in age but in social and political status): the proper targets of his sexual desire included, specifically, women of any age, free males past the age of puberty who were not yet old enough to be citizens (I'll call them "boys," for short), as well as foreigners and slaves of either sex.[12]

Moreover, the physical act of sex between a citizen and a statutory minor was stylized in such a way as to mirror in the minute details of its hierarchical arrangement the relation of structured inequality that governed the wider social interaction of the two lovers. What an Athenian did in bed was determined by the differential in status that distinguished him or her from his or her sexual partner; the (male) citizen's superior prestige and authority expressed themselves in his sexual precedence—in his power to initiate a sexual act, his right to obtain pleasure from it, and his assumption of an insertive rather than a receptive sexual role. Different social actors had different sexual roles: to assimilate both the superordinate and the subordinate member of a sexual relationship to the same "sexuality" would have been as bizarre, in Athenian eyes, as classifying burglar as an "active criminal," his victim as a "passive criminal," and the two of them alike as partners in crime—it would have been to confuse what, in reality, were supposedly separate and distinct identities.[13] Each act of sex was no doubt an expression of real, personal desire on the part of the sexual actors involved, but their very desires had already been shaped by the shared cultural definition of sex as an activity that generally occurred only between a citizen and a noncitizen, between a person invested with full civil status and a statutory minor.

The "sexuality" of the classical Athenians, then, far from being independent of "politics" (each construed as an autonomous sphere) *was constituted by the very principles* on which Athenian public life was organized. In fact, the correspondences in classical Athens between sexual norms and social practices were so strict that an inquiry into Athenian "sexuality" *per se* would be nonsensical: such an inquiry could only obscure the phenomenon it was intended to elucidate, for it would conceal the sole context in which the sexual protocols of the classical Athenians make any sense—namely, the structure of the Athenian polity. The social articulation of sexual desire in classical Athens thus furnishes a telling illustration of the interdependence in culture of social practices and subjective experiences. Indeed, the classical Greek record strongly supports the conclusion drawn (from a quite different body, of evidence) by the French anthropologist Maurice Godelier: "it is not sexuality which haunts society, but society which haunts the body's sexuality."[14]

For those inhabitants of the ancient world about whom it is possible to generalize, sexuality did not hold the key to the secrets or the human personality. (In fact, the very concept of and set of practices centering on "the human personality"—the physical and social sciences of the blank individual—belong to a much later era and bespeak the modern social and economic conditions that accompanied their rise.) In the Hellenic world, by contrast, the measure of a free male was most often taken by observing how he fared when tested in public competition against other free males, not by scrutinizing his sexual constitution. War (and other agonistic contests), not love, served to reveal the inner man, the stuff a free Greek male was made of.[15] A striking instance of this emphasis on public life as the primary locus of signification can be found in the work of Artemidorus, a master dream-interpreter who lived and wrote in the second century of our era and whose testimony, there is good reason to believe, accurately represents the sexual norms of ancient Mediterranean culture.[16] Artemidorus saw public life, not erotic life, as the principal tenor of dreams. Even sexual dreams, in Artemidorus's system, are seldom *really* about sex: rather, they are about the rise and fall of the dreamer's public fortunes, the vicissitudes of his domestic economy.[17] If a man dreams of having sex with his mother, for example, his dream signifies to Artemidorus nothing in particular about the dreamer's own sexual psychology, his fantasy life, or the history of his relations with his parents; it's a very common dream, and so it's a bit tricky to interpret precisely, but basically it's a lucky dream: it may signify—depending on the family's circumstances at the time, the postures of the partners in the dream, and the mode of penetration—that the dreamer will be successful in politics ("success" meaning, evidently, the power to screw one's country), that he will go into exile or return from exile, that he will win his lawsuit, obtain a rich harvest from his lands, or change professions, among many other things (1.79). Artemidorus's system of dream interpretation resembles the indigenous dream-lore of certain Amazonian tribes who, despite their quite different sociosexual systems, share with the ancient Greeks a belief in the predictive value of dreams. Like Artemidorus, these Amazonian peoples reverse what modern bourgeois Westerners take to be the natural flow of signification in dreams (from images of public and social events to private and sexual meanings): in both Kagwahiv and Mehinaku culture, for example, dreaming about the female genitalia portends a wound (and so a man who has such a dream is especially careful when he handles axes or other sharp instruments the next day); dreamt wounds do not symbolize the female genitalia.[18] Both these ancient and modern dream-interpreters, then, are innocent of "sexuality": what is fundamental to their experience of sex is not anything *we* would regard as essentially sexual;[19] it is instead something essentially outward, public, and social. "Sexuality," for cultures not shaped by some very recent European and American bourgeois developments, is not a cause but an effect. The social body precedes the sexual body.

*   *   *

I now come to the second of my two themes—namely, the individuating function of sexuality, its role in generating individual sexual identities. The connection between the modern interpretation of sexuality as an autonomous domain
and the modern construction of individual sexual identities has been well analyzed, once again, by Robert Padgug:

> the most commonly held twentieth-century assumptions about sexuality imply
> that it is a separate category of existence (like "the economy," or "the state,"
> other supposedly independent spheres of reality), almost identical with the
> sphere of private life. Such a view necessitates the location of sexuality within
> the individual as a fixed essence, leading to a classic division of individual and
> society and to a variety of psychological determinisms, and, often enough, to
> a full-blown biological determinism as well. These in turn involve the
> enshrinement of contemporary sexual categories as universal, static, and per-
> manent, suitable for the analysis of all human beings and all societies.[20]

The study of ancient Mediterranean societies clearly exposes the defects in any
such essentialist conceptualization of sexuality. Because, as we have seen in the
case of classical Athens, erotic desires and sexual object-choices in antiquity
were generally not determined by a typology of anatomical sexes (male versus
female), but rather by the social articulation of power (superordinate versus subordinate), the currently fashionable distinction between homosexuality and heterosexuality (and, similarly, between "homosexuals" and "heterosexuals" as
individual types) had no meaning for the classical Athenians: there were not, so
far as they knew, two different kinds of "sexuality," two differently structured
psychosexual states or modes of affective orientation, but a single form of
sexual experience which all free adult males shared—making due allowance for
variations in individual tastes, as one might make for individual palates.[21]

Thus, in the Third Dithyramb by the classical poet Bacchylides, the
Athenian hero Theseus, voyaging to Crete among the seven youths and seven
maidens destined for the Minotaur and defending one of the maidens from the
advances of the libidinous Cretan commander, warns him vehemently against
molesting *any one* of the Athenian youths (*tin' ëïtheôn:* 43)—that is, any girl *or
boy*. Conversely, the antiquarian *littérateur* Athenaeus, writing six or seven hundred years later, is amazed that Polycrates, the tyrant of Samos in the sixth century B.C., did not send for any boys *or women* along with the other luxury articles he imported to Samos for his personal use during his reign, "despite his passion for relations with males" (12.540c–e).[22] Now *both* the notion that an act of
heterosexual aggression in itself makes the aggressor suspect of homosexual
tendencies *and* the mirror-opposite notion that a person with marked homosexual tendencies is bound to hanker after heterosexual contacts are nonsensical
to us, associating as we do sexual object-choice with a determinate kind of "sex-

uality," a fixed sexual nature, but it would be a monumental task indeed to enumerate all the ancient documents in which the alternative "boy or woman"
occurs with perfect nonchalance in an erotic context, as if the two were functionally interchangeable.[23]

A particularly striking testimony to the imaginable extent of male indifference to the sex of sexual objects can be found in a marriage-contract from Hellenistic Egypt dating to 92 B.C.[24] This not untypical document stipulates that "it
shall not be lawful for Philiscus [the prospective husband] to bring home
another wife in addition to Apollonia or to have a concubine *or boy-lover*. . . ."[25]
The possibility that one's husband might take it into his head at some point
during one's marriage to set up another household with his boyfriend evidently
figured among the various potential domestic disasters that a prudent fiancée
would be sure to anticipate and to indemnify herself against. A somewhat similar expectation is articulated in an entirely different context by Dio
Chrysostom, a moralizing Greek orator from the late first century A.D. In a
speech denouncing the corrupt morals of city life, Dio asserts that even
respectable women are so easy to seduce nowadays that men will soon tire of
them and will turn their attention to boys instead—just as addicts progress inex-
orably from wine to hard drugs (7.150–152). According to Dio, then, pederasty
is not simply a second best; it is not "caused," as many modern historians of the
ancient Mediterranean appear to believe, by the supposed seclusion of women,
by the practice (it was more likely an ideal) of locking them away in the inner
rooms of their fathers' or husbands' houses and thereby preventing them from
serving as sexual targets for adult men. In Dio's fantasy, at least, pederasty
springs not from the insufficient but from the superabundant supply of sexually
available women; the easier it is to have sex with women, on his view, the less
desirable sex with women becomes, and the more likely men are to seek sexual
pleasure with boys. Scholars sometimes describe the cultural formation underlying this apparent refusal by Greek males to discriminate categorically among
sexual objects on the basis of anatomical sex as a bisexuality of penetration[26]
or—even more intriguingly—as a heterosexuality indifferent to its object,[27] but
I think it would be advisable not to speak of it as a sexuality at all but to describe
it, rather, as a more generalized ethos of penetration and domination,[28] a sociosexual discourse structured by the presence or absence of its central term: the
phallus.[29] It may be worth pausing now to examine one text in particular which
clearly indicates how thoroughly ancient cultures were able to dispense with the
notion of sexual identity.

The document in question is the ninth chapter in the Fourth Book of the *De
morbis chronicis,* a mid-fifth-century A.D. Latin translation and adaptation by
the African writer Caelius Aurelianus of a now largely lost work on chronic diseases by the Greek physician Soranus, who practiced and taught in Rome during
the early part of the second century A.D. Caelius's work is not much read nowadays, and it is almost entirely neglected by modern historians of "sexuality";[30]
its date is late, its text is corrupt, and, far from being a self-conscious literary

artifact, it belongs to the despised genre of Roman technical writing. But, despite all these drawbacks, it repays close attention, and I have chosen to discuss it here partly in order to show what can be learned about the ancient world from works that lie outside the received canon of classical authors.

The topic of this passage is *molles* (*malthakoi* in Greek)—that is, "soft" or unmasculine men, men who depart from the cultural norm of manliness insofar as they actively desire to be subjected by other men to a "feminine" (that is, receptive) role in sexual intercourse.[31] Caelius begins with an implicit defense of his own unimpeachable masculinity by noting how difficult it is to believe that such people actually exist;[32] he then goes on to observe that the cause of their affliction is not natural (that is, organic) but is rather their own excessive desire, which—in a desperate and foredoomed attempt to satisfy itself—drives out their sense of shame and forcibly converts parts of their bodies to sexual uses not intended by nature. These men willingly adopt the dress, gait, and other characteristics of women, thereby confirming that they suffer not from a bodily disease but from a mental (or moral) defect. After some further arguments in support of that point, Caelius draws an interesting comparison: "For just as the women called *tribades* [in Greek], because they practice both kinds of sex, are more eager to have sexual intercourse with women than with men and pursue women with an almost masculine jealousy . . . so they too [i.e., the *molles*] are afflicted by a mental disease" (132–33). The mental disease in question, which strikes both men and women alike and seems to be defined as a perversion of sexual desire, would certainly appear to be nothing other than homosexuality as it is often understood today.

Several considerations combine to prohibit that interpretation, however. First of all, what Caelius treats as a pathological phenomenon is not the desire on the part of either men or women for sexual contact with a person of the same sex; quite the contrary: elsewhere, in discussing the treatment of satyriasis (a state of abnormally elevated sexual desire accompanied by itching or tension in the genitals), he issues the following advice to those who suffer from it (*De morbis acutis*, 3.18.180–81).[33]

> Do not admit visitors and particularly young women and boys. For the attractiveness of such visitors would again kindle the feeling of desire in the patient. Indeed, *even healthy persons,* seeing them, would in many cases seek sexual gratification, stimulated by the tension produced in the parts [i.e., in their own genitals].[34]

There is nothing medically problematical, then, about a desire on the part of males to obtain sexual pleasure from contact with males—so long as the proper phallocentric protocols are observed; what is of concern to Caelius,[35] as well as to other ancient moralists,[36] is the male desire to be sexually penetrated by males, for such a desire represents a voluntary abandonment of the culturally constructed masculine identity in favor of the culturally constructed feminine one. It is sex-role reversal, or gender-deviance, that is problematized here and that also furnishes part of the basis for Caelius's comparison of unmasculine men to masculine women, who assume a supposedly masculine role in their relations with other women and actively "pursue women with an almost *masculine* jealousy."

Moreover, the ground of the similitude between these male and female gender-deviants is not that they are both homosexual but rather that they are both *bi*sexual (in our terms), although in that respect at least they do not depart from the ancient sexual norm. The tribads "are [*relatively*] more eager to have sexual intercourse with women *than with men*" and "practice both kind of sex"—that is, they have sex with both men and women.[37] As for the *molles,* Caelius's earlier remarks about their extraordinarily intense sexual desire implies that they turn to receptive sex because, although they try, they are not able to satisfy themselves by means of more conventionally masculine sorts of sexual activity, including insertive sex with women.[38] Far from having desires that are structured differently from those of normal folk, these gender-deviants desire sexual pleasure just as most people do, but they have such strong and intense desires that they are driven to devise some unusual and disreputable (though ultimately futile) ways of gratifying them. This diagnosis becomes explicit at the conclusion of the chapter when Caelius explains why the disease responsible for turning men into *molles* is the only chronic disease that becomes stronger as the body grows older.

> For in other years when the body is still strong and can perform the normal functions of love, the sexual desire [of these persons] assumes a dual aspect, in which the soul is excited sometimes while playing a passive and sometimes while playing an active role. But in the case of old men who have lost their virile powers, all their sexual desire is turned in the opposite direction and consequently exerts a stronger demand for the feminine role in love. In fact, many infer that this is the reason why boys too are victims of this affliction. For, like old men, they do not possess virile powers; that is, they have not yet attained those powers which have already deserted the aged [137].[39]

"Soft" or unmasculine men, far from being a fixed and determinate sexual species with a specifically sexual identity, are evidently either men who once experienced an orthodoxly masculine sexual desire in the past or who will eventually experience such a desire in the future. They may well be men with a constitutional tendency to gender-deviance, according to Caelius, but they are not homosexuals: being a womanish man, or a mannish woman, after all, is not the same thing as being a homosexual. Furthermore, all the other ancient texts known to me, which assimilate both males who enjoy sexual contact with males and females who enjoy sexual contact with females to the same category, do so—in conformity with the two taxonomic strategies employed by Caelius Aurelianus—either because such males and females both *reverse* their proper sex-roles and adopt the sexual styles, postures, and modes of copulation conventionally associated with the opposite gender, or because they both *alternate* between the personal characteristics and sexual practices proper, respectively, to men and to women.[40]

Caelius's testimony makes an important historical point. Before the scientific construction of "sexuality" as a positive, distinct, and constitutive feature of individual human beings—an autonomous system within the physiological and psychological economy of the human organism—certain kinds of sexual *acts* could be individually evaluated and categorized, and so could certain sexual tastes or inclinations, but there was no conceptual apparatus available for identifying a person's fixed and determinate sexual *orientation,* much less for assessing and classifying it.[41] That human beings differ, often markedly, from one another in their sexual tastes in a great variety of ways (including sexual object-choice), is an unexceptionable and, indeed, an ancient observation[42]: Plato's Aristophanes invents a myth to explain why some men like women, why some men like boys, why some women like men, and why some women like women *(Symposium* 189c–193d). But it is not immediately evident that patterns of sexual object-choice are by their very nature more revealing about the temperament of individual human beings, more significant determinants of personal *identity,* than, for example, patterns of dietary object-choice.[43] And yet, it would never occur to us to refer a person's dietary preference to some innate, characterological disposition,[44] to see in his or her strongly expressed and even unvarying preference for the white meat of chicken the symptom of a profound psychophysical orientation, leading us to identify him or her in contexts quite removed from that of the eating of food as, say, a "pectoriphage" or a "stethovore"; nor would we be likely to inquire further, making nicer discriminations according to whether an individual's predilection for chicken breasts expressed itself in a tendency to eat them quickly or slowly, seldom or often, alone or in company, under normal circumstances or only in periods of great stress, with a clear or a guilty conscience ("ego-dystonic pectoriphagia"), beginning in earliest childhood or originating with a gastronomic trauma suffered in adolescence. If such questions did occur to us, moreover, I very much doubt whether we would turn to the academic disciplines of anatomy, neurology, clinical psychology, genetics, or sociobiology in the hope of obtaining a clear causal solution to them. That is because (1) we regard the liking for certain foods as a matter of taste; (2) we currently lack a theory of taste; and (3) in the absence of a theory we do not normally subject our behavior to intense, scientific or aetiological, scrutiny.

In the same way, it never occurred to the ancients to ascribe a person's sexual tastes to some positive, structural, or constitutive sexual feature of his or her personality. Just as we tend to assume that human beings are not individuated at the level of dietary preference and that we all, despite many pronounced and frankly acknowledged differences from one another in dietary habits, share the same fundamental set of alimentary appetites, and hence the same "dieticity" or "edility," so most premodern and non-Western cultures, despite an awareness of the range of possible variations in human sexual behavior, refuse to individuate human beings at the level of sexual preference and assume, instead, that we all share the same fundamental set of sexual appetites, the same "sexuality." For most of the world's inhabitants, in other words, "sexuality" is no more a "fact of life" than "dieticity." Far from being a necessary or intrinsic constituent of human life, "sexuality" seems indeed to be a uniquely modern, Western, even bourgeois production—one of those cultural fictions which in every society give human beings access to themselves as meaningful actors in their world, and which are thereby objectivated.

If there is a lesson that we should draw from this picture of ancient sexual attitudes and behaviors, it is that we need to de-center *sexuality* from the focus of the cultural interpretation of sexual experience—and not only ancient varieties of sexual experience. Just because modern bourgeois Westerners are so obsessed with sexuality, so convinced that it holds the key to the hermeneutics of the self (and hence to social psychology as an object of historical study), we ought not therefore to conclude that everyone has always considered sexuality a basic and irreducible element in, or a central feature of, human life. Indeed, there are even sectors of our own societies to which the ideology of "sexuality" has failed to penetrate. A sociosexual system that coincides with the Greek system, insofar as it features a rigid hierarchy of sexual roles based on a set of socially articulated power-relations, has been documented in contemporary America by Jack Abbott, in one of his infamous letters written to Norman Mailer from a federal penitentiary; because the text is now quite inaccessible (it was not reprinted in Abbott's book), and stunningly apropos, I have decided to quote it here at length.

> It really was years, many years, before I began to actually realize that the women in my life—the prostitutes as well as the soft, pretty girls who giggled and teased me so much, my several wives and those of my friends—it was years before I realized that they were not women, but men; years before I assimilated the notion that this was unnatural. I still only know this intellectually, for the most part—but for the small part that remains to my ken, I know it is like a hammer blow to my temple and the shame I feel is profound. Not because of the thing itself, the sexual love I have enjoyed with these women (some so devoted it aches to recall it), but because of shame—and anger—that the world could so intimately betray me; so profoundly touch and move me—and then laugh at me and accuse my soul of a sickness, when that sickness has rescued me from mental derangement and despairs so black as to cast this night that surrounds us in prison into day. I do not mean to say I never knew the physical difference—no one but an imbecile could make such a claim. I took it, without reflection or the slightest doubt, that this was a natural sex that emerged within the society of men, with attributes that naturally complemented masculine attributes. I thought it was a natural phenomenon in the society of women as well. The attributes were feminine and so there seemed

no gross misrepresentation of facts to call them (among us men) "women." . . .
Many of my "women" had merely the appearance of handsome, extremely
neat, and polite young men. I have learned, analyzing my feelings today, that
those attributes I called feminine a moment ago were not feminine in any way
as it appears in the real female sex. These attributes seem now merely a tendency to need, to depend on another man; to need never to become a rival or
to compete with other men in the pursuits men, among themselves, engage in.
It was, it occurs to me now, almost boyish—not really feminine at all.

This is the way it always was, even in the State industrial School for
Boys—a penal institution for juvenile delinquents—where I served five years,
from age twelve to age seventeen. They were the possession and sign of manhood and it never occurred to any of us that this was strange and unnatural. It
is how I grew up—a natural part of my life in prison.

It was difficult for me to grasp the definition of the clinical term "homosexual"—and when I finally did it devastated me, as I said.[45]

Abbott's society surpasses classical Athenian society in the extent to which
power relations are gendered. Instead of the Greek system which preserves the
distinction between males and females but overrides it when articulating categories of the desirable and undesirable in favor of a distinction between dominant and submissive persons, the system described by Abbott wholly assimilates
categories of sociosexual identity to categories of gender identity—in order, no
doubt, to preserve the association in Abbott's world between "masculinity" and
the love of "women." What determines gender, for Abbott, is not anatomical sex
but social status and personal style. "Men" are defined as those who "compete
with other men in the pursuits men, among themselves, engage in," whereas
"women" are characterized by the possession of "attributes that naturally complement masculine attributes"—namely, a "tendency to need, to depend on
another man" for the various benefits won by the victors in "male" competition.
In this way "a natural sex emerges within the society of men" and qualifies, by
virtue of its exclusion from the domain of "male" precedence and autonomy, as
a legitimate target of "male" desire.

The salient features of Abbott's society are uncannily reminiscent of those
features of classical Athenian society with which we are already familiar. Most
notable is the division of the society into superordinate and subordinate groups
and *the production of desire* for members of the subordinate group in members
of the superordinate one. Desire is sparked in this system, as in classical Athens,
only when it arcs across the political divide, only when it traverses the boundary
that marks out the limits of intramural competition among the élite and that
thereby distinguishes subjects from objects of sexual desire. Sex between
"men"—and, therefore, "homosexuality"—remains unthinkable in Abbott's society (even though sex between anatomical males is an accepted and intrinsic
part of the system), just as sex between citizens, between members of the
empowered social caste, is practically inconceivable in classical Athenian
society. Similarly, sex between "men" and "women" in Abbott's world is not a

private experience in which social identities are lost or submerged; rather, in Abbott's society as in classical Athens, the act of sex—instead of implicating both sexual partners in a common "sexuality"—helps to articulate, to define, and to actualize the differences in status between them.

To discover and to write the history of sexuality has long seemed to many a sufficiently radical undertaking in itself, inasmuch as its effect (if not always the intention behind it) is to call into question the very naturalness of what we currently take to be essential to our individual natures. But in the course of implementing that ostensibly radical project many historians of sexuality seem to have reversed—perhaps unwittingly—its radical design: by preserving "sexuality" as a stable category of historical analysis not only have they not denaturalized it but, on the contrary, they have newly idealized it.[46] To the extent, in fact, that histories of "sexuality" succeed in concerning themselves with *sexuality,* to just that extent are they doomed to fall as *histories* (Foucault himself taught us that much), unless they also include as an essential part of their proper enterprise the task of demonstrating the historicity, conditions of emergence, modes of construction, and ideological contingencies of the very categories of analysis that undergird their own practice.[47] Instead of concentrating our attention specifically on the history of sexuality, then, we need to define and refine a new, and radical, historical sociology of psychology, an intellectual discipline designed to analyze the cultural poetics of desire, by which I mean the processes whereby sexual desires are constructed, mass-produced, and distributed among the various members of human living-groups.[48] We must train ourselves to recognize conventions of feeling as well as conventions of behavior and to interpret the intricate texture of personal life as an artifact, as the determinate outcome, of a complex and arbitrary constellation of cultural processes. We must, in short, be willing to admit that what seem to be our most inward, authentic, and private experiences are actually, in Adrienne Rich's admirable phrase, "shared, unnecessary/and political."[49]

A little less than fifty years ago W. H. Auden asked, in the opening lines of a canzone, "When shall we learn, what should be clear as day, We cannot choose what we are free to love?"[50] It is a characteristically judicious formulation: love, if it is to be love, must be a free act, but it is also inscribed within a larger circle of constraint, within conditions that make possible the exercise of that "freedom." The task of distinguishing freedom from constraint in love, of learning to trace the shifting and uncertain boundaries between the self and the world, is a dizzying and, indeed, an endless undertaking. If I have not significantly advanced this project here, I hope at least to have encouraged others not to abandon it.

Notes

1. Or, if it does, that history is a matter for the evolutionary biologist, not for the historian; see Lynn Margulis and Dorion Sagan, *The Origins of Sex* (New Haven: Yale University Press, 1985).

2. I adapt this formulation from a passage in Louis Adrian Montrose, "'Shaping Fantasies': Figurations of Gender and Power in Elizabethan Culture," *Representations* 2 (1983): 61–94 (passage on p. 62), which describes in turn the concept of the "sex/gender system" introduced by Gayle Rubin, "The Traffic in Women: Notes on the 'Political Economy' of Sex." In *Toward an Anthropology of Women,* ed. Rayna R. Reiter (New York, 1975), pp. 157–210.

3. Volumes Two and Three of Foucault's *History of Sexuality,* published shortly before his death, depart significantly from the theoretical orientation of his earlier work in favor of a more concrete interpretative practice; see my remarks in "No Views of Greek Love: Harald Patzer and Michel Foucault," *One Hundred Years of Homosexuality,* pp. 62–71, esp. p. 64.

4. Michel Foucault, *The History of Sexuality, Volume I: An Introduction,* trans. Robert Hurley (New York, 1978), p. 127. See Teresa de Lauretis, *Technologies of Gender: Essays on Theory, Film, and Fiction* (Bloomington: Indiana University Press, 1987), pp. 1–30, esp. p. 3, who extends Foucault's critique of sexuality to gender.

5. Foucault, *The History of Sexuality*, pp. 105–6.

6. Of special relevance are: Robert A. Padgug, "Sexual Matters: On Conceptualizing Sexuality in History," *Radical History Review* 20 (1979): 3–23; George Chauncey Jr., "From Sexual Inversion to Homosexuality: Medicine and the Changing Conceptualization of Female Deviance," in *Homosexuality: Sacrilege, Vision, Politics*, ed. Robert Boyers and George Steiner = *Salmagundi* 58–59 (1982–1983): 114–46; Arnold I. Davidson, "Sex and the Emergence of Sexuality," *Critical Inquiry* 14 (1987–1988): 16–48. See *also The Cultural Construction of Sexuality*, ed. Pat Caplan (London, 1987); T. Dunbar Moodie, "Migrancy and Male sexuality on the South African Gold Mines," *Journal of Southern African Studies* 14 (1987–1988): 228–56; George Chauncey Jr., "Christian Brotherhood or Sexual Perversion? Homosexual Identities and the Construction of Sexual Boundaries in the World War One Era," *Journal of Social History* 19 (1985–1986): 189–211.

7. E.g., Michel Foucault, *The Use of Pleasure. The History of Sexuality,* vol. 2, trans. Robert Hurley (New York, 1985), pp. 92, 253.

8. In applying the term "ideological" to sexual experience, I have been influenced by the formulation of Stuart Hall, "Culture, the Media, and the 'Ideological Effect,' " in *Mass Communication and Society*, ed. James Curran, Michael Gurevitch, Janet Woolacott, et al. (London, 1977), pp. 315–48, esp. p. 330: "ideology as a *social practice* consists of the 'subject' positioning himself in the specific complex, the objectivated field of discourses and codes which are available to him in language and culture at a particular historical conjuncture" (quoted by Ken Tucker and Andrew Treno, "The Culture of Narcissism and the Critical Tradition: An Interpretative Essay," *Berkeley Journal of Sociology* 25 [1980]: 341–55 [quotation on p. 351]); see also Hall's trenchant discussion of the constitutive role of ideology in "Deviance, Politics, and the Media," in *Deviance and Social Control,* ed. Paul Rock and Mary McIntosh, Explorations in Sociology 3 (London, 1974), pp. 261–305.

9. Padgug, "Sexual Matters," p. 16.

10. I say "phallus" rather than "penis" because (1) what qualifies as a phallus in this discursive system does not always turn out to be a penis (see note 29, below) and (2) even when phallus and penis have the same extension, or reference, they still do not have the same intension, or meaning: "phallus" betokens not a specific item of the male anatomy *simpliciter* but that same item *taken under the description* of a cultural signifier; (3) hence, the meaning of "phallus" is ultimately determined by its function in the larger sociosexual discourse; i.e., it is that which penetrates, that

which enables its possessor to play an "active" sexual role, and so forth: see Rubin, "The Traffic in Women," pp. 190–92.

11. Foucault, *The Use of Pleasure,* p. 215, puts it very well: "sexual relations—always conceived in terms of the model act of penetration, assuming a polarity that opposed activity and passivity—were seen as being of the same type as the relationship between a superior and a subordinate, an individual who dominates and one who is dominated, one who commands and one who complies, one who vanquishes and one who is vanquished."

12. In order to avoid misunderstanding, I should emphasize that by calling all persons belonging to these four groups "statutory minors," I do not wish either to suggest that they enjoyed the *same* status as one another or to obscure the many differences in status that could obtain between members of a single group—e.g., between a wife and a courtesan—differences that may not have been perfectly isomorphic with the legitimate modes of their sexual use. Nonetheless, what is striking about Athenian social usage is the tendency to collapse such distinctions as did indeed obtain between different categories of social subordinates and to create a simple opposition between them all, *en masse,* and the class of adult male citizens: on this point, see Mark Golden, "*Pais,* 'Child' and 'Slave,'" *L'Antiquité classique* 54 (1985): 91–104, esp. pp. 101 and 102, n. 38.

13. I have borrowed this analogy from Arno Schmitt, who uses it to convey what the modern sexual categories would look like from a traditional Islamic perspective: see Gianni De Martino and Arno Schmitt, *Kleine Schriften zu zwischenmännlicher Sexualität und Erotik in der muslimischen Gesellschaft* (Berlin, 1985), p. 19. Note that even the category of anatomical sex, defined in such a way as to include both men and women, seems to be absent from Greek thought for similar reasons: the complementarity of men and women as sexual partners implies to the Greeks a polarity, a difference in species, too extreme to be bridged by a single sexual concept equally applicable to each. In Greek medical writings, therefore, "the notion of sex never gets formalized as a functional identity of male and female, but is expressed solely through the representation of asymmetry and of complementarity between male and female, indicated constantly by abstract adjectives *(to thêly* ['the feminine'], *to arren* ['the masculine'])," according to Paola Manuli, "Donne mascoline, femmine sterili, vergini perpetue: La ginecologia greca tra Ippocrate e Sorano," in Silvia Campese, Paola Manuli, and Giulia Sissa, *Madre materia: Sociologia e biologia della donna greca* (Turin, 1983), pp. 147–92, esp. pp. 151 and 201n.

14. Maurice Godelier, "The Origins of Male Domination," *New Left Review* 127 (May–June 1981): 3–17 (quotation on p. 17); cf. Maurice Godelier, "Le sexe comme fondement ultime de l'ordre social et cosmique chez les Baruya de Nouvelle—Guinée. Mythe et réalité," in *Sexualité et pouvoir,* ed. Armando Verdiglione (Paris, 1976), pp. 268–306, esp. pp. 295–96.

15. I am indebted for this observation to Professor Peter M. Smith of the University of North Carolina at Chapel Hill, who notes that Sappho and Plato are the chief exceptions to this general rule.

16. See John J. Winkler, "Unnatural Acts: Erotic Protocols in Artemidoros' *Dream Analysis,*" *Constraints of Desire: The Anthropology of Sex and Gender in Ancient Greece* (New York, 1989), pp. 17–44, 221–24.

17. S. R. F. Price, "The Future of Dreams: From Freud to Artemidorus," *Past and Present* 113 (November 1986): 3–37, abridged in *Before Sexuality: The Construction of Erotic Experience in the Ancient Greek World,* ed. David M. Halperin, John J. Winkler and Froma I. Zeitlin (Princeton, N.J.: Princeton University Press, 1990), pp. 365–87; see also Michel Foucault, *The Care of the Self, The History of Sexuality,* vol. 3, trans. Robert Hurley (New York, 1986), pp. 3–36, esp. pp. 26–34.

18. See Waud H. Kracke, "Dreaming in Kagwahiv: Dream Beliefs and Their Psychic Uses in an Amazonian Indian Culture," *The Psychoanalytic Study of Society* 8 (1979): 119–71, esp. pp. 130–32, 163 (on the predictive value of dreams) and pp. 130–31, 142–45, 163–64, 168 (on the reversal of the Freudian direction of signification—which Kracke takes to be a culturally constituted defense mechanism and which he accordingly undervalues); Thomas Gregor, "'Far, Far Away My Shadow Wandered. . .': The Dream Symbolism and Dream Theories of the Mehinaku Indians

of Brazil," *American Ethnologist* 8 (1981): 709–20, esp. pp. 712–13 (on predictive value) and 714 (on the reversal of signification), largely recapitulated in Thomas Gregor, *Anxious Pleasures: The Sexual Lives of an Amazonian People* (Chicago, 1985), pp. 152–61, esp. p. 153. Foucault's comments on Artemidorus, in *The Care of the Self,* pp. 35–36, are relevant here: "The movement of analysis and the procedures of valuation do not go from the act to a domain such as sexuality or the flesh, a domain whose divine, civil, or natural laws would delineate the permitted forms; they go from the subject as a sexual actor to the other areas of life in which he pursues his [familial, social, and economic] activity. And it is in the relationship between these different forms of activity that the principles of evaluation of a sexual behavior are essentially, but not exclusively, situated."

19. Note that even the human genitals themselves do not necessarily figure as sexual signifiers in all cultural or representational contexts: for example, Caroline Walker Bynum. "The Body of Christ in the Later Middle Ages: A Reply to Leo Steinberg," *Renaissance Quarterly* 39 (1986): 399–439, argues in considerable detail that there is "reason to think that medieval people saw Christ's penis not primarily as a sexual organ but a the object of circumcision and therefore as the wounded, bleeding flesh with which it was associated in painting and in text" (p. 407).

20. Padgug, "Sexual Matters," p. 8.

21. Paul Veyne, in "La famille et l'amour sous le Haut-Empire romain," *Annales* (E. S. C) 33 (1978): 35–63, remarks (p. 50) that Seneca's *Phaedra* is the earliest text to associate homosexual inclinations with a distinct type of subjectivity. The question is more complex than that, however, and a thorough exploration of it would require scrutinizing more closely the ancient figure of the *kinaidos,* a now-defunct sexual life-form: for details, see Maud W. Gleason, "The Semiotics of Gender: Physiognomy and Self-Fashioning in the Second Century C.E.," in *Before Sexuality,* pp. 389–415; John J. Winkler, "Laying Down the Law: The Oversight of Men's Sexual Behavior in Classical Athens," *Constraints of Desire,* pp. 45–70, 224–26.

22. See Padgug, "Sexual Matters," 3, who mistakenly ascribes Athenaeus's comment to Alexis of Samos (Jacoby, *Fragmente der griechischen Historiker* 539, fr. 2).

23. See K. J. Dover, *Greek Homosexuality* (London, 1978), pp. 63–67, for an extensive, but admittedly partial, list; also, Robert Parker, *Miasma: Pollution and Purification in Early Greek Religion* (Oxford, 1983), p. 94. For some Roman examples, see T. Wade Richardson, "Homosexuality in the Satyricon," *Classica et Mediaevalia* 35 (1984): 105–27, esp. p. 111.

24. I wish to emphasize that I am *not* claiming that all Greek men must have felt such indifference: on the contrary, plenty of ancient evidence testifies to the strength of individual preferences for a sexual object of one sex rather than another (see note 42, below). But many ancient documents bear witness to a certain constitutional reluctance on the part of the Greeks to predict, in any given instance, the sex of another man's beloved merely on the basis of that man's past sexual behavior or previous pattern of sexual object-choice.

25. *P. Tebtunis* I 104, translated by A. S. Hunt and C. C. Edgar, in *Women's Life in Greece and Rome,* ed. Mary Lefkowitz and Maureen B. Fant (Baltimore, 1982), pp. 59–60; another translation is provided, along with a helpful discussion of the document and its typicality, by Sarah B. Pomeroy, *Women in Hellenistic Egypt from Alexander to Cleopatra* (New York, 1984), pp. 87–89.

26. "Une bisexualité de sabrage": Veyne, 50–55; see the critique by Ramsay MacMullen, "Roman Attitudes to Greek Love," *Histôria* 32 (1983): 484–502, esp. pp. 491–97. Other scholars who describe the ancient behavioral phenomenon as "bisexuality" include Luc Brisson, "Bisexualité et médiation en Grèce ancienne," *Nouvelle revue de psychoanalyse* 7 (1973): 27–48; Alain Schnapp, "Une autre image de l'homosexualité en Grèce ancienne," *Le Débat* 10 (1981): 107–17, esp. pp. 116–17: Lawrence Stone, "Sex in the West," *The New Republic* (July 8, 1985): 25–37, esp. pp. 30–32 (with doubts). Contra, Padgug, "Sexual Matters," p. 13: "to speak, as is common, of the Greeks as 'bisexual' is illegitimate as well, since that merely adds a new, intermediate category, whereas it was precisely the categories themselves which had no meaning in antiquity."

27. T. M. Robinson, [Review of Dover's *Greek Homosexuality*], *Phoenix* 35 (1981): 160–63, esp. p. 162: "the reason why a heterosexual majority might have looked with a tolerant eye on 'active' homosexual practice among the minority, and even in some measure within their own group [!], . . .

is predictably a sexist one: to the heterosexual majority, to whom (in a man's universe) the 'good' woman is *kata physin* [i.e., naturally] passive, obedient, and submissive, the 'role' of the 'active' homosexual will be tolerable precisely because his goings-on can, without too much difficulty, be equated with the 'role' of the male *hetero*sexual, i.e., to dominate and subdue; what the two have in common is greater than what divides them." But this seems to me to beg the very question that the distinction between heterosexuality and homosexuality is supposedly designed to solve.

28. An excellent analysis of the contemporary Mediterranean version of this ethos has been provided by David Gilmore, "Introduction: The Shame of Dishonor," in *Honor and Shame and the Unity of the Mediterranean*, ed. Gilmore, Special Publication of the American Anthropological Association, 22 (Washington, D.C., 1987), pp. 2–21, esp. pp. 8–16.

29. By "phallus" I mean a culturally constructed signifier of social power: for the terminology, see note 10, above. I call Greek sexual discourse phallic because (1) sexual contacts are polarized around phallic action—i.e., they are defined by who has the phallus and by what is done with it; (2) sexual pleasures other than phallic pleasures do not count in categorizing sexual contacts; (3) in order for a contact to qualify as sexual, one—and no more than one—of the two partners is required to have a phallus (boys are treated in pederastic contexts as essentially unphallused (see Martial, 11.22; but cf. *Palatine Anthology* 12.3, 7, 197, 207, 216, 222, 242) and tend to be assimilated to women; in the case of sex between women, one partner—the "tribad"—is assumed to possess a phallus-equivalent (an overdeveloped clitoris) and to penetrate the other: sources for the ancient conceptualization of the tribad—no complete modern study of this fascinating and long-lived fictional type, which survived into the early decades of the twentieth century, is known to me—have been assembled by Friedrich Karl Forberg, *Manual of Classical Erotology*, trans. Julian Smithson [Manchester, 1884; repr. New York, 1966], pp. 11, 108–67; Paul Brandt [pseud. "Hans Licht"], *Sexual Life in Ancient Greece*, trans. J. H. Freese, ed. Lawrence H. Dawson [London, 1932], pp. 316–28; Gaston Vorberg, *Glossarium eroticum* [Hanau, 1965], pp. 654–55; and Werner A. Krenkel, "Masturbation in der Antike," *Wissenschaftliche Zeitschrift der Wilhelm-Pieck-Universität Rostock* 28 [1979], pp. 159–78, esp. p. 171. For a recent discussion, see Judith P. Hallett, "Female Homoeroticism and the Denial of Roman Reality in Latin Literature," *Yale Journal of Criticism* 3.1 [1989].

30. Exceptions include Vern L. Bullough, *Homosexuality: A History* (New York, 1979), pp. 3–5, and John Boswell *Christianity, Social Tolerance, and Homosexuality: Gay People in Western Europe from the Beginning of the Christian Era to the Fourteenth Century* (Chicago, 1980), pp. 53n., 75n.

31. For an earlier use of *mollis* in this almost technical sense, see Juvenal, 9.38.

32. See P. H. Schrijvers, *Eine medizinische Erklärung der männlichen Homosexualität aus der Antike (Caelius Aurelianus De Morbis Chronicis IV 9)* (Amsterdam, 1985), p. 11.

33. I have borrowed this entire argument from Schrijvers, *Eine medizinische Erklärung*, pp. 7–8; the same point about the passage from *De morbis acutis* had been made earlier—unbeknownst to Schrijvers, apparently—by Boswell, *Christianity, Social Tolerance, and Homosexuality*, pp. 53, n. 33; 75, n. 67.

34. Translation (with my emphasis and amplification) by I. F. Drabkin, ed. and trans., *Caelius Aurelianus On Acute Diseases and On Chronic Diseases* (Chicago, 1950), p. 413.

35. As his chapter title, "De mollibus sive subactis," implies.

36. See especially the pseudo-Aristotelian *Problemata* 4.26, well discussed by Dover, *Greek Homosexuality*, pp. 168–70, and by Winkler, "Laying Down the Law," pp. 67–69; generally, Boswell, *Christianity, Social Tolerance, and Homosexuality*, p. 53; Foucault, *The Use of Pleasure*, pp. 204–14.

37. The Latin phrase *quod utramque Venerem exerceant* is so interpreted by both Drabkin, *Caelius Aurelianus*, p. 901n., and Schrijvers, *Eine medizinische Erklärung*, pp. 32–33, who secures this reading by citing Ovid, *Metamorphoses* 3.323, where Teiresias, who had been both a man and a woman, is described as being learned in the field of *Venus utraque* Compare Petronius, *Satyricon* 43.8: *omnis minervae homo.*

38. I follow, once again, the insightful commentary by Schrijvers, *Eine medizinische Erklärung*, p. 15.

39. I quote from the translation by Drabkin, *Caelius Aurelianus*, p. 905, which is based on his plausible, but nonetheless speculative, reconstruction (accepted by Schrijvers, *Eine medizinische Erklärung*, p. 50) of a desperately corrupt text. For the notion expressed in it, compare Marcel Proust, *À la recherche du temps perdu*, ed. Pierre Clatac and André Ferré (Paris, 1954), III: 204, 212; *Remembrance of Things Past*, trans. C. K. Scott Moncrieff and Terence Kilmartin (New York, 1981), III: 203, 209; discussion by Eve Kosofsky Sedgwick, "Epistemology of the Closet (II)," *Raritan* 8 (Summer 1988): 102–30.

40. Anon., *De physiognomonia* 85 (vol. ii, p. 114.5–14 Förster); Vettius Valens, 2.16 (p. 76.3–8 Kroll); Clement of Alexandria, *Paedagogus* 3.21.3; Firmicus Maternus, *Mathesis* 6.30.15–16 and 7.25.3–23 (esp. 7.25.5).

41. See Foucault, *The History of Sexuality*, p. 43: "As defined by the ancient civil or canonical codes, sodomy was a category of forbidden acts; their perpetrator was nothing more than the juridical subject of them. The nineteenth-century homosexual became a personage, a past, a case history, and a childhood, in addition to being a type of life, a life form, and a morphology, with an indiscreet anatomy and possibly a mysterious physiology. Nothing that went into his total composition was unaffected by his sexuality. It was everywhere present in him: at the root of all his actions because it was their insidious and indefinitely active principle; written immodestly on his face and body because it was a secret that always gave itself away. It was consubstantial with him, less as a habitual sin than as a singular nature." See also Randolph Trumbach, "London's Sodomites: Homosexual Behavior and Western Culture in the 18th Century," *Journal of Social History* 11 (1977): 1–33, esp. p. 9; Richard Sennett, *The Fall of Public Man* (New York, 1977), pp. 6–8; Padgug, "Sexual Matters," pp. 13–14; Jean-Claude Féray, "Une histoire critique du mot homosexualité, [IV]," *Arcadie* 28, no. 328 (1981): 246–58, esp. pp. 246–47; Schnapp (note 26, above), p. 116 (speaking of Attic vase-paintings): "One does not paint acts that characterize persons so much as behaviors that distinguish groups"; Pierre J. Payer, *Sex and the Penitentials: The Development of a Sexual Code 550–1150* (Toronto, 1984), pp. 40–44, esp. pp. 40–41: "there is no word in general usage in the penitentials for homosexuality as a category. . . . Furthermore, the distinction between homosexual acts and people who might be called homosexuals does not seem to be operative in these manuals" (also, pp. 14–15, 140–53); Bynum, "The Body of Christ," p. 406.

42. For attestations to the strength of individual preferences (even to the point of exclusivity) on the part of Greek males for a sexual partner of one sex rather than another, see Theognis, 1367–68; Euripides, *Cyclops* 583–84; Xenophon, *Anabasis* 7.4.7–8; Aeschines, 1.41, 195; the *Life of Zeno* by Antigonus of Carystus, cited by Athenaeus, 13.563e; the fragment of Seleucus quoted by Athenaeus, 15.697de (= *Collectanea Alexandrina*, ed. J. U. Powell [Oxford, 1925], p. 176); an anonymous dramatic fragment cited by Plutarch, *Moralla*, pp. 766f–767a (= *Tragicorum Graecorum Fragmenta*, ed. August Nauck, 2d ed. [Leipzig, 1926], p. 906, #355; also in Theodor Kock, *Comicorum Atticorum Fragmenta* [Leipzig, 1880–1888], III: 467, #360); Athenaeus, 12.540e, 13.60le and ff.; Achilles Tatius, 2.35.2–3; pseudo-Lucian, *Erôtes 9–10;* Firmicus Maternus, *Mathesis* 7.15.1–2; and a number of epigrams by various hands contained in the *Palatine Anthology* 5.19, 65, 116, 208, 277, 278; 11.216; 12.7, 17, 41, 87, 145, 192, 198, and *passim* (cf. P. G. Maxwell-Stuart, "Strato and the Musa Puerilis," *Hermes* 100 [1972]: 215–40). See, generally, Dover, *Greek Homosexuality*, pp. 62–63; John Boswell, "Revolutions, Universals and Sexual Categories," in *Homosexuality: Sacrilege, Vision, Politics* (note 6, above), pp. 89–113, esp. pp. 98–101; Winkler, "Laying Down the Law"; and, for a list of passages, Claude Courouve, *Tableau synoptique de références à l'amour masculin: Auteurs grecs et latins* (Paris, 1986).

43. Hilary Putnam, in *Reason, Truth, and History* (Cambridge, Eng., 1981), pp. 150–55, in the course of analyzing the various criteria by which we judge matters of taste to be "subjective," implies that we are right to consider sexual preferences more thoroughly constitutive of the human personality than dietary preferences, but his argument remains circumscribed, as Putnam himself points out, by highly culture-specific assumptions about sex, food, and personhood.

44. Foucault, *The Use of Pleasure*, pp. 51–52, remarks that it would be interesting to determine exactly when in the evolving course of Western cultural history sex became more morally problematic than eating; he seems to think that sex won out only at the turn of the eighteenth century, after a long period of relative equilibrium during the middle ages: see also *The Use of Pleasure*, p. 10; *The Care of the Self*, p. 143; "On the Genealogy of Ethics: An Overview of Work in Progress," in Hubert L. Dreyfus and Paul Rabinow, *Michel Foucault: Beyond Structuralism and Hermeneutics*, 2d ed. (Chicago, 1983), pp. 229–52, esp. p. 229. The evidence lately assembled by Stephen Nissenbaum, *Sex, Diet, and Debility in Jacksonian America: Sylvester Graham and Health Reform*, Contributions in Medical History, 4 (Westport, Conn., 1980), and by Caroline Walker Bynum. *Holy Feast and Holy Fast: The Religious Significance of Food to Medieval Women* (Berkeley, 1987), suggests that moral evolution may not have been quite such a continuously linear affair as Foucault appears to imagine.

45. Jack H. Abbott, "On 'Women,'" *New York Review of Books* 28:10 (June 11, 1981): 17. It should perhaps be pointed out that this lyrical confession is somewhat at odds with the more gritty account contained in the edited excerpts from Abbott's letters that were published a year earlier in the *New York Review of Books* 27:11 (June 26, 1980): 34–37. (One might compare Abbott's statement with some remarks uttered by Bernard Boursicot in a similarly apologetic context and quoted by Richard Bernstein, "France Jails Two in a Bizarre Case of Espionage," *New York Times* [May 11, 1986]: "I was shattered to learn that he [Boursicot's lover of twenty years] is a man, but my conviction remains unshakable that for me at that time he was really a woman and was the first love of my life.")

46. See Davidson (note 6, above), p. 16.

47. I wish to thank Kostas Demelis for helping me with this formulation. Compare Padgug, "Sexual Matters," p. 5: "In any approach that takes as predetermined and universal the categories of sexuality, real history disappears."

48. Stephen Greenblatt, "Fiction and Friction," in *Reconstructing Individualism: Autonomy, Individuality, and the Self in Western Thought*, ed. Thomas C. Heller, Morton Sosna, and David E. Wellbery, with Arnold I. Davidson, Ann Swidler, and Ian Watt (Stanford, 1986), pp. 30–52, 329–32, esp. p. 34, makes a similar point; arguing that "a culture's sexual discourse plays a critical role in shaping individuality," he goes on to say, "It does so by helping to implant in each person an internalized set of dispositions and orientations that governs individual improvisations." See also Padgug, Sexual Matters"; generally, Julian Henriques, Wendy Holloway, Cathy Urwin, Venn Couze, and Valerie Walkerdine, *Changing the Subject: Psychology, Social Regulation and Subjectivity* (London, 1984).

49. "Translations" (1972), lines 32–33, in Adrienne Rich, *Diving into the Wreck: Poems 1971–1972* (New York, 1973), pp. 40–41 (quotation on p. 41).

50. "Canzone" (1942), lines 1–2, in W. H. Auden, *Collected Poems*, ed. Edward Mendelson (New York, 1976), pp. 256–57 (quotation on p. 256).

30

Sexual Matters:
On Conceptualizing Sexuality in History

Robert Padgug

Sexuality—the subject matter seems so obvious that it hardly appears to need comment. An immense and ever-increasing number of "discourses" has been devoted to its exploration and control during the last few centuries, and their very production has, as Foucault points out,[1] been a major characteristic of bourgeois society. Yet, ironically, as soon as we attempt to apply the concept to history, apparently insurmountable problems confront us.

To take a relatively simple example, relevant to one aspect of sexuality only, what are we to make of the ancient Greek historian Alexis's curious description of Polykrates, sixth-century B.C. ruler of Samos?[2] In the course of his account of the luxurious habits of Polykrates, Alexis stresses his numerous imports of foreign goods, and adds: "Because of all this there is good reason to marvel at the fact that the tyrant is not mentioned as having sent for women or boys from anywhere, despite his passion for liaisons with males. . . . Now, that Polykrates did not "send for women" would seem to us to be a direct corollary of "his passion for liaisons with males." But to Alexis—and we know that his attitude was shared by all of Greek antiquity[3]—sexual passion in any form implied sexual passion in all forms. Sexual categories which seem so obvious to us, those which divide humanity into "heterosexuals" and "homosexuals," seem unknown to the ancient Greeks.

A problem thus emerges at the start: the categories which most historians normally use to analyze sexual matters do not seem adequate when we deal with Greek antiquity. We might, of course, simply dismiss the Greeks as "peculiar"— a procedure as common as it is unenlightening—but we would confront similar problems with respect to most other societies. Or, we might recognize the difference between Greek sexuality and our own, but not admit that it creates a problem in conceptualization. Freud, for example, writes:

This article originally appeared in *Radical History Review* 20 (Spring/Summer 1979), pp. 3–23. Reprinted with the permission of Cambridge University Press.

The most striking distinction between the erotic life of antiquity and our own no doubt lies in the fact that the ancients laid the stress upon the instinct itself, whereas we emphasize its object. The ancients glorified the instinct and were prepared on its account to honor even an inferior object; while we despise the instinctual activity in itself, and find excuses for it only in the merit of the object.[4]

Having made this perceptive comment, he lets the subject drop: so striking a contrast is, for him, a curiosity, rather than the starting point for serious critique of the very categories of sexuality.

Most investigators into sexuality in history have in fact treated their subject as so many variations on a single theme, whose contents were already broadly known. This is not only true of those who openly treat the history of sexuality as a species of entertainment, but even of those whose purpose is more serious and whose work is considered more significant from an historical point of view. One example chosen from the much-admired *The Other Victorians* of Steven Marcus,[5] is typical. Marcus describes a very Victorian flagellation scene which appears in the anonymous *My Secret Life*. After describing its contents, he states categorically:

But the representation in *My Secret Life* does something which pornography cannot. It demonstrates how truly and literally childish such behavior is; it shows us, as nothing else that I know does, the pathos of perversity, how deeply sad, how cheerless a condemnation it really is. It is more than a condemnation; it is—or was—an imprisonment for life. For if it is bad enough that we are all imprisoned within our own sexuality, how much sadder must it be to be still further confined within this foreshortened, abridged and parodically grotesque version of it.

Marcus already *knows* the content and meaning of sexuality, Victorian or otherwise. It was not *My Secret Life* which gave him his knowledge, but rather his predetermined and prejudged "knowledge" which allowed him to use *My Secret Life* to create a catalogue of examples of a generalized and universal sexuality, a sexuality which was not the result but the organizing principle of his study. Given this preknowledge, sexuality in history could hardly become a problem—it was simply a given.

Not surprisingly, for Marcus as well as for many other "sex researchers"— from Freudians to positivists—the sexuality which is "given," which is sexuality *tout court,* is what they perceive to be the sexuality of their own century, culture, and class, whether it bears a fundamentally "popular" stamp or comes decked out in full scientific garb.

In any approach that takes as predetermined and universal the categories of sexuality, real history disappears. Sexual practice becomes a more or less sophisticated selection of curiosities, whose meaning and validity can be gauged by that truth—or rather truths, since there are many competitors—which we, in our enlightened age, have discovered. This procedure is reminiscent of the political economy of the period before, and all too often after, Marx, but it is not purely bourgeois failing. Many of the chief sinners are Marxists.

A surprising lack of a properly historical approach to the subject of sexuality has allowed a fundamentally bourgeois view of sexuality and its subdivisions to deform twentieth-century Marxism. Marx and Engels themselves tended to neglect the subject and even Engels's *Origins of the Family, Private Property and the State* by no means succeeded in making it a concern central to historical materialism. The Marxism of the Second International, trapped to so great a degree within a narrow economism, mainly dismissed sexuality as merely superstructural. Most later Marxist thought and practice, with a few notable exceptions—Alexandra Kollontai, Wilhelm Reich, and Frankfurt School—has in one way or another accepted this judgment.

In recent years questions concerning the nature of sexuality have been re-placed on the Marxist agenda by the force of events and movements. The women's movement, and, to an increasing degree, the gay movement, have made it clear that a politics without sexuality is doomed to failure or deformation; the strong offensive of the American right-wing which combines class and sexual politics can only reinforce this view.[6] The feminist insistence that "the personal *is* political," itself a product of ongoing struggle, represents an immense step forward in the understanding of social reality, one which must be absorbed as a living part of Marxist attitudes toward sexuality. The important comprehension that sexuality, class, and politics cannot easily be disengaged from one another must serve as the basis of a materialist view of sexuality in historical perspective as well.

Sexuality As Ideology

The contemporary view of sexuality which underlies most historical work in this field is the major stumbling block preventing further progress into the nature of sexuality in history. A brief account of it can be provided here, largely in the light of feminist work, which has begun to discredit so much of it. What follows is a composite picture, not meant to apply as a whole or in detail to specific movements and theories. But the general assumptions which inform this view appear at the center of the dominant ideologies of sexuality in twentieth-century capitalist societies, and it is against these assumptions that alternative theories and practices must be gauged and opposed.

In spite of the elaborate discourses and analyses devoted to it, and the continual stress on its centrality to human reality, this modern concept of sexuality remains difficult to define. Dictionaries and encyclopedias refer simply to the division of most species into males and females for purposes of reproduction; beyond that, specifically human sexuality is only described, never defined. What the ideologists of sexuality describe, in fact, are only the supposed spheres of its operation: gender, reproduction, the family, and socialization; love and intercourse. To be sure, each of these spheres is thought by them to have its own essence and forms ("*the* family," for example), but together they are taken to define the arena in which sexuality operates.

Within this arena, sexuality as a general, overarching category is used to define and delimit a large part of the world in which we exist. The almost perfect congruence between those spheres of existence which are said to be sexual and what is viewed as the "private sphere" of life is striking. As Carroll Smith-Rosenberg, working partly within this view of sexuality, puts it, "The most significant and intriguing historical questions relate to the events, the causal patterns, the psychodynamics of private places: the household, the family, the bed, the nursery, and kinship systems."[7] Indeed, a general definition of the most widely accepted notion of sexuality in the later twentieth century might easily be "that which pertains to the private, to the individual," as opposed to the allegedly "public" spheres of work, production, and politics.

This broad understanding of sexuality as "the private" involves other significant dualities, which, while not simply translations of the general division into private and public spheres, do present obvious analogies to it in the minds of those who accept it. Briefly, the sexual sphere is seen as the realm of psychology, while the public sphere is seen as the realm of politics and economics; Marx and Freud are often taken as symbolic of this division. The sexual sphere is considered the realm of consumption, the public sphere that of production; the former is sometimes viewed as the site of use value and the latter as that of exchange value. Sexuality is the realm of "nature," of the individual, and of biology; the public sphere is the realm of culture, society, and history. Finally, sexuality tends to be identified most closely with the female and the homosexual, while the public sphere is conceived of as male and heterosexual.

The intertwined dualities are not absolute, for those who believe in them are certain that although sexuality properly belongs to an identifiable private sphere, it slips over, legitimately or, more usually, illegitimately, into other spheres as well, spheres which otherwise would be definitely desexualized. Sexuality appears at one and the same time as narrow and limited and as universal and ubiquitous. Its role is both overestimated as the very core of being and underestimated as a merely private reality.

Both views refer sexuality to the individual, whom it is used to define. As Richard Sennett suggests:

> Sexuality we imagine to define a large territory of who we are and what we feel. . . . Whatever we experience must in some way touch on our sexuality, but sexuality *is*. We uncover it, we discover it, we come to terms with it, but we do not master it.[8]

Or, as Foucault rather more succinctly states, "In the space of a few centuries, a certain inclination has led us to direct the question of what we are to sex."[9] This is, after all, why we write about it, talk about it, worry about it so continuously.

Under the impulse of these assumptions, individuals are encouraged to see themselves in terms of their sexuality. This is most easily seen in such examples of "popular wisdom" as that one must love people for their inner, that is, sexual, selves, and not for "mere incidentals," like class, work, and wealth, and in the apparently widespread belief that the "real me" emerges only in private life, in the supposedly sexual spheres of intercourse and family, that is, outside of class, work, and public life. Sexuality is thereby detached from socioeconomic and class realities, which appear, in contrast, as external and imposed.

The location of sexuality as the innermost reality of the individual defines it, in Sennett's phrase, as an "expressive state," rather than an "expressive act."[10] For those who accept the foregoing assumptions, it appears as a *thing,* a fixed essence, which we possess as part of our very being; it simply *is.* And because sexuality is itself seen as a thing, it can be identified, for certain purposes at least, as inherent in particular objects, such as the sex organs, which are then seen as, in some sense, sexuality itself.

But modern sexual ideologues do not simply argue that sexuality is a *single* essence; they proclaim, rather, that it is a *group* of essences. For although they tell us that sexuality as a general category is universally shared by all of humanity, they insist that subcategories appear within it. There are thus said to be sexual essences appropriate to "the male," "the female," "the child," "the homosexual," "the heterosexual" (and indeed to "the foot-fetishist," "the child-molester," and on and on). In this view, identifiable and analytically discrete groups emerge, each bearing an appropriate sexual essence, capable of being analyzed as a "case history," and given a normative value. Krafft-Ebing's *Psychopathia Sexualis* of 1886 may still stand as the *logical* high point of this type of analysis, but the underlying attitude seems to permeate most of contemporary thought on the subject.

In sum, the most commonly held twentieth-century assumptions about sexuality imply that it is a separate category of existence (like "the economy," or "the state," other supposedly independent spheres of reality), almost identical with the sphere of private life. Such a view necessitates the location of sexuality within the individual as a fixed essence, leading to a classic division of individual and society and to a variety of psychological determinisms, and, often enough, to a full-blown biological determinism as well. These in turn involve the enshrinement of contemporary sexual categories as universal, static, and permanent, suitable for the analysis of all human beings and all societies. Finally, the consequences of this view are to restrict class struggle to nonsexual realms, since that which is private, sexual, and static is not a proper arena for public social action and change.

Biology and Society

The inadequacies of this dominant ideology require us to look at sexuality from a very different perspective, a perspective which can serve both as an implicit critique of the contemporary view as well as the starting point for a specific Marxist conceptualization.

If we compare human sexuality with that of other species, we are immediately struck by its richness, its vast scope, and the degree to which its potentialities can seemingly be built upon endlessly, implicating the entire human world. Animal sexuality, by contrast, appears limited, constricted, and predefined in a narrow physical sphere.

This is not to deny that human sexuality, like animal sexuality, is deeply involved with physical reproduction and with intercourse and its pleasures. Biological sexuality is the necessary precondition for human sexuality. But biological sexuality is only a precondition, a set of potentialities, which is never unmediated by human reality, and which becomes transformed in qualitatively new ways in human society. The rich and ever-varying nature of such concepts and institutions as marriage, kinship, "love," "eroticism," in a variety of physical senses and as a component of fantasy and religious, social, and even economic reality, and the general human ability to extend the range of sexuality far beyond the physical body, all bear witness to this transformation.

Even this bare catalogue of examples demonstrates that sexuality is closely involved in *social* reality. Marshall Sahlins makes the point clearly, when he argues that sexual reproduction and intercourse must not be

> considered *a priori* as a biological fact, characterized as an urge of human nature independent of the relations between social persons . . . [and] acting *upon* society from without (or below). [Uniquely among human beings] the process of "conception" is always a double entendre, since no satisfaction can occur without the act and the partners as socially defined and contemplated, that is, according to a symbolic code of persons, practices and proprieties.[11]

Such an approach does not seek to eliminate biology from human life, but to absorb it into a unity with social reality. Biology as a set of potentialities and insuperable necessities[12] provides the material of social interpretations and extensions; it does not *cause* human behavior, but conditions and limits it. Biology is not a narrow set of absolute imperatives. That it is malleable and broad is as obvious for animals, whose nature is altered with changing environment, as for human beings.[13] The uniqueness of human beings lies in their ability to create the environment which alters their own—and indeed other animals'— biological nature.

Human biology and culture are both necessary for the creation of human society. It is as important to avoid a rigid separation of "Nature" and "Culture" as it is to avoid reducing one to the other, or simply uniting them as an undifferentiated reality. Human beings are doubly determined by a permanent (but not immutable) natural base and by a permanent social mediation and transformation of it. An attempt to eliminate the biological aspect is misleading because it denies that social behavior takes place within nature and by extension of natural processes. Marx's insistence that "men make their own history but they do not make it just as they please" applies as well to biological as to inherited social realities.[14] An attempt—as in such disparate movements as Reichian analysis or the currently fashionable "sociobiology"—to absorb culture into biology is equally misleading, because, as Sahlins puts it:

> Biology, while it is an absolutely necessary condition for culture, is equally and absolutely insufficient, it is completely unable to specify the cultural properties of human behavior or their variations from one human group to another.[15]

It is clear that, with certain limits, human beings have no fixed, inherited nature. We *become* human only in human society. Lucien Malson may overstate his case when he writes, "The idea that man has no nature is now beyond dispute. He has or rather is a history,"[16] but he is correct to focus on history and change in the creation of human culture and personality. Social reality cannot simply be "peeled off" to reveal "natural man" lurking beneath.[17]

This is true of sexuality in all its forms, from what seem to be the most purely "natural" acts of intercourse[18] or gender differentiation and hierarchy to the most elaborated forms of fantasy or kinship relations. Contrary to a common belief that sexuality is simply "natural" behavior, "nothing is more essentially transmitted by a social process of learning than sexual behavior," as Mary Douglas notes.[19]

Even an act which is apparently so purely physical, individual, and biological as masturbation illustrates this point. Doubtless we stroke our genitals because the act is pleasurable and the pleasure is physiologically rooted, but from that to masturbation, with its large element of fantasy, is a social leap, mediated by a vast set of definitions, meanings, connotations, learned behavior, shared and learned fantasies.

Sexual reality is variable, and it is so in several senses. It changes within individuals, within genders, and within societies, just as it differs from gender to gender, from class to class, and from society to society. Even the very meaning and content of sexual arousal varies according to these categories.[20] Above all, there is continuous *development and transformation* of its realities. What Marx suggests for hunger is equally true of the social forms of sexuality: "Hunger is hunger, but the hunger gratified by cooked meat eaten with a knife and fork is a different hunger from that which bolts down raw meat with the aid of hand, nail and tooth."[21]

There do exist certain sexual forms which, at least at a high level of generality, are common to all human societies: life, intercourse, kinship, can be understood universally on a very general level. But that both "saint and sinner" have erotic impulses, as George Bataille rightly claims,[22] or that Greece, medieval Europe, and modern capitalist societies share general sexual forms, do not make the contents and meaning of these impulses and forms identical or undifferentiated. They must be carefully distinguished and separately understood, since their inner structures and social meanings and articulations are very different. The content and meaning of the eroticism of Christian mysticism is by no means reducible to that of Henry Miller, nor is the asceticism of the monk identical to that of the Irish peasants who delay their marriages to a relatively late age.[23]

The forms, content, and context of sexuality always differ. There is no abstract and universal category of "the erotic" or "the sexual" applicable without change to all societies. Any view which suggests otherwise is hopelessly mired in one or another form of biologism, and biologism is easily put forth as the basis of normative attitudes toward sexuality, which, if deviated from, may be seen as rendering the deviant behavior "unhealthy" and "abnormal." Such views are as unenlightening when dealing with Christian celibacy as when discussing Greek homosexual behavior.

Sexuality as Praxis (I)

When we look more directly at the social world itself, it becomes apparent that the general distinguishing mark of human sexuality, as of all social reality, is the unique role played in its construction by language, consciousness, symbolism, and labor, which, taken together—as they must be—are *praxis,* the production and reproduction of material life. Through *praxis* human beings produce an ever-changing human world within nature and give order and meaning to it, just as they come to know and give meaning to, and, to a degree, change, the realities of their own bodies, their physiology.[24] The content of sexuality is ultimately provided by human social relations, human productive activities, and human consciousness. The *history* of sexuality is therefore the history of a subject whose meaning and contents are in a continual process of change. It is the history of social relations.

For sexuality, although part of material reality, is not itself an object or thing. It is rather a group of social relations, of human interactions. Marx writes in the *Grundrisse* that "Society does not consist of individuals, but expresses the sum of interrelations, the relations within which these individuals stand."[25] This seems to put the emphasis precisely where it should be: individuals do exist as the constituent elements of society, but society is not the simple multiplication of isolated individuals. It is constituted only by the relationships between those individuals. On the other hand, society does not stand outside of and beyond the individuals who exist within it, but is the expression of their complex activity.

The emphasis is on activity and relationships, which individuals ultimately create and through which, in turn, they are themselves created and modified. Particular individuals are both subjects and objects within the process, although in class societies the subjective aspect tends to be lost to sight and the processes tend to become reified as objective conditions working from outside.

Sexuality is relational.[26] It consists of activity and interactions—active social relations—and not simply "acts," as if sexuality were the enumeration and typology of an individual's orgasms (as it sometimes appears to be conceived of in, for example, the work of Kinsey and others), a position which puts the emphasis back within the individual alone. "It" does not do anything, combine with anything, appear anywhere; only people acting within specific relationships create what we call sexuality. This is a significant aspect of what Marx means when he claims, in the famous Sixth Thesis on Feuerbach, that "the essence of man is no abstraction inherent in each single individual. In its reality it is the ensemble of the social relations."[27] Social relations, like the biological inheritance, at once create, condition, and limit the possibilities of individual activity and personality.

Praxis is fully meaningful only at the level of sociohistorical reality. The particular interrelations and activities which exist at any moment in a specific society create sexual and other categories which, ultimately, determine the broad range of modes of behavior available to individuals who are born within that society. In turn, the social categories and interrelations are themselves altered over time by the activities and changing relationships of individuals. Sexual categories do not make manifest essences implicit within individuals, but are the expression of the active relationships of the members of entire groups and collectives.

We can understand this most clearly by examining particular categories. We speak, for example, of homosexuals and heterosexuals as distinct categories of people, each with its sexual essence and personal behavioral characteristics. That these are not "natural" categories is evident. Freud, especially in the *Three Essays on the Theory of Sexuality,* and other psychologists have demonstrated that the boundaries between the two groups in our own society are fluid and difficult to define. And, as a result of everyday experience as well as the material collected in surveys like the Kinsey reports, we know that the categories of heterosexuality and homosexuality are by no means coextensive with the activities and personalities of heterosexuals and homosexuals. Individuals belonging to either group are capable of performing and, on more or less numerous occasions, do perform acts and have behavioral characteristics and display social relationships thought specific to the other group.

The categories in fact take what are no more than a group of more or less closely related acts ("homosexual"/"heterosexual" behavior) and convert them into case studies of people ("homosexuals"/"heterosexuals"). This conversion of acts into roles/personalities, and ultimately into entire subcultures, cannot be said to have been accomplished before at least the seventeenth century, and, as a firm belief and more or less close approximation of reality, the late nineteenth century.[28] What we call "homosexuality" (in the sense of the distinguishing traits of "homosexuals"), for example, was not considered a unified set of acts, much less a set of qualities defining particular persons, in precapitalist societies. Jeffrey Weeks, in discussing the act of Henry VIII of 1533, brought sodomy within the purview of statute law, argues that

> the central point was that the law was directed against a series of sexual acts, not a particular type of person. There was no concept of the homosexual in law, and homosexuality was regarded not as a particular attribute of a certain type of person but as a potential in all sinful creatures.[29]

The Greeks of the classical period would have agreed with the general principle, if not with the moral attitude. Homosexuality and heterosexuality for them were indeed groups of not necessarily very closely related acts, each of which could be performed by any person, depending upon his or her gender, status, or class.[30] "Homosexuals" and "heterosexuals" in the modern sense did not exist in their world, and to speak, as is common, of the Greeks, as "bisexual" is illegitimate as well, since that merely adds a new, intermediate category, whereas it was precisely the categories themselves which had no meaning in antiquity.

Heterosexuals and homosexuals are involved in social "roles" and attitudes which pertain to a particular society, modern capitalism. These roles do have something in common with very different roles known in other societies— modern homosexuality and ancient pederasty, for example, share at least one feature: that the participants were of the same sex and that sexual intercourse is often involved—but the significant features are those that are not shared, including the entire range of symbolic, social, economic, and political meanings and functions each group of roles possesses.

"Homosexual" and "heterosexual" *behavior* may be universal; homosexual and heterosexual *identity and consciousness* are modern realities. These identities are not inherent in the individual. In order to be gay, for example, more than individual inclinations (however we might conceive of those) or homosexual activity is required; entire ranges of social attitudes and the construction of particular cultures, subcultures, and social relations are first necessary. To "commit" a homosexual act is one thing: to *be* a homosexual is something entirely different.

By the same token, of course, these are changeable and changing roles. The emergence of a gay movement (like that of the women's movement) has meant major alterations in homosexual and heterosexual realities and self-perceptions. Indeed it is abundantly clear that there has always existed in the modern world a dialectical interplay between those social categories and activities which ascribe to certain people a homosexual identity and the activities of those who are so categorized. The result is the complex constitution of "the homosexual" as a social being within bourgeois society. The same is, of course, true of "the heterosexual," although the processes and details vary.[31]

The example of homosexuality/heterosexuality is particularly striking, since it involves a categorization which appears limited to modern societies. But even categories with an apparently more general application demonstrate the same social construction.

For example, as feminists have made abundantly clear, while every society does divide its members into "men" and "women," what is meant by these divisions and the roles played by those defined by these terms varies significantly from society to society and even within each society by class, estate, or social position. The same is true of kinship relations. All societies have some conception of kinship, and use it for a variety of purposes, but the conceptions differ widely and the institutions based on them are not necessarily directly comparable. Above all, the modern nuclear family, with its particular social and economic roles, does not appear to exist in other societies, which have no institution truly analogous to our own, either in conception, membership, or in articulation with other institutions and activities. Even within any single society, family/kinship patterns, perceptions, and activity vary considerably by class and gender.[32]

The point is clear: the members of each society create all of the sexual categories and roles within which they act and define themselves. The categories and the significance of the activity involved will vary widely as do the societies within whose general social relations they occur, and categories appropriate to each society must be discovered by historians.

Not only must the categories of any single society or period not be hypostatized as universal, but even the categories which are appropriate to each society must be treated with care. Ultimately, they are only parameters within which sexual activity occurs or, indeed, against which it may be brought to bear. They tend to be normative—and ideological—in nature, that is, they are presented as the categories within which members of particular societies *ought* to act. The realities of any society only approximate the normative categories, as our homosexual/heterosexual example most clearly showed. It is both as norms, which determine the status of all sexual activity, and as approximations to actual social reality that they must be defined and explored.

Sexuality as Praxis (II)

Within this broad approach, the relationship between sexual activity and its categories and those that are nonsexual, especially those that are economic in nature, become of great importance. Too many Marxists have tried to solve this problem by placing it within a simplified version of the "base/superstructure" model of society, in which the base is considered simply as "the economy," narrowly defined, while sexuality is relegated to the superstructure; that is, sexuality is seen as a "reflex" of an economic base.[33] Aside from the problems

inherent in the base/superstructure model itself,[34] this approach not only reproduces the classic bourgeois division of society into private and public spheres,
enshrining capitalist ideology as universal reality, but loses the basic insights
inherent in viewing sexuality as social relations and activity.

Recently, many theorists, mainly working within a feminist perspective,
began to develop a more sophisticated point of view, aiming, as Gayle Rubin put
it in an important article,[35] "to introduce a distinction between 'economic'
system and 'sexual' system, and to indicate that sexual systems have a certain
autonomy and cannot always be explained in terms of economic forces." This
view, which represented a great advance, nonetheless still partially accepted the
contemporary distinction between a sphere of work and a sphere of sexuality.

The latest developments of socialist-feminist theory and practice have
brought us still further, by demonstrating clearly that both sexuality in all its
aspects and work/production are equally involved in the production and reproduction of *all* aspects of social reality, and cannot be easily separated out from
one another.[36] Above all, elements of class and sexuality do not contradict one
another or exist on different planes, but produce and reproduce each other's
realities in complex ways, and both often take the form of activity carried out
by the same persons working within the same institutions.

This means, among other things, that what we consider "sexuality" was, in
the prebourgeois world, a group of acts and institutions not necessarily linked to
one another, or, if they were linked, combined in ways very different from our
own. Intercourse, kinship, and the family, and gender, did not form anything like
a "field" of sexuality. Rather, each group of sexual acts was connected directly
or indirectly—that is, formed a part of—institutions and thought patterns which
we tend to view as political, economic, or social in nature, and the connections
cut across our idea of sexuality as a thing, detachable from other things, and as
a separate sphere of private existence.

The Greeks, for example, would not have known how, and would not have
thought, to detach "sexuality" from the household (*oikos*), with its economic,
political, and religious functions; from the state (especially as the reproduction
of citizenship); from religion (as the fertility cults or ancestor worship, for
example); or from class and estate (as the determiner of the propriety of sexual
acts, and the like). Nor would they have been able to distinguish a private realm
of "sexuality"; the Greek *oikos* or household unit was as much or more a public
institution as a private one.[37] This is even more true of so-called primitive societies, where sexuality (mediated through kinship, the dominant form of social
relations) seems to permeate all aspects of life uniformly.

It was only with the development of capitalist societies that "sexuality" and
"the economy" became separable from other spheres of society and could be
counterposed to one another as realities of different sorts.[38] To be sure, the reality
of that separation is, in the fullest sense of the word, ideological; that is, the
spheres do have a certain reality as autonomous areas of activity and consciousness, but the links between them are innumerable, and both remain sig-

nificant in the production and reproduction of social reality in the fullest sense. The actual connections between sexuality and the economy must be studied in greater detail, as must the specific relations between class, gender, family, and intercourse,[39] if the Marxist and sexual liberation movements are to work in a cooperative and fruitful, rather than antagonistic and harmful, manner.

A second major problem-area stands in the way of a fuller understanding of sexuality as *praxis*. The approach to sexuality we have outlined does not overcome the apparently insurmountable opposition between society and the individual which marks the ideological views with which we began our discussion. But it overcomes it at a general level, leaving many specific problems unsolved. The most important of these is the large and thorny problem of the determination of the specific ways in which specific individuals react to existing sexual categories and act within or against them. To deal with this vast subject fully, Marxists need to develop a psychology—or a set of psychologies—compatible with their social and economic analyses.[40]

Much the most common approach among western Marxists in the last fifty years toward creating a Marxist psychology has been an attempt, in one manner or another, to combine Marx and Freud. Whether in the sophisticated and dialectical versions of the Frankfurt School, Herbert Marcuse, or Wilhelm Reich, or in what Richard Lichtman has called "the popular view that Freud analyzed the individual while Marx uncovered the structure of social reality,"[41] these attempts arose out of the felt need for a more fully developed Marxist psychology in light of the failure of socialist revolutions in the West.

None of these attempts has, ultimately, been a success, and their failure seems to lie in real contradictions between Marxist and Freudian theory. Both present theories of the relationship between individual and society, theories which contradict each other at fundamental levels.

Freud does accept the importance of social relations for individual psychology. For him, sexuality has its roots in physiology, especially in the anatomical differences between the sexes, but these distinctions are not in themselves constitutive of our sexuality. Sexuality is indeed a process of development in which the unconscious takes account of biology as well as of society (mediated through the family) to produce an individual's sexuality.[42]

The problems begin here. Society, for Freud, is the medium in which the individual psyche grows and operates, but it is also in fundamental ways antipathetical to the individual, forcing him or her to repress instinctual desires. Freud's theory preserves the bourgeois division between society and the individual, and ultimately gives primacy to inborn drives within an essentially ahistorical individual over social reality. In a revealing passage, Freud argues:

> Human civilization rests upon two pillars, of which one is the control of natural forces and the other the restriction of our instincts. The ruler's throne rests upon fettered slaves. Among the instinctual component which are thus brought into service, the sexual instincts, in the narrow sense of the word, are conspic-

uous for their strength and savagery. Woe if they should be set loose! The throne would be overturned and the ruler trampled under foot.[43]

In spite of the fact that Freud does not view instincts as purely biological in nature,[44] he certainly sees sexuality as an internal, biologically based force, a thing inherent in the individual. This is a view which makes it difficult to use Freud alongside of Marx in the elucidation of the nature of sexuality. This is not to say that we need necessarily discard all of Freud. The general theory of the unconscious remains a powerful one. Zillah Eisenstein pointed in a useful direction when she wrote, "Whether there can be a meaningful synthesis of Marx and Freud depends on whether it is possible to understand how the unconscious is reproduced and maintained by the relations of the society."[45] But it is uncertain whether the Freudian theory of the unconscious can be stripped of so much of its specific content and remain useful for Marxist purposes. The work of Lacan, which attempts to "debiologize" the Freudian unconscious by focusing on the role of language, and that of Deleuze and Guattari, in the *Anti-Oedipus,* which attempts to provide it with a more full sociohistorical content, are significant beginnings in this process."[46]

At the present time, however, Marxism still awaits a psychology fully adequate to its needs, although some recent developments are promising, such as the publication in English of the important non-Freudian work of the early Soviet psychologist L. S. Vygotskii.[47] But if psychology is to play a significant role in Marxist thought, as a science whose object is one of the dialectical poles of the individual/society unity, then it must have a finer grasp of the nature of that object. At this point, we can only agree with Lucien Seve that the object of psychology has not yet been adequately explored.[48]

Notes

1. Michel Foucault, *The History of Sexuality, Volume 1: An Introduction,* Robert Hurley, trans. (New York: Pantheon, 1978).

2. As reported in Athenaeus, *Deipnosophistae* 12.450, in Felix Jacoby, *Fragmente der griechischen Historiker* (Leiden: Brill, 1954–1964) no. 539, fragment no. 2.

3. For other examples, see Lucian, "The Ship," in Loeb Classical Library edition of Lucian, volume VI, p. 481, or Plutarch, "The Love Stories," in *Moralia* 771E–775E, which provides pairs of similar love tales, each consisting of one involving heterosexual love and one involving homosexual love.

4. Sigmund Freud, *Three Essays on the Theory of Sexuality,* trans. James Strachey (New York Basic Books, 1964), p. 38; the footnote was added in the 1910 edition.

5. Steven Marcus, *The Other Victorians: A Study of Sexuality and Pornography in Mid-Nineteenth Century England,* 2d ed. (New York: Basic Books, 1974), p. 127.

6. See Linda Gordon and Allen Hunter, "Sex, Family and the New Right," *Radical America* 11/12 (November 1977/February 1978): 9–26.

7. Carroll Smith-Rosenberg, "The New Woman and the New History," *Feminist Studies* 3 (1976): 185.

8. Richard Sennett, *The Fall of the Public Man* (New York: Random House, 1977), p. 7.

9. Foucault, *History of Sexuality,* p. 78.

10. Sennett, *Fall of the Public Man,* p. 7.

11. Marshall Sahlins, *New York Review of Books* (November 23, 1978), p. 51.

12. On biology as a realm of necessary, see Sebastiano Timpanaro, *On Materialism* (London: NLB, 1978).

13. Helen H. Lambert, "Biology and Equality," *Signs* 4 (1978): 97–117, especially p. 104.

14. These points are strongly insisted upon by Timpanaro, *On Materialism.* See also Raymond Wilson, "Problems of Materialism," *New Left Review* 109 (1978): 3–18.

15. M. Sahlins, *The Use and Abuse of Biology* (Ann Arbor: University of Michigan Press, 1976), p. xi.

16. L. Malson, *Wolf Children and the Problem of Human Nature* (New York: Monthly Review Press, 1972), p. 9.

17. Ibid., p. 10.

18. Ibid., p. 48.

19. Mary Douglas, *Natural Symbols: Explorations in Cosmology,* (New York: Pantheon Books, 1973), p. 93.

20. W. H. Davenport, "Sex in Cross-Cultural Perspective," in F. Beach, ed., *Human Sexuality in Four Perspectives* (Baltimore: Wiley, 1977), chapter 5.

21. Karl Marx, *Grundrisse,* ed. Martin Nicolaus (New York: Random House, 1973), p. 92.

22. Georges Bataille, *Death and Sensuality: A Study of Eroticism and Taboo* (New York: Arno Press, 1962).

23. See the important analysis of this and similar points in Denis de Rougemont, *Love in the Western World* (New York: Pantheon, 1956), pp. 159ff.

24. See Adolfo Sanchez Vazques, *The Philosophy of Praxis,* trans. Mike Gonzales (London: Merlin Press, 1977).

25. Marx, *Grundrisse,* p. 265.

26. See the work of the so-called "symbolic interactionists," best exemplified by Kenneth Plummer, *Sexual Stigma* (London: Routledge and Kegan Paul, 1975). Their work, although not Marxist and too focused on individuals *per se,* does represent a major step forward in our understanding of sexuality as interpersonal.

27. Karl Marx, "Sixth Thesis on Feuerbach," in Karl Marx and Friedrich Engels, *Collected Works* (New York: International Publishers, 1976) 5: 4.

28. Mary McIntosh, "The Homosexual Role," *Social Problems* 16 (1968): 182–93, the pioneer work in this field, suggests the seventeenth century for the emergence of the first homosexual subculture. Randolph Trumbach, "London's Sodomites: Homosexual Behavior and Western Culture in the Eighteenth Century," *Journal of Social History* 11 (1977/1978):1–33, argues for the eighteenth century. Jeffrey Weeks, in two important works, " 'Sins and Diseases': Some Notes on Homosexuality in the Nineteenth Century," *History Workshop* 1 (1976): 211–19, and *Coming Out: Homosexual Politics in Britain from the Nineteenth Century to the Present* (London: Quartet Books, 1977), argues, correctly, I think, that the full emergence of homosexual role and subculture occurs only in the second half of the nineteenth century. See also Bert Hansen, "Historical Construction of Homosexuality," *Radical History Review* 20 (1979): 66–73, and Jeffrey Weeks, "Movements of Affirmation: Sexual Meaning and Homosexual Identities," *Radical History Review* 20 (1979): 164–80. All of these works deal with England, but there is little reason to suspect that the general phenomenon, at least, varies considerably in other bourgeois countries.

29. Weeks, *Coming Out,* p. 12.

30. The best work available on Greek homosexual behavior is K. J. Dover, *Greek Homosexuality* (Cambridge: Harvard University Press, 1975), which contains further bibliography.

31. See *History of Sexuality,* parts 4–5, as well as Guy Hocquenghem, *Homosexual Desire,* trans. Dangoor Daniella (New York: Schocken, 1980).

32. On the conceptualization of family, kinship and household, see the important collective

work by Rayna Rapp, Ellen Ross, and Renate Bridenthal, "Examining Family History," *Feminist Studies* 5 (1979): 174–200, as well as Rayna Rapp, "Family Class in Contemporary America," *Science and Society* 42 (1978): 278–300. Also see Mark Poster, *Critical Theory of the Family* (New York: Seabury Press, 1978), and the critique of it by Ellen Ross, "Rethinking The Family,'" *Radical History Review* 20 (1979): 76–84.

33. This appears to be true even of such relatively unorthodox thinkers as Louis Althusser, *Lenin and Philosophy* (New York: Monthly Review Press, 1971), pp. 127–86; E. Balibar and Louis Althusser, *Reading Capital* (London: NLB, 1970), part III; P. Hindess and B. Hirst, *Pre-Capitalist Modes of Production* (London: Routledge and Kegan Paul, 1975), especially chapter 1; and Claude Meillassoux, *Maidens, Meal, and Money: Capitalism and the Domestic Community,* (New York: Cambridge University Press, 1981), part I.

34. See Raymond Williams, *Marxism and Literature* (New York: Oxford University Press, 1977), especially part II.

35. Gayle Rubin, "The Traffic in Women: Notes on the 'Political Economy' of Sex," in *Towards an Anthropology of Women*, ed. Rayna Reiter (New York: Monthly Review, 1975), p. 167. For other similar views, on this point at least, see R. Bridenthal, "The Dialectics of Production and Reproduction in History," *Radical America* 10:2 (1976): 3–11; Nancy Chodorow, "Mothering, Male Dominance and Capitalism," in *Capitalist Patriarchy and the Case for Social Feminism*, ed. Z. Eisenstein (New York: Monthly Review Press, 1979), pp. 83–106; and Juliet Mitchell, *Woman's Estate* (New York: Pantheon Books, 1972).

36. Among recent works which come to this conclusion, and whose bibliographies and notes are useful for further study, see Joan Kelly, "The Doubled Vision of Feminist Theory," *Feminist Studies* 5 (1979): 216–27; Lisa Vogel, "Questions on the Woman Question," *Monthly Review* (June 1979): 39–60; Renate Bridenthal, "Family and Reproduction," the third part of a joint essay cited in note 32 above; Eli Zaretsky, *Capitalism and Personal Life* (New York: Harper and Row, 1976), pp. 24ff.; and Ann Forman, *Femininity as Alienation: Women and the Family in Marxism and Psychoanalysis* (London: Pluto, 1977).

37. On the *oikos* and related institutions, see W. K. Lacey, *The Family in Classical Greece* (London: Thames and Hudson, 1968).

38. See Foucault, *History of Sexuality,* and Zaretsky, *Capitalism and Personal Life,* for attempts to conceptualize the emergence of these categories. On the nonemergence of a separate sphere of the economy in noncapitalist societies, see Georg Lukacs, *History and Class Consciousness*, trans. Rodney Livingstone (Cambridge: MIT Press, 1972), and Samir Amin, "In Praise of Socialism," in *Imperialism and Unequal Development* (New York: Monthly Review Press, 1979), pp. 73–85.

39. For the works which begin this process, see those cited in notes 35 and 26 above, plus the articles collected in Eisenstein, *Capitalist Patriarchy*.

40. For a full discussion of this need and what it involves, see Lucien Seve, *Marxism and the Theory of Human Personality* (London: Lawrence and Wishart, 1975). Seve is the best on the social conditioning of individual psychology and weakest on individual psychic processes themselves.

41. "Marx and Freud," part 1, *Socialist Review* 30 (1976): 5. This article, along with its two successors in *Socialist Review* 33 (1977): 59–84 and 36 (1977): 37–78, forms a good introduction to the study of the relationship between Marx and Freud, arguing for their incompatibility.

42. An important recent attempt to demonstrate the social underpinnings of Freud's thought is Juliet Mitchell, *Psychoanalysis and Feminism* (New York: Pantheon, 1974). Eli Zaretsky, "Male Supremacy and the Unconscious," *Socialist Review* 21/22 (1975): 7–55, demonstrates several defects in Freud's understanding of sociohistorical reality, but suggests that they are remediable.

43. Sigmund Freud, "The Resistance to Psychoanalysis," *The Standard Edition of the Complete Psychological Works of Sigmund Freud*, ed. and trans. James Strachey (London: Hogarth Press, 1953–1974), 19: 218.

44. See Freud, "Instincts and Their Vicissitudes," *The Standard Edition,* 14: 105–40.

45. Eisenstein, *Capitalist Patriarchy*, p. 3.

46. G. Deleuze and F. Guattari, *Anti-Oedipus: Capitalism and Schizophrenia* (New York: Viking Press, 1977). See also the work of Herbert Marcuse, especially *Eros and Civilization* (Boston: Beacon Press, *1955),* and Norman O. Brown, *Life against Death* (Middletown, Conn.: Wesleyan University Press, 1959).

47. L. S. Vygotskii, *Mind in Society: The Development of Higher Psychological Processes* (Cambridge, Mass.: Harvard University Press, 1977). See also Stephen Toulmin's essay on Vygotskii, "The Mozart in Psychology," *New York Review of Books,* September 28, 1978, pp. 51–57.

48. This essay represents a condensed and reworked version of the introduction to a much longer work on the nature of sexuality in history. The author wishes to thank Betsy Blackmar, Edwin Burrows, Victoria de Grazia, Elizabeth Fee, Joseph Interrante, Michael Merrill, David Varas, and Michael Wallace for their invaluable comments on earlier drafts. He dedicates the essay to David Varas, without whose help and encouragement it would have been impossible to write it.

31

Sex and the Logic of Late Capitalism

Linda Singer

A few words about the chapter title. It should be clear that when I invoke the term "sex," I am not referring to some innate or ahistorically given set of biological or instinctual predispositions, but to a set of practices, techniques, behavior, language, signs that are already, from the very outset, social, i.e., they presuppose or are emergent with reference to the Other. The conjunction of terms in the title should not, therefore, be read as a promise to produce that which might emerge by a separation of the two terms conjoined, i.e., as a retrieval of some pristine sexuality from the grips of capitalist logic, or the re-invention of some post-capitalist form. By use of the conjunction I hope to call attention to what I read as a relationship of reciprocal constitution between them, i.e., the terms opposed then conjoined are really correlatives, like play and work, each of which comes to take on its signification in and through this relationship, a relationship that, as I hope to show, is not seamless, i.e., is not without its points of contradiction, opposition, and contest.

There is an extensive literature documenting this dynamic with two key figures circulating prominently within it, the philosophers of play and work, Freud and Marx. There are the various rereadings of their intersecting points and divergences (Reich, Fromm, Marcuse, Slater) and those that seek in some sense to inaugurate a post discourse (Althusser, Lacan, Nancy, Lyotard). Although this work depends and relies on this literature, my aim here is far less ambitious; i.e., I am not attempting to give a systemic or genetic account of this relationship, but rather, I intend to focus on some specific contradictions emergent as a consequence or as strategic responses to the sexual epidemic.

One of the linking tropes derived from the literature is that of economy— i.e., sexuality or libido can be thought of as a political economy, a systemic grid of differences which produce, circulate, and order value. In a capitalist logic, the primary value to be produced and accumulated is surplus value or profit. Late capitalism, by which I mean the historical form now operative in first world industrial and postindustrial nations, represents a specific development of this logic, and is a system of such significant complexity that I cannot do justice to it in this context. But from this complexity I am interested in extracting certain agenda, priority, and strategies following from the transformation of value to that of profit, and to show how sexual epidemic provides both occasions for its extension and points at which the contradictions which are also produced provide special problems for the projects of sexual management.

In late capitalist economies, profit is generated less from the primary production of material goods, and far more from the production of services—a move from an economy geared toward production to a knowledge and service economy, or, as Baudrillard claims, simulation. Furthermore, the basic strategies for maximizing profitability (i.e., cost-effectiveness) are now being applied to the accumulation of capital as such (the intensification of profitability through the manipulation of the markers of profitability: currencies, stocks, foreign exchange, etc.). The aforementioned shift can be explained vis-à-vis this kind of cost-effectiveness, i.e., primary production is no longer the most efficient way to accumulate profit.

Because the accumulation of profit depends upon extracting the value of what the worker produces and transferring it to someone else, and because work is organized in a way to make the most profitable use of the worker's time (that is, it is already alienated), capitalism has always demanded a disciplined work force, a body of workers capable of working their bodies in a way responsive to social demands and utilities.[1] Following this logic through the strategic mediations provided by Foucault, sexuality emerges in the capitalist discipline as both that which is to be disciplined, and that which remains as excess or resistance to discipline and therefore must also be pacified, accommodated, indulged. It is also, consequently, that which must also be socially managed and coordinated to maximize its social utility, i.e., its profitability.

Logic of capitalism depends not only on control over surplus or production, but also on the production of scarcity, or controlled scarcity. The notion of scarcity is crucial to capitalism—both as its justification (there's not enough, especially now, of what we need to survive; therefore, let's control it so that the maximum number of people benefit by it—production of surplus) and sometimes, at least, as that for which capitalism is the remedy. Without scarcity, there would be no value. But scarcity must always be articulated: it must be constructed usually by reference to a nexus of needs and desires. Hence, capitalism must also be perpetually creating needs—and here later capitalism, not of primary production but reproductions and simulations—has developed in a way that significantly diverges from the classic form represented in Marx.

When the profit logic is applied to sexuality understood in this sense, a clear difference emerges as two separable but not necessarily oppositional profit centers useful for generating negotiable social currency, sectors I will summarily term the reproductive and the erotic. The utility of reproduction for a system dependent upon perpetual expansion is obvious. Profit accumulation will always depend upon the production of workers, preferably more than are necessary at any given time so as to keep wages down, and upon an ever-expanding body of consumers and heirs. The development of sciences like demographics, fertility and contraceptive technology, and population control provide clear evidence that this crucially vital social function is not being left to chance. But profitability is not limited to a question of numbers and distribution. Following the principle of both multiplying and extending profit centers, reproduction is organized to be done in the most profitable way, i.e., with the least investment of social resources. Where reproduction generates profits in the form of commodity consumption, this results in a shift in the signification of the reproductive unit (the biological family) from a site of production to that of consumption.

But this strategy depends on mobilizing that which is excluded, namely, the erotic excess, the nonutilitarian dimensions of sexuality which are often summarized under the sign of pleasure. As many thinkers from Marcuse to Foucault have pointed out, capitalism works not only by opposing itself to the pleasure principle, but by finding strategic ways to mobilize it, a form of control by incitement, not by the repression but by the perpetual promise of pleasure, i.e., of that which is denied by the profit-producing process. The genius of late capitalism is the development of strategies for managing and profiting by its own excess. Two basic strategies are condensation and displacement, which correspond to genital primacy and commodity fetishism.

As a consequence of its success, late capitalism has largely succeeded in establishing the articulation of needs and desires along two basic axes—genital gratification and satisfaction through consumption. These two elements converge in the construct of leisure, that sphere of time which is not work. In the contemporary organization of time, leisure functions as that which is both compensatory and inciting, viz., work (when one is unemployed, one is not at leisure). But as the product of discipline, it also functions as a site of resistance. Leisure time is certainly a major profit sector.

Although the logic of late capitalism would demand an enlargement of erotic and reproductive commodities, this logic does not operate seamlessly but finds its limits regarding an oppositional profit logic in terms of which sexual labor, reproductive and erotic, must also remain the only form of labor which is unpaid and uncompensated. This opposition and the contradictions it produces are not without strategic value, a value that is both economic and psychological/ideological. Although that value will become clearer as things proceed, one point of contradiction proper to capitalism needs to be emphasized from the outset: on the one hand, paid labor under capitalism marks that labor as alienated; on the other hand, capitalist sexual political economy seeks to preserve the status of sex work as unalienated labor, allowing the disciplinary dimensions to recede or be displaced by its mobilizing functions as a mechanism for resistance, transgression, opposition to the sphere of demand. As a consequence, sexuality functions in a late capitalist economy as a prototype or emblem not only of alienation, but also of freedom, and that in the name of which demands can be made of an alienating social system.[2] But this depends precisely on setting limits to the process of commodification. Sexual commodities depend for their value on the existence of a sphere of uncommodified sexuality, as the demand for the segregation of sexual work from the compensatory economy of wage labor only makes sense once sexuality has been constituted as that which is always subject to the logic of the commodity.

The management and construction of these boundaries has always been a complicated process which has generated any number of systems of knowledge, surveillance, incitement, and punishment. The management problems posed specifically by a sexuality that is constituted as epidemic are significant, and my intent in this chapter is to try to trace out some of those that emerge from the attempt both to expand the ways and forms in which sexuality both reproductive and erotic can be commodified and to preserve sexual labor as that which is ideally unpaid.

Because epidemic conditions arouse concern about the exchange of bodily fluids, various strategic agendas have been offered as inducements to genital deintensification, to which one should, under most circumstances, "just say no." In this sense, as I have previously suggested, the epidemic sex-pol economy might currently be described as being in a state of recession or stagflation, discouraged by a prudential logic in terms of which genital sexuality is a high-risk investment, prompting a move toward libidinal diversification. Not surprisingly, one form of diversification/displacement will be perpetually offered in the forms of commodities, many of which are being marketed rather explicitly as compensatory, safe-sex substitutes. (I will discuss some of the particulars here shortly.) But one ironic consequence of the sexual epidemic is that sexual services and commodities have been a real growth area in the 1980s. At a time when uncommodified sexuality has been constituted as a high-risk zone, the zone of sexual commodification expands as a profit center.

Within late capitalism, there exist strategic connections between advertising, marketing, and pornography; each represents and enacts a strategy of seduction. Although advertising and pornography are differentiated by their strategies and styles, they exist in a relation of mutual incitement. Within the contemporary erotic economy, it is necessary to trace the transformational logic and grammar that effect the transferential network by which erotic desire is constituted as commodity fetish.

These connections are necessarily made at the level of language, signs, spectacles. The effectivity by which advertising creates erotic needs demands a reinscription of the body, where the body in question is designed precisely to be spectacle, on display—a mirroring simulacra—another site for induced misrecognition (*mésconnaissance* in the Lacanian sense). Such representations constitute sites of erotic satisfaction and release. In both advertising and pornography, the goal is to incite arousal and satisfaction serially, that is, to displace erotic investment on to other commodities, other items within the genre. Both modes of incitement depend on signs and reading; they are phantasmatic constructions, images, whose value consists in not being real (in the Lacanian sense). Here we encounter the limits of any narrow sociological or representational theory of reading, for the power to incite, to produce erotic need, here depends on the incestuous slippage of signs, the variability of positions in a system of ungrounded differences, i.e., language. In this sense, then, pornography is not the discourse by which one body is represented to another body: it is a phenomenon of literacy, addressed to a reader of signs. Advertising is the mechanism for mobilizing this transferential network in the direction of particular commodities. In pornography, the commodity is a sexual semiotic, that is, a phenomenon of sex without bodies. This is part of what makes pornography an appropriate site for erotic investment in the age of sexual epidemic.

Advertising depends on marketing, which is the science of constructing, dividing, targeting, and mobilizing consumers. Marketing entails the transformation of an audience from one of potential to actual consumers. This is accomplished through a series of interrelated strategies, most saliently, market segmenting and establishing tactical specificity, which involves recognizing, producing, and proliferating differentiated needs in the service of profitability. The goal of marketing, to facilitate consumption, involves the intensification and extensification of profits. This means to create for (of) the commodity an existential necessity which, in many cases, does not preexist the commodity and which is inseparable from it. In light of this logic, then, the production of addiction serves as the ultimate success of marketing strategy. For the addict is the most loyal of customers, one of whom the provider can be sure will be a repeat purchaser. For the addict, the object has become quite literally an existential necessity, an object or commodity which functions both to satiate and to expand the needs it also creates (one has to have had a drink or a cigarette in order to need one). Addiction can be read as the ultimate extension of the logic of discipline—the production and regulation of needs—through this double-gesture of incitement and enslavement in the name of pleasure.

The regulatory or disciplinary mechanisms of the market seek to control and cure the very addictions they themselves have produced. There are specific sites of addiction that are produced and controlled by the regulatory mechanisms that have emerged to address the epidemic of AIDS. One site of strategic intersection is the war on drugs, since intravenous drug usage is one medium for the transmission of the virus. In the name of health, we are witnessing the remobilization of sentiments in favor of regulating the ingestion of substances of various kinds, which appears not only in the crackdown on those substances already under legal control (illegal recreational drugs), but in the proliferation of testing for an ever-expanding list of prescription drugs: tranquilizers, steroids, hormones. What constitutes acceptable addiction is now subject to redefinition. We have seen a switch from policies which encourage addiction to tobacco to policies designed to limit tobacco consumption through prohibition. This prohibition has been extended spatially to include planes, restaurants, and the workplace. Both sugar and caffeine have been produced as new controlled substances.

The prohibitions against addiction, however, are strengthened by the preservation of the very addictive behavior they ostensibly seek to limit. Addictive behavior helps to produce a disciplinary subject; addictive behavior is routinized and repetitive and, to that extent, predictable. Addictive exchange structures are also useful insofar as the agency of control is displaced onto the object: regulations are dissimulated and rewritten as the language of need and desire.

The convergence of marketing, pornography, and epidemic logic produces now widely distributed images of sickness and health as new forms of pornography. We get the double production of AIDS photographs contrasted with new versions of the body beautiful. The logic of addiction also encourages the routinized and repetitive behavior of the "health addict," the workaholic who makes sure to make time for that morning workout at the gym. This disciplinary logic of addiction works in yet another direction to intensify the phenomenon of ritualistic repetition in domestic work and childrearing practices.

Many factors not specific to epidemic conditions also contribute to motivate this expansion. In some sense, sex work has specific characteristics that would make it attractive as a source of potential profit intensification. Excluding from consideration for the moment reproductive technology, most forms of sex work are rather capitally deintensive, relative to other industries. Here profitability is also intensified by its resistance—i.e., most forms of sexual wage labor are also considered taboo. This allows for a higher profit margin, a lower paid and more manipulable/vulnerable labor force, and a particular set of expectations, viz., satisfaction from its clientele. Those ways of capitalizing on sexuality that have been most enduring are those which maximize this margin most efficiently. (Not a long time has to be spent training workers, designing/maintaining complicated equipment, or any real concern given to quality control.)

Three major institutional forms for capitalizing on sexuality as the marker of desire in late capitalism (though not specifically its inventions) are *prostitution, addiction,* and *pornography.* All three are strategies for maximizing and consolidating the socially useful, profitable excess produced as sexual energy, excess desire. These institutional forms have dual functions compatible with the dual strategy of discipline and incitement. They function as strategic safety valves, compensatory indulgences, selective circumscribed sites of transgression on the one hand, while they also function as limits against which coordinated and acceptable forms can be mobilized and maintained. In other words, the existence of commodified forms of sexuality capitalizes both by turning sex into capital, and by preserving sexuality from it.

These three institutions are certainly not specific to late capitalism. Not for nothing is prostitution referred to as the oldest profession. If we are to believe Lévi-Strauss, prostitution was the original form of exchange, where the objects exchanged are the bodies of women. But in the phase of development described alternatively as one-dimensional (Marcuse) or the consumer society of simulations (Baudrillard), these institutions take on connotative and productive values that are specific to that mode of organization. Further dynamics of overdetermination are induced by conditions of sexual epidemic which encourage, at least at the level of prescriptive ideology and prudential reason (which are obviously not the whole story), a more wary relation to other bodies, suggesting sublimatory strategies of displacement onto objects, images, commodities. Those in our culture are already commodity-competent. We cannot help but be. The socially inscribed circuitry which allows for the displacement of erotic significance onto subjects has already been well trained by advertising and the cinema. In the age of epidemic, however, what had been a system of subliminal seductions has now been promoted to the status of an explicit prescription, and not only from marketers.

The point is that epidemic sexuality has been constructed not coincidentally as a window of opportunity for capital, a period of growth, producing new and enlarged mechanisms for commodifying the sexual body, erotic and reproductive, and for profit by the fact that in catastrophic conditions which place the sexual body in question, value is intensified. The panic induced by the epidemic construct induces precisely the kind of free-floating anxiety that, precisely because it has no object, can be transferred onto any object, and from object to object in series. The kind of symptomatic hysteria that expresses itself through intensified consumption is the kind of hysteria that is good enough for business to become hegemonized as rational prudence.

The lesson that late capitalism has chosen to draw from its own production can be summarized by the slogan "Sex costs." AIDS provided an occasion for the cost-benefit logic in which sexuality had been constituted as the sphere of primary satisfaction to become an explicit articulation. It is not that sex has not always had its price. It is just that in the age of sexual epidemic, which is also the age of late capitalism, the joint efforts of the commodity system, the medical profession, and the media have found a way to make that ideological construct profitable. At one level this is a moment in which capital seems to be tipping its hand, but it is more like the dance of the seven veils. This cost-benefit logic leaves in place the profit and possession logic underlying that which is offered as the alternative—monogamous marriage.

Entrepreneurs like Hugh Hefner found ways to package promiscuous sexuality as an occasion, indeed, a rationalization for conspicuous consumption. Now its opposite, i.e., the risk of sexual promiscuity, is also represented in a way that necessitates consumption. Codes of opposition have now become interchangeably a rationalization for consumption and for accumulation as profit.

The surplus produced by this neutralization takes on particular strategic value given the intensification of affect operative in epidemic conditions. In this context, the homogeneity and substitutability of commodities takes on the added connotations of safety and comfort. The very attention to surfaces, the temporality of perpetual seduction, the slick and glossy thinness of the image take on added appeal when the depth of the body and history have come to be thought of as explosions ready to happen, a depth which is a phenomenon now linked with despair and with death. The distraction induced by the sheer speed with which the series of commodities is presented can in this context come to seem the most innocent and least threatening form of seduction. Absence of finality becomes a virtue. Disappointment is never irrevocable. If it's bad, just throw it away.

The sexual epidemic in which the prospect of "liberated spontaneous sexuality" is represented as no longer possible, or in the process of slipping away, provides a context in which the myth of scarcity, so central to the creation of needs and demands upon which capitalist production depends, can be rewritten and recirculated. If "free sex" is scarce, one will have to pay. Sex costs. If the cost of contact with bodies is too high in the currency of risks, one will have to pay in another currency for something else. The myth of scarcity circulating in this epidemic is not only a tale of the scarcity of bodies, it is a tale about the scarcity of time as well. The sexual epidemic temporalizes the erotic and eroticizes the temporal in the direction of profit intensification, similar in strategy and effect to the profit intensification of spatiality in the 1970s under the name of the "condominium," where space is divided into the smallest marketable units and then sold as equity investments. The foreshortening of time provided by dyadic linkage of death and desire is conducive to the incitement of multiple episodic consumption encounters. Why not now, since you can't take it with you? Brevity is conducive to seriality and the patterns of repetition upon which the market economy depends.

The isolation induced by epidemic conditions, symptomatized by the fear of contagion, is also conducive to seduction by commodities. As Baudrillard suggests, "consumption is primarily organized as a discourse to oneself." Indeed, a number of advertisements for sexual services address a consumer explicitly constructed at home, in bed, alone—e.g., the phone sex industry. What is produced here is an auto-eroticism mediated by objects or, better, telephonic projections which are at once commodities and services on the market. (One calls in, as it were, to gain access to a discourse that one fantasizes is for oneself; in other words, one pays to turn erotic discourse on/for oneself.)

The hegemony of the sexual epidemic is instructive in the ways it induces the very anxieties it also promises to allay, constructs the deprivations for which it can then rationalize its productions as compensation. Baudrillard points out the ways in which "consumer society substitutes a social order of values and classifications for a contingent world of needs and pleasure."[3] This substitution is facilitated by the hegemony of sexual epidemic in which the possibility of such contingent pleasure is also represented as slipping away, dying out.

Baudrillard remarks, "It is not political will that breaks the monopoly of the market . . . it is the fact that every unitary system, if it wants to survive, has to evolve a binary system of regulation . . . power is only absolute if it knows how to refract itself in equivalent variations; that is, if it knows how to redouble itself through this doubling."[4] Within contemporary epidemic conditions, regulation works through the installation of a set of binary relations that entail the legalization and normalization of some practices at the same time that others are criminalized. This binary system of regulation functions to fetishize and target specific institutional forms for regulation by leaving the larger structures of power to circulate and proliferate. That which is prohibited works to sustain hegemonic social structures: the regulation of prostitution preserves marriage and the sexual and reproductive exploitation of women; pornography preserves advertising; addiction preserves brand loyalty and repeat-purchasing consumer patterns. Regulation inescapably takes place within a system of capital, commodities, and the asymmetrical figuration of differences, including sexual difference, that reproduces hegemonic lines of privilege, dominance, and power.

Although criminality is regularly figured as that which threatens the smooth functioning of this system, criminal behavior is itself the paradigm for behavior which maximizes profits. Criminality generates profits directly in the form of a higher profit margin, i.e., higher prices, lower labor costs, no taxes, benefits, deductions. As the paradigm for profit making, criminality assumes its most public form in the way that international capital "launders" its "dirty" drug money. Here the system which creates and seeks to manage a criminal class turns out to be the most blatant criminal. The crimes of international capital— e.g., laundering drug money through international transfers—work the possibilities of capitalism for its own constitutive criminality. Moreover, crimes of such global magnitude—e.g., the U.S.-Noriega affair—justify the production of a discourse of outrage that also allows for the maintenance of homologous forms of exploitation under other names. Most important among these latter forms is the institution of marriage as a form of sex work, legalized prostitution, which remains largely unpaid and not for profit. That social form makes sure that women do not control or profit from the surplus value already imposed on them by the construction of "woman" as eroticized commodity. Indeed, that social arrangement makes sure that any negotiable profits derived from her work go somewhere else. The other way that such value-laden social forms get put into false contrast with criminality and exploitation is through the circulation of a notion of "safe sex" as synonymous with the family, preserving and protecting incest and intramarital rape as forms of safe sex. The profitability of illicit sexualities and institutions that provide services and commodities, regulation, therapy, punishment, offers further justification for surveillance. One of the consequences of sexual epidemic is a kind of social urgency about discovering sexual criminals—most notably those that sexually exploit children. There seems to be an epidemic in reported cases of child sexual exploitation—by parents, child-care workers, baby-sitters, as well as strangers. What social surplus is produced in these search-and-destroy missions?

This is also an era of high-visibility sex crimes—Jennifer Levin, Tawana Brawley. Certainly the twenty years American feminists worked to increase public awareness and sensitivity to the very ubiquity of sexual assault, as well as the context they provided for reinterpreting its significance, are partly responsible for the attention which the public has been willing to give to these incidents. But as the media attention given these two particular cases has clearly shown, the pursuit of legal or social remedies for such offenses also always has the ironic effect of producing two victims, while placing both parties to the encounter on trial.

What is the ideological/social utility that results from the production of surplus victims and defendants?

Certainly, one immediate and proximal result of the number of child abuse cases recently making headlines is to raise parental and especially maternal concerns regarding day care and the safety of their children. Compounding an already existing social guilt, these recent cases help to reinvent the myth of the nuclear family as the optimum social space for children and, by contrast, any collective social alternatives are correlated with implicit risk and danger.

Attention to criminal sexuality is also useful as part of the larger effort to minimize recognition of class difference. Sex crimes do cut across classes. One of the reasons so many of these cases have received coverage is that it was middle-class women and children, like Jennifer Levin and Lisa Steinberg, who were victimized. Publicizing social problematics that seem immune to class differences has a certain utility in reducing class resentment, and in inducing more sympathetic reactions toward social regulations, even when these are class-differentiated (issues like abortion). This publicity allows also for social coding of the private as a sphere of greater control, protection, and safety, which will have serious implications for social issues like day care.

The creation of a criminal class conceived as outside the system of capital and regulatory management justifies the mobilization of social power as militaristic force, e.g., fight crime, war on drugs, wipe out porn. There seems to be at work here a figuration of criminality as disease, and a reverse association of disease with criminal—i.e., high-risk—activity (crimes like drug addiction are likened to diseases like cancer, where AIDS appears to be the unnamed associative link between them). Both criminality and disease are conceived as outlaws, invaders with secret ways, as well as forces of disorder. Both criminality and disease (and their postulated equivalence) are used to rationalize forms of power in the name of maintaining a healthier, that is, crime-free and disease-free, society. Both rationalize power as management. As Susan Sontag remarks, "Society is presumed to be in basically good health; disease (disorder) is, in principle, always manageable."[5]

Criminalization normalizes that which it opposes—it also creates a highly marketable excess. Hence, we witness the proliferation of sex-crime dramas on television and on film, the blurring of fictional and informational genres, the "typing" of such narratives: day care abuse, child abuse, incest, family murders, murders of parents by children, violence against women who have strayed outside the marital norm.

As in the production of addiction, then, regulatory power preserves and increases the very criminality that it claims to oppose, becoming the paradigm for the contagious criminality that justifies its own interventionist strategies ad infinitum.

Part of the point of this whole discussion is that the revisions, reconsolidation, and expansions of these institutions also change or ought to change the political issues surrounding them—what is significant about these phenomena gets recast, as do the terms of contest. Specifically, they decenter what have been the primary competing social agendas/discourses in terms of an opposition between a logic of repression, prohibition, and punishment (criminality) and those which seek to mainstream, normalize, enlarge the scope of such practices. Questions tend to center either around a juridical rhetoric (legalization vs. criminalization), or a moral one of sin and sanctity, or a political one of rights and freedoms. The limits of legislative and prescriptive approaches to these institutions dramatically show the limits of prohibition as a strategy. They also miss the obvious strategy value of the attempt at prohibition to the intensification of their profitability (exhibited focally in all the cases where being banned in Boston prompts increased sales everywhere else). Criminalization also reduces protection for both service providers and customers. Transgressiveness comes at a high price, and is indeed part of what contributes to its market value and high profit margin.

Political questions regarding these institutions ought not to be posed in a way that misrecognizes or confuses the socially constructive with the legislatively elective. The question in late capitalism cannot be whether or not there ought be prostitution, as though such a matter could be decided. To pose the question this way is to miss what prostitution is, and in some sense, if one is prone to speak this way, what is wrong or at least problematic about it. Part of what is problematic is the hegemonic utility of that which it mobilizes as resistance—like the fetishizing of sexual labor as unpaid, the noncompensatory economy which maintains reproduction as alienated and undervalued, and the system of heterosexist and male domination it justifies. The excess represented by these institutions also tells us a great deal about the lack constituting that which is situated as the prescribed, the normal, the acceptable.

It is also to assume the suturability of needs to the social. A better strategy would be to see needs as that demand which can never be socially accommodated, hence a site of resistance to regulatory seductions. These are desires which are explicitly placed in a sphere of transferable differences that are available only through explicit efforts of articulation and contestation. To see pornography as some special set of representations is to miss the extent to which pornography is the master genre for late capitalism, the literature for a society of perpetual incitement. In this sense, pornography is not an aberration, but an intensification of its productive logic, its generative grammar. Similarly with respect to addiction—it is not an aberration, deviance, but a success story, a model for modifications and transfer.

In an epidemic context, the limits of frontiers/boundaries legislative and otherwise are obvious. Epidemic is defined by its indifference to those boundaries and prescriptions. It is that which cannot be willed away, individually or collectively. In this sense ours is the age of epidemic prostitution, pornography, and addiction, or these have become epidemic and not by accident. Hence these forms are neither marginal nor optional, but are the modes by which sexuality is histor-ically institutionalized in our age. They are that against which the hubris of elim-ination logic shows itself. The law will also always produce that which stands out-side it. Sexual epidemic mediated through the logic of late capitalism operates to produce contradictory ideological, institutional, and technological effects, viz., the project of sexual management. On the one hand, there is the attempt to market "selective refusal" as a preferred social response—e.g., the "just say no" cam-paign, which is both an official campaign, and a recurring motif available through a variety of popular cultural outlets, in film, popular fiction, television.

At the same time that this foray in the aesthetics of discretion is being designed and circulated, the range, availability, and outlets for producing and marketing sexual apparatuses and services proliferate. Needless to say, the com-modification of sexual services is not itself a new development. Prostitution and wet-nursing are practices that have long and extensive histories. There is also an extensive tradition of cultures producing apparatuses designed either to facilitate or to stimulate sexual contact, enhance its pleasures while precluding pregnancy or sexual contact (chastity belts, genital mutilations). Such apparatuses, as well as the workers who produce and/or use these items in the performance of sexual ser-vices, may be classed into two basic categories: *reproductive technology* (contra-ception, abortion, birthing instruments and services) and *erotic technology and services*. Whereas neither category is a product of capitalism per se (such prac-tices predate its emergence historically), strategies and mechanisms specific to late capitalism have helped contribute to the fact that sexual products and services are a growth area in the contemporary economy even at a time when there is an explicit cultural agenda to limit sexual circulation. Indeed, one of the ironies of the contemporary situation is that many products and services are being marketed as safer alternatives to genital sex, or as safeguards against epidemic conditions. Correlatively, the expansion of sexual services facilitated by technological devel-opments (in areas like medical, communication. and other technologies) expands the number and nature of sexual workers, especially expanding the numbers of workers outside the sphere of primary production (which in this case would mean genital contact). Reproductive and fertility technology expand the potential reproductive and medical brigades. Expansion of the therapeutic sexual service areas has also opened new occupations as sexual counselors and surrogates. New forms of erotica—phone services, special-interest sex clubs (S & M, swapping), the current trend for clubs catering to women (Chippendales)—expand the forms sexual work can take, and therefore the potential sources of profit.

Expansion of the profitability of the sex industry has been accomplished, in part. by incorporation of strategies and mechanisms that have been successful in maximizing profit in other areas. These strategies (which will be discussed later and in greater detail) include mass-marketing tactics like advertising, market segmenting, specialization of functions, deskilling of labor as a conse-quence of its division into relatively anonymous, interchangeable functions (the essential characteristic of any call girl or phone sex operation, as well as of the porn theaters which run features continually throughout the day with the audience entering and leaving at will). As an example of the strategic utility of mass-marketing techniques, consider the ways in which strategies of mass marketing and market segmenting have been used to expand the audience for pornographic films and texts. The traditional pornography audience was overwhelmingly male, and the usual conditions for spectatorship (which usually involved going to a specialized zone where such publications and theaters were housed) meant that men usually indulged in pornography either alone or at male-dominated events, like stag or fraternity parties or gay male clubs. The relative inaccessibility of pornographic publications, traditionally concealed in brown paper wrappers in stores with blacked-out windows, and the clandestine conditions under which they have been sold, presumably contributed to part of their transgressive appeal—outside the mainstream mass market, so hot they have to be kept under wraps. This aesthetic has not been entirely displaced. But it is now supplemented by subsidiary forms and outlets aimed at other audiences—most notably, heterosexual women—which make pornography available in home video form (therefore available for viewing privately in a domestic context) or marketed through mail order in women's magazines. Barbara Ehrenreich also points to an emerging genre of "Christian fundamentalist" erotica, sex manuals, and marriage guides designed to eroticize relationships within that moral and normative framework. Some particular items like Marabel Morgan's *The Total Woman* are given the full benefit of advertising and promotion through the mainstream media. Erotic paraphernalia are now being marketed like Tupperware, to women in their homes, where they are presumably more at ease, and where exploration of such products may occur under conditions more discreet than in a store. Erotic material can also be sampled on cable television stations, which are also major outlets for advertising phone sex, call girl, and other services and establishments. The marketing of such material in the home and through conventional media like television not only increases the potential market saturation for such messages but also alters the signification attached to them. Taking sexual services out of the red light district and bringing them into the home has the function of normalizing and destigmatizing them, encouraging the viewer to consider them as commodities like any others that are also advertised in such formats. With the expansion of in-home buying services, the decision to respond to an advertisement run by one of the numerous "escort services" that advertise in New York City is accomplished in the same manner as one buys a lawn mower, with the added benefit that one's companion will arrive far more quickly than the lawn mower. In this instance, we have a case of a new marketing strategy for a fairly traditional sexual service.

But part of the proliferative genius of late capitalism is to find ever more profit-intensive areas of investment (more profit-intensive than the weekly importation, as one service promises, of "submissive oriental women right [*sic*] trained to fill our every need and desire"). The latest and most ingenious development in the area, from the perspective of cost effectiveness, are the new series of phone sex services known as "party lines." Such services, which charge the caller by the minute, differ from services in which the caller is connected with a paid employee of the service (usually female) with whom to converse. The new services, by contrast, are not nearly so labor-intensive, since the caller pays only to talk with other paying callers. The obvious benefit here is that such ventures are relatively capital-deintensive, with costs limited to setting up the telephone system, and labor-deintensive, since the only employee with whom a client is likely to come into contact is an operator, who, at least it is claimed, monitors calls, eliminating abusive or offensive callers, and in some cases is able to arrange private lines for two parties who want to speak free from auditory surveillance by others on the line. For the most part, however, the clients entertain, solicit, titillate one another. In this case, the sexual service for which one pays is really the technology that allows callers to contact others, often anonymously, privately, without being seen. This is the perfect cost-effective enterprise for the society that Foucault has dubbed the society of "talking sex."

Telephonic promiscuity is marketed as a safer and more discrete alternative or compensation in an age where other forms of sexual contact are being represented as far more risky. It also makes possible a form of social contact appropriate to mass culture—reaching out and touching someone telephonically—highly mediated, simulated, coded, anonymous, and expensive. For the consumer, such services have the advantage of being easily accessible and easy to use, as well as being malleable enough to accommodate a range of agendas, styles, and presumably outcomes. There are special services for gay men, lesbians, teens, blacks. Such services can also be enjoyed under conditions that are relatively discreet, and involve no advance planning and relatively little risk—conditions of use can be controlled by the user (one can hang up when one wants to, one can speak or not, etc.). Such services expand the range of consumers to those classes of people—teenagers, single mothers, housebound women, for example—who would not be likely or even able to enter the sexual commodity system otherwise. The obvious benefit from the viewpoint of the service provider is that the users are also the show. The service is made profitable by low labor costs and high profit margins.

Market segmenting has also been a useful strategy for expanding the market for sexual services. Part of this involves a logic of specialized sexualities, each of which can then be fetishized in its differences through a capital- and commodity-intensive erotic aesthetic. Barbara Ehrenreich remarks on the popularity of S & M as a particularly capital-intensive form of sex (requiring elaborate paraphernalia as well as technical discourses and service providers, tops, bottoms, clubs, magazines, etc.). The economic advantage of specialized sexuality is not only proliferation (more kinds of sex, more kinds of supportive instrumentation), but the creation of a differential economy of access and availability, a kind of erotics of supply and demand, which allows certain sexual practices to be proferred at premium prices, given their presumed relatively limited availability.

Here, again, the culture of sadomasochism is a good example, but other contemporary practices come to mind: specialized dating services that place a premium on very young prostitutes—male and female—or so-called secret or special practices. The multiplication of erotic possibility also maximizes possibilities for demand and desire. The very division of sexualities becomes an erotic mechanism of perpetual stimulation and incitement and also maximizes sites of profitability, positions within the economy from which profits can be made: experts, aesthetes, procurers, and proselytizers. Such mechanisms also work to produce a kind of compensatory optimism. At a time when certain sexual possibilities are being cut off, the market economy can always promise satisfaction in the form of next year's model, the market's way of producing a "revolutionary" development and sustaining a sense of apparent freedom through the proliferation of a range of erotic options, styles, and scenes.

Mass marketing of sexual apparatuses and services, not only erotica but also contraception devices, sexual accessories, and hygiene products, helps normalize the commodification of sexual functions and the integration of sexuality into a capitalist market system. One of the linking figures which helps to accomplish this social suturing is that of power, which is easily transferred from the economic to the sexual realm and back again. It is the very strategic versatility of this figure that allows those who pay for sex to feel empowered in that gesture: one can always get some sex by paying for it, one can be in control of the conditions for satisfying one's needs, desires, and thereby be less vulnerable. Those who receive payment also feel as though they have the upper hand precisely because they are in the position of benefiting in a clearly marked social way from this transaction, and hence are less vulnerable. The irony here is in the way that the mediation by the economic, specifically the monetary, is linked or recoded in the currency of personal control and autonomy.[6] Self-employed prostitutes, for example, often represent this explicitly as an occupational benefit, and as a positive distinction between their position and that occupied by most other women, who are disempowered by having to give it away for free (or the price of meal, or in concert with unpaid domestic labor). On the other hand, it comes as no surprise that one of the pleasures of prostitution for many men is precisely their feeling of superiority to those whose services they consume. In this configuration, power is associated precisely with not having to sell oneself, but rather in being so vested with excess that one can use it to elicit what one wants from another on demand. When one pays the piper, one can also call the tune.

The figure of the female prostitute, especially, also helps to empower men not only by testifying to their superior economic position, but also because such a figure is used, in reverse, to discipline "straight" women in a way that also works to male economic advantage, by normalizing or valorizing the dispensation of women's sexual services (erotic and reproductive) without economic compensation. If men can represent prostitution as the debased and exploitative form of sexual exchange, the appropriation of women's services without compensatory benefit can be sold to women in the name of their own autonomy, dignity. The same forms of economic privilege which have always sustained prostitution are also those which sustain it as a segment of sexual forms, and a relatively marginal one. The maintenance of this relative marginality is crucial for maintaining a larger economy in which the majority of women can be said to choose to do sex work for free. By maintaining sex for money as a distinct segment or sexual subset, the largely "free market" in sexuality, which would include all forms of uncompensated sexual exchanges, is hegemonized and naturalized in a way that sustains dominant class and gender interests, and is ultimately exploitative of its practitioners, especially relative to the consumers. This differentiates sex work from most other industries, where laws tend to favor the producer.

The figure of the prostitute can also be used to manipulate women psychically as a regulatory device in relation to other women: she is available as the ever-present, threatening other. If his needs are not accommodated at home, he can easily pay for sex elsewhere. This figure also produces a kind of sentimentalization which obscures the dynamics of the sexual political economy, and encourages women strategically to misidentify the nature of their interests in such transactions. One is debased by the receipt of some kind of clearly discernible and negotiable currency or benefit. Love, appreciation, admiration are not, in this context, considered negotiable currencies, though they could and certainly are marketed as not only compensatory but superior benefits. Gold diggers, women willing to use sexual liaison as a vehicle for improving their economic and social positions, are usually, most amusingly, represented as dumb rather than as particularly canny, clever readers of the heterosexual market system, strategic investors of their own sexual and social capital for maximum benefit. Part of the paradox of prostitution is that its mechanisms work not only to place women but also to lead them to identify with positions negatively, oppositionally defined (regarding other women), while preserving without question the entitlement of men to occupy both. Women are ultimately both self- and socially defined in terms of an opposition in which the best sex is both paid and unpaid.

Another paradox raised by the figure and institution of prostitution (in its contemporary incarnation) concerns contradictory relations between power and knowledge, and between economic and sexual value. Although the routes by which women enter the institution vary widely, from explicit coercion[7] to explicit choice (as a preferable occupation to others considered), it is an occupation in which there are no standards of certification, valuation, accreditation, norms of expertise. At most, there are informal reference networks, recommendations from consumers, and the pimp's or prostitute's promotional discourse. But the very economic transaction transfers to the prostitute the signification attached to being a professional, i.e., of being expert, up on the latest developments, providing the quality of service for which others are willing to pay. She must be good if she can get people to pay for it.

It is important to discuss prostitution as a specific set of social practices and institutions which are socially coded as marginal, discrete in the sense of being determinate, ghettoized and thereby or therefore carrying the markers of transgression and to a certain extent, taboo—witness the Jim Bakker episode. It must be emphasized that prostitution certainly exists, in another sense, on a continuum with other ways of socially organizing and transacting sexual relationships where relationships are already mediated by a logic of profit and loss. Radical lesbian critiques of marriage (like Ti-Grace Atkinson's) and of heterosexual relationships in general (as in Firestone and Beauvoir) depend on a linkage between traditional bourgeois marriage and courtship with prostitution. The similarities are that of exchange of sex for some form of material and/or in many cases softer currency—like love, romance, social legitimacy or recognition.

In the traditional male-female exchange, women are in the position, often emphasized only for a short period of time, of having to barter their social currency—sexual attractiveness and fertility—for the prospect of economic support/security and legitimacy for their offspring. Just what is objectionable about this transaction varies with particular feminist theorists, but central to all of these is the assumption that the very conditions which necessitate/encourage such transactions are already sufficiently asymmetrical as to disadvantage women in such exchanges. Disadvantages are coded in multiple currencies. Because a woman's future in patriarchy is so much a function of the man with whom she is officially linked through marriage, women's affectivity and eroticism are always infused by strategic considerations that infringe upon the spontaneity of her eroticism, and which impose upon the very structures of her desires a dependency that abridges her autonomy and capacities for self-transcendence (Beauvoir). Like the prostitute, her linkages are based not on a calculus of desire but rather on the basis of the best exchange rate. Considered in this light, marriage and prostitution come to look less different and more structurally similar. In both cases, social necessity demands that women put themselves on the market, present the most attractive packaging possible, and wait for the bids to come in. Success in either enterprise depends in different degrees on the woman's willingness and ability to incarnate the desires of the other with superior purchasing power (or some other currency in which the woman is invested or intending to invest), to provide those services which he is willing to support materially. In both cases her value is determined relationally, i.e., by her exchange value assessed in terms of the market, even though much of the labor in performing such services demands precisely autonomous creativity, imagination, cleverness, and craft.

Further linking their situations are the conditions that make questions of choice and autonomy highly ambiguous and problematic. On the one hand, the choice between mother and whore is one of the primary figures of differentiation for women. The difference between the good and the bad, the respectable and the illicit, the revered and the exploited. Feminist analysis, however, which emphasizes the exploited condition of all women, forces a reconsideration of the political economy of heterosexuality in a way that problematizes the nature and the significance of these oppositions. If prostitution is objectionable, as many liberals and feminists argue, it is because it is exploitative (either of women or the sacredness of sexual relationships, or of the clients), especially under conditions where men such as pimps and club owners end up with the lion's share of a woman's earnings, and where her work only enhances the forms of control he has over her. Many Marxist and lesbians-feminists have argued that marriage operates, especially economically but also psychologically, in much the same way, and therefore that marriage, motherhood, even heterosexual relationships as such, are paradigmatic cases of the alienation and exploitation of women's labor.

The traditional marriage contract, and the conduct of contemporary marital relationships, assumes and in fact depends upon vast contributions of women's unpaid labor. This includes domestic service which, as survey after survey indicates, is still women's responsibility whether or not they are also engaged in wage labor. (Women who do not do their own household tasks are more than likely to be paying another woman to do it for them.) Reproduction is also similarly organized so that the majority of labor not only in birthing but more importantly childrearing falls disproportionately to women, as does the burden of economic support in the growing number of cases in which fathers either do not acknowledge paternity, divorce the child's mother, or fail to marry her in the first place. Whereas cases of elective paternity are socially rewarded, there has been historically very little effort made to hold men economically accountable for the children they produce. If they choose to, men can use their children, and by extension the women who produce them, as legitimate heirs, points for consolidating or marking their social wealth, authority, and power. If not, women are often left, as divorce statistics indicate, economically impoverished by the children whose absent father's name they still carry, often leaving that same man free to begin the very same process with another woman. Ironically, in light of the contemporary statistics on the longevity of marriages, the rate of paternal child support, the number of single mother households, one of the primary benefits of marriage over prostitution, namely, the prospect of legitimacy, economic support (at least partial), and a coparent for one's children, is rapidly eroding. Given statistical probabilities, one of the strategic considerations that enters choices about marriage and childbirth is the prospect that as a woman one is likely, at least at some point and for some period of time, to do this alone, with male participation largely elective and selective.

What has also been called "the displaced homemaker syndrome" is another example of the ways in which the political economy of marriage parallels the more exploitative dimensions of the prostitutive exchange. Much of the currency that women both invest in their marriage, and more importantly in the context in which they are paid, is the relatively nonnegotiable currency of love, affection nurture, and attention. Through such transactions, men are able to exact from their wives vast amounts of unpaid and often unacknowledged labor as typists, researchers, translators, editors, secretaries, etc., that not only enhances their professional status and work, but also puts them in a better position to abandon their wives when their services are no longer necessary or are available elsewhere. There is also evidence that men benefit professionally and economically from the attention wives give to their husbands' needs, not only by creating a comfortable environment in which he can work or retreat from work, but also by giving him the psychological nurturance and space to concentrate on his work, knowing that his daily needs are being taken care of, leaving him more available and open to the very possibilities of which women in performing these functions are deprived. Given the current ways of organizing the biological time clock, women are often in the position of interrupting or abridging their careers to raise families at the very time that men are most professionally active, and are likely to be making the most rapid advances in their careers. Given this, it is not surprising that even in cases where both parties engage in wage labor, women are still the ones economically disadvantaged by divorce. The position of many divorced women is like that of the worker in the company town whose one plant has just closed. Paid in the company scrip of affection, she is now left with a bunch of worthless investments because the contract in which they had some currency no longer exists.[8]

Feminist analysis of the sixties and seventies has the effect of both problematizing and making more complex the question of what prostitution is and, by extension, what if any sexual exchange, given the logic of late capitalism, mediated through a sexual politics of male and heterosexist privilege, could be nonexploitative, noncommodified, not productive of some alienated stratification of dominance.

The effect of this kind of feminist analysis is radically to disrupt the logic of stabilized opposition by virtue of which the category of prostitution is socially constructed as some unique sphere of a specifically commodified sexual relationship, thereby allowing for the implication that all other forms of sexual exchanges are not commodified, do not exist, operate, function within a market economy. By extension, it calls into question not only just what/where prostitution is not (if not marriage, then maybe romance) but also just what the nature of such nonexploitative relationships is supposed to be.

When Ti-Grace Atkinson made the claim that marriage was legalized prostitution, that statement forced a reconsideration not only of prostitution, but also of marriage and of the legal system which constructs and enforces a materially reinforced symbolic difference between the two practices. Several lines of questioning and construction are prompted by this crucial insight, but none of them take what might be described as the hegemonic interrogation of oppositions—either marriage or prostitution, yes or no to prostitution, particularly on the basis of the opposition of good and bad. The productive effect of the irony operative in Atkinson's statement is both to elicit the embedded social investments in these signifiers, and at the same time to problematize the moral and evaluative mystifications that divide these choices and the women who identify themselves and one another in terms of their relationships to them. In doing so, it displaces judgmental considerations with strategic ones of relative and situational advantage, while at the same time pointing toward the limits of such strategic machinations in a context already organized in a way to secure their circumscription and domination.

One obvious line following from Atkinson's conjunction of marriage and prostitution is a very definite critique of marriage and of the assumptions which both produce and condemn prostitution as an institution. If, as one line of argument suggests, prostitution is wrong because it exploits sexual desire, degrading it by turning it into a material exchange, marriage is wrong for the same reasons. Men are still forced to pay for sex and women to sell it. If prostitution exploits women, especially their youthful bodies and spirits, often leaving them with very little to show for their efforts, married women are often in the same position. The differences that prompt the morally self-righteous superior positions often underlying critiques of prostitution must get recast in light of the recognition that, in relation to economic exploitation, good women, women who marry, are frequently not that much better off. Considered strategically, as a response to what is an essentially exploitative heterosexual politics, it might be argued, as some feminists have done, that at least in principle the prostitute may very well be in a better position, economically and otherwise, than the married woman (especially if she is in a position to control her own money, i.e., works freelance). As against the situation of the married woman, her services are compensated in negotiable currency rather than in more mystical forms like love and affection. The transaction is therefore more straightforward, demystified, honest. Furthermore, because she is on the open market (or at least on a market with multiple points for consumption of her services), she is in a better position both to barter and to increase the profitability of her assets, making not one deal, but many.

What is considered obligatory behavior for a wife, and is thereby often entirely uncompensated, becomes for the prostitute one more occasion for negotiations and profit potential. She can charge separately for each sexual act she performs, with other amenities like costume or talk-time charged at separate rates. Rather than being trapped in the impossible project of attempting to fulfill the needs and desire of a single person on whom one depends for one's very survival, the prostitute can often profit by the very *unfulfillability* of those needs which both motivate her clients to seek her out, and allow her to profit, whether or not at least most of the promises she makes are ever fulfilled. If he is not satisfied with her performance, he will simply find someone else, as will she. The prostitute may be also thought to be advantaged by being divested of much of the romantic mythology that mystifies other women. She, more than other women, is clear about what she wants from such an encounter, and in most cases is more likely to get it—up front. She is also in a better position than most women, especially wives, to determine the time, circumstances, and conditions under which the encounter will take place, as well as to be in charge of establishing its limits, temporally and substantively. What she will and won't do is much more subject to explicit bargaining. Furthermore, while her performances may often be rather theatrically elaborate (a tactic, ironically enough, that Marabel Morgan recommends for wives to keep their husbands home), she is also more discreet and performatively specific about what is expected from her, in contrast with wives who in addition to performing sexual functions are also expected to meet psychological and emotional needs for nurture.

In what was probably a largely unintended irony, the liberal feminist advocacy of the prenuptial contract stipulating the precise terms and conditions of exchange (popular in the 1970s) was an effort to secure some of the benefits of the prostitute's situation for married women. And while both kinds of agreements can be and are often breached, it can be argued that at least the durational limits of the prostitute's connection with her client offers some measure of self-protection. Precisely because such contracts have no legal status, they are also easier to escape.

Atkinson's statement therefore gives a different picture of the alternatives, at least for women who take themselves to be heterosexual. It is not a choice between selling or not selling oneself, being exploited or not, but rather a question of the form and social valence given to the form such exchanges take. A woman can sell herself to one man (or at least to one man at a time) or to many. She can trade sex or fertility or nurturance or domestic service. She can do her work in the kitchen, or on the street, in a bedroom or a bathhouse. But the larger conditions which alienate labor are the same, empowering men both because they do and do not have to pay for sex, and they control and have far superior access to the currencies of social value.

What does separate marriage and prostitution, and by extension the women who identify themselves and one another in terms of these markers, is the legal mark of difference which establishes these institutions' identities within differential calculus of value. Marriage is that form of alienated heterosexual exchange that is not only legally sanctioned but also socially rewarded, celebrated, and promoted. Prostitutes, by contrast, are selectively harassed, punished, and forced to run the risk of those in marginal enterprises, often having to pay for protection both from the regulations and from the risks of clients and pimps whose behavior is also unregulated. Although there may be strategic advantages in presenting oneself as available to any man rather than as the possession of one, there are also clearly risks and dangers precisely in that availability—the risk of being raped, hurt, killed, or ripped off with little likelihood of any legal remedies or social compensation for one's losses. Furthermore, the moral surplus attached to the differences in legal status functions both to dismiss the harm done to prostitutes, either because they are bad women or because they have somehow gotten what they deserve, and to induce women to enter into what Dworkin calls the protection racket of the heterosexual couple. In this racket, women, to some extent like the figures in Hobbes's imagined social contact, agree to give up some of their mobility and autonomy in exchange for the protection of one man against the exploitative intrusions of other men. The debased fate of the prostitute is then used as a part of a construction in which marriage can come to be seen by many women as the strategically preferable choice.

The question now becomes, which strategic utilities are being operationalized in the legal distinction between marriage and prostitution? What is it specifically about marital relationships that, from the point of view of the masculinist capitalist legal system, make them the strategically preferred social arrangement? One way to begin to answer this question is to remember that the purpose of the legal system is to protect the consolidation of hegemonic interests. Considered from the point of view of a cost-benefit logic, marriage is the most cost-effective way to maximize the profit potential of women for men, while maintaining a ceiling on the level of male capitalization. The marriage contract institutionalizes the expropriation of women's labor and love (or at least conjugal duties), along with an asymmetrical series of rights and obligations. Considered by heterosexual men, marriage is constructed less as an either/or alternative to prostitution than as a strategically and situationally beneficial alternative to it. The benefits are for men who can pay for sex when it suits them while otherwise having greater access to a woman from whom they frequently receive far more extensive and higher-quality service at a much lower price. The utility of this construction is both that it mobilizes a majority of women into what is from their standpoint the least advantageous exchange system, and subjects them to a logic of opposition, psychologically and politically, that men are and always have been free to cross. The occasions for prostitution are numerous, considered from both the sides of supply and demand, and the needs or desires it activates are those which have been represented as relatively foundational or basic. The very limits of this kind of arrangement, temporally and functionally, are also instrumental to its proliferation as well as to the promise embedded in this institution.

That is why the logic of repression is ultimately both inadequate and uninteresting when it comes to discussions of the politics, value, or utility of prostitution. Such discussions are often misleading, homogenizing what are rather diverse enterprises, and depending upon a set of assumptions, both about social particulars and about larger epistemic issues like the status/possibility of free will and choice. Arguments that attempt to advocate for prostitution through the language of legalization miss the point of what prostitution is for. Strategically, given the existing local logic, legalized prostitution is something of an oxymoron. It fails to get at the heart of the issue in terms of exploitation, since, as has been argued, legality and selective exploitation are certainly compatible, as evidenced by the legal construction of marriage, and the capitalist definition of free employment.

Arguments made in favor of legalizing or decriminalizing prostitution often depend upon the kind of strategic analysis I have been talking about. According to this position, given the relatively limited opportunities available for well-paid work open to most women, choosing to sell sexual service which is more highly valued than a woman's other skills can be seen as a reasonable strategic option, and certainly should not be socially precluded or punished, especially without similar treatment being given to those who choose to avail themselves of it. Precluding sexual service as an occupational choice is therefore not only arbitrary, but also reflects a basic and intolerable social hypocrisy by virtue of which sexuality is that which is both most highly valued in women, and also that which can never be activated in a way that enriches or benefits the party who is valued. The argument is therefore based on a situation that assumes choice—with the decision to enter prostitution a strategic determination of where an individual's best opportunities lie—and therefore should, like other occupational choices, be protected. Furthermore, since money is a primary currency of social value, there is no prima facie reason to exempt sexual exchanges. In capitalism, workers are constantly in the position of having to exchange their bodily capacities for wages or marriage. Given that the moral differences between these economies are negligible, there is no good reason to punish women for behavior that in other circumstances would be socially rewarded and recognized—namely, the activity of maximizing one's powers and capacities for one's own benefit through the accumulation of surplus value. If heterosexual relationships in patriarchy all have the effect of exploiting women, women at least ought to be in a position to decide how best strategically to navigate this situation. Prostitution thereby becomes defensible as a choice which women ought to be able to make without fear of organized social reprisal, especially on the grounds of moral self-righteousness.

While such arguments have the effect of restoring to the prostitute some dignity beyond that of the hapless victim, as well as pointing up the connection between prostitution and other socially exploitative exchange systems, such positions ultimately depend upon a set of assumptions precisely about choice that may be true for some women who find themselves in the sex industry, but are certainly not generalizable as a model. As a number of feminist works, including *Female Sexual Slavery*,[9] have shown, the strategic model is simply not descriptive of the conditions under which many women end up as prostitutes. There is certainly much documentation of the various forms of coercion used to procure prostitutes, including abduction, sale by parents or husbands (mostly in the third world), violence or the threat thereof, and various forms of chemical and psychological manipulation, as well as the exploitation of women in vulnerable positions—because they are poor, or young, runaways, abandoned, addicted, etc., which leave them without other choices in any meaningful sense. Hence, while it may be important, at least within the limits of a capitalist patriarchal sexual economy, to argue for the rights of women to choose to sell their sexual services, it is a mistake to think that this is coextensive with a defense of prostitution as such. Legalizing prostitution would do little more than provide conditions that would support, encourage, and likely multiply such coercive practices by legalizing and normalizing them. Legalizing prostitution because marriage is legal is to miss the point of what is wrong with both of them, while creating further conditions that will allow social responsibility for its fallout to be placed yet again on the backs of its victims.

On the other hand, any effort to limit/eradicate prostitution through the imposition of increased punitive measures flies in the face of the larger developments in both technology and marketing which allow for an expansion of the possibilities for making sexual exchanges economically profitable. This is especially clear in the area of reproductive technologies, where it is already possible for a man to sell his sperm (a right which has never been contested or claimed to be exploitative) and where a woman could, although recent legal developments suggest otherwise, conceivably be in a position either to sell eggs for

implantation in the body of another woman, or to sell her egg and uterus for artificial insemination, or just her uterus for carrying another woman's fertilized
ovum. There may also very well be a market in eggs for medical research or for
any other medical or other benefit that may be extracted from them. Certainly,
the commodification of reproductive functions is not an entirely unprecedented
phenomenon historically. The practice of kings with infertile wives taking mis-
tresses or disposing of wives for other ones has a long history, as does the practice by which economically privileged women contract the services of wet-
nurses. But developments not only in technology but also in ideology, the legal
system, and social expectations about the nature of families, maximize the occasions and the sheer number of such transactions.

Beyond those factors encouraging wider use of such services, the fact that
such procedures are profitable for those with control of the technology and professional expertise means that it is likely that such tendencies will intensify.
Such practices, buttressed by supportive marketing and promotional techniques,
are likely to reduce whatever resistance might exist in the marketplace to paid
sexual services, both erotic and reproductive.

These circumstances, I believe, change the shape and nature of the questions and of the discourse that seeks to resist the exploitative consequences of
sexual commodification, forcing a strategic consideration of just what exchange
forms can be legitimately juxtaposed to it—in other words, what would nonexploitative sexual exchanges be like, how would they function, and what
would be the prospective consequences of such transactions, especially in light
of the historically specific conditions brought about by the hegemony of sexual
epidemic, which preclude or otherwise change the terms of what had been culturally figured as the model of liberated sexuality?

One significant pre-epidemic vision of sexual freedom consisted in the promotion of a series of multiple encounters considered nonexploitative by virtue
of resisting the model of monogamy, possession, commitment and by remaining
without expectations, episodic, an exchange in kind of sex for sex. Not only
have conditions of epidemic made such strategies less viable, but so has feminist critique, which has problematized this vision of liberation by asking
whether it is not a different modality of regulation, given the ways in which
these sexual exchanges are sutured into a logic of profit and loss. (This may be
the place to recuperate the critique of models of sexual liberation founded on the
noncommitted multiple ejaculatory economy of adolescent males.)

Prostitution, the selling of recreational sexual services, related products and
accoutrements, is only one dimension of the capitalization of sexuality—its social
mobilization and organization for the production of profit. Sexuality is also organized through other disciplinary mechanisms—like the medical and the therapeutic which also allow for further interventions by the commodity system.

As a recent article in the *West Side Spirit* by Janet Grady Sullivan an-
nounces, the "AIDS business" is "booming." Out of a situation of death and
despair, cagey entrepreneurs are developing services and technologies designed

precisely to address these new circumstances, including "drugs for treatment and prevention, blood storage centers, detection techniques and nutritional supplements." One might also add, dating services that provide contacts with only prescreened clients as well as other kinds of social services designed to reduce risks of random encounters. AIDS also has had an effect on how existing products like condoms are being marketed—television ads are now aimed at women. Another social service: a Long Island–based Safecom aimed at gay men—which offers clients "safe company cards" after they have had two negative tests three months apart.

The AIDS epidemic was certainly not the first intersection of the medical commodity and sexual market systems. Selling sexual aids and services—contraceptive devices, aphrodisiacs, and love potions—has a long history. But the capital intensification of sexuality began in earnest with the medicalization of sexuality at the end of the nineteenth century, which generated, along with a catalogue of sexual dysfunctions and diseases, a series of medical, psychological, and pharmaceutical technologies, therapies, and therapists with which to address them, along with a supportive research and scholarly apparatus as well as a popular (self-help) literature. Whereas the imposition of the medical discourse has had profound effects on the social structures of sexuality, I want to concentrate here on those which show how this historical process has helped to manage and transform the social currency of sexual exchange in a way that maximizes profit, both in terms of the consolidation of economic capital, and in terms of social profitability, i.e., its utility. This is important because such logic affects and will affect the social strategies developed for addressing the AIDS epidemic as well as the forms such therapeutic technologies and the discourse about them will take.

Both Foucault and Marcuse addressed the intersections between sexuality and the dominant strategies imposed by hegemonic institutional utilities. Foucault's discussion emphasizes the strategic utility of sexuality as a site for intervention into the lives of populations and individuals. Dominant utilities include those of producing populations (and regulating that production) and coordinating the lives and behaviors of individuals. Marcuse's analysis (as well as that of feminists like Diana Dinsmore) emphasizes the specific utility of sexuality for two other crucial social functions—one of which is the creation of socially useful desires, i.e., desires which the existing social system is designed to meet, and the fulfillment of which will serve to enhance the power and authority exerted by the hegemonic forms of organization, most notably, the organization of social labor for private profit, and the organization of reproduction and kinship in patrilineal, male-dominated forms. What increases the ideological potency of sexuality as a mechanism of social control is that regulation ultimately becomes translated into the currency of self-regulation, because sexuality has already been constructed as that which is or belongs to the realm of the private, i.e., opposed to the social. The regulatory force is represented and enacted through a currency not of coercion but of desire, in a way that encourages its individuation or personalization.

If desire is paradigmatically sexual, and the sexual is paradigmatically private, then individuals are far more likely to project expectations for their own fulfillment (and resentment over the lack of it) onto the private sphere than to articulate those expectations as an organized social demand, a demand for an organized social response, such as the redistribution and reorganization of basic institutions. The social logic which propels the cultural tendency (at least in the last one hundred years) both to talk more about sex and to increase the desire for it (control by incitement), can be attributed at least in part to its success as a mechanism of both pacification and mystification. That is, it provides a way to provide satisfaction to individuals in a way that not only preserves existing power structures, but also entails a minimum of capital or social investment to maintain. (Though there are indications in the recent and ongoing discussion of day care that the social cost of maintaining the nuclear family may very well be going up. In the resistance to day care, the existing assumptions about low costs are made obvious: why pay for what we've always gotten for free and, to show the beauty of this tactic, have freely chosen?)

Mechanisms work both to reduce the demands individuals are likely to make on the social and to encourage paradigmatic identification of themselves with a private rather than class affiliation, a move which works to mislead individuals about the source of much of their distress. One of the great ironies that feminists, especially American, drew from the so-called sexual revolution was that human tragedies follow from the discourse which made sexuality, especially genital sexual contact, the primary bearer or marker of human well-being, a burden it could not and does not bear well. Overinvestment in sexuality is also a way of avoiding or minimizing the demand for investments in other areas, specifically the demand that other enterprises, like work, also be organized with an expectation of the possibility of satisfaction.

One of the other strategic benefits of overinvestment in sexuality and the consequent centrality of notions of sexual identity is that it encourages divisions that make populations ultimately easier to regulate (gay ghettos, red-light districts) and also easier to target as consumers (market segmenting). The phallus is the primary commodity fetish.

Sex being so central to the very conception of human well-being, mechanisms are now in place and being mobilized which will justify (or be represented a justified by) the concern for protecting this very sexuality (and its freedom) from the threats imposed by disease. In the name of sexual health all sorts of means to control populations that would ordinarily seem unacceptable now seem to be justified as lesser evils: recent suggestions for quarantining, tattooing people with AIDS, and other proposed legislation which would treat the disease as a justifiable cause for denying citizens what would otherwise be their rights.

These issues force a consideration of the ways in which the AIDS epidemic is producing a social surplus, negotiable even though it is not only or primarily monetary currency. The AIDS epidemic also provides justification for the state's intervention into the bodies of all kinds of individuals—gays, military recruits, pregnant women, prisoners, maybe applicants for federal jobs, and IV drug users. Clearly, AIDS discourse is supplemental to an existing trend by virtue of which social control and surveillance of the behavior of human beings is progressively normalized and rationalized by increased use of routine screening of potential employees for drugs and alcohol, no-smoking legislation, changes in liability laws regarding drunk driving. All of these procedures are designed to intervene in cases where the self-regulatory logic of "just say no" has failed. Such practices share a common justification in the terms of benevolence—either paternalistic ("We want our employees to get help or protection") toward clients and others, or, to a much lesser degree, punitive. More important than the substantive effects of these particular procedures is the social recoding of practices that have been understood as the invasion of privacy, surveillance, intrusion, to what is currently regarded as benevolent protection.

Notes

1. See Sigmund Freud, *Civilization and its Discontents,* ed. and trans. James Strachey (New York: Norton, 1963); Herbert Marcuse, *Eros and Civilization: A Philosophical Inquiry into Freud* (Boston: Beacon Press, 1955).

2. One might consider in this regard the sexual politics of Wilhelm Reich, and the theory of pansexualism. See Wilhelm Reich, *Sex-pol, Essays, 1929–34,* ed. Lee Baxandall (New York: Vintage, 1972).

3. Jean Baudrillard, "Consumer Society," in *Jean Baudrillard: Selected Writings,* ed. Mark Poster (Stanford: Stanford University Press, 1988), p. 43.

4. Ibid.

5. Susan Sontag, *AIDS and Its Metaphors* (New York: Farrar, Straus, & Giroux, 1989).

6. *Sex Work: Writings by Women in the Sex Industry,* ed. Frederique Delacoste and Priscilla Alexander (Pittsburgh: Cleis Press, 1987).

7. Kathleen Barry, *Female Sexual Slavery* (New York: New York University Press, 1985).

8. See Shulamith Firestone, *The Dialectic of Sex* (New York: Morrow, 1970).

9. Kathleen Barry, *Female Sexual Slavery* (Englewood Cliffs, N.J.: Prentice-Hall, 1979).

32

Conceptual History and Conceptions of Perversion*

Arnold I. Davidson

. . . One purpose of conceptual history lies in showing us that our concepts and their organization are marked by their historical origins, that we will not really understand the problems that many of our concepts give rise to, unless we trace out the conditions of their emergence, however remote from us those conditions may appear to be. In attempting to understand psychiatry's emergence, in the nineteenth century, as an autonomous medical discipline, and specifically its conceptual autonomy from neurology and cerebral pathology, I have been led, in other writings, to focus on the emergence of new disease categories. I have especially emphasized the decline of pathological anatomy as either an explanatory theory for so-called mental diseases and disorders, or the foundation for the classification and description of these diseases. The birth of psychiatry as a distinct medical discipline is simultaneous with the emergence of a new class of functional diseases, of which sexual perversion and hysteria were perhaps the two most prominent examples. Ultimately, these functional diseases were fully describable simply as functional deviations of some kind, diseases that did not have an anatomically localizable pathology. Elsewhere, I have tried to show some of the changes in styles of reasoning that were necessary in order for true-or-false statements about such functional diseases to become possible, and I have tried to write a history of the modern medical concept of perversion, which required showing the conditions under which perversion emerged as an object of medical knowledge.[1] Although I have claimed that there were no perverts before the later part of the nineteenth century, I do not want to repeat the arguments for that claim now. Rather, I would just like to summarize some of the

---

*This is an edited and shortened version of Arnold I. Davidson, "Styles of Reasoning, Conceptual History, and the Emergence of Psychiatry," which originally appeared in *The Disunity of Science: Boundaries, Contexts and Power,* edited by Peter Galison and David J. Stump (Stanford University Press, 1996). Reprinted by permission of the author and publisher.

results of my conceptual history of perversion, first, to show, as it were, the methodology in action, and, second, to indicate some of its advantages over the kind of conceptual analysis philosophers are accustomed to.

The best way to understand the nineteenth-century obsession with perversion is to examine the concept of the sexual instinct, for the actual conception of perversion underlying clinical thought was that of a functional disease of this instinct. That is to say, the class of diseases that affected the sexual instinct was precisely the sexual perversions. A functional understanding of the instinct allowed one to isolate a set of disorders or diseases that were disturbances of the special functions of the instinct. Moreau (du Tours), in a book that influenced the first edition of Krafft-Ebing's *Psychopathia Sexualis,* argued that the clinical facts forced one to accept, as absolutely demonstrated, the psychic existence of a sixth sense, which he called the genital sense.[2] Although the notion of a genital sense may appear ludicrous, Moreau's characterization was adopted by subsequent French clinicians, and his phrase "sens génital" was preserved, by Charcot among others, as a translation of our "sexual instinct." The genital sense is just the sexual instinct, masquerading in different words. Its characterization as a sixth sense was a useful analogy. Just as one could become blind, or have acute vision, or be able to discriminate only a part of the color spectrum, and just as one might go deaf, or have abnormally sensitive hearing, or be able to hear only certain pitches, so too this sixth sense might be diminished, augmented, or perverted. What Moreau hoped to demonstrate was that this genital sense had special functions, distinct from the functions served by other organs, and that just as with the other senses, this sixth sense could be psychically disturbed without the proper working of other mental functions, either affective or intellectual, being harmed.[3] A demonstration such as Moreau's was essential in isolating diseases of sexuality as distinct morbid entities.

The *Oxford English Dictionary* reports that the first modern medical use in English of the concept of perversion occurred in 1842 in Dunglison's *Medical Lexicon*: "*Perversion,* one of the four modifications of function in disease: the three others being augmentation, diminution, and abolition."[4] The notions of perversion and function are inextricably intertwined. Once one offers a functional characterization of the sexual instinct, perversions become a natural class of diseases, and without this characterization there is really no conceptual room for this kind of disease. Whatever words of pathological anatomy he and others offered, it is clear that Krafft-Ebing understood the sexual instinct in a functional way. In his *Textbook on Insanity* Krafft-Ebing is unequivocal in his claim that life presents two instincts, those of self-preservation and sexuality; he insists that abnormal life presents no new instincts, although the instincts of self-preservation and sexuality "may be lessened, increased or manifested with perversion."[5] The sexual instinct was often compared with the instinct of self-preservation, which manifested itself in appetite. In his section "Disturbances of the Instincts," Krafft-Ebing first discusses the anomalies of the appetites, which he divides into three different kinds. There are increases of the appetite (hyperorexia), lessening of the appetite (anorexia), and perversions of the appetite, such as a "true impulse to eat spiders, toads, worms, human blood, etc."[6] Such a classification is exactly what one should expect on a functional understanding of the instinct. Anomalies of the sexual instinct are similarly classified as lessened or entirely wanting (anesthesia), abnormally increased (hyperaesthesia), and perverse expression (paraesthesia); in addition there is a fourth class of anomalies of the sexual instinct, which consists in its manifestation outside the period of anatomical and physiological processes in the reproductive organs (paradoxia).[7] In both his *Textbook on Insanity* and *Psychopathia Sexualis,* Krafft-Ebing further divides the perversions into sadism, masochism, fetishism, and contrary sexual instinct.[8]

In order to be able to determine precisely what phenomena are functional disturbances or diseases of the sexual instinct, one must also, of course, specify what the normal or natural function of this instinct consists in. Without knowing what the normal function of the instinct is, everything and nothing could count as a functional disturbance. There would be no principled criterion to include or exclude any behavior from the disease category of perversion. So one must first believe that there is a natural function of the sexual instinct and then believe that this function is quite determinate. One might have thought that questions as momentous as these would have received extensive discussion during the nineteenth-century heyday of perversion. But, remarkably enough, no such discussion appears. There is virtually *unargued unaminity* both on the fact that this instinct does have a natural function and on what that function is. Krafft-Ebing's view is representative here:

> During the time of the maturation of physiological processes in the reproductive glands, desires arise in the consciousness of the individual which have for their purpose the perpetuation of the species (sexual instinct). . . . With opportunity for the natural satisfaction of the sexual instinct, every expression of it that does not correspond with the purpose of nature—i.e., propagation—must be regarded as perverse.[9]

Nineteenth-century psychiatry silently adopted this conception of the function of the sexual instinct, and it was often taken as so natural as not to need explicit statement. It is not at all obvious why sadism, masochism, fetishism, and homosexuality should be treated as species of the same disease, for they appear to have no essential features in common. Yet if one takes the natural function of the sexual instinct to be propagation, it becomes possible to see why they were all classified together as perversions. They all manifest the same kind of perverse expression, the same basic kind of functional deviation. Thus this understanding of the instinct permits a *unified* treatment of perversion, allows one to place an apparently heterogeneous group of phenomena under the same natural disease-kind. Had anyone denied either that the sexual instinct has a natural function or that this function is procreation, diseases of perversion, as we understand them, would not have entered psychiatric nosology.

Although this truncates a long, convoluted story, it is enough for my purposes here. What I want to do now is contrast this kind of archaeology of the concept of perversion . . . with a justly famous, methodologically standard conceptual analysis. Thomas Nagel's "Sexual Perversion," published in 1969 and interestingly revised ten years later for inclusion in his collection *Mortal Questions,** is one of our most famous conceptual analyses, having spawned by itself almost an entire literature. Nagel's paper seems to me, even after all these years, still to be the best of its kind, and I would like to use it as an example of the methodological limitations of its kind of approach. Nagel's analysis proceeds, through an extraordinary coupling of Jean-Paul Sartre and Paul Grice, by way of an analysis of sexual desire, which "in the paradigm case of mutual desire . . . is a complex system of superimposed mutual perceptions."[10] Roughly put, and without any of Nagel's imaginative examples, he argues that in mutual sexual desire, X desires that Y desires that X desires $Y,$ and Y desires that X desires that Y desires X—"It involves a desire that one's partner be aroused by the recognition of one's desire that he or she be aroused."[11] Nagel continues, "I believe that some version of this overlapping system of distinct sexual perceptions and interactions is the basic framework of any full-fledged sexual relation and that relations involving only part of the complex are significantly incomplete";[12] and finally "various familiar deviations constitute truncated or incomplete versions of the complete configuration, and may be regarded as perversions of the central impulse."[13] Reading this article, one is struck by the fact that, despite its interest, it seems to have very little to do with the concept of perversion. One's perplexity is increased by the first sentence of the article—"There is something to be learned about sex from the fact that we possess a concept of perversion"— and by Nagel's insistence that "if there are any sexual perversions, they will have to be sexual desires or practices that are in some sense unnatural, though the explanation of this natural/unnatural distinction is of course the main problem."[14] This latter claim showed that Nagel inhabited the same conceptual space as late nineteenth-century psychiatry, which was able to solve the main problem by offering a conceptually determinate and unambiguous distinction between the natural and unnatural; the theory of the sexual instinct played precisely this role. But when Nagel comes to give his account of perversion as a truncated or incomplete version of the system of superimposed mutual perceptions, the main problem of characterizing the natural/unnatural distinction seems to disappear. Indeed, in the original version of this paper, this distinction plays almost no role at all, even though Nagel also says there that it is the main problem. In the later version of the paper, an extremely interesting extra paragraph and a half is added. Nagel repeats his claim that familiar deviations constitute truncated or incomplete versions of the complete configuration of mutual perceptions, and then immediately adds: "The concept of perversion implies that a *normal* sexual development has been turned aside by distorting influ-

---

*Chapter 22 in this volume.

ences. I have little to say about this causal condition. But if perversions are in some sense *unnatural,* they must result from interference with the development of a capacity that is there potentially."[15] The next paragraph is concerned with how difficult it is to determine what causal influences are distorting, and Nagel eventually concludes, "We appear to need an independent [noncircular] criterion for a distorting influence, and we do not have one."[16] But if we cannot say what a distorting influence of normal sexual development is, then we cannot say what is natural or unnatural. And if we cannot distinguish the natural from the unnatural, then, by Nagel's own admission, we cannot make sense of the concept of perversion. Again, the theory of the sexual instinct, which was part of nineteenth-century psychiatry, was meant to serve precisely this role.

Consider finally what Nagel says about homosexuality. In the 1969 version of his paper he says, "It is not clear whether homosexuality is a perversion if that is measured by the standard of the described configuration, but it seems unlikely";[17] after a brief further discussion he concludes, "Certainly if homosexuality is a perversion, it is so in a very different sense from that in which shoe-fetishism is a perversion, for some version of the full range of interpersonal perceptions seems perfectly possible between two persons of the same sex."[18] Here is what he says in 1979: "Homosexuality cannot similarly be classed as a perversion on phenomenological grounds. Nothing rules out the full range of interpersonal perceptions between persons of the same sex. The issue then depends on whether homosexuality is produced by distorting influences that block or displace a natural tendency to heterosexual development. . . . The question is whether heterosexuality is the natural expression of male and female sexual dispositions that have not been distorted. It is an unclear question, and I do not know how to approach it."[19] I think it is clear what is going on here. Nagel wants to analyze the concept of perversion, and he is determined by the conceptual space of which that concept is part. In order to do what he claims he wants to do he must say something about the concepts of the natural and unnatural, normal sexual development, and distorting influences. These are concepts without which there is no space for the concept of sexual perversion. But what Nagel in fact does is to present a phenomenological account of ideal sexuality that has nothing to do with the concept of perversion, that makes no real use of the concepts of the natural and unnatural (and related concepts). According to the phenomenological account, certain kinds of sexual behavior need not fall short of the ideal. But it is an entirely different question as to whether they are perversions. Hence Nagel's difficulties in dealing with homosexuality. If we examine the historical conditions under which the concept of perversion emerged, we see that Nagel's claims are determined by those conditions of emergence. On the other hand, his positive account ignores those conditions of emergence and offers us a description of sexuality that actually seems to have no room for the concept of perversion. This is no matter of mere words. Nagel's account is almost internally incoherent, purporting to analyze the concept of perversion but employing unrelated concepts; this creates deep theoretical problems for his account, as indicated by the differences in the two versions of his paper. If we undertake a conceptual history of perversion, we can explain why he has the theoretical difficulties that he does have. Both determined by the conditions of emergence of the concept and attempting to ignore them, he produces an account that cannot do what he wants it to do. Nagel is "shaped by pre-history, and only archeology can display its shape."[20]

I hope that this contrast between two methods for analyzing the concept of perversion begins to show what the significance and philosophical advantages of conceptual history are. Of course, in my own account here, I have only just begun to detail the conceptual space of psychiatry, and so to show which concepts make up the psychiatric style of reasoning. In previous work, I have discussed some of the differences between the anatomical and psychiatric styles of representing sexual diseases, and I have tried to supplement my conceptual history with a discussion of the distinctive habits of inference and analogy, and the different forms of explanation that characterize the two styles.* But since I want to follow Heinrich Wölfflin's lead in understanding style, let me just assert that if we look at the history of neurology and psychiatry in the nineteenth century, we can begin to reconstruct some of the polar concepts that make up the two opposed styles. For example, we are presented with the polarities between organ and instinct, structure and function, and anatomical defect and perversion. The first of each of these pairs of concepts partially makes up the anatomical style of reasoning about disease, while the second of each of these pairs helps constitute the psychiatric style of reasoning. Just as Wölfflin's polarities differentiate two visual modes of representation, so these polarities distinguish two conceptual modes of representation. By figuring out exactly how the concepts combine with one another in determinate ways to form possible true-or-false statements, and by understanding the kinds of inference, analogy, evidence, and explanation that are linked to these conceptual combinations, we can reconstitute a full-fledged style of reasoning. It is only by engaging in this historical task that we will understand the nature of many of the philosophical problems we face. Crombie has described his enterprise as "a kind of comparative intellectual anthropology,"[21] and I have suggested that we understand it, in the first instance, as a comparative anthropology of concepts, sometimes labeled by its French practitioners not as anthropology but as archaeology. Call it what one will, I think it ought to play a crucial role in philosophical analysis.

Let me proceed to give some examples that I think will show how radically different anatomical and psychiatric styles of reasoning about disease actually were and still are. Like Foucault, I am concerned with how systems of knowledge shape us as subjects, how these systems literally make us subjects. Our categories and conceptualizations of the self determine not only how others view us,

---

*In the first half of this essay, not reproduced here, I discuss and make use of the notion of style found in Heinrich Wölfflin, *Principles of Art History: The Problem of the Development of Style in Later Art,* 7th ed. (New York: Dover, 1950).

but also how each person conceives of him- or herself. I am interested in the history of sexuality because I think that, in modern times, categories of sexuality have partially determined how we think of ourselves, have partially determined the shape of ourselves as subjects. Moreover, it is strategically useful to focus on the history of sexuality when discussing the emergence of psychiatric reasoning, since this history allows one clearly to exhibit two distinctive styles of reasoning. If we take the example of sexual identity and its disorders, we can see two systems of knowledge exhibiting two styles of reasoning, as they are constituted in the nineteenth century. I will consider only one particular case of the anatomical style of reasoning, a case that Foucault has made famous with his publication of the memoirs of the nineteenth-century French hermaphrodite Herculine Barbin. As Foucault points out in his introduction to the case of Herculine Barbin, in the Middle Ages both canon and civil law designated those people "hermaphrodites" in whom the two sexes were juxtaposed, in variable proportions. In some of these cases the father or godfather determined at the time of baptism which sex was to be retained. However, later, when it was time for these hermaphrodites to marry, they could decide for themselves whether they wished to retain the sex that had been assigned them, or whether they preferred instead the opposite sex. The only constraint was that they could not change their minds again, but had to keep the sex that they had chosen until the end of their lives.[22]

However, gradually in the eighteenth century, and into the nineteenth century, it came to be thought that everybody had one and only one real sex, and it became the task of the medical expert to decipher "the true sex that was hidden beneath ambiguous appearances,"[23] to find the one true sex of the so-called hermaphrodite. It is in this context that the case of Herculine Barbin must be placed. Adelaide Herculine Barbin, also known as Alexina or Abel Barbin, was raised as a girl, but was eventually recognized as really being a man. Given this determination of his true sexual identity, Barbin's civil status was changed, and being unable to adapt to his new identity, he committed suicide. The details of the case are fascinating, but my concern is with how medical science determined Herculine's real sexual identity. Here are some remarks from the doctor who first examined Barbin, and who published a report in 1860 in the *Annales d'hygiène publique et de médicine légale*. After describing Barbin's genital area, Dr. Chesnet asks:

> What shall we conclude from the above facts? Is Alexina a woman? She has a vulva, labia majora, and a feminine urethra. . . . She has a vagina. True, it is very short, very narrow; but after all, what is it if not a vagina? These are completely feminine attributes. Yes, but Alexina has never menstruated; the whole outer part of her body is that of a man, and my explorations did not enable me to find a womb. . . . Finally, to sum up the matter, ovoid bodies and spermatic cords are found by touch in a divided scrotum. *These are the real proofs of sex.* We can now conclude and say: Alexina is a man, hermaphroditic, no doubt, but with an obvious predominance of masculine sexual characteristics.[24]

Notice that the real proofs of sex are to be found in the anatomical structure of Barbin's sexual organs.

Writing nine years later in the *Journal de l'anatomie et de la physiologie de l'homme,* Dr. E. Goujon definitively confirms Chesnet's conclusions by using that great technique of pathological anatomy, the autopsy. After discussing Barbin's external genital organs, Goujon offers a detailed account of his internal genital organs:

> Upon opening the body, one saw that the epididymis of the left testicle had passed through the ring; it was smaller than the right one; the vase deferentia drew near each other behind and slightly below the bladder, and had normal connections with the seminal vesicles. Two ejaculatory canals, one on each side of the vagina, protruded from beneath the mucous membrane of the vagina and traveled from the vesicles to the vulvar orifice. The seminal vesicles, the right one being a little larger than the left, were distended by sperm that had a normal consistency.[25]

All of medical science, with its style of pathological anatomy, agreed with August Tardieu when he claimed in his revealingly titled book *Question médico-légale de l'identité dans ses rapports avec les vices de conformation des organes sexuels* that, "to be sure, the appearances that are typical of the feminine sex were carried very far in his case, but both science and the law were nevertheless obliged to recognize the error and to recognize the true sex of this young man."[26]

Let me now bypass a number of decades. The year is 1913, and the great psychologist of sex Havelock Ellis has written a paper called "Sexo-Aesthetic Inversion" that appears in *Alienist and Neurologist.*[27] It begins as follows:

> By "sexual inversion," we mean exclusively such a change in a person's sexual impulses, the result of inborn constitution, that the impulse is turned towards individuals of the same sex, while all the other impulses and tastes may remain those of the sex to which the person by anatomical configuration belongs. There is, however, a wider kind of inversion, which not only covers much more than the direction of the sexual impulses, but may not, and indeed frequently does not, include the sexual impulse at all. This inversion is that by which a person's tastes and impulses arc so altered that, if a man, he emphasizes and even exaggerates the feminine characteristics in his own person, delights in manifesting feminine aptitudes and very especially, finds peculiar satisfaction in dressing himself as a woman and adopting a woman's ways. Yet the subject of this perversion experiences the normal sexual attraction, though in some cases the general inversion of tastes may extend, it may be gradually, to the sexual impulses.[28]

After describing some cases, Ellis writes further:

> The precise nature of aesthetic inversion can only be ascertained by presenting illustrative examples. There are at least two types of such cases; one, the most common kind, in which the inversion is mainly confined to the sphere of

clothing, and another, less common but more complete, in which cross-dressing is regarded with comparative indifference but the subject so identifies himself with those of his physical and psychic traits which recall the opposite sex that he feels really to belong to that sex, although he has no delusion regarding his anatomical conformation.[29]

It is significant that one name Ellis considers for this disorder, although he rejects it in favor of "sexo-aesthetic inversion," is "psychical hermaphroditism," but he believes that this latter designation is not quite accurate, because people who suffer from this anomaly "are not usually conscious of possessing the psychic dispositions of both sexes but only of one, the opposite sex."[30]

Ellis's discussion descends from the psychiatric style of reasoning that began, roughly speaking, in the second half of the nineteenth century. Sexual identity is no longer exclusively linked to the anatomical structure of one's internal and external genital organs. It is now a matter of impulses, tastes, aptitudes, satisfactions, and psychic traits. There is a whole new set of concepts that makes it possible to detach questions of sexual identity from facts about anatomy, a possibility that came about only with the emergence of a new style of reasoning. And with this new style of reasoning came entirely new kinds of sexual diseases and disorders. Psychiatric theories of sexual identity disorders were not false, but were rather not even candidates for truth-or-falsehood as little as a hundred and fifty years ago. Only with the birth of a psychiatric style of reasoning were there categories of evidence, verification, explanation, and so on, that allowed such theories to be either true or false. Rules for the production of true discourses about sexuality radically changed in the mid- to late nineteenth century. And lest you think that Ellis's discussion is anachronistic, I should point out that the third edition of the *Diagnostic and Statistical Manual of Mental Disorders* of the American Psychiatric Association discussed disorders of sexual identity in terms that are almost conceptually identical to those of Ellis. It calls these disorders, "characterized by the individual's feelings of discomfort and inappropriateness about his or her anatomic sex and by persistent behaviors generally associated with the other sex," Gender Identity Disorders.[31] We live with the legacy of this relatively recent psychiatric style of reasoning, so foreign to earlier medical theories of sex. So-called sex-change operations were not only technologically impossible in earlier centuries; they were conceptually unintelligible as well.

Here is one final piece of evidence about stylistic changes in representing diseases, this time some visual evidence. It was not uncommon for eighteenth- and nineteenth-century medical textbooks to include drawings depicting hermaphrodites. These poor creatures were shown exhibiting their defective anatomy, the pathological structure of their organs revealing, for all to see, the condition of their diseased sexual identity. Their ambiguous status was an ambiguous anatomical status. But not too many decades later, a new iconography of sexual diseases was to appear. It is exemplified in the frontispiece to

D. M. Rozier's tract on female masturbation.[32] When one opens this book, one is confronted by a drawing of a young woman. She is pale and looks as if she is in a state of mental and physical exhaustion. Her head is stiffly tilted toward her left, and her eyes are rolled back, unfocused, the pupils barely visible. She is a habitual masturbator; her body looks normal, but you can see her psyche, her personality, disintegrating before your very eyes. She stands as an emblem of psychiatric disorders, so distinct from her anatomically represented predecessors. Stanley Cavell has accurately captured the depth of the changes that have taken place between these two styles of representation when, concerning the natural and conventional, he writes, "Perhaps the idea of a new historical period is an idea of a generation whose natural reactions—not merely whose ideas or mores— diverge from the old; it is an idea of new (human) nature."[33] And thus I want to claim that we should understand the emergence of perversion as itself part of an idea of new (human) nature.

Notes

1. Arnold I. Davidson, "Closing Up the Corpses," in G. Boulos, ed., *Meaning and Method* (Cambridge: Cambridge University Press, 1990). More detailed historical documentation for my claims can be found in that chapter.

2. Paul Moreau (du Tours), *Des aberrations du sens génésique* (Paris: Asselin, 1880), p. 2.

3. Ibid., p. 3.

4. *Oxford English Dictionary* (Oxford: Clarendon Press, 1933) s.v., vol. 7, p. 739.

5. Richard von Krafft-Ebing, *Textbook on Insanity* (Philadelphia: Davis, 1904), p. 79. Krafft-Ebing considers abolition to be the extreme case of diminution.

6. Ibid., pp. 77–81.

7. Ibid., p. 81. This same classification is given in Richard von Krafft-Ebing, *Psychopathia Sexualis* (New York: Stein and Day, 1965), p. 34.

8. Krafft-Ebing, *Textbook,* pp. 83–86; *Psychopathia,* 34–36.

9. Krafft-Ebing, *Psychopathia,* pp. 16, 62–63; see also *Textbook,* p. 81. For other representative statements, see Albert Moll, *Perversions of the Sex Instinct* (Newark: Julian Press, 1931), pp. 172, 182 (originally published in German in 1891); and Dr. Laupts (pseudonym of G. Saint-Paul), *L'homosexualité et les types homosexuels: Nouvelle édition de perversion et perversités sexuelles* (Paris: Vigot, 1910).

10. Thomas Nagel, "Sexual Perversion," in *Mortal Questions* (Cambridge: Cambridge University Press, 1979), p. 44.

11. Ibid., p. 47.

12. Ibid., p. 46.

13. Ibid., p. 48.

14. Ibid, p. 39.

15. Ibid, p. 48 (my emphasis).

16. Ibid., p. 50.

17. Thomas Nagel, "Sexual Perversion," *Journal of Philosophy* 66, no. 1 (January 16, 1969): 15.

18. Ibid., p. 16.

19. Nagel, *Mortal Questions,* pp. 50–51.

20. Hacking, "Proof," p. 179.

21. A. C. Crombie, "Philosophical Presuppositions and Shifting Interpretations of Galileo," in Jaakko Hintikka, David Gruedner, and Evandro Agazzi, eds., *Theory Change, Ancient Axiomatics, and Galileo's Methodology: Proceedings of teh 1978 Pisa Conference on the History and Philosophy of Science* (Dordrecht: Reidel, 1981), p. 283.

22. Michel Foucault, *Herculine Barbin, Being the Recently Discovered Memoirs of a Nineteenth-Century French Hermaphrodite* (New York: Pantheon, 1980), pp. vii–viii.

23. Ibid., p. viii.

24. Ibid., pp. 127–28 (my emphasis).

25. Ibid., pp. 135–36.

26. Ibid., p. 123. Tardieu's book was published in 1874. Parts of it had previously appeared in the *Annales d'hygiène publique* in 1872. A fuller discussion of questions of sexual identity would have to consider this document in detail.

27. Havelock Ellis, "Sexo-Aesthetic Inversion," *Alienist and Neurologist* 34 (1913): 156–67

28. Ibid., p. 156.

29. Ibid., p. 159.

30. Ibid., p. 158, n. 7.

31. American Psychiatric Association, *Diagnostic and Statistical Manual Of Mental Disorders,* 3d ed. (Washington, D.C.: American Psychiatric Association, 1980), p. 261.

32. D. M. Rozier, *Des habitudes secrètes ou des maladies produites par l'onanisme chez les femmes* (Paris: Audin, 1830). For a discussion of the changing iconography of the insane, see Sander L. Gilman, *Seeing the Insane* (New York: Wiley, 1982).

33. Stanley Cavell, *The Claim of Reason: Wittgenstein, Skepticism, Morality, and Tragedy* (Oxford: Clarendon Press, 1979), p. 121.

33

Making Up People

Ian Hacking

Were there any perverts before the latter part of the nineteenth century? According to Arnold Davidson, "The answer is NO. . . . Perversion was not a disease that lurked about in nature, waiting for a psychiatrist with especially acute powers of observation to discover it hiding everywhere. It was a disease created by a new (functional) understanding of disease."[1] Davidson is not denying that there have been odd people at all times. He is asserting that perversion, as a disease, and the pervert, as a diseased person, were created in the late nineteenth century. Davidson's claim, one of many now in circulation, illustrates what I call making up people.

I have three aims: I want a better understanding of claims as curious as Davidson's; I would like to know if there could be a general theory of making up people, or whether each example is so peculiar that it demands its own non-generalizable story; and I want to know how this idea "making up people" affects our very idea of what it is to be an individual. I should warn that my concern is philosophical and abstract; I look more at what people might be than at what we are. I imagine a philosophical notion I call dynamic nominalism, and reflect too little on the ordinary dynamics of human interaction.

First we need more examples. I study the dullest of subjects, the official statistics of the nineteenth century. They range, of course, over agriculture, education, trade, births, and military might, but there is one especially striking feature of the avalanche of numbers that begins around 1820. It is obsessed with *analyse morale,* namely, the statistics of deviance. It is the numerical analysis of suicide, prostitution, drunkenness, vagrancy, madness, crime, *les misérables.* Counting generated its own subdivisions and rearrangements. We find classifi-

Reprinted from *Reconstructing Individualism: Autonomy, Individuality and the Self in Western Thought,* Thomas Heller, Morton Sosna, and David Wellbery, eds., with the permission of Stanford University Press. © 1986 by the Board of Trustees of the Leland Stanford Junior University.

cations of over four thousand different crisscrossing motives for murder and requests that the police classify each individual suicide in twenty-one different ways. I do not believe that motives of these sorts or suicides of these kinds existed until the practice of counting them came into being.[2]

New slots were created in which to fit and enumerate people. Even national and provincial censuses amazingly show that the categories into which people fall change every ten years. Social change creates new categories of people, but the counting is no mere report of developments. It elaborately, often philanthropically, creates new ways for people to be.

People spontaneously come to fit their categories. When factory inspectors in England and Wales went to the mills, they found various kinds of people there, loosely sorted according to tasks and wages. But when they had finished their reports, millhands had precise ways in which to work, and the owner had a clear set of concepts about how to employ workers according to the ways in which he was obliged to classify them.

I am more familiar with the creation of kinds among the masses than with interventions that act upon individuals, though I did look into one rare kind of insanity. I claim that multiple personality as an idea and as a clinical phenomenon was invented around 1875: only one or two possible cases per generation had been recorded before that time, but a whole flock of them came after. I also found that the clinical history of split personality parodies itself—the one clear case of classic symptoms was long recorded as two, quite distinct, human beings, each of which was multiple. There was "the lady of MacNish," so called after a report in *The Philosophy of Sleep,* written by the Edinburgh physician Robert MacNish in 1832, and there was one Mary R. The two would be reported in successive paragraphs as two different cases, although in fact Mary Reynolds was the very split-personality lady reported by MacNish.[3]

Mary Reynolds died long before 1875, but she was not taken up as a case of multiple personality until then. Not she but one Félida X got the split-personality industry under way. As the great French psychiatrist Pierre Janet remarked at Harvard in 1906, Félida's history "was the great argument of which the positivist psychologists made use at the time of the heroic struggles against the dogmatism of Cousin's school. But for Félida it is not certain that there would be a professorship of psychology at the Collège de France."[4] Janet held precisely that chair. The "heroic struggles" were important for our passing conceptions of the self, and for individuality, because the split Félida was held to refute the dogmatic transcendental unity of apperception that made the self prior to all knowledge.

After Félida came a rush of multiples. The syndrome bloomed in France and later flourished in America, which is still its home. Do I mean that there were no multiples before Félida? Yes. Except for a very few earlier examples, which after 1875 were reinterpreted as classic multiples, there was no such syndrome for a disturbed person to display or to adopt.

I do not deny that there are other behaviors in other cultures that resemble multiple personality. Possession is our most familiar example—a common form of Renaissance behavior that died long ago, though it was curiously hardy in isolated German villages even late in the nineteenth century. Possession was not split personality, but if you balk at my implication that a few people (in committee with their medical or moral advisers) almost choose to become splits, recall that tormented souls in the past have often been said to have in some way chosen to be possessed, to have been seeking attention, exorcism, and tranquility.

I should give one all-too-tidy example of how a new person can be made up. Once again I quote from Janet, whom I find the most open and honorable of the psychiatrists. He is speaking to Lucie, who had the once fashionable but now forgotten habit of automatic writing. Lucie replies to Janet in writing without her normal self's awareness:

> *Janet.* Do you understand me?
> *Lucie (writes).* No.
> *J.* But to reply you must understand me.
> *L.* Oh yes, absolutely.
> *J.* Then what are you doing?
> *L.* I don't know.
> *J.* it is certain that someone is understanding me.
> *L.* Yes.
> *J.* Who is that?
> *L.* Somebody besides Lucie.
> *J.* Another person. Would you like to give her a name?
> *L.* No.
> *J.* Yes. It would be far easier that way.
> *L.* Oh well. If you want: Adrienne.
> *J.* Then, Adrienne, do you understand me?
> *L.* Yes.[5]

If you think this is what people used to do in the bad old days, consider poor Charles, who was given a whole page of *Time* magazine on October 25, 1982 (p. 70). He was picked up wandering aimlessly and was placed in the care of Dr. Malcolm Graham of Daytona Beach, who in turn consulted with Dr. William Rothstein, a notable student of multiple personality at the University Hospital in Columbia, South Carolina. Here is what is said to have happened:

> After listening to a tape recording made in June of the character Mark, Graham became convinced he was dealing with a multiple personality. Graham began consulting with Rothstein, who recommended hypnosis. Under the spell, Eric began calling his characters. Most of the personalities have been purged, although there are three or four being treated, officials say. It was the real personality that signed a consent form that allowed Graham to comment on the case.[6]

Hypnosis elicited Charles, Eric, Mark, and some twenty-four other personalities. When I read of such present-day manipulations of character, I pine a little for Mollie Fancher, who gloried in the personalities of Sunbeam, Idol, Rosebud, Pearl, and Ruby. She became somewhat split after being dragged a mile by a horse car. She was not regarded as especially deranged, nor in much need of "cure." She was much loved by her friends, who memorialized her in 1894 in a book with the title *Mollie Fancher, The Brooklyn Enigma: An Authentic Statement of Facts in the Life of Mollie J. Fancher, The Psychological Marvel of the Nineteenth Century.*[7] The idea of making up people has, I said, become quite widespread. *The Making of the Modern Homosexual* is a good example; 'Making' in this title is close to my 'making up.'[8] The contributors by and large accept that the homosexual and the heterosexual as kinds of persons (as ways to be persons, or as conditions of personhood), came into being only toward the end of the nineteenth century. There has been plenty of same-sex activity in all ages, but not, *Making* argues, same-sex people and different-sex people. I do not wish to enter the complexities of that idea, but will quote a typical passage from this anthology to show what is intended:

> One difficulty in transcending the theme of gender inversion as the basis of the specialized homosexual identity was the rather late historical development of more precise conceptions of components of sexual identity. [Footnote:] It is not suggested that these components are 'real' entities, which awaited scientific 'discovery.' However once the distinctions were made, new realities effectively came into being.[9]

Note how the language here resembles my opening quotation: "not a disease . . . in nature, waiting for . . . observation to discover it" versus "not . . . 'real' entities, which awaited scientific 'discovery.'" Moreover, this author too suggests that "once the distinctions were made, new realities effectively came into being."

This theme, the homosexual as a kind of person, is often traced to a paper by Mary McIntosh, "The Homosexual Role" which she published in 1968 in *Social Problems.*[10] That journal was much devoted to "labeling theory," which asserts that social reality is conditioned, stabilized, or even created by the labels we apply to people, actions, and communities. Already in 1963 "A Note on the Uses of Official Statistics" in the same journal anticipated my own inferences about counting.[11] But there is a currently more fashionable source of the idea of making up people, namely, Michel Foucault, to whom both Davidson and I are indebted. A quotation from Foucault provides the epigraph—following one from Nietzsche—for *The Making of the Modern Homosexual;* and although its authors cite some 450 sources, they refer to Foucault more than anyone else. Since I shall be primarily concerned with labeling, let me state at once that for all his famous fascination with discourse, naming is only one element in what Foucault calls the "constitution of subjects" (in context a pun, but in one sense the making up of the subject): "We should try to discover how it is that subjects are gradually, progressively, really and materially constituted through a multiplicity of organisms, forces, energies, materials, desires, thoughts, etc."[12]

Since so many of us have been influenced by Foucault, our choice of topic and time may be biased. My examples dwell in the nineteenth century and are obsessed with deviation and control. Thus among the questions on a complete agenda, we should include these two: is making up people intimately linked to control? Is making up people itself of recent origin? The answer to both questions might conceivably be yes. We may be observing a particular medico-forensic-political language of individual and social control. Likewise, the sheer proliferation of labels in that domain may have engendered vastly more kinds of people than the world had ever known before.

Partly in order to distance myself for a moment from issues of repression, and partly for intrinsic interest, I would like to abstract from my examples. If there were some truth in the descriptions I and others have furnished, then making up people would bear on one of the great traditional questions of philosophy, namely, the debate between nominalists and realists.[13] The author I quoted who rejects the idea that the components of the homosexual identity are real entities, has taken a timeworn nominalist suggestion and made it interesting by the thought that "once the distinctions were made, new realities effectively came into being." You will recall that a traditional nominalist says that stars (or algae, or justice) have nothing in common except our names ('stars', 'algae', 'justice'). The traditional realist in contrast finds it amazing that the world could so kindly sort itself into our categories. He protests that there are definite sorts of objects in it, at least stars and algae, which we have painstakingly come to recognize and classify correctly. The robust realist does not have to argue very hard that people also come sorted. Some are thick, some thin, some dead, some alive. It may be a fact about human beings that we notice who is fat and who is dead, but the fact itself that some of our fellows are fat and others are dead has nothing to do with our schemes of classification.

The realist continues: consumption was not only a sickness but also a moral failing, caused by defects of character. That is an important nineteenth-century social fact about TB. We discovered in due course, however, that the disease is transmitted by bacilli that divide very slowly and that we can kill. It is a fact about us that we were first moralistic and later made this discovery, but it is a brute fact about tuberculosis that it is a specific disease transmitted by microbes. The nominalist is left rather weakly contending that even though a particular kind of person, the consumptive, may have been an artifact of the nineteenth century, the disease itself is an entity in its own right, independently of how we classify. It would be foolhardy, at this conference ["Reconstructing Individualism," Stanford University, February 18–20, 1984], to have an opinion about one of the more stable human dichotomies, male and female. But very roughly, the robust realist will agree that there may be what really are physiological borderline cases, once called "hermaphrodites." The existence of vague boundaries is normal: most of us are neither tall nor short, fat nor thin. Sexual physiology is unusually abrupt in its divisions. The realist will take the occasional compulsive fascination with transvestism, or horror about hermaphrodites (so well described by Stephen Greenblatt in . . . [*Reconstructing Individualism*][14]), as human (nominalist) resistance to nature's putative aberrations. Likewise the realist will assert that even though our attitudes to gender are almost entirely nonobjective and culturally ordained, gender itself is a real distinction.

I do not know if there were thoroughgoing, consistent, hard-line nominalists who held that every classification is of our own making. I might pick that great British nominalist Hobbes out of context: "How can any man imagine that the names of things were imposed by their natures?"[15] or I might pick Nelson Goodman.[16]

Let me take even the vibrant Hobbes, Goodman, and their scholastic predecessors as pale reflections of a perhaps nonexistent static nominalist, who thinks that all categories, classes, and taxonomies are given by human beings rather than by nature and that these categories are essentially fixed throughout the several eras of humankind. I believe that static nominalism is doubly wrong: I think that many categories come from nature, not from the human mind, and I think our categories are not static. A different kind of nominalism—I call it dynamic nominalism—attracts my realist self, spurred on by theories about the making of the homosexual and the heterosexual as kinds of persons or by my observations about official statistics. The claim of dynamic nominalism is not that there was a kind of person who came increasingly to be recognized by bureaucrats or by students of human nature but rather that a kind of person came into being at the same time as the kind itself was being invented. In some cases, that is, our classifications and our classes conspire to emerge hand in hand, each egging the other on.

Take four categories: horse, planet, glove, and multiple personality. It would be preposterous to suggest that the only thing horses have in common is that we call them horses. We may draw the boundaries to admit or to exclude Shetland ponies, but the similarities and difference are real enough. The planets furnish one of T. S. Kuhn's examples of conceptual change.[17] Arguably the heavens looked different after we grouped Earth with the other planets and excluded Moon and Sun, but I am sure that acute thinkers had discovered a real difference. I hold (most of the time) that strict nominalism is unintelligible for horses and the planets. How could horses and planets be so obedient to our minds? Gloves are something else: we manufacture them. I know not which came first, the thought or the mitten, but they have evolved hand in hand. That the concept "glove" fits gloves so well is no surprise: we made them that way. My claim about making up people is that in a few interesting respects multiple personalities (and much else) are more like gloves than like horses. The category and the people in it emerged hand in hand.

How might a dynamic nominalism affect the concept of the individual person? One answer has to do with possibility. Who we are is not only what we did, do, and will do but also what we might have done and may do. Making up people changes the space of possibilities for personhood. Even the dead are more than their deeds, for we make sense of a finished life only within its sphere of former possibilities.

But our possibilities, although inexhaustible, are also bounded. If the nominalist thesis about sexuality were correct, it simply wasn't possible to be a heterosexual kind of person before the nineteenth century, for that kind of person was not there to choose. What could that mean? What could it mean in general to say that possible ways to be a person can from time to time come into being or disappear? Such queries force us to be careful about the idea of possibility itself.

We have a folk picture of the gradations of possibility. Some things, for example, are easy to do, some hard, and some plain impossible. What is impossible for one person is possible for another. At the limit we have the statement: "With men it is impossible, but not with God, for with God, all things are possible" (Mark 10:27). (Christ had been saying that it is easier for a camel to pass through the eye of a needle than for a rich man to enter the kingdom of heaven.) Degrees of possibility are degrees in the ability of some agent to do or make something. The more ability, the more possibility, and omnipotence makes anything possible. At that point, logicians have stumbled, worrying about what were once called "the eternal truths," and are now called "logical necessities." Even God cannot make a five-sided square, or so mathematicians say, except for a few such eminent dissenters as Descartes. Often this limitation on omnipotence is explained linguistically, being said to reflect our unwillingness to call anything a five-sided square.

There is something more interesting that God can't do. Suppose that Arnold Davidson, in my opening quotation about perversion, is literally correct. Then it was not possible for God to make George Washington a pervert. God could have delayed Washington's birth by over a century, but would that have been the same man? God could have moved the medical discourse back one-hundred-odd years. But God could not have simply made him a pervert, the way He could have made him freckled or had him captured and hung for treachery. This may seem all the more surprising since Washington was but eight years older than the Marquis de Sade—and Krafft-Ebing has sadomasochism among the four chief categories of perversion. But it follows from Davidson's doctrine that de Sade was not afflicted by the disease of perversion, nor even the disease of sadomasochism either.

Such strange claims are more trivial than they seem: they result from a contrast between people and things. Except when we interfere, what things are doing, and indeed what camels are doing, does not depend on how we describe them. But some of the things that we ourselves do are intimately connected to our descriptions. Many philosophers follow Elizabeth Anscombe and say that intentional human actions must be "actions under a description."[18] This is not mere lingualism, for descriptions are embedded in our practices and lives. But if a description is not there, then intentional actions under that description cannot be there either: that, apparently, is a fact of logic.

Elaborating on this difference between people and things: what camels, mountains, and microbes are doing does not depend on our words. What happens to tuberculosis bacilli depends on whether or not we poison them with

BCG vaccine, but it does not depend upon how we describe them. Of course we poison them with a certain vaccine in part because we describe them in certain ways, but it is the vaccine that kills, not our words. Human action is more closely linked to human description than bacterial action is. A century ago I would have said that consumption is caused by bad air and sent the patient to the Alps. Today, I may say that TB is caused by microbes and prescribe a two-year course of injections. But what is happening to the microbes and the patient is entirely independent of my correct or incorrect description, even though it is not independent of the medication prescribed. The microbes' possibilities are delimited by nature, not by words. What is curious about human action is that by and large what I am deliberately doing depends on the possibilities of description. To repeat, this is a tautological inference from what is now a philosopher's commonplace, that all intentional acts are acts under a description. Hence if new modes of description come into being, new possibilities for action come into being in consequence.

Let us now add an example to our repertoire; let it have nothing to do with deviancy, let it be rich in connotations of human practices, and let it help furnish the end of a spectrum of making up people opposite from the multiple personality. I take it from Jean-Paul Sartre, partly for the well-deserved fame of his description, partly for its excellence as description, partly because Sartre is our premium philosopher of choice, and partly because recalling Sartre will recall an example that returns me to my origin. Let us first look at Sartre's magnificent humdrum example. Many among us might have chosen to be a waiter or waitress and several have been one for a time. A few men might have chosen to be something more specific, a Parisian *garçon de café,* about whom Sartre writes in his immortal discussion of bad faith:

> His movement is quick and forward, a little too precise, a little too rapid. He comes toward the patrons with a step a little too quick. He bends forward a little too eagerly, his eyes express an interest too solicitous for the order of the customer.[19]

Psychiatrists and medical people in general try to be extremely specific in describing, but no description of the several classical kinds of split personality is as precise (or as recognizable) as this. Imagine for a moment that we are reading not the words of a philosopher who writes his books in *cafés* but those of a doctor who writes them in a clinic. Has the *garçon de café* a chance of escaping treatment by experts? Was Sartre showing or merely anticipating when he concluded this very paragraph with the words: "There are indeed many precautions to imprison a man in what he is, as if we lived in perpetual fear that he might escape from it, that he might break away and suddenly elude his condition." That is a good reminder of Sartre's teaching: possibility, project, and prison are one of a piece.

Sartre's antihero chose to be a waiter. Evidently that was not a possible choice in other places, other times. There are servile people in most societies, and servants in many, but a waiter is something specific, and a *garçon de café* more specific. Sartre remarks that the waiter is doing something different when he pretends to play at being a sailor or a diplomat than when he plays at being a waiter in order to be a waiter. I think that in most parts of, let us say, Saskatchewan (or in a McDonald's anywhere), a waiter playing at being a *garçon de café* would miss the mark as surely as if he were playing at being a diplomat while passing over the french fries. As with almost every way in which it is possible to be a person, it is possible to be a *garçon de café* only at a certain time, in a certain place, in a certain social setting. The feudal serf putting food on my lady's table can no more choose to be a *garçon de café* than he can choose to be lord of the manor. But the impossibility is evidently different in kind.

It is not a technical impossibility. Serfs may once have dreamed of travel to the moon; certainly their lettered betters wrote or read adventures of moon travel. But moon travel was impossible for them, whereas it is not quite impossible for today's young waiter. One young waiter will, in a few years, be serving steaks in a satellite. Sartre is at pains to say that even technical limitations do not mean that you have fewer possibilities. For every person, in every era, the world is a plenitude of possibilities. "Of course," Sartre writes, "a contemporary of Duns Scotus is ignorant of the use of the automobile or the aeroplane. . . . For the one who has no relation of any kind to these objects and the techniques that refer to them, there is a kind of absolute, unthinkable and undecipherable nothingness. Such a nothing can in no way limit the For-itself that is choosing itself; it cannot be apprehended as a lack, no matter how we consider it." Passing to a different example, he continues, "The feudal world offered to the vassal lord of Raymond VI infinite possibilities of choice; we do not possess more."[20]

"Absolute, unthinkable and undecipherable nothingness" is a great phrase. That is exactly what being a multiple personality, or being a *garçon de* café, was to Raymond's vassal. Many of you could, in truth, be neither a Parisian waiter nor a split, but both are thinkable, decipherable somethingnesses. It would be possible for God to have made you one or the other or both, leaving the rest of the world more or less intact. That means, to me, that the outer reaches of your space as an individual are essentially different from what they would have been had these possibilities not come into being.

Thus the idea of making up people is enriched; it applies not to the unfortunate elect but to all of us. It is not just the making up of people of a kind that did not exist before: not only are the split and the waiter made up, but each of us is made up. We are not only what we are but what we might have been, and the possibilities for what we might have been are transformed.

Hence anyone who thinks about the individual, the person, must reflect on this strange idea, of making up people. Do my stories tell a uniform tale? Manifestly not. The multiple personality, the homosexual or heterosexual person, and the waiter form one spectrum among many that may color our perception here. Suppose there is some truth in the labeling theory of the modern homosexual.

It cannot be the whole truth, and this for several reasons, including one that is future-directed and one that is past-directed. The future-directed fact is that after the institutionalization of the homosexual person in law and official morality, the people involved had a life of their own, individually and collectively. As gay liberation has amply proved, that life was no simple product of the labeling.

The past-directed fact is that the labeling did not occur in a social vacuum, in which those identified as homosexual people passively accepted the format. There was a complex social life that is only now revealing itself in the annals of academic social history. It is quite clear that the internal life of innumerable clubs and associations interacted with the medico-forensic-journalistic labeling. At the risk of giving offense, I suggest that the quickest way to see the contrast between making up homosexuals and making up multiple personalities is to try to imagine split-personality bars. Splits, insofar as they are declared, are under care, and the syndrome, the form of behavior, is orchestrated by a team of experts. Whatever the medico-forensic experts tried to do with their categories, the homosexual person became autonomous of the labeling, but the split is not.

The *garçon de café* is at the opposite extreme. There is of course a social history of waiters in Paris. Some of this will be as anecdotal as the fact that croissants originated in the cafés of Vienna after the Turkish siege was lifted in 1653: the pastries in the shape of a crescent were a mockery of Islam. Other parts of the story will be structurally connected with numerous French institutions. But the class of waiters is autonomous of any act of labeling. At most the name *garçon de café* can continue to ensure both the inferior position of the waiter and the fact that he is male. Sartre's precise description does not fit the *garçon de café* that is a different role.

I do not believe there is a general story to be told about making up people. Each category has its own history. If we wish to present a partial framework in which to describe such events, we might think of two vectors. One is the vector of labeling from above, from a community of experts who create a "reality" that some people make their own. Different from this is the vector of the autonomous behavior of the person so labeled, which presses from below, creating a reality every expert must face. The second vector is negligible for the split but powerful for the homosexual person. People who write about the history of homosexuality seem to disagree about the relative importance of the two vectors. My scheme at best highlights what the dispute is about. It provides no answers.

The scheme is also too narrow. I began by mentioning my own dusty studies in official statistics and asserted that these also, in a less melodramatic way, contribute to making up people. There is a story to tell here, even about Parisian waiters, who surface in the official statistics of Paris surprisingly late, in 1881. However, I shall conclude with yet another way of making up people and human acts, one of notorious interest to the existentialist culture of a couple of generations past. I mean suicide, the option that Sartre always left open to the For-itself. Suicide sounds like a timeless option. It is not. Indeed it might be better described as a French obsession.

There have been cultures, including some in recent European history, that knew no suicide. It is said that there were no suicides in Venice when it was the noblest city of Europe. But can I seriously propose that suicide is a concept that has been made up? Oddly, that is exactly what is said by the deeply influential Esquirol in his 1823 medical-encyclopedia article on suicide.[21] He mistakenly asserts that the very word was devised by his predecessor Sauvages. What is true is this: suicide was made the property of medics only at the beginning of the nineteenth century, and a major fight it was too.[22] It was generally allowed that there was the noble suicide, the suicide of honor or of state, but all the rest had to be regarded as part of the new medicine of insanity. By mid-century it would be contended that there was no case of suicide that was not preceded by symptoms of insanity.[23]

This literature concerns the doctors and their patients. It exactly parallels a statistical story. Foucault suggests we think in terms of "two poles of development linked together by a whole cluster of intermediary relations."[24] One pole centers on the individual as a speaking, working, procreating entity he calls an "anatomo-politics of the human body." The second pole, "focused on the species body," serves as the "basis of the biological processes: propagation, births, and mortality, the level of health, life expectancy and longevity." He calls this polarity a "biopolitics of the population." Suicide aptly illustrates patterns of connection between both poles. The medical men comment on the bodies and their past, which led to self-destruction; the statisticians count and classify the bodies. Every fact about the suicide becomes fascinating. The statisticians compose forms to be completed by doctors and police, recording everything from the time of death to the objects found in the pockets of the corpse. The various ways of killing oneself are abruptly characterized and become symbols of national character. The French favor carbon monoxide and drowning; the English hang or shoot themselves.

By the end of the nineteenth century there was so much information about French suicides that Durkheim could use suicide to measure social pathology. Earlier, a rapid increase in the rate of suicide in all European countries had caused great concern. More recently authors have suggested that the growth may have been largely apparent, a consequence of improved systems of reporting.[25] It was thought that there were more suicides because more care was taken to report them. But such a remark is unwittingly ambiguous: reporting brought about more suicides. I do not refer to suicide epidemics that follow a sensational case, like that of von Kleist, who shot his lover and then himself on the Wannsee in 1811—an event vigorously reported in every European capital. I mean instead that the systems of reporting positively created an entire ethos of suicide, right down to the suicide note, an art form that previously was virtually unknown apart from the rare noble suicide of state. Suicide has of course attracted attention in all times and has invited such distinguished essayists as Cicero and Hume. But the distinctively European and American pattern of suicide is a historical artifact. Even the unmaking of people has been made up.

Naturally my kinds of making up people are far from exhaustive. Individuals serve as role models and sometimes thereby create new roles. We have only to think of James Clifford's . . . "On Ethnographic Self-Fashioning: Conrad and Malinowski."[26] Malinowski's book largely created the participant-observer cultural-relativist ethnographer, even if Malinowski himself did not truly conform to that role in the field. He did something more important—he made up a kind of scholar. The advertising industry relies on our susceptibilities to role models and is largely engaged in trying to make up people. But here nominalism, even of a dynamic kind, is not the key. Often we have no name for the very role a model entices us to adopt.

Dynamic nominalism remains an intriguing doctrine, arguing that numerous kinds of human beings and human acts come into being hand in hand with our invention of the categories labeling them. It is for me the only intelligible species of nominalism, the only one that can even gesture at an account of how common names and the named could so tidily fit together. It is of more human interest than the arid and scholastic forms of nominalism because it contends that our spheres of possibility, and hence ourselves, are to some extent made up by our naming and what that entails. But let us not be overly optimistic about the future of dynamic nominalism. It has the merit of bypassing abstract hand waving and inviting us to do serious philosophy, namely, to examine the intricate origin of our ideas of multiple personality or of suicide. It is, we might say, putting some flesh on that wizened figure, John Locke, who wrote about the origin of ideas while introspecting at his desk. But just because it invites us to examine the intricacies of real life, it has little chance of being a general philosophical theory. Although we may find it useful to arrange influences according to Foucault's poles and my vectors, such metaphors are mere suggestions of what to look for next. I see no reason to suppose that we shall ever tell two identical stories of two different instances of making up people.

Notes

1. Arnold Davidson, "Closing Up the Corpses: Diseases of Sexuality and the Emergence of the Psychiatric Style of Reasoning," in *Meaning and Method: Essays in Honor of Hilary Putnam,* ed. George Boolos (Cambridge: Cambridge University Press, 1990).

2. Ian Hacking. "Biopower and the Avalanche of Printed Numbers," *Humanities in Society* 5 (1982): 279–95; "The Autonomy of Statistical Law," in *Scientific Explanation and Understanding: Essays on Reasoning and Rationality in Science*, ed. N. Rescher (Lanham, Md.: University Press of America, 1983), pp. 3–20; "How Should We Do the History of Statistics?" *Ideology & Consciousness* 11.

3. Ian Hacking, "The Invention of Split Personalities," in *Human Nature and Natural Knowledge*, eds. Alan Donagan, Anthony Perovich Jr., and Michael Wedin (Dordrecht: D. Reidel, 1986), pp. 63–85.

4. Pierre Janet, *The Major Symptom of Hysteria* (New York: Hafner, 1965), p. 78.

5. Pierre Janet, "Les Actes inconsistents et le dedoublement de la personnalité pendant le somnambulisme provoqué," *Revue Philosophique* 22 (1886): 581.

6. *The State,* Columbia, S.C., October 4, 1982, p. 3A. I apologize for using a newspaper story, but the doctors involved created this story for the papers and do not reply to my letters requesting more information.

7. Abraham H. Dailey, *Mollie Fancher, the Brooklyn Enigma* (Brooklyn: Eagle Book Printing Department, 1894).

8. K. Plummer, ed., *The Making of the Modern Homosexual* (Totowa, N.J.: Barnes and Noble).

9. John Marshall, "Pansies, Perverts and Macho Men: Changing Conceptions of the Modern Homosexual," in *The Making of the Modern Homosexual,* pp. 150, 249, note 6.

10. Reprinted in *The Making of the Modern Homosexual,* pp. 30–43, with postscript; originally published in *Social Problems* 16 (1968): 182–92.

11. John Kituse and Aaron V. Cewrel, "A Note on the Uses of Official Statistics," *Social Problems* 11 (1963): 131–39.

12. Michel Foucault, *Power/Knowledge,* ed. C. Gordon (New York: Pantheon, 1980), p. 97. The translation of this passage is by Alessandro Fontana and Pasquale Pasquino.

13. After the conference, my colleague Bert Hansen (who has helped me a number of times with this paper) remarked that the relation of the nominalist/realist dispute to homosexuality is used by John Boswell, "Revolutions, Universal and Sexual Categories," *Salmagundi* 58–59 (1982–83): 89–114.

14. Stephen Greenblatt, "Fiction and Friction," in Thomas Heller, et al., *Reconstructing Individualism: Autonomy, Individuality, and the Self in Western Thought* (Stanford: Stanford University Press), pp. 30–52.

15. Thomas Hobbes, *Elements of Philosophy,* II, 4.

16. Trendy, self-styled modem nominalists might refer to his *Ways of Worldmaking* (Indianapolis: Hackett, 1978), but the real hard line is his *Fact, Fiction and Forecast* (Cambridge, Mass.: Harvard University Press, 1955)—a line so hard that few philosophers who write about the "new riddle of induction," of that book appear even to see the point. Goodman is saying that the only reason to project the hypothesis that all emeralds are green rather than grue—the latter implying that those emeralds, which are in the future examined for the first time, will prove to be blue—is that the word 'green' is entrenched, i.e., it is a word and a classification that we have been using. Where the inductive skeptic Hume allowed that there is a real quality, greenness, that we project out of habit, for Goodman there is only our practice of using the word 'green' *(Fact, Fiction and Forecast,* chapter 4).

17. T. S. Kuhn, *The Structure of Scientific Revolutions* (Chicago: University of Chicago Press, 1962), p. 115.

18. G. E. M. Anscombe, *Intention* (Oxford: Oxford University Press, 1957).

19. Jean-Paul Sartre, *Being and Nothingness,* trans. Hazel E. Barnes (London: Methuen, 1957), p. 59.

20. Ibid., p. 522.

21. E. Esquirol, "Suicide," *Dictionnare des Science Medicales* (Paris, 1823). LIII:213.

22. Ian Hacking, "Suicide au XIXᵉ siècle," in *Medicine et probabilitiès,* ed. A. Fagot (Paris, 1982), pp. 165–86.

23. C. E. Bourdin, *Du suicide considéré comme maladie* (Batignolles, 1845), p. 19. The first sentence of this book asserts in bold letters: *Le suicide est une monomanie.*

24. Michel Foucault, *The History of Sexuality,* trans. Robert Hurley (New York: Random House, 1978), 1:139

25. A classic statement of this idea is Jack Douglas, *The Social Meanings of Suicide* (Princeton: Princeton University Press, 1967), chapter 3.

26. Clifford, "On Ethnographic Self-Fashioning: Conrad and Malinowski" in *Reconstructing Individualism: Autonomy, Individuality, and the Self in Western Thought,* ed. Thomas Heller, Morton Sosna, and David Wellbery (Stanford: Stanford University Press, 1986), pp. 140–62.

34

Dangerous Pleasures:
Foucault and the Politics of Pedophilia

Linda Martín Alcoff

> The use of the word ["sexuality"] was established in connection with other
> phenomena: the development of diverse fields of knowledge . . . ; the estab-
> lishment of a set of rules and norms . . . and changes in the way individuals
> were led to assign meaning and value to their conduct, their duties, their plea-
> sures, their feelings and sensations, their dreams.
>
> —Foucault, *Use of Pleasure*

In a post-Foucauldian academic world, most of the traditional theoretical
grounds for evaluating sexual practices are no longer viable. If we accept Foucault's account of the discursive constitution of sexuality, his counterargument
to the thesis that "sex constitutes our innermost truth," and his reconfiguration
of the relationship between domination and discourse, then we are forced to
question many standard theoretical and methodological approaches to the study
and evaluation of the politics of sexual practices.[1] Foucault argues compellingly
against the assumption that bringing sexual activity into discourse and studying
it "scientifically" will stay the hand of prejudice and liberate sexual desire. He
argues against any general presumption about the liberatory nature of discourse
and the law, or the belief that theoretical and legal discourses will reveal injustice and champion the needs of victims. Given his critique of the way even liberatory discourses impose order through constructing norms of identity and
practice, one may wonder whether Foucault would reject *any* project to develop
a normative account of sexual practices.

For theorists who work on issues of sexual violence, Foucault's arguments
challenge us to reassess our previous framing of sexual issues, including sexual

First published in *Feminist Interpretations of Michel Foucault*, ed. Susan J. Heckman (University
Park: The Pennsylvania State University Press, 1996), pp. 99–135. Copyright © 1996 by The
Pennsylvania State University Press. Reproduced by permission of the Pennsylvania State Uni-
versity Press.

violence. The notion that the sexual aggressor is pathological or has a personality disorder hearkens back to a pre-Foucauldian reliance on a discourse of essential identity. And on the basis of the view quoted from Foucault above—that the meaning of sexual experience is discursively constructed—theorists such as Gayle Rubin have argued that in our culture, "sexual acts are burdened with an excess of significance."[2] Following this logic, we might wonder whether the labeling of some acts as sexual violence or sexual abuse is produced by just such an "excess of significance."

Now on the one hand, it may seem that Foucault could not countenance such a concept as "excess of significance"; it implies that there exists a norm of significance that has been exceeded. And his work consistently declines to prescribe or vindicate, preferring instead to suggest new questions rather than answer old ones. On the other hand, there are places in which Foucault would seem to agree with Rubin. For example, although Foucault never sanctioned coercive acts against children, he rejected the view that sexual relations between adults and children are always harmful for the children involved. He argued against legal interventions in such relations, and against the consensus position held by psychiatric institutions that such relations, in whatever form they take, inevitably produce trauma for children and indicate pathological problems in the adult. In one passage in volume 1 (*An Introduction*) of his *History of Sexuality,* Foucault relates an incident in nineteenth-century France in which a farmhand sexually molested a small child and was brought before the legal and medical experts for analysis. For Foucault, the principal significance of this event was:

> The pettiness of it all; the fact that this everyday occurrence in the life of village sexuality, these inconsequential bucolic pleasures, could become, from a certain time, the object not only of a collective intolerance but of a judicial action, a medical intervention, a careful clinical examination, and an entire theoretical elaboration. . . . So it was that our society . . . assembled around these timeless gestures, these barely furtive pleasures between simple-minded adults and alert children, a whole machinery for speechifying, analyzing, and investigating.[3]

For many of his feminist readers, Foucault's insightful work in uncovering new mechanisms of domination appears painfully at odds with his stated positions on sexual relations between adults and children, in which he renders such relations "inconsequential" and "petty," and presents the children involved as simply "alert" or "precocious." How can we make sense of such positions given his general work? Is there a conflict between his critique of domination and his analysis of sexuality? What are the implications of his declaration that "sexuality" does not exist for an account of sexual violence? *Has* our culture attributed an excessive significance to sex with children?

In this essay I shall explore Foucault's position on sexual relations between adults and children and try to make sense of it in the context of his other relevant theoretical work. While agreeing with a significant part of Foucault's account of sexuality in its relationship to discourse and the law, I shall also challenge Foucault's position on pedophilia but seek a post-Foucauldian or Foucauldian-informed manner in which to analyze sexual relations between adults and children. The goal of this essay, therefore, is not simply to charge Foucault with an incorrect, politically dangerous position on adult-child sex, but to explain the connection between his position on pedophilia with his larger account of sexuality and to attempt to use Foucault's own insights about the relationships between discourse, power, and pleasure to advance our theoretical analysis and evaluation of these sexual practices.

Foucault on Pedophilia

> Every morality, in the broad sense, comprises codes of behavior and forms of subjectivation.
>
> —Foucault, *Use of Pleasure*

We have two principal sources through which to hear Foucault's views on this topic. One is the striking (but ignored) passage already cited, the "village simpleton" story. The other is a transcript from an interview conducted on the topic with Foucault, Guy Hocquenghem, and Jean Danet, broadcast by France-Culture in 1978. In this section I shall analyze both these texts and explore how the positions they articulate could emerge out of Foucault's work. In the next section, I shall consider an essay by Gayle Rubin that represents, I believe, her version of an "applied Foucault"; that is, an application of Foucault's views toward the development of a radical politics of sexual diversity.

The interview with Foucault, Hocquenghem, and Danet has been published under the title "La Loi de la Pudeur" and also as "Sexual Morality and the Law."[4] The topic of the interview was the question of legal jurisdiction over sexual practices between adults and children or youths, and the panelists' support of a petition campaign in France against several specific laws that criminalized acts between adults and children "below the age of fifteen" (Guy Hocquenghem, *PPC*, 273). Since all three panel participants were in major accord on this issue, I shall discuss the text in full rather than only Foucault's contributions to it, though I will indicate the specific author of each passage quoted.

Foucault's interest and concern with this issue resulted from his critique of the relationship between the institutions of psychiatry and psychology on the one hand and the law on the other. The former institutions, acting in their capacity as expert discourses, have been implicated in the negotiation of relations of power between the state, the law, and the individual, usually (or in his view, perhaps always) with the effect of increasing and consolidating structures of domination. One of the principal examples of this is the construction of criminal identities, in which juridical procedures take as their object of evaluation not the crime but the criminal. The goal becomes to understand, categorize, and, where possible, reform the "criminal mind." It is Foucault's argument that highly contentious species of subjectivity are theoretically and in some cases experientially constituted in this way. Foucault's concern is thus with the unchallenged and increasing hegemony of both psychological discourses and practices and the law via their mutual association on the topic of pedophilia.

Foucault is very much troubled by the view that sexuality is "the business of the law" (*PPC*, 271) for two reasons. The first is that the law has instituted outrageous repressive maneuvers against homosexuality and something it calls "sodomy" through a contrived association with pedophilia and through its presumption to judge and intervene in the sexual practices of its citizens, as well as through a widespread and officially sanctioned heterosexism and homophobia. Second, Foucault is concerned about the fact that the law presumes to make judgments, not of practices or acts, but of individuals, based on so-called objective facts about how individuals can and should be categorized. Foucault uses the Jouy case* to suggest that the designation "pedophile" was historically the paradigm category of "dangerous individuals." Pedophilia has thus played a key role in justifying the view that sexuality is the "business of the law." Moreover, Foucault argues that children have their own sexuality over which historically the law has imposed an absolute repression. And finally, Foucault finds incredible the psychiatric establishment's claim to "know" the "nature" of childhood sexuality. He therefore suggests that we reject their assertion that childhood sexuality "is a territory with its own geography that the adult must not enter" or that "the child must be protected from his own desires, even when his desires orientate him towards an adult" (*PPC,* 276).

The general position of the panelists is, then, to call into question the paternalism adopted by the law and psychiatry over children's sexuality. A key aspect of this paternalism involves the refusal to accept the possibility that a child may authentically consent to sex with adults. The panelists point to the fact that children may not have the ability to articulate what they are feeling or wanting, and when they are unable to formulate their own desires the courts unfailingly presume to speak for them. Foucault characterizes this as the imposition of hegemonic discourses on the subjugated discourse of the child. Demanding that the child be able to articulate her or his consent involves bringing sex "into discourse," which will entail bringing it into the dominant discourse and subjecting it to the dominant discourse's codes of normality. The concept of consent itself implies that sex is a contractual relationship, a view that the panelists find absurd. Children cannot always articulate their desires in a form that can be represented as legal consent, and even when they can the authorities interpret their consent as an inauthentic or otherwise unreliable expression. In contrast to this form of discursive paternalism and control, the panelists accept the authenticity of chil-

---

* I.e., the case of the "simple-minded farmhand." See below. (Ed.)

dren's stated consent, and they advocate listening to the children themselves without assuming that we can know their "true" desires. But the panelists also express reservations about the use of consent as a criterion of judgment in these cases because it may be difficult for a child to articulate his or her own desire and because the consensual/contractual model is unsuitable for sexual relations.

The members of the panel were careful to distinguish their views on this topic from the issue of (adult) rape, although they bemoan the fact that feminists' agitation around rape has reinforced the power of the state over sexuality. Foucault expressed the concern that "sexuality will become a threat in all social relations" (*PPC*, 281); that is, that sex will always be seen as a potential danger, which will then authorize the state to constitute "dangerous individuals" and "vulnerable populations" and to enforce massive policies of oversight and intervention. The result will be, in Foucault's words, "a new regime for the supervision of sexuality" (*PPC*, 281), or a new totalitarianism. In order to avert this result, sexual practices, in whatever form they take, should not be within the punitive jurisdiction of the state. As Hocquenghem warned, "The constitution of this type of criminal [the "pedophile"], the constitution of this individual perverse enough to do a thing that hitherto had always been done without anybody thinking it right to stick his nose into it, is an extremely grave step from a political point of view."[5]

In the above I reconstituted in summary form the panel's general argument in its most persuasive light. But there are some other passages in the interview that, perhaps, reveal more about the panelists' views (and desires) than the above thematic synopsis, though the last statement quoted suggests that their primary motivation may not be the protection of children from unfair discursive and sexual subordination. For example, an important recurring theme is the deflation of adult-child sex itself as an event of any significance. In the panelists' view, dominant society has inflated these acts far beyond their true significance (as is suggested by Hocquenghem's point that these are things that "had always been done"), but now adult-child sex is being sensationalized by authoritative institutions for their own opportunistic reasons. At another point in the discussion Hocquenghem derided the emphasis put on child pornography as a priority for political action over other issues such as racist violence, clearly rejecting the view that such issues have equal importance. Danet also takes issue with the current hierarchy of heinous crimes: "A lawyer will be quite happy to defend someone accused of murdering ten old ladies. That doesn't bother him in the least. But to defend someone who has touched some kid's cock for a second, that's a real problem" (*PPC*, 279). Danet's point is that it is very difficult to get good legal defense for those accused of pedophilia, but his ironic phrasing and his reference to "some kid" indicates the almost laughable insignificance he accords to sex acts between adults and children. Foucault's use of terms such as "petty," "inconsequential," and "everyday," in reference to the farmhand incident demonstrates a similar desire to deflate the importance of these acts. In their view, sexual acts of any type between adults and children or youths have been invested with inordinate meaning and "fabricated" as a crime, when in reality it "is quite simply the erotic or sensual relationship between a child and an adult" (Hocquenghem, *PPC,* 277). Thus sometimes, though not always, such sexual relations have nothing criminal or harmful about them, and those accused of pedophilia have been unfairly hounded and vilified by vigilante mobs as well as state functionaries in a manner disproportionate to their crimes, if indeed any crime occurred at all.

Despite the problems they have with applying the notion of consent to sexual practices, the panelists rely on just such a notion in their argument that not all sexual relations between adults and children are violent or exploitative. Foucault says that we must "listen to children" and that "the child may be trusted to say whether or not he was subjected to violence" (*PPC,* 284). The way Hocquenghem puts it is more ambiguous:

> When we say that children are "consenting" in these cases, all we intend to say is this: in any case, there was no violence, or organized manipulation in order to gain affective or erotic relations. . . . The public affirmation of consents to such acts is extremely difficult, as we know. Everybody—judges, doctors, the defendant—knows that the child was consenting, but nobody says anything, because, apart from anything else, there's no way it can be introduced. It's not the effect of the prohibition by law: it's really impossible to express a very complete relationship between a child and an adult—a relation that is progressive, long, goes through all kinds of stages, which are not all exclusively sexual, through all kinds of affective contacts. To express this in terms of legal consent is an absurdity. In any case, if one listens to what a child says and if he says "I didn't mind," that doesn't have the legal value of a consent. (*PPC,* 285)

This passage is telling on a number of counts. Hocquenghem evidently holds the position that a "very complete" relationship between a child and an adult will include sexual relations. On the one hand, he points out rightly that consent should indicate the absence not only of violence but also of organized manipulation, but on the other hand, his articulation of the "authentic" consent is not at all reassuring. When does one use the phrase "I didn't mind"? When someone is *doing something* to *me,* without my participation. This hardly sounds like an expression of spontaneous desire on the child's part, or the description of a reciprocal relationship. It sounds much more like the child is willing to put up with something the adult wants to do.

We can next turn to take a closer look at the passage in *An Introduction* in which Foucault introduces a case of what would now be commonly called child molesting as an illustration of his thesis about the connection between discourse and sexuality. Contra the repressive hypothesis, which holds that sexuality has been repressed in Victorian discourse, Foucault argues, convincingly, that in the last two centuries sexuality has been less repressed than produced and managed, and that the primary mechanism for this has been precisely bringing sexual practices into the realm of discourse. Behaviors that had heretofore received scant attention came to be extracted orally in the confessional, analyzed in detail, painstakingly related in autobiographical form, and articulated into "expert discourses" in the human sciences. And the sexuality of children came into view as a "problem" of increasing importance within a context organized around the control of populations and the production of docile bodies. Children's masturbation was subjected to parental, religious, and scientific observation and monitoring, and a host of discourses were developed to analyze, explain, and provide "solutions" to the problem.

It was in connection to this development that sexual relations between adults and children, Foucault intimates, became the subject of scrutiny as well as punitive judgments. The change was clearly evident by 1867, where a "simple-minded" farmhand was turned in to the authorities after having

> obtained a few caresses from a little girl, just as he had done before and seen done by the village urchins round about him; for, at the edge of the wood, or in the ditch by the road leading to Saint-Nicolas, they would play the familiar game called "curdled milk." . . . [and] this village half-wit . . . would give a few pennies to the little girls for favors the older ones refused him.[6]

But this time, Foucault relates, the familiar, ordinary incident in the life of the village, the "everyday occurrence [of] inconsequential bucolic pleasures" became the subject of judicial and medical intervention. The farmhand was subjected to detailed, invasive questioning about his "thoughts, inclinations, habits, sensations, and opinions" (31). The "experts" inspected his anatomy to the point of studying his "facial bone structure" and measuring his "brainpan" for signs of "degenerescence" (31). In the end, he was shut away at a hospital.

Foucault's object in discussing this case is to mark that moment in the history of sexuality in which sex is brought under the jurisdiction of expert discourses in the human sciences. But his goal is not merely to develop a more accurate history of the West: he wants to defamiliarize his readers to this alignment between sexual practices and the will to truth. Thus his use of this particular case is intended to suggest that the medical and legal responses were odd and inappropriate; that is, that they exceeded the significance of the event. Given the disparate juxtaposition between the insignificance of the event itself and the portentous response it received from the authorities, what he refers to as the overlay of an "everyday bit of theatre with their solemn discourse" (32), Foucault's implication is that the responses were involved in discursive structures of domination. This argumentative strategy is also evident in the full passage that was partly quoted earlier:

> So it was that our society—and it was doubtless the first in history to take such measures—assembled around these timeless gestures, these barely furtive pleasures between simple-minded adults and alert children, a whole machinery for speechifying, analyzing, and investigating. (32)

Foucault relates with irony the fact that the farmhand's name was Jouy, a word that resonates in French with the verb "jouir" meaning to enjoy, delight in, and to have an orgasm. This suggests the fact that, for Foucault, before the intervention of the authorities the principal meaning of this event was pleasure.

Foucault clearly wants to disrupt any easy assurance that we "know" the true meaning of this event or the quality of its felt experience for the participants. Yet his construction of this narrative paradoxically works to replicate without critical reflection most of our own culture's presumptions (in his term, its "historical a priori") about such sexual practices. Foucault's narrative encourages the view that they are primarily committed by adults whom he unfeelingly characterizes as "half-wits," and thus that adults who engage in these acts are motivated by sexual needs, being incapable of achieving sexual satisfaction with their peers. And by characterizing the children who participate in these acts as especially "alert" and "precocious," Foucault reinforces the common view that these children take an active and willing role, uncoerced, and may even be seductive.[7] It hardly need be said that Foucault lacked sufficient evidence to warrant his claims about the girl's participation in or feelings about the event. His quickness to assume such knowledge manifests unfortunately typical male and adult patterns of epistemic arrogance. If such relations were reciprocally desired and pleasurable for both parties, why did there need to be an exchange of a "few pennies" to ensure the girl's participation? Whose point of view is silently assumed when one determines that the prostituting of small girls is a petty and trivial event? For whom are such "bucolic" pleasures inconsequential? Thus, here we have an apparent contradiction: Foucault seeks to problematize and deessentialize sexuality and sexual experience; yet the rhetorical strategy he uses to subvert standard assumptions simply invokes an alternative set, arguably more patriarchal than the first.

The point of view Foucault adopts in the Jouy example is one curiously at odds with his principal thesis in *An Introduction*. It is a picture in which pleasure stands on one side, in almost pure form, innocent and harmless, and on the other side stands discourse, power, and domination. On the basis of such a picture we are led through the analysis to posit pleasure as antithetical to power, even as exempt from its discursive constitutions and machinations. But in other places in this book Foucault takes pains to reveal precisely the way in which power effects its domination not simply or primarily through the repression of pleasures or through negation, but through productive maneuvers (which include the production of pleasure itself). This is what prompts Judith Butler to say in her commentary on this book that for Foucault, "If the repressive law constitutes the desire it is meant to control, then it makes no sense to appeal to that constituted desire as the emancipatory opposite of repression."[8] Yet clearly he is doing so in this passage.

This apparent inconsistency begins to recede once we realize that, for Foucault pleasure is a force that can be taken up, used, incited, fomented, and manipulated, but is not itself discursively constituted. Foucault's concern is with the relationship among pleasure, discourse, and power, and the way in which pleasures can get used and taken up by institutional discourses and aligned with power/knowledges. Thus, he is concerned about the way in which various sexual pleasures get categorized and correlated to specified personality profiles and identities that can then be managed and disciplined. And he is also concerned with the way in which institutional discourses and disciplinary regimes are proliferated, disseminated, and consolidated through their complicated relationships with pleasure. The model of opportunism I alluded to earlier is strictly speaking inaccurate, as Foucault attributes no conscious strategy of self-maximization to discourses; still, the streams of circulating discourse are made wider and stronger to the extent they can merge with streams of pleasure. The intersection between knowledges and pleasures occurs through such codifications as "the pedophile." To the extent that the pedophile can be characterized as an ever-present threat, a "dangerous individual," detectable only through the expert analysis of "signs" by recognized authorities, the discursive focus on the pleasures of the pedophile serve to enlarge the scope of institutional discourses.

There are also ways in which such discourses not only take up preexisting pleasures, but create the structural arrangements necessary for new pleasures to be formed, such as the pleasure the priest or therapist enjoys through the process of extracting a confession that details some sexual practice, or the pleasure the general public can now enjoy in reading about sexuality, whether in "objective" studies, autobiographical narratives, or "how-to" manuals. But in all of these analyses pleasure itself remains, in an important sense, untouched. Foucault does not engage in, and in fact argues against, the practice of doing a political and/or moral evaluation of various forms of pleasure. He never condemns the priest, for example, for achieving pleasure through a practice that involves the humiliation and shaming of the penitent, but simply shows the role that voyeuristic sadism plays in the construction of various discursive arrangements and distributions of power. Like Marx, for whom everything was included in the realm of the dialectical movement of history except for the "natural" heterosexual relations regarding childbirth and childcare, Foucault demonstrates a similar blindspot by exempting his own favored entity from his theory of discursive constitution and flux: pleasure. Pleasures are vulnerable to social shifts in the sense that different discourses and different societies allow for differing arrangements between bodies, or what he refers to in *An Introduction* as "a different economy of bodies and pleasures" (159). But the variability in the distributions of bodies and pleasures is not the same as their constitution by a discourse. Intriguingly, then, *The History of Sexuality* ends up naturalizing pleasure, as outside the domain of the discursively constituted ontological realm and as an inappropriate subject for social and political evaluation as well as sanction by the state or any legislative body. It is for this reason that Foucault can end the book declaring that "the rallying point for the counterattack against the deployment of sexuality ought not to be sex-desire, but bodies and pleasures" (157).

Butler grapples with this problem in Foucault as well in relationship to his account of discourse and desire. She initially reads him as holding that there is no desire outside of discourse, which is the apparent theme of this volume. But she also finds a moment of contradiction in his account. Foucault posits, according to Butler, a more fundamental form of desire that exists below discourse, prior to history, and reminiscent of the basic life-affirming energy found in both Hegel's mythology of the lord and bondsman and in Nietzsche's positive variation on Schopenhauer's will-to-power. This "productive desire seems less an historically *determined* than a historically *occasioned* desire which, in its origins, is an ontological invariant of human life."[9] This would seem to solve our puzzle, if it allows for a level of desire/pleasure free from discursive construction that can then indeed stand as the innocent other to power. But can it allow for this? I would say it cannot if Butler is right (as I think she is) that for Foucault all desire is historically occasioned. Desires and pleasures are not identical, but they are connected, and if there is no desire that is not historically occasioned, then there can be no pleasure innocent of history, where history especially for Foucault is the very site of the movements and developments of discursive regimes. But if this is the case, then how can any pleasure, such as the pleasure of Jouy, exist on the other side of power/knowledge, apart from or prior to the structured relations between discourses and power? And how can Foucault end with a rallying cry for bodies and pleasures presented as if in contrast to the discursive deployment of desire?

My argument is, then, that, despite appearances to the contrary, Foucault in fact does not hold that pleasure is ontologically constituted by discourse and exists in intrinsic and not only extrinsic relationship to structures such as patriarchy. Such a view would have allowed him to consider the ways in which certain pleasures are not merely redistributed but produced, such as the pleasure of violating, the pleasure of harming, and the pleasure in vastly unequal and non-reciprocal sexual relations. And most important, it would also work against the possibility that pleasure, in all its various forms, could serve as the haven or bulwark against the mechanisms of dominant power/knowledges. If pleasure is itself the product of discursive constitution, it cannot play the role of innocent outsider. It is because Foucault sees pleasure as playing this latter role that he repudiates the view that pleasures can and should be open to political and moral evaluation and assessment. Foucault argues that this would simply increase the hegemony of dominant discourses to intervene in minute practices of everyday life, which in his view is the principal feature of contemporary domination.

But here we have a true note of discord between conflicting tendencies in his own work: on the one hand, the uncovering of the machinations of power at work in the multiple sites of "personal life"; on the other, the fear of striking a judgmental pose with respect to individual practice in any form. Despite the significant dangers of the latter, given that we live in a period of more efficient social discipline than perhaps the West has ever experienced, I would argue that a feminist Foucauldian cannot afford to repeat Foucault's own disenabling ambivalence. If we are persuaded by his (and others') account of domination in "everyday life," we must risk putting forward our judgments about when and where it occurs. It is a mistake to think that putting forward such judgments will necessarily result in an overall increase in repression: the repression of adult-child sex may effect a decrease in the constraints by which children's own sexual energies are policed, managed, and deflected.

There is no necessary contradiction between a view that takes seriously the connection, among discourse, power, and sexuality, and a politics of sexuality that repudiates various sexual pleasures. Why does Foucault presume such a conflict? Most likely because he has seen such a discourse of repudiation itself integrated within the currently dominant discourses of power/knowledge. Certainly, too, his concern with the strategies by which homosexual practices have been condemned is evident here, though the connection between homosexuality and pedophilia is again discursively constituted rather than "natural." A further reason, as I have suggested, is that pleasure figures too innocently in Foucault's own discourse, connected to power only in what might be called extrinsic rather than intrinsic ways. Thus, my reading of Foucault suggests that his position on pedophilia results from his conflict about evaluative judgments, his overriding concern with the persecutions inflicted by the currently dominant discourses of sexuality, and from his assumption that, when disinvested of its relation to discourse, pleasure is necessarily resistant to domination. This account of pleasure as an intrinsic good is what drives the sexual politics developed by Gayle Rubin.

Rubin's "Applied" Foucault

Like communists and homosexuals of the 1950's, boy-lovers are so stigmatized that it is difficult to find defenders of their civil liberties, let alone for their erotic orientation. . . . In twenty years or so, it will be much easier to show that these men have been the victims of a savage and undeserved witchhunt.

—Gayle Rubin, "Thinking Sex"

In her powerful and influential essay, "Thinking Sex: Notes for a Radical Theory of the Politics of Sexuality," Rubin develops and extends Foucault's insights about the disciplining of erotic life to develop a new politics of sexual practices. Rubin's interpretation of Foucault is not above contention, but her use of Foucault to develop a "descriptive and conceptual framework for thinking about sex and its politics" is suggestive of the kind of practical, applicable politics on contemporary issues that at least one influential reading of Foucault can engender (275).

Rubin uses Foucault's analyses of the nonessentialist status of sexuality, the fictional character of sexual identities, and the role sexuality has played both discursively and nondiscursively in the consolidation of dominating structures, to advance what she calls a "radical thought about sex" (274). She starts by giving an overview of the contemporary crusade against sexual diversity and shows how this "anti-sex backlash" is connected to a hierarchical categorization of sexual acts and sexual identities (which themselves imply essentialist understandings of sexuality) and to a Christian-inspired assumption that sex is "negative"; that is, guilty until proved innocent.[10] She details the chilling degree of persecution inflicted on what she calls "erotic minorities" and makes an analogy between such "systems of sexual judgement" (282) and racism and anti-Semitism. She convincingly argues that the acceptance of an excessively narrow, officially sanctioned form of sexual activity and the condemnation of all other possible variations "rationalize[s] the well-being of the sexually privileged and the adversity of the sexual rabble" and manifests one of the major forms of unacknowledged oppression existent in our society (280).

Her counterargument is more problematic. She argues for a "pluralistic sexual ethics" that borrows the concept of "benign variation" from evolutionary biology. But for evolutionary biology, of course, variation is not only neutral, it is necessary. Thus in Rubin's view variation is inherently morally positive (as implied in the very term "benign"). Moreover, in her evocation of evolutionary arguments to theorize the diversity of sexual practices, Rubin resuscitates a naturalistic account of sexuality once again, repeating Foucault's own tendencies (283). The implication of the argument is that evaluative analyses and moral hierarchies are no more appropriate for sexual practices than for plant diversity. The only appropriate value system is the one she borrows again from evolutionary biology, in which more and different is inherently better, and freedom equals variety and proliferation. Her account succeeds in effacing the role of power in constructing and proliferating all social relations including sexual practices; thus she ends by endorsing a form of moral relativism, or perhaps moral equivalency, in which power disappears from the frame.

Such a position would be obviously implausible when applied to sexual violence, but Rubin stipulates that her account does not apply to "sexual coercion, sexual assault, or rape" though it does apply to "the 'status' offenses such as statutory rape" as well as to what she calls consensual adult-child sex (288). Thus, her benign variations are meant to exclude acts of coercion and violence. And though she neglects to theorize such acts, her proposal for a "democratic morality" evidences a concern for them: "A democratic morality should judge sexual acts by the way partners treat one another, the level of mutual consideration, the presence or absence of coercion, and the quantity and quality of the pleasures they provide" (283).

I find this last proposal very promising, and I also agree that most sexual variation is benign and that many sexual practices are inappropriately categorized in a hierarchy of value. But there are at least three major problems with Rubin's formulation of a radical sexual politics, and each of these problems bear crucially on the issue of adult-child sexual relations.

In her category of benign sexual variations that face unfair repression Rubin includes "fetishism, sadism, masochism, transsexuality, transvestism, exhibitionism, voyeurism and pedophilia" as well as promiscuous homosexuality and commercial sex (280, 281, 283). She lumps together all these activities into one monolithic unity, and assumes they can be adequately analyzed in a single account. But adult-child sex and, for example, transvestism involve extremely different moral as well as political issues, and cannot be usefully placed in the same category for the purpose of political or moral analysis. Rubin not only lumps them together, but maintains that the persecution of transvestites is no more outrageous than the persecution of pedophiles, both of whom suffer from a "prejudice" inflicted against them that she likens to "racism, ethnocentrism, and religious chauvinism" (280).

Second, it is a grave error for Rubin to believe, along with Foucault, Danet, and Hocquenghem, as discussed above, that the issue of sexual violence can be excluded from any theory of the politics of sexuality. This is an error not simply because of the importance of understanding sexual violence, but because the way in which we identify sexual violence will affect the way in which we will come to understand and analyze all other sexual practices (and vice versa). For example, I think it can be shown that there is an intrinsic relationship between the persecution of "sodomy" and the acceptance of the violation of young children. Both of these are connected to an institution of patriarchy that has legitimated itself through a macho heterosexuality founded in part on the ownership and control of children. The particular version of macho heterosexuality found in Christianity justifies the absolute power and authoritarianism of elite men, which includes their right to determine the treatment of all subordinates, on the basis of each being the father of a heterosexual family unit, and thus a provider and progenitor of the species. This schema pits both homosexuality and the rights of children in direct conflict with the legitimation of patriarchal power, which is here defined as a form of heterosexual paternalism.[11] Therefore, to understand both the persecution of homosexuality as well as the violation of children, we need to understand these phenomena in the complex details of their interrelationship.

Moreover, where Rubin tosses off the categories of "sexual coercion, sexual assault and rape" as if these are unambiguously defined, in actual fact their scope of application is constantly being contested and their definition is nowhere clear or unchallenged. In nineteenth-century U.S. culture, sex between a white woman and an African-American man was defined as a violation whether or not she consented. Within heterosexual marriage, rape has usually been considered impossible, by virtue of the terms of the marriage contract. And there are further arguments today about how to construe "date rape" and statutory rape. Thus, the line of demarcation between the practices that are considered violent and those thought to be harmless is not at all clear and is being incessantly redrawn. Rubin's own account of "benign" sexual practices will have a direct effect on where that line can be located within her own theory, whether or not she acknowledges this fact. No account of sexuality can present itself as inapplicable or irrelevant to sexual violence because each account will influence the way in which sexual violence is conceptualized and identified.

Finally, Rubin's specific discussion of adult-child sex is itself extremely problematic. Her very use of the term "cross-generational sex" lumps together such disparate issues as the social disapproval of relations between older women and younger men with the relations between adults and children. The term "cross-generational sex" is becoming more and more widely used in discourses of sexual libertarianism, even though the specific analyses usually center around sex between adults and children or youths. For example, the average age of membership of England's Pedophile Information Exchange is 37, and they describe themselves as "chiefly interested" in males between the ages of 14 and 19. Pedophilic interest in girls is focused primarily on the ages from 8 to 10.[12] The René Guyon Society advocates sex without intercourse with girls up to the age of 12, and then "initiation" at the age of 13.[13] When the statistics focus on incest and exclude incidents with strangers or acquaintances, the *average* age of the child drops to 7. The all-inclusive notion of "cross-generational sex" to discuss these events together with relations between differently aged adults tends toward obscuring the specificity of the issues involved in sexual relations between fully matured adults and dependent children.

Rubin has nothing but sympathy for the "men [who] have been the victims of a savage and undeserved witchhunt" ("Thinking Sex," 273). She likens pedophiles to African-Americans and to Jews in suffering unjust persecution (298). She sympathizes with their vulnerability to exposure and points out that "having to maintain such absolute secrecy is a considerable burden" (292). Nowhere in the article does she mention or cite references to victims of child sexual abuse, or their own accounts of these events in their lives and the impact it has had on their adult sexuality.

Rubin also asserts that "cross-generational" sex is the "lowliest category on the hierarchy of sex" (279). This is hardly the case. Cross-generational relations between old men and young women are the subject of so many approving cultural representations that they may seem to typify one of the normative scenarios for "romance." It is only sex with children that receives a pretension of condemnation, but even here the facts concerning prosecution belie this stated concern. Rubin is mistaken to claim that children are "ferociously" protected from adult sexuality when the reality is that actions are generally only taken when more than the violation of children is at stake: to justify the persecution of homosexuals, to enable a criticism of "working mothers," or to extend and legitimate the paternalistic power of the repressive apparatus of the state.

Rubin's "applied Foucault," while it follows his valorization of pleasure as an intrinsic good, misses the better parts of Foucault's analysis, which insists on the constitutive relationship among desire, discourse, and power. I find it remarkable, for example, that Rubin refuses to interrogate the desire of a thirty-seven-year-old man for a fourteen-year-old boy, or the systematic preferences of some adults for children who are physically much weaker and emotionally and intellectually much less articulate (and more flexible and responsive to adult influence than a peer would be). This critical absence seems to follow from an

unacknowledged premise that where there is desire, pleasure, and any semblance of consent, there is a good that deserves to be defended. In Rubin's "sex-
positive" view, all sexual practices should be considered innocent until proven
guilty. This type of "pro" attitude toward sexual pleasure may be correlated with
what Eric Presland calls the "want/have syndrome" (if I want it then I automatically have a right to it), endemic to both masculinist ideology and consumer
capitalism.[14] If Rubin had consulted the growing literature written by survivors
of childhood abuse and assault, she might have changed her view about the
innocent status of pedophilia. In the next section I shall try to develop a new
articulation of pedophilia that can avert the homophobic effect of its perceived
tie to homosexuality, avoid a naturalistic account of pleasure, and retain a
"metaphysics of suspicion" with respect not only to puritan condemnations but
likewise to adult assurances that the children "don't mind."

A "Countersentence"

> A demand rather than a method, a morality more than a theory.
> —Georges Canguilhem

Both children and youths, or young teenagers, have been discussed throughout
this analysis. Putting age limits on these categories is obviously arbitrary, since
children reach puberty and attain maturity at very different ages due to sex and
glandular differences or other idiosyncratic variables. Dissimilar cultures can
also significantly affect empowerment by imposing diverse social expectations
and practices. The concept of childhood is culturally and historically variable,
and currently dependent on controversial developmental theories. The concept
of the teenager is even more recent. For all of these reasons it is impossible to
devise a categorization by age that will be applicable across sexual identity, culture, historical period, and the individual differences. Clearly the best approach
would be as local as possible, and thus specific to a group of children or youths
who have most of these variables in common.

There is no resolution to the inherent complexity involved in establishing
age demarcations for such categories as children and youth. Still, we might be
able to identify the critical determinants by which such categories would be
developed, such as basic motor skills for running away; language skills for articulating questions, desires, and commands; the onset of puberty; and economic
independence. The most common distinction used to separate children and
youths is puberty, although puberty itself is an elastic concept. But even after
puberty most youths in Western societies are economically dependent and emotionally vulnerable to adult manipulation and coercion. In the following analysis
I am relying on literature and data from Western countries; based on this, I shall

assume that at least one broad analysis of pedophilia can be made in regard to all children and youths under the age of sixteen, though there will be obvious differences that need to be taken into account within this grouping in relation to specific issues and practices. The virtue of a general account is not that it can deal with every single case, but that it can shed light on general features of a class of cases.

Perhaps the most crucial distinction besides age that needs to be made is that between homosexual and heterosexual practices. Pedophilic practices vary enormously; some prefer only girls, some have sex with boys while married or otherwise sexually engaged with adult women, and some focus on boys alone. Florence Rush claims that no such distinction is relevant: that the impulse to engage with children sexually transcends any distinction of sexual orientation.[15] This view seems shortsighted, however. Given the enormous difference in social attitudes toward homosexual and heterosexual practices, and given the real differences between these respective sexual communities, surely one must avoid generalizations that would subsume these practices into a single account.

On the one hand, plausible arguments can be made that in a homophobic context, same-sex relations between youths of the same age are structurally impractical, and older men or women can play a useful role in making it possible to express homosexual desire. As Foucault suggests, sexual pleasures and sensations can be assigned different meanings and values with different affective components, from which it surely follows that it is unwise to make inferences from a heterosexual context to a homosexual one or vice versa. However, it is not necessarily useless to theorize pedophilia (as the adult desire for children) and pederasty (as the desire of men for adolescent boys) in the same account.[16] Across the significant differences lies at least one important similarity: unequal, nonreciprocal relations of power and desire. Tom Reeves, founder of the North American Man/Boy Love Association (NAMBLA), stresses that he has no interest in children or in molestation, but he also says that it is the boys' intermediate status as not-yet-adults that holds his attraction. He likes their freedom and rebelliousness, their mixture of "rough yet innocent," and admits that he likes to be in charge of things, even though he repudiates the notion that in relationships with boys he always is.[17] I am certain that he is correct to say that he is not always in control, but in his affairs with boys from the ages of thirteen to eighteen I doubt the power is ever equal. Reeves's argument is that it is the repressive laws against such relationships that create the furtive situations that produce prostitution and the unethical and manipulative treatment of boys by men. The law may well exacerbate some problems well beyond what they would be otherwise. But it is not the law alone that is responsible for the inequalities of independence, emotional and psychic development, and susceptibility to manipulation between boys and men.

Pat Califia defends relations between adults and children or youth on similar libertarian grounds. She argues that "there is nothing wrong with a more privileged adult offering a young person money, privacy, freedom of movement, new ideas and sexual pleasure."[18] The "and" in this list suggests that the first four are tied to the last, turning what may appear to be a beneficent relationship into a form of opportunist manipulation where an adult procures sex by providing important benefits the child or youth wants or needs. But this is precisely the common scenario of pedophilia, in which there is seduction and manipulation rather than overt violence, and in which the young person is taught to use sex to get her other needs met, and so learns to offer sex for attention, for companionship, for money, and so on. When sex is exchanged for an adult's "goods" that the young person or child wants or needs, how can this indicate an authentic consent to the sex itself, much less a desire?

In preparation for writing this essay I have been reading two very disparate sets of literature, one set concerned with the crisis of childhood sexual abuse and a second set focused on the increasing problems of homophobia and rightist sexual repression. No one seems to be able to share a concern with both of these issues as equal priorities, or to attempt an account of the relationship between them.[19] Sexual libertarians always make a point of condemning abuse and coercion, but never explore the reasons for the epidemic proportions and prevalence of these sexual events. Advocates for child victims usually espouse a condemnation of homophobia and often distance themselves from statist, legalistic solutions, but their analyses rarely employ social criticisms of the role of law in discourse, such as Foucault offers. Both sides thus perceive the other as guilty of bad faith. Child advocates wonder if the libertarians are really concerned about child abuse or if they believe that the statistics (and even the trauma) are produced by a moralistic climate of discourse. Libertarians wonder if every child advocate harbors an anti-sex authoritarian attitude and a tendency to invest in sexual acts "an excess of significance," perhaps ultimately motivated by their participation in the profitable self-help institutions.

What is needed, it seems to me, is an account that can bring together these disparate concerns in full equality. This is not to deny that in local contexts certain elements may pose a greater danger, and merit more extensive attention and intervention. A perfectly evenhanded approach in all situations would achieve only an abstract, superficial justice, and would likely result in many all too concrete injustices. What is needed, rather, is an approach that puts all of these considerations into play—that is, concern with sexual violence, abuse, patriarchy, homophobia, disciplinary forms of domination (though not always in equal measure)—while remaining attentive to the fallibility and indeterminateness of any account of sexual life. The following account attempts to enact this charge insofar as it can apply to a general analysis of pedophilia.

Let us assume for the sake of argument that the position articulated by Foucault, Hocquenghem, Danet, and Rubin is grounded in a genuine concern to transform the conditions of sexual oppression in which children live. In the context of the United States where a brilliant surgeon general can be fired merely for mentioning masturbation and sex education in the same sentence, we should all share this concern. The question then becomes, What is the best way to enact this transformation?

In their view, the liberation of children's sexuality must necessarily include an end to the repression of consensual sexual relations between adults and children. This assumes that we can demarcate sexual relations based on physical violence and overt manipulation from sexual relations that are in some sense consented to by the children themselves. But this assumption is difficult to maintain. Verbal consent can be easily produced by background structural conditions such as economic and emotional dependence. When children are involved there is also a significant possibility of real confusion about how to describe the experience. Many adult survivors from childhood assaults recall that in the beginning they were not clear on what was happening to them or what the other person was doing; this further complicates consent. One man relates, "He showered me with gifts and attention. And he knew how to get both of us going. . . . I fought him at first. But he excited me. And soon I was hooked."[20] When such a seduction is practiced not on an adult but on a child, the effect is a manipulation that takes advantage of the child's susceptibility and confusion.

Consent can be produced in a variety of ways, from seductive manipulation to coercion. A woman writes:

> Then one afternoon when I was just waking up from a nap, he sat next to me on the side of the bed. He put his big heavy fingers in my pants and began rubbing my clitoris. I had no idea what he was trying to do. He asked, yet sort of told me, "It feels good, doesn't it?" All I knew was I couldn't say no. I felt powerless to move. I said Yes. . . . He told me never to tell anyone. But I already knew I wouldn't say a word. My mother adored him, idealized him, and I felt I needed to protect our image of our great Daddy.[21]

Consent alone can never serve as a sufficient means to ensure that the child or young person is safe.

I would agree with Foucault that a consensual/contractual model makes little sense when applied to sexual relations, no more than applied to love. This is not because desire does not admit of a yes or no expression, but because the nature of sexual expression is not an exchange or a trade, but (ideally) a mutual engagement. Desire is enacted and enhanced in the performance of sexual practices, and not simply lying there inert beforehand ready to be exchanged. The concept of consent is a sometimes useful abstraction that can help to clarify what happened and to articulate the presence or absence of coercion, but it has only a limited ability to capture the nature of sexual experience.

Furthermore, from a position of moral concern over the well-being of the participants in a sexual encounter, what one needs to know is not whether there was stated consent, but whether the actions performed represented the authentic desires of each participant. I fully acknowledge how problematic the concept of authenticity is, given the fact that neither desires nor selves are ontologically independent in the way the concept has historically implied, and yet it is the authenticity of the children's desires that is at stake here. A concern with the presence or absence of consent is derivative on this more basic consideration. If a child does express consent, we must still ask whether or not it is an "authentic" expression.

The concept of authenticity may imply that there is an essential sexual desire (or lack of desire), intrinsic to an individual prior to social interactions or cultural influence. Such an implication is highly dubious, but it is not a necessary part of any and all accounts of authenticity. The criticism of old accounts of authenticity is that they presume an essential self with essential desires and needs prior to the cultural, social, and discursive insertion of the individual; but this criticism is directed at concepts of essentialism, not authenticity. For example, a distinction between authentic and inauthentic forms of consent might be based not on a concept of the essential or the natural but on the particular configuration of the existent relationship among power, desire, and discourse in a given situation. Such a configuration as typically exists in a psychiatric relationship, for example, suggests to many of us that the desire of the patient for her therapist (or vice versa) is in some sense problematic. The concept of authenticity captures this sense, by suggesting that without that configuration of power and discourse, the desire would not be the same. This argument presumes no essentialism.

Foucault's analysis suggests that desire must be analyzed in terms of its location with respect to power and discourse, and he implies, even on a critical reading, that there is no desire that is not "historically occasioned," to use Butler's words. The problem with the desire of the patient for her therapist is not that it is historically occasioned, but the kind of occasion that prompted it. Given this, the question we must ask is, What are the kinds of historical occasions that prompt desires between adults and children? This question calls for an exploration of the interconnections between adult-child sexual practices, discourse and power, or a genealogy of particular occasions of pedophilia.

It is obvious that children are disempowered relative to adults in both discursive and extradiscursive ways. Their discourse is subordinate and subjugated, and their actions are constrained within systems of possibility set out beforehand without their participation. This is not to say that they cannot resist or articulate new positions discordant with dominant regimes, but that they are positioned differently than adults and subject to more strenuous and invasive techniques of domination.

In every culture that exists children are dependent on adults for their very survival, though this dependence can vary in degree and form. Children are usually most dependent on the adults in their family or the adults who care for them but they are also dependent on the adults in their community generally. Their position vis-à-vis adults can therefore be characterized by its dependency, vulnerability, and relative powerlessness. This results not simply from the fact that children are usually smaller and physically weaker but because they are economically dependent on adults for their livelihood, and for a thousand other things like the quality of their education, the adjudication of their fights with other children, their sense of security and well-being, their hygiene, and their health. The very range of actions within which they may maneuver is set out for them, though children continually contest this range, sometimes successfully. Their relationship with adults is not reciprocal, mutually interdependent, or equal: children have a vastly reduced ability to get away or fight back, to talk or argue back, and to maintain their sense of self against adult mediation. Most children are not complete victims of adult power, but neither is their power equal to ours, either individually or collectively. As one survivor wrote, "a victim doesn't know he has a choice. That's the problem. If nobody else knows what's going on, then we don't know what to do."[22]

Some have argued that all of the above is correct but remediable. For example, Jamie Gough uses a Marxist analysis of oppression to suggest that children's subordination is socially constructed, and therefore the solution should be empowerment rather than paternalism.[23] It is true that the position of children is analogous in important respects to the position of slaves, insofar as both are disempowered, vulnerable, and dependent with respect to the adult or master. Would Rubin or Foucault countenance a view that masters can have sex with their slaves when the slaves "truly" desire it? Does the notion of a slave's authentic desire for sex with her master make any sense or have any credibility? If we are against sexual relations coerced through manipulation, the structural features of a master-slave relationship calls into question any assertion of desire for the master on the part of the slave, since such an expression may be too easily overdetermined by her position of dependence, either economic or psychological dependence or both in combination. Gough is certainly right that the solution to this situation is to eradicate the position of the slave through eradicating slavery, but here is where slavery and childhood are disanalogous. The institution of childhood can be radically altered, and children can become significantly more empowered than at present, but the vulnerability, dependency, and relative powerlessness of children vis-à-vis adults cannot ever be completely eradicated.[24]

Despite this, the analogy Gough suggests between children and other oppressed groups remains instructive. For example, the laws and social structures designed (purportedly) to protect women from violation have resulted in an increase in women's vulnerability. Those women who were "protected" from the dangerous public sphere of waged work were left more vulnerable to male violence in the home, without an effective escape route. Such "protections" of children have often had similar results. The lesson here is that children's rights must be extended, not curtailed, and they must have access to power outside the scope of their family or immediate caregivers.

The issue of power is precisely, though oddly, what Foucault leaves out of his analysis. When he speaks of "precocious little girls" he is blind to the way in which young girls who are often subject to multiple forms of domination based on their class, race, and gender have very few avenues by which to get their basic needs met. Sexual behavior is a common avenue that the dominant structures which favor adult men provide for girls and sometimes for boys as well. The "seductive," coy, or coquettish behavior of young girls must be analyzed in the context of a system of differential power relations and domination. When we leave the constitutive role of power aside we end up with the version of liberal or libertarian pluralism Rubin adopts, where sexual practices are treated under a descriptive model like a natural variety of plant species.

Power, as Foucault helped us to see, is not only often linked to discourse; it is constitutive of discourse. When adults interpret children's behavior, verbal or otherwise, as expressions of desire to have sex with them, the adults are assimilating that behavior within an economy of meaning to which it may very well not conform. They are interpreting the children within an economy based on sameness, incorporating the child's expressions within a system of meaning based on the adult's. Grubman-Black puts this point as follows:

> We were children whose rights and needs were denied. We were required to meet someone else's definition of us and of him. We were unable to escape the dream that was not of our making or choice. Whatever we sought, for whatever reason, we were met with one fixated response. I needed to be held and hugged, not fondled or aroused. We needed companionship and guidance, not sexual initiation. For many of us, there was emptiness in our lives. The offender chose to fill his own emptiness, his own needs, leaving us to feel even more barren.[25]

Grubman-Black describes a scenario too many of us can remember and identify with: a situation in which a child's entreaty is met with a kind of misresponse from an adult. The child wants and needs one thing, perhaps affection, attention, closeness, warmth, love, companionship, guidance, or affirmation, and the adult responds with his or her own agenda involving genital stimulation and erotic desire. Such missed communications may of course result from willful ignorance and manipulation on the adult's part, but they are also exacerbated by the disparate economies of meaning between the discursive and gestural practices of children and adults.

My claim is not that the world of children and the world of adults is absolutely incommensurable. It is not necessary to claim that children and adults can never communicate with each other in order to argue that every communicative interaction between them is mediated by the vulnerability, dependence, and relative powerlessness of children. My point is that the adult interpretation of children's behavior and expressions will always be structured by this ubiquitous inequality, and given the intrinsic connections among meaning, power, and truth, the discourse of children will always be distinct in significant ways from the discourse of adults, structured as it is around a different set of relationships.

Linguistic styles and practices emerge out of lived realities, which are themselves structured and filtered through language. But significantly different lived realities will correspond to significant differences in the metaphysics and epistemologies embedded in language; that is, the ontological assumptions and patterns of discursive authorization operative in a language. Who gets to speak, who will be accorded authority or at least presumption in their favor, what it is possible to express and what ontological objects (such as "desire") it is possible to entertain will all vary between such linguistic practices as exist among, say, Western scientists, gay Latinos, or lower-class children. These group demarcations can be drawn in multiple ways, as discrete, as overlapping, through the crisscrossing grids that can exist within the complexity of group exchange and relations in multivocal and multilayered societies. But substantive epistemic and semantic demarcations persist among adults, youth, and children. Adults who interpret children's behavior and linguistic practices as "consent" are imposing their own usage of "consent" across a linguistic border over which meanings can change drastically. Children certainly have the ability to consent to any number of things, but the meaning of that consent may shift in important respects when it is transported from an adult's to a child's context. We can use Foucault's expanded conception of a discourse, as embodying both meanings and ontological commitments as well as practices to identify the existence of a different discourse between adults and children, not incommensurable discourses but organized around a different set of strategic rules. Once we follow Foucault in acknowledging the relationship between power and discourse, we must also acknowledge that a significant difference in one's positioning with respect to dominant structures of power will result in a significant difference in the strategic rules by which discursive moves can be made.

When we incorporate the discourse of children with our own, and translate their desires within an economy of adult sexuality characterized by genital, orgasmic sex, we are exerting our force once again to eradicate any possible difference that may be there. The only way to avoid this is to leave children alone sexually, and thus allow the development and maintenance of their own sexual differences, either with themselves or with each other.

The possibility remains that children sometimes authentically consent to sex with adults, and this possibility is real, not merely logical or technical. Indeed, the male survivor literature often includes some accounts of pleasure. In my own experience of support groups, I remember one woman who said that she enjoyed her sexual relationship with her older brother. The simple infrequency of such narratives should not cause us to deny their validity and might in fact be the result of the current discursive prohibition against such statements. There are also victims of childhood sexual abuse that appear to be asymptomatic of traumatic aftereffects. This apparent absence of trauma is a difficult issue for those of us who are symptomatic survivors to face.

The existence of asymptomatic victims (whose status as "victims" is obviously problematic here) is insufficient to establish that adult-child sex is nonharming. There might be any number of alternative explanations before we confirm this hasty conclusion. For example, we need to look carefully at the widely variable context of sexual abuse, from sustained activity with a family member to a brief incident with a stranger. The type and degree of sexual interaction is relevant, as are the relations between those involved, the child's prior state of self-esteem, the general context of her security and well-being, her ability to be heard and believed about the incident soon afterward, her age, and so forth. In some cases negative aftereffects are immediate but responded to so effectively that they quickly diminish. Or the child herself is strong and secure enough to incorporate the event without being traumatized by it. Sexual experiences that children have with adults are so variable that the existence of some asymptomatic adult survivors in and of itself does not disconfirm the general harm of adult-child sex unless we were to find out more information about the patterns and contexts of symptomatic responses.

The issue of stated consent or felt pleasure needs to be assessed separately. There are several different ways one might understand such reports: (1) on the Freudian model, that the child is enacting an authentic desire of its own for a parent or parent figure; (2) that such stories indicate the possibility that adult-child sex is innocuous, and it is only the feminist or psychological literature that influences adults to reconstruct their experiences as damaging, painful, and coercive (in which case the narratives I have drawn from will be held invalid); (3) that no analytic model can account for all cases, and these are the exceptions to the rule; (4) that such accounts represent a kind of false consciousness where the survivor is still participating in the common tendency among children to protect the adult and rationalize his or her behavior. Taking (1), (2), or (4) as the full story strikes me as too simplistic, each assuming a monolithic analysis. The problem with (3) is that, while not assuming a monolithic analysis, it offers no explanation of the variability. And none of these options address the issue that desire and pleasure can be structurally and discursively constituted.

An alternative option would be one that allowed for variability in lived experience, but that also maintained that pleasure and damage can coexist in a single event. Children often "authentically" ask for things which would harm them if they got them. A desire for x does not make it harmless. This is not to say that the question of children's authentic desires is no longer relevant, but that it must be supplemented by an exploration of the issue of harm. In the narratives contained in *Broken Boys/Mending Men,* for example, the instances where pleasure and desire on the part of the boy are reported present seem to in no way mitigate against the trauma and harm that resulted. "It felt good," and yet the negative aftereffects make a long list: fear of trusting anyone, feeling like everyone who expresses concern ultimately wants only sex, self-destructiveness, self-loathing, shame, humiliation, fear of abandonment, and a host of pathological emotional and psychic disorders.[26]

Foucault argued that codes of morality comprise forms of subjectivation; I would argue the same for sexual practices. Sexual practices are self-constituting; that is, they affect the constitution of psychic life, the imaginary construction of one's self, and the structure of internal experience. A child's sexual practices with an adult will have an effect on that child's psychic structuring and subjectivity. All such constituting effects occur within specific discursive contexts, and for this reason some might claim that the harm of adult-child sex results from a disapproving social context rather than the event itself. But this claim is implausible if only because of the phenomenology of sex itself, which involves uniquely sensitive, vulnerable. and psychically important areas of body, a fact that persists across cultural differences. Thus sexual experiences have the capacity to impart crucial meanings concerning one's body and, therefore, one's self. This capacity does not establish that sexual acts have uniform meanings, but that they have in any case significant subject-constituting meanings rather than an absence of meaning. It is not social context alone that makes sexual acts significant, but social context in relation to the phenomenology of embodiment.

Moreover, sexual practices are profoundly intersubjective and relational, and impart meanings also about the limits and possibilities of one's relationship to others. (Given the role of fantasy in masturbation, even it can be seen as intersubjective, though of course one cannot harm others in an act of private masturbation.) NAMBLA argues (similarly to Rubin) that the state is motivated to repress sexuality because sex represents the ultimate individualism, and thus a kind of inherent resistance to state control.[27] But this argument betrays NAMBLA's own belief that sexual practices are fundamentally a sphere of the individual rather than the social. I believe the truth is exactly the reverse: the fact that sexual practices are intersubjective rather than individual suggests that the intersubjective and relational aspects of sexual practices can never be set aside in one's analysis.

In my own case a relatively brief series of assaults at a young age led to fairly fundamental alterations in my sense of self, my construction of intersubjective relations, and my experience of embodiment. I had many of the negative feelings discussed above, including a deep sense of shame (despite the fact that, in my case, there was no semblance of consent). It was terrifying to be dragged about against my will, to have my body poked and prodded and used for purposes I only dimly perceived, to have my screams and pleas ignored, and to have all this done to me with impunity. This gave me a profound message about my status as a social subject in the community. If I could be harmed to this degree with no one seeming to care, I thought it must be because I deserved it. Thus I came away from this experience with a self-image of worthlessness that I have struggled with ever since.

Such a narrative as I just gave is, of course, a reconstruction. At the time of the events, I remember clearly feeling only terror, pain, confusion, and a kind of shock. My grades went from A's to D's, I became withdrawn, and I cried so incessantly that my parents thought I had started puberty (at nine!). My current understanding of both the events and their full effect on me was produced through therapy, feminist consciousness, talking with others who had had similar experiences, and a number of other experiences and readings. Such processes of reconstructing and reassessing events is an inevitable part of any childhood traumatic experience (indeed, of any childhood). One alters one's understanding of events on the basis of the enlarged discursive domain one develops and on the basis of a constantly changing self. The point is not to suspect all such reconstructions as fictional overlays, nor to posit a pre-discursive, pre-theoretical experience that can be simply discovered once and for all when one is an adult. Experience is always reconstructed in memory, and memories are not pure representations, but we can make evaluative distinctions between better and worse reconstructions.

What I resist is the notion that it is possible to "interpret away" sexual trauma. Psychic harm is not a spiritual substance that can remain locked away as if in Descartes's pineal gland. If it exists, it makes itself manifest, though of course the "signs" of such manifestation will themselves require interpretation, admittedly a fallible and difficult enterprise. One man writes, "It took me years before I realized that I had been lied to, manipulated, and taken advantage of. . . . I avoided most people, had no friends, and I was a mess."[28] Such phenomenological descriptions belie the claim that trauma is produced after the fact. It is certainly possible for reconstructed narratives to be adversely influenced by dubitable theories or even political motivations. But we cannot reduce this possibility by denying that reconstructions are an inevitable part of all childhood memories. A better approach would be to explore the ties between institutional discourses of knowledge and power, using Foucault's critique as a starting place.

For all the reasons given above, I believe that the dangers of adult-child sex are significant enough to warrant a general prohibition. I realize that my position might be seen to validate an undesirable maternalism (or paternalism, but I will use the feminine form since there seems to be no neutral equivalent) that would reinforce the powerlessness of children. The concern here is that, if we do not allow for children's authentic consent to sex with adults, and always interpret children as not "truly" or "authentically" desiring to have sex with adults, perhaps we are silencing them once again, and restricting their desires. But we must disentangle a repudiation of sex between adults and children with a repudiation of children's sexuality. These have usually been linked. "Unnatural" sexual relations between children have often been theorized as the result of sexual relations with adults, and therefore the former were condemned as deviations caused by adult violation. Although this may be the case some of the time, it is clearly not the case that all sexual relations between children (even genital ones) are a deviation brought on by adults. Separating these issues will help to avoid an unnecessarily restrictive maternalism that would police and repress all sexual practices by children. I would argue that the latter would not be a true maternalism but rather, as Foucault suggests, a domination of children aligned with pleasure—the pleasure of observing their sexual actions and forcing their confessions—and the regulation of children as a population of docile, manipulable bodies. The intervention into children's own sexual behavior should be restricted to violent or coercive behavior or sexual relations between children from disparate ages, in which case a power differential exists analogous to the one between adults and children.

M(p)aternalism is a relationship between unequals, and so is often rejected by feminists and anticolonialists on the grounds that maternalistic support can never bring about or instantiate relations of equality or freedom. I agree with that analysis. But relations between adults and children can never achieve complete equality and freedom, and children require care from adults in order to survive and flourish. It is a self-serving illusion for adults to believe that we can completely avoid maternalistic relations toward children or renounce the responsibility that all adults have toward all children.

It might be objected that if we dismiss our ability to interpret accurately the linguistic utterances of children we will restrict their ability to have any input into our behavior toward them. I would agree that such a result is highly undesirable, and despite the arguments I made above, I would disagree with the view that our languages are so different that any communication is unreliable. And yet when the risks are exceedingly high, as in the case of sexual abuse given the depth and longevity of its traumatic aftereffects, and when the possible gains are almost inversely low, surely the best course of action is to hedge our bets and prevent the possibility of such aftereffects from occurring.

The problem of adult sexual relations with children is not a problem of the "violation of innocence." This is one of the most prevalent traditional reasons given, and it is linked to the notion that the rape of a virgin is somehow worse than the rape of women who are not virgins, so that the rape of prostitutes and of married women by their husbands is not accorded the seriousness of the rape of "innocents." Historically, the concern with sexual "innocents" was a result of the commodification of virgins: once raped, they stood to lose substantial market value as marriageable property. The rape of women already deflowered was therefore of less importance because it would not alter their market value.

The argument that adult child sexual relations are wrong because children are "innocent" is also mistaken for at least two reasons. First, it puts a presumption of value on the absence of sexual experience over its presence, such that "innocence" should be maintained as long as possible because it is inherently desirable. Such a presumption is surely false, and makes sense only when one has a negative orientation toward sexual experience generally, as for example, in Christian dogma. Moreover, the argument assumes, and mandates, that children are properly asexual. This is again patently false, and in that sense children are not innocent. Children have a variety of sexual feelings and some act on them in various ways. Therefore, the reason for opposing adult-child sex should not be the innocence of children. It is that logic which leads to the practice of asking rape victims about their sexual past, of taking the rape of sexually active persons less seriously, and of judging sexually active or knowledgeable children as "bad" and therefore necessarily complicit in their violation.

But to the extent that the concern with "innocence" includes a concern with those who are especially vulnerable, there is a kernel of truth here. Children are not innocent of sexuality, though their sexuality may significantly diverge from adult manifestations. But children are more vulnerable, whether or not they have acted out sexual feelings and desires. Children are still in the process of forming their sense of themselves, of sexuality, and of embodied relations with others. This process never stops completely, but it is more significant and dramatic during childhood, with more longlasting effects. Because children have less experience, they are more flexible and suggestive to mediations that would construct their subjectivities. It is easier to "season" a young girl and turn her into a prostitute than an older woman. Therefore, when children are raped and violated, it is likely that such an experience will more deeply and profoundly affect their sense of their self, their worth, their future possibilities, their relations with others, and their sexuality. This has nothing to do with their innocence of sexuality; it results from the fact that they are more actively and intensely engaged in self-creation and world-interpretation than adults, and that their developing account of themselves and their world is more open, fluid, and flexible, since it has enjoyed fewer repetitions and developed less into a practiced habit of belief.

Some might object to the line of reasoning presented here on the grounds that, if this argument stands that power differentials adversely affect the possibility of "authentic" consent, then a lot of adult-adult sex should not be engaged in either, such as student-teacher, husband-housewife, employer-employee, and so on. I would agree: all such sex is extremely dangerous, though we can note that in adult-adult situations in many cases, the subordinate adult will still have more options to fight back and get away than a child would.

Michael Alhonte has written an interesting essay, as an eighteen-year-old "boy" in a man-boy relationship who began his involvement with men at the age of thirteen, defending his legal right to man-boy love.[29] He argues instructively against an ageism that stereotypes both boys and men and works against perceiving individual differences. But his article spends most of its time criticizing problems in man-boy relationships. He talks about the problems of inequality, the "unpleasant unbalance" caused by finances, and says that boys in such relationships come to feel embarrassed and irritated by their own maturation processes, which diminish the source of their attractiveness to men. He points out that in most of these relationships the boy is expected to play a submissive role. And he offers a rather negative portrait of "the problem of objectification":

> Too many men adore boys as abstract sexual beings, but refuse (or are unable) to deal with them as people. If they *do* pretend to show interest in what a boy has to say after sex, it is usually in a patronizing, superior manner; often it is punctuated with degrading estimations of the boy's sexual value—as if this were the only level on which a boy can be valuable—perhaps intended as sincere compliments but more likely to be the only statements the man can honestly make, since he is not bothered in the slightest to get to know something about the boy. (158)

He also argues that a desire based solely on youth is damaging:

> one must never allow the desire for youthfulness to obstruct the avenues for growth and self-expression in a relationship. To identify the factor that

enchants a man with a boy as merely the boy's youth is to ageistically negate the whole range of positive traits that the boy has. (159)

He says that the result of such attractions based solely on youth is to keep the relationship from evolving as the boy matures and even to stagnate the boy's metamorphosis into an adult in order to retain the basis of desire. In the cases Alhonte discusses, the youth in the relationship is not a child and is hardly powerless. Such cases might seem to be best-case scenarios, least likely to inflict psychic damage on the youths involved. Perhaps the damage is small in some instances, but Alhonte's descriptions actually support many of my concerns.

I have tried to show that the problem with the "excess of significance" view is that it assumes a more primordial sexual experience below the discursive overlay of power/knowledges, and it assumes that at this deeper level sex is light, inconsequential, relatively trivial. But sexual practices, like codes of morality, comprise forms of subjectivation: that is, they are self-constituting. A normative account of sexual practices such as pedophilia could begin here, not with an attempt, like Rubin's, to disinvest pleasure from power (a hopeless project), but with an analysis of the modes of subjectivation produced by various configurations of pleasure, power, and discourse.

In the first blush of the second wave of feminism, there was a period in which it was very important to begin to envision the contours of a future nonsexist society, to create a new imaginary possibility for women. During this period, feminist theorists such as Andrea Dworkin, Shulamith Firestone, and Kate Millett envisioned a future utopia in which children would be empowered enough to choose who they lived with, what kind of lives they would lead, and to engage in sexual relations with each other as well as with adults and family members. These works were written from an impulse toward envisioning a better future for children. But it is not transformative to posit a future where children have sex with adults: this is our uninterrupted past and present. A truly transformative future would be one in which children could be, for the first time, free from the economy of adult sexual desire and adult sexual demands. Only this future will be truly new and unknown, and the sexuality of children that emerges from it, and that we indeed have no way to predict, will be determined then and only then by children themselves.

Notes

1. I thank Raja Halwani, Joy Rouse, Margaret Himley, Robert Praeger, Steven Seidman, Tom Wartenburg, Linda Nicholson, Laura Gray, and Ingeborg Majer O'Sickey for their helpful criticisms and comments on this paper.

2. Gayle Rubin, "Thinking Sex: Notes for a Radical Theory of the Politics of Sexuality," in *Pleasure and Danger: Exploring Female Sexuality,* ed. Carole S. Vance (Boston: Routledge and Kegan Paul, 1984), p. 279. [This article will be referred to hereinafter simply by page number.]

3. Foucault, *The History of Sexuality*, vol. 1, *An Introduction*, trans. Robert Hurley (New York: Pantheon, 1978), pp. 31–32.

4. The first title appeared in *Recherches* 37 (April 1979): 69–82; the second, in *Michel Foucault: Politics, Philosophy, Culture: Interviews and Other Writings, 1977–1984*, ed. Lawrence D. Kritzman, trans. Alan Sheridan et al. (New York: Routledge, 1988), pp. 271–85. Subsequent references will be to the second text, cited as *PPC*.

5. *PPC*, p. 278. Perhaps one of the working assumptions here is that discourses of sexuality must always or necessarily end up constituting figures of identity: for example, the "pedophile," the "homosexual." But consider the efforts of (some of the) safer-sex discourses to resist such identity-talk in favor of practices-talk; for example, "anal sex" rather than "the gay male."

6. Foucault, *An Introduction*, pp. 31–32.

7. Foucault refers to "precocious little girls" on page 40, "The Perverse Imagination."

8. Judith P. Butler, *Subjects of Desire: Hegelian Reflections in Twentieth-Century France* (New York: Columbia University Press, 1987), p. 218.

9. Ibid., p. 228 (emphases in original).

10. Here is an issue where I find her reading of Foucault implausible: she interprets the right-wing crusade as simply anti-sex, whereas Foucault would surely say, at the very least, that a more complicated relationship between desire and rightist discourses exists than one characterized by a flat negation.

11. See, for example the justifications of patriarchy used by Rousseau in Linda Bell, *Visions of Women* (Clifton, N.J.: Humana, 1983), esp. p. 196. Here he tells us, "the husband ought to be able to superintend his wife's conduct, because it is of importance to him to be assured that the children, whom he is obliged to acknowledge and maintain, belong to no one but himself."

12. Jeffrey Weeks, *Sexuality and Its Discontents: Meanings, Myths, and Modern Sexualities* (New York: Routledge, 1985), p. 228.

13. Ellen Bass and Louise Thornton, eds., *I Never Told Anyone: Writings by Women Survivors of Child Sexual Abuse* (New York: Harper and Row, 1983), pp. 30–31.

14. Eric Presland, "Whose Power? Whose Consent?" in *The Age Taboo: Gay Male Sexuality, Power, and Consent*, ed. Daniel Tsang (London and Boston: Gay Men's Press and Alyson Publications, 1981), p. 75.

15. Florence Rush, *The Best-Kept Secret: Sexual Abuse of Children* (New York: McGraw-Hill, 1980), p. 173.

16. Do adult women practice pedophilia and pederasty? Yes, certainly. To the same degree as adult men? It is doubtful. Jamie Gough suggests that the general denial of women's sexuality accounts for the fact that women are rarely considered capable of pedophilia. It could also be that women's sexuality is different or has developed differently from men's; it certainly has been treated differently by societies. See Gough, "Childhood Sexuality and Pedophilia," in *The Age Taboo: Gay Male Sexuality, Power, and Consent*, ed. Daniel Tsang (London and Boston: Gay Men's Press and Alyson Publications, 1981), p. 67.

17. See Tom Reeves, "Loving Boys," in *The Age Taboo: Gay Male Sexuality, Power, and Consent*, pp. 25–37.

18. Pat Califia, "Man/Boy Love and the Lesbian/Gay Movement," in *The Age Taboo: Gay Male Sexuality, Power, and Consent*, p. 138.

19. An impressive exception is Steven Seidman's *Embattled Eros: Sexual Politics and Ethics in Contemporary America* (New York: Routledge, 1992).

20. Stephen D. Grubman-Black, *Broken Boy/Mending Men Recovery from Childhood Sexual Abuse* (Blue Ridge Summit, Pa.: Tab Books, 1990), p. 25.

21. Bass and Thornton, *I Never Told Anyone*, pp. 180–81.

22. Grubman-Black, *Broken Boys/Mending Men*, p. 92.

23. Gough, "Childhood Sexuality and Pedophilia," pp. 65–71.

24. I make this case for classes, not for every individual. Consider the child of a slaveowning plantation master vis-à-vis an adult slave. Even though power in this case may reside more with the child, she or he is still developmentally unequal.

25. Grubman-Black, *Broken Boys/Mending Men*, pp. 15–16.

26. See Grubman-Black, *Broken Boys/Mending Men*.

27. NAMBLA, "The Case for Abolishing the Age of Consent Laws," in *The Age Taboo: Gay Male Sexuality, Power, and Consent*, esp. p. 95.

28. Grubman-Black, *Broken Boys/Mending Men*, p. 90.

29. Michael Alhonte, "Confronting Ageism," in *The Age Taboo: Gay Male Sexuality, Power, and Consent*, pp. 156–60.

PART THREE

DESIRE, PORNOGRAPHY, and RAPE

35

Patriarchal Sex

Robert Jensen

Patriarchal sex (example 1): Four male undergraduates at Cornell University post on the Internet the "Top 75 reasons why women (bitches) should not have freedom of speech." Reason #20: "This is my dick. I'm gonna fuck you. No more stupid questions."[1]

Patriarchal sex (example 2): Rhonda was separated from her husband but was on generally friendly terms with him. One night he entered her home. For the next seven hours, he raped her. "It was like something just snapped in him. He grabbed me and said, "We gonna have sex, I need to fuck.'"[2]

I begin with a working definition of patriarchal sex: Sex is fucking.[3] In patriarchy, there is an imperative to fuck—in rape and in "normal" sex, with strangers and girlfriends and wives and estranged wives and children. What matters in patriarchal sex is the male need to fuck. When that need presents itself, sex occurs.

From that, a working definition of what it means to be a man in this culture: A man is a male human who fucks.[4]

What I'm Trying to Do and What I'm Not Trying to Do

In this essay I want to analyze patriarchal sex and theorize about strategies for moving away from it. In simple terms, I want to think about how we males might stop fucking and stop being men.

First published in the *International Journal of Sociology and Social Policy* 17, nos. 1–2 (1987). Reprinted with the permission of the publisher.

I draw on the work of radical feminist theorists and activists, my research on pornography and sexuality, and my experience as a man in U.S. culture in the last half of the twentieth century. I move without apology between personal narrative and reflection, and more formal scholarly writing. I reject the conventional academic obsession with splitting off mind and body, reason and emotion, objective and subjective, scholarship and activism. One of the ways I know about the world is by living in it, and the knowledge I have gained has led me to a political position that makes certain actions on my part morally necessary. Decades of feminist and other critical work more than adequately justify this kind of engaged scholarship.[5]

What follows is part of my longterm project of trying to make sense of a system into which I was born, a system that privileges certain people with certain attributes (e.g., white, male, heterosexual, educated—all of which I have or have had at one point in my life) and works to maintain the concentration of power in the hands of a relatively small group of people.

This essay is not a "men's studies" or "gender studies" project. It is a feminist-inspired project.[6] I am a man working within feminist theory to try to understand the nature of oppression, specifically in this essay the nature of gender oppression and the role of sexuality in that oppression. My goal is to be a traitor to my gender, as well as to my race and my class. I routinely fail at this goal, though sometimes I get glimpses of what success looks like. I am fortunate to have the support of many feminist women[7] and a few like-minded male colleagues.[8] Integral to that support is their willingness to hold me accountable for my actions and words; the critique is a key part of the support.

Also, this essay is not an attempt to tell women what they should think or how they should behave. I am trying to talk primarily to other men about my struggle and what I have learned from it. I do this work both out of a yearning for justice for those oppressed in patriarchy (women, particularly lesbians, children, and to some extent gay men) and out of self-interest (the desire to live a more fulfilling life in a more just, humane, and compassionate world). I work both out of hope for the future and out of fear.

The Fear

"What's your problem—are you afraid of sex?"

That question has been posed to me often as I have been involved in anti-pornography work. For a long time, my answer was no, of course not. Me, afraid? I'm no prude.

I am not a prude, but I have come to realize that I am very much afraid of sex. I am afraid of sex as sex is defined by the dominant culture, practiced all around me, and projected onto magazine pages, billboards, and movie screens.

I am afraid of sex because I am afraid of domination, cruelty, violence, and death. I am afraid of sex became sex has hurt me and hurt lots of people I know, and because I have hurt others with sex in the past. I know that there are people out there who have been hurt by sex in ways that are beyond my words, who have experienced a depth of pain that I will never fully understand. And I know there are people who are dead because of sex.

Yes, I am afraid of sex. How could I not be?[9]

A common response from people when I say things like that is, "You're nuts." Sometimes, when I'm feeling shaky, a voice in the back of my head asks, "Am I nuts?"

I have been doing research and writing on pornography and sexuality for about eight years.[10] In the past few years, I have been trying to figure out how to talk to people who think I am crazy and how to deal with my own fear that they may be right. I have been trying to understand why the attack on the feminist critique of patriarchal sex has been so strong and so successful, and how it connects to the backlash against feminist work on sexual violence.

Here's one tentative explanation: It is too scary to be afraid of sex. To go too far down the road with the radical critique of sexuality means, inevitably, acknowledging a fear of patriarchal sex. And if all the sex around us is patriarchal, then we are going to live daily with that fear. And if patriarchal sex seems to be so overwhelmingly dominant that it sometimes is difficult to believe that any other sex is possible, then maybe we are always going to be afraid. Maybe it's easier to not be afraid, or at least to repress the fear. Maybe that's the only way to survive.

But maybe not. Maybe being afraid of sex is the first step toward something new. Maybe things that seem impossible now will be possible someday. Or maybe we will find that we won't need what we thought we needed.[11] Maybe being afraid is the first step out of the fear and into something else that we cannot yet name.

Expanding the Working Definition of Patriarchal Sex

I was born in 1958 in a small city in the upper Midwest to white parents who, after some years of struggle, settled into the middle class. I went to a Protestant church and public school. I had friends, mostly other boys. We talked about sex and we begged, borrowed, and stole pornography. I watched a lot of television and went to a lot of movies. I had a G. I. Joe doll and toy guns. I played sports. I was a quirky kid in some respects, physically smaller than most and a bit of an egghead from an early age. Maybe my family was a little more emotionally abusive than most, but maybe not. In many regards, I grew up "normal." And I got a normal education in sex.

Here is the curriculum for sex education for a normal American boy: Fuck women.

Here is the sexual grammar lesson I received. "Man fucks women; subject verb object."[12]

The specifics varied depending on the instructor.

Some people said, "Fuck as many women as often as you can for as long as you can get away with it." Others said, "Fuck a lot of women until you get tired of it, and then find one to marry and just fuck her." And some said, "Don't fuck any women until you find one to marry, and then fuck her for the rest of your life and never fuck anyone else."

Some said, "Women are special; put them on a pedestal before and after you fuck them." Others said, "Women are shit; do what you have to do to fuck them, and then get away from them."

Most said, "Only fuck women." A few said, "Fuck other men if you want to."

The basic concepts were clear: Sex is fucking. Fucking is penetration. The things you do before you penetrate are just warm-up exercises. If you don't penetrate, you haven't fucked, and if you haven't fucked, you haven't had sex. Frye defines this kind of heterosexual, and heterosexist, intercourse as, "male-dominant-female-subordinate-copulation-whose-completion-and-purpose-is-the-male's-ejaculation."[13] That is sex in patriarchy.

All the teachers (parents, friends, ministers, celebrities, pornographers, movie directors, etc.) tend to agree on the one primary rule about sex in patriarchy: You gotta get it. You have to fuck something at some point in your life. If you don't get it, there's something wrong with you. You aren't normal. You aren't really alive. You certainly aren't a man.

When I was a kid, I'm not sure I really wanted to fuck anyone. But eventually I figured out that if didn't learn to do it, I was going to be an outcast. So I learned, though later than most of my peers.

My first sex was with pornography. I was about six years old the first time I saw it. For the next two decades, it was part of my life on an irregular basis. I had sex with women in person, and I had sex with women in magazines and movies (masturbating to pornography is a way of having sex, of sexually using the women in it). As far as I can tell from research and conversations with men, I had a fairly typical sex life. I learned to like being in control. That was pare of the appeal of sex with pornography: I had control over when I used it, and I was in control of the women in it.[14] That was part of the appeal of sex with women: I was the man, and I was in control because men "naturally" take control of sex. Once the details of access with a particular woman were negotiated, I was in control. Patriarchal sex practices vary from person to person, from attempts at more egalitarian interaction to the sadomasochistic. My preferred practices, on the surface, leaned more toward the egalitarian, but when I think about my sexual history I can connect every practice to a need for control, either of the woman or of the woman's pleasure.

When I started to realize that, I realized I was in trouble. When I realized that most everyone around me was in trouble, I started to get scared. When I got real scared, I stopped having patriarchal sex. That meant I stopped having sex with other people, including the people in pornography. At first, I didn't do this consciously. I just found it more and more difficult to have sex. At some point, I consciously made a decision to quit. As I began to understand more about how deeply I had been trained in the rules of patriarchal sex, it became more clear that I would have to stop participating in that system. I would have to stop fucking. I could no longer pretend that I was "working it out" by trying to put into practice new ideas about sex. Patriarchal sex was too deeply rooted in my body and my psyche. Before I could reconstruct my sexuality, I needed time to deconstruct, free of the pressure to have sex.

The Radical Feminist Critique

By the time I came to understand that I wanted, and needed, to stop having patriarchal sex, I had a framework within which to understand what was happening to me. Radical feminist critiques of pornography and patriarchal sex gave me a vocabulary, a way to make coherent in words what was happening in my body and mind. That made it possible though by no means easy, to begin the process. Many feminist activists and theorists have contributed to this critique.[15] Here's my summary:

Men in contemporary American culture (I make no claim to cross-cultural or historical critique; I am writing about the world in which I live) are trained through a variety of cultural institutions to view sex as the acquisition of pleasure by the taking of women. Sex is a sphere in which men (by this I don't mean that every man believes this, but that many men believe this is true for all men) believe themselves to be naturally dominant and women naturally passive. Women are objectified and women's sexuality is commodified. Sex is sexy because men are dominant and women are subordinate; power is eroticized. In certain limited situations, those roles can be reversed (men can play at being sexually subordinate and women dominant), so long as power remains sexualized and power relations outside the bedroom are unchanged.

Summed up by Andrea Dworkin:

> The normal fuck by a normal man is taken to be an act of invasion and ownership undertaken in a mode of predation; colonializing, forceful (manly) or nearly violent; the sexual that by its nature makes her his.[16]

One of the key sites in which these sexual values are reflected, reinforced, and normalized is pornography. Domination and subordination are sexualized, sometimes in explicit representations of rape and violence against women, but always in the objectification and commodification of women and their sexuality.[17] This results in several kinds of harms to women and children: (1) the harm caused in the production of pornography; (2) the harm in having pornography forced on them; (3) the harm in being sexually assaulted by men who use pornography and (4) the harm in living in a culture which pornography reinforces and sexualizes women's subordinate status.

In a world in which men hold most of the social, economic, and political power, the result of the patriarchal sexual system is widespread violence, sexualized violence, and violence-by-sex against women and children. This includes physical assault, emotional abuse, and rape by family members and acquaintances as well as strangers. Along with the experience of violence, women and children live with the knowledge that they are always targets.

Attention to the meaning of the central male slang term for sexual intercourse—"fuck"—is instructive. To fuck a woman is to have sex with her. To fuck someone in another context ("he really fucked me over on that deal") means to hurt or cheat a person. And when hurled as a simple insult ("fuck you") the intent is denigration and the remark is often prelude to violence or the threat of violence. Sex in patriarchy is fucking. That we live in a world in which people continue to use the same word for sex and violence, and then resist the notion that sex is routinely violent and claim to be outraged when becomes overtly violent, is testament to the power of patriarchy. In this society, sex and violence are fused to the point of being indistinguishable. Yet to say this out loud is to risk being labeled crazy: "What's wrong with you—are you afraid of sex? Are you nuts?"

The Wrong Ways Out of This Problem

1. All women and most men I've met are against rape. That is, they are against those acts the law defines as rape. But most aren't against fucking, because fucking is sex and how can you be against sex, which is seen as natural? This view is summed up in the phrase "Rape is a crime of violence, not of sex." But rape is a crime of sex; to de-sex rape is to turn away from the possibility of understanding rape. This is not to say that men don't seek power over women through rape and that the power isn't expressed violently; it is to acknowledge that men seek power over women through sex of all kinds, including rape.

I think people, men and women, want to believe that rape is violence-not-sex because to acknowledge that rape is sex requires that we ask how it is that so many men can decide that rape is an acceptable way to get sex. Rape is not the result of the aberrant behavior of a limited number of pathological men, but is "normal" within the logic of the system. When sex is about power and control, and men are socially, and typically physically, more powerful than women and children, then sexual violence is the inevitable outcome. As Dworkin argues, "Rape is no excess, no aberration, no accident, no mistake—it embodies sexuality as the culture defines it."[18]

This does not mean that every man is a rapist in legal terms. It means that we live in a society in which men, both legally designated rapists and non-rapists, are raised with rapist ethics.[19] Raping is a particularly brutal kind of fucking, but the difference between "deviant" rape and the "normal" fuck is often difficult to see.[20] Timothy Beneke, looking at how metaphors frame sex as an expression of male power and conquest, concludes:

> [E]very man who grows up in America and learns American English learns all too much to think like a rapist, to structure his experience of women and sex in terms of status, hostility, control, and dominance.[21]

So, the conventional view is that rape can't be about sex and has to be about violence, because if it's about sex then each one of us has to ask how deeply into our bodies the norms of patriarchal sex have settled. Men have to ask about how sexy dominance is to them, and women have to ask how sexy submission is to them. And if we think too long about that, we face the question of why we're still having patriarchal sex. And if we face that question, we may have to consider the possibility of stopping. And if we aren't having sex, then we have to face the dominant culture's assumption that we aren't really alive because we aren't having sex.

2. Women aren't victims, some say, and radical feminism has tried to turn women into victims by focusing on the harms of patriarchal sex.[22] This is a deceptively appealing rhetorical move. When members of one class (women) identify a way that members of another class (men) routinely hurt them, those who are hurt are told they are responsible for the injury because they identified it. If women would stop talking about these injuries, the logic seems to be, then the injuries would stop. This strategy seems popular with some women and lots of men lately. I understand why men take this stance; it relieves them of any obligation to evaluate their own behavior and be responsible. And I understand why women don't want to see themselves as always at risk of men's violence and sexual aggression. But saying you aren't at risk because you don't want to be at risk doesn't take the risk away.

What does the word "victim" mean? Dworkin writes:

> It's a true word. If you were raped, you were victimized. You damned well were. You were a victim. It doesn't mean that you are a victim in the metaphysical sense, in your state of being, as an intrinsic part of your essence and existence. It means somebody hurt you. They injured you. . . . And if it happens to you systematically because you are born a woman, it means that you live in a political system that uses pain and humiliation to control and to hurt you.[23]

Understanding one's victimization is not the same as playing the victim. Acknowledging that women often are victimized is not an admission of weaknesses or a retreat from responsibility. Instead, it makes possible organized and sustained resistance to the power that causes the injuries. By clearly identifying the victimizers (most always men) and the system within which the injury is ignored or trivialized (patriarchy), political change becomes possible.

We live in a world in which some people exercise their power in a way that hurts others. It has become popular to pretend the injuries are the product of the overactive imaginations of whiners. White people routinely tell nonwhite people that racism is not a big problem and that if the nonwhites would stop complaining, all would be fine. Rich people tell poor and working people that there is no such thing as class in the United States and that if we all would just work hard together everything would be fine. Straight people tell lesbian and gay people that if they would just stop making such a public nuisance to themselves everyone would leave them alone and things would be fine. But things aren't fine. We live in racism. Poor and working people are being crushed by a cruel economic system. Heterosexism oppresses lesbians and gays. And men keep fucking women.

Why Try?

If patriarchy is this dominant and patriarchal sex this colonizing, one might ask what hope there is in resistance. Would it not make more sense to go along and get along?

No system, no matter how overwhelming and oppressive, is beyond challenge. Borrowing a metaphor from Naomi Scheman, we can think of patriarchy as being like concrete in the city. It covers almost everything. It is heavy and seemingly unmovable, and it paves the world. But the daily wear and tear produces cracks, and in those cracks, plants grow—weeds, grass, sometimes a flower. Living things have no business growing up out of concrete, but they do. They resist the totality of the concrete.

No system of power can obliterate all resistance. All systems yield space in which things can grow. I have seen resistance to patriarchal sex grow, even flourish, in the cracks. I have friends, the people who helped me sort these things out and move forward, who continue to survive and grow in resistance to patriarchal sex. In my life I have met few people interested in this project of resistance, but it doesn't take many people for me to feel as if resistance is worthwhile. But I also seek more than just a few friends who are scattered around the country. I would like to be part of an epistemic community in which these questions can be explored.

Epistemic Communities

What kind of investigation is required for confronting patriarchal sex? I am not after THE solution to the problem. At times, I am not entirely sure about the questions. Lorraine Code suggests that when epistemology is construed as a quest for understanding, the appropriate question becomes not "What can I know?" but "What sort(s) of discourse does the situation really call for?"[24] It is from conversation and the sharing of richly detailed narratives that understanding, not definitive answers, can begin to emerge.

While we are all individually accountable for our actions, the effort to understand sexuality is not solely an individual task; we have a responsibility to create collectively the tools for this investigation. As Code suggests:

> Thinking individuals have a responsibility to monitor and watch over shifts in, changes in, and efforts to preserve good intellectual practice. . . . In principle, everyone is responsible, to the of his or her ability, for the quality of cognitive practice in a community.[25]

Such community can be difficult to form and maintain. Pressures from the dominant ideology, combined with the routine human failings, can make the task seem overwhelming. My experience is that there are different levels of community at which different levels of conversation can happen. I have done most of this work in a fairly small group that includes a core of five to ten trusted friends, colleagues, and students (fellow students when I was in graduate school, and on rare occasions now, students whom I meet as a professor). Beyond that, I sometimes meet others with similar interests and convictions with whom I have important, though perhaps not ongoing, conversations. There is no recipe for how these conversations develop and no criteria for whom I connect with. The conversations cross lines of, among other things, gender, race, age, and sexual orientation, though not without great effort and occasional stress.

But one thing that is constant for me in these conversations is an understanding—sometimes stated but often simply understood—that we won't have sex, now or in the foreseeable future. These kinds of conversations can involve strong emotions and physical responses, and it is easy to want to channel that energy into sex. Also, there are ways in which talking-about-sex can be a type of having-sex. It takes constant monitoring to reject patriarchy's rule and not engage in sex. But I believe it is essential to resist the imperative to have sex because we do not always learn more about our desire by acting on it. I believe that having sex and talking-having sex in my core epistemic community would undermine progress. It would erode trust, not just between the people involved in the sex but in the whole community, and would make it difficult, if not impossible, for the conversation to continue.[26] Such activity suggests that no matter how much one tries to redefine sexuality or talks about change, in the end we're all just interested in fucking each other.

Beyond those small communities in which we are likely to feel most safe in searching to understand sexuality, important conversations can, and must, go on in a larger context. This essay is one attempt to create an epistemic community; implicit (and now explicit) is an invitation for others to engage me in conversation. My search for community at this level happens at conferences, in the classroom, in anti-pornography and anti-rape public presentations, and in conversations with a variety of people I meet. Most often, I am sharing things I have learned in my core community with others and asking for feedback. These conversations are unpredictable but always, in some sense, productive for me.[27]

The Work of Women and Men

In her discussion of epistemic responsibility, Code asserts that "knowing well" is of considerable moral significance.[28] On matters of sexuality, knowing well requires attention not just to what our desires are but to where those desires come from. To simply *know*, "This is what arouses me," without attempting to understand *why* it does is epistemically irresponsible. Code reminds us that it can be easier "to believe that a favorite theory is true and to suppress nagging doubts than to pursue the implications of those doubts and risk having to modify the theory."[29] Being epistemically responsible requires that we investigate those nagging doubts.

In this and other work, I tend to focus on the objectification, aggression, and violence that is central to the dominant construction of male sexuality in this culture. I believe this focus is proper, especially because I am a man and I work from my experience as a man. However, these questions about the construction of our sexuality are as crucial for women as men.[30] This does not mean I claim the right to tell women what their sexuality should look like. It means that we all must acknowledge that, to varying degrees, our lives have been shaped by patriarchy and men's values, and that we must examine the effects.

An example: While having sex, a man finds it sexy to put a woman's arms behind her head and hold them down at the wrists, rendering her fairly immobile and intensifying the experience of intercourse for him. The man should consider: How did he come to develop this practice? What is it about rendering a woman immobile that feels sexy? Why does having control over a woman in such a manner intensify his orgasm? All of those questions are central to epistemic responsibility; to act morally, he needs to know. But what if the woman in that scenario also finds the practice exciting? What if the sensation of being unable to move her arms while having intercourse intensifies her sexual response? What is it about being immobile that feels sexy?

I believe women have the same epistemic responsibility as men. However, in a society where women are often blamed for being in some way responsible for the injuries that men inflict on them, such a call for epistemic responsibility can appear to be asking women to blame themselves for the ways in which they may have internalized patriarchy's values. But this is not about blame or guilt; it is about the search for understanding, for freedom. Just as pornography teaches men to rape, romance novels teach women to be rape victims. Just as fathers often instill rapist values in sons, mothers often teach daughters how to submit to the boys. I believe there are compelling moral and political arguments for men to change. It also seems clear that to survive, women must change.

Hetero and Homo

By the way, I am gay. I lived most of my thirty-eight years as a heterosexual. I was once married, and I have a son. I am out, although what exactly that means for me—beyond a public rejection of heterosexuality and its institutions—is unclear at the moment. But gay-or-straight doesn't much matter. The question of resistance to patriarchal sex is just as important in the gay male world as it is for straight men. As far as I can tell, the majority of gay men fuck in about the same way as straight men do. We all received pretty much the same training. In fact, the term "fucking" is thrown around in many gay male conversations with frequency and ease, in a celebratory way. Fucking is taken to be the thing that gay men do; some might even argue that if you aren't fucking, you aren't gay.

If that's the case, then I'm not gay. And I'm not straight. I'm trying to live in the cracks in the concrete.

Imagining Not-Sex

In early versions of this essay, I wrote about the task of imagining what a new kind of sex, a nonpatriarchal sex, might look like. I suggested that one of the main problems in this project of resistance is that we lack a language in which to imagine what that sex might be. I felt the need to imagine things beyond our experience, in words that we have yet to find.

I still believe that we lack the vocabulary to talk about this and that creative imagination is at the center of this project. But I no longer think that imagining a new kind of sex is crucial, or even helpful, at this point. I fear that a rush to fill the void left when one starts to disengage from patriarchal sex can ultimately keep us from moving forward; we risk trying to reconstruct before we have adequately deconstructed, before we understand enough about how the norms of patriarchal sex live in our bodies. Obviously, this is not like the flushing of a system to get the toxins out, not a mechanical task that has a dear beginning and end. I expect to struggle for the rest of my life to understand how patriarchy has shaped my identity and sexuality. If I waited for the magic moment of pure clarity to begin a reconstruction project, I would be waiting forever. But I want to guard against beginning the reconstruction process prematurely.

There is an important lesson in my rush to want to fill the void with new imagined conceptions of nonpatriarchal sex. Although I claimed to have been willing to stop having sex for some period of time, my first instinct was to rush toward a reconstruction. That is, in trying to resist the imperative to have sex, I gave in to the imperative to create a new kind of sex so that I could have it. I told myself that because we are humans with bodies and needs for intimacy, that the task of imagining something new was crucial. I do have a body, and I need love and intimacy. But the question remains: Would any sex I could imagine at this moment really be nonpatriarchal? Have I disentangled myself from patriarchy enough to even begin that task?

The answer for me is clearly no, that I am not in a good position to imagine something new. That is my judgment about myself, and I don't pretend to have the answer for others. I come to this moment with a specific history that shapes what is possible for me. I do not know what is possible for others, and I expect that many men who share the values I describe decide to take other paths toward a similar goal. My point is not to persuade everyone that not-sex is their only option, but to suggest that it is a relevant question for everyone—that it is an option and that there is a compelling argument to be made for that choice. If we want to leave behind patriarchal sex, not only must we confront the likelihood that we might need to stop having sex for some period of time, but we must be willing to accept that we may not have any idea of what will take the place of patriarchal sex for quite some time. In other words, we have to be willing to live a life without sex for the sake of justice, for the sake of ourselves.

So, for the time being, I want to imagine not-sex. I reject sex in the hope that someday, maybe in my lifetime and maybe not, I can find a way to be physically intimate outside of patriarchy. Maybe we will call it sex, maybe not. At this point, it's not a terribly important question for me.

This move to embrace not-sex may seem a drastic, or even silly, rhetorical move. But I think the gravity of the situation justifies the deployment of new language. As Susan Cole puts it:

> We have a long way to go before we uncover the full extent of the damage. We may not see the full repair in our lifetimes and it may not be possible to chart the entire course for change.[31]

I no longer trust myself to chart the course for change, to refashion sex into something I can trust. So, I seek not-sex, something different than what "sex" means in the dominant culture. I want intimacy, trust, and respect from other people, and I hope that it is possible for those things to be expressed physically. But I don't want sex.[32]

To say that I don't want sex is not to deny my sexuality nor cut myself off from my erotic power, as Audre Lorde uses that term.[33] Lorde talks about the way in which women's erotic power is falsely cordoned off in the bedroom, made into "plasticized sensation," and confused with the pornographic.[34] For Lorde, the erotic is a life-force, a creative energy:

those physical, emotional, and psychic expressions of what is deepest and strongest and richest within each of us, being shared: the passions of love, in its deepest meanings.[35]

Lorde writes about expressing her erotic power in some ways that the culture does not define as sexual and others that the culture might call sexual; she writes of the erotic power flowing both in the act of writing a good poem and in "moving into sunlight against the body of a woman I love." My expression of the erotic at this point my life need not include such movement against the body of another. What is crucial is not channeling my erotic energy into sex, but finding other ways to feel that power. Lorde writes:

Recognizing the power of the erotic within our lives can give us the energy to pursue genuine change within our world, rather than merely settling for a shift of characters in the same weary drama.[36]

To be more specific, what does it mean to say that in my intimate (broadly defined) relationships I want to tap my erotic power while practicing not-sex? Does it mean a ban on touch that produces an erection for me? A ban on touch of another person's body in areas that are typically sexualized (genitals, breasts, buttocks)? Is there any way to achieve not-sex intimacy that involves touch?

For me, not-sex is intimacy that resists or transcends oppression. In practice, that has meant different things with different people, depending on my relationship with them and the level of trust. For example, one female friend and I hug frequently, and I feel as if that touch is not-sex and a loving intimacy. A gay male friend and I tend to hug when we greet and say goodbye, and each of us knows that if the other needed emotionally supportive not-sex physical contact we would provide it. But we are not routinely physical out of a commitment to not-sex. In both relationships, there is an erotic element; in neither case is it made sexual.

Masturbation is a more difficult issue for me in thinking through not-sex. I sometimes do it, though I am aware that the fantasies that fuel that masturbation are almost exclusively scripted by patriarchy. There is a difference between self-touch that is motivated by self-love, and self-touch that is rooted in those scripts. My struggle with this issue (not to be confused with adolescent guilt over masturbation) remains unresolved, and is one reminder that perhaps I am further from imagining a nonpatriarchal sex than I once thought.

Jim Koplin once said to me that it is at the moment when a man can no longer achieve an erection—when all the old ways of sparking sexual pleasure have failed—that something new is possible. That moment, he said, may be the most creative point in our lives. "Impotence" becomes not a failure or a problem, but the point from which something new becomes possible. In this sense, I strive for impotency; that may be the point at which I am doing something more than shuffling characters in "the same weary drama."

Heat and Light

As I have said, I am not interested in writing a recipe book for nonpatriarchal sex. I do not want to imagine new practices or create new rules for sex at this point in my life. But is there anything one can say about a new path, about where not-sex might lead me?

There is a cliché that when an argument is of little value, it produces "more heat than light." One of the ways this culture talks about sex is in terms of heat: She's hot, he's hot, we had hot sex. Sex is bump-and-grind; the friction produces the heat, and the heat makes the sex good. Fucking produces heat. Fucking is hot.

But what if our embodied connections could be less about heat and more about light? What if instead of desperately seeking hot sex, we searched for a way to produce light when we touch? What if such touch were about finding a way to create light between people so that we could see ourselves and each other better? If the goal is knowing ourselves and other like that, then what we need is not heat but light to illuminate the path. How do we touch and talk to each other to shine that light? I'm not sure. There are lots of ways to produce light in the world, and some are better than others. Light that draws its power from rechargeable solar cells for example, is better than light that draws on throwaway batteries. Likewise, there will be lots of ways to imagine nonpatriarchal sex. Some will be better than others, depending on the values on which they are based. The task ahead is not just imagining something new, but being alert to how things that seem new can be rooted in old ideas.

Conclusion

A possible response to this from other men (and women): "Not-sex. Striving for impotency. Are you crazy?"

Sometimes I wonder. But I don't think I am crazy. I feel as if I may be going sane.

Notes

1. A copy of the message was posted on several Internet discussion lists and widely circulated, and criticized, in November 1995.

2. Raquel Kennedy Bergen, "Surviving Wife Rape: How Women Define and Cope with the Violence," *Violence against Women* 1, no. 2 (1995):125.

3. I don't use the word "fuck" without hesitation and concern. The word carries with it incredible violence, and I realize that it can feel assaultive to some people, especially women. But in this case I believe that it is the word that most accurately represents what I am trying describe.

4. My focus will remain on heterosexual men and their sex with women, though much of what I will say here has relevance for gay men. More on that later.

5. E.g., Lorraine Code, *What Can She Know?* (Ithaca, N.Y.: Cornell University Press, 1991), and Camilla Stivers, "Reflections on the Role of Personal Narrative in Social Science," *Signs* 18, no. 2 (1992): 408–25.

6. See also Robert Jensen, "Men's Lives and Feminist Theory," *Race, Gender and Class* 2, no. 2 (1995): 111–25.

7. Thanks specifically to Elvia Arriola, Rebecca Bennett, Donna McNamara, Nancy Potter, and Naomi Scheman for their roles in helping me understand these issues.

8. Thanks to Jim Koplin, a friend, intellectual partner, and colleague in the anti-pornography movement. Much of what I write here was first spoken by Jim and by me in conversation. I can no longer trace the origin of some of the ideas; many are as much Jim's as mine. His affection, support, and wisdom inform this essay.

9. There is another kind of fear that I believe most, if not all, men live with: the fear of not meeting the imagined standard of masculinity, of never being a skilled enough sexual performer to be a "real" man—the stud, the man in total control. That fear is real, as is the alienation from self and partner that results. However, the fear I am describing here is a deeper fear, a realization of how thoroughly sexuality in this culture eroticizes domination and subordination. More on that later.

10. Robert Jensen, "Knowing Pornography," *Violence against Women* 2, no. 1 (1996): 82–102, "Pornographic Lives," *Violence against Women* 1, no. 1 (1995): 32–54, "Pornographic Novels and the Ideology of Male Supremacy," *Howard Journal of Communications* 5, nos. 1–2 (1994): 92–107, and "Pornography and the Limits of Experimental Research," in Gail Dines and Jean M. Humez, eds., *Gender, Race and Class in Media: A Text-Reader* (Thousand Oaks, Calif.: Sage, 1994), pp. 298–306.

11. This has proved to be the case in other parts of my life. I live without a car, a television, or meat. At earlier times in my life, I would have thought that impossible. Now I find my life immeasurably enriched by the absence of those things.

12. Catherine A. MacKinnon, *Toward a Feminist Theory of the State* (Cambridge, Mass.: Harvard University Press, 1989), p. 124.

13. Marilyn Frye, *Willful Virgin* (Freedom, Calif.: Crossing Press, 1992), p. 113.

14. Jensen, "Knowing Pornography."

15. Susan Cole, *Pornography and the Sex Crisis* (Toronto: Amanita, 1989); Andrea Dworkin, *Pornography: Men Possessing Women* (New York: Perigee, 1981), *Intercourse* (New York: Free Press, 1987), and *Letters from a War Zone* (London: Secker and Warburg, 1988); Sheila Jeffreys, *Anticlimax: A Feminist Perspective on the Sexual Revolution* (New York: New York University Press, 1990); Catherine MacKinnon, *Feminism Unmodified: Discourses on Life and Law* (Cambridge, Mass.: Harvard University Press, 1987), and *Toward A Feminist Theory of the State*; Diane E. H. Russell, ed., *Making Violence Sexy: Feminist Views on Pornography* (New York: Teachers College Press, 1993).

16. Dworkin, *Intercourse*, p. 63.

17. Dworkin, *Pornography: Men Possessing Women* and *Letters from a War Zone*; Mac-

Kinnon, *Feminism Unmodified*; Catharine MacKinnon, *Only Words* (Cambridge, Mass.: Harvard University Press, 1993).

18. Andrea Dworkin, *Our Blood* (New York: Harper & Row, 1976) p. 46.

19. John Stoltenberg, *Refusing to Be a Man: Essays on Sexual Justice* (Portland, Ore.: Brettenbush Books, 1989).

20. MacKinnon, *Toward a Feminist Theory of the State*.

21. Timothy Beneke, *Men on Rape* (New York: St. Martin's Press, 1982), p. 16.

22. One popular female writer argues that such "victim feminism" needs to be replaced with "power feminism" (Naomi Wolf, *Fire with Fire: The New Female Power and How It Will Change the 21st Century* [New York: Random House, 1993]). Another claims that radical feminists, or "gender feminists," have hijacked the women's movement and betrayed the real interests of women (Christina Hoff Sommers, *Who Stole Feminism? How Women Have Betrayed Women* [New York: Simon and Schuster, 1994]).

23. Andrea Dworkin, "Women-Hating Right and Left," in *The Sexual Liberals and the Attack on Feminism* (New York: Pergamon Press, 1990), pp. 38–39.

24. Lorraine Code, *Epistemic Responsibility* (Hanover, N.H.: University Press of New England, 1987), p. 165.

25. Ibid., p. 245.

26. This is especially true when the sex happens across differences in status that reflect potential power imbalances, such as a large age gap, significant wealth or class gaps, and gender. Most devastating, I believe, is sexual contact between people in institutionalized roles of unequal power, such as student/teacher, client/therapist, parishioner/clergy, etc. I believe that sexual activity in such situations is always wrong.

27. I don't want to appear naive about this wider community. As troubling and divisive as these investigations can be in communities committed to feminism and liberatory politics, they can be dangerous in mainstream and reactionary political circles, where people may want to ignore or undermine a feminist analysis. My goal, and the goal of the feminists whose work informs my analysis, is the exploration and celebration of diversity, but the goal of those to the right is often the suppression of diversity. These political realities are important to consider. The kind of open discussion that is crucial to expanding our understanding may be safe in some contexts but not in others, and more safe for some than others. But it is important that the conversation continue.

28. Code, *Epistemic Responsibility*.

29. Ibid., p. 59. This is not to say that every individual in every situation need engage in discussions about these matters. People whose sexuality is under attack by the established social structure—lesbians gay men and, in some sense, many heterosexual women—might feel that social conditions make it unsafe to engage in such open discussion. For example, a lesbian high school teacher in a small town may not be able to be part of a discussion about sexual practices in that community. Still, the idea of epistemic responsibility does suggest we should make whatever efforts are possible to pursue knowledge about sexuality and its social construction.

30. Thanks to Rebecca Bennett for reminding me of the importance of discussing this.

31. Cole, *Pornography and the Sex Crisis*, p. 132.

32. In response to a draft of this essay, Jim Koplin suggested that labeling this "not-sex" is reactive rather than inventive and offered alternative terms such as "body-play," "body-connection," or "creative touch." I understand his point, but I think that at this stage in my project I want to hold onto a clear break from sex. At some point in the future, I may shift to such language, but my gut tells me it is too early for me to do that.

33. See also Carter Heyward, *Touching Our Strength: The Erotic as Power and the Love of God* (San Francisco: Harper & Row, 1989).

34. Audre Lorde, "Uses of the Erotic: The Erotic as Power," in *Sister Outsider* (Freedom, Calif.: Crossing Press, 1984), p. 54.

35. Ibid., p. 56.

36. Ibid., p. 59.

36

This Sex Which Is Not One

Luce Irigaray

Female sexuality has always been theorized within masculine parameters. Thus, the opposition "virile" clitoral activity/"feminine" vaginal passivity which Freud—and many others—claims are alternative behaviors or steps in the process of becoming a sexually normal woman, seems prescribed more by the practice of masculine sexuality than by anything else. For the clitoris is thought of as a little penis which is pleasurable to masturbate, as long as the anxiety of castration does not exist (for the little boy), while the vagina derives its value from the "home" it offers the male penis when the now forbidden hand must find a substitute to take its place in giving pleasure.

According to these theorists, woman's erogenous zones are no more than a clitoris-sex, which cannot stand up in comparison with the valued phallic organ; or a hole-envelope, a sheath which surrounds and rubs the penis during coition; a nonsex organ or a masculine sex organ turned inside out in order to caress itself.

Woman and her pleasure are not mentioned in this conception of the sexual relationship. Her fate is one of "lack," "atrophy" (of her genitals), and "penis envy," since the penis is the only recognized sex organ of any worth. Therefore she tries to appropriate it for herself, by all the means at her disposal: by her somewhat servile love of the father-husband capable of giving it to her; by her desire of a penis-child, preferably male; by gaining access to those cultural values which are still "by right" reserved for males alone and are therefore always masculine, etc. Woman lives her desire only as an attempt to possess at long last the equivalent of the male sex organ.

All of that seems rather foreign to her pleasure, however, unless she remains within the dominant phallic economy. Thus, for example, woman's autoeroticism is very different from man's. He needs an instrument in order to touch himself: his hand, woman's genitals, language—And this self-stimulation requires a minimum of activity. But a woman touches herself by and within herself directly, without mediation, and before any distinction between activity and passivity is possible. A woman "touches herself" constantly without anyone being able to forbid her to do so, for her sex is composed of two lips which embrace continually. Thus, within herself she is already two—but not divisible into ones—who stimulate each other.

This autoeroticism, which she needs in order not to risk the disappearance of her pleasure in the sex act, is interrupted by a violent intrusion: the brutal spreading of these two lips by a violating penis. If, in order to assure an articulation between autoeroticism and heteroeroticism in coition (the encounter with the absolute other which always signifies death), the vagina must also, but not only, substitute for the little boy's hand, how can woman's autoeroticism possibly be perpetuated in the classic representation of sexuality? Will she not indeed be left the impossible choice between defensive virginity, fiercely turned back upon itself, or a body open for penetration, which no longer recognizes in its "hole" of a sex organ the pleasure of retouching itself? The almost exclusive, and ever so anxious, attention accorded the erection in Occidental sexuality proves to what extent the imaginary that commands it is foreign to everything female. For the most part, one finds in Occidental sexuality nothing more than imperatives dictated by rivalry among males: the "strongest" being the one who "gets it up the most," who has the longest, thickest, hardest penis or indeed the one who "pisses the farthest" (cf. little boys' games). These imperatives can also be dictated by sadomasochist fantasies, which in turn are ordered by the relationship between man and mother: his desire to force open, to penetrate, to appropriate for himself the mystery of the stomach in which he was conceived, the secret of his conception, of his "origin." Desire-need, also, once again, to make blood flow in order to revive a very ancient—intrauterine, undoubtedly, but also prehistoric—relation to the maternal.

Woman, in this sexual imaginary, is only a more or less complacent facilitator for the working out of man's fantasies. It is possible, and even certain, that she experiences vicarious pleasure there, but this pleasure is above all a masochistic prostitution of her body to a desire that is not her own and that leaves her in her well-known state of dependency. Not knowing what she wants, ready for anything, even asking for more, if only he will "take" her as the "object" of *his* pleasure, she will not say what she wants. Moreover, she does not know, or no longer knows, what she wants. As Freud admits, the beginnings of the sexual life of the little girl are so "obscure," so "faded by the years," that one would have to dig very deep in order to find, behind the traces of this civilization, this history, the vestiges of a more archaic civilization which could give some indication as to what woman's sexuality is all about. This very ancient civilization undoubtedly would not have the same language, the same alphabet—

Woman's desire most likely does not speak the same language as man's desire, and it probably has been covered over by the logic that has dominated the West since the Greeks.

In this logic, the prevalence of the gaze, discrimination of form, and individualization of form is particularly foreign to female eroticism. Woman finds pleasure more in touch than in sight and her entrance into a dominant scopic economy signifies, once again, her relegation to passivity: she will be the beautiful object. Although her body is in this way eroticized and solicited to a double movement between exhibition and pudic retreat in order to excite the instincts of the "subject," her sex organ represents the horror of having nothing to see. In this system of representation and desire, the vagina is a flaw, a hole in the representation's scoptophilic objective. It was admitted already in Greek statuary that this "nothing to be seen" must be excluded, rejected, from such a scene of representation. Woman's sexual organs are simply absent from this scene: they are masked and her "slit" is sewn up.

In addition, this sex organ which offers nothing to the view has no distinctive form of its own. Although woman finds pleasure precisely in this incompleteness of the form of her sex organ, which is why it retouches itself indefinitely, her pleasure is denied by a civilization that privileges phallomorphism. The value accorded to the only definable form excludes the form involved in female autoeroticism. The *one* of form, the individual sex, proper name, literal meaning—supersedes, by spreading apart and dividing, this touching of *at least two* (lips) which keeps woman in contact with herself, although it would be impossible to distinguish exactly what "parts" are touching each other.

Whence the mystery that she represents in a culture that claims to enumerate everything, cipher everything by units, inventory everything by individualities. *She is neither one nor two.* She cannot, strictly speaking, be determined either as one person or as two. She renders any definition inadequate. Moreover, she has no "proper" name. And her sex organ, which is not *a* sex organ, is counted as *no* sex organ. It is the negative, the opposite, the reverse, the counterpart, of the only visible and morphologically designatable sex organ (even if it does pose a few problems in its passage from erection to detumescence): the penis.

But woman holds the secret of the "thickness" of this "form," its many-layered volume, its metamorphosis from smaller to larger and vice versa, and even the intervals at which this change takes place. Without even knowing it. When she is asked to maintain, to revive, man's desire, what this means in terms of the value of her own desire is neglected. Moreover, she is not aware of her desire, at least not explicitly. But the force and continuity of her desire are capable of nurturing all the "feminine" masquerades that are expected of her for a long time.

It is true that she still has the child, with whom her appetite for touching, for contact, is given free reign, unless this appetite is already lost, or alienated by the taboo placed upon touching in a largely obsessional civilization. In her relation to the child she finds compensatory pleasure for the frustrations she encounters all too often in sexual relations proper. Thus maternity supplants the deficiencies of repressed female sexuality. Is it possible that man and woman no longer even caress each other except indirectly through the mediation between them represented by the child? Preferably male. Man, identified with his son, rediscovers the pleasure of maternal coddling; woman retouches herself in fondling that part of her body: her baby-penis-clitoris.

What that entails for the amorous trio has been clearly spelled out. The Oedipal interdict seems, however, a rather artificial and imprecise law—even though it is the very means of perpetuating the authoritarian discourse of father—when it is decreed in a culture where sexual relations are impracticable, since the desire of man and the desire of woman are so foreign to each other. Each of them is forced to search for some common meeting ground by indirect means: either an archaic, sensory relation to the mother's body, or a current, active or passive prolongation of the law of the father. Their attempts are characterized by regressive emotional behavior and the exchange of words so far from the realm of the sexual that they are completely exiled from it. "Mother" and "father" dominate the couple's functioning, but only as social roles. The division of labor prevents them from making love. They produce or reproduce. Not knowing too well how to use their leisure. If indeed they have any, if moreover they want to have any leisure. For what can be done with leisure? What substitute for amorous invention can be created?

We could go on and on—but perhaps we should return to the repressed female imaginary? Thus woman does not have a sex. She has at least two of them, but they cannot be identified as ones. Indeed, she has many more of them than that. Her sexuality, always at least double, is in fact *plural*. Plural as culture now wishes to be plural? Plural as the manner in which current texts are written, with very little knowledge of the censorship from which they arise? Indeed, woman's pleasure does not have to choose between clitoral activity and vaginal passivity, for example. The pleasure of the vaginal caress does not have to substitute itself for the pleasure of the clitoral caress. Both contribute irreplaceably to woman's pleasure but they are only two caresses among many to do so. Caressing the breasts, touching the vulva, opening the lips, gently stroking the posterior wall of the vagina, lightly massaging the cervix, etc., evoke a few of the most specifically female pleasures. They remain rather unfamiliar pleasures in the sexual difference as it is currently imagined, or rather as it is currently ignored: the other sex being only the indispensable complement of the only sex.

But *woman has sex organs just about everywhere*. She experiences pleasure almost everywhere. Even without speaking of the hysterization of her entire body, one can say that the geography of her pleasure is much more diversified, more multiple in its differences, more complex, more subtle, than is imagined— in an imaginary centered a bit too much on one and the same.

"She" is indefinitely other in herself. That is undoubtedly the reason she is called temperamental incomprehensible, perturbed, capricious—not to mention her language in which "she" goes off in all directions and in which "he" is unable to discern the coherence of any meaning. Contradictory words seem a little crazy to the logic of reason, and inaudible for him who listens with ready-made grids, a code prepared in advance. In her statements—at least when she dares to speak out—woman retouches herself constantly. She just barely separates from herself some chatter, an exclamation, a half-secret, a sentence left in suspense—When she returns to it, it is only to set out again from another point of pleasure or pain. One must listen to her differently in order to hear an *"other meaning" which is constantly in the process of weaving itself, at the same time ceaselessly embracing words and yet casting them off to avoid becoming fixed, immobilized.* For when "she" says something, it is already no longer identical to what she means. Moreover, her statements are never identical to anything. Their distinguishing feature is one of contiguity. They touch (*upon*). And when they wander too far from this nearness, she stops and begins again from "zero": her body-sex organ.

It is therefore useless to trap women into giving an exact definition of what they mean, to make them repeat (themselves) so the meaning will be clear. They are already elsewhere than in this discursive machinery where you claim to take them by surprise. They have turned back within themselves, which does not mean the same thing as "within yourself." They do not experience the same inferiority that you do and which perhaps you mistakenly presume they share. "Within themselves" means *in the privacy of this silent, multiple, diffuse tact.* If you ask them insistently what they are thinking about, they can only reply: nothing. Everything.

Thus they desire at the same time nothing and everything. It is always more and other than this *one*—of sex, for example—that you give them, that you attribute to them and which is often interpreted, and feared, as a sort of insatiable hunger, a voracity which will engulf you entirely. While in fact it is really a question of another economy which diverts the linearity of a project, undermines the target object of a desire, explodes the polarization of desire on only one pleasure, and disconcerts fidelity to only one discourse—

Must the multiple nature of female desire and language be understood as the fragmentary, scattered remains of a raped or denied sexuality? This is not an easy question to answer. The rejection, the exclusion of a female imaginary undoubtedly places woman in a position where she can experience herself only fragmentarily as waste or as excess in the little structured margins of a dominant ideology, this mirror entrusted by the (masculine) "subject" with the task of reflecting and redoubling himself. The role of "femininity" is. prescribed moreover by this masculine specula(riza)tion and corresponds only slightly to woman's desire, which is recuperated only secretly, in hiding, and in a disturbing and unpardonable manner.

But if the female imaginary happened to unfold, if it happened to come into play other than as pieces, scraps, deprived of their assemblage, would it present itself for all that as *a* universe? Would it indeed be volume rather than surface? No. Unless female imaginary is taken to mean, once again, the prerogative of the maternal over the female. This maternal would be phallic in nature, however, closed in upon the jealous possession of its valuable product, and competing with man in his esteem for surplus. In this race for power, woman loses the uniqueness of her pleasure. By diminishing herself in volume, she renounces the pleasure derived from the nonsuture of her lips: she is a mother certainly, but she is a virgin mother. Mythology long ago assigned this role to her in which she is allowed a certain social power as long as she is reduced, with her own complicity, to sexual impotence.

Thus a woman's (re)discovery of herself can only signify the possibility of not sacrificing any of her pleasures to another, of not identifying with anyone in particular, of never being simply one. It is a sort of universe in expansion for which no limits could be fixed and which, for all that, would not be incoherency. Nor would it be the polymorphic perversion of the infant during which its erogenous zones await their consolidation under the primacy of the phallus.

Woman would always remain multiple, but she would be protected from dispersion because the other is a part of her, and is autoerotically familiar to her. That does not mean that she would appropriate the other for herself, that she would make it her property. Property and propriety are undoubtedly rather foreign to all that is female. At least sexually. *Nearness,* however, is not foreign to woman, a nearness so close that any identification of one or the other, and therefore any form of property, is impossible. Woman enjoys a closeness with the other that is *so near she cannot possess it, any more than she can possess herself.* She constantly trades herself for the other without any possible identification of either one of them. Woman's pleasure, which grows indefinitely from its passage in/through the other, poses a problem for any current economy in that all computations that attempt to account for woman's incalculable pleasure are irremediably destined to fail.

However, in order for woman to arrive at the point where she can enjoy her pleasure as a woman, a long detour by the analysis of the various systems of oppression which affect her is certainly necessary. By claiming to resort to pleasure alone as the solution to her problem, she runs the risk of missing the reconsideration of a social practice upon which *her* pleasure depends.

For woman is traditionally use-value for man, exchange-value among men. Merchandise, then. This makes her the guardian of matter whose price will be determined by "subjects": workers, tradesmen, consumers, according to the standard of their work and their need-desire. Woman are marked phallically by their fathers, husbands, procurers. This stamp(ing) determines their value in sexual commerce Woman is never anything more than the scene of more or less rival exchange between two men, even when they are competing for the possession of mother-earth.

How can this object of transaction assert a right to pleasure without extricating itself from the established commercial system? How can this merchandise relate to other goods on the market other than with aggressive jealousy? How can raw materials possess themselves without provoking in the consumer fear of the disappearance of his nourishing soil? How can this exchange in noth-ingness that can be defined in "proper" terms of woman's desire not seem to be pure enticement, folly, all too quickly covered over by a more sensible discourse and an apparently more tangible system of values?

A woman's evolution, however radical it might seek to be, would not suf-fice then to liberate woman's desire. Neither political theory nor political prac-tice has yet resolved nor sufficiently taken into account this historical problem, although Marxism has announced its importance. But women are not, strictly speaking, a class and their dispersion in several classes makes their political struggle complex and their demands sometimes contradictory.

Their underdeveloped condition stemming from their submission by/to a culture which oppresses them, uses them, cashes in on them, still remains. Woman reap no advantage from this situation except that of their quasi-monopoly of masochistic pleasure, housework, and reproduction. The power of slaves? It is considerable since the master is not necessarily well served in mat-ters of pleasure. Therefore, the inversion of the relationship, especially in sexual economy, does not seem to be an enviable objective.

But if women are to preserve their autoeroticism, their homo-sexuality, and let it flourish, would not the renunciation of heterosexual pleasure simply be another form of this amputation of power that is traditionally associated with women? Would this renunciation not be new incarceration, a new cloister that women would willingly build? Let women tacitly go on strike, avoid men long enough to learn to defend their desire notably by their speech, let them discover the love of other women protected from that imperious choice of men which puts them in a position of rival goods, let them forge a social status which demands recognition, let them earn their living in order to leave behind their condition of prostitute—These are certainly indispensable steps in their effort to escape their proletarization on the trade market. But, if their goal is to reverse the existing order—even if that were possible—history would simply repeat itself and return to phallocratism, where neither women's sex, their imaginary, nor their language can exist.

—Translated by Claudia Reeder

37

Why Do Men Enjoy Pornography?

Alan Soble

Under stress of hatred, of boredom, of sudden panic, great gaps open. It is as if a man and a woman then heard each other for the first time and knew, with sickening conviction, that they share no common language, that their previous understanding had been based on a trivial pidgin which had left the heart of meaning untouched. Abruptly the wires are down and the nervous pulse under the skin is laid bare in mutual incomprehension.

—George Steiner, "After Babel"

Why do men enjoy pornography? I want to offer a partial explanation, in Marxist terms, of why men in capitalism consume pornography and why pornography has the characteristics it has. To accomplish this goal we need to consider why male sexuality in capitalism elevates the visual and downgrades the tactile, why it separates sex and affection, and what effects it has on women and their sexuality.

In Byron's *Don Juan* (I, 194) Donna Julia utters these infamous words:

> Man's love is of man's life a thing apart,
> 'Tis Woman's whole existence.

Of course, Byron could not have foreseen that the pattern he saw as normal and unproblematic would eventually be the subject of political economy and that Freud would make it the theme of one of his most ambitious ventures in social psychology.[1] Byron could not have recognized the irony in his choice of the word "apart" (a-part, a part); but in one stroke he captured the essence of atomistic bourgeois society and the effect of its mode of production on male sexu-

Alan Soble, "Why Do Men Enjoy Pornography?" from *Rethinking Masculinity: Philosophical Explorations in Light of Feminism,* eds. Larry May and Robert A. Strikwerda (Lanham, Md.: Rowman and Littlefield Publishers, Inc., 1992). Reprinted by permission of Yale University Press.

ality. Similarly, there is a world of irony in his word "whole," which expresses the effect that women's confinement to the spheres of reproduction and holistic service production has on their sexuality. The difference recognized by Byron is the leitmotif of this chapter.[2] . . .

Pornography in Capitalism: Consumerism

I begin with the observation that most pornography (with the exception, say, of the pornography collected at the Kinsey Institute for Sex Research) is consumed in order to experience sexual arousal, to gratify sexual curiosity, to generate sexual fantasies, or otherwise to satisfy desires, with or without masturbation. Pornography is designed and produced with these consumer purposes in mind. It is a mass-produced commodity, vast quantities made possible primarily by a photographic technology that employs negatives and a publishing technology that can churn out inexpensive paperbacks. As a commodity, pornography represents the expansion of capital into another area of life. A useful idea, although not a new one, is that sexuality in capitalism has been commodified; the best examples are prostitution and the "circulation" and "exchange" of sexuality in promiscuity. But commodification applies as well to "normal" sexual relations. Pornography makes sexual arousal and pleasure into a commodity. Moreover, pornography replicates the commodification of sexual activity and women's bodies.[3]

When sexual feelings and sexual activity become commodified, they are governed by the same principles that control commodities in capitalism: the desire for sexual experiences is manipulated and encouraged, their availability is restricted to create scarcity, the cost of high-quality or esoteric activities increases inversely with supply, and the whole process is passed off as the inevitable result of natural law.[4] In short, the commodification of sexuality represents the imposition of a demand on consumers. Without further details, this account does not take us very far. It only repeats the Marxist idea that the desire for consumer goods in capitalism is as much the result of the needs of capitalist production, as mediated by the sales effort, as it is of an independently existing consumer need. Why has the imposition of demand in this case been so successful? Factors beyond the pornography industry must be invoked.[5]

The commodification of sexual experiences involves both its *actual* scarcity, created by cultural elements that perpetuate restrictive sexual standards (what I call the Victorian element), and its *perceived* scarcity, manufactured by cultural elements that perpetuate norms of health or morality defined in terms of sexual freedom (the liberal health and psychology industry). The Victorian element creates scarcity through its norms of premarital chastity, monogamous marriage, and especially the regulation of women's sexuality, and it relies on guilt and anxiety to establish conformity with these norms. The liberal health element creates the perception of scarcity, not only by bringing to attention the "irrational" restrictive norms of the Victorian element, but also by promising a world rich in sexual experience; the imagined wealth of this sexual utopia makes the actual scarcity appear worse than it is. The liberal health element, paradoxically, also uses guilt and anxiety to establish conformity with its norms (for example, some women feel anxiety if they are not clitoral *enough,* or do not masturbate, or do not have multiple orgasms); one feels guilty if one is not living up to "enlightened" norms of sexual health, rather than feeling guilty because one is too weak-willed to obey Victorian prohibitions.[6] The Victorian element and the liberal element are battling each other for social power. They are competitors in the business of selling another commodity—judgment-norms—and consumers are in the unenviable position of having to decide which corporation offers the best buy.

Persons who hear *both* that sex is wrong except in certain approved situations *and* that a mark of mental, physical, and social well-being is an active sex life are torn between contradictory pronouncements. The consumption of pornography by men during the last twenty-five years is partially explainable as the result of the forces of liberal sexual health vanquishing the forces of Victorian sexual prohibition. Liberals recognized the connection between pornography and their sexual-freedom norms, and they fought for relaxation of legal controls on pornography; the liberalization of the law surely made the production and distribution of pornography possible (especially hard-core pornography), but it does not exactly explain why this pornography has been consumed. The liberal health industry, with its own set of products and services and its own style of generating institutional power, has been replacing the Victorian religion-theology industry as the supplier of sexual judgment-norms. This partially explains the consumption of pornography. It can also be seen as an attempt by men to escape the conflict between these opposing pronouncements. The use of pornography in masturbatory sexuality satisfies, in a convoluted way, both conservative prohibitions (no "real" sexual activity is engaged in; one is not literally unfaithful to one's wife) and liberal norms ("if it feels good, do it"). One of the attractive features of this explanation is that it does not appeal to a hydraulic model of sexuality; that is, the consumption of pornography is not the result of sexual energy spilling out of a container that tries valiantly but unsuccessfully to hold it. Both the avoidance of sexuality and the search for sexual experience result from the commodification of sexuality and the imposition of demands: desire to avoid sexual activity, created by the Victorians, and desire to engage in sexual activity created by the competing liberals.[7]

Men's interest in pornography is also produced by the desensitization of the male body. In limiting the erotic range of smell, taste, and touch, the desensitization of the body makes the visual component of male sexuality a central source of sexual arousal and pleasure. Men's consumption of pornography has consisted mostly of photographic magazines, films, and videos. In leaving only the penis sensitive, desensitization provides what must appear to the consumer to be a natural link between visual pornography and genital masturbation. This causal connection between the mode of production, its effects on the laborer, and the consumption of pornography operates in tandem with other features of capitalist society. In particular, visual pornography allows the consumer to walk the line between the conservative prohibition and the liberal encouragement of sexual activity. Sexual pleasure induced by visual stimuli is not derived from genuine intimate contact, and therefore visual sexuality does not literally violate conservative prohibitions ("look, but don't touch"); at the same time, the consumer vicariously participates in a broader range of sexual activity and thereby satisfies the liberal pronouncement that he should feel free to enjoy whatever sexual experiences are available. That the use of pornography is not consistent with the *spirit* of either pronouncement is ignored by the rationalizing consumer. A common Victorian criticism of pornography is that the voyeurism encouraged by pornography undermines intimacy. The liberal, too, doubts the mental adjustment of those who derive too much pleasure from vicarious sexuality and not enough from "real" sexual activity. The use of pornography is the consumer's semirational response to being caught between these quite different standards.

The consumption of pornography can be partially understood in terms of men's visual sexuality, the genital primacy of the desensitized consumer, and the victory of liberal health professionals over religious and other conservatives (or as the consumer's response to the contradiction between the two), in addition to the commodity imposition carried out by the pornography industry. A full explanation, however, must make intelligible not just the consumption of pornography, but its *vast* consumption. I doubt that this consumption is only the result of mass production, marketing techniques, expanded visual sexuality, and penile hypersensitivity. Men must be terribly dissatisfied with their sexual lives, or they must believe that pornography adds something to their sexual lives, or they must be otherwise motivated by a sense that pornography is important. People whose wants have been created and manipulated do spend large amounts of money on items they admit are frivolous. But the consumption of pornography is not the consumption of hula-hoops, nor is it viewed that way by the men who use it. The fiery legal battles, the secrecy and persistence of male consumers, and the millions spent annually on pornography show that men take pornography seriously. We might almost say that men have found out, not merely that they enjoy it, but that they need it.

Pornography in Capitalism: Powerlessness

My explanation for the vast consumption of pornography appeals to both the boredom and the powerlessness yielded by capitalist work relations, the nature of labor, and the centralization of economics and politics. Pornography is a diversion, an escape from the dull, predictable world of work. Continued boredom also partially explains the quantity of pornography consumed. The sexual experience that involves visual stimuli, fantasies, and masturbation is intense (because of the hypersensitized penis), but it is short-lived and requires repetition. Visual stimuli arouse quickly but they need to be replaced with new stimuli, hence the quantity of pornography consumed and the attendant "throwaway commodification of women's bodies. Powerlessness, however, is the more important factor. Being bored with one's wife or lover, or with life in general, is only a small part of the story. And the boredom is just a form of powerlessness or derived from it.

A common view holds that pornography causes men to have sexual thoughts, ideas, or fantasies that they otherwise would not have.[8] To a certain extent this is true; no one reading de Sade's *120 Days of Sodom* is likely to finish the book without a handful of new ideas. But probably closer to the truth is the view that pornography allows men a great deal of autonomy in constructing sexual images. Goldstein and Kant defend the idea that pornography merely causes men to have sexual ideas when they distinguish between erotic daydreaming and pornography:

> In our view erotic pictures, stories, and movies simply serve as a substitute for the self-generating daydreams of the pornography user. . . . The daydream comes apparently from some inner stimulation to one's imagination. In the case of erotica, the theme portrayed comes from someone else's imagination, is depicted in tangible form, and can be thought of as separate from one's own wishes and motivations.[9]

To be sure, there is a difference between sexual daydreaming and the fantasies men have when using pornography, but Goldstein and Kant's suggestion, that in the former case the ideas come from "inside" and in the latter they come from "outside," is an oversimplification. Some of the content of our sexual daydreams comes ultimately from "outside," and the ideas entertained by users of pornography are not merely imprints from the "outside," transferred, as it were, directly and without modification from the pornographic magazine into the mind. The crude view is succinctly put by George Steiner: "Sexual relations are . . . one of the citadels of privacy. . . . The new pornographers subvert this last, vital privacy: they do our imagining for us."[10] Curiously, a defender of pornography responds to Steiner by claiming that *this* "is exactly what all good writers have done since the birth of literature. The measure of their talent has . . . been their ability to *make* us see the world through their eyes."[11] But writers of good literature, even as they do show us another view of the world, do not make us— force us—to think anything, and they do not do our imagining for us.[12] One might want to insist that here we have a nice distinction between pornography and good literature: the former does our imagining for us; the latter does not.[13]

For example, Joseph Slade claims that photographic and filmed pornography leave "nothing . . . to the imagination."[14] But Slade exposes the defect of this crude view when he later writes that "the cameraman cannot get inside the performers' minds."[15] He concludes from this that the consumers of pornography "do not know what" the performers are thinking. But it is in virtue of this feature of the camera that the consumer has freedom in actively filling in the thoughts, sensations, or feelings of the performers. The viewer can also add details or activities in his mind to those depicted.

To emphasize the causal determination of ideas by pornography is therefore one-sided. It overlooks the fact that pornography presents a partial picture of a fantasy world, that pornographic literature leaves gaps for the reader to fill in, and that pornographic films and especially photographs leave even larger gaps for the viewer to fill in.[16] The consumer of pornography uses the material not so much to learn of sexual variations but to obtain the visual and descriptive foundation upon which to build a fantasy. The brute facts provided by the photograph are transformed into a fantastic scenario, and the consumer creates a drama in which he is director, participant, or member of the audience at will. Pornography appeals to the user in virtue this dramatic scenario; indeed, its partially undefined content, waiting to be expanded into a full script, explains why men consume it in vast quantities.

Pornography allows men to gain a sense of control. In his fantasy world the consumer of pornography is the boss: Mr. X shall screw Ms. Y in position P and at time t while she wears/disrobes/reveals/lubricates/laughs/exclaims/resists/seduces/pouts/farts in exactly the way the consumer wants. (This explanation also illuminates the appeal of prostitution: with a woman he has hired, a man can experience what he wants when he wants it.) Pornographic fantasies provide sexual experiences without the entanglements, mistakes, imperfections, hassles, and misunderstandings that interfere with pleasure and that accompany sex with a wife, lover, girlfriend, or stranger. Or, if there are to be complications, pornographic fantasy allows men to imagine the particular complications that they find arousing. Of course, no mode of sexual activity is ideal: all forms—masturbation with pornography, paying a prostitute, getting married, having sex with strange women—have their advantages and disadvantages. The vast consumption of pornography over the last twenty-five years implies that men perceive the relative benefits of masturbation with pornography as increasingly significant, enough to make that mode of sexuality a contender equal with the others.[17] And the pleasure of fantasized sexuality is not limited to the pleasure of wanting the fantasized activity to actually occur.[18] The pornographic sexual experience is not always a mere substitute for "real" sexual activity; it is often "an authentic, autonomous sexual activity."[19]

In a sense, the grab at control through fantasized arrangements is literally infantile,[20] especially if we understand maturity as a willingness to work out problems with the people one associates with. But the male user of pornography has decided, at least implicitly and for certain times or places, that maturity in this sense is not worth the loss of pleasure.[21] Men want these particular pleasures here and now, and in fantasy they have things exactly the way they want them.[22] We would be expecting far too much of people raised in an infantilizing society were we to complain about such regressions; we would be blaming the victims. The use of pornography is an attempt to recoup in the domain of sexual fantasy what is denied to men in production and politics; in this sense the use of pornography in capitalism provides substitute gratification. Pornographic fantasy gives men the opportunity which they otherwise rarely have, to order the world and conduct its events according to their individual tastes. In the fantasy world permitted by pornography men can be safely selfish and totalitarian. The illusion of omnipotence is a relief from the estranged conditions of their lives and, with a little rationalization, can make existence in that real world, in which they have substantially less power, bearable. Men use pornography as compensation for their dire lack of power; pornography is therefore not so much an expression of male power as it is an expression of their lack of power.

The powerlessness for which pornographic fantasy compensates is not simply productive, political, and economic powerlessness. This powerlessness in capitalism can explain a tendency for people to fantasize, and it does contribute to pornographic fantasizing.[23] But if this general powerlessness were the only cause of fantasizing, we would expect not specifically sexual fantasies but Walter Mitty fantasies of astounding successes in business and politics. This kind of powerlessness explains the appeal of adventure stories and Dirty Harry movies, but it doesn't take us far enough in understanding pornography.[24] In addition, pornography compensates specifically for sexual powerlessness, the powerlessness of males in their sexual relationships with women.

In his discussion of the effects of industrialization in the early nineteenth century, Edward Shorter tells us about the

> shift toward powerlessness for men in the arena of real-world politics, whereby all the little people who had possessed some tiny stake—and feeble voice—in the governance of the traditional village community now became completely disenfranchised politically, until the advent of universal male voting toward the century's end. There has been no end of speculation, though little evidence, that the political powerlessness which men perceive is expressed in their resentment of women. If that is true, we might have further grounds for anticipating an increase in rapes in these factory-industrial regions.[25]

Supposing that the speculation contains some truth, I do not find altogether convincing the idea that an increase in rape, if understood as a *sexual* crime, is mostly due to men's *political* powerlessness. Political powerlessness should (*ceteris paribus*) lead to a political response. Therefore, to connect rape and men's powerlessness one must invoke at some point either sexual powerlessness or a reconception of rape. Shorter begins to provide the requisite sort of analysis when he discusses the increase in rape beginning in the 1960s in the Anglo-

Saxon countries.[26] He suggests that rape became a political act directed at women, a response to the feminist-inspired challenge to male power. In this case the connection is made by reconceptualizing rape.

But in the case of pornography today, invoking men's sexual powerlessness is better than ignoring the sexual nature of men's interest in pornography. There are at least two sources of men's dissatisfaction in their relationships with women, dissatisfactions that can be dealt with by recouping a sense of power in the fantasy world made possible by pornography. First, men tend to be more interested in sex for its own sake than women, and they emphasize the sexual over the affectionate aspects of their relationships with women. Men who have this interest in sexual activity for its own sake to a certain extent lack control over their sexual lives and recoup this perceived loss of power in a fantasy world. There is some truth to the folk-wisdom that women can often find a sexual partner more easily than men, and that women decline an invitation to engage in sexual activity more readily than men. Pornography restores men's sense that they have control over their sexuality, by allowing them to populate their fantasy world with women who are equally interested in sex for its own sake.[27]

Second, women's accommodation to male sexuality has never been complete and is becoming less so. Earlier I explained some of women's alienation in terms of the requirements of male sexuality and the practices that socialize women or lead to their accommodation. But socialization is not omnipotent, and women can simply refuse to accommodate. Refusals to accommodate may even be entirely rational. To the extent that women refuse to fit the requirements of male sexuality, men experience frustration and powerlessness. Socialization is less effective as a mechanism for producing what men want, so they have less control over the sexuality of women. A decrease in the accommodation of women to male sexuality, which has resulted from an increase in feminist and quasi-feminist consciousness over the last twenty-five years, has contributed to male powerlessness, specifically sexual powerlessness.[28] Men whose sexual partners have not sufficiently accommodated to male sexuality, and who become sexually bored with partners over whom they have less control, turn to pornographic fantasy in which their sexual desires are satisfied by fully accommodating women.[29] If Shorter is right that rape has increased in response to the women's movement, rape can be construed as a counteroffensive, as backlash. But men who turn to pornography in response to the decreased accommodation of women are retreating, not attacking. The attempt to gain a sense of sexual control in the realm of fantasy is an admission of defeat, a resignation to the way the women's movement has changed the world.[30]

On the one hand, the use of pornography is an attempt to retain in the world of fantasy the prerogatives of masculinity that are being eroded. If sex has been, but is no longer, "a domain of activity where the individual male can conceive of himself as being plausibly efficacious,"[31] then the flight to pornography can be seen as an attempt to establish a new domain for sexual prowess under the *same* prevailing notion of masculinity. But, on the other hand, one can detect in the consumption of pornography a rejection of the prevailing notion of masculinity.[32] Masturbation violates the prevailing standards of masculinity: the real man screws real women, he does not jerk off. If the vast consumption of pornography implies that a good deal of masturbation is going on, then men are rejecting the prevailing standards of masculinity. The consumption of pornography suggests, therefore, that men are abandoning the idea that, to prove themselves, they need to seduce women. Furthermore, for men who are living alone, who are postponing or avoiding marriage, or who realize, from divorce statistics, that relationships are not the stabilizing and secure retreats from the world they once might have been, masturbation with pornography is a useful and pleasurable activity that complements the new, evolving masculine role. If pornography is used in these two ways—as adherence in the realm of fantasy to the old style of masculinity, and as embracing the trend toward a new style of masculinity—then we can again understand the consumption of pornography as a balancing act that attempts to satisfy the demands of competing pronouncements: the conservative pronouncement to be a man, and the liberal pronouncement to reject old-fashioned notions of manhood.

Notes

1. Sigmund Freud, "The Most Prevalent Form of Degradation in Erotic Life," in Phillip Rieff, ed., *Sexuality and the Psychology of Love* (New York: Collier, 1963), pp. 58–60.

2. My thesis, that the sexuality of men is atomistic and that of women holistic, is of course a generalization: there are complications, exceptions, and recent changes in the pattern, some of which I discuss later. Carol Gilligan's *In a Different Voice* (Cambridge, Mass.: Harvard University Press, 1982) has found a parallel difference between men and women's conceptions of self and approaches to morality. For men, separateness from others (atomism) is the significant feature, while for women it is interdependence and connection (holism).

3. For the former, see Douglas Stewart, "Pornography, Obscenity, and Capitalism," *Antioch Review* 35 (Fall 1977): 395. For the latter, see (one of many examples) Peter Michelson, *The Aesthetics of Pornography* (New York; Herder and Herder, 1971), p. 217.

4. See Richard Lichtman, "Marx and Freud, Part 3: Marx's Theory of Human Nature," *Socialist Revolution* 7, no. 6 (1977): 57.

5. In her explanation of the consumption of romances by women, Janice Radway takes a different slant. She wants to make sure we understand that this consumption is not only a function of the needs of women, but "equally a function of . . . production, distribution, advertising, and marketing techniques." *Reading the Romance* (Chapel Hill: University of North Carolina Press, 1984), p. 20.

6. Using the terminology of "Jehovanist" and "Naturalist," Murray Davis (*Smut: Erotic Reality/Obscene Ideology* [Chicago: University of Chicago Press, 1983], p. 194) makes a similar point: "Naturalists have managed to replace the old 'sin' of giving into sexual desire with the new 'sickness' of not having enough sexual desire to give into."

7. Rather than speaking about the manipulation of women's sexuality by these competing social forces, Christine Pickard reasserts a repression model in bemoaning Victorian influences on women: "The fact that so many women 'fell by the wayside' bears testimony to the presence of

strong sexual urges that could not always be submerged despite strong forces inducing her to do so." ("A Perspective on Female Responses to Sexual Material," in Yaffe and Nelson, eds., *The Influence of Pornography on Behavior* [London: Academic Press, 1982], pp. 91–117, at p. 98.) Why not say that the fact that so many women "stayed the course" bears testimony to the absence of strong sexual urges that could not always be created despite the strong liberal forces inducing them to do so?

8. For example, Diana Russell, "Pornography and Violence: What Does the New Research Say?" in Lederer, ed., *Take Back the Night* (New York: Morrow, 1980), pp. 218–38.

9. Michael Goldstein and Harold Kant, *Pornography and Sexual Deviance* (Berkeley and Los Angeles: University of California Press, 1973), pp. 135–36.

10. George Steiner, "Night Words," in David Holbrook, ed., *The Case against Pornography* (LaSalle: Open Court, 1973), pp. 227–36, at pp. 234–35.

11. Kenneth Tynan, "Dirty Books Can Stay," in Douglas Hughes, ed., *Perspectives on Pornography* (New York: St. Martin's, 1970), pp. 109–21, at p. 119 (italics added).

12. "The good writer creates character by a cunning combination of the said and the unsaid." (Felix Pollack, "Pornography: A Trip around the Halfworld," in Hughes, *Perspectives on Pornography*, pp. 170–96, at p. 194). Pollack defends pornography by arguing that it, too, allows the active participation of the user. See also Gore Vidal, "On Pornography," *The New York Review of Books*, March 31, May 12, 1966, p. 6.

13. See Davis, *Smut*, pp. 136–37.

14. Joseph Slade, "Pornographic Theaters off Times Square," in Ray Rist, ed., *The Pornography Controversy* (New Brunswick, N.J.: Transaction Books, 1975), pp. 119–39, at p. 129.

15. Ibid., p. 130.

16. See Susan Sontag, *On Photography* (New York: Farrar, Straus and Giroux, 1973), pp. 106–9.

17. Leslie Farber's reading of Masters and Johnson concludes that the perfect orgasm is "wholly subject to its owner's will, wholly indifferent to human contingency or context. Clearly, this perfect orgasm is the orgasm achieved on one's own," through masturbation (*Lying, Despair, Jealousy, Envy, Sex, Suicide, Drugs, and the Good Life* [New York: Basic Books, 1976], p. 140). If the perfect orgasm is the one achieved in masturbation, then the important question is not "why do men consume so much pornography?" but rather "why do men ever bother with sex with prostitutes, wives, girlfriends, strangers?" Davis remarks, "Considering the obstacles, one wonders how two people ever manage to copulate at all" (*Smut*, p. 20), and he answers: "Plainly, human beings must possess something sexually arousing that animal species, natural phenomena, and technological products lack. That something else is a social self" (p. 106). But one need not wax so metaphysical to explain why masturbation with pornography does not replace other modes of sexuality altogether. Pornography cannot reproduce certain sexual sensations that can be experienced only with another person. Indeed, the ability of pornography to provide satisfaction is reduced if a person cannot use the material to conjure up fantasies based on memories of "real" sexual activity.

18. See Susan Feagin, "Some Pleasures of Imagination," *Journal of Aesthetics and Art Criticism* 43, no. 1, (1984): 51.

19. Susan Barrowclough, review of "Not a Love Story," *Screen* 23, no. 5 (1982): 33.

20. Ann Snitow discusses pornography as satisfying the desire to reexperience the omnipotence of childhood, in "Mass Market Romance: Pornography for Women Is Different," *Radical History Review* 20 (1979): 153–54.

21. Nancy Hartsock argues that men enjoy pornography because it allows them to avoid the dangers of intimacy with women, that men's "fear" of intimacy drives them to reassert control through pornography (*Money, Sex and Power* [New York: Longman, 1983], pp. 169–70, 176, 252). But this thesis rules out altogether that for some men masturbation with pornography is a sexual activity in its own right with its own advantages. Hartsock also magnifies men's perceptions of relationships when she says they "fear" intimacy. We should not forget that "a woman without a man is like a fish without a bicycle" works both ways.

22. Molly Haskell makes the same point about women's fantasies ("Rape Fantasy," *Ms.,* November 1976, p. 85).

23. Lawrence Rosenfield explains the consumption of pornography in capitalism *entirely* as a function of political powerlessness and the powerlessness derived from noncollectivized labor ("Politics and Pornography," *Quarterly Journal of Speech* 59 (1973), especially pp. 414–19).

24. Geoffrey Gorer argues that pornography is best understood by including it with "the literature of fear, the ghost story, the horror story, the thriller," and for example, "books of wine connoisseurship," all of which invoke physical responses (The Danger of Equality [New York: Weybright and Talley, 1966], pp. 222–24).

25. Edward Shorter, "On Writing the History of Rape," *Signs* 3, no. 2 (1977): 479.

26. Ibid., p. 481.

27. David Chute agrees that pornography is "a symptom of impotence rather than power," but he insists that pornography is largely consumed by young, shy, and unattractive men; hence, he believes that pornography is an expression only of *their* powerlessness to entice partners." ("Dirty Pillow Talk," *The Boston Phoenix*, September 23, 1980, p. 5). But consumption by these men does not explain the billions of dollars spent on pornography. Sexually active men also consume pornography, and the explanation I offer applies to them as well. Note that the President's Commission found that most patrons of adult bookstores and movie theaters were white, middle-aged, middle-class men *(Report on the Commission on Obscenity and Pornography* [New York: Bantam, 1970], pp. 25–26, 157–63).

28. Consciousness-raising groups, feminist psychotherapy, and the media (e.g., *Ms.*) undoubtedly undermine socialization and encourage refusals to accommodate.

29. Heidi Hartmann ("The Family as the Locus of Gender, Class, and Political Struggle," *Signs*, 6 [1981]: 377ff.) argues against the view that the power of men over women in the home has recently been weakened. But she shows only that men have retained power over women's domestic labor, not their sexuality.

30. I think Michele Barrett and Mary McIntosh get it backward when they write (*The Anti-Social Family* [London: NLB, 1982], p. 76) "Men would not be willing to pay prostitutes if it were not for the fact that their heterosexual desires have been indulged and accorded legitimacy and women's constructed as weak and receptive, in the interests of a male-dominated marriage system. The same applies to pornography." On my account it is precisely because men's sexuality has *not* been "indulged" by not fully accommodating women that they find both prostitution and pornography inviting. (I can imagine Woody Allen's reply: men do not use pornography because there are not enough good women lovers; rather, men sleep with women because they cannot get enough good pornography.)

31. John Gagnon and William Simon, *Sexual Conduct: The Social Sources of Human Sexuality* (Chicago: Aldine, 1973), p. 272.

32. Barbara Ehrenreich (*The Hearts of Men: American Dreams and the Flight from Commitment,* [Garden City, N.Y.: Anchor Press, 1983], pp. 125–26) argues that men's "revolt" against the male sex role can be perceived in male-submissive sadomasochistic pornography. I extend her insight by suggesting that all pornography can be understood this way.

38

Surviving Sexual Violence: A Philosophical Perspective

Susan J. Brison

This is an unorthodox philosophy article, in both style and subject matter. Its primary aim is not to defend a thesis by means of argumentation, but rather to give the reader imaginative access to what is, for some, an unimaginable experience, that of a survivor of rape. The fact that there is so little philosophical writing about violence against women results not only from a lack of understanding of its prevalence and of the severity of its effects, but also from the mistaken view that it is not a properly philosophical subject. I hope in this essay to illuminate the nature and extent of the harm done by sexual violence and to show why philosophers should start taking this problem more seriously.

On July 4, 1990, at 10:30 in the morning, I went for a walk along a peaceful-looking country road in a village outside Grenoble, France. It was a gorgeous day, and I didn't envy my husband, Tom, who had to stay inside and work on a manuscript with a French colleague of his. I sang to myself as I set out, stopping to pet a goat and pick a few wild strawberries along the way. About an hour and a half later, I was lying face down in a muddy creek bed at the bottom of a dark ravine, struggling to stay alive. I had been grabbed from behind, pulled into the bushes, beaten, and sexually assaulted. Feeling absolutely helpless and entirely at my assailant's mercy, I talked to him, calling him "sir." I tried to appeal to his humanity, and, when that failed, I addressed myself to his self-interest. He called me a whore and told me to shut up. Although I had said I'd do whatever he wanted, as the sexual assault began I instinctively fought back, which so enraged my attacker that he strangled me until I lost consciousness. When I awoke, I was being dragged by my feet down into the ravine. I had often, while dreaming, thought I was awake, but now I was awake and con-

First published in the *Journal of Social Philosophy* 24, no. 1 (Spring 1993). Reprinted by permission of the *Journal of Social Philosophy*.

vinced I was having a nightmare. But it was no dream. After ordering me, in a gruff, Gestapo-like voice, to get on my hands and knees, my assailant strangled me again. I wish I could convey the horror of losing consciousness while my animal instincts desperately fought the effects of strangulation. This time I was sure I was dying. But I revived, just in time to see him lunging toward me with a rock. He smashed it into my forehead, knocking me out, and eventually, after another strangulation attempt, he left me for dead.

After my assailant left, I managed to climb out of the ravine, and was rescued by a farmer who called the police, a doctor, and an ambulance. I was taken to emergency at the Grenoble hospital, where I underwent neurological tests, x-rays, blood tests, and a gynecological exam. Leaves and twigs were taken from my hair for evidence, my fingernails were scraped, and my mouth was swabbed for samples. I had multiple head injuries, my eyes were swollen shut, and I had a fractured trachea, which made breathing difficult. I was not permitted to drink or eat anything for the first thirty hours, though Tom, who never left my side, was allowed to dab my blood-encrusted lips with a wet towel. The next day, I was transferred out of emergency and into my own room. But I could not be left alone even for a few minutes. I was terrified my assailant would find me and finish the job. When someone later brought in the local paper with a story about my attack, I was greatly relieved that it referred to me as *Mlle. M. R.* and didn't mention that I was an American. Even by the time I left the hospital, eleven days later, I was so concerned about my assailant tracking me down that I put only my lawyer's address on the hospital records.

Although fears for my safety may have initially explained why I wanted to remain anonymous, by that time my assailant had been apprehended, indicted for rape and attempted murder, and incarcerated without possibility of bail. Still, I didn't want people to know that I had been sexually assaulted. I don't know whether this was because I could still hardly believe it myself, because keeping this information confidential was one of the few ways I could feel in control of my life, or because, in spite of my conviction that I had done nothing wrong, I felt ashamed.

When I started telling people about the attack, I said, simply, that I was the victim of an attempted murder. People typically asked, in horror, "What was the motivation? Were you mugged?" and when I replied "No, it started as a sexual assault," most inquirers were satisfied with that as an explanation of why some man wanted to murder me. I would have thought that a murder attempt *plus* a sexual assault would require more, not less, of an explanation than a murder attempt by itself. (After all, there are *two* criminal acts to explain here.)

One reason sexual violence is taken for granted by many is because it is so very prevalent. The FBI, notorious for underestimating the frequency of sex crimes, notes that, in the United States, a rape occurs on an average of every six minutes.[2] But this figure covers only the reported cases of rape, and some researchers claim that only about 10 percent of all rapes get reported.[3] Every fifteen seconds, a woman is beaten.[4] The everydayness of sexual violence, as evidenced by these mind-numbing statistics, leads many to think that male violence against women is natural, a given, something not in need of explanation, and not amenable to change. And yet, through some extraordinary mental gymnastics, while most people take sexual violence for granted, they simultaneously manage to deny that it really exists—or, rather, that it could happen to them. We continue to think that we—and the women we love—are immune to it, provided, that is, that we don't do anything 'foolish.' How many of us have swallowed the potentially lethal lie that 'If you don't do anything wrong, if you're just careful enough, you'll be safe'? How many of us have believed its damaging, victim-blaming corollary: 'If you are attacked, it's because *you* did something wrong'? These are lies, and in telling my story I hope to expose them, as well as to help bridge the gap between those of us who have been victimized and those who have not.

But what, you may be thinking, does this have to do with philosophy? Why tell my story in this academic forum? Judging from the virtual lack of philosophical writing on sexual violence, one might well conclude there is nothing here of interest to philosophers. Certainly, I came across nothing in my search for philosophical help with explaining what had happened to me and putting my shattered world back together.[5] Yet sexual violence and its aftermath raise numerous philosophical issues in a variety of areas in our discipline. The disintegration of the self experienced by victims of violence challenges our notions of personal identity over time, a major preoccupation of metaphysics. A victim's seemingly justified skepticism about everyone and everything is pertinent to epistemology, especially if the goal of epistemology is, as Wilfrid Sellars put it, that of feeling at home in the world. In aesthetics—as well as in philosophy of law—the discussion of sexual violence in—or as—art could use the illumination provided by a victim's perspective. Perhaps the most important issues posed by sexual violence are in the areas of social, political, and legal philosophy, and insight into these, as well, requires an understanding of what it's like to be a victim of such violence.

One of the very few articles written by philosophers on violence against women is Ross Harrison's "Rape: A Case Study in Political Philosophy."[6] In this article Harrison argues that not only do utilitarians need to assess the harmfulness of rape in order to decide whether the harm to the victim outweighs the benefit to the rapist, but even on a rights-based approach to criminal justice we need to be able to assess the benefits and harms involved in criminalizing and punishing violent acts such as rape. On his view, it is not always the case, contra Ronald Dworkin, that rights trump considerations of utility, so, even on a rights-based account of justice, we need to give an account of why, in the case of rape, the pleasure gained by the perpetrator (or by multiple perpetrators, in the case of gang-rape) is always outweighed by the harm done to the victim. He points out the peculiar difficulty most of us have in imagining the pleasure a rapist gets out of an assault, but, he asserts confidently, "There is no problem imagining what it is like to be a victim. . . ."[7] To his credit, he acknowledges the importance, to political philosophy, of trying to imagine others' experience, for otherwise we could not compare harms and benefits, which he argues must be done even in cases of conflicts of rights in order to decide which of competing rights should take priority. But imagining what it is like to be a rape victim is no simple matter, since much of what a victim goes through is unimaginable. Still, it's essential to try to convey it.

In my efforts to tell the victim's story—my story, our story—I've been inspired and instructed not only by feminist philosophers who have refused to accept the dichotomy between the personal and the political, but also by critical race theorists such as Patricia Williams, Mari Matsuda, and Charles Lawrence who have incorporated first-person narrative accounts into their discussions of the law. In writing about hate speech, they have argued persuasively that one cannot do justice to the issues involved in debates about restrictions on speech without listening to the victims' stories.[8] In describing the effects of racial harassment on victims, they have departed from the academic convention of speaking in the impersonal, 'universal,' voice and related incidents they themselves experienced. In her ground-breaking book, *The Alchemy of Race and Rights,* Williams describes how it felt to learn about her great-great-grandmother who was purchased at age eleven by a slave owner who raped and impregnated her the following year. And in describing instances of everyday racism she herself has lived through, she gives us imaginative access to what it's like to be the victim of racial discrimination. Some may consider such first person accounts in academic writing to be self-indulgent, but I consider them a welcome antidote to the arrogance of those who write in a magisterial voice that in the guise of 'universality' silences those who most need to be heard.

Philosophers are far behind legal theorists in acknowledging the need for a diversity of voices. We are trained to write in an abstract, universal voice and to shun first-person narratives as biased and inappropriate for academic discourse. Some topics, however, such as the impact of racial and sexual violence on victims, cannot even be broached unless those affected by such crimes can tell of their experiences in their own words. Unwittingly further illustrating the need for the victim's perspective, Harrison writes, elsewhere in his article on rape, "What principally distinguishes rape from normal sexual activity is the consent of the raped woman."[9] There is no parallel to this in the case of other crimes, such as theft or murder. Try "What principally distinguishes theft from normal gift-giving is the consent of the person stolen from." We don't think of theft as "gift-giving minus consent." We don't think of murder as "assisted suicide minus consent." Why not? In the latter case, it could be because assisted suicide is relatively rare (even compared with murder) and so it's odd to use it as the more familiar thing to which we are analogizing. But in the former case, gift-giving is presumably more prevalent than theft (at least in academic circles) and yet it still sounds odd to explicate theft in terms of gift-giving minus consent. In the cases of both theft and murder, the notion of violation seems built into our conceptions of the physical acts constituting the crimes, so it is inconceivable that one could consent to the act in question. Why is it so easy for a philosopher such as Harrison to think of rape, however, as "normal sexual activity minus consent"? This may be because the nature of the violation in the case of rape hasn't been all that obvious. Witness the phenomenon of rape jokes, the prevalence of pornography glorifying rape, the common attitude that, in the case of women, 'no' means 'yes,' that women really want it.[10]

Since I was assaulted by a stranger, in a "safe" place, and was so visibly injured when I encountered the police and medical personnel, I was, throughout my hospitalization and my dealings with the police, spared the insult, suffered by so many rape victims, of not being believed or of being said to have asked for the attack. However, it became clear to me as I gave my deposition from my hospital bed that this would still be an issue in my assailant's trial. During my deposition, I recalled being on the verge of giving up my struggle to live when I was galvanized by a sudden, piercing image of Tom's future pain on finding my corpse in that ravine. At this point in my deposition, I paused, glanced over at the police officer who was typing the transcript, and asked whether it was appropriate to include this image of my husband in my recounting of the facts. The *gendarme* replied that it definitely was and that it was a very good thing I mentioned my husband, since my assailant, who had confessed to the sexual assault, was claiming I had provoked it. As serious as the occasion was, and as much as it hurt to laugh, I couldn't help it—the suggestion was so ludicrous. Could it have been those baggy Gap jeans I was wearing that morning? Or was it the heavy sweatshirt? My maddeningly seductive jogging shoes? Or was it simply my walking along minding my own business that had provoked his murderous rage?

After I completed my deposition, which lasted eight hours, the police officer asked me to read and sign the transcript he'd typed to certify that it was accurate. I was surprised to see that it began with the words, *"Comme je suis sportive . . ."*—"Since I am athletic . . ."—added by the police to explain to the court just what possessed me to go for a walk by myself that fine morning. I was too exhausted by this point to protest "no, I'm not an athlete, I'm a philosophy professor," and I figured the officer knew what he was doing, so I let it stand. That evening, my assailant confessed to the assault. I retained a lawyer, and met him along with the investigating magistrate, when I gave my second deposition toward the end of my hospitalization. Although what occurred was officially a crime against the state, not against me, I was advised to pursue a civil suit in order to recover unreimbursed medical expenses, and, in any case, I needed an advocate to explain the French legal system to me. I was told that since this was an "easy" case, the trial would occur within a year. In fact, the trial took place two and a half years after the assault, due to the delaying tactics of my assailant's lawyer, who was trying to get him off on an insanity defense. According to Article 64 of the French criminal code, if the defendant is determined to have been insane at the time, then, legally, there was *"ni crime, ni délit"*—neither crime nor offense. The jury, however, did not accept the insanity plea and found my assailant guilty of rape and attempted murder, sentencing him to ten years in prison.

As things turned out, my experience with the criminal justice system was better than that of most sexual assault victims. I did, however, occasionally get glimpses of the humiliating insensitivity victims routinely endure. Before I could be released from the hospital, for example, I had to undergo a second forensic examination at a different hospital. I was taken in a wheelchair out to a hospital van, driven to another hospital, taken to an office where there were no receptionists and where I was greeted by two male doctors I had never seen before. When they told me to take off my clothes and stand in the middle of the room, I refused. I had to ask for a hospital gown to put on. For about an hour the two of them went over me like a piece of meat, calling out measurements of bruises and other assessments of damage, as if they were performing an autopsy. This was just the first of many incidents in which I felt as if I was experiencing things posthumously. When the inconceivable happens, one starts to doubt even the most mundane, realistic perceptions. Perhaps I'm not really here, I thought, perhaps I did die in that ravine. The line between life and death, once so clear and sustaining, now seemed carelessly drawn and easily erased.

For the first several months after my attack, I led a spectral existence, not quite sure whether I had died and the world went on without me, or whether I was alive but in a totally alien world. Tom and I returned to the States, and I continued to convalesce, but I felt as though I'd somehow outlived myself. I sat in our apartment and stared outside for hours, through the blur of a detached vitreous, feeling like Robert Lowell's newly widowed mother, described in one of his poems as mooning in a window "as if she had stayed on a train / one stop past her destination."[11]

My sense of unreality was fed by the massive denial of those around me—a reaction I learned is an almost universal response to rape. Where the facts would appear to be incontrovertible, denial takes the shape of attempts to explain the assault in ways that leave the observers' worldview unscathed. Even those who are able to acknowledge the existence of violence try to protect themselves from the realization that the world in which it occurs is their world and so they find it hard to identify with the victim. They cannot allow themselves to imagine the victim's shattered life, or else their illusions about their own safety and control over their lives might begin to crumble. The most well-meaning individuals, caught up in the myth of their own immunity, can inadvertently add to the victim's suffering by suggesting that the attack was avoidable or somehow her fault. One victims' assistance coordinator, whom I had phoned for legal advice, stressed that she herself had never been a victim and said that I would benefit from the experience by learning not to be so trusting of people and to take basic safety precautions like not going out alone late at night. She didn't pause long enough during her lecture for me to point out that I was attacked suddenly, from behind, in broad daylight.

We are not taught to empathize with victims. In crime novels and detective films, it is the villain, or the one who solves the murder mystery, who attracts our attention; the victim, a merely passive pretext for our entertainment, is conveniently disposed of—and forgotten—early on. We identify with the agents' strength and skill, for good or evil, and join the victim, if at all, only in our nightmares. Though one might say, as did Clarence Thomas, looking at convicted criminals on their way to jail, "but for the grace of God, there go I,"[12] a victim's fate prompts an almost instinctive "it could never happen to me." This may explain why there is, in our criminal justice system, so little concern for justice for victims—especially rape victims. They have no constitutionally protected rights *qua* victims. They have no right to a speedy trial or to compensation for damages (though states have been changing this in recent years), or to privacy vis-à-vis the press. As a result of their victimization, they often lose their jobs, their homes, their spouses—in addition to losing a great deal of money, time, sleep, self-esteem, and peace of mind. The rights to "life, liberty, and the pursuit of happiness," possessed, in the abstract, by all of us, are of little use to victims who can lose years of their lives, the freedom to move about in the world without debilitating fear, and any hope of returning to the pleasures of life as they once knew it.

People also fail to recognize that if a victim could not have anticipated an attack, she can have no assurance that she will be able to avoid one in the future. More to reassure themselves than to comfort the victim, some deny that such a thing could happen again. One friend, succumbing to the gambler's fallacy, pointed out that my having had such extraordinary bad luck meant that the odds of my being attacked again were now quite slim (as if fate, though not completely benign, would surely give me a break now, perhaps in the interest of fairness). Others thought it would be most comforting to pretend nothing had happened. The first card I received from my mother, while I was still in the hospital, made no mention of the attack or of my pain and featured the "bluebird of happiness," sent to keep me ever cheerful. The second had an illustration of a bright, summery scene with the greeting: "Isn't the sun nice? Isn't the wind nice? Isn't everything nice?" Weeks passed before I learned, what I should have been able to guess, that after she and my father received Tom's first call from the hospital they held each other and sobbed. They didn't want to burden me with their pain—a pain which I now realize must have been greater than my own.

Some devout relatives were quick to give God all the credit for my survival but none of the blame for what I had to endure. Others acknowledged the suffering that had been inflicted on me, but as no more than a blip on the graph of God's benevolence—a necessary, fleeting, evil, there to make possible an even greater show of good. An aunt, with whom I have been close since childhood, did not write or call at all until three months after the attack, and then sent a belated birthday card with a note saying that she was sorry to hear about my "horrible experience" but pleased to think that as a result I "will become stronger and will be able to help so many people. A real blessing from above for sure." Such attempts at a theodicy discounted the horror I had to endure. But I learned that everyone needs to try and make sense, in however inadequate a way, of such senseless violence. I watched my own seesawing attempts to find something for which to be grateful, something to redeem the unmitigated awfulness: I was glad I didn't have to reproach myself (or endure others' reproaches) for having done something careless, but I wished I had done something I could consider reckless so that I could simply refrain from doing it in the future. I was glad I did not yet have a child, who would have to grow up with the knowledge that even the protector could not be protected, but I felt an inexpressible loss when I recalled how much Tom and I had wanted a baby and how joyful were our attempts to conceive. It is difficult, even now, to imagine getting pregnant, because it is so hard to let even my husband near me, and because it would be harder still to let a child leave my side.

It might be gathered, from this litany of complaints, that I was the recipient of constant, if misguided, attempts at consolation during the first few months of my recovery. This was not the case. It seemed to me that the half-life of most people's concern was less than that of the sleeping pills I took to ward off flashbacks and nightmares—just long enough to allow the construction of a comforting illusion that lulls the shock to sleep. During the first few months after my assault, most of the aunts, uncles, cousins, and friends of the family notified by my parents almost immediately after the attack didn't phone, write, or even send a get well card, in spite of my extended hospital stay. These are all caring, decent people who would have sent wishes for a speedy recovery if I'd had, say, an appendectomy. Their early lack of response was so striking that I wondered whether it was the result of self-protective denial, a reluctance to mention something so unspeakable, or a symptom of our society's widespread emotional illiteracy that prevents most people from conveying any feeling that can't be expressed in a Hallmark card.

In the case of rape, the intersection of multiple taboos—against talking openly about trauma, about violence, about sex—causes conversational gridlock, paralyzing the would-be supporter. We lack the vocabulary for expressing appropriate concern, and we have no social conventions to ease the awkwardness. Ronald de Sousa has written persuasively about the importance of grasping paradigm scenarios in early childhood in order to learn appropriate emotional responses to situations.[13] We do not learn—early or later in life—how to react to a rape. What typically results from this ignorance is bewilderment on the part of victims and silence on the part of others, often the result of misguided caution. When, on entering the angry phase of my recovery period, I railed at my parents: "Why haven't my relatives called or written? Why hasn't my own brother phoned?" They replied, "They all expressed their concern to us, but they didn't want to remind you of what happened." Didn't they realize I thought about the attack every minute of every day and that their inability to respond made me feel as though I had, in fact, died and no one had bothered to come to the funeral?

For the next several months, I felt angry, scared, and helpless, and I wished I could blame myself for what had happened so that I would feel less vulnerable, more in control of my life. Those who haven't been sexually violated may have difficulty understanding why women who survive assault often blame themselves, and may wrongly attribute it to a sex-linked trait of masochism or lack of self-esteem. They don't know that it can be less painful to believe that you did something blameworthy than it is to think that you live in a world where you can be attacked at any time, in any place, simply because you are a woman. It is hard to go on after an attack that is both random—and thus completely unpredictable—and not random, that is, a crime of hatred towards the group to which you happen to belong. If I hadn't been the one who was attacked on that road in France, it would have been the next woman to come along. But had my husband walked down that road instead, he would have been safe.

Although I didn't blame myself for the attack, neither could I blame my attacker. Tom wanted to kill him, but I, like other rape victims I came to know, found it almost impossible to get angry with my assailant. I think the terror I still felt precluded the appropriate angry response. It may be that experiencing anger toward an attacker requires imagining oneself in proximity to him, a prospect too frightening for a victim in the early stages of recovery to conjure up. As Aristotle observed in the *Rhetoric*, Book I, "no one grows angry with a person on whom there is no prospect of taking vengeance, and we feel comparatively little anger, or none at all, with those who are much our superiors in power."[14] The anger was still there, however, but it got directed toward safer targets: my family and closest friends. My anger spread, giving me painful shooting signs that I was coming back to life. I could not accept what had happened to me. What was I supposed to do now? How could everyone else carry on with their lives when women were dying? How could Tom go on teaching his classes, seeing students, chatting with colleagues . . . and why should he be able to walk down the street when I couldn't?

The incompatibility of fear of my assailant and appropriate anger toward him became most apparent after I began taking a women's self-defense class. It became clear that the way to break out of the double bind of self-blame versus powerlessness was through empowerment—physical as well as political. Learning to fight back is a crucial part of this process, not only because it enables us to experience justified, healing rage, but also because, as Iris Young has observed in her essay "Throwing Like a Girl," "women in sexist society are physically handicapped," moving about hesitantly, fearfully, in a constricted lived space, routinely underestimating what strength we actually have.[15] We have to learn to feel entitled to occupy space, to defend ourselves. The hardest thing for most of the women in my self-defense class to do was simply to yell 'No!' Women have been taught not to fight back when being attacked, to rely instead on placating or pleading with one's assailant—strategies that researchers have found to be least effective in resisting rape.[16]

The instructor of the class, a survivor herself, helped me through the difficult first sessions, through the flashbacks and the fear, and showed me I could be tougher than ever. As I was leaving after one session, I saw a student arrive for the next class—with a guide dog. I was furious that, in addition to everything else this woman had to struggle with, she had to worry about being raped. I thought I understood something of her fear since I felt, for the first time in my life, like I had a perceptual deficit—not the blurred vision from the detached vitreous, but, rather, the more hazardous lack of eyes in the back of my head. I tried to compensate for this on my walks by looking over my shoulder a lot and punctuating my purposeful, straight-ahead stride with an occasional pirouette, which must have made me look more whimsical than terrified.

The confidence I gained from learning how to fight back effectively not only enabled me to walk down the street again, it gave me back my life. But it was a changed life. A paradoxical life. I began to feel stronger than ever before, and more vulnerable, more determined to fight to change the world, but in need of several naps a day. News that friends found distressing in a less visceral way—the trials of the defendants in the Central Park jogger case, the controversy over *American Psycho,* the Gulf war, the Kennedy rape case, the Tyson trial, the fatal stabbing of law professor Mary Jo Frug near Harvard Square, the ax murders of two women graduate students at Dartmouth College—triggered debilitating flashbacks in me. Unlike survivors of wars or earthquakes, who inhabit a common shattered world, rape victims face the cataclysmic destruction of their world alone, surrounded by people who find it hard to understand what's so distressing. I realized that I exhibited every symptom of post-traumatic stress disorder—dissociation, flashbacks, hypervigilance, exaggerated startle response, sleep disorders, inability to concentrate, diminished interest in significant activities, and a sense of a foreshortened future.[17] I could understand why children exposed to urban violence have such trouble envisioning their futures. Although I had always been career-oriented, always planning for my future, I could no longer imagine how I would get through each day, let alone what I might be doing in a year's time. I didn't think I would ever write or teach philosophy again.

The American Psychiatric Association's *Diagnostic and Statistical Manual* defines post-traumatic stress disorder, in part, as the result of "an event that is outside the range of usual human experience."[18] Because the trauma is, to most people, inconceivable, it's also unspeakable. Even when I managed to find the words—and the strength—to describe my ordeal, it was hard for others to hear about it. They would have preferred me to just "buck up," as one friend urged me to do. But it's essential to talk about it, again and again. It's a way of remastering the trauma, although it can be retraumatizing when people refuse to listen. In my case, each time someone failed to respond it felt as though I were alone again in the ravine, dying, screaming. And still no one could hear me. Or, worse, they heard me, but refused to help.

I now know they were trying to help, but that recovering from trauma takes time, patience, and, most of all, determination on the part of the survivor. After about six months, I began to be able to take more responsibility for my own recovery, and stopped expecting others to pull me through. I entered the final stage of my recovery, a period of gradual acceptance and integration of what had happened. I joined a rape survivors' support group, I got a great deal of therapy, and I became involved in political activities, such as promoting S.15: the Violence against Women Act of 1991. . . .[19] Gradually, I was able to get back to work.

When I resumed teaching at Dartmouth in the fall of 1991, the first student who came to see me in my office during freshman orientation week told me that she had been raped. Last spring four Dartmouth students reported sexual assaults to the local police. In the aftermath of these recent reports, the women students on my campus have been told to use their heads, lock their doors, not go out after dark without a male escort. They have been advised: just don't do anything stupid.

Although colleges are eager to "protect" women by limiting their freedom of movement or providing them with male escorts, they continue to be reluctant to teach women to protect themselves. After months of lobbying the administration at my college, we were able to convince them to offer a women's self-defense and rape prevention course. It was offered last winter as a physical education course, and nearly one hundred students and employees signed up for it. Shortly after the course began, I was informed that the women students were not going to be allowed to get P.E. credit for it, since the administration had determined that it discriminated against men. I was told that granting credit for the course was in violation of Title IX, which prohibits sex-discrimination in education programs receiving federal funding—even though granting credit to men for being on the football team was not, even though Title IX law makes an explicit exception for P.E. classes involving substantial bodily contact, and even though every term the college offers several martial arts courses, for credit, that are open to men, geared to men's physiques and needs, and taken predominantly by men. I was told by an administrator that, even if Title IX permitted it, offering a women's self-defense course for credit violated "the College's nondiscrimination clause—a clause which, I hope, all reasonable men and women support as good policy." The implication that I was not a "reasonable woman" didn't sit well with me as a philosopher, so I wrote a letter to the appropriate administrative committee criticizing my college's position that single-sex sports, male-only fraternities, female-only sororities, and pregnancy leave policies are not discriminatory, in any invidious sense, while a women's self-defense class is. The administration has finally agreed to grant P.E. credit for the course, but shortly after that battle was over, I read in the *New York Times* that "a rape prevention ride service offered to women in the city of Madison and on the University of Wisconsin campus may lose its university financing because it discriminates against men."[20] The dean of students at Wisconsin said that this group—the Women's Transit Authority—which has been providing free nighttime rides to women students for nineteen years—must change its policy to allow male drivers and passengers. These are, in my view, examples of the application of what Catharine MacKinnon refers to as "the stupid theory of equality."[21] To argue that rape prevention policies for women discriminate against men is like arguing that money spent making university buildings more accessible to disabled persons discriminates against those able-bodied persons who do not benefit from these improvements.[22]

Sexual violence victimizes not only those women who are directly attacked, but *all* women. The fear of rape has long functioned to keep women in their place. Whether or not one agrees with the claims of those, such as Susan Brownmiller, who argue that rape is a means by which *all* men keep *all* women subordinate,[23] the fact that all women's lives are restricted by sexual violence is indisputable. The authors of *The Female Fear,* Margaret Gordon and Stephanie Riger, cite studies substantiating what every woman already knows—that the fear of rape prevents women from enjoying what men consider to be their birthright. Fifty percent of women never use public transportation after dark because of fear of rape. Women are eight times more likely than men to avoid walking in their own neighborhoods after dark, for the same reason.[24] In the seminar I taught last spring on Violence against Women, the men in the class were stunned by the extent to which the women in the class took precautions against assault every day—locking doors and windows, checking the back seat of the car, not walking alone at night, looking in closets on returning home. And this is at a 'safe,' rural New England campus.

Although women still have their work and leisure opportunities unfairly restricted by their relative lack of safety, paternalistic legislation excluding women from some of the 'riskier' forms of employment (e.g., bartending[25]) has, thankfully, disappeared, except, that is, in the military. We are still debating whether women should be permitted to engage in combat, and the latest rationale for keeping women out of battle is that they are more vulnerable than men to sexual violence. Those wanting to limit women's role in the military are now using the reported indecent assaults on the two female American prisoners of war in Iraq as evidence for women's unsuitability for combat.[26] One might as well argue that the fact that women are much more likely than men to be sexually assaulted on college campuses is evidence that women are not suited to post-secondary education. No one, to my knowledge, has proposed returning Ivy League colleges to their former all-male status as a solution to the problem of campus rape. Some have, however, seriously proposed enacting after-dark curfews for women, in spite of the fact that men are the perpetrators of the assaults. This is yet another indication of how natural it still seems to many people to address the problem of sexual violence by curtailing women's lives. The absurdity of this approach becomes apparent once one realizes that a woman can be sexually assaulted anywhere, at any time—in 'safe' places, in broad daylight, even in her own home.

For months after my assault, I was afraid of people finding out about it— afraid of their reactions and of their inability to respond. I was afraid that my professional work would be discredited, that I would be viewed as 'biased,' or, even worse, not properly 'philosophical.' Now I am no longer afraid of what might happen if I speak out about sexual violence. I'm much more afraid of what *will* continue to happen if I don't. Sexual violence is a problem of catastrophic proportions—a fact obscured by its mundanity, by its relentless occurrence, by the fact that so many of us have been victims of it. Imagine the moral outrage, the emergency response we would surely mobilize, if all of these everyday assaults occurred at the same time or were restricted to one geographical region? But why should the spatiotemporal coordinates of the vast numbers of sexual assaults be considered to be morally relevant? From the victim's point of view, the fact that she is isolated in her rape and her recovery, combined with the ordinariness of the crime that leads to its trivialization, makes the assault and its aftermath even more traumatic.

As devastating as sexual violence is, however, I want to stress that it is possible to survive it, and even to flourish after it, although it doesn't seem that way at the time. Whenever I see a survivor struggling with the overwhelming anger and sadness, I'm reminded of a sweet, motherly woman in my survivors' support group who sat silently throughout the group's first meeting. At the end of the hour she finally asked, softly, through tears: "Can anyone tell me if it ever stops hurting?" At the time I had the same question, and wasn't satisfied with any answer. Now I can say, yes, it does stop hurting, at least for longer periods of time. A year ago, I was pleased to discover that I could go for fifteen minutes without thinking about my attack. Now I can go for hours at a stretch without a flashback. That's on a good day. On a bad day, I may still take to my bed with lead in my veins, unable to find one good reason to go on.

Our group facilitator told us that first meeting: "You will never be the same. But you can be better." I protested that I had lost so much: my security, my self-esteem, my love and my work. I had been happy with the way things were. How could they ever be better now? As a survivor, she knew how I felt, but she also knew that, as she put it, "When your life is shattered, you're forced to pick up the pieces, and you have a chance to stop and examine them. You can say 'I don't want this one anymore' or 'I think I'll work on that one.'" I have had to give up more than I would ever have chosen to. But I have gained important skills and insights, and I no longer feel tainted by my victimization. Granted, those of us who live through sexual assault aren't given ticker tape parades or the keys to our cities, but it's an honor to be a survivor. Although it's not exactly the sort of thing I can put on my résumé, it's the accomplishment of which I'm most proud.

Now, more than two years after the assault, I can acknowledge the good things that have come from the recovery process—the clarity, the confidence, the determination, the many supporters and survivors who have brought meaning back into my world. This is not to say that the attack and its aftermath were, on balance, a good thing or, as one aunt put it, "a real blessing from above." I would rather not have gone down that road. It's been hard for me, as a philosopher, to learn the lesson that knowledge isn't always desirable, that the truth doesn't always set you free. Sometimes, it fills you with incapacitating terror and, then, uncontrollable rage. But I suppose you should embrace it anyway, for the reason Nietzsche exhorts you to love your enemies: if it doesn't kill you, it makes you stronger.

People ask me if I'm recovered now, and I reply that it depends on what that means. If they mean "am I back to where I was before the attack"? I have to say, no, and I never will be. I am not the same person who set off, singing, on that sunny Fourth of July in the French countryside. I left her—and her trust, her innocence, her *joie de vivre*—in a rocky creek bed at the bottom of a ravine. I had to in order to survive. I now understand what a friend described to me as a Jewish custom of giving those who have outlived a brush with death new names. The trauma has changed me forever, and if I insist too often that my friends and family acknowledge it, that's because I'm afraid they don't know who I am.

But if recovery means being able to incorporate this awful knowledge into my life and carry on, then, yes, I'm recovered. I don't wake each day with a start, thinking: "this can't have happened to me!" It happened. I have no guarantee that it won't happen again, although my self-defense classes have given me the confidence to move about in the world and to go for longer and longer walks—with my two dogs. Sometimes I even manage to enjoy myself. And I no longer cringe when I see a woman jogging alone on the country road where I live, though I may still have a slight urge to rush out and protect her, to tell her to come inside where she'll be safe. But I catch myself, like a mother learning to let go, and cheer her on, thinking, may she always be so carefree, so at home in her world. She has every right to be.

Notes

1. I would like to thank the North American Society for Social Philosophy for inviting me to give this paper as a plenary address at the Eighth International Social Philosophy Conference, Davidson College, August 1, 1992. I am also grateful to the Franklin J. Matchette Foundation for sponsoring this talk.

2. Federal Bureau of Investigation, *Uniform Crime Reports for the United States,* 1989, p. 6.

3. Robin Warshaw notes that "[g]overnment estimates find that anywhere from three to ten rapes are committed for every one rape reported. And while rapes by strangers are still underreported, rapes by acquaintances are virtually nonreported. Yet, based on intake observations made by staff at various rape counseling centers (where victims come for treatment, but do not have to file police reports), 70–80 percent of all rape crimes are acquaintance rapes." See Robin Warshaw, *I Never Called It Rape* (New York: Harper & Row, 1988), p. 12.

4. National Coalition against Domestic Violence, fact sheet, in "Report on Proposed Legislation S.15: The Violence against Women Act," p. 9. On file with the Senate Judiciary Committee.

5. After I presented this paper at Davidson College, Iris Young drew my attention to Jeffner Allen's discussion of her rape in Jeffner Allen, *Lesbian Philosophy: Explorations* (Palo Alto, Calif.: Institute of Lesbian Studies, 1986).

6. Another, much more perceptive, article is Lois Pineau's "Date Rape: A Feminist Analysis," *Law and Philosophy* 8 (1989): 217–43. In addition, an excellent book on the causes of male violence was written by a scholar trained as a philosopher, Myriam Miedzian. See Myriam Miedzian, *Boys Will Be Boys: Breaking the Link between Masculinity and Violence* (New York:

Doubleday, 1991). Philosophical discussions of the problem of evil, even recent ones such as that in Robert Nozick, *The Examined Life: Philosophical Meditations* (New York: Touchstone Books, 1989), don't mention the massive problem of sexual violence. Even Nell Noddings' book, *Women and Evil* (Berkeley and Los Angeles: University of California Press, 1989), which is an "attempt to describe evil from the perspective of women's experience," mentions rape only twice, briefly, and in neither instance from the victim's point of view.

7. Ross Harrison, "Rape—A Study in Political Philosophy," in *Rape: An Historical and Cultural Inquiry*, ed. Sylvana Tomaselli and Roy Porter (New York: Basil Blackwell, 1986), p. 51.

8. See especially Patricia Williams's discussion of the Ujaama House incident in *The Alchemy of Race and Rights* (Cambridge, Mass.: Harvard University Press, 1991), pp. 110–16; Mari Matsuda, "Public Response to Racist Speech: Considering the Victim's Story," *Michigan Law Review* 87, no. 8 (1989): 2320–81; and Charles Lawrence, "If He Hollers, Let Him Go: Regulating Racist Speech on Campus," *Duke Law Journal* (1990): 481–83.

9. Harrison, "Rape," p. 52.

10. As the authors of *The Female Fear* note: "The requirement of proof of the victim's non-consent is unique to the crime of forcible rape. A robbery victim, for example, is usually not considered as having 'consented' to the crime if he or she hands money over to an assailant [especially if there was use of force or threat of force]." See Margaret T. Gordon and Stephanie Riger, *The Female Fear: The Social Cost of Rape* (Chicago: University of Illinois Press, 1991), p. 59.

11. Robert Lowell, *Selected Poems* (New York: Farrar, Straus and Giroux, 1977), p. 82.

12. Quoted in *The New York Times*, September 13, 1991, p. A18. Although Judge Thomas made this statement during his confirmation hearings, Justice Thomas's actions while on the Supreme Court have belied his professed empathy with criminal defendants.

13. Ronald de Souza, *The Rationality of Emotion* (Cambridge, Mass.: MIT Press, 1987).

14. In Jonathan Barnes, ed., *The Complete Works of Aristotle* (Princeton: Princeton University Press, 1984), 2:2181–82. I thank John Cooper for drawing my attention to this aspect of Aristotle's theory of the emotions.

15. Iris Marion Young, *Throwing Like a Girl and Other Essays in Feminist Philosophy and Social Theory* (Indianapolis: Indiana University Press, 1990), p. 153.

16. See Pauline B. Bart and Patricia H. O'Brien, "Stopping Rape: Effective Avoidance Strategies," *Signs* 10, no. 1 (1984): 83–101.

17. For a clinical description of Post-traumatic Stress Disorder (or PTSD), see the *Diagnostic and Statistical Manual*, 3rd ed., rev., (American Psychiatric Association, 1987). Excellent discussions of the recovery process undergone by rape survivors can be found in Morton Bard and Dawn Sangrey, *The Crime Victim's Book* (New York: Brunner/Mazel, 1986); Helen Benedict, *Recovery: How to Survive Sexual Assault—for Women, Men, Teenagers, Their Friends and Families* (Garden City, New York: Doubleday, 1985); Judith Lewis Herman, *Trauma and Recovery* (New York: Basic Books, 1992); and Ronnie Janoff-Bulman, *Shattered Assumptions: Towards a New Psychology of Trauma* (New York: The Free Press, 1992). I have also found it very therapeutic to read first-person accounts by rape survivors such as Susan Estrich, *Real Rape* (Cambridge, Mass.: Harvard University Press, 1987), and Nancy Ziegenmeyer, *Taking Back My Life* (New York: Summit Books, 1992).

18. *Diagnostic and Statistical Manual*, 3rd ed., rev. (Washington, D.C.: American Psychiatric Association, 1987), p. 247.

19. S.15, sponsored by Sen. Joseph Biden, D-Del., was drafted largely by Victoria Nourse, Special Counsel for Criminal Law, Office of the Senate Judiciary Committee. I am particularly interested in Title III, which would reclassify gender-motivated assaults as bias crimes. From the victim's perspective this reconceptualization is important. What was most difficult for me to recover from was the knowledge that some man wanted to kill me simply because I am a woman. This aspect of the harm inflicted in hate crimes (or bias crimes) is similar to the harm caused by hate speech. One cannot make a sharp distinction between physical and psychological harm in the case of PTSD sufferers. Most of the symptoms are physiological. I find it odd that in philosophy of law, so many theorists are devoted to a kind of Cartesian dualism that most philosophers of mind rejected long ago.

20. *The New York Times,* April 19, 1992, p. 36.

21. She characterized a certain theory of equality in this way during the discussion after a Gauss seminar she gave at Princeton University, April 9, 1992.

22. For an illuminating discussion of the ways in which we need to treat people differently in order to achieve genuine equality see Martha Minnow, *Making All the Difference: Inclusion, Exclusion, and American Law* (Ithaca, N.Y.: Cornell University Press, 1990).

23. See Susan Brownmiller, *Against Our Will: Men, Women, and Rape* (New York: Bantam Books, 1975).

24. Gordon and Riger, *The Female Fear.*

25. As recently as 1948, the United States Supreme Court upheld a state law prohibiting the licensing of any woman as a bartender (unless she was the wife or daughter of the bar owner where she was applying to work). *Goesaert v. Cleary,* 335 U.S. 464 (1948).

26. *The New York Times,* June 19, 1992, p. 1, A13.

39

What's Wrong with Rape

Pamela Foa

It is clear that rape is wrong. It is equally clear that the wrongness of rape is not completely explained by its status as a criminal assault. Dispute begins, however, when we attempt to account for the special features of rape, the ways in which its wrongness goes beyond its criminal character. I shall argue against those who maintain that the special wrongness of rape arises from and is completely explained by a societal refusal to recognize women as *people*. I shall offer a different explanation: The special wrongness of rape is due to, and is only an exaggeration of, the wrongness of our sexual interactions in general. Thus, a clear analysis of the special wrongness of rape will help indicate some of the essential features of healthy, nonrapine sexual interactions.

I. The Wrongness of Rape Goes Beyond Its Criminality

It is to be expected during this period of resurgent feminism that rape will be seen primarily as a manifestation of how women are mistreated in our society. For example, consider these remarks of Simone de Beauvoir:

> All men are drawn to B[rigitte] B[ardot]'s seductiveness, but that does not mean that they are kindly disposed towards her. . . . They are unwilling to give up their role of lord and master. . . . Freedom and full consciousness remain their [the men's] right and privilege. . . . In the game of love BB is as much a hunter as she is a prey. The male is an object to her, just as she is to him, and

From *Feminism and Philosophy* (Totowa, N.J.: Littlefield, Adams & Company, 1977). Reprinted by permission.

that is precisely what wounds the masculine pride. In the Latin countries where men cling to "the myth of woman as object," BB's naturalness seems to them more perverse than any possible sophistication. It is to assert that one is man's fellow and equal, to recognize that between the woman and him there is a mutual desire and pleasure. . . .

But the male feels uncomfortable if, instead of a doll of flesh and blood, he holds in his arms a conscious being who is sizing him up. "You realize," an average Frenchman once said to me, "that when a man finds a woman attractive, he wants to be able to pinch her behind." A ribald gesture reduces a woman to a thing that a man can do with as he pleases without worrying about what goes on in her mind and heart and body.[1]

And rape is apparently the quintessential instance of women being viewed as objects, of women being treated as entities other than, and morally inferior to, men. It is implicit in this object-view that if men, and therefore society, viewed women as full moral equals, rape would be an assault no different in kind than any other. Thus, it is a consequence of this view that the special wrongness of rape is to be found in the nonsexual aspects of the act.

To this end, Marilyn Frye and Carolyn Shafer suggest in their paper "Rape and Respect" that the wrongness of rape is twofold: first, it is the use of a person without her consent in the performance of an act or event which is against her own best interests; and second, it is a social means of reinforcing the status of women as kinds of entities who lack and ought to lack the full privileges of personhood—importantly, the freedom to move as they will through what is rightfully their domain.[2] What is good about this account is that it provides one way of understanding the sense of essential violation of one's *person* (and not mere sexual abuse), which seems to be the natural concomitant of rape.

This account, further, gives one explanation for the continuous social denial of the common fact of criminal rape. On this view, to recognize rape as a criminal act, one must recognize the domains of women. But if domains are inextricably connected with personhood—if personhood, in fact, is to be analyzed in terms of domains—then it ought to be obvious that where there is no domain there can be no criminal trespass of domain; there can only be misperceptions or misunderstandings. To recognize domains of consent is to recognize the existence of people at their centers. Without such centers, there can be no rape.

Unfortunately, I do not believe that this kind of account can serve as an adequate explanation of what's wrong with rape. I find irrelevant its emphasis on the ontological status of women as persons of the first rank. It is granted that in any act of rape a person is used without proper regard to her personhood, but this is true of every kind of assault. If there is an additional wrongness to rape, it must be that more is wrong than the mere treatment of a person by another person without proper regard for her personhood. Later in this essay, I shall show that there is no need to differentiate ontologically between victim and assailant in order to explain the special wrongness of rape. However, it is important to recognize that rape is profoundly wrong even if it is not an act between ontological equals.

The special wrongness of rape cannot be traced to the fact that in this act men are not recognizing the full array of moral and legal rights and privileges which accrue to someone of equal status. Rape of children is at least as heinous as rape of adults, though few actually believe that children have or ought to have the same large domain of consent adults (male and female) ought to have. In part, this is what is so disturbing about a recent English decision I shall discuss in a moment: it seems to confuse the ontological with the moral. Men's wishes, intentions, and beliefs are given a different (and more important) weight, just because they are (wrongly in this case, perhaps rightly in the case of children) viewed as different kinds of entities than women.

But even if one thinks that women are not people, or that all people (for example, children), do not have the same rights or, prima facie, the same domains of consent, it seems that rape is still especially horrible, awful in a way that other assaults are not. There is, for example, something deeply distressing, though not necessarily criminal, about raping one's pet dog. It is disturbing in ways no ordinary assault, even upon a person, seems to be disturbing. It may here be objected that what accounts for the moral outrage in these two cases is that the first is an instance of pedophilia, and the second of bestiality. That is, the special wrongness of these acts is due to the "unnatural" direction of the sexual impulse, rather than to the abusive circumstances of the fulfillment of a "natural" sexual impulse.

I would argue in response that outrage at "unnatural" acts is misdirected and inappropriate. The notion that acting "against" nature is immoral stems from the false belief that how things are in the majority of cases is, morally speaking, how things always ought to be. Acting unnaturally is not acting immorally unless there is a moral design to the natural order—and there is no such structure to it. This means, then, that if it is reasonable to feel that something very wrong has occurred in the above two cases, then it must be because they are rape and not because they are "unnatural acts." However, even if this argument is not conclusive, it must be agreed that the random raping of a mentally retarded adult is clearly wrong even though such an individual does not, in our society, have all the legal and moral rights of normal people.[3]

Of course, another very reasonable point to make here may well be that it is not just people who have domains, and that what's wrong with rape is the invasion by one being into another's domain without consent or right. But if something like this is true, then rape would be wrong because it was an "incursion" into a domain. This would make it wrong in the same way that other assaults are wrong. The closer the incursion comes to the center of a person's identity, the worse is the act.

The problem here is that such an argument suggests that rape is wrong the same way, and only the same way, that other assaults are wrong. And yet the evidence contradicts this. There is an emotional concomitant to this assault, one that is lacking in nonsexual criminal assaults. What must be realized is that when it comes to sexual matters, people—in full recognition of the equal ontological status of their partners—treat each other abominably. Contrary to the Frye/Shafer theory, I believe that liberated men and women—people who have no doubts about the moral or ontological equality of the sexes—can and do have essentially rapelike sexual lives.

The following case is sufficient to establish that it is not just the assault upon one's person, or the intrusion into one's domain, that makes for the special features of rape. In New York twenty or so years ago, there was a man who went around Manhattan slashing people with a very sharp knife. He did not do this as part of any robbery or other further bodily assault. His end was simply to stab people. Although he was using people against their own best interests, and without their consent—that is, although he is broadly violating domains—to be the victim of the Mad Slasher was not to have been demeaned or dirtied as a person in the way that the victim of rape is demeaned or dirtied. It was not to be wronged or devalued in the same way that to be raped is to be wronged or devalued. No one ever accused any of the victims of provoking, initiating, or enjoying the attack.

Yet the public morality about rape suggests that unless one is somehow mutilated, broken, or killed in addition to being raped, one is suspected of having provoked, initiated, complied in, consented to, or oven enjoyed the act. It is this public response, the fear of such a response and the belief (often) in the rationality of such a response (even from those who do unequivocally view you as a person) that scorns to make rape especially horrible.

Thus, what is especially bad about rape is a function of its place in our society's sexual views, not in our ontological views. There is, of course, nothing necessary about these views, but until they change, no matter what progress is made in the fight for equality between the sexes, rape will remain an especially awful act.

II. Sex, Intimacy, and Pleasure

Our response to rape brings into focus our inner feelings about the nature, purpose, and morality of all sexual encounters and of ourselves as sexual beings. Two areas which seem immediately problematic are the relation between sex and intimacy and the relation between sex and pleasure.

Our Victorian ancestors believed that sex in the absence of (at least marital) intimacy was morally wrong and that the only women who experienced sexual pleasure were nymphomaniacs.[4] Freud's work was revolutionary in part just because he challenged the view of "good" women and children as asexual creatures.[5] Only with Masters and Johnson's work, however, has there been a full scientific recognition of the capacity of ordinary women for sexual pleasure.[6] But though it is now recognized that sexual pleasure exists for all people at all stages of life and is, in its own right, a morally permissible goal, this contemporary attitude is still dominated by a Victorian atmosphere. It remains the common feeling that it is a kind of pleasure which should be experienced only in private and only between people who are and intend to be otherwise intimate. Genital pleasure is private not only in our description of its physical location, but also in our conception of its occurrence or occasion.

For the rape victim, the special problem created by the discovery of pleasure in sex is that now some people believe that *every* sex act must be pleasurable to some extent, including rape.[7] Thus, it is believed by some that the victim in a rape must at some level be enjoying herself—and that this enjoyment in a nonintimate, nonprivate environment is shameful. What is especially wrong about rape, therefore, is that it makes evident the essentially sexual nature of women, and this has been viewed, from the time of Eve through the time of Victoria, as cause for their humiliation. Note that on this view the special evil of rape is due to the feminine character and not to that of her attacker.[8]

The additional societal attitude that sex is moral only between intimates creates a further dilemma in assessing the situation of the rape victim. On the one hand, if it is believed that the sex act itself creates an intimate relationship between two people, then, by necessity, the rape victim experiences intimacy with her assailant. This may incline one to deny the fact of the rape by pointing to the fact of the intimacy. If one does not believe that sex itself creates intimacy between the actors, but nonetheless believes that sex is immoral in the absence of intimacy, then the event of sex in the absence of an intimate relationship, even though involuntary, is cause for public scorn and humiliation. For the rape victim, to acknowledge the rape is to acknowledge one's immorality. Either way, the victim has violated the social sexual taboos and she must therefore be ostracized.

What is important is no longer that one is the victim of an assault, but rather that one is the survivor of a social transgression. This is the special burden that the victim carries.

There is support for my view in Gary Wills's review of Tom Wicker's book about the Attica prisoners' revolt.[9] What needs to be explained is the apparently peculiar way in which the safety of the prisoners' hostages was ignored in the preparations for the assault on the prison and in the assault itself. What strikes me as especially important in this event is that those outside the prison walls treated the *guards* exactly like the *prisoners*. The critical similarity is the alleged participation in taboo sexual activity, where such activity is seen as a paradigm of humiliating behavior. In his review Wills says,

> Sexual fantasy played around Attica's walls like invisible lightning. Guards told their families that all the inmates were animals. . . .
> When the assault finally came, and officers mowed down the hostages along with the inmates, an almost religious faith kept faked stories alive

against all the evidence—that the hostages were found castrated; that those still living had been raped. . . . None of it was true, but the guards knew what degradation the prisoners had been submitted to, and the kind of response that might call for. . . .

One has to go very far down into the human psyche to understand what went on in that placid town. . . . The bloodthirsty hate of the local community was so obvious by the time of the assault that even Rockefeller . . . ordered that no correction personnel join the attack. . . . [Nonetheless] eleven men managed to go in. . . . Did they come to save the hostages, showing more care for them than outsiders could? Far from it. They fired as early and indiscriminately as the rest. Why? I am afraid Mr. Wicker is a bit too decent to understand what was happening, though his own cultural background gives us a clue. Whenever a white girl was caught with a black in the old South, myth demanded that a charge of rape be brought and the "boy" be lynched. But a shadowy ostracism was inflicted on the girl. Did she fight back? Might she undermine the myth with a blurted tale or a repeated episode? At any rate, she was tainted. She had, willed she or nilled she, touched the untouchable and acquired her own evil halo of contamination. Taboos take little account of "intention." In the same way, guards caught in that yard were tainted goods. . . . They were an embarrassment. The white girl may sincerely have struggled with her black assailant; but even to imagine that resistance was defiling—and her presence made people imagine it. She was a public pollution—to be purged. Is this [comparison] fanciful? Even Wicker . . . cannot understand the attitude of those in charge who brought no special medical units to Attica before the attack began. . . . The lynch mob may kill the girl in its urgency to get at the boy—and it will regret this less than it admits.[10]

Accounts like the one offered by Frye and Shafer might explain why the *prisoners* were treated so callously by the assaulting troops, but they cannot explain the brutal treatment of the hostages. Surely they cannot say that the guards who were hostages were not and had never been viewed as people, as ontological equals, by the general society. And yet there was the same special horror in being a hostage at Attica as there is for a woman who has been raped. In both cases the *victim* has acquired a "halo of contamination" which permanently taints. And this cannot be explained by claiming that in both cases society is denying personhood or domains of consent to the victim.

The victim in sexual assault cases is as much a victim of our confused beliefs about sex as of the assault itself. The tremendous strains we put on such victims are a cruel result of our deep confusion about the place of, and need for, sexual relationships and the role of pleasure and intimacy in those relationships.

In spite of the fact, I believe, that as a society we share the *belief* that sex is only justified in intimate relationships, we act to avoid real intimacy at almost any cost. We seem to be as baffled as our predecessors were about the place of intimacy in our sexual and social lives. And this is, I think, because we are afraid that real intimacy creates or unleashes sexually wanton relationships, licentious lives—and this we view as morally repugnant. At the same time, we believe that sex in the absence of an intimate relationship is whoring and is therefore also morally repugnant. It is this impossible conflict which I think shows us that we will be able to make sense of our response to rape only if we look at rape as the model of all our sexual interactions, not as its antithesis.

III. The Model of Sex: Rape

Though we may sometimes speak as though sexual activity is most pleasurable between friends, we do not teach each other to treat our sexual partners as friends. Middle-class children, whom I take to be our cultural models, are instructed from the earliest possible time to ignore their sexual feelings. Long before intercourse can be a central issue, when children are prepubescent, boys are instructed to lunge for a kiss and girls are instructed to permit nothing more than a peck on the cheek. This encouragement of miniature adult sexual behavior is instructive on several levels.

It teaches the child that courting behavior is rarely spontaneous and rarely something which gives pleasure to the people involved—that is, it is not like typical playing with friends. It gives the child a glimpse of how adults do behave, or are expected to behave, and therefore of what is expected in future life and social interactions. Importantly, boys are instructed *not* to be attentive to the claims of girls with respect to their desires and needs. And girls are instructed *not* to consult their feelings as a means of or at least a check on what behavior they should engage in.

Every American girl, be she philosopher-to-be or not, is well acquainted with the slippery-slope argument by the time she is ten. She is told that if she permits herself to become involved in anything more than a peck on the cheek, anything but the most innocent type of sexual behavior, she will inevitably become involved in behavior that will result in intercourse and pregnancy. And such behavior is wrong. That is, she is told that if she acquiesces to any degree to her feelings, then she will be doing something immoral.

Meanwhile, every American boy is instructed, whether explicitly or not, that the girls have been given this argument (as a weapon) and that therefore, since everything that a girl says will be a reflection of this argument (and not of her feelings), they are to ignore everything that she says.

Girls are told never to consult their feelings (they can only induce them to the edge of the slippery slope); they are always to say "no." Boys are told that it is a sign of their growing manhood to be able to get a girl way beyond the edge of the slope, and that it is standard procedure for girls to say "no" independently of their feelings. Thus, reasonably enough, boys act as far as one can tell independently of the explicit information they are currently receiving from the girl.

For women, it is very disconcerting to find that from the age of eight or nine or ten, one's reports of one's feelings are no longer viewed as accurate, truthful, important, or interesting R. D. Laing, the English psychiatrist and theorist, claims that it is this type of adult behavior which creates the environment in which insanity best finds its roots.[11] It is clear, at least, that such behavior is not a model of rationality or health. In any event, rape is a case where only the pretense of listening has been stripped away. It is the essence of what we have all been trained to expect.

In a sexually healthier society, men and women might he told to engage in that behavior which gives them pleasure as long as that pleasure is not (does not involve actions) against anyone's will (including coerced actions) and does not involve them with responsibilities they cannot on will not meet (emotional, physical, or financial).

But as things are now, boys and girls have no way to tell each other what gives them pleasure and what not, what frightens them and what not; there are only violence, threats of violence, and appeals to informing on one or the other to some dreaded peer or parental group. This is a very high-risk, high-stake game, which women and girls, at least, often feel may easily become rape (even though it is usually played for little more than a quick feel in the back seat of the car or corner of the family sofa). But the ultimate consequences of this type of instruction are not so petty. Consider, for example, the effects of a recent English high-court decision:

> Now, according to the new interpretation, no matter how much a woman screams and fights, the accused rapist can be cleared by claiming he believed the victim consented, even though his belief may be considered unreasonable or irrational.
>
> On a rainy night seven months ago, a London housewife and mother of three claims she was dragged into this dilapidated shed. Annie Baker says she screamed for help and she fought but she was raped. Mrs. Baker lost her case in court because the man claimed he thought when she said no, she meant yes.
>
> One member of Parliament [predicts juries will] "now have the rapist saying that the woman asked for what she got and she wanted what they [sic] gave her."
>
> However, the Head of the British Law Society maintains, "Today juries are prepared to accept that the relationship between the sexes has become much more promiscuous, and they have to look much more carefully to see whether the woman has consented under modern conditions. . . . One mustn't readily assume that a woman did not consent, because all indications are that there is a greater willingness to consent today than there was thirty years ago."[12]
>
> "The question to be answered in this case," said Lord Cross of Chelsea, "as I see it, is whether, according to the ordinary use of the English language, a man can be said to have committed rape if he believed that the woman was consenting to the intercourse. I do not think he can."[13]

This is the most macabre extension imaginable of our early instruction. It is one which makes initially implausible and bizarre any suggestion that the recent philosophical analyses of sexuality as the product of a mutual desire for communication—or even for orgasm or sexual satisfaction—bear any but the most tangential relation to reality.[14]

As we are taught, sexual desires are desires women ought not to have and men must have. This is the model which makes necessary an eternal battle of the sexes. It is the model which explains why rape is the prevalent model of sexuality. It has the further virtue of explaining the otherwise puzzling attitude of many that women will cry "rape" falsely at the slightest provocation. It explains, too, why men believe that no woman can be raped. It is as though what was mildly unsatisfactory at first (a girl's saying "no") becomes, overtime, increasingly erotic, until the ultimate turn-on becomes a woman's cry of "rape!"

IV. An Alternative: Sex between Friends

Understanding what's wrong with rape is difficult just because it is a member of the most common species of social encounter. To establish how rape is wrong is to establish that we have *all* been stepping to the wrong beat. Rape is only different in degree from the quintessential sexual relationship: marriage.

As Janice Moulton has noted, recent philosophical attention to theories of sexuality seem primarily concerned with sex between strangers.[15] On my view, we can explain this primary interest by noticing that our courting procedures are structured so that the couple must remain essentially estranged from each other. They do not ever talk or listen to each other with the respect and charity of friends. Instead, what is taken as the height of the erotic is sex without intimacy.

As long as we remain uncertain of the legitimacy of sexual pleasure, it will be impossible to give up our rape model of sexuality. For it can only be given up when we are willing to talk openly to each other without shame, embarrassment, or coyness about sex. Because only then will we not be too afraid to listen to each other.

Fortunately, to give this up requires us to make friends of our lovers.[16] Once we understand that intimacy enlarges the field of friendship, we can use some of the essential features of friendship as part of the model for sexual interaction, and we can present the pleasures of friendship as a real alternative to predatory pleasures.

I am not here committing myself to the view that the correct model for lovers is that of friends. Though I believe lovers involved in a healthy relationship have a fairly complex friendship, and though I am at a loss to find any important feature of a relationship between lovers which is not also one between friends, it may well be that the two relationships are merely closely related and not, in the end, explainable with the identical model.

It remains an enormously difficult task to throw over our anachronistic beliefs, and to resolve the conflict we feel about the sexual aspects of ourselves. But once this is done, not only will there be the obvious benefits of being able to exchange ignorance and denial of ourselves and others for knowledge, and fear for friendship, but we will also be able to remove the taboo from sex—even from rape. There will be no revelation, no reminder in the act of rape which we will need so badly to repress or deny that we must transform the victim into a guilt-bearing survivor. An act of rape will no longer remind us of the "true" nature of sex and our sexual desires.

Where there is nothing essentially forbidden about the fact of our sexual desires, the victim of rape will no longer be subject to a taboo or be regarded as dirty and in need of societal estrangement. The victim can then be regarded as having been grievously insulted, without simultaneously and necessarily having been permanently injured.

Further, if the model of sexual encounters is altered, there will no longer be any motivation for blaming the victim of rape. Since sex and rape will no longer be equated, there will be no motive for covering our own guilt or shame about the rapine nature of sex in general by transferring our guilt to the victim and ostracizing her. Rape will become an unfortunate aberration, the act of a criminal individual, rather than a symbol of our systematic ill-treatment and denial of each other.

Notes

1. Simone de Beauvoir, *Brigitte Bardot and the Lolita Syndrome* (London: New English Library, 1962), pp. 28, 30, 32.

2. Frye and Shafer characterize a domain as "where . . . a person . . . lives. . . . Since biological life and health are prerequisites for the pursuit of any other interests and goals, . . . everything necessary for their maintenance and sustenance evidently will fall very close to the center of the domain. Anything which exerts an influence on . . . a person's will or dulls its intelligence or affects its own sense of its identity . . . also comes very near the center of the domain. Whatever has a relatively permanent effect on the person, whatever affects its relatively constant surroundings, whatever causes it discomfort or distress—in short, whatever a person has to live with—is likely to fall squarely within its domain" ("Rape and Respect," [in *Feminism and Philosophy* (Totowa, N.J.: Littlefield, Adams, 1977)], p. 337).

3. This societal attitude, however, that the mentally retarded are not the equals of normal people is not one with which I associate myself.

4. Françoise Basch, *Relative Creatures: Victorian Women and Society in the Novel* (New York: Schocken Books, 1974), pp. 8–9, 270–71.

5. See *The Basic Writings of Sigmund Freud*, ed. A. A. Brill (New York: Random House, 1948), pp. 553–633.

6. William H. Masters and Virginia E. Johnson, *Human Sexual Response* (Boston: Little, Brown, 1966).

7. It may well be that Freud's theory of human sexuality is mistakenly taken to support this

view. See Sigmund Freud, *A General Introduction to Psychoanalysis* (New York: Washington Square Press, 1962), pp. 329–47.

8. What is a complete non sequitur, of course, is that the presence of such pleasure is sufficient to establish that no criminal assault has occurred. The two events are completely independent.

9. Tom Wicker, *A Time to Die* (New York: Quadrangle Books, 1975).

10. Gary Wills, "The Human Sewer," *New York Review of Books*, April 3, 1975, p. 4.

11. See, for example, R. D. Laing and A. Esterson, *Sanity, Madness and the Family* (Baltimore: Penguin, Pelican Books, 1970).

12. "CBS Evening News with Walter Cronkite," May 22, 1975.

13. *New American Movement Newspaper,* May 1975, p. 8.

14. See R. C. Solomon, "Sex and Perversion," Tom Nagel, "Sexual Perversion," and Janice Moulton, "Sex and Reference," in *Philosophy and Sex*, 1st ed., ed. Robert Baker and Frederick Elliston (Amherst, N.Y.: Prometheus Books, 1975).

15. Janice Moulton, "Sex and Sex," unpublished manuscript.

16. See Lyla O'Driscoll, "On the Nature and Value of Marriage" [in *Feminism and Philosophy*]. She argues that marriage and the sexual relations it entails should be based on friendship rather than romantic love.

40

Men in Groups:
Collective Responsibility for Rape

Larry May and Robert Strikwerda

As teenagers, we ran in a crowd that incessantly talked about sex. Since most of us were quite afraid of discovering our own sexual inadequacies, we were quite afraid of women's sexuality. To mask our fear, of which we were quite ashamed, we maintained a posture of bravado, which we were able to sustain through mutual reinforcement when in small groups or packs. Riding from shopping mall to fast food establishment, we would tell each other stories about our sexual exploits, stories we all secretly believed to be pure fictions. We drew strength from the camaraderie we felt during these experiences. Some members of our group would yell obscenities at women on the street as we drove by. Over time, conversation turned more and more to group sex, especially forced sex with women we passed on the road. To give it its proper name, our conversation turned increasingly to rape. At a certain stage, we tired of it all and stopped associating with this group of men, or perhaps they were in most ways still boys. The reason we left was not that we disagreed with what was going on but, if this decision to leave was reasoned at all, it was that the posturing (the endless attempts to impress one another by our daring ways) simply became very tiresome. Only much later in life did we think that there was anything wrong, morally, socially, or politically, with what went on in that group of adolescents who seemed so ready to engage in rape. Only later still did we wonder whether we shared in responsibility for the rapes that are perpetrated by those men who had similar experiences to ours.[1]

Catharine MacKinnon has recently documented the link between violence and rape in the war in Bosnia. Young Serbian soldiers, some with no previous sexual experience, seemed quite willing to rape Muslim and Croatian women as their reward for "winning" the war. These young men were often encouraged in

Originally published in *Hypatia* 9, no. 2 (Spring 1994). © by Larry May and Robert Strikwerda. Reprinted with permission of the authors.

these acts by groups of fellow soldiers, and even sometimes by their commanding officers. Indeed, gang rape in concentration camps, at least at the beginning of the war, seems to have been common.[2] The situation in Bosnia is by no means unique in the history of war.[3] But rape historically has never been considered a war crime. MacKinnon suggests that this is because "Rape in war has so often been treated as extracurricular, as just something men do, as a product rather than a policy of war."[4]

War crimes are collective acts taken against humanity; whereas rape has almost always been viewed as a despicable "private" act. In this essay we wish to challenge the view that rape is the responsibility only of the rapists by challenging the notion that rape is best understood as an individual, private act. This is an essay about the relationship between the shared experiences of men in groups, especially experiences that make rape more likely in Western culture, and the shared responsibility of men for the prevalence of rape in that culture. The claim of the essay is that in some societies men are collectively responsible for rape in that most if not all men contribute in various ways to the prevalence of rape, and as a result these men should share in responsibility for rape.

Most men do very little at all to oppose rape in their societies; does this make them something like co-conspirators with the men who rape? In Canada, a number of men have founded the "White Ribbon Campaign." This is a program of fund-raising, consciousness-raising, and symbolic wearing of white ribbons during the week ending on December 6th, the anniversary of the murder of fourteen women at a Montreal engineering school by a man shouting "I hate feminists." Should men in U.S. society start a similar campaign? If they do not, do they deserve the "co-conspirator" label? If they do, is this symbolic act enough to diminish their responsibility? Should men be speaking out against the program of rape in the war in Bosnia? What should they tell their sons about such rapes, and about rapes that occur in their home towns? If men remain silent, are they not complicitous with the rapists?

We will argue that insofar as male bonding and socialization in groups contributes to the prevalence of rape in Western societies, men in those societies should feel responsible for the prevalence of rape and should feel motivated to counteract such violence and rape. In addition, we will argue that rape should be seen as something that men, as a group, are collectively responsible for, in a way which parallels the collective responsibility of a society for crimes against humanity perpetrated by some members of their society. Rape is indeed a crime against humanity, not merely a crime against a particular woman. And rape is a crime perpetrated by men as a group, not merely by the individual rapist.

To support our claims we will criticize four other ways to understand responsibility for rape. First, it is sometimes said that only the rapist is responsible since he alone intentionally committed the act of rape. Second, it is sometimes said that no one is responsible since rape is merely a biologically oriented response to stimuli that men have little or no control over. Third, it is sometimes said that everyone, women and men alike, contribute to the violent environment which produces rape so both women and men are equally responsible for rape, and hence it is a mistake to single men out. Fourth, it is sometimes said that it is "patriarchy," rather than individual men or men as a group, which is responsible for rape.[5] After examining each of these views we will conclude by briefly offering our own positive reasons for thinking that men are collectively responsible for the prevalence of rape in Western society.

I. The Rapist As Loner or Demon

Joyce Carol Oates has recently described the sport of boxing, where men are encouraged to violate the social rule against harming one another, as "a highly organized ritual that violates taboo."

> The paradox of the boxer is that, in the ring, he experiences himself as a living conduit for the inchoate, demonic will of the crowd: the expression of their collective desire, which is to pound another human being into absolute submission.[6]

Oates makes the connection here between boxing and rape. The former boxing heavyweight champion of the world, Mike Tyson, epitomizes this connection both because he is a convicted rapist, and also because, according to Oates, in his fights he regularly used the pre-fight taunt "I'll make you into my girlfriend," clearly the "boast of a rapist."[7]

Just after being convicted of rape, Mike Tyson gave a twisted declaration of his innocence:

> I didn't rape anyone. I didn't hurt anyone—no black eyes, no broken ribs. When I'm in the ring, I break their ribs, I break their jaws. To me, that's hurting someone.[8]

In the ring, Tyson had a license to break ribs and jaws; and interestingly he understood that this was a case of hurting another person. It was just that in the ring it was acceptable. He knew that he was not supposed to hurt people outside the ring. But since he didn't break any ribs or jaws, how could anyone say that he hurt his accuser, Desiree Washington? Having sex with a woman could not be construed as having hurt her, for Tyson apparently, unless ribs or jaws were broken.

Tyson's lawyer, attempting to excuse Tyson's behavior, said that the boxer grew up in a "male-dominated world." And this is surely true. He was plucked from a home for juvenile delinquents and raised by boxing promoters. Few American males had been so richly imbued with male tradition, or more richly rewarded for living up to the male stereotype of the aggressive, indomitable fighter. Whether or not he recognized it as a genuine insight, Tyson's lawyer points us toward the heart of the matter in American culture: misbehavior, especially sexual misbehavior of males toward females is, however mixed the messages, something that many men condone. This has given rise to the use of the term "the rape culture" to describe the climate of attitudes that exists in the contemporary American male-dominated world.[9]

While noting all of this, Joyce Carol Oates ends her *Newsweek* essay on Tyson's rape trial by concluding that "no one is to blame except the perpetrator himself." She absolves the "culture" at large of any blame for Tyson's behavior. Oates regards Tyson as a sadist who took pleasure in inflicting pain both in and out of the boxing ring. She comes very close to demonizing him when, at the end of her essay, she suggests that Tyson is an outlaw or even a sociopath. And while she is surely right to paint Tyson's deed in the most horrific colors, she is less convincing when she suggests that Tyson is very different from other males in our society. In one telling statement in her essay, however, Oates opens the door for a less individualistic view of rape by acknowledging that the boxing community had built up in Tyson a "grandiose sense of entitlement, fueled by the insecurities and emotions of adolescence."[10]

Rape is normally committed by individual men; but, in our view, rape is not best understood in individualistic terms. The chief reasons for this are that individual men are more likely to engage in rape when they are in groups, and men receive strong encouragement to rape from the way they are socialized as men, that is, in the way they come to see themselves as instantiations of what it means to be a man. Both the "climate" that encourages rape and the "socialization" patterns which instill negative attitudes about women are difficult to understand or assess when one focuses on the isolated individual perpetrator of a rape. There are significant social dimensions to rape that are best understood as group-oriented.

As parents, we have observed that male schoolchildren are much more likely to misbehave (and subsequently to be punished by being sent to "time out") than are female schoolchildren. This fact is not particularly remarkable, for boys are widely believed to be more active than girls. What is remarkable is that school-teachers, in our experience, are much more likely to condone the misbehavior of boys than the misbehavior of girls. "Boys will be boys" is heard as often today as it was in previous times.[11] (See Robert Lipsyte's essay about the Glen Ridge, New Jersey, rape trial where the defense attorney used just these words to defend the star high school football players who raped a retarded girl.) From their earliest experience with authority figures, little boys are given mixed signals about misbehavior. Yes, they are punished, but they are also treated as if their misbehavior is expected, even welcome. It is for some boys, as it was for us, a "badge of honor" to be sent to detention or "time out." From older boys and from their peers, boys learn that they often will be ostracized for being "too goody-goody." It is as if part of the mixed message is that boys are given a license to misbehave.

And which of these boys will turn out to be rapists is often as much a matter of luck as it is a matter of choice. Recent estimates have it that in the first few months of the war "30,000 to 50,000 women, most of them Muslim" were raped by Serbian soldiers.[12] The data on date rape suggest that young men in our society engage in much more rape that anyone previously anticipated. It is a serious mistake in psychological categorization to think that all of these rapes are committed by sadists. (Studies by Amir show that the average rapist is not psychologically "abnormal."[13]) Given our own experiences and similar reports from others, it is also a serious mistake to think that those who rape are significantly different from the rest of the male population. (Studies by Smithyman indicate that rapists "seemed not to differ markedly from the majority of males in our culture."[14]) Our conclusion is that the typical rapist is not a demon or sadist, but, in some sense, could have been many men.

Most of those who engage in rape are at least partially responsible for these rapes, but the question we have posed is this: are those who perpetrate rape the *only* ones who are responsible for rape? Contrary to what Joyce Carol Oates contends, we believe that it is a serious mistake to think that only the perpetrators are responsible. The interactions of men, especially in all-male groups, contribute to a pattern of socialization that also plays a major role in the incidence of rape. In urging that more than the individual perpetrators be seen as responsible for rape, we do not mean to suggest that the responsibility of the perpetrator be diminished. When responsibility for harm is shared it need not be true that the perpetrators of harm find their responsibility relieved or even diminished. Rather, shared responsibility for harms merely means that the range of people who are implicated in these harms is extended. (More will be said on this point in the final section.)

II. The Rapist As Victim of Biology

The most recent psychological study of rape is that done by Randy Thornhill and Nancy Wilmsen Thornhill, "The Evolutionary Psychology of Men's Coercive Sexuality."[15] In this work, any contention that coercion or rape may be socially or culturally learned is derisively dismissed, as is any feminist argument for changing men's attitudes through changing especially group-based socialization. The general hypothesis they support is that

> sexual coercion by men reflects a sex-specific, species-typical psychological adaptation to rape: Men have certain psychological traits that evolved by natural selection specifically in the context of coercive sex and made rape adaptive during human evolution.[16]

They claim that rape is an adaptive response to biological differences between men and women.

Thornhill and Thornhill contend that the costs to women to engage in sex ("nine months of pregnancy") greatly exceed the costs to men ("a few minutes of time and an energetically cheap ejaculate"). As a result women and men come very early in evolutionary time to adapt quite differently sexually.

> Because women are more selective about mates and more interested in evaluating them and delaying copulation, men, to get sexual access, must often break through feminine barriers of hesitation, equivocation, and resistance.[17]

Males who adapted by developing a proclivity to rape and thus who "solved the problem" by forcing sex on a partner, were able to "out-reproduce" other, more passive males and gain an evolutionary advantage.

In one paragraph, Thornhill and Thornhill dismiss feminists who support a "social learning theory of rape" by pointing out that males of several "species with an evolutionary history of polygyny" are also "more aggressive, sexually assertive and eager to copulate." Yet, in "the vast majority of these species there is no sexual training of juveniles by other members of the group." This evidence, they conclude, thoroughly discredits the social learning theory and means that such theories "are never alternatives to evolutionary hypotheses about psychological adaptation."[18] In response to their critics, Thornhill and Thornhill go so far as to say that the feminist project of changing socialization patterns is pernicious.

> The sociocultural view does seem to offer hope and a simple remedy in that it implies that we need only fix the way that boys are socialized and rape will disappear. This naive solution is widespread. . . . As Hartung points out, those who feel that the social problem of rape can be solved by changing the nature of men through naive and arbitrary social adjustments should "get real about rape" because their perspective is a danger to us all.[19]

According to the Thornhills, feminists and other social theorists need to focus instead on what are called the "cues that affect the use of rape by adult males."[20]

The evolutionary biological account of rape we have rehearsed above would seemingly suggest that no one is responsible for rape. After all, if rape is an adaptive response to different sexual development in males and females, particular individuals who engage in rape are merely doing what they are naturally adapted to do. Rape is something to be controlled by those who control the "cues" that stimulate the natural rapist instincts in all men. It is for this reason that the Thornhills urge that more attention be given to male arousal and female stimulation patterns in laboratory settings.[21] Notice that even on the Thornhills' own terms, those who provide the cues may be responsible for the prevalence of rape, even if the perpetrators are not. But Thornhill and Thornhill deny that there are any normative conclusions that follow from their research and criticize those who wish to draw out such implications as committing the "naturalistic fallacy."[22]

In contrast to the Thornhills, a more plausible sociobiological account is given by Lionel Tiger. Tiger is often cited as someone who attempted to excuse male aggression. In his important study he defines aggression as distinct from violence, but nonetheless sees violence as one possible outcome of the natural aggressive tendencies, especially in men.

> Aggression occurs when an individual or group see their interest, their honor, or their job bound up with coercing the animal, human, or physical environ- ment to achieve their own ends rather than (or in spite of) the goals of the object of their action. Violence may occur in the process of interaction.[23]

For Tiger, aggression is intentional behavior which is goal-directed and based on procuring something which is necessary for survival. Aggression is a "'normal' feature of the human biologically based repertoire." [24] Violence, "coercion involving physical force to resolve conflict," [25] on the other hand, is not necessarily a normal response to one's environment, although in some cir- cumstances it may be. Thus, while human males are evolutionarily adapted to be aggressive, they are not necessarily adapted to be violent.

Tiger provided an account that linked aggression in males with their bio- logical evolution.

> Human aggression is in part a function of the fact that hunting was vitally important to human evolution and that aggression is typically undertaken by males in the framework of a unisexual social bond of which participants are aware and with which they are concerned. It is implied, therefore, that aggres- sion is 'instinctive' but also must occur within an explicit social context varying from culture to culture and to be learned by members of any community. . . .
> Men in continuous association aggress against the environment in much the same way as men and women in continuous association have sexual relations.[26]

And while men are thus predisposed to engage in aggression, in ways that women are not, it is not true in Tiger's view that a predisposition to engage in violent acts is a normal part of this difference.

Thornhill and Thornhill fail to consider Tiger's contention that men are evo- lutionarily adapted to be aggressive, but not necessarily to be violent. With Tiger's distinction in mind it may be said that human males, especially in asso- ciation with other males, are adapted to aggress against women in certain social environments. But this aggressive response need not lead to violence, or the threat of violence, of the sort epitomized by rape; rather it may merely affect noncoercive mating rituals. On a related point, Tiger argues that the fact that war has historically been "virtually a male monopoly" is due to both male bonding patterns and evolutionary adaptation. [27] Evolutionary biology provides only part of the story since male aggressiveness need not result in such violent encoun- ters as occur in war or rape. After all, many men do not rape or go to war; the cultural cues provided by socialization must be considered at least as important as evolutionary adaptation.

We side with Tiger against the Thornhills in focusing on the way that all-male groups socialize their members and provide "cues" for violence. Tiger has recently allied himself with feminists such as Catharine MacKinnon and others who have suggested that male attitudes need to be radically altered in order to have a major impact on the incidence of rape (see the preface to the second edition of *Men in Groups*). One of the implications of Tiger's research is that rape and other forms of male aggressive behavior are not best understood as isolated acts of individuals. Rather than simply seeing violent aggression as merely a biologically predetermined response, Tiger places violent aggressiveness squarely into the group dynamics of men's interactions—a result of his research not well appreciated.

In a preface to the second edition of his book, Tiger corrects an unfortunate misinterpretation of his work.

> One of the stigmas which burdened this book was an interpretation of it as an apology for male aggression and even a potential stimulus of it—after all, boys will be boys. However I clearly said the opposite: "This is not to say that . . . hurtful and destructive relations between groups of men are inevitable. . . . It may be possible, as many writers have suggested, to alter social conceptions of maleness so that gentility and equivocation rather than toughness and more or less arbitrary decisiveness are highly valued." [28]

If Tiger is right, and the most important "cues" are those which young boys and men get while in the company of other boys and men, then the feminist project of changing male socialization patterns may be seen as consistent with, rather than opposed to, the sociobiological hypotheses. Indeed, other evidence may be cited to buttress the feminist social learning perspective against the Thornhills. Different human societies have quite different rates of rape. In her anthropological research among the Minangkabau of West Sumatra, Peggy Reeves Sanday has found that this society is relatively rape-free. Rape does occur, but at such a low rate—28 per 3 million in 1981–82 for example—as to be virtually nonexistent. [29] In light of such research, men, rather than women, are the ones who would need to change their behavior. This is because it is the socialization of men by men in their bonding-groups, and the view of women that is engendered, that provides the strongest cues toward rape. Since there may indeed be something that males could and should be doing differently that would affect the prevalence of rape, it does not seem unreasonable to continue to investigate the claim that men are collectively responsible for the prevalence of rape.

III. The Rapist As Victim of Society

It is also possible to acknowledge that men are responsible for the prevalence of rape in our society but nonetheless to argue that women are equally responsible. Rape is often portrayed as a sex crime perpetrated largely by men against women. But importantly, rape is also a crime of violence, and many factors in our society have increased the prevalence of violence. This prevalence of violence is the cause of both rape and war in Western societies. Our view, that violence of both sorts is increased in likelihood by patterns of male socialization which then creates collective male responsibility, may be countered by pointing out that socialization patterns are created by both men and women, thereby seemingly implicating both men and women in collective responsibility for rape and war.

Sam Keen has contended that it is violence that we should be focusing on rather than sex or gender, in order to understand the causes and remedies for the prevalence of rape. According to Keen,

> Men are violent because of the systematic violence done to their bodies and spirits. Being hurt they become hurters. In the overall picture, male violence toward women is far less than male violence toward other males . . . these outrages are a structural part of a warfare system that victimizes both men and women.[30]

Keen sees both men and women conspiring together to perpetuate this system of violence, especially in the way they impart to their male children an acceptance of violence.

Women are singled out by Keen as those who have not come to terms with their share of responsibility for our violent culture. And men have been so guilt-tripped on the issue of rape that they have become desensitized to it. Keen thinks that it is mistake to single out men, and not women also, as responsible for rape.

> Until women are willing to weep for and accept equal responsibility for the systematic violence done to the male body and spirit by the war system, it is not likely that men will lose enough of their guilt and regain enough of their sensitivity to accept responsibility for women who are raped. [31]

Even though women are equally responsible for the rape culture, in Keen's view, women should be singled out because they have not previously accepted their share of responsibility for the creation of a violent society.

Keen is at least partially right insofar as he insists that issues of rape and war be understood as arising from the same source, namely the socialization of men to be violent in Western cultures. We agree with Keen that rape is part of a larger set of violent practices that injure both men and women. He is right to point out that men are murdering other men in our society in increasing numbers, and that this incidence of violence probably has something to do with the society's general condoning, even celebrating, of violence, especially in war.

Keen fails to note though that it is men, not women, who are the vast majority of both rapists and murderers in our society. And even if some women do act in ways which trigger violent reactions in men, nevertheless, in our opinion this pales in comparison with the way that men socialize each other to be open to violence. As Tiger and others have suggested, aggressive violence results primarily from male-bonding experiences. In any event, both fathers and mothers engage in early childhood socialization. Men influence the rape culture both through early childhood socialization and through male-bonding socialization of older male children. But women only contribute to this culture, when they do, through individual acts of early childhood socialization. For this reason Keen is surely wrong to think that women share responsibility *equally* with men for our rape culture.

In our view, some women could prevent some rapes; and some women do contribute to the patterns of socialization of both men and women that increase the incidence of rape. For these reasons, it would not be inappropriate to say that women share responsibility for rape as well as men. But we believe that it is a mistake to think that women share equally in this responsibility with men. For one thing, women are different from men in that they are, in general, made worse off by the prevalence of rape in our society. As we will next see, there is a sense in which men, but not women, benefit from the prevalence of rape, and this fact means that men have more of a stake in the rape culture, and hence have more to gain by its continued existence.

In general, our conclusion is that women share responsibility, but to a far lesser extent than men, for the prevalence of rape. We do not support those who try to "blame the victim" by holding women responsible for rape because of not taking adequate precautions, or dressing seductively, etc. Instead, the key for us is the role that women, as mothers, friends, and lovers, play in the overall process of male socialization that creates the rape culture. It should come as no surprise that few members of Western society can be relieved of responsibility for this rape culture given the overwhelming pervasiveness of that culture. But such considerations should not deter us from looking to men, first and foremost, as being collectively responsible for the prevalence of rape. The women who do contribute to aggressive male socialization do so as individuals; women have no involvement parallel to the male-bonding group.

IV. The Rapist As Group Member

Popular literature tends to portray the rapist as a demonic character, as the "Other." What we find interesting about the research of Thornhill and Thornhill is that it operates unwittingly to support the feminist slogan that "all men are rapists," that the rapist is not male "Other" but male "Self." What is so unsettling about the tens of thousands of rapes in Bosnia is the suggestion that what ordinary men have been doing is not significantly different from what the "sex-fiends" did. The thesis that men are adapted to be predisposed to be rapists, regardless of what else we think of the thesis, should give us pause and make us less rather than more likely to reject the feminist slogan. From this vantage point, the work of Tiger as well as Thornhill and Thornhill sets the stage for a serious reconsideration of the view that men are collectively responsible for rape.

There are two things that might be meant by saying that men are collectively responsible for the prevalence of rape in Western culture. First, seeing men as collectively responsible may mean that men as a group are responsible in that they form some sort of super-entity that causes, or at least supports, the prevalence of rape. When some feminists talk of "patriarchy," what they seem to mean is a kind of institution that operates through, but also behind, the backs of individual men to oppress women. Here it may be that men are collectively responsible for the prevalence of rape and yet no men are individually responsible. We call this *nondistributive collective responsibility* [italics added]. Second, seeing men as collectively responsible may mean that men form a group in which there are so many features that the members share in common, such as attitudes or dispositions to engage in harm, that what holds true for one man also holds true for all other men. Because of the common features of the members of the group men, when one man is responsible for a particular harm, other men are implicated. Each member of the group has a share in the responsibility for a harm such as rape. We call this *distributive collective responsibility* [italics added].[32] In what follows we will criticize the first way of understanding men's collective responsibility, and offer reasons to support the second.

When collective responsibility is understood in the first (nondistributive) sense, this form of responsibility is assigned to those groups that have the capacity to act. Here there are two paradigmatic examples: the corporation and the mob.[33] The corporation has the kind of organizational structure that allows for the group to form intentions and carry out those intentions, almost as if the corporation were itself a person. Since men, qua men, are too amorphous a group to be able to act in an organized fashion, we will not be interested in whether they are collectively responsible in this way. But it may be that men can act in the way that mobs act, that is, not through a highly organized structure but through something such as like-mindedness. If there is enough commonality of belief, disposition, and interest of all men, or at least all men within a particular culture, then the group may be able to act just as a mob is able to respond to a commonly perceived enemy.

It is possible to think of patriarchy as the oppressive practices of men coordinated by the common interests of men, but not organized intentionally. It is also productive to think of rape as resulting from patriarchy. For if there is a "collective" that is supporting or creating the prevalence of rape it is not a highly organized one, since there is nothing like a corporation that intentionally plans the rape of women in Western culture. If the current Serbian army has engaged in the systematic and organized rape of Muslim women as a strategy of war, then this would be an example of nondistributive responsibility for rape. But the kind of oppression characterized by the prevalence of rape in most cultures appears to be systematic but not organized. How does this affect our understanding of whether men are collectively responsible for rape?

If patriarchy is understood merely as a system of coordination that operates behind the backs of individual men, then it may be that no single man is responsible for any harms that are caused by patriarchy. But if patriarchy is understood as something which is based on common interests, as well as common benefits, extended to all or most men in a particular culture, then it may be that men are collectively responsible for the harms of patriarchy in a way which distributes out to all men, making each man in a particular culture at least partially responsible for the harms attributable to patriarchy. This latter strategy is consistent with our own view of men's responsibility for rape. In the remainder of this essay we will offer support for this conceptualization of the collective responsibility of men for the prevalence of rape.

Our positive assessment, going beyond our criticism of the faulty responses in earlier sections of our paper, is that men in Western culture are collectively responsible in the distributive sense, that is, they each share responsibility, for the prevalence of rape in that culture. This claim rests on five points: (1) Insofar as most perpetrators of rape are men, then these men are responsible, in most cases, for the rapes they committed. (2) Insofar as some men, by the way they interact with other (especially younger) men, contribute to a climate in our society where rape is made more prevalent, then they are collaborators in the rape culture and for this reason share in responsibility for rapes committed in that culture. (3) Also, insofar as some men are not unlike the rapist, since they would be rapists if they had the opportunity to be placed into a situation where their inhibitions against rape were removed, then these men share responsibility with actual rapists for the harms of rape. (4) In addition, insofar as many other men could have prevented fellow men from raping, but did not act to prevent these actual rapes, then these men also share responsibility along with the rapists. (5) Finally, insofar as some men benefit from the existence of rape in our society, these men also share responsibility along with the rapists.

It seems to us unlikely that many, if any, men in our society fail to fit into one or another of these categories. Hence, we think that it is not unreasonable to say that men in our society are collectively responsible (in the distributive sense) for rape. We expect some male readers to respond as follows:

> I am adamantly opposed to rape, and though when I was younger I might have tolerated rape-conductive comments from friends of mine, I don't now, so I'm not a collaborator in the rape culture. And I would never be a rapist whatever the situation, and I would certainly act to prevent any rape that I could. I'm

pretty sure I don't benefit from rape. So how can I be responsible for the prevalence of rape?

In reply we would point out that nearly all men in a given Western society meet the third and fifth conditions above (concerning similarity and benefit). But women generally fail to meet either of these conditions, or the first. So, the involvement of women in the rape culture is much less than is true for men. In what follows we will concentrate on these similarity and benefit issues.

In our discussion above, we questioned the view that rapists are "other." Diane Scully, in her study of convicted rapists, turns the view around, suggesting that it is women who are "other." She argues that rapists in America are not pathological, but instead

> that men who rape have something to tell us about the cultural roots of sexual violence. . . . They tell us that some men use rape as a means of revenge and punishment. Implicit in revenge rape is the collective liability of women. In some cases, victims are substitutes for significant women on whom men desire to take revenge. In other cases, victims represent all women. . . . In either case, women are seen as objects, a category, but not as individuals with rights. For some men, rape is an afterthought or bonus they add to burglary or robbery. In other words, rape is "no big deal." . . . Some men rape in groups as a male bonding activity—for them it's just something to do. . . . Convicted rapists tell us that in this culture, sexual violence is rewarding . . . these men perceived rape as a rewarding, low-risk act. [34]

It is the prevalent perception of women as "other" by men in our culture that fuels the prevalence of rape in American society.

Turning to the issue of benefit, we believe that Lionel Tiger's work illustrates the important source of strength that men derive from the all-male groups they form. There is a strong sense in which men benefit from the all-male groups that they form in our culture. What is distinctly lacking is any sense that men have responsibility for the social conditions, especially the socialization of younger men which diminishes inhibitions toward rape, that are created in those groups. Male bonding is made easier because there is an "Other" that males can bond "against." And this other is the highly sexualized stereotype of the "female." Here is a benefit for men in these groups—but there is a social cost: from the evidence we have examined there is an increased prevalence of rape. Men need to consider this in reviewing their own role in a culture that supports so much rape.

There is another sense in which benefit is related to the issue of responsibility for rape. There is a sense in which many men in our society benefit from the prevalence of rape in ways many of us are quite unaware. Consider this example:

> Several years ago, at a social occasion in which male and female professors were present, I asked off-handedly whether people agreed with me that the

campus was looking especially pretty at night these days. Many of the men responded positively. But all of the women responded that this was not something that they had even thought about, since they were normally too anxious about being on campus at night, especially given the increase in reported rapes recently.[35]

We men benefited in that, relative to our female colleagues, we were in an advantageous position vis-a-vis travel around campus. And there were surely other comparative benefits that befell us as a result of this advantage concerning travel, such as our ability to gain academically by being able to use the library at any hour we chose.

In a larger sense, men benefit from the prevalence of rape in that many women are made to feel dependent on men for protection against potential rapists. It is hard to overestimate the benefit here for it potentially affects all aspects of one's life. One study found that 87 percent of women in a borough of London felt that they had to take precautions against potential rapists, with a large number reporting that they never went out at night alone.[36] Whenever one group is made to feel dependent on another group, and this dependency is not reciprocal, then there is a strong comparative benefit to the group that is not in the dependent position. Such a benefit, along with the specific benefits mentioned above, support the view that men as a group have a stake in perpetuating the rape culture in ways that women do not. And just as the benefit to men distributes throughout the male population in a given society, so the responsibility should distribute as well.

V. Conclusions

When people respond to conflict with violence, they coerce one another and thereby fail to treat one another with respect as fellow autonomous beings. Rape and murder, especially in war, victimize members of various groups simply because they are group members. These two factors combine to create a form of dehumanization that can warrant the charge of being a crime against humanity. What makes an act of violence more than just a private individual act in wartime is that killing and rape are perpetrated not against the individual for his or her unique characteristics, but solely because the individual instantiates a group characteristic, for example, being Jewish, or Muslim, or being a woman. Such identification fails to respect what is unique about each of us.

Our point is not that all men everywhere are responsible for the prevalence of rape. Rather, we have been arguing that in Western societies, rape is deeply embedded in a wider culture of male socialization. Those who have the most to do with sustaining that culture must also recognize that they are responsible for

PART THREE: DESIRE, PORNOGRAPHY, and RAPE

the harmful aspects of that culture.[37] And when rape is conjoined with war, especially as an organized strategy, then there is a sense that men are collectively responsible for the rapes that occur in that war,[38] just as groups of people are held responsible for the crimes of genocide, where the victims are persecuted simply because they fall into a certain category of low-risk people who are ripe for assault.

Rape, especially in times of war, is an act of violence perpetrated against a person merely for being an instantiation of a type. Insofar as rape in times of war is a systematically organized form of terror, it is not inappropriate to call rape a war crime, a crime against humanity. Insofar as rape in times of peace is also part of a pattern of terror against women to the collective benefit of men, then rape in times of peace is also a crime against humanity.[39] Rape, in war or in peace, is rarely a personal act of aggression by one person toward another person. It is an act of hostility and a complete failure to show basic human respect.[40] And more than this, rape is made more likely by the collective actions, or inactions, of men in a particular society. Insofar as men in a particular society contribute to the prevalence of rape, they participate in a crime against humanity for which they are collectively responsible.

The feminist slogan "all men are rapists" seems much stronger than the claim "all men contribute to the prevalence of rape." Is the feminist slogan merely hyperbole? It is if what is meant is that each time a rape occurs, every man did it, or that only men are ever responsible for rape. But, as we have seen, each time a rape occurs, there is a sense in which many men could have done it, or made it less likely to have occurred, or benefited from it. By direct contribution, or by negligence or by similarity of disposition, or by benefiting, most if not all men do share in each rape in a particular society. This is the link between being responsible for the prevalence of rape and being responsible, at least to some extent, for the harms of each rape.

The purpose of these arguments has been to make men aware of the various ways that they are implicated in the rape culture in general as well as in particular rapes. And while we believe that men should feel some shame for their group's complicity in the prevalence of rape, our aim is not to shame men but rather to stimulate men to take responsibility for resocializing themselves and their fellow men. How much should any particular man do? Answering this question would require another paper, although participating in the Canadian White Ribbon Campaign, or in anti-sexism education programs, would be a good first step.[41] Suffice it to say that the status quo, namely doing nothing, individually or as a group, is not satisfactory, and will merely further compound our collective and shared responsibility for the harms caused by our fellow male members who engage in rape.[42]

Notes

1. This paragraph is based on Larry May's experiences growing up in an upper middle class suburban U.S. society. While our experiences differ somewhat in this respect, these experiences are so common that we have referred to them in the first person plural.

2. Tony Post et al., "A Pattern of Rape," *Newsweek*, January 4, 1993, pp. 32–36.

3. Susan Brownmiller, "Making Female Bodies the Battlefield," *Newsweek*, January 4, 1993, p. 37.

4. Catherine A. MacKinnon, "Turning Rape into Pornography: Postmodern Genocide," *Ms.*, July/August 1993, p. 30.

5. There is a fifth response, namely, that women alone are somehow responsible for being raped. This response will be largely ignored in our essay since we regard it as merely another case of "blaming the victim." See Diana Scully, *Understanding Sexual Violence* (Boston: Unwin Hyman, 1990) for a critical discussion of this response. Undoubtedly there are yet other responses. We have tried to focus our attention on the most common responses we have seen in the literature on rape.

6. Joyce Carol Oates, "Rape and the Boxing Ring," *Newsweek*, February 24, 1992, p. 60.

7. Ibid., p. 61.

8. *St. Louis Post-Dispatch*, March 27, 1992, p. 20A.

9. See Susan Griffin, "Rape: The All-American Crime," *Ramparts*, September 1971, pp. 26–35; reprinted in *Women and Values: Readings in Feminist Philosophy*, ed. Marilyn Pearsall (Belmont, Calif.: Wadsworth, 1986).

10. Oates, "Rape and the Boxing Ring," p. 61.

11. Robert Lipsyte, "An Ethics Trial: Must Boys Always Be Boys?" *New York Times*, March 12, 1993, p. B-11.

12. Post et al., "A Pattern of Rape," p. 32.

13. Cited in Griffin, "Rape: The All-American Crime," p. 178.

14. Cited in Scully, *Understanding Sexual Violence*, p. 75.

15. *Behavioral and Brain Sciences* 15 (1992): 36–75.

16. Ibid., p. 363.

17. Ibid., p. 366.

18. Ibid., p. 364.

19. Ibid., p. 416.

20. Ibid.

21. Ibid., p. 375.

22. Ibid., p. 407.

23. Lionel Tiger, *Men in Groups*, 2d ed. (New York: Marion Boyars Publishers, 1984), pp. 158–59. (The first edition appeared in 1969.)

24. Ibid., p. 159.

25. Ibid.

26. Ibid., pp. 159–60.

27. Ibid., p. 81.

28. Ibid., p. 191.

29. Peggy Reeves Sanday, "Rape and the Silencing of the Feminine," in *Rape: An Historical and Social Enquiry*, ed. Sylvana Tomaselli and Roy Porter (Oxford: Basil Blackwell, 1986), p. 85; and Sanday, "Androcentric and Matrifocal Gender Representation in Minangkabau Ideology," in *Beyond the Second Sex*, ed. Peggy Reeves Sanday and Ruth Gallagher Goodenough (Philadelphia: University of Pennsylvania Press, 1990). See also Maria Lepowsky, "Gender in an Egalitarian Society," in *Beyond the Second Sex*.

30. Sam Keen, *Fire in the Belly* (New York: Bantam Books, 1991), p. 47.

31. Ibid.

32. Larry May, *The Morality of Groups* (Notre Dame, Ind.: University of Notre Dame Press, 1987), chap. 2.

33. Ibid., chaps. 2 and 4.

34. Scully, *Understanding Sexual Violence*, pp. 162–63.

35. In his fascinating study of the climate of rape in American culture, Timothy Beneke also reports as one of his conclusions that the fear of rape at night "inhibits the freedom of the eye, hurts women economically, undercuts women's independence, destroys solitude, and restricts expressiveness." Such curtailments of freedom, he argues, "must be acknowledged as part of the crime." Timothy Beneke, *Men on Rape* (New York: St. Martin's Press, 1982), p. 170.

36. See Jill Radford, "Policing Male Violence, Policing Women," in *Women, Violence and Social Control*, ed. Valna Hammer and Mary Maynard (Atlantic Highlands, N.J.: Humanities Press, 1987), p. 33.

37. Roy Porter, "Does Rape Have a Historical Meaning?" in *Rape: An Historical and Social Enquiry*, pp. 222–23.

38. The European Community's preliminary investigation into the reports of widespread Bosnian rapes of Muslim women by Serbian soldiers concluded that "Rape is part of a pattern of abuse, usually perpetrated with the conscious intention of demoralizing and terrorizing communities, driving them from their homes and demonstrating the power of the invading forces. Viewed in this way, rape cannot be seen as incidental to the main purpose of the aggression but as serving a strategic purpose in itself" (*St. Louis Post-Dispatch*, January 9, 1993, 8A).

39. See Claudia Card, "Rape as a Terrorist Institution," in *Violence, Terrorism, and Justice*, ed. R. G. Frey and Christopher Morris (New York: Cambridge University Press, 1991).

40. See Carolyn M. Shafer and Marilyn Frye, "Rape and Respect, " in *Feminism and Philosophy*, ed. Mary Vetterling-Braggin, Frederick Elliston, and Jane English (Totowa, N.J.: Littlefield Adams, 1977).

41. We would also recommend recent essays by philosophers who are trying to come to terms with their masculinity. See our essay on friendship as well as the essay by Hugh LaFollette in our anthology *Rethinking Masculinity*, ed., Larry May and Robert Strikwerda (Lanham, Md.: Rowen & Littlefield, 1992).

42. We would like to thank Virginia Ingram, Jason Clevenger, Victoria Davion, Karen Warren, Duane Cady, and Marilyn Friedman for providing us with critical comments on earlier drafts of this essay.

41

The Rape Crisis,
or "Is Dating Dangerous?"

Katie Roiphe

Radical feminists aren't the only ones talking about the rape crisis anymore. Since the mid-eighties the media have been kindling public interest in rape with a series of alarming revelations. In 1985, *Ms.* magazine published the startling results of an early study on rape in universities in a story dramatically entitled "Date Rape: The Story of an Epidemic and Those Who Deny It."[1] That same year, the *New York Times* ran an article called "A New Recognition of the Realities of 'Date Rape.' "[2] After William Kennedy Smith's televised date-rape trial, in 1991, there was a flurry of articles and editorials about rape. As everyone waited to see what would happen to the Kennedy name and his word against hers, a new discussion of the rape crisis opened up on the front pages, capturing public attention.

According to the widely quoted *Ms.* survey, one in four college women is the victim of rape or attempted rape. One in four. I remember standing outside the dining hall in college looking at a purple poster with this statistic written in bold letters. It didn't seem right. If sexual assault was really so pervasive, it seemed strange that the intricate gossip networks hadn't picked up more than one or two shadowy instances of rape. If I was really standing in the middle of an epidemic, a crisis, if 25 percent of my female friends were really being raped, wouldn't I know it? The answer is not that there is a conspiracy of silence. The answer is that measuring rape is not as straightforward as it seems.

Neil Gilbert, professor of social welfare at the University of California at Berkeley, has written several articles attacking the two sociological studies that are cornerstones of the rape-crisis movement, the *Ms.* magazine study and one done in the early eighties by Diana Russell. Having taken a closer look at the numbers, he questions the validity of the one-in-four statistic. He points out that

Reprinted from Katie Roiphe, *The Morning After: Sex, Fear, and Feminism on Campus* (Boston: Little, Brown and Co., 1993).

in the *Ms.* study, which is the one most frequently quoted, 73 percent of the women categorized as rape victims did not define their experience as "rape."[3] It was Dr. Mary Koss, the psychologist conducting the study, who did. These are not self-proclaimed victims, then—these are victims according to someone else. From Koss's point of view, these women were suffering from what they used to call false consciousness. The way it is usually and tactfully phrased these days is that they don't recognize what has really happened to them.

Gilbert also points out that 42 percent of the women identified in this study as rape victims later had sex with the man who supposedly raped them *after* the supposed rape.[4] As Gilbert delves further into the numbers, he does not necessarily disprove the one-in-four statistic, but he does help clarify what it means. He reveals that the so-called "rape epidemic" on campuses is more a way of interpreting, a way of seeing, than a physical phenomenon. It is more about a change in sexual politics than a change in sexual behavior. . . .

As Gilbert points out, at Berkeley, a campus with fourteen thousand female students, only two rapes were reported to the police in 1990, and between forty and eighty students sought assistance from the campus rape-counseling service. Even if we assume that many students don't report rapes, even to the sympathetic rape-crisis center, the one-in-four statistic would still leave thousands of rapes unaccounted for.

No matter how one feels about Gilbert's perspective, his research shows that these figures are subjective, that what is being called rape is not a clear-cut issue of common sense. Whether or not one in four college women has been raped, then, is a matter of opinion, not a matter of mathematical fact. Everyone agrees that rape is a terrible thing, but we don't agree on what rape is. There is a gray area in which someone's rape may be another person's bad night. Definitions become entangled in passionate ideological battles. There hasn't been a remarkable change in the number of women being raped, it seems, just a change in how receptive the political climate is to those numbers. As Koss herself phrased it, "In the past these cases would not have come to light. But today more women are willing to recognize that the problem exists."[5] Clearly, from her perspective not enough women are "recognizing" the problem, since most of the women in her own study didn't recognize that, by Koss's standards, they had been raped.

The next questions, then, are who is identifying this epidemic and why. Somebody is "finding" this rape crisis, and finding it for a reason. Asserting the prevalence of rape lends urgency, authority, to a broader critique of culture. In a dramatic description of the rape crisis, Naomi Wolf writes in *The Beauty Myth,* "Cultural representation of glamorized degradation has created a situation among the young in which boys rape and girls get raped as a *normal course of events* [Wolf's italics]."[6] Whether or not she really believes rape is part of the "normal course of events" these days, Wolf is making a larger point. She is talking about the whole cultural climate surrounding sex. Wolf's rhetorical excess serves her polemic about sexual politics. Her dramatic prose is a call to arms. She is trying to rally the feminist troops. Wolf uses rape as a red flag, an undeniable sign that things are falling apart.

Back in 1975, Susan Brownmiller's best-selling, encyclopedic discussion of rape, *Against Our Will: Men, Women and Rape,* carried the issue into the mainstream. Brownmiller writes that "from prehistoric times to the present, I believe, rape has played a critical function. It is nothing more or less than a conscious process of intimidation by which *all men* keep *all women* in a state of fear [Brownmiller's italics]."[7] As Brownmiller's argument demonstrates, discussions of rape often extend beyond discussions of a physical act. With her grand, sometimes paranoid strokes, Brownmiller portrays rape as the central mechanism of oppression. She is describing rape as something originary, something that defines relations between men and women.

From Susan Brownmiller to Naomi Wolf, feminist prophets of the rape crisis are talking about something more than forced penetration. They are talking about rape as part of what is often referred to as "rape culture." Even a commonly circulated pamphlet about acquaintance rape giving practical advice includes this overtly ideological statement: "The images we see in advertisements, on television, and in movies portray forced sex as somehow natural and permissible, especially if it involves two people who know each other. These images reflect society's tolerance of acquaintance rape—an epidemic of violent crime."[8] Even in the most pragmatic of contexts, numbers are marshaled behind a cause, and statistics about rape become more than just statistics about rape.

Rape is a natural trump card for feminism. Arguments about rape can be used to sequester feminism in the teary province of trauma and crisis. They can block analysis with statements like "You can't possibly understand what I've been through." Declarations of rape are used as an insurmountable obstacle, a point beyond which no questions are allowed.

Invoking the rape crisis, as Wolf and Brownmiller do, strengthens an argument by infusing it with heightened emotional appeal. For many feminists, then, rape becomes a vehicle, a way to get from here to there. By blocking analysis with its claims to unique pandemic suffering, the rape crisis becomes a powerful source of authority.

The idea of a rape epidemic has swollen beyond a few polemical passages. Although the rhetoric and statistics may be the stuff of airy political visions, they also affect real students and real financial decisions on college campuses. Universities channel money and resources, rooms, energy, and ideas into rape-counseling and education programs.

The fear of rape is not confined to university officials. It is not the kind of administrative worry that barely catches the attention of the average freshman. Students shout about it at Take Back the Night marches. They talk about it over coffee. At a party, standing in the corner, one can hear two college sophomores talking about the danger of being raped by friends. One of them says a male friend of hers recently confessed that he was infatuated with her. Afterward, she let him drive her home, she trusted him. Nothing happened, thank God, she tells her friend over her plastic cup of red punch, but it scares me to think of what could have, it scares me to think that I trusted him after I knew how he felt about me. Yeah, the other one agrees, you have to stay in public places in situations like that.

Dead serious, eyes wide with concern, one college senior tells me that she believes one in four is too conservative an estimate. This is not the first time I've heard this. She tells me the right statistic is closer to one in two. That means one in two women is raped. It's amazing, she says, amazing that so many of us are sexually assaulted every day.

What is amazing is that this student actually believes 50 percent of women are raped. This is the true crisis: that there are a not insignificant number of young women walking around with this alarming belief. This hyperbole contains within it a state of perpetual fear. A young woman asks a male friend to walk her three blocks back to her dorm at eight o'clock in the evening. Half of all women are raped in their lifetime, and she cannot walk outside at night without that thought hovering in the windblown leaves, the shadowy corners, the empty cars. She says she is glad they have those blue lights all over campus, although, she adds grimly, they may not do any good—this is the chorus of the rape crisis. And we certainly are in a state of crisis if these college students really believe, as they walk around, as they go to parties and lectures and late-night movies, that they have a 50 percent chance of being raped.

"Acquaintance Rape: Is Dating Dangerous?"—a pamphlet commonly found at counseling centers—gives a sample date-rape scenario. On the cover, the title rises from the shards of a shattered photograph of a boy and girl dancing. The pamphlet tells us what "she" is thinking and what "he" is thinking as the date progresses. She thinks: "He was really handsome and he had a great smile. We talked and found we had a lot in common. When he asked me over to his place for a drink I thought it would be OK. He was such a good listener and I wanted him to ask me out again." She's just looking for a sensitive boy, a good listener with a great smile, but unfortunately his intentions are not as pure as hers.

Beneath his great smile, he is thinking: "She looked really hot, wearing a sexy dress that showed off her great body." They start talking right away. He knows that she likes him because she keeps smiling and touching his arm while she's speaking. He notes, "She seemed pretty relaxed so I asked her back to my place for a drink . . . when she said 'yes' I knew that I was going to be lucky."

When they get to his room the bed turns out to be the only place to sit. Our innocent heroine thinks, "I didn't want him to get the wrong idea but what else could I do?" They talk for a while and then he makes his move. She is startled. He begins by kissing. She says she really liked him so the kissing was nice. But then he pushes her down on the bed. She tries to get up and tells him to stop, but "he was so much bigger and stronger."[9]

These cardboard stereotypes are not just educating freshmen about rape, they are also educating them about "dates" and about sexual desire. With titles like "Friends Raping Friends: Could It Happen to You?" date-rape pamphlets call into question all relationships between men and women. Beyond just warning students about rape, this movement produces its own images of sexual behavior, in which men exert pressure and women resist. By defining the dangerous date in these terms—with this type of male and this type of female, and their different types of expectations—these pamphlets promote their own perspective on how men and women feel about sex: men are lascivious, women are innocent.

Although it is not always an explicit part of their agenda, feminists involved in the rape-crisis movement educate young women according to certain beliefs about sexual behavior, both real and ideal. The sleek images of pressure and resistance projected in movies, videotapes, pamphlets, and speeches create their own model of what is acceptable sexual behavior. The don'ts imply their own set of do's. The movement against rape, then, not only dictates the way sex *shouldn't be* but also the way it *should be.* Sex should be gentle, it should not be aggressive; it should be absolutely equal, it should not involve domination and submission; it should be tender, not ambivalent; it should communicate respect, not consuming desire. . . .

The American College Health Association's pamphlet tells men: "Your desires may be beyond your control, but your actions are within your control." And it warns the female student to "communicate your limits clearly." According to this picture of sexual relations, her desires are never beyond her control. The assumption embedded in the movement against date rape is our grandmothers' assumption: men want sex, women don't. In emphasizing this struggle—he pushing, she resisting—the rape-crisis movement recycles and promotes an old model of sexuality.

In her recent book, *Feminism without Illusions,* Elizabeth Fox-Genovese describes the "epidemic" in these terms:

> Although the sexual revolution has "liberated" young women from many of the older constraints of propriety, it has also deprived them of the attendant protections. . . . [They] have cause to worry that when they choose not to have sexual relations with a particular man, their "no" may not be respected. The ensuing confusion has given rise to the epidemic of "acquaintance rape" on campuses.[10]

Fox-Genovese's analysis is tinged with regret. She notes that along with freedom comes risk. Broken taboos are broken locks: they leave female experience open to new dangers.

Robin Warshaw, in *I Never Called It Rape,* expresses her nostalgia for days of greater social control:

> Up until the 1970s, colleges adopted a "substitute parent" attitude toward their students, complete with curfews (often more strict for females than males), liquor bans, and stringent disciplinary punishments. In that era, students were punished for violating the three-feet-on-the-floor rules during coed visiting hours in dormitories or being caught with alcohol on school property. Although those regulations did not prevent acquaintance rape, they undoubtedly kept

down the numbers of incidents by making women's dorms havens of no-men-allowed safety.[11]

While sequestering women in "havens of no-men-allowed safety" may seem undesirable to most of us, later in her book Warshaw recommends creating single-sex dorms and redesigning coed dorms to separate the sexes more effectively.[12] Her recommendations push college life back into the fifties. William Bennett, Ronald Reagan's conservative secretary of education, also pushed for the university to act "in loco parentis." He called for universities to not stay neutral in the choice between "decent morality and decadence."[13] The rhetoric of feminists and conservatives blurs and overlaps in this desire to keep our youth safe and pure. . . .

By viewing rape as encompassing more than the use or threat of physical violence to coerce someone into sex, rape-crisis feminists reinforce traditional views about the fragility of the female body and will. Today's definition of date or acquaintance rape stretches beyond acts of violence or physical force. According to common definitions of date rape, even verbal coercion or manipulation constitutes rape. Verbal coercion is defined as "a woman's consenting to unwanted sexual activity because of a man's verbal arguments not including verbal threats of force."[14] The belief that verbal coercion is rape extends beyond official definitions; it pervades workshops, counseling sessions, and student opinion pieces. In Harvard's moderate feminist magazine, the *Lighthouse,* a student wrote an impassioned piece about the prevalence of what she considered emotional rape.

In an essay entitled "Nonviolent Sexual Coercion," psychologists Charlene Muehlenhard and Jennifer Schrag include the remarks "He said he'd break up with me if I didn't," "He said I was frigid," and "He said everyone's doing it" in the category of verbal coercion. They go on to explain that "a woman with low self-esteem might feel that if she refuses her partner's sexual advances she will lose him, and her value will be lessened because she is no longer associated with him."[15] This is a portrait of the cowering woman, knocked on her back by the barest feather of peer pressure. Solidifying this image of women into policy implies an acceptance of the passive role. By protecting women against verbal coercion, these feminists are promoting the view of women as weak-willed, alabaster bodies, whose virtue must be protected from the cunning encroachments of the outside world. The idea that women can't withstand verbal or emotional pressure infantilizes them. The suggestion lurking beneath this definition of rape is that men are not just physically but intellectually and emotionally more powerful than women. Printing pamphlets about verbal coercion institutionalizes an unacceptable female position.

We should not nurture this woman on her back, her will so mutable, so easily shaped; we should not support her in her passivity. We are not this woman on her back. We do not have the mind of an eleven-year-old in the body of a twenty-year-old. All competent female college students are compromised by the association of gullibility, low self-esteem, and the inability to assert ourselves with our position in relation to men. We should not be pressured and intimidated by words like "I'll break up with you if you don't"—and anyone who is intimidated should be recognized as the exception, not the rule. Allowing verbal coercion to constitute rape is a sign of tolerance toward the ultrafeminine stance of passivity. The brand of "low self-esteem" these psychologists describe should not be tolerated, it should be changed. Whether or not we feel pressured, regardless of our level of self-esteem, the responsibility for our actions is still our own.

Imagine men sitting around in a circle talking about how she called him impotent and how she manipulated him into sex, how violated and dirty he felt afterward, how coercive she was, how she got him drunk first, how he hated his body and couldn't eat for three weeks afterward. Imagine him calling this rape. Everyone feels the weight of emotional pressure at one time or another. The question is not whether people pressure each other, but how that pressure is transformed in our mind and culture into full-blown assault. There would never be a rule or a law, or even a pamphlet or peer-counseling group, for men who claimed to have been emotionally raped or verbally pressured into sex. And for the same reasons—assumptions of basic competence, free will, and strength of character—there should be no such rules or groups or pamphlets for women.

A manners guide from 1848 warns young women about the perils of verbally coercive men:

> The more attractive his exterior, the more dangerous he is as a companion for
> a young and inexperienced girl, and the more likely to dazzle and bewilder her
> mind. . . . He can with a subtlety almost beyond the power of her detection,
> change her ordinary views of things, confuse her judgments, and destroy her
> rational confidence in discriminating the powers of her own mind.[16]

The fear of verbal coercion, then, does not have its origins in modern feminism. The idea that young girls will be swayed, their judgment overturned, their mind dazzled and bewildered, by the sheer force of masculine logic has been included in date-rape pamphlets for more than a century.

Any value there may be in promoting this idea about female passivity and gullibility is eclipsed by its negative effects. Feminist educators should keep track of the images they project: women can't take care of themselves, they can't make their own decisions with a clear head. . . .

People have asked me if I have ever been date-raped. And thinking back on complicated nights, on too many glasses of wine, on strange and familiar beds, I would have to say yes. With such a sweeping definition of rape, I wonder how many people there are, male or female, who haven't been date-raped at one point or another. People pressure and manipulate and cajole each other into all sorts of things all the time. As Susan Sontag writes, "Since Christianity upped the ante and concentrated on sexual behavior as the root of virtue, everything pertaining to sex has been a 'special case' in our culture, evoking peculiarly inconsistent attitudes."[17] No human interactions are free from pressure, and the idea that sex is, or can be, makes it what Sontag calls a "special case," vulnerable to the inconsistent expectations of double standard.

With their expansive version of rape, rape-crisis feminists invent a kinder, gentler sexuality. Beneath the broad definition of rape, these feminists are endorsing their own utopian vision of sexual relations: sex without struggle, sex without power, sex without persuasion, sex without pursuit. If verbal coercion constitutes rape, then the word "rape" itself expands to include any kind of sex a woman experiences as negative. . . .

Going against the current of much rape-crisis feminism, Marjorie Metsch, Columbia's director of peer education, . . . distinguishes between rape and bad sex. "Most of the time when someone comes in and says 'I was really really drunk and I shouldn't have had sex last night,' it is not the same as saying 'I was raped.' My attitude is that you do not use language that the person herself is not using. It could be that it was just bad sex." Metsch reasons that the social and psychological weight of the word "rape" eclipses its descriptive value in cases of regretted sex. With this approach, she avoids injecting everyday college life with the melodrama of the rape crisis.

But some people want that melodrama. They want the absolute value placed on experience by absolute words. Words like "rape" and "verbal coercion" sculpt the confusing mass of experience into something easy to understand. The idea of date rape comes at us fast and coherent. It comes at us when we've just left home and haven't yet figured out where to put our new futon or how to organize our new social life. The rhetoric about date rape defines the terms, gives names to nameless confusions, and sorts through mixed feelings with a sort of insistent consistency. In the first rush of sexual experience, the fear of date rape offers a tangible framework in which to locate fears that are essentially abstract.

When my mother was young, navigating her way through dates, there was a definite social compass. There were places not to let him put his hands. There were invisible lines. The pill wasn't available, abortion wasn't legal, and sex was just wrong. Her mother gave her "mad money" to take out on dates in case her date got drunk and she needed to escape. She had to go far enough to hold his interest, and not far enough to endanger her reputation.

Now the rape-crisis feminists are offering new rules. They are giving a new political weight to the same old no. My mother's mother told her to drink sloe gin fizzes so she wouldn't drink too much and get too drunk and go too far. Now the date-rape pamphlets tell us, "Avoid excessive use of alcohol and drugs. Alcohol and drugs interfere with clear thinking and effective communication."[18]

My mother's mother told her to stay away from empty rooms and dimly lit streets. In her guidelines about rape prevention, Robin Warshaw writes, "Especially with a recent acquaintance, women should insist on going only to public places such as restaurants and movie theaters."[19]

There is a danger in these new rules. We shouldn't need to be reminded that the rigidly conformist fifties were not the heyday of women's power. Barbara

Ehrenreich writes of "re-making love," but there is a danger in remaking love in its old image. While the terms may have changed, attitudes about sex and women's bodies have not. Rape-crisis feminists threaten the progress that's been made. They are chasing the same stereotypes our mothers spent so much energy running away from.

One day I was looking through my mother's bookshelves, and I found her old, battered copy of Germaine Greer's feminist classic, *The Female Eunuch.* The pages were dog-eared, and whole passages were marked with penciled notes. It was 1971 when Germaine Greer fanned the fires with *The Female Eunuch,* and it was 1971 when my mother read it, brand-new, explosive, a tough and sexy terrorism for the early stirrings of the feminist movement.

Today's rape-crisis feminists threaten to create their own version of the desexualized woman Greer complained of twenty years ago. Her comments need to be recycled for present-day feminism. "It is often falsely assumed," Greer writes,

> even by feminists, that sexuality is the enemy of the female who really wants to develop these aspects of her personality. . . . It was not the insistence on her sex that weakened the American woman student's desire to make something of her education, but the insistence upon a *passive* sexual *role* [Greer's italics]. In fact, the chief instrument in the deflection and perversion of female energy is the denial of female sexuality for the substitution of femininity or sexlessness.[20]

It is the passive sexual role that threatens us still, and it is the denial of female sexual agency that threatens to propel us backward.

Notes

1. *Ms.,* October 1985.
2. *New York Times,* October 23, 1985.
3. Neil Gilbert, "Realities and Mythologies of Rape," *Society* 29 (May–June 1992).
4. Ibid.
5. *New York Times,* October 23, 1985.
6. Naomi Wolf, *The Beauty Myth* (New York: William Morrow, 1991), p. 167.
7. Susan Brownmiller, *Against Our Will: Men, Women and Rape* (New York: Bantam, 1975), p. 5.
8. "Acquaintance Rape." Rockville, Md.: American College Health Association, 1992.
9. "Acquaintance Rape: Is Dating Dangerous?" Rockville, Md.: American College Health Association, 1987.
10. Elizabeth Fox-Genovese, *Feminism without Illusions* (Chapel Hill: University of North Carolina Press, 1991), p. 21.
11. Robin Warshaw, *I Never Called It Rape* (New York: Harper and Row, 1988), p. 24.
12. Ibid., p. 174.
13. *Chronicle of Higher Education,* March 26, 1986.

14. Charlene L. Muehlenhard and Jennifer L Schrag, "Nonviolent Sexual Coercion," in Andrea Parrot and Laurie Bechhofer, eds., *Acquaintance Rape: The Hidden Crime* (New York: John Wiley, 1991), p. 122.

15. Ibid., p. 123.

16. T. S. Arthur, *Advice to Young Ladies* (Boston: Phillips and Sampson, 1848), p. 151.

17. Susan Sontag, *Styles of Radical Will* (New York: Farrar, Straus and Giroux 1976), p. 46.

18. "Acquaintance Rape: 'Is Dating Dangerous?' " Rockville, Md.: American College Health Association, 1991.

19. Warshaw, *I Never Called It Rape,* p. 153.

20. Germaine Greer, *The Female Eunuch* (New York: McGraw-Hill, 1971), p. 59.

42

Is Rape Sex or Violence?
Conceptual Issues and Implications

Charlene L. Muehlenhard, Sharon Danoff-Burg, and Irene G. Powch

Say you have a man who believes a woman is attractive. He feels encouraged by her and he's so motivated by that encouragement that he rips her clothes off and has sex with her against her will. Now let's say you have another man who grabs a woman off some lonely road and in the process of raping her says words like, "You're wearing a skirt! You're a woman! I hate women! I'm going to show you, you woman!" Now, the first one's terrible. But the other's much worse. If a man rapes a woman while telling her he loves her, that's a far cry from saying he hates her. A lust factor does not spring from animus.

—Orrin Hatch, U.S. Senate[1]

Rape is never an act of lust. Mr. Hatch just doesn't get it.

—Eleanor Smeal, Fund for a Feminist Majority[2]

The above debate regarding the Violence against Women Act of 1993 focused on how rape is to be conceptualized: Is rape sex, motivated by lust, or is rape violence? This question has emerged in numerous contexts, including political, scientific, clinical, and interpersonal contexts.

A simplistic answer to the question—Is rape sex or violence?—would be that nonfeminists view rape as sex, whereas feminists view rape as violence.[3] As we show, however, this simplistic answer is incorrect. Both feminists and nonfeminists have taken a variety of positions on this question. Furthermore, neither a "rape is sex" nor a "rape is violence" position has solely positive or negative implications for rape victims or for all women.

The purpose of this essay is not to answer the question, "Is rape sex or violence?" Rather, our purpose is to examine thoughtfully the conceptual issues behind this question. These conceptual issues include the following: Is rape sex or violence from whose perspective? From the perspective of the victim? The perpetrator? All women and men in our society?

What is rape? That is, what is it that we are characterizing as sex or violence? What is sex? That is, what characteristics would rape need to have before we could say that rape "was" sex? Similarly, what is violence? What characteristics would rape need to have before we could say that rape "was" violence?

Finally, what are the implications of different positions on this debate? What are the social, scientific, and legal implications for rape victims and perpetrators, as well as for all women and men?

From Whose Perspective?

The question—"Is rape sex or violence?"—implies that rape is a monolithic entity, similar from any perspective. Rape, however, is experienced from numerous perspectives. In fact, Spender suggested that the experience of rape from the victim's perspective is so different from the perpetrator's experience that we need two different words to describe these totally different experiences.[4]

In this section, we discuss rape from the perspectives of victims, perpetrators, and all women and men in this culture.[5] Paradoxically, however, when we turn to the literature for insights, what we find are the perspectives of various writers about the perspectives of victims, perpetrators, and all women and men. Historically, many of these writers have expressed views consistent with the interests of those in power, such as those scientists who attempted to justify or trivialize rape by writing that rape was unconsciously desired by female victims. Before we conclude that the least biased approach is for persons involved to speak for themselves, however, we should ask ourselves if we would take perpetrators' accounts at face value, knowing that even incarcerated perpetrators often deny engaging in sexual coercion.[6]

Furthermore, as we discuss this question from different perspectives, it will become clear that the meaning of the question—"Is rape sex or violence?"—is ambiguous. It could refer to motivation, to consequences, or to how one experiences, conceptualizes, and labels the experience. Thus, when someone says, "Rape is sex to the rapist and violence to the victim," they often are referring to the motivation and experience of the rapist but to the experience of and consequences for the victim.

With these complexities in mind, we now discuss the perspectives of victims, perpetrators, and all women and men.

The Victim's Perspective

In the scientific literature published through the mid-1970s, experts' conceptualizations of victims' perspectives could be characterized as follows: To the extent that these experts regarded rape as a "real" phenomenon rather than as false charges made up by hysterical women,[7] they frequently viewed rape as a sexual experience that the victim unconsciously desired[8] and that the victim invited by being unconsciously seductive[9] or blatantly provocative to the rapist.[10]

Beginning in the 1970s this scientific analysis of rape as sexually desirable for victims was challenged by feminist writers. These feminists focused an unprecedented amount of attention on rape, engaging in political activism and advocating new theoretical perspectives. Although the grassroots nature of feminist activism makes a complete record impossible to compile, existent records indicate that feminist activists held the first speak-outs on rape and organized the first rape crisis centers in the early 1970s.[11] Feminist theorists such as Brownmiller,[12] Greer,[13] Griffin,[14] and Millett[15] emphasized the violent nature of rape and conceptualized rape as a form of social control of women. For example, in her classic article, "Rape: The All-American Crime," Susan Griffin wrote,

> Rape is an act of aggression in which the victim is denied her self-determination. It is an act of violence which, if not actually followed by beatings or murder, nevertheless always carries with it the threat of death. And finally, rape is a form of mass terrorism, for the victims of rape are chosen indiscriminately.[16]

Since the 1970s, research has documented the devastating consequences experienced by rape victims. Currently, even persons who argue that rape is sex from the perpetrator's perspective often say that rape is violence from the victim's perspective. For example, Palmer, in an article arguing that rapists are frequently motivated by sexual desire, wrote, "Thanks to the feminist movement, no one any longer defends the dangerous claim that rape is a sexually arousing or sought-after experience on the part of the *victim*."[17] Symons, who also argued that sexual desire motivates rapists, commented, "What has, of course, been shown is that rape very rarely is a sexual experience for the victim."[18]

It would be overly simplistic, however, to say that rape is never sex from the victim's perspective. The definition of rape and who labels the act become an issue here. For example, Koss, Dinero, Seibel, and Cox used a definition of rape based on a legal definition. They found that women who had been raped (based on Koss et al.'s definition) did not always consider themselves to have been raped. This was especially likely in the context of a dating relationship: Women labeled the incident rape in 55.0 percent of cases involving strangers, in 27.7 percent of cases involving nonromantic acquaintances, and in 18.3 percent of cases involving steady dating partners. Some of the women viewed the incident as a crime other than rape (this was the case for 15.6 percent of the incidents involving strangers and 15.0 percent of the incidents involving acquaintances). Other women viewed the incident as miscommunication (this was the case for 21.5 percent of the incidents involving strangers and 50.9 percent of the incidents involving acquaintances). Still other women reported not feeling victimized (this was the case for 7.9 percent of the incidents involving strangers and 11.1 percent of the incidents involving acquaintances).[19] Although Koss et al. did not specifically ask women if they viewed the incident as violence or sex, it seems probable that women who viewed the incident as rape or some other crime probably regarded it as violence (they may or may not also have viewed the incident as sex). Conversely, it seems likely that women who viewed the incident as miscommunication and women who did not feel victimized probably were more likely to have viewed the incident as sex and less likely to have viewed it as violence.

Victims' conceptualizations of their experiences are influenced by what they learn from the popular culture. The law, depictions of rape in the media, and what others say about rape influence victims' ideas of what events constitute rape and how they should interpret these events. The dominant culture sends us powerful messages about rape, sex, and violence: that "real rape" is a narrowly defined set of events (e.g., a stranger with a weapon forcing a woman to have penile-vaginal intercourse); that men cannot control their sexual urges if women "get them" aroused; that "real men" may use force to get what they want; and that, under certain circumstances, one is obligated to have sex whether one wants to or not.[20] To the extent that rape victims (as defined by researchers, the law, etc.) have internalized these messages, they may or may not interpret their experiences as rape, sex, or violence. How victims label an incident is not necessarily related to the seriousness of the consequences, however. For example, Koss et al. found that, although victims of acquaintance rape (as the researchers defined it) were less likely than victims of stranger rape to label their experience as rape, the two groups did not differ significantly in their subsequent depression, anxiety, problems with relationships, problems with sex, or thoughts of suicide (over one-fourth of both groups reported considering suicide).

The Perpetrator's Perspective

Cultural messages that influence how victims label their experiences also influence how perpetrators experience and conceptualize their behavior. The question of whether rape is sex or violence to a perpetrator, however, frequently refers to motivation. Motivational questions could be addressed by investigating what perpetrators say about their motivation; however, this approach is likely to be complicated by perpetrators' desire to view their behavior in a positive light, as well as by the illegality of rape and the possibility (albeit a minute possibility) of criminal sanctions. Motivational questions could also be addressed by investigating perpetrators' underlying motivations—unconscious motivations (from a psychodynamic perspective) or behavioral contingencies (from an operant perspective). An observer's conclusions about such underlying motivations may be very different from perpetrators' explanations of their own behavior.

In asking about perpetrators' motivations, we also must keep in mind that different rapists have different motivations;[21] in fact, even the same rapist may be motivated by different factors at different times. Thus to say that rape is motivated by sex or violence or by any other single factor is likely to be overly simplistic.

The Perspectives of All Women and Men

One feature that distinguished feminists' analyses of rape from previous scientific accounts was feminists' focus on the perspectives of all women and all men. Recall Griffin's statement, quoted above, that "rape is a form of mass terrorism, for the victims of rape are chosen indiscriminately."[22] Brownmiller also considered the perspective of all women and men: "From prehistoric times to the present, I believe, rape has played a critical function. It is nothing more or less than a conscious process of intimidation by which *all men* keep *all women* in a state of fear."[23]

Feminist theorists noted similarities in the impact of rape and other forms of violence: similarities in consequences for victims and similarities in producing fear that forces potential victims to alter their behavior. Thus they argued for the utility of conceptualizing rape as violence. In such an analysis, one could ask about "society's"[24] motives for perpetuating rape myths that blame women for rape, for advocating rape prevention strategies that limit women's freedom, and for establishing a legal system that shields rapists by making a charge of rape almost impossible to prove. This system benefits men at the expense of women.

People who do not rape are likely to have different motives for perpetuating this system than do rapists. For example, even men who do not rape might benefit by having access to occupational, educational, leisure, and other opportunities that women are afraid to pursue.[25] "Any one man might not rape to preserve the patriarchy,"[26] but preserving the patriarchy might well be the motivation of those who benefit from a system that forces women to restrict their sexual behavior, their dress, their mobility—in short, their freedom.

The Impact of Definitions

The question—"Is rape sex or violence?"—depends on how rape, sex, and violence are defined and conceptualized. Often, these terms are used as if their definitions were obvious, and most English-speaking people would report knowing the definitions of these terms. Beneath the surface understandings of these terms, however, the boundaries of people's definitions are fuzzy. Although people often can provide examples of acts that would definitely be construed as rape or sex or violence, they often have difficulty giving precise definitions or saying whether certain acts would or would not fit into these categories. Different people also disagree about how these terms should be defined.

We do not intend to provide the "true" or "accurate" definitions of these terms; in fact, we regard a true definition as a meaningless concept. Instead, we approach these definitional issues from a social constructionist perspective. "Social constructionism is principally concerned with elucidating the processes by which people come to describe, explain or otherwise account for the world in which they live."[27] Of primary interest to us here is to note that the words that we use are created by people: "The terms in which the world is understood are social artifacts, products of historically situated interchanges among people."[28] The meanings that we assign to words are made up by people and change over time and place. The meanings of words reflect the power relations among people; people dominant in the culture define words from their perspective, usually in ways that benefit themselves.[29] Because language does not merely name reality but actually shapes reality, it can be an act of resistance for less powerful groups to point out who benefits and who loses from commonly accepted definitions and conceptualizations and to develop their own definitions and conceptualizations.

What Is Rape?

There is no single correct definition of *rape*. Commonly used definitions of rape all include the notion of nonconsensual sexual behavior, but definitions differ dramatically along several dimensions.[30] Depending on how sex and violence are conceptualized, the differences in various definitions may influence our thinking about whether rape is sex or violence.

In the stereotypic rape, the rapist is either threatening the victim with a weapon or hitting her with his fists; the victim is crying, pleading, and perhaps struggling. Consistent with this stereotype, some definitions of rape—for example, some legal definitions—require a great deal of force by the perpetrator.[31] Similarly, some definitions require that the victim fight, cry, scream, or plead.[32]

Other definitions do not require force; the fact that the perpetrator initiated sexual behavior without the victim's consent makes the act rape. Consent, however, is itself a complicated concept. Sometimes consent occurs in the context of limited options. For example, if a woman consents to sex because the alternative is to be physically beaten, most people would regard her consent as meaningless and would regard the sex as rape even though she "consented." What if she consents to sex with her husband because the alternative is divorce and poverty, perhaps even homelessness, for herself and her children? In this case, would her consent be regarded as meaningless and would sex with her husband be regarded as rape? In this society and others, sex within marriage is regarded as the norm—a spouse's entitlement.[33] A husband who expects sex in his marriage is likely to be motivated by sex, as he understands it, rather than by violence.

Some feminist theorists' definitions of rape are much broader than traditional definitions. For example, MacKinnon wrote, "Politically, I call it rape whenever a woman has sex and feels violated."[34] This would include situations in which women have sex due to economic pressure, fear of being raped if they refuse, or other sorts of pressure. Robin Morgan wrote, *"I would claim that rape exists any time sexual intercourse occurs when it has not been initiated by the woman, out of her own genuine affection and desire."*[35] Robin Morgan's definition would even include some situations in which the woman herself initiated sex, given the pressures on women to initiate sex out of "fear of losing the guy, fear of being thought a prude, fear of hurting his fragile feelings, *fear.*"[36] Gavey wrote that

Dominant discourses on heterosexuality position women as relatively passive subjects who are encouraged to comply with sex with men, irrespective of their own sexual desire. Through the operation of disciplinary power, male dominance can be maintained in heterosexual practice often in the absence of direct force or violence. The discursive processes that maintain these sets of power relationships can be thought of as "technologies of heterosexual coercion."[37]

Such technologies include the tyranny of normality, which dictates how often and under what circumstances "normal" women must engage in sex; the ideology of permissive, meaningless sex, which deprives women of reasons to refuse; and negative labeling, such as a woman's being taunted as "sexually uptight"[38] or "a ball-breaking feminist"[39] if she refuses. Thus these technologies of heterosexual coercion can hide sexual coercion from both those who coerce and those who are coerced.

Some writers contend that in our patriarchal culture women can never truly consent to sex.[40] They argue that, in a patriarchal culture, even if women desire sex, this desire is likely to have been constructed by the patriarchal culture. Furthermore, the Southern Women's Writing Collective argued that in this culture sex is part of a package that includes love, security, and emotional support; giving up sex would result in giving up all this. For these reasons, they argued, women in this culture can never freely consent to sex.

Levine highlighted the culturally constructed nature of rape when he defined rape as the *"culturally disvalued* use of coercion by a male to achieve the submission of a female to sexual intercourse."[41] If the cultural norm is to regard certain types of coercion as appropriate, then those behaviors, however unwanted, will not be considered rape. Thus rape generally is not defined as broadly as the definitions just discussed; it has been in the interest of people with power to define rape as requiring blatant acts of force rather than subtle uses of power. As we move away from definitions requiring blatant force by the perpetrator and vehement reactions by the victim to more subtle uses of power, however, the distinction between rape and "normal sex" becomes blurred. Motivations for rape can become indistinguishable from motivations for sex.

What Is Sex?

In order to address the question—"Is rape sex or violence?"—we need to consider the definition of *sex*. That is, what criteria would rape need to meet to be considered sex?

In his article arguing that rape is sexually motivated, Palmer criticized the following argument:

Sex includes tenderness, affection, and joy.
Rape does not include these qualities.
Therefore, rape is not sex.

Palmer argued that "the validity of this argument depends on the accuracy of its definition of 'sex,' and there appears to be considerable evidence that this definition of sex is unduly limiting."[42] Apparently Palmer meant unduly limiting to men, for he proceeded to give examples of how men can divorce sex from love. Palmer's statement about the "accuracy" of a definition suggests that he believes that there is an accurate definition of sex. We, on the other hand, take the position that there is no accurate definition of sex. Using a social constructionist perspective, we view sex as a fluid, socially negotiated concept.

Although conceptualizing sex as "tenderness, affection, and joy" differentiates sex from rape, other conceptualizations of sex make sex and rape indistinguishable and thus make rape appear normal, invisible as rape and visible only as sex. For instance, psychoanalytic theorists traditionally have conceptualized women's sexuality as inextricably linked to pain and violence.[43] Deutsch described masochism as a fundamental trait of femininity and a component of mature sexual intercourse. She wrote that, because women's vaginas are "passive," women need to be overpowered by men in order to experience sexual pleasure. Bonaparte wrote that "In coitus, the woman, in effect, is subjected to a sort of beating by the man's penis. She receives its blows and often, even, loves their violence."[44] Some, though not all, contemporary psychoanalysts have similar attitudes. Adams-Silvan discussed her patient's wish to be raped and "her wish for sexually gratifying masochistic submission."[45] If one conceptualizes women as masochistic and violence as a necessary component of women's sexuality, then one might conclude that women could experience rape as sex or perhaps as both sex and violence.

Feminist writers also have discussed links between sex and violence. Rather than viewing these links as essential components of femininity or female sexuality, however, feminists have emphasized the dominant culture's construction of sex as violence and the role of this construction in perpetuating male dominance. In her article emphasizing the violent nature of rape, Griffin described rape as "the perfect combination of sex and violence."[46] She wrote that "erotic pleasure cannot be separated from culture, and in our culture male eroticism is wedded to power. . . . For in our culture heterosexual love finds an erotic expression through male dominance and female submission."[47] Dworkin also wrote about the merging of sex and violence for men:

> When feminists say *rape is violence, not sex,* we mean to say that from our perspective as victims of forced sex, we do not get sexual pleasure from rape; contrary to the rapist's view, the pornographer's view, and the law's view, rape is not a good time for us. This is a valiant effort at crosscultural communication, but it is only half the story: because for men, rape and sex are not different species of event. Domination is sexual for most men, and rape, battery, incest, use of prostitutes and pornography, and sexual harassment are modes of domination imbued with sexual meaning.[48]

Beneke discussed parallels between rape and sex as conceptualized by "ordinary men." He analyzed metaphors that men use to discuss sex: sex as a hunt or conquest (e.g., "I'm going *to go out and get a piece of ass tonight*"[49]); sex as war (e.g., "I tried to get her into bed but *got shot down.* . . . He's always *hitting on* women"[50]); sex as hitting women's genitals (e.g., "I'd like to *bang* her *box*"[51]); the penis as a gun and sperm as ammunition (e.g., "*He shot his load* into her"[52]); impregnation as violence (e.g., "He *knocked her up,*"[53]); sex as aggressive degradation (e.g., "I'd like to *screw* her. I want *to fuck* her"[54]). Beneke concluded that, for many men, seeking sex has more to do with status, hostility, control, and dominance than with sensual pleasure or sexual satisfaction. He drew parallels between these motivations of normal men for normal sex and Groth's discussion of rapists' motivations:

> Rape, then, is a pseudosexual act, a pattern of sexual behavior that is concerned much more with *status, hostility, control, and dominance* [italics added] than with sensual pleasure or sexual satisfaction. It is sexual behavior in the primary service of nonsexual needs.[55]

Beneke concluded,

> If we are going to say that, for a man, rape has little to do with sex, we may as well add that sex itself often has little to do with sex, or, if you like, that rape has plenty to do with sex as it is often understood and spoken about by men.[56]

What Is Violence?

In order to consider whether rape is sex or violence, we need to consider how violence is conceptualized. D. H. J. Morgan discussed the process by which acts are labeled as violence. Generally, he argued, acts of "legitimated" violence are labeled *force* or *restraint* rather than violence (he preferred to discuss legitimated violence rather than "legitimate" violence because the former term emphasizes the legitimation process rather than implying "fixed structures or uncontested essences"[57]). In some cases (e.g., corporal punishment), the legitimation process is so effective that the violence almost disappears.

Along these lines, Greenblatt discussed two kinds of cultural rules: (1) prescriptive and proscriptive rules, which tell members of a society what they should and should not do, and (2) interpretive rules, which "tell societal members how to interpret and make sense of what someone (oneself or another) has done."[58] These two kinds of rules are related in that interpretive rules determine which prescriptive and proscriptive rules apply in a given situation. Some people have more power than others to influence society's interpretive rules, including rules about whether a behavior should be considered sex or violence. "The fact is, anything that anybody with power experiences as sex is considered ipso facto not violence, because someone who matters enjoyed it."[59]

Violence can be understood in many ways. Theorists writing about aggression, a concept closely related to violence, have found it useful to distinguish between hostile, angry, or affective aggression and instrumental aggression.[60] In this conceptualization, *hostile aggression* arises from anger; the goal is to injure. *Instrumental aggression,* on the other hand, is aggression employed as a means to attain some goal; injury may occur, but it is not the goal in and of itself.

This distinction is important when we think about rape and violence. Sometimes when rape is conceptualized as violence, hostile aggression is implicit, such as in the statement, "Rape is about power and anger. Often, a man rapes to overpower or express anger at a woman—to get back at her."[61] Campbell, however, argued that, for men, aggression is usually instrumental. "Men see aggression as a means of exerting control over other people when they feel the need to reclaim power and self-esteem."[62]

> The point of men's instrumental aggression is not to signal emotional upset or to let off steam but to control the behavior of another person, and this can be done as effectively, if not more effectively, when anger does not get in the way. . . . Such cold and calculated aggression finds its most sinister expressions in the exclusively male crime of rape and the predominantly male crime of robbery, both of which nearly always demand an aggressor who feels no anger toward the target of his violence.[63]

Thus, we could conceptualize rape as instrumental aggression regardless of the rapists' level of anger as long as we could show that violence or force is being used as a means of obtaining some goal.

Within this framework of instrumental aggression, the goal to be obtained through the act of rape varies according to different theorists and according to one's perspective. One could conceptualize rape as instrumental aggression in which a rapist uses force to achieve the goal of sex, in which a rapist uses sex to achieve the goal of dominating the victim, or in which powerful people perpetuate rape myths and the legal system to achieve the goal of controlling women, keeping women locked in their homes, afraid, dependent on men for protection.

In general, nonfeminist theorists have emphasized the goal of sex, and feminist theorists have emphasized the goals of dominating and controlling rape victims and women in general. It would be inaccurate, however, to say that feminists claim that sex is never the goal of rape. In Diana Russell's classic book on marital rape, she outlined several reasons why a husband might rape his wife. She regarded marital rape as most frequently motivated by a husband's desire to dominate his wife—that is, as instrumental aggression in which he uses rape to achieve the goal of dominance. She regarded some cases of marital rape as motivated by sex, however—instrumental aggression in which a husband uses force to achieve the goal of sex:

> Implicit in my typology, particularly the . . . category of husbands who prefer consensual sex with their wives but who have raped them when their sexual advances are refused, is the notion that rape in marriage can be sexually motivated. . . . Some husbands have sex whenever and however they wish, regardless of whether or not their wives are willing, since, they, like the law, see this as their right. They are *exercising* power when they do this, but they are not necessarily *motivated* by the desire for power.[64]

So far, our discussion of violence has been consistent with the *American Heritage Dictionary* definition, "physical force exerted for the purpose of violating, damaging, or abusing."[65] This dictionary also defines violence as "the abusive or unjust exercise of power."[66] Using this definition, what counts as violence broadens considerably. Theorists in the field of domestic violence have identified a variety of forms of violence that a batterer can use, including not only physical abuse but also emotional abuse, economic abuse, sexual abuse, isolating the victim from friends and family, and intimidating the victim.[67] Pinthus also defined violence broadly in terms of its function: "Violence should be understood as any action or structure that diminishes another human being."[68] Such definitions come more from the perspective of victims than of perpetrators. They highlight the fact that both blatant physical force and more subtle acts that do not appear brutal on the surface all may be equally devastating in their effects on victims.

Implications

The question of how to conceptualize rape has important legal, scientific, clinical, and interpersonal implications. It has sometimes been assumed that conceptualizing rape as sex has solely negative implications for women, whereas conceptualizing rape as violence has solely positive implications. We believe, however, that the situation is considerably more complex.

Rape As Sex Rather Than Violence

Prior to the feminist reanalysis of rape beginning in the 1970s, influential segments of both the scientific community and the public conceptualized all but the most narrowly defined acts of rape as sex that was desired by female victims.[69] This led to blaming rape victims for inviting rape, either unconsciously or consciously, and it led to solutions that entailed restricting women's freedom.

The feminist reanalysis has certainly had an impact, and today it is less acceptable than before to state publicly that women enjoy or invite rape. Such beliefs still exist, however. For example, in a March 24, 1990, speech, Texas Republican gubernatorial nominee Clayton Williams compared foul weather to rape, saying, "If it's inevitable, just relax and enjoy it."[70] The idea that women "ask for" or "invite" rape by getting men sexually aroused also still persists. Advice columnist Ann Landers, for example, wrote that "the woman who 'repairs to some private place for a few drinks and a little shared affection' has, by her acceptance of such a cozy invitation, given the man reason to believe that she is a candidate for whatever he might have in mind."[71] She also agreed with a reader who argued that women "invite trouble" by "telling raw jokes and using street language. Bouncing around (no bra) in low-cut sweaters and see-through blouses. Wearing skirts slit to the city limits up the sides, back or front."[72] Such attitudes serve as a form of social control of women, dictating that women refrain from any behavior that might sexually arouse men. Furthermore, such attitudes suggest that if a women is raped, she is likely to have enjoyed it, and, in any case, she is to blame for the rape.

Clearly, then, conceptualizing rape as sex can have negative consequences for rape victims and for all women. There can also be positive consequences, however. To the extent that men's sexual arousal to rape cues precipitates rape, assessment and treatment of such sexual arousal may help prevent rape.[73] Furthermore, analyses of the similarities between rape and normal sex have highlighted the coercive nature of many socially acceptable forms of sex.[74] Such analyses have led to a critique of how sex is constructed in our society and how such constructions serve to make sexual coercion invisible or to make it appear to be trivial or the fault of the victim.[75] Challenges to normal forms of coercive sexuality will ultimately benefit rape victims and all women.

Rape As Violence Rather Than Sex

Five years after Brownmiller's 1975 publication of *Against Our Will*, Warner wrote, "It is now generally accepted by criminologists, psychologists, and other professionals working with rapists and rape victims that rape is not primarily a sexual crime, it is a crime of violence."[76] The implications of this reconceptualization were profound. Rape crisis centers, rape law reform, and a new courage of rape victims to speak out were among the positive effects of this change in how rape was conceptualized. The lives of many rape victims were improved because, when rape is regarded primarily as violence rather than as sex "invited" by the victim, a rape victim is less likely to be retraumatized by victim-blaming questions and attitudes from family, friends, and the legal system. The blame is more clearly placed where it belongs—on the perpetrator. When rape is regarded as primarily an act of violence, rape victims are granted a framework for understanding feelings of rage, fear, and depression as normal reactions. For example, rape victims' reactions can be conceptualized as posttraumatic stress disorder, similar to reactions of others who have experienced violence (e.g., Vietnam veterans), rather than as signs of being "crazy." Rape victims are empowered to work through their anger in constructive ways through counseling and activism. All this would help a person to move through recovery stages from victim to survivor.

Viewing rape as an act of violence also allows for a recognition of the fear of rape that is pervasive among women as a group and hence allows for the recognition that the ever-present threat of rape serves as a powerful social control of women's behavior, restricting women and keeping women in the home, which was supposed to be safe.[77] This, in turn, highlights the sociopolitical conditions that create a rape-prone culture, which connects the problem of rape with the more general problem of the subjugation of women.[78] In other words, conceptualizing rape as violence contributes to an understanding of rape within its social context. This conceptualization has had heuristic value, suggesting new sets of variables to be investigated.

In some cases, however, conceptualizing rape as violence rather than sex has shortcomings that may fail rape victims. Estrich argued that, if rape is understood as violence rather than sex, it is difficult to convince a jury that coercive sex is rape if it did not involve a great deal of extrinsic violence.[79]

Even if the prosecutor can prove that sex was nonconsensual, the jury may be unlikely to convict if the case did not include a great deal of violence as the jury understands it. If a jury is unlikely to convict, a prosecutor may be dissuaded from prosecuting. Equating rape with violence could lead to policies exemplified by the advice a detective sergeant gave to fellow officers in a 1975 issue of *Police Review*:

> It should be borne in mind that except in the case of a very young child, the offense of rape is extremely unlikely to have been committed against a woman

who does not immediately show signs of *extreme violence* (italics added). If a woman walks into a police station and complains of rape with no such signs of violence she must be closely interrogated. Allow her to make her statement to a policewoman and then drive a horse and cart through it. It is always advisable if there is any doubt of the truthfulness of her allegations to call her an outright liar.[80]

Not only are juries and judges subject to this difficulty, victims themselves may not define what was done to them as violence and hence may not define it as rape. Rapists frequently use intimidation or the weight of their bodies; they take advantage of the victim's confusion, shock, fear, or intoxication; they ignore the victim's refusal; or they act without the victims' consent. Many rapists do not use weapons, punches, or other actions that people readily identify as violence. Thus, rape victims who understand rape as violence, not sex, might not think of their experience as rape. They might feel out of place going to a rape crisis center and thus never seek help. Or, if they seek help and are told that rape is "not sex," they might not feel understood if to them the act seemed like sex. This might cause problems especially for rape victims who experienced a physiological sexual response during the rape. Not conceptualizing what was done to them as rape may result in the victim becoming stuck in a cycle of desperately trying to make something tolerable out of a horrible experience, especially if this is a first sexual experience for a young person.[81]

Regarding rape as violence, not sex, was "a breakthrough at a time when labeling virtually any act sex was considered exonerating."[82] When we say that sex is separate from rape and violence, however, "we fail to criticize what has been made of *sex,* what has been done to us *through* sex, because we leave the line between rape and intercourse . . . right where it is."[83] We now turn to another conceptualization that views rape as both sex and violence and that critiques how sex, as well as rape and violence, has been constructed in our culture.

Rape As Sex and Violence

Rather than regarding rape as sex *or* violence, rape can be conceptualized as sex *and* violence, with an understanding that these concepts are socially constructed rather than essential and that in this culture violence against women is eroticized.[84] Such a conceptualization could make it easier for rape victims to identify their experience as rape, even if it felt like sex, albeit unwanted sex, and even if they experienced a sexual response. This conceptualization might make it easier for them to seek the support they need.

A conceptualization of rape as sex and violence could also be useful for rape prevention programs, such as programs sponsored by junior high schools, high schools, and universities. Students could be told that even if behavior feels like sex to them, it could still be rape; sex and rape are not mutually exclusive. The current emphasis on sexual harassment in the schools[85] is fertile ground for a discussion of the links between violence and sexuality.

Such a conceptualization also highlights the links between sex and violence found not only in pornography, but also in mainstream narratives ranging from fairy tales to beer commercials to romance novels in which "a brute male sexuality is magically converted to romance."[86] Thus, conceptualizing rape as both sex and violence has positive implications not only for understanding rape, but also for critiquing the socially constructed links between sex and violence.

Control: Beyond Sex and Violence

Ultimately, we would like to see this discussion move beyond sex versus violence to one of control. Control is a broader, more encompassing concept than violence; if someone is powerful enough, they can control others without having to resort to violence as it is commonly understood. A focus on control would lead us to ask questions such as, Who controls women's sexuality? Who controls men's sexuality? How free are women and men to control their own sexuality? How free are women and men to refuse to engage in unwanted sex, to engage in sex with the partner of their choice, or to engage in the type of consensual sexuality that they would like?

Using such a conceptualization, the criterion for sexual coercion would not be whether someone had experienced violence, it would be whether someone had freely consented to the sexual activity. Rape prevention programs would not merely tell students to avoid violence; they would tell students to refrain from sexual behavior with anyone who had not freely consented. Jurors would not focus on whether an incident involved violence; they would ask themselves whether the victim had freely consented.

Such a conceptualization would ultimately need to move beyond the level of individual behavior to the level of constraints that inhibit people's ability to consent or refuse freely. This would include critiquing economic disadvantage that make women as a group dependent on men. It would include critiquing the "technologies of heterosexual coercion,"[87] such as the tyranny of normality, ideologies that deprive women and men of reasons to refuse, and negative labeling of women and men who refuse sex. It would include critiquing laws, such as sodomy laws, that restrict consenting adults from freely consenting to the kind of consensual sex they want and thus force them to choose between sex that they do not want and no sex at all. Until women and men have the ability and the resources to freely refuse or consent to have sex, no one—especially the less powerful people in our society—can truly control their own sexuality.

Notes

1. Quoted by R. Shalit, "Is Rape a Crime?" *San Jose Mercury News*, June 28, 1993, p. 7B.

2. Ibid.

3. There is no one definition of feminism; in fact, diversity is inherent in feminism. Our view of feminism includes the beliefs "that women are valuable and that social change to benefit women is needed" (R. Unger and M. Crawford, *Women and Gender: A Feminist Psychology* [New York: McGraw-Hill, 1992], p. 9; see R. Tong, *Feminist Thought: A Comprehensive Introduction* [Boulder, Colo.: Westview Press, 1989]).

4. D. Spender, *Man Made Language* (London: Routledge and Kegan Paul, 1980).

5. We acknowledge that it is problematic to presume to speak for "all women and men" in this culture. When we refer to the perspectives of all women and men regarding rape, we are referring to the impact of rape on how gender is constructed in this society.

6. J. Wolfe and V. Baker, "Characteristics of Imprisoned Rapists and Circumstances of the Rape," in *Rape and Sexual Assault: Management and Intervention* (Germantown, Md.: Aspen Systems, 1980).

7. E.g., H. Deutsch, *The Psychology of Women* (New York: Grune and Stratton, 1944).

8. E.g., M. Factor, "A Woman's Psychological Reaction to Attempted Rape," *Psychoanalytic Quarterly* 23 (1954): 243–44, and W. S. Wille, "Case Study of a Rapist: An Analysis of the Causation of Criminal Behavior," *Journal of Social Therapy* 7 (1961): 10–21.

9. E.g., W. H. Blanchard, "The Group Process in Gang Rape," *Journal of Social Psychology*, 49 (1959): 259–66.

10. E.g., M. Amir, *Patterns in Forcible Rape* (Chicago: University of Chicago Press, 1971); J. M. MacDonald, *Rape Offenders and Their Victims* (Springfield, Ill.: Thomas, 1971); for further discussion see C. L. Muehlenhard, P. A. Harney, and J. M. Jones, "From 'Victim-Precipitated' Rape to 'Date Rape': How Far Have We Come?" *Annual Review of Sex Research* 3 (1992): 219–53.

11. B. S. Deckard, *The Women's Movement: Political, Socioeconomic, and Psychological Issues*, 3d ed. (New York: Harper and Row, 1983); Rape Victim Support Service, "History," unpublished manuscript (Lawrence, Kans., n.d.).

12. S. Brownmiller, *Against Our Will: Men, Women, and Rape* (New York: Bantam, 1975).

13. G. Greer, *The Female Eunuch* (New York: McGraw-Hill, 1970).

14. S. Griffin, "Rape: The All-American Crime," *Ramparts* 10 (1971): 26–35.

15. K. Millett, *Sexual Politics* (New York: Ballantine, 1969).

16. S. Griffin, "Rape: The All-American Crime," p. 35.

17. C. T. Palmer, "Twelve Reasons Why Rape Is Not Sexually Motivated: A Skeptical Examination," *Journal of Sex Research* 25 (1988): 514 (italics in original).

18. D. Symons, *The Evolution of Human Sexuality* (New York: Oxford University Press, 1979) p. 35.

19. M. P. Koss, T. E. Dinero, C. A. Seibel, and S. L. Cox, "Stranger and Acquaintance Rape: Are There Differences in the Victim's Experience?" *Psychology of Women Quarterly* 12 (1988): 1–23.

20. T. Beneke, *Men on Rape* (New York: St. Martin's Press, 1982); S. Estrich, *Real Rape: How the Legal System Victimizes Women Who Say No* (Cambridge, Mass.: Harvard University Press, 1987); R. K. Reinholtz, C. L. Meuhlenhard, J. L. Phelps, and A. T. Satterfield, "Sexual Discourse and Sexual Intercourse: How the Way We Communicate Affects the Way We Think about Sexual Coercion," in *Gender, Power, and Communication in Human Relationships* (Hillsdale, N.J.: Lawrence Erlbaum Associates, 1995), pp. 141–62.

21. A. N. Groth, *Men Who Rape: The Psychology of the Offender* (New York: Plenum, 1979); G. C. N. Hall and R. Hirschman, "Toward a Theory of Sexual Aggression: A Quadripartite Model." *Journal of Consulting and Clinical Psychology* 59 (1991): 662–69; R. A. Prentky and R.

A. Knight, "Identifying Critical Dimensions for Discriminating Among Rapists," *Journal of Consulting and Clinical Psychology* 59 (1991): 643–61; and D. E. H. Russell, ed., *Making Violence Sexy: Feminist Views on Pornography* (New York: Teachers College Press, 1990).

22. Griffin, "Rape: The All-American Crime," p. 35.

23. Brownmiller, *Against Our Will*, p. 5 (italics in original).

24. We are using the term *society* to refer to the entire social system that affects us. This includes our customs, governments, laws, religions, and sciences; our conversations and media depictions; our mutually accepted ways of understanding the world; and so forth. We have some reservations about using this term. It is convenient, but it also renders individuals' actions and responsibilities invisible. It becomes too easy to say that rape is no one's fault; society is to blame (see B. Pope, "Agency—Who Is to Blame?" in *The Knowledge Explosion*, ed., C. Kramarae and D. Spender (New York: Teachers College Press, 1992), pp. 413–22.

25. Brownmiller, *Against Our Will*; E. Green, S. Hebron, and D. Woodward, "Women, Leisure, and Social Control," in *Women, Violence, and Social Control*, ed. J. Hanmer and M. Maynard (Atlantic Heights, N.J.: Humanities Press International, 1987), pp. 75–92; Griffin, "Rape: The All-American Crime."

26. Muehlenhard et al., "From 'Victim-Precipitated' Rape to 'Date Rape,'" p. 240.

27. K. G. Gergen, "Social Constructionist Inquiry: Context and Implications," in *The Social Construction of the Person*, ed. K. J. Gergen and K. E. Davis (New York: Springer-Verlag, 1985), pp. 3–4.

28. Ibid., p. 5.

29. G. Lerner, *The Lesson of Patriarchy* (New York: Oxford University Press, 1986); Spender, *Man Made Language*.

30. See C. L. Muehlenhard, I. G. Powch, J. L. Phelps, and L. M. Giusti, "Definitions of Rape: Scientific and Political Implications," *Journal of Social Issues* 48 (1992): 23–44, for further discussion.

31. Estrich, *Real Rape*.

32. E.g., C. Alder, "An Exploration of Self-Reported Sexually Aggressive Behavior," *Crime and Delinquency* 31 (1985): 306–31; E. J. Kanin, "An Examination of Sexual Aggression as a Response to Sexual Frustration," *Journal of Marriage and the Family*, 29 (1967): 428–33.

33. D. Finkelhor and K. Yllo, *License to Rape: Sexual Abuse of Wives* (New York: Holt, Rhinehart and Winston, 1985); D. E. H. Russell, *Rape in Marriage*, rev. ed. (Bloomington, Ind.: Indiana University Press, 1990).

34. C. MacKinnon, *Feminism Unmodified: Discourses on Life and Law* (Cambridge, Mass.: Harvard University Press, 1987), p. 8.

35. R. Morgan, "Theory and Practice: Pornography and Rape" (1974), in R. Morgan, *The Word of a Woman: Feminist Dispatches, 1968–1992*, p. 84 (italics in original).

36. Ibid.

37. N. Gavey, "Technologies and Effects of Heterosexual Coercion," *Feminism and Psychology* 2 (1992): 325–51.

38. Ibid., p. 340.

39. Ibid., p. 347.

40. A Southern Women's Writing Collective, "Sex Resistance in Heterosexual Arrangements," in *The Sexual Liberals and the Attack on Feminism,* ed. D. Leidholdt and J. Raymond (New York: Pergamon, 1990), pp. 140–47.

41. R. A. Levine, "Gusii Sex Offenses: A Study in Social Control," *American Anthropologist* 61 (1959): 965 (italics added).

42. Palmer, "Twelve Reasons Why Rape Is Not Sexually Motivated," p. 516.

43. See Muehlenhard et al., "From 'Victim-Precipitated Rape' to 'Date Rape,' " for further discussion.

44. M. Bonaparte, *Female Sexuality* (New York: Grove Press, 1965 [1953]), p. 87.

45. A. Adams-Silvan, "The Active and Passive Fantasy of Rape as a Specific Determinant in a Case of Acrophobia," *International Journal of Psycho-Analysis* 67 (1986): 470.

46. Griffin, "Rape: The All-American Crime," p. 109.

47. Ibid., pp. 29–30.

48. A. Dworkin, *Letters from a War Zone* (London: Secker and Warburg, 1988), pp. 179–80 (italics in original).

49. Beneke, *Men on Rape,* p. 13 (italics in original).

50. Ibid. (italics in original).

51. Ibid., p. 14 (italics in original).

52. Ibid. (italics in original).

53. Ibid. (italics in original).

54. Ibid., p. 17 (italics in original).

55. Groth, *Men Who Rape,* p. 13.

56. Beneke, *Men on Rape,* p. 16.

57. D. H. J. Morgan, "Masculinity and Violence," in *Women, Violence, and Social Ccontrol,* p. 182.

58. C. S. Greenblatt, "A Hit Is a Hit Is a Hit . . . Or Is It? Approval and Tolerance of the Use of Physical Force by Spouses," in *The Dark Side of Families: Current Family Violence Research,* ed. D. Finkelbor, R. J. Gelles, G. T. Hotaling, and M. A. Straus (Beverly Hills, Calif.: Sage, 1982), p. 235.

59. MacKinnon, "Feminism Unmodified," p. 233.

60. R. G. Geen, *Human Aggression* (Pacific Grove, Calif.: Brooks/Cole, 1990); R. A. Jones, C. Hendrick, and Y. M. Epstein, *Introduction to Social Psychology* (Sunderland, Mass.: Sinauer Associates, 1979); D. G. Myers, *Social Psychology* (New York: McGraw-Hill, 1983).

61. American College Health Association, *Acquaintance Rape* [brochure] (Baltimore: Author, 1992).

62. A. Campbell, *Women, Men, and Aggression* (New York: Basic Books, 1993), p. viii.

63. Ibid., p. 72.

64. Russell, *Rape in Marriage,* p. 142 (italics in original).

65. *American Heritage Dictionary of the English Language,* ed. W. Morris (Boston: American Heritage/Houghton Mifflin, 1975), p. 1431.

66. Ibid.

67. Domestic Abuse Intervention Project, *Power and Control* (Duluth, Minn.: Abuse Intervention Project, n.d.).

68. As quoted in C. Ramazanoglu, "Sex and Violence in Academic Life Or You Can Keep a Good Woman Down," in *Women, Violence, and Social Control,* p. 64.

69. Muehlenhard et al., "Definitions of Rape."

70. "Victim Says Rapist Quoted Williams," *Bryan-College Station Eagle,* April 2, 1990, p. la.

71. A. Landers, " 'Date Rape' Not Always Clear-Cut," *Houston Chronicle,* July 29, 1985, sec. 4, p. 2.

72. A. Landers, "Many Actions Tend to Invite Trouble: Women Should Convey Right Messages to Their Dates," *Houston Chronicle,* August 12, 1985, p. B6.

73. H. E. Barbaree and W. L. Marshall, "The Role of Male Sexual Arousal in Rape: Six Models," *Journal of Consulting and Clinical Psychology* 59 (1991): 621–30.

74. Gavey, "Technologies and Effects of Heterosexual Coercion"; MacKinnon, "Feminism Unmodified"; C. L. Muehlenhard and J. Schrag, "Nonviolent Sexual Coercion," in *Acquaintance Rape: The Hidden Crime,* ed. A. Parrot and L. Bechhofer (New York: John Wiley and Sons, 1991), pp. 115–28; Russell, *Rape in Marriage.*

75. Beneke, *Men on Rape*; Reinholtz et al., "Sexual Discourse and Sexual Intercourse"; Russell, *Rape in Marriage.*

76. C. G. Warner, ed., *Rape and Sexual Assault: Management and Interventioin* (Germantown, Md,: Aspen Systems, 1980), p. 94.

77. M. T. Gordon and S. Riger, *The Female Fear* (New York: Free Press, 1989); E. A.

Stanko, "Fear of Crime and the Myth of the Safe Home: A Feminist Critique of Criminology," in *Feminist Perspectives on Wife Abuse,* ed. K. Yllo and M. Bograd (Newbury Park, Calif.: Sage, 1988), pp. 75–88.

78. P. R. Sanday, "The Socio-Cultural Context of Rape: A Cross-Cultural Study," *Journal* of *Social Issues* 37 (1981): 5–27.

79. Estrich, *Real Rape.*

80. J. Temkin, "Women, Rape, and Law Reform," in *Rape: An Historical and Social Enquiry,* ed. S. Tomaselli and R. Porter (New York: Basil Blackwell, 1986), p. 12.

81. E. Bass and L. Davis, *The Courage to Heal: A Guide for Women Survivors of Child Sexual Abuse* (New York: Harper and Row, 1988).

82. MacKinnon, *Feminism Unmodified,* p. 233.

83. Ibid., pp. 86–87 (italics in original).

84. Beneke, *Men on Rape*; Dworkin, *Letters from a War Zone*; Griffin, "Rape: The All-American Crime"; Russell, *Making Violence Sexy.*

85. F. Barringer, "School Hallways as a Gauntlet of Sexual Taunts," *New York Times,* June 2, 1993, education sec., p.7.

86. A. B. Snitow, "Mass Market Romance: Pornography for Women Is Different," in *Powers of Desire: The Politics of Sexuality,* ed. A. Snitow, C. Stansell, and S. Thompson (New York: Monthly Review Press, 1983), p. 253.

87. Gavey, "Technologies and Effects of Heterosexual Coercion," p. 325.

43

The Antioch College
Sexual Offense Prevention Policy

Antioch College

Approved by the Board of Trustees on June 8, 1996

[Editor's Note: The Antioch College Sexual Offense Policy was adopted in February 1991 by the Administrative Council (AdCil), which is composed of faculty, students, administrators, and staff. The policy is currently in the process of being revised. The policy is currently in its third revised form.

The policy is reprinted here with the permission of Antioch College. It consists of a preface and the policy itself.

Antioch College is a small, residential liberal arts college in Ohio; it is now part of Antioch University, which has campuses in a number of urban areas. The policy applies to the College only, not to the other campuses, which are largely nonresidential and serve many nontraditional students.

Preface

Antioch College has made a strong commitment to the issue of respect, including respect for each individual's personal and sexual boundaries. Sexual offenses are dehumanizing. They are not just a violation of the individual, but of the Antioch community.

Some of the principles fundamental to this policy are:

1) All sexual behavior occurring between Antioch community members on or off the Antioch College campus must be consensual.

Reprinted by permission of the Antioch College Sexual Offense Prevention and Survivors' Advocacy Program.

2) When a sexual offense, as defined herein, is committed by a community member, such action will not be tolerated.

3) While Antioch exists within a larger society governed by existing laws, it is also part of Antioch's mission to strive for the betterment of both the individual and society. Thus, our standards for behavior may be broader than currently exist under state and federal laws. Community members are expected to respect and uphold these standards. These community standards are part of Antioch's educational mission. Any educational community which does not recognize the potentially devastating effects of sexual offenses and does not work for an atmosphere of mutual respect and safety risks undermining their educational mission.

4) When state or federal laws may be violated, the College urges the complainant to take the matter to the appropriate governmental body. . . .

5) This policy is gender neutral, and applies equally to women and men of all sexual orientations, recognizing that both women and men commit sexual offenses, and both women and men may be sexually offended.

6) Community members need to be respectful and honor the confidentiality of participants as matters proceed under this policy.

7) This policy is not intended to suggest that community members should engage in sexual behavior. Rather, it is intended to encourage and support community members to make and place appropriate physical and sexual boundaries where they choose. Community members who choose to be sexually active should practice safer sex.

This policy is a crucial part of our educational and prevention efforts but represents only a part of our commitment to the safety and well-being of our community members.

A support network exists that consists of the Sexual Offense Prevention and Survivors' Advocacy Program, including its director who is an advocate for both the policy and survivors; the Peer Advocacy Program; a 24-hour crisis and support line; and other support services available through both the Program and the Counseling Center. The Program Director/Advocate (or other designated administrator) shall be responsible for initiation and coordination of measures required by this policy, unless otherwise specified.

Antioch College provides and maintains educational programs for all community members, some aspects of which are required. The educational aspects of this policy are intended to prevent sexual offenses and ultimately heighten community awareness. Each community member must also contribute their efforts to insure the proper implementation of this policy.

The implementation of this policy also utilizes established Antioch governance structures and adheres to contractual obligations.

Seeking to reduce the amount of sexual offenses occurring on campus, students in fall 1990 and winter 1991 drafted Antioch's first Sexual Offense Policy. The first revision was written in winter 1992 and included the definition of consent as "willing and verbal." The second revision, written in the winter and spring of 1996, strengthens the policy based on accumulated experience. This policy has come from students with the support of faculty, staff, and administrators. This policy applies to every member of the Antioch community.

Consent

1. For the purpose of this policy, "consent" shall be defined as follows:

the act of willingly and verbally agreeing to engage in specific sexual behavior.

See (4) below when sexual behavior is mutually and simultaneously initiated.

Because of the importance of communication and the potential dangers when misunderstanding exists in a sexual situation, those involved in any sexual interaction need to share enough of a common understanding to be able to adequately communicate: (1) requests for consent; and, (2) when consent is given, denied, or withdrawn.

Note: Recognized American and international sign languages are considered a form of verbal language for the purpose of this policy.

2. When sexual behavior is not mutually and simultaneously initiated, then the person who initiates sexual behavior is responsible for verbally asking for the consent of the other individual(s) involved.

3. The person with whom sexual contact/conduct is initiated shall verbally express his/her willingness or must verbally express consent, and/or express his/her lack of willingness by words, actions, gestures, or any other previously agreed-upon communication.

Silence and/or noncommunication must never be interpreted as consent.

4. When sexual behavior is mutually and simultaneously initiated, then the persons involved share responsibility for getting/giving or refusing/denying consent by words, actions, gestures or by any other previously agreed-upon communication.

5. Obtaining consent is an ongoing process in any sexual interaction. Verbal consent should be obtained with each new level of physical and/or sexual behavior in any given interaction, regardless of who initiates it. Asking "Do you want to have sex with me?" is not enough. The request for consent must be specific to each act.

6. If someone has initially consented but then stops consenting during a sexual interaction, she/he should communicate withdrawal of consent verbally

(example: saying "no" or "stop") and/or through physical resistance (example: pushing away). The other individual(s) must stop immediately.

    7. In order for consent to be meaningful and valid under this policy:

       a) the person not initiating must have judgment and control unimpaired by any drug or intoxicant administered to prevent her/his resistance, and/or which has been administered surreptitiously, by force or threat of force, or by deception;

       b) the person not initiating must have judgment and control unimpaired by mental dysfunction which is known to the person initiating;

       c) the person not initiating must not be asleep or unconscious;

       d) the person initiating must not have forced, threatened, coerced, or intimidated the other individual(s) into engaging in sexual behavior.

    8. To knowingly take advantage of someone who is under the influence of alcohol, drugs, prescribed or over-the-counter medication is not acceptable behavior in the Antioch community.

Offenses of the Sexual Offense Prevention Policy Defined

Our standards of behavior may be broader than currently exist under state and federal laws. These community standards are part of Antioch's educational mission, to be dealt with through on-campus administrative means as part of the educational process. When state or federal laws may be violated, the College urges a complainant to take the matter to the appropriate governmental body. . . .

    The following actions are prohibited under Antioch College's Sexual Offense Prevention Policy and, in addition to possible criminal prosecution, may result in sanctions up to and including expulsion or termination of employment.

Nonconsensual Sexual Conduct

Nonconsensual sexual conduct. "Sexual conduct" means vaginal intercourse, anal intercourse, fellatio and cunnilingus between persons regardless of sex. Penetration, however slight, is sufficient to complete vaginal or anal intercourse. This category includes, but is not limited to, rape and sexual battery as defined in Ohio Revised Code.

Nonconsensual Sexual Comportment

Nonconsensual sexual comportment, exclusive of sexual conduct as defined above, means any sexual behavior which includes the insertion of any part of the body or any instrument, apparatus, or other object into the body cavity of another. This category includes, but is not limited to, felonious sexual penetration as defined in Ohio Revised Code.

Nonconsensual Sexual Contact I

Nonconsensual sexual contact I includes when a person has nonconsensual contact with another; causes another to have nonconsensual sexual contact with the offender; causes another without her/his consent to sexually touch her/himself; causes two or more other persons to have nonconsensual sexual contact; when, for the purpose of preventing resistance, the offender substantially impairs the other person's or one of the other persons' judgment or control by administering any drug or intoxicant to the other person, surreptitiously, deceptively, or by force or threat of force. "Sexual contact" means the touching of an erogenous zone of another, including but not limited to the thigh, genitals, buttock, pubic region, or breast, for the purpose of sexually arousing or gratifying either person. This category includes, but is not limited to, gross sexual imposition as defined in Ohio Revised Code.

Nonconsensual Sexual Contact II

Nonconsensual sexual contact II includes when a person has nonconsensual contact; causes another to have nonconsensual contact with the offender; causes another without her/his consent to sexually touch her/himself; causes two or more other persons to have nonconsensual sexual contact; when any of the following applies: (1) the offender knows that the sexual contact is likely to be offensive to the other person, or one of the other persons, or is reckless in that regard; (2) the offended knows that the other person's ability to appraise the nature of or control the offender's or touching person's conduct is substantially impaired; (3) the offender knows that the other person, or one of the other persons, is unaware of the sexual contact. "Sexual contact" means the touching of an erogenous zone of another, including but not limited to the thigh, genitals, buttock, pubic region, or breast, for the purpose of sexually arousing or gratifying either person. This category includes, but is not limited to, sexual imposition as defined in Ohio Revised Code.

Insistent and/or Persistent Sexual Harassment

Any insistent and/or persistent intimidation or abuse considered sexually threatening and/or offensive according to the standards of the Antioch community. This includes, but is not limited to, unwelcome and irrelevant comments, references, gestures, or other forms of personal attention which are inappropriate and which may be perceived as persistent sexual overtones or denigration.

Unnecessarily Endangering the Health of Another

If someone knows or reasonably should know that she/he is infected with a disease or condition which can be transmitted sexually, that person must not engage in any sexual behavior with another individual in any manner which would put that individual at risk of contracting the disease or condition.

Before engaging in any behavior considered "high risk" for transmission, the person who is infected has an obligation to inform the other individual so that an informed choice regarding safety can be made. This category acknowledges an individual's right to privacy regarding personal health matters, but holds that in balance with concern for individual and community safety.

Options If A Violation May Have Occurred

1. To make our community as safe as possible for all community members, community members who are suspected of violating this policy should be made aware of the concern about their behavior. The other provisions of this policy provide channels and guidelines for such education. Sometimes people are not aware that their behavior is sexually offensive, threatening, or hurtful. Awareness of the effects of their behavior may cause them to change their behavior.

2. If someone suspects that a violation of this Sexual Offense Prevention Policy may have occurred, she/he should contact a member of the Sexual Offense Prevention and Survivors' Advocacy Program, or the Dean of Students.

A 24-hour Crisis and Support Line has been established. From on campus, call PBX 6458, or 767-6458. From off campus, call 1-800-841-1314.

Any discussion of a suspected violation with a member of the Sexual Offense Prevention and Survivors' Advocacy Program or the Dean of Students will be treated as confidential.

3. Options

When a suspected violation of this policy is reported, the person who receives the report should explain to the person reporting all of the options which are appropriate in responding to the suspected offense.

Those options include, in no particular order, and are not limited to:

- directly confronting the alleged offender;
- having appropriate mediation with the alleged offender;
- having the Dean of Students or Associate Dean of Students talk with the alleged offender;
- filing a formal complaint;
- filing an anonymous or confidential complaint with a member of the Sexual Offense Prevention and Survivors' Advocacy Program so the alleged action is recorded;
- getting counseling or crisis intervention;
- getting appropriate medical treatment;
- filing a police report if the alleged offense is against the law;
- taking a concern to the Community Standards Board;
- choosing to do nothing further.

More than one of these options may be used by the person alleging she/he was violated (hereafter referred to as the "primary witness").

4. Criminal Complaints

It is strongly encouraged that suspected violations be reported, and that they be reported as soon as is reasonable after a suspected violation has occurred. Where criminal misconduct is involved (see . . . Ohio Revised Code for definitions), reporting the misconduct to the local law enforcement agency is strongly recommended.

Because of the need to collect physical evidence for criminal complaints, if the primary witness is giving any consideration to filing a criminal complaint, the primary witness should, as soon as possible, go to the hospital, ideally in the jurisdiction where the alleged crime occurred (for example, if the incident occurred on campus, the complainant should go to Greene Memorial Hospital in Xenia).

The primary witness is not charged for the administration of a rape evidence collection kit. A peer advocate, the Advocate, or a member of the Greene County Victim-Witness Program can accompany the primary witness to the hospital to provide information and support.

5. Mediation

If the person reporting a suspected policy violation wishes to arrange for mediation, then the Advocate, the Dean of Students, or a staff member of the Sexual Offense Prevention and Survivors' Advocacy Program shall arrange for mediation consistent with the mediation guidelines used by the Sexual Offense Prevention and Survivors' Advocacy Program. Options available include: (1) mediation arranged through an off-campus program or agency; (2) mediation arranged and/or facilitated by the Advocate or the Dean of Students.

a) If the Dean of Students arranges or facilitates mediation, or mediation occurs through an off-campus program or agency, then for statistical purposes, the Dean shall notify the Advocate of the mediation session.
b) A written agreement with educational and/or behavioral requirements may be part of the outcome of a mediation session. Copies of this agreement shall be given to the parties involved, the Dean of Students, and either the Advocate or the Director of the Counseling Center. The Dean of Students shall be responsible for handling violations of written mediated agreements, and shall have the right to act as she/he sees fit.
c) Should a student persist in sexually threatening or offensive behavior after mediation has been attempted, the primary witness, Advocate, or Dean of Students may refer the case to the Hearing Board.
d) If a satisfactory conclusion is not reached through mediation, or if the mediation agreement is not adhered to by any of its participants, other options may be pursued as listed above, including referral to the Hearing Board.

6. In the event that an action taken by the Dean of Students regarding a sexual offense is appealed, the appeal shall be made to the Hearing Board.

7. Complaint by a Student Involving a College Employee

Any student who feels that an employee has violated this policy should contact the Advocate or the Dean of Students as soon as possible. Contacting the Advocate does not mean the student will be required to file a formal complaint. Discussion with the Advocate will be considered confidential.

When a written complaint is filed, if the alleged offender (hereafter known as "the respondent") is an employee, the Advocate shall inform the President or the Director of Human Resources of the reported violation of he Sexual Offense Prevention Policy. The matter will be promptly investigated by the appropriate administrator or other supervisor with the assistance of the Advocate. If whatever review process appropriate to the employee results in a determination that the policy has been violated, then the remedy should be commensurate with the seriousness of the violation, and procedures specified in College and University policies should be followed.

8. Complaint by a College Employee toward Another Employee

Any employee who feels that another employee has violated this policy should contact the Advocate or their appropriate supervisor or union designee. Contacting the Advocate does not mean the employee will be required to file a formal complaint. Discussion with the Advocate or the employee's supervisor will be considered confidential.

When a written complaint is filed, if the respondent is an employee, the Advocate shall inform the President or the Director of Human Resources of the reported violation of the Sexual Offense Prevention Policy. The matter will be promptly investigated by the appropriate administrator or other supervisor. If whatever review process appropriate to the employee results in a determination that the policy has been violated, then the remedy should be commensurate with the seriousness of the violation, and procedures specified in College and University policies should be followed.

9. Complaints Involving a Noncommunity Member and a Community Member

In the event that a noncommunity member feels that a community member has violated this policy with her/him, the noncommunity member may seek out the Advocate, the Dean of Students, or contact the Crisis and Support Line for an appropriate referral. Complaints regarding employees will be handled as in (7) above, Complaint by a Student Involving a College Employee. If the respondent is a student, the complaint may be referred to the Dean of Students, who has the authority to handle it according to her/his discretion. The Hearing Board will not be utilized in these complaints.

If a community member feels violated by a noncommunity member, the community member should bring the matter to the attention of the Advocate, the Dean of Students, and/or the community member's supervisor. Offenses which may be violations of Ohio Revised Code should be reported to the local law enforcement agency immediately. While the jurisdiction of the policy does not extend to violations by noncommunity members, the Advocate and/or the

Sexual Offense Prevention and Survivors' Advocacy Program may provide advocacy and support to the community member. The College will not provide legal counsel in these circumstances.

10. Filing a Formal Complaint with the Intent to Go to the Hearing Board

If the primary witness wishes the Hearing Board to make a finding regarding an alleged policy violation, the primary witness must file a written complaint with the Advocate. The Advocate shall inform the primary witness of her/his rights regarding procedure and appeal under this policy.

When a formal complaint is filed, if the respondent is a student, then the following procedures shall be followed:

A. The Advocate shall notify the Dean of Students, or another senior College official in the Dean of Students' absence, who shall have the respondent report to the Dean of Students' office within a reasonable period of time, not to exceed the next business day the College is open that the respondent is on campus. When the respondent reports, the respondent will then be informed by the Advocate and/or the Dean of Students of the report of the sexual offense, the policy violation which is being alleged, and her/his rights regarding procedure and appeal. The respondent will be given an opportunity to present their side of the story at that time. If the respondent does not report as directed, then implementation of this policy shall proceed.

B. Based on the information available, the Dean of Students, or another senior College official appointed by the President in the Dean of Students' absence will determine whether there is reasonable cause to believe that a policy violation may have occurred and whether a hearing should be scheduled.

C. In cases where nonconsensual sexual conduct or nonconsensual sexual comportment are alleged, the following steps may be taken for the protection of the primary witness, the respondent, and the community. These steps should in no way be perceived as implying either that the primary witness is not believed nor that the respondent is in violation of the policy.

If the respondent and/or the primary witness are living on campus at the time of the complaint, then the Dean will discuss the option of relocating off campus within eight hours of being notified that a decision has been made to hold a hearing (unless otherwise determined by the Dean of Students). They will reside off campus until such time that the Hearing Board has heard the case and rendered its decision.

If the respondent and/or primary witness are unable to locate alternate housing off campus, then the Dean of Students shall arrange for housing in different locations at the College's expense. Similarly, if the primary witness and/or respondent have a cafeteria meal plan, then the Dean shall schedule different times for them to be in the cafeteria or provide them with funds sufficient to buy food off campus. Other scheduling may also be arranged, such as classes and access to the library.

If either the respondent or the primary witness refuses to leave on-campus residential housing, and the Dean of Students feels it is in both their interest and the interest of the community, then the Dean may require that they leave campus. If either party refuses to adhere to any decision by the Dean regarding their housing or scheduling, then an appeal may be made to the voting members of the Hearing Board.

The education of any student who is either a primary witness or respondent should be interrupted as little as possible. Therefore, if attending classes on campus is not determined by the Dean of Students to be appropriate for either or both parties, alternate instruction shall be arranged off campus by their faculty members in a way which, pending appropriate completion, will ensure there is no negative impact on their evaluations as students.

D. The Hearing Board will then convene for a hearing, to hear the case. Consistent with this policy, the Hearing Board will take into account the primary witness's story, the respondent's story, witnesses, the past history of the respondent, and other relevant evidence, and will determine whether or not a policy violation has occurred and which aspect of the policy has been violated.

E. The Hearing shall take place as soon thereafter as is reasonable, no longer than seven days from the date of filing or the notification of the respondent, unless the Hearing Board Chair determines that reasonable cause exists for convening the meeting at a later, still reasonable time, in which event the Chair shall so notify all appropriate parties. If the hearing cannot occur for reasons such as co-op or illness, it will convene when both parties involved return to campus.

If a formal complaint is filed within the last two weeks of the term, the Hearing Board may decide to postpone the hearing until such time that both parties have returned to campus. However, if the complaint involves behavior alleged to have occurred during the current term, the Hearing may be held that term.

If a hearing is delayed beyond the term in which the case is filed, then the Hearing Board is to consider all likely complications of the delay, such as a student going on co-op, and may institute temporary changes in a student's plan until such time that the complaint is resolved.

F. If the primary witness chooses, she/he may have a representative at all hearings of the Hearing Board and/or through any appeals process. The primary witness's representative may provide both advocacy and emotional support for the primary witness. When appropriate, if the primary witness chooses, then the primary witness's representative may act on her/his behalf during portions of the hearing and any appeals process which do not require the immediate presence of the primary witness. Choosing a representative from within the Antioch community is encouraged.

The Dean of Students will maintain a list of community members, including faculty, staff, and administrators, with qualifications to serve as the primary witness's representative. Qualifications include, but are not limited to, a willingness to serve, familiarity with this policy, support for the student, and if a faculty member, then preferably a tenured faculty member. In addition, if the primary witness chooses, she/he may have a lawyer present during those portions of the hearing where the primary witness is allowed to be present. The primary witness shall have this privilege provided that the attorney does not interfere with the educational process of the hearing, interrupt or otherwise intrude upon the process.

G. If the respondent chooses, she/he may have a representative at all hearings of the Hearing Board and/or through any appeals process. The respondent's representative may provide both advocacy and emotional support for the respondent. When appropriate, if the respondent chooses, then the respondent's representative may act on her/his behalf during portions of the hearing and any appeals process which do not require the immediate presence of the respondent. Choosing a representative from within the Antioch community is encouraged.

The Dean of Students will maintain a list of community members, including faculty, staff, and administrators, with qualifications to serve as the respondent's representative. Qualifications include, but are not limited to, a willingness to serve, familiarity with this policy, support for the student, and if a faculty member, then preferably a tenured faculty member. In addition, if the respondent chooses, she/he may have a lawyer present during those portions of the hearing where the respondent is allowed to be present. The respondent shall have this privilege provided that the attorney does not interfere with the educational process of the hearing, interrupt or otherwise intrude upon the process.

9. The Hearing Board and any appellate body which hears a case under this policy shall administer its proceedings according to these fundamental assumptions:

A. There will be no reference to the past consensual, nonviolent sexual behavior of either the primary witness or respondent.

B. No physical evidence of a sexual offense is necessary to determine that one has occurred, nor is a visit to the hospital or the administration of a rape kit. Physical evidence may, however, be accepted by the Hearing Board. It is the primary witness's decision as to whether or not to offer physical evidence to the Hearing Board regarding her/his personal body.

C. The fact that a respondent was under the influence of drugs or alcohol or mental dysfunction at the time of the sexual offense will not excuse or justify the commission of any sexual offense as defined herein, and shall not be used as a defense. While such circumstances may not affect the decision of the Hearing Board regarding if a violation did occur, the Hearing Board may consider the impairment when determining the remedy in the event a policy violation is found.

10. The policy is intended to deal with sexual offenses which occurred between Antioch community members on or off the Antioch College campus on or after February 7, 1991. Sexual offenses which occurred prior to that date

were still a violation of community standards, and should be addressed through the policies and governance structures which were in effect at the time of the offense.

The Hearing Board

1. The Hearing Board's duties are:
    a) to hear all sides of the story;
    b) to investigate as appropriate;
    c) to determine if a violation of this policy has occurred;
    d) to develop, in consultation with the Dean of Students and the Advocate, an appropriate remedy in cases where mandatory remedies are not prescribed in this policy;
    e) to prepare a written report setting forth its findings which it distributes to the parties involved and the Dean of Students.

2. The Hearing Board will consist of four community representatives as voting members, the Dean of Students as a nonvoting ex-officio member, and the Advocate to monitor the proceedings of the hearing and to assist the Hearing Board in fairly implementing the hearing process.

3. A. A Hearing Board Pool will be appointed by AdCil (Administrative Council) by the end of each spring term, to begin serving at the beginning of the next academic year, for the duration of that academic year. The Pool will of twelve community members: six students, three faculty members, and three administrators/staff members.
   The twelve members of the Hearing Board Pool shall be appointed by AdCil from the following recommended candidates:
    1) The six student members will be chosen from the ten student candidates recommended nominated by ComCil (Community Council);
    2) The three faculty members will be chosen from six faculty candidates nominated by the Dean of Faculty;
    3) The three administrators/staff members will be chosen from six candidates nominated by the President of the College.
   The membership of the Hearing Board Pool shall be divided equally between women and men, and shall reflect the diversity that exists within the Antioch community, including race, ethnicity, and sexual orientation.
   B. Four of the members of the Hearing Board Pool shall be appointed by AdCil to serve each year as a Hearing Board. Two of the Hearing Board members must be students, one must be a faculty member, and one must be an administrator/staff person.

The composition of the Hearing Board shall include both women and men and shall reflect the diversity of the Antioch community.

C. One member of the Hearing Board shall be designated by AdCil to serve as Chair. The Chair shall preside for all Hearing Board meetings that term, and shall make the necessary arrangements to convene the Hearing Board (i.e., contact Hearing Board members, notify all parties involved of date, time, place, etc.).

D. The eight representatives who are not serving in a particular term shall be alternates in case an active member is not available or has a conflict of interest.

E. If an active member of the Hearing Board has a conflict of interest in the case, the conflict should be reported to the Hearing Board Chair or the Advocate as soon as possible. The President shall be responsible to determine if the conflict requires replacing the member with an alternate from the pool of twelve approved by AdCil.

If additional members need to be appointed to the Hearing Board pool in the course of the year, AdCil must approve them. If AdCil is not in session (i.e., between terms), then the President may, in consultation with the Dean of Faculty and the Dean of Students, act in place of AdCil to appoint an appropriate Hearing Board, pool, or replacement Board member.

If the President is unavailable to make these appointments, then the Dean of Faculty shall make them; if the Dean of Faculty is unavailable, then the Dean of Administration and Finance should make them; if the Dean of Administration and Finance is also unavailable, then the Community Manager(s) should make the appointments.

4. All members of the Hearing Board pool shall receive training by the Advocate and the College attorney regarding this policy and pertinent legal issues before participating in any hearings, and receive a copy of the entire policy and appropriate appendices. These training sessions shall be conducted at least once a year.

5. ... Any procedures not covered in this policy ... shall be determined according to the discretion of the Hearing Board.

Remedies

1. When a policy violation by a student is found by the Hearing Board, the Hearing Board shall also determine a remedy which is commensurate with the offense, except in those cases where mandatory remedies are prescribed in this policy.

When a remedy is not prescribed, the Hearing Board shall determine the remedy in consultation with the Dean of Students and the Advocate, and shall include an educational and/or rehabilitation component as part of the remedy.

2. *For Nonconsensual Sexual Conduct:* In the event that the Hearing Board determines that a violation of nonconsensual sexual conduct has occurred, as defined under this policy, the recommended remedy is immediate expulsion or removal from the campus.

3. *For Nonconsensual Sexual Comportment:* In the event that the Hearing Board determines that a violation of nonconsensual sexual comportment has occurred, as defined under this policy, then the respondent should: (a) be suspended immediately for a period of no less than six months; (b) successfully complete a treatment program for sexual offenders approved by the Director of Counseling Services before returning to campus; and (c) upon return to campus, be subject to mandatory class and co-op scheduling so that the respondent and primary witness avoid, to the greatest extent possible, all contact, unless the primary witness agrees otherwise.

In the event that the Hearing Board determines that a second violation of nonconsensual sexual comportment has occurred, with the same respondent, then the respondent must be expelled immediately.

4. *For Nonconsensual Sexual Contact I:* In the event that the Hearing Board determines that a violation of nonconsensual sexual contact I has occurred, as defined under this policy, then the recommended remedy is that the respondent: (a) be suspended immediately for a period of no less than six months; (b) successfully complete a treatment program for sexual offenders approved by the Director of Counseling Services before returning to campus; and (c) upon return to campus, be subject to mandatory class and co-op scheduling so that the respondent and primary witness avoid, to the greatest extent possible, all contact, unless the primary witness agrees otherwise.

In the event that the Hearing Board determines that a second violation of nonconsensual sexual contact I has occurred, with the same respondent, then the respondent must be expelled immediately.

5. *For Nonconsensual Sexual Contact II:* In the event that the Hearing Board determines that a violation of nonconsensual sexual contact II has occurred, as defined under this policy, then the recommended remedy is that the respondent: (a) be suspended immediately for a period of no less than three months; (b) successfully complete a treatment program for sexual offenders approved by the Director of Counseling Services before returning to campus; and (c) upon return to campus, be subject to mandatory class and co-op scheduling so that the respondent and primary witness avoid, to the greatest extent possible, all contact, unless the primary witness agrees otherwise.

In the event that the Hearing Board determines that a second violation of nonconsensual sexual contact II has occurred, with the same respondent, then the respondent must be expelled immediately.

6. *For Insistent and/or Persistent Sexual Harassment:* In the event that the Hearing Board determines that the violation of insistent and/or persistent sexual harassment has occurred, as defined under this policy, then the recommended remedy is that the respondent: (a) be suspended immediately for a period of no less than six months; (b) successfully complete a treatment program for sexual offenders approved by the Director of Counseling Services before returning to campus; and (c) upon return to campus, be subject to mandatory class and co-op scheduling so that the respondent and primary witness avoid, to the greatest extent possible, all contact, unless the primary witness agrees otherwise.

In the event that the Hearing Board determines that a second violation of insistent and/or persistent sexual harassment has occurred, with the same respondent, then the respondent must be expelled immediately.

7. *For Unnecessarily Endangering the Health of Another:* In the event that the Hearing Board determines that a violation of Unnecessarily Endangering the Health of Another has occurred, as defined under this policy, then the remedy is left to the discretion of the Hearing Board.

8. In all cases, a *second offense* under this policy, regardless of category, must receive a more severe consequence than did the first offense if the second offense occurred after the Hearing Board's first finding of a respondent's violation of this policy.

9. The remedy for a *third offense*, regardless of category, must be expulsion, if the third offense occurred after the Hearing Board's first or second finding of a respondent's violation of this policy.

10. It is the responsibility of the Dean of Students to ensure that the Hearing Board's remedies are carried out.

The Appeals Process

1. In the event that the respondent or primary witness is not satisfied with the decision of the Hearing Board, then she/he shall have the right to appeal the Hearing Board's decision within seventy-two hours of receiving that decision.

2. In the event of an appeal, the College shall secure the services of a hearing review officer with experience in conducting arbitrations or administrative

agency or other informal hearings. A hearing review officer, who is not a current member of the Antioch College community, shall be selected by AdCil in consultation with the Advocate for the purpose of handling such appeals.

3. The hearing review officer shall review the record(s) and/or written report(s) of the hearing, any other written materials supplied to her/him by any of the involved parties, and meet with any of the involved parties which she/he determines appropriate to determine if there was fundamental fairness in the hearing process.

The hearing review officer's analysis shall include a determination of whether the respondent was fully apprised of the charges against her/him; that the appealing party had a full and fair opportunity to tell her/his side of the story; and whether there was any malfeasance by the Hearing Board. The hearing review officer will present her/his finding and recommendation for action, if any, to the President of the College.

Confidentiality

1. Community members need to be respectful and honor the confidentiality of participants as matters proceed under this policy.

   A. Once someone feels that a violation of this policy has occurred, then it is crucial that all persons involved be treated with respect and that the complaint be handled confidentially.

   B. Any violations of confidentiality will be considered a serious breach of Antioch College's community standards, and may be handled by the Dean of Students, an employee's supervisor, or presented to the Community Standards Board for debate. If the Dean of Students or Community Standards Board feels the matter may be best handled by the Sexual Offense Hearing Board, the violation may be referred to the Hearing Board. The Hearing Board has the authority to handle alleged breaches of confidentiality of Sexual Offense Prevention Policy matters, and to issue remedies as it sees fit.

   C. Any appeal of a decision by the Community Standards Board will be appealed to the Hearing Board.

   D. Publicly accusing someone of violating this policy, if the person accused has not been appropriately confronted under this policy (see "Options") or charged under state or federal law, shall be considered a serious breach of community standards and will be referred to the Dean of Students or Community Standards Board for action.

2. For all matters under this policy:

   a) The name of the primary witness shall not be considered public knowledge until such time that the primary witness releases her/his name publicly.

b) The name of the respondent shall not be considered public knowledge until such time that the respondent releases her/his name publicly, unless the respondent is found in violation of the policy, at which time the release of the respondent's name may be included with the release of the Hearing Board's findings. The name of the respondent should be released with the Hearing Board's findings if a violation is found and the remedy includes the suspension or expulsion of the respondent.

c) The names of any witnesses shall not be released publicly until such time that each witness chooses to release her/his own name publicly.

3. All of the proceedings of the Hearing Board, and all testimony given, shall be kept confidential.

A. For the duration of the hearing process and any appeals process, the primary witness, the respondent, and any witnesses coming forward shall have the right to determine when and if their names are publicly released. No one shall make a public release of a name not their own while the process is under way. Any public breach of confidentiality may constitute a violation of community standards and be presented to the Community Standards Board for debate.

B. In the event of an appeal, the appealing party (or the party considering the appeal) shall have the right to review any written and/or audio records of the hearing. Such review shall take place on the Antioch campus with a member of the Hearing Board present. No materials are to be duplicated by any party; no materials are to be removed from the Antioch campus except to be given to the hearing review officer or to the College attorneys.

C. All members of the Hearing Board, including any notetakers, are bound to keep the contents of the proceedings confidential.

D. All written and/or audio records of the process which are kept by the Hearing Board are to be turned over to the College Attorneys at the conclusion of the appeals process, and shall be stored in their offices, to be disposed of when and as they see fit.

Educational and Support Implementation Procedures

1. The Sexual Offense Prevention and Survivors' Advocacy Program will serve as the central collection point on campus of all reports of sexual offenses involving community members. Anyone on campus who learns of a sexual offense should confidentially report that offense to the Advocate and/or the Dean of Students.

PART THREE: DESIRE, PORNOGRAPHY, and RAPE

2. A minimum of one educational workshop about consent, sexuality, sexual offenses, personal safety, and the Sexual Offense Prevention Policy will be incorporated into each Orientation program for new students. The Dean of Students will appoint a committee each year to facilitate the development and presentation of the fall workshop. This committee should include, but not be limited to, representatives from Community Government, the Dean of Students' Office, and the Sexual Offense Prevention and Survivors' Advocacy Program. Attendance shall be required of all students new to the Antioch community.

3. To further confirm each student's understanding of this policy, each student who attends Antioch College must sign a statement that they have read and understand the Sexual Offense Prevention Policy at the beginning of their first term. Students currently enrolled before September 1996 must sign the statement at the beginning of their next term either studying or living on campus. The Registrar and Dean of Students will share responsibility for making sure each student has a signed statement on file.

4. Workshops on consent, sexuality, sexual offenses, personal safety and this policy will also be offered during all study terms. The Advocate, in consultation with Community Government, shall arrange to have at least one speaker from off campus to address those issues each fall and spring term.

5. New faculty members, including adjunct faculty and teaching assistants, must attend an orientation session on the Sexual Offense Prevention Policy and similar policies dealing with student-faculty boundaries no later than the end of their first month on campus.

The Dean of Faculty and FEC (Faculty Executive Committee) is responsible for scheduling these sessions in consultation with the Advocate. Further, it is recommended to the College administration that all employees working on the Antioch College campus be encouraged to attend workshops on sexual offense and personal safety issues.

Supervisors in all areas are responsible for scheduling orientation sessions with all new and continuing employees on related policies, maintaining appropriate boundaries with students, and personal safety.

6. It is recommended that the faculty integrate the educational resources of the Sexual Offense Prevention and Survivors' Advocacy Program into their courses whenever it is appropriate.

A one-credit P.E. self-defense course will be offered each term. This course must include self-defense and self-protection skills that can be immediately utilized and must be open to all Antioch community members free of charge. The implementation of this requirement is the responsibility of the Dean of Faculty. The Advocate must be consulted in the hiring of the instructor.

Intensive language study courses and orientations for AEA (Antioch Education Abroad) programs are strongly encouraged to include a role play relevant to sexual harassment or a similar boundary violation, so students can learn appropriate language and ways of responding. Cultural values around personal boundaries and sexual violence should also be explored.

7. A Peer Advocacy Program will be maintained by the Sexual Offense Prevention and Survivors' Advocacy Program and the Counseling Center.

The Peer Advocates serve a variety of functions in the community, within the limits of their training. These may include: (1) serving as educators and resources about sexual offenses, options available to survivors, personal safety, and the Sexual Offense Prevention Policy; (2) advocating for survivors and their significant others on campus, as well as in appropriate medical and legal settings off campus; (3) providing crisis intervention; (4) staffing the crisis and support line; (5) making appropriate referrals with the assistance of the Advocate to the Counseling Center, the Sexual Offense Prevention and Survivors' Advocacy Program, local mental health practitioners and other health care providers.

Peer Advocates are not "counselors" or "therapists" and should not be used as a person's primary means of support on campus.

The Dean of Students is responsible for ensuring that Peer Advocates receive adequate training and support, and are qualified to serve. . . .

8. Support services for female and male community members who identify as survivors of sexual offenses will be offered through Counseling Services and/or the Sexual Offense Prevention and Survivors' Advocacy Program.

9. A support network for students who are on co-op will be maintained by the Advocate and the Sexual Offense Prevention and Survivors' Advocacy Program, with access to trained crisis contact people.

10. A brochure about safety on co-op will be kept available through the Center for Cooperative Education, the Dean of Students, and the Sexual Offense Prevention and Survivors' Advocacy Program.

11. Condoms and other safer sex supplies will be made available free through Community Government. Every term, the Counseling Center and Community Government will sponsor free and anonymous HIV testing to all community members.

Some sexual behaviors and practices are deemed "high risk" for the transmission of certain sexually transmitted diseases and health conditions. As the medical establishment gains more knowledge about these diseases and conditions, the list of behaviors considered high risk for transmission is updated. Information about what is currently considered "high risk" will be kept available through the College's Infirmary and the Counseling Center. Because the

College's physicians may have the most recent information, the infirmary, the Counseling Center, and the Hearing Board are encouraged to consult with them as appropriate.

12. The Advocate, in consultation with the Dean of Students Office, will be responsible for supplying the community with a summary of all educational and programmatic activities on a regular basis. The summary shall include, but not be limited to, the following information:
   a) the number of reported incidents and complaints from the previous term, and the outcomes whenever possible.
   b) the schedule of planned events as outlined in the Policy for the upcoming term.
   c) an evaluation of the actual activities (including the required self-defense class) that took place the previous term.

This summary will be shared with AdCil each term and will be published in the Record no later than the second issue of the term. A file of all the summaries will be kept by the Library, Dean of Students, Community Government, and the Sexual Offense Prevention and Survivors' Advocacy Program.

In addition, a summary of the findings that the Hearing Board chooses to release to the community will also be kept on file by the Library, the Dean of Students, and the Sexual Offense Prevention and Survivors' Advocacy Program.

13. The Center for Cooperative Education, Antioch Education Abroad, and the Environmental Field Program should all work with the Sexual Offense Prevention and Survivors' Advocacy Program in educating students about personal safety, and how to contact resources should the need arise. The Advocate should be notified confidentially of any sexual violation which occurs on or off campus involving a community member as soon as possible.

14. Copies of this policy and its appendices will be kept available by the Dean of Students, the Sexual Offense Prevention and Survivors' Advocacy Program, Community Government, and the Library.

44

The Antioch Policy, a Community Experiment in Communicative Sexuality

Matthew C. Silliman

Antioch College, a small residential liberal arts college in Yellow Springs, Ohio, recently instituted a campus policy aimed at developing, in a social context, principles intriguingly similar to those Lois Pineau applies to legal remedies for date rape.[1] It is appropriate, even necessary, to survey that experiment here, for the success of any proactive legal strategy, such as Pineau's, would depend on a concomitant development of social attitudes in practice. The law itself can certainly have an educative role, but given the amazing cacophony of ridicule, abuse, and aggressive ignorance which greeted news of the Antioch policy, Pineau's conclusion is probably too sanguine about the effectiveness of a mass media campaign for making such simple yet fundamental change. Educational institutions which address themselves to widespread social problems by developing community-based responses perform a critical function in trying out solutions, independently of whether those strategies could apply unmodified to the society as a whole.

This essay aims briefly to defend the reasonableness of the Antioch policy against several of the charges which have been leveled against it. My principal thesis is that anyone who subscribes to a minimalist version of the Enlightenment Liberal conceptions of freedom, consent, choice, and individual liberty ought to welcome both the process and the product of Antioch's efforts to confront the problem of sexual exploitation and acquaintance rape. It is an understatement to say that the policy has not, however, been received with welcome, leading to the suspicion either that its detractors do *not* subscribe to such principles or that it has been systematically misunderstood.

Among many criticisms, the policy has been called paternalistic and authoritarian, puritanical and neo-Victorian, an attempt to reduce sexual intimacy to contractual relations, artificial or anti-romantic, and unenforceable. These are not simple criticisms, but vigorous denunciations, and many of them come from alleged representatives of so-called mainstream culture. It is instructive to note the ferocity with which they are issued, for it may be an indication that the policy touches a nerve worthy of further probing. I will address each of these charges in turn; the more delicate task of examining deeper philosophical objections, specifically those concerns stemming from the problematicity of the above liberal concepts, I will forgo in the present essay, except to indicate some of them in passing.

Paternalism

Detractors of the Antioch policy, which provides for a system of adjudication and sanctions for offenses ranging from nondisclosure of a known sexually transmitted disease to rape, have termed it paternalistic, even authoritarian, in scope and content. Those making such charges are apparently under the impression that the policy was imposed on the campus community by an administration excessively concerned with the personal morality of its students, and a particular concern to "protect" women from unwelcome sexual contact.

It is worth observing that to the extent that the policy is correctly described as paternalistic, it is certainly not more so than is the society at large with respect to those serious offenses (we do not usually speak of laws against battery, rape, murder, etc., as paternalistic). Antioch has at most slightly redefined the criteria for determining whether such an offense has been committed. However, the charge of paternalism misses a very important feature of Antioch's procedure in adopting the policy, a feature which suggests that it is actually much less paternalistic than is the wider society. The policy is the product of a long and inclusive process of community deliberation, initiated by students and giving all members of the college community a full and thorough deliberative role. Debate and discussion on committees, task forces, and open forums over a significant period of time were designed to ensure that the policy was not imposed autocratically and that its function in the community was more educative than punitive (in fact, few alleged violations have reached the point of implementing punishment).

Moreover, the policy makes a rare and important point of insisting, from the point of the original complaint, that the adjudicative process ". . . honor[s] the wishes of the victim regarding what is done (or not done)." This provision is expressly not a threat to the rights of the accused (who is also given specific protections), but is an attempt to ensure both that the victim is not revictimized by an impersonal process, and that the inherently autocratic process of enforcement avoids, to the extent possible, aggravating an already difficult situation.

The charge of paternalism or authoritarianism is, therefore, either rooted in ignorance of the policy itself, or based on a misunderstanding of the community process which gave rise to it. To make such a charge would thus be to confuse thoughtful decisions of an interactive community with anonymous dictates of an impersonal state. This is not to suggest that large-scale governments are incapable of thoughtful policy, or that Antioch is a utopian community without problematic power relations. Paternalism is probably alive and well at Antioch; in this policy it seems to be at low ebb.

Puritanism

Related to the charge of paternalism is the claim that the policy is puritanical or neo-Victorian, a return to the putative bad old days of colleges and universities serving *in loco parentis* to regulate the sexual behavior of their students. Several obvious features of the Antioch policy contradict this rather odd criticism. In the first place, the policy does not forbid any legal sexual practice; it does not attempt to tell students when, whether, or with whom to have or not to have sex. Although the policy was developed in response to serious concerns about the prevalence of women being raped by men, it acknowledges that sexual misconduct is possible in any intimate context, and is written so as to apply generically to women and men, lesbians, straights, bisexuals, and gays.

The policy simply and eloquently insists that consent—which is, after all, already required by existing state and federal law (and widely assented to as an appropriate principle in such matters)—be overt.[2] The college's motivation for this requirement is neither the prudish regulation of students' sexual lives nor a misguided attempt to regulate behavior "for their own good": it stems instead from the collectively perceived threats to members of the community of rape and sexually transmitted disease. It is thus an essentially respectful attempt to address, in particular ways, the enormous and highly intractable social problem, which is also a *criminal* problem, of acquaintance rape, by the reasonable expedient of insisting that consent be verbally expressed and be an ongoing verbal process.

Contractualization of Intimacy

The Antioch policy does not, as many charge, make sexual relations contractual in the legal sense, thus illegitimately importing contract relations into putatively private, intimate spaces. Rather, what the requirement to solicit and verbalize consent or nonconsent at various stages of intimacy does is short-circuit a process whereby, in the prevailing mythology of sexual relations, a woman is presumed to have made a quasi-contractual (usually nonverbal) commitment to have sex by agreeing to one stage of physical intimacy, or by not actively resisting (thereby doing what she may believe will place her at further risk). As Pineau argues, socially (and even legally) a woman is often presumed to have generated a sort of contractual obligation to follow through sexually, even when her attire or behavior is merely interpreted (by someone else) as seductive. Under the Antioch principles, whether a rape victim did or did not "ask for it" becomes purely a matter of whether the defendant can plausibly claim that words to that effect were actually spoken, and not at all a matter of what mythological delusions were operative in the perpetrator's imagination. Such a claim, or its counterclaim, is significantly easier to test for plausibility in case a complaint requires adjudication.

The prevailing presumption of contractual obligation, which Antioch calls into question with its policy, is indefensible, both on the grounds that the law does not equate even a promise with a binding contract, and because it is rooted in a common but false empirical belief that male sexuality is not subject to rational or moral control. By insisting not only on verbal consent, but on a series of verbal consents at different stages of intimacy, the Antioch policy implicitly denies both the false belief about male sexuality and the invidious presumption of an obligation arising from a woman's prior words or actions. It is, as Pineau argues, the criterion of consent as it is presently interpreted which sets up a sexual encounter as contractually obligatory; the Antioch policy does the opposite.

Artificiality

The specific requirement that consensual sexual acts involve both a verbalization of consent and a process of renewed verbalization at subsequent levels of intimacy have led several observers to object that it seems to take all the spontaneity out of intimacy, that it seems somehow "artificial." It seems more than strange that any thoughtful person living in the present decade can still imagine sexual relations as having an obviously "natural," and thereby normative, pattern. This is strange not only because of what we have learned about cultural and historical differences in the construction of sexual meaning and practice, but also because what might have seemed natural a few years ago is now potentially lethal. Real changes in society and biology must lead to changes in how we live and love, and these changes will seem "artificial" only to those who do not acknowledge that the world is different from when they were younger.

That otherwise thoughtful people have expressed this as a criticism is, however, powerful testimony to the durability of patriarchal mythmaking about "human nature." As is usual when such claims are made, the rhetoric of nature here serves to enshrine the sexual status quo—a sexual double standard which undermines attempts to pose substantive solutions to serious social problems, such as the prevalence of acquaintance rape (shocking even by conservative estimates). Such an argument reveals itself to assume that these very real problems, especially those facing women, are simply not very important.

Associated with the charge of artificiality is the sense that being required to talk about intimacy while pursuing it is antiromantic and destructive of spontaneity. Several things might be said about this, ranging from the concern that romance and spontaneity may in some cases be inconsistent with adequate safety and respect for one's sexual partner(s), to the assertion that, in practice, once new habits are developed, sex in accordance with the Antioch policy need be no less spontaneous or emotionally affecting than otherwise, and perhaps more so, since possible ambiguities of communication between partners, relating to whether one or the other does or does not actually wish to be doing what they are doing, become significantly less likely.

It is difficult to imagine, however, what motivates the concern about spontaneity if not a fear of being held accountable for whether one's partner actually consents to a sexual act or not (one student at a state university was reported to protest, revealingly, that if he had to get verbal consent he would "never get to have sex"). Active and ongoing communication about sex certainly cannot eliminate the ambiguities, risks, doubts, and anxieties of sexuality in our society. It does, however, neutralize some of the guesswork, and it effectively undercuts much cultural mythology that is operative in sexual relations. This gives some reason to believe that such a practice could in fact lead to a *more* romantic and (in other ways) spontaneous experience.[3]

Unenforceability

Some have criticized the policy for being difficult or impossible to enforce, given that sexual acts normally occur in private. This is in one sense another species of the objection raised above about autocratic attempts to control personal morality, the replies to which I will not repeat. It also suggests a naiveté about the function in our lives of laws and rules generally.

Enforcement of any regulation is always a sort of rear-guard action, serving at best to remind potential violators of the risks of noncooperation as an adjunct to the many other motivations for obedience (habit, respect for authority, sense of community, perceived self-interest, etc.). Regulations work best when they merely codify an already nearly universal practice, or when their principal function is more educative than punitive, which the Antioch policy (as noted above) emphatically is. The policy itself provides for formal introduction to its terms and purposes for every new member of the community, and all indications so far are that the initiative has been overwhelmingly well received by the student body.

Moreover, when we reflect that existing rape, sexual assault, and sexual harassment laws (which Antioch's policy supplements) are among the most difficult laws to enforce, precisely because the court must decide whether to believe the plaintiff or the defendant in the absence of much supporting evidence, the objection is once again turned on its head. By specifying overt, clear, verbal communication as the criterion by which the presence or absence of consent is to be measured, the policy dramatically clarifies for people, in advance, what needs to have occurred for the defendant honestly to presume consent. With this clarification, it ought to be much more difficult for either party to lie plausibly about the specific dialogue accompanying the disputed encounter, and considerably easier to determine whether the event was a sexual offense or an honest misunderstanding. To the extent that enforceability is not merely a red herring, therefore, the Antioch policy should actually improve just enforcement.

Conclusion

It would be foolish to pretend that verbalizing consent eliminates the possibility (even, under patriarchy, the probability) of various forms of pressure and coercion, from threats and emotional manipulation to social conditioning and the emotional depredations of prior abuse (the Antioch policy makes specific reference to such abuse and provides for counseling and other resources to address it). This granted, however, who would argue that verbal consent, solicited and obtained, can have *no effect whatever* in relieving deep communicative ambiguity and undercutting damaging sexual mythology? That clear, direct language is an antidote to superstition and confusion is a basic tenet of the liberal heritage, and although its efficacy can certainly be exaggerated, it would be difficult to argue that it has no place at all.

The Antioch policy seems to me also to go one step beyond this liberal doctrine, in attempting to reformulate the meaning and power dynamic of consent in social practice, but it does so without undermining any commonly held liberal principle other than the indefensible myths of explicit patriarchy. It is not by any stretch of the imagination a conclusive solution to the social and criminal problems involved in sexual relations, but it does begin to address some real issues, in ways that building more prisons, prescribing harsh sentences for convicted rapists, and seeking to further restrict women's freedom of movement, the most common of proposed antidotes to rape, do not.

Antioch has long been recognized for its respectfulness of students making their own choices in social as well as academic areas, so it is not surprising, or a change of direction, as some allege, that this experiment arose at such an institution (an Antioch alumna of my acquaintance has gleefully nicknamed the college "U. Ask!"). Far from being a reversal of a respectful tradition or a threat to liberty, the new policy seems to be real, if incremental, progress toward the same ideal. If Antioch's policy impinges upon anyone's "liberty," it does so only in that it undermines the presumptive privilege of men to have their needs met without concern for the needs and feelings of women. This seems a small loss compared to the enormous probable gain in substantive freedom—from harassment and misunderstanding—for all members of the community.[4]

Notes

1. Pineau, "Date Rape: A Feminist Analysis," chapter 1 in *Date Rape: Feminism, Philosophy, and the Law,* ed. Leslie Francis (University Park: The Pennsylvania State University Press, 1996).

2. Among the most problematic of liberal concepts, of course, are those of consent and informed consent. I will not here defend them against the radical criticism that gendered socialization so circumscribes the lives, of women especially, that to speak of their free consent, particularly to heterosexual acts, is meaningless. This is a topic for a different essay. For the present I will say only (a) that consent is a powerful idea with which it is politic to work even as we critique it, and (b) that a charge of false consciousness logically implies that we can in principle distinguish it from some truer consciousness—that is, that it must be *possible* to overcome one's social programming (at least incrementally) and become freer, if never entirely free, of overwhelming socializing forces. Thus, while it makes eminent sense to question the "freedom" of a woman's "choice" to engage in heterosexual sex under patriarchy, we must also admit that such constraint admits of varying degrees and that the concept of consent is therefore merely complicated, not vacuous.

3. It is legitimate to object that this begs important questions about what constitutes or ought to constitute spontaneous, romantic, or desirable sex. Some would argue that whatever sex a person desires (or alternatively, *authentically* desires) is ipso facto desirable, and that it would be prima facie wrong to specify, even negatively, what forms this should take. This, again, is an issue I must decline to address in the present essay, except to say that if the person making such an objection has agreed with me that we have an identifiable problem of *bad* sex, that is, sex which is exploitative in one of a number of specifiable ways, then that person has already conceded at least a negative prescriptive criterion for sexuality. On the other hand, to deny that exploitative sex is a problem would entail denying even the conceptual possibility of rape.

4. I am grateful to Leslie Francis, Greta Phinney, David K. Johnson, and Lisa Tessman for their advice and encouragement on this project.

List of Contributors

Linda Martín Alcoff leaches philosophy at Syracuse University.

Thomas Aquinas (1225–1274), Italian religious and philosopher, taught at the University of Paris.

Robert B. Baker teaches philosophy at Union College.

Michael D. Bayles (deceased) taught philosophy at the University of Kentucky, and was a fellow in law and philosophy at Harvard Law School, 1974–75.

Jeremy Bentham (1748–1832), English jurist and philosopher, taught at the University of London.

Susan J. Brison teaches philosophy at Dartmouth College.

Hélène Cixous is a philosopher and linguist at the Centre National de la Recherche Scientifique, Paris.

Stephen R. L. Clark teaches philosophy at the University of Liverpool.

Sharon Danoff-Burg teaches at the University of Kansas.

Arnold I. Davidson teaches philosophy at the University of Chicago.

Frederick A. Elliston (deceased) taught philosophy at the University of Hawaii.

Shulamith Firestone is the author of *The Dialectic of Sex* (New York, 1970).

Pamela Foa authored the article "What's Wrong with Rape?" which appeared in *Feminism and Philosophy,* ed. M. Vetterling-Braggin, F. A. Elliston, and J. English (Totowa, N.J., 1977).

Michel Foucault (1926–1984) was chair of the history of systems of thought at the Collège de France.

Ian Hacking teaches philosophy at Victoria College, the University of Toronto.

David M. Halperin teaches in the Department of Sociology, Culture, and Communication at the University of New South Wales.

Luce Irigaray teaches at the Université de Paris, the Sorbonne, and the Université de Bordeaux.

Robert Jensen teaches at the University of Texas at Austin.

Jeff Jordan teaches philosophy at the University of Delaware.

Michael Levin teaches in the philosophy program at CUNY Graduate School and University Center.

Mike W. Martin teaches philosophy at Chapman University in Orange, California.

Larry May and Robert Strikwerda teach at Washington University in St. Louis, Missouri.

Susan Mendus teaches political philosophy at the University of York, England.

Richard D. Mohr teaches at the University of Illinois at Urbana-Champaign.

Charlene L Muehlenhard has a joint appointment in psychology and women's studies at the University of Kansas.

Thomas Nagel teaches philosophy at New York University.

Margaret M. Nash teaches philosophy at the State University of New York, Cortland.

Robert Padgug is an independent scholar living in New York City.

Paul VI (b. Giovanni Battista Montini, 1897) reigned as pope from 1963 to 1978.

Irene G. Powch is author of the article "Wilderness Therapy" in *Women & Therapy* 15, nos. 3–4 (1994).

Jeffrey Reiman teaches in the Department of Philosophy and Religion at American University in Washington, D.C.

Katie Roiphe is the author of *The Morning After: Fear, Sex & Feminism on College Campuses* (New York, 1993).

Matthew R Silliman teaches philosophy at North Adams State College in Massachusetts.

Linda Singer (deceased) taught at Miami University.

Alan Soble teaches in the philosophy department at the University of New Orleans.

Robert C. Solomon teaches philosophy at the University of Texas at Austin.

Edward Stein teaches philosophy at Yale University.

Judith Jarvis Thomson teaches in the Department of Linguistics and Philosophy at the Massachusetts Institute of Technology.

Joyce Trebilcot teaches philosophy at Washington University in St. Louis, Missouri.

Mary Anne Warren teaches philosophy at San Francisco State University.

Richard Wasserstrom is emeritus professor of philosophy at Phil Board/ Cowell College, the University of California, Santa Cruz.

Ralph Wedgwood teaches in the Department of Linguistics and Philosophy at the Massachusetts Institute of Technology.